dti
Department of Trade and Industry

Mirror Group Newspapers plc

Investigations under Sections 432(2) and 442 of the Companies Act 1985

Report by

The Honourable Sir Roger John Laugharne Thomas

and

Raymond Thomas Turner FCA

(Inspectors appointed by the Secretary of State for Trade and Industry)

Volume One

LONDON: The Stationery Office

Published with the permission of the Department of Trade and Industry on behalf of the Controller of Her Majesty's Stationery Office.

First published 2001

ISBN 0 11 515481 7

Printed in the United Kingdom for The Stationery Office.
TJ3759 C30 03/01 19585 605041

MIRROR GROUP NEWSPAPERS plc

CONTENTS

VOLUME ONE

The appendices to the Report are contained in Volume Two

OUTLINE CHRONOLOGY OF SIGNIFICANT EVENTS

1971/73	DTI Reports on Pergamon Press Ltd. Robert Maxwell severely criticised "...not... a person who can be relied on to exercise proper stewardship of a publicly quoted company".
1974	Robert Maxwell's private companies re-acquired Pergamon Press Ltd.
1980	Robert Maxwell's private companies obtained a controlling interest in British Printing Corporation; Robert Maxwell became chief executive. Company subsequently renamed Maxwell Communication Corporation (MCC).
1984	July: Robert Maxwell's companies (private side) acquired Mirror Group Newspapers (MGN) for £113m.
From 1984	Robert Maxwell ended restrictive labour practices at MGN and introduced modern technology; MGN became highly profitable and was able to provide over £300m to the private side between 1984 and 1990.
1985-1988	MCC and the private side's period of expansion; a number of companies of substantial worth and potential acquired.
1985	Pension funds commenced lending monies to private side.
1987	Private side incurred over £300m in borrowings taking up rights issue in MCC.
1988	MCC borrowed $3 billion and acquired Macmillan and Official Airlines Guides.
	Autumn: Pension funds commenced lending shares to provide collateral for bank loans to private side.
1989	Private side bank borrowing approached £1 billion. Robert Maxwell began selling assets but also continued acquiring companies.
1990	Robert Maxwell spent £130m (some through offshore entities) on MCC shares.
	Robert Maxwell's companies faced a financial crisis in late summer as MCC had to repay part of $3 billion borrowings.
	Decision made to float 49 per cent. of MGN.
	Private companies only survived 31 December year end through borrowings from pension funds and unauthorised overdrafts; bank borrowings remained at about £1 billion.
1991	January to April : Advisers worked on the flotation.
	: Robert Maxwell spent £105m (some through offshore entities) on MCC shares.
	30 April: MGN floated – produced £210m to reduce MGN bank borrowing. At the time private side owed pension funds £100m and was using £270m of their assets as collateral; private side bank borrowings remained at about £1 billion.
	May to July: Robert Maxwell spent £72m through offshore entities on MCC shares and £26m on MGN shares.
	April to November: MGN supported private side through provision of cash and use of its bank borrowings.
	5 November: Robert Maxwell died. Empire thereafter collapsed and MGN sought support of bankers.

SUMMARY

In June 1992 we were appointed by the Secretary of State for Trade and Industry as Inspectors to investigate the affairs of Mirror Group Newspapers plc.

In 1995:
- we had completed most of our enquiries into the complex events.
- we provided to the Secretary of State an Information Memorandum in two volumes setting out a detailed account of the information we had then obtained.
- we would have been able to complete our Report that year if it had not been for the criminal proceedings arising out of the collapse of the company empire controlled by the late Mr Robert Maxwell.
- we submitted to the Secretary of State some recommendations.

Those criminal proceedings and problems surrounding and following from them thereafter substantially delayed the completion of our enquiry.

As requested on our appointment, the focus of our Report is on the flotation of Mirror Group Newspapers on 30 April 1991. We have sought to explain:
- why Mirror Group Newspapers was floated by Mr Robert Maxwell;
- what the due diligence procedures carried out did not reveal, particularly about the pension funds and why the abuse of the pension funds was not discovered earlier;
- what was not done at the flotation, but ought to have been;
- why within seven months of April 1991 the support of Mirror Group Newspapers bankers was necessary.

To do this we have had to describe some earlier events at Mirror Group Newspapers and its pension funds and, as Mr Robert Maxwell ran his financial empire (including the pension funds) as one, some of the events elsewhere in the empire until his death in November 1991. The Report must not, however, be seen as an account of all Mr Robert Maxwell's activities at MGN or elsewhere, or of all the circumstances surrounding the collapse of his empire and the ftermath.

At the outset of our Report, we provide below a brief summary of the events, the responsibility for what happened and our main recommendations and lessons from the events.

Summary of events

The 1971 DTI Report

1. In 1971 Inspectors appointed by the DTI produced a Report on Pergamon Press Ltd which was severely critical of Mr Robert Maxwell. They concluded:

> "We regret having to conclude that, notwithstanding Mr Maxwell's acknowledged abilities and energy, he is not in our opinion a person who can be relied on to exercise proper stewardship of a publicly quoted company."

In two subsequent Reports on Pergamon Press Ltd and related companies in 1972/73 the same Inspectors detailed and criticised Mr Robert Maxwell's business methods.

The rebuilding of Mr Robert Maxwell's fortunes and his acquisition of Mirror Group Newspapers

2. After the events that had led to those Reports, Mr Robert Maxwell spent his time rebuilding his businesses. The two most significant events were:

- He re-acquired in 1974 Pergamon Press Ltd and its scientific journal publishing business which he made highly profitable.

- He obtained in 1980 a controlling interest in British Printing Corporation plc which was on the brink of insolvency. It was a listed company, but, despite the views expressed in 1971, he became its chief executive and subsequently its chairman. He restored the company to profitability and re-established himself in the eyes of many bankers and ensured their support for future expansion. This company was renamed by him Maxwell Communication Corporation plc.

He placed the ultimate ownership of these companies in the Maxwell Foundation, a Liechtenstein entity that he secretly controlled though a Swiss lawyer; this was characteristic of the "need to know" basis on which he ran his businesses. He was the only person in a position to have a full picture of all his interests.

3. On 12 July 1984 Mr Robert Maxwell's private companies (known as the "private side") acquired Mirror Group Newspapers from Reed International plc for £113m. At the time of the purchase Mr Robert Maxwell undertook to make a partial flotation of the Company. He assumed complete control over its management and finances and gradually restored Mirror Group Newspapers to profitability by ending restrictive labour practices and introducing modern technology.

The period of expansion

4. Both Mirror Group Newspapers and Pergamon Press' scientific journals business had strong cash flow. Over £300m of the cash generated by Mirror Group Newspapers was, by December 1990, transferred by Mr Robert Maxwell and used to finance other businesses. The scientific journals business was transferred from the private side to Maxwell Communication Corporation in early 1986. On the strength of those sources of cash, Mr Robert Maxwell announced in April 1986 his intention of achieving through Maxwell Communication Corporation a global communications and information company with revenues of £3-£5 billion by the end of the 1980s; he saw himself competing with Mr Rupert Murdoch and his News Group Newspapers. Mr Robert Maxwell began a frenetic period of corporate expansion in the UK, Europe and North America and acquired companies of substantial worth and potential. On 1 July 1986 Maxwell Communication Corporation became a FTSE 100 company.

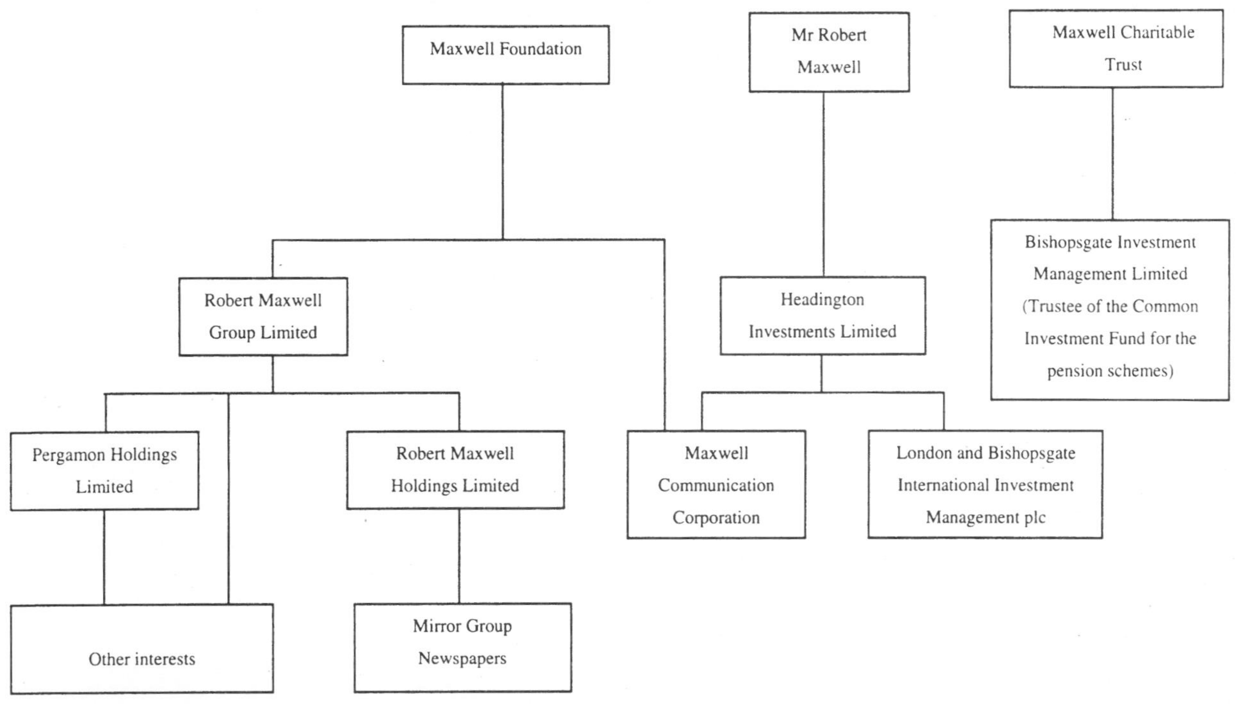

**Simplified ownership structure of Mr Robert Maxwell's main companies.
The structure varied; this chart shows it at the time of the flotation**

5. In the course of this expansion, Mr Robert Maxwell was courted by many leading professional advisers and investment banks who were eager to lend money to him or advise on corporate acquisitions which provided them with significant fees. He entertained and was entertained by leading politicians and world statesmen. The fact that leading professional advisers and banks were prepared to act for him or do business with him was used by him further to re-establish his reputation. It was during this period that Mr Robert Maxwell's youngest son, Mr Kevin Maxwell, became an important member of the management of his businesses.

Mr Robert Maxwell's management of the companies and his use of the pension funds from 1985

6. During this period of expansion significant practices developed in relation to Mr Robert Maxwell's companies and the pension funds:

- Mr Robert Maxwell dominated the management of all these companies. He gradually took over the management of a substantial part of the investments of their pension funds, save for those governed by US legislation.

- Mr Robert Maxwell personally controlled through a central treasury the movement of cash within and between his companies (including having sole signatory authority for an unlimited amount over the bank accounts including those of his main listed company Maxwell Communication Corporation).

- Cash was borrowed by the private side on a regular and unsecured basis from the pension funds beginning in 1985. This did not become known to the trustees of the funds. The accounts were "window dressed" with balances brought to nil at the financial year end to avoid disclosure.

- The pension funds were used on a regular basis to assist in the corporate strategy of the empire and to provide cash in exchange for investments which Maxwell Communication Corporation or other businesses needed to sell.

- The pension funds made substantial investments in Maxwell Communication Corporation shares.

- The presentation of the financial position of Mr Robert Maxwell's companies and the pension funds in the annual accounts was carefully managed and the minimum disclosure made.

- An in-house nominee company, Bishopsgate Investment Trust plc, was established to hold some of the assets of the public companies and private side as well as the pension funds; there were delays in recording the beneficial ownership. This meant that some of those dealing with Mr Robert Maxwell did not necessarily know who in fact owned the shares and the similarity in names of the various "Bishopsgate" companies caused confusion.

These practices were known to Mr Kevin Maxwell and those close to Mr Robert Maxwell in the management of his companies as well as to Coopers & Lybrand Deloitte. Coopers & Lybrand Deloitte were the auditors of the public companies and private side companies and pension funds and provided advisory services to Mr Robert Maxwell in connection with the acquisition and disposal of companies.

7. Although during the period of expansion some of the pension funds benefited from Mr Robert Maxwell's investment skill and the extra income derived from lending to the private side, even during this period there were losses.

- When Mirror Group Newspapers needed £34m cash in 1986, this was provided by the pension funds in return for shares held by Mirror Group Newspapers in Reuters. When these shares were transferred back in 1989, the pension funds not only made a loss on the transaction, but never obtained any part of the significant profits which the private side earned when the Reuters' share price increased very shortly thereafter.

- The pension funds were used to purchase Maxwell House in Holborn, London in 1986, but it was the private side that obtained the real benefits on the transaction.

8. In 1988, two investment management companies controlled by Mr Robert Maxwell, Bishopsgate Investment Management Ltd (BIM) and London and Bishopsgate International Investment Management plc (LBI), were authorised by IMRO, the regulator. Despite doubts expressed as to whether Mr Robert Maxwell was "fit and proper", it was considered that there was insufficient evidence against him to deny approval. BIM and LBI managed a significant proportion of the investments of the pension funds and LBI became the investment managers of an investment trust, First Tokyo Index Trust plc. Subsequent inspections by IMRO failed to uncover the use being made of the pension funds.

The developing financial pressures on Mr Robert Maxwell's companies

9. As a result of a rights issue by Maxwell Communication Corporation in 1987 which was intended to finance acquisitions, the private side assumed, in taking up the rights, a very substantial debt burden of over £300m; the debt grew with further acquisitions by the private side, including the acquisition of AGB Research plc in October 1988 for £134m. All that borrowing was secured on property or shares; most of the shares used as security were shares in Maxwell Communication Corporation. By the beginning of 1989 the bank borrowing of the private side approached £1 billion. In addition, Maxwell Communication Corporation itself also made very substantial borrowings of $3 billion to finance, in 1988, the purchase of Macmillan Inc. and Official Airlines Guide Inc. for which Mr Robert Maxwell overpaid.

10. As Mr Robert Maxwell had always regarded the pension funds as his, when financial pressures on his companies became greater in 1988, he made greater use of the pension funds through the practices identified in paragraph 6. Some banks became reluctant to accept Maxwell Communication Corporation shares as collateral for loans to the private side, because they would in effect be taking for a loan to one group of companies controlled by Mr Robert Maxwell, collateral from another company controlled by him. From November 1988, Mr Robert Maxwell therefore began to make use of the more marketable blue chip shares held by the pension funds and First Tokyo Index Trust as collateral for bank borrowings to the private side; this was described as 'stocklending' to make it appear to be the legitimate practice of lending securities to market makers as part of ordinary share dealing activities. Cash continued to be borrowed from the pension funds by the private side without providing any collateral to the pension funds for these loans. A significant part of the shares of the pension funds and First Tokyo Index Trust which were used as collateral were held by an independent custodian.

11. Mr Robert Maxwell ran his companies and the pension funds as if they were one. He moved assets between them as best suited his overall interests. However, the complex ownership and financial structure of his empire and the concealment of the use of the

pension funds made it difficult for banks to gain a clear picture of the financial strength of his empire. The practice was to be "economic with the information" supplied to them. Although all the groups of companies and pension funds within Mr Robert Maxwell's empire were audited, they were not audited at a common date. Nor was there any overview of the empire as a whole.

12. Although Mr Robert Maxwell began an asset disposal programme in 1989 to ease the financial pressures, he went on acquiring companies and would not contemplate approaching the banks for re-negotiation of the debt.

Mr Robert Maxwell and Maxwell Communication Corporation shares

13. Mr Robert Maxwell was obsessed by the Maxwell Communication Corporation share price; it was also important as it affected the amount of collateral he had to provide when Maxwell Communication Corporation shares were used to secure loans to the private side. Although, as can be seen from the chart, he always held more than 50 per cent. of Maxwell Communication Corporation, he continued to buy Maxwell Communication Corporation shares to be held by his private companies and the pension funds. From May 1989 he manipulated the market, principally by buying shares secretly through overseas entities.

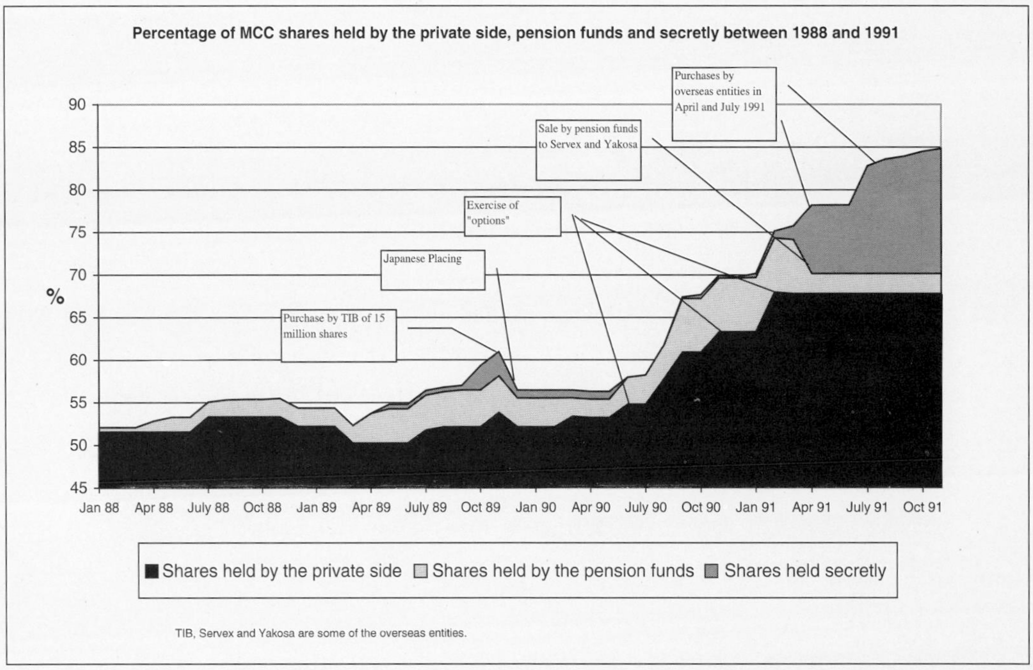

The investment bank with whom he principally dealt was Goldman Sachs. The extent of Mr Robert Maxwell's activity was known to Mr Kevin Maxwell and some of those closely associated with Mr Robert Maxwell. However, the true extent of these activities was unknown to the regulatory authorities in the UK or the USA. The expenditure on Maxwell Communication Corporation shares contributed to the declining financial condition of the private side.

The financial crisis in the summer of 1990

14. By the summer of 1990, in a less favourable economic climate, Mr Robert Maxwell's private companies and Maxwell Communication Corporation faced a substantial financial crisis as part of Maxwell Communication Corporation's debt was scheduled to be repaid in the autumn and the prices which could be obtained for businesses owned by Maxwell Communication Corporation were not as high as had been hoped. £100m was borrowed by the private side from the pension funds in May and June 1990, much of which was provided from the sale of pension fund investments. To provide cash for Maxwell Communication Corporation, two Canadian assets owned by Maxwell Communication Corporation were transferred to Mirror Group Newspapers in October 1990 for £129m which Mirror Group Newspapers financed by borrowing. Maxwell Communication Corporation's share price also came under pressure; significant purchases of Maxwell Communication Corporation shares were made by Mr Robert Maxwell; during 1990 he spent £130m on these. Two of the purchases from Goldman Sachs in 1990 were announced as "options".

15 The private side was able to survive the financial year ended 31 December 1990 only through a carefully planned series of transactions involving the use of pension fund assets and unauthorised overdrafts obtained by LBI from Morgan Stanley Trust Company of \$135m (£74m) and Lloyds Bank plc of £52m. \$56m (£31m) of the overdraft from Morgan Stanley Trust Company was on a pension fund account.

16. The financial crisis of 1990 was the catalyst for the decision to float Mirror Group Newspapers on the Stock Exchange in London by selling 49 per cent. of the shares. This was intended not only to raise money to reduce the overall bank borrowings but to provide Mr Robert Maxwell with shares in a second listed company for use as further collateral for bank borrowings.

17. It was initially hoped that the price obtained on the flotation, together with the sale of other assets, might significantly alleviate the financial crisis faced by Mr Robert Maxwell's empire. However it became clear that the proceeds which would be obtained from the sale of 49 per cent. of Mirror Group Newspapers would not compensate the private side for the loss of its use of Mirror Group Newspapers' cash flow; the sale by Maxwell Communication Corporation of the scientific journals business to Elsevier in April 1991 ended that source of cash flow to Maxwell Communication Corporation. It is apparent therefore that Mr Robert Maxwell knew that, when Mirror Group Newspapers was floated, he had to go on using the cash and other resources of Mirror Group Newspapers and its pension funds after the flotation to support his empire as had been done in the past.

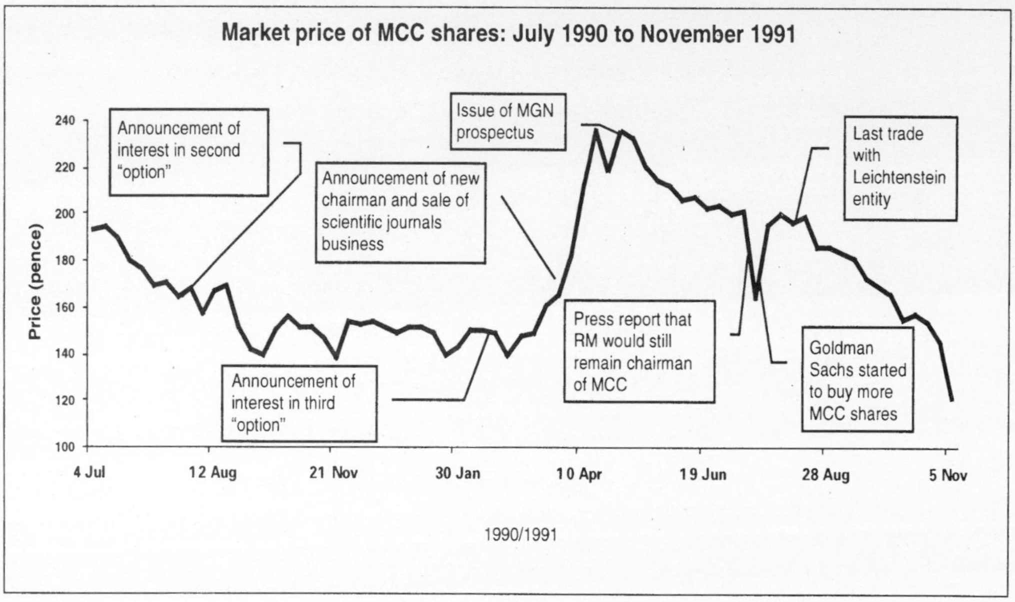

18. Mr Robert Maxwell spent a further £105m on the purchase of Maxwell Communication Corporation shares between January and April 1991, largely through a third "option" and the use of overseas entities. As can be seen from the chart, the Maxwell Communication Corporation share price rose and this was thought to be helpful to the flotation. Most of the purchases were from Goldman Sachs. By the 30 April 1991, the disclosed holding of Mr Robert Maxwell, his family, the private side and the Maxwell Foundation in Maxwell Communication Corporation was 68 per cent.; through the secret purchases by other entities he controlled a further 8 per cent. bringing his total holding to 76 per cent.

The flotation of Mirror Group Newspapers on 30 April 1991

19. Mr Robert Maxwell appointed advisers of the highest reputation to act for Mirror Group Newspapers for the purposes of the flotation – Samuel Montagu & Co Limited, Smith New Court plc, Coopers & Lybrand Deloitte, Clifford Chance, and Salomon Brothers International Limited (who were appointed to market the issue in the USA and Continent). Linklaters & Paines were appointed solicitors to the issue. The advisers were paid a total of £9m in fees. The flotation in London was accompanied by extensive marketing in the USA and on the Continent.

20. On the flotation of Mirror Group Newspapers on 30 April 1991, Mirror Group Newspapers had a modernised and profitable newspaper business. The nature and extent of Mr Robert Maxwell's interest in Mirror Group Newspapers, after a reorganisation of the ownership structure, was properly disclosed. However, we have not discovered any evidence that Mr Robert Maxwell had "changed his spots" as regards his stewardship of a publicly listed company:

- No proper consideration was given to the way Mr Robert Maxwell had run Mirror Group Newspapers nor to the financial controls in place at the time.

- No proper system of corporate governance was put in place although two distinguished non-executive directors were appointed to the board of Mirror Group Newspapers. Mr Robert Maxwell was permitted to be executive chairman.

- No change was made to the financial controls. Mr Robert Maxwell had sole signatory authority over the bank accounts for an unlimited amount, the central treasury remained in control and on 29 and 30 April 1991 (the day before and the day of the publication of the prospectus), £30m was paid from Mirror Group Newspapers' funds for the benefit of Maxwell Communication Corporation and the private side.

- The abuses of the pension funds were neither discovered nor brought to an end:

    - On 30 April 1991 cash loans from the pension funds amounted to £100m and shares to the value of £270m were being used as collateral for bank borrowings.

    - The similar use being made of the shares in the portfolio of First Tokyo Index Trust was discovered by the independent directors on its board, but Mr Robert Maxwell offered to purchase First Tokyo Index Trust on 30 April 1991 to prevent that use being made public.

    - The size of the pension funds' holding in Maxwell Communication Corporation shares (which should have been disclosed in a circular issued by Maxwell Communication Corporation in October 1990) was reduced by a sale for £55m to two overseas entities controlled by Mr Robert Maxwell on 25 April 1991; that amount was never paid to the pension funds. The sale was effected through Goldman Sachs as an agency sale in New York; it did not come to the attention of the market in London.

- The limited financial review of the private side undertaken by Coopers & Lybrand Deloitte at the time of the flotation did not take into account the borrowing of cash from the pension funds or the use of their shares as collateral for bank borrowings. The review did not reveal the serious financial position of the private side. Although Mirror Group Newspapers was meant to be a stand alone company, its fortunes were inextricably linked to those of the private side whose bank borrowings remained at about £1 billion.

21. For these principal reasons, Mirror Group Newspapers was not suitable for listing and the prospectus was materially inaccurate and misleading.

The use made of Mirror Group Newspapers' assets after flotation

22. Mr Robert Maxwell remained, after the flotation, in a position to continue, as he had intended, to use Mirror Group Newspapers' cash flow and to use its pension funds for the benefit of his other businesses. Nothing in reality changed. There was no effective "ring fence".

23. The flotation raised £235m after payment of fees and commissions. £210m was used to reduce the increased bank borrowing Mirror Group Newspapers had undertaken when it had acquired the Canadian assets from Maxwell Communication Corporation and £18m was paid to the private side. However, the private side and Maxwell Communication Corporation remained under severe financial pressure, despite the continued disposal of other assets.

24. Mirror Group Newspapers and its pension funds continued to be used therefore to support the other businesses. There were no proper corporate or financial controls in place to prevent this. Money was regularly borrowed and foreign exchange transactions carried out to provide short term liquidity. In September and October 1991, Mirror Group Newspapers borrowed a total of £80m from banks so that it could be lent to the private side. Mirror Group Newspapers also took a new lease of the Mirror Building which was held by a private side company to enable that company to refinance a loan.

The purchase of Maxwell Communication Corporation and Mirror Group Newspapers shares

25. Mr Robert Maxwell had agreed not to buy or sell Mirror Group Newspapers shares at the time of flotation without the consent of Samuel Montagu. When the share price declined he sought, but was refused, permission to buy. He therefore used the same overseas entities as he had used for the purchase of Maxwell Communication Corporation shares to buy Mirror Group Newspapers shares to the value of £26m from Goldman Sachs.

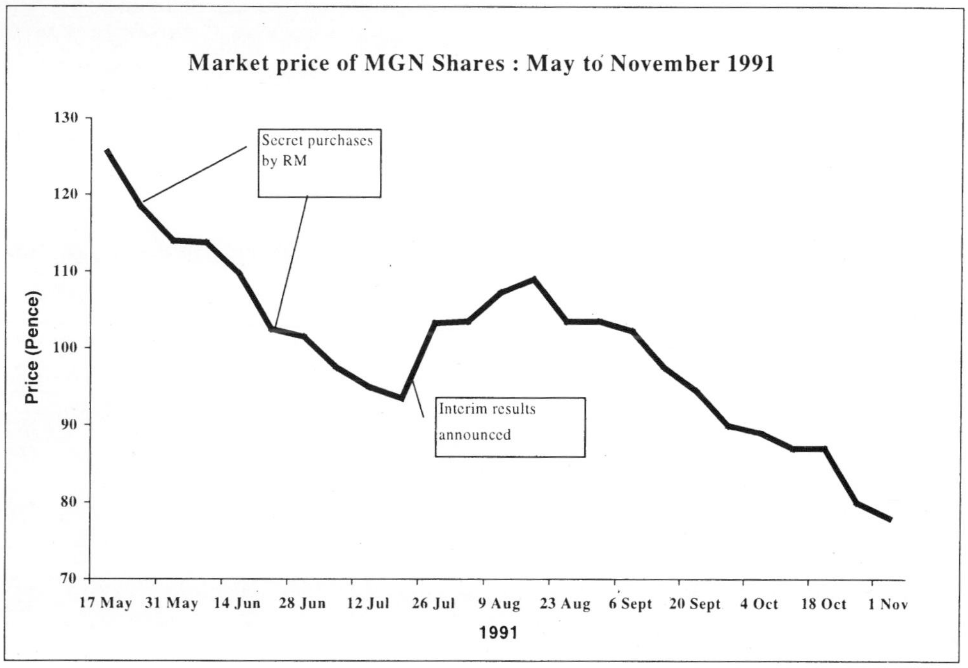

26. When in July and August 1991 the price of Maxwell Communication Corporation shares was under pressure, Mr Robert Maxwell spent a further £75m purchasing Maxwell Communication Corporation shares through the overseas entities from Goldman Sachs in pursuit of the same strategy. His total expenditure on the purchase of Maxwell Communication Corporation and Mirror Group Newspapers shares in 1990 and 1991 was £344m.

27. By August 1991, the 51 per cent. shareholding in Mirror Group Newspapers owned by the private side and shares acquired secretly had been pledged to banks to secure loans made to the private side.

The collapse and the aftermath

28. By the end of October 1991, the private side, having made significant disposals, had no substantial assets other than shares in Mirror Group Newspapers and Maxwell Communication Corporation and property. At that time the pressures became severe. For example, Goldman Sachs required repayment of two loans. When repayment was not made, they began selling Maxwell Communication Corporation shares provided as collateral; the share price fell substantially. The directors of Mirror Group Newspapers were examining the use being made of about £40m of Mirror Group Newspapers' assets. Lehmans demanded repayment of their financing. It is apparent that Mr Robert Maxwell could not seek the support of his bankers to save his empire without disclosing the true state of affairs and the use he had made of the pension funds. The imminent collapse of the empire was inevitable.

29. That collapse occurred shortly after Mr Robert Maxwell's death on 5 November 1991. Mirror Group Newspapers also had to seek the support of its bankers because of the use that had been made of the assets of Mirror Group Newspapers and its pension funds.

30. As a result of the collapse, many pensioners suffered anxiety and loss and the employees of Mr Robert Maxwell's companies suffered uncertainty and redundancy. Mr Kevin Maxwell and others associated with Mr Robert Maxwell faced a long criminal trial in which they were acquitted. Disciplinary proceedings were brought by self regulatory organisations.

The responsibility

In view of the acquittals in the criminal proceedings, we decided that we would proceed in a manner that did not, and would not be seen to, call the acquittals into question. Nonetheless conduct can be blameworthy without being criminal. Furthermore, because our functions as Inspectors are essentially investigative so as to ascertain and record facts and we are not a court of law, we do not make legal determinations on any issue. Where therefore we attribute responsibility, we do so in that context and in terms of blame.

The primary responsibility rests with Mr Robert Maxwell. In addition Mr Kevin Maxwell bears a heavy responsibility in respect of many of the events. Some of those in Mr Robert Maxwell's management team also bear a significant responsibility in respect of these events. We have set this out in chapter 22.

The practices in the pension funds which we have identified were known to Coopers & Lybrand Deloitte. They and other professional advisers and houses were closely involved with the directors of Mirror Group Newspapers in preparing Mirror Group Newspapers for flotation; all these bear to the extent we have ascribed in chapter 22 responsibilities for the failure to make Mirror Group Newspapers suitable for listing and the inaccuracies in the prospectus.

Goldman Sachs were the Investment bank with whom Mr Robert Maxwell principally dealt when purchasing Maxwell Communication Corporation and Mirror Group Newspapers shares and bear a substantial responsibility in respect of the manipulation that occurred in the market.

There was also a failure in three distinct areas of regulation:

- protection of the pensioners
- the flotation of new companies on the Stock Exchange
- trading in shares in transnational markets.

Main recommendations and lessons from the events

Although we submitted some recommendations to the Secretary of State for Trade and Industry in 1995, we have reviewed the position in the light of the considerable developments that have occurred since then.

Many of the deficiencies in legislation and regulation which permitted the events at Mirror Group Newspapers to occur have been rectified, but there remain some important matters which still require to be addressed or considered including:

1. Building on the work carried out by the Occupational Pensions Regulatory Authority in providing more assistance to and encouraging training for trustees who perform the vital role of the stewardship and investment of Occupational Pension Schemes.

2. Providing a statement of Guidance on the role and duties of advisers on a flotation.

3. Building on the radical changes made by the Financial Services Authority, in particular by imposition of severe sanctions against companies who do not report fraud and by encouraging secondment of staff from leading firms to regulatory bodies as a normal part of a City career.

4. Addressing the regulation of markets in securities to provide more effective control over firms that operate on a transnational basis to ensure the fair, open and transparent conduct of such markets and more effective investor protection.

5. Providing more detailed guidance on the audit of business "empires".

6. Addressing the issues relating to auditor independence with a view to maintaining public confidence in the audit and discouraging a firm which provides audit services to a company from acting as reporting accountants on that company.

7. Making non-executive directors more accountable, separating the offices of chairman and chief executive, and providing extra statutory Guidance on the duties of all directors to amplify the general principles that it is proposed be incorporated into the Companies Act.

8. Avoiding an "expectations gap" by making the public aware that regulation cannot entirely eliminate fraud, malpractice or manipulation of the markets.

The most important lesson from all the events is that high ethical and professional standards must always be put before commercial advantage. The reputation of the financial markets depends on it.

MIRROR GROUP NEWSPAPERS plc

REPORT

TABLE OF CONTENTS

PART TWO: THE FLOTATION

PART THREE: THE EVENTS AFTER THE FLOTATION

PART FOUR: CONCLUSIONS, RECOMMENDATIONS AND LESSONS FROM THE EVENTS

Index of Plans, Figures, Graphs and Tables

LIST OF APPENDICES

PREFACE : The course and scope of our enquiry

The course of the enquiry

The events we have investigated are complex and a considerable time has elapsed since our appointment. However, the course of the enquiry has been substantially affected by the problems surrounding and following from the criminal proceedings arising out of the collapse of the company empire controlled by the late Mr Robert Maxwell (RM). It is therefore necessary to set out a short account of the enquiry.

Our Appointment

Shares in Mirror Group Newspapers (MGN) were offered to the public and listed on the London Stock Exchange in April/May 1991. Within seven months of that flotation, MGN had to seek the support of its bankers in the light of unusual payments which had been made from the company and the use that had been made of its pension funds.

On 8 June 1992 we were appointed by the Secretary of State for Trade and Industry as Inspectors under Sections 432 and 442 of the Companies Act 1985 to investigate the affairs of MGN (and to have particular regard to the flotation) and also to investigate the membership of the company for the purpose of determining those persons interested in its success or failure.

The Information Memorandum

During the course of our enquiry, we were requested by the Secretary of State for Trade and Industry under Section 437(1A) of the Companies Act 1985 (as amended) to provide to him with a memorandum setting out an account of the information we had obtained as a result of our investigations.

We prepared a memorandum in draft which covered the entire scope of the Inspection and supplied parts for comment to some of those who had given evidence to us. The draft was revised in the light of comments received and submitted to the Secretary of State in February 1995 as an Information Memorandum under Section 437(1A). It comprised two volumes, one containing our narrative account and the other 18 appendices.

We also submitted to the Secretary of State in 1995 various recommendations arising out of the matters we had investigated.

The Criminal Proceedings

At the time of the submission of the Information Memorandum, criminal proceedings were pending against (amongst others) Mr Kevin Maxwell (KM), Mr Ian Maxwell (IM) and Mr Trachtenberg. A trial in respect of some of the matters with which they had been charged was imminent. The remaining charges were to be heard, separately, in later trials. We were therefore unable to interview KM, IM and Mr Trachtenberg at this time, but the Information Memorandum and certain evidence we had obtained was made available to them for the purposes of the first trial.

In the first trial, KM faced two charges of conspiracy to defraud. IM, Mr Trachtenberg and Mr Bunn each faced a single charge of conspiracy to defraud. KM was accused of conspiring between 3 July 1991 and

10 December 1991 with RM to defraud the trustees and beneficiaries of the pension schemes which participated in the Common Investment Fund (CIF) by dishonestly using shares in Scitex for the purposes of one of RM's private companies. In a separate charge, KM was accused of conspiring between 5 and 21 November 1991 with Mr Bunn, Mr Trachtenberg and IM to defraud the trustees and beneficiaries of the pension schemes which participated in the CIF by dishonestly using shares in Teva for the benefit of one of RM's private companies. This second charge was the one upon which IM, Mr Trachtenberg and Mr Bunn also stood trial.

The first trial started on 31 May 1995; on 19 January 1996, KM, IM and Mr Trachtenberg were acquitted. Mr Bunn had been taken ill during the course of the trial and the prosecution decided not to proceed against him.

In April and May 1996, with the knowledge of the trial judge, Phillips J, we sent out to some of those whose conduct we had examined provisional criticisms. We received responses to those provisional criticisms, but were unable to proceed to complete our enquiry because the prosecution had expressed an intention to continue the criminal proceedings in a second trial of three further charges, which would have involved KM, Mr Trachtenberg and Mr Fuller. Further proceedings against IM had been abandoned.

Under the 3 further charges KM, Mr Trachtenberg and Mr Fuller were accused of conspiring to defraud certain banks to whom shares in Berlitz had been pledged in support of loans provided by the banks to RM's private companies between 1 July 1990 and 6 December 1991.

Mr Stoney had been charged in the criminal proceedings with conspiring between 1 August 1991 and 3 December 1991, with KM, to defraud MGN in connection with a loan by Bankers Trust to MGN and false accounting in relation to that loan. The charges against Mr Stoney were not to be included in the prospective second trial that was to take place.

An application was made by KM and Mr Trachtenberg (supported by Mr Fuller) to stay the further proceedings against them. In September 1996 that application succeeded. In his ruling at that time Mr Justice Buckley said that the common thread running between the charges in the first and prospective second trial was one of the dishonest misuse of others' assets. The Judge described the charges which had already been tried as "no doubt... the most serious examples the prosecution had of the fraudulent course of conduct alleged". He went on:

> "I wish to make plain, I am not suggesting that an acquittal even after a long trial necessarily means that severed counts cannot be tried. Each case will turn on its own particular circumstances; there are many factors to be considered as I have already observed. I am suggesting that if all parties have played their part and the essential criminality alleged has been placed before a jury who have acquitted, it should be unusual for a second trial to take place. The reason is that it would be very likely to appear to the public that the authorities were not prepared to accept the verdict of a jury and were determined to pursue the defendant at whatever cost to the public purse, court time or disruption of the defendant's personal life, business or professional career. That must not happen. . . .
>
> Mr Kevin Maxwell's dealings with various banks and alleged lies or misleading statements to them featured at length in the trial. Mr Justice Phillips dealt with it carefully in his summing up. It took some time. It was part of the overall picture of illiquidity, risk and the defendants' appreciation of risk. Berlitz, to a limited extent, was canvassed with Mr Kevin Maxwell in cross examination. Even if, as [the prosecution] urged on me, I consider the prospective trial only as [they present] it, it would be unreal to

> pigeonhole the Berlitz counts as wholly separate matters. They are separate charges in law. They are separate examples of the defendants', in particular Mr Kevin Maxwell's, dealings with banks. However, they remain, unarguably to my mind, further but clearly less serious examples of the overall dishonesty alleged. The most serious examples have been tried. The defendants were acquitted. . . .
>
> The factors that have influenced me most are that the essential criminality of the prosecution's case was before the jury in the first trial. The defendants' alleged dishonesty was the central issue, as it always had been in the prosecution's presentation of the course of conduct upon which all the charges were based. I have no doubt that the alleged misuse of pension funds was always regarded as the most serious example of that conduct. Broadly speaking, if any jury was going to convict in this case surely it would have been on the pension counts. In the words of the trial judge - "*I doubt if there have been many criminal cases where the jury have had a better opportunity to study the demeanour of a witness*". - The result was acquittal. In the circumstances of this case, to override all consideration for the Defendants and their families and what they must have endured over the last few years and to launch another long trial at enormous expense would, in my judgment, run a grave risk of suggesting to the public that the authorities did not accept the verdict of a jury. I do not propose to run that risk."

The further progress of the enquiry in the light of the acquittals and Buckley J's ruling

The reasoning apparent from the ruling of Buckley J is the concept that the "essential criminality" in the matters which had already been tried and the matters which the prosecution were proposing should be tried was essentially the same, that of dishonestly misusing others' assets. The alleged dishonesty was, Buckley J said, the central issue.

It is clear from that summing up of Phillips J in the first trial that dishonesty was at the heart of the allegations and the jury were being directed to acquit unless they were sure that the defendants engaged in a course of dishonest conduct. He directed the jury that dishonesty involved appreciation of the fact that the assets being employed were the property of the pension funds and appreciation of the substantial risks attached to the use of the assets. Dishonesty also involved two mental elements. First, the prosecution would have to prove that any reasonable or honest person would regard it as dishonest to put the pension fund's property at risk in the manner alleged. Secondly, the prosecution would have to prove that the defendants knew that an honest and reasonable person would so regard it. Phillips J drew attention to the fact that, in this connection, KM had given evidence about the culture which had developed within the Maxwell organisation and asked the jury:

> "Had it become so much the norm to use assets of any member of the Group and the assets of the pension funds for the benefit of other members of the Group, that a defendant may have lost sight of the implications of such conduct; lost sight of the duty of the trustee of a pension fund to put the interests of the fund before any private interests; and done just that without appreciating that someone who had not been exposed to this culture would regard such conduct as dishonest?"

Phillips J told the jury:

> "...you have to consider whether the defendant's conduct was, to his own knowledge, dishonest. This means that if you conclude that it was dishonest by your standards, you must go on to consider whether the defendants have been so infected by the Group culture that they no longer knew right from wrong where use of pension fund assets were concerned."

We carefully considered all the directions given to the jury in the first trial, the ruling of Buckley J and the effect of the acquittals on the charges relating to shares in Scitex and Teva (which had not been the subject of our enquiry) and we took advice from Lord Neill of Bladon QC and Professor Beatson QC. We decided that we should proceed in a manner which did not, and which would not be seen to, call the acquittals into question or cast doubt on the conclusions of the jury on the honesty of the defendants as regards their course of conduct. Nonetheless conduct can be blameworthy without being criminal.

It is our duty to produce a candid report setting out the facts, our views of the respective responsibility of those concerned, our criticisms where we considered them to be justified, and our recommendations. Our functions are essentially investigative so as to ascertain and record facts. We are not a Court of Law and we do not make legal determinations on any issue[a]. Where, therefore, we attribute responsibility in our report we do so in that context and in terms of blame.

Some of the directors of MGN and some of the advisers have, in their responses to our provisional criticisms of them, sought to attribute to the actions of some of those charged in the criminal proceedings conduct which would question the verdict by attributing to them dishonest conduct and have suggested that such dishonest conduct would have nullified any action they might have taken. However, even if such directors and advisers were correct about such conduct, it would not have caused us to revise our conclusions as to their responsibility.

The completion of our enquiries

In December 1996, we interviewed IM and in March 1997 we interviewed Mr Trachtenberg.

In September 1996, we sought to interview KM whose evidence we considered very important as he had played a significant rol̀e in many of the events. For 2½ years KM raised objections of principle to assisting us. He maintained that we were acting oppressively and unfairly and made a number of demands including that the Secretary of State for Trade and Industry should pay for his legal representation and for his time to prepare for and attend interviews; that he should not be questioned on topics explored at other interviews which had taken place over many days before office-holders and the Serious Fraud Office (SFO), and at the trial; that he be released from any obligation of confidentiality and that an undertaking be given that he would not face further civil and criminal proceedings. He also made a formal request to the Secretary of State for Trade and Industry (then the Rt Hon Margaret Beckett MP) that she direct the Inspectors to take no further steps in the enquiry.

We or the Secretary of State for Trade and Industry (as appropriate) attempted to meet KM's concerns in relation to each of these matters. In the end, KM was not satisfied and when he continued to maintain his stance, and also at his invitation, we certified him to the Court under section 436 of the Companies Act 1985.

Sir Richard Scott VC decided[b] in March 1999 that KM need not give an undertaking of confidentiality and that if we restricted the topics on which he was to be questioned and provided him with certain materials, KM should answer our questions. After, and as a result of that judgment, KM agreed to co-operate with our inquiries. Nonetheless, there was still lengthy correspondence between ourselves and KM (concerning, for example, KM's objections to the scope of our interviews and the absence of lists of questions) before KM came for interview. Finally, he attended for 9 days in July and August 2000. He

---

a See *Fayed v the United Kingdom* (1994) 18 EHRR 393.

b In *Re An inquiry into Mirror Group Newspapers plc* [2000] Ch.194.

was not legally represented. He was provided with ample opportunity to reflect on his evidence and raise other matters. The interviews raised further matters which required investigation and enquiries. Our interviews did not cover those topics on which he had been extensively examined at the criminal trial or by the office-holders of the companies that had been under RM's control; although we have referred to that evidence (where relevant) in our Report, our investigation on those topics is not as complete as we would have wished.

When KM gave his evidence to us he answered all the questions we put, gave us additional information and drew our attention to paragraphs in the Information Memorandum which he considered did not convey the right balance. It is a matter of regret that he did not respond to our questions and provide to us this assistance earlier in our enquiry. To the extent that we were unable to ask him all the questions we would have wished our Report may be incomplete.

We would have completed our Report in 1995 had it not been for the criminal trial. We would have finished our report in 1997 had we been able to obtain KM's evidence at that time.

The evidence and enquiries

We have obviously not had the benefit of any evidence RM might have given to us and his account of the events will never be known. To that extent the information available to us is incomplete. On some matters KM has been able to give us his understanding of his father's views and, where appropriate, these have been included.

We have

- interviewed 176 witnesses;
- obtained written evidence from 111 other persons; and
- sought information from 46 banks and financial institutions.

These are listed in Appendix 1. In the time since the events described in the Report, many entities have changed their names; we have used the names which were in use during the relevant period.

We received the fullest co-operation from MGN who provided us with all the documentation we requested, including much that would otherwise have been the subject of legal professional privilege.

Our team and our advisers

In the first phase of our enquiry from our appointment in 1992 until the completion of the Information Memorandum in 1995 we had the support of a large and gifted team from Mazars Neville Russell; although it is not possible to name them all, we would like to thank them for their very significant contribution.

We would not have been able to carry out the enquiry without the professionalism and dedication of the Secretaries to the Inspection, Glyn Williams FCA and Warwick Sabey FCA of Mazars Neville Russell, and of Counsel to the Inspectors, Nicholas Peacock, together with the efficient support of our personal assistant, Jennifer Schoon and our shorthand writers, Susan Solomon and Miriam Weisinger. We are most grateful to them for their invaluable assistance throughout the entire period of the enquiry.

We are also much indebted to Lord Neill of Bladon QC, Professor Beatson QC and Catherine Newman QC who have advised us and to the DTI for their assistance and guidance.

Other proceedings

Apart from the criminal proceedings to which we have referred, civil proceedings were brought against several of those involved including KM and IM. KM was made a bankrupt in September 1992 and discharged in September 1995. Disciplinary proceedings were brought by self-regulatory organisations against those firms we identify in Appendix 20.

The scope of the Investigation and the Report

To understand the flotation, what needed to be done to prepare MGN for flotation and what happened thereafter, it has been necessary for us to consider

- the circumstances in which RM acquired MGN and his role in the company and its pension funds up to the time of the flotation; and

- the development of RM's other principal businesses, as the fortunes of MGN were inextricably linked to those other businesses and they had a significant impact on what happened to MGN and its pension schemes over the period 1984 to 1991.

We have not examined events that have occurred in connection with MGN[a] after the death of RM on 5 November 1991, save where necessary to obtain an understanding of what happened prior to that time. Events relating to the pension funds that occurred after 30 April 1991 were outside the scope of our enquiry. We were asked not to enquire into events which were the subject matter of the main charges in the criminal proceedings. The principal matters covered in the first trial concerned events relating to the pension funds after 30 April 1991. It is clear from our investigations that the abuses of the pension funds were well established long before 30 April 1991. However, we have referred to events involving the pension funds after 30 April 1991 where they directly affected MGN.

For the reasons set out above:

- the first part of this Report contains an account covering the period to the end of 1990, when a final decision to proceed with the flotation was made. This part sets out the development of MGN and its pension schemes under RM's ownership and their interrelation to RM's other businesses. We only deal with those other businesses in so far as they relate to MGN and we have not attempted to tell the story of those other businesses; an investigation of those other businesses as well as Maxwell Communication Corporation plc (MCC), another listed company controlled by RM, was outside the scope of our enquiry.
- the second part examines what was done to prepare MGN for flotation.
- the third part covers what happened at MGN after flotation until RM's death.
- the fourth part sets out our conclusions, our views as to the responsibility for what happened and recommendations and lessons from the events.

---

[a] The company that was MGN (No 00168660) at the time of our appointment changed its name to Mirror Group PLC on 21 April 1994. Following a merger in September 1999 the company became a wholly owned subsidiary of Trinity Mirror Plc. On 10 December 1999 the company re-registered as a private company to become Mirror Group Limited.

We enquired into the membership of MGN, and in particular the use of an offshore entity, the Maxwell Foundation. We are satisfied that proper disclosure was made in the prospectus of the persons interested in the success or failure of MGN and that there are no adverse matters to which we should draw attention.

More detailed information on certain topics is contained in the Appendices. Two of these provide detailed accounts of the most complex events that had a material bearing on what happened to MGN:

- Appendix 7: Dealings in MCC shares from 1989 and the market for MCC and MGN shares in 1991
- Appendix 8: The use of the assets of the pension funds to April 1991

Hindsight

We have sought, wherever possible, to rely on contemporary documents and endeavoured in our interviews with witnesses to assess their evidence without the benefit of hindsight. We have done this not only in respect of what became known after the death of RM but also in respect of the development of standards of conduct since 1991. Some, in their responses to provisional criticisms, have said we have reached our conclusions with the benefit of hindsight. We have examined those observations carefully and reviewed our conclusions. Where we have not changed them, we have satisfied ourselves that we have excluded hindsight.

Some witnesses whom we have criticised have made submissions to us that their conduct at the time of the events is excusable since RM's probity was generally accepted at the time and that they, like many others, were unaware of the irregularities which came to light later. In giving careful attention to this proposition we have also had to take into account other evidence. Some believed that the 1971/73 Reports had accurately concluded that RM was untrustworthy, some had direct experience of his unscrupulous behaviour and others, including some regulators, simply believed that he was not a man to be trusted. Our final conclusions take into account all this evidence.

Completeness

We must emphasise that this Report cannot and does not give a complete picture of all the matters involving RM. Consequently it will not refer to all persons who, at various times, were associated with him, for example as directors or employees of his companies. We have concentrated on what we considered the most important and most relevant matters within the terms of our appointment.

The Honourable Sir R J L Thomas

R T Turner FCA

5 March 2001

PART ONE
1984 to 1990

1. THE ACQUISITION OF MGN

The 1971 DTI Report

1.1 On 13 July 1971, Mr Owen Stable QC and Sir Ronald Leach, Inspectors appointed by the Department of Trade and Industry (DTI), in presenting their Interim Report on the affairs of Pergamon Press Limited (PPL)[a] concluded[b]:

> "We regret having to conclude that, notwithstanding Mr Maxwell's acknowledged abilities and energy, he is not in our opinion a person who can be relied on to exercise proper stewardship of a publicly quoted company."

The detailed findings of that Report, to which we will refer when considering the issues that arose on the flotation in 1991, are as significant to any understanding of RM's business methods as this well-known conclusion[c].

1.2 It is not necessary to describe the events that led to that Report or the effect that had on RM's position. It is sufficient to say that in the period to 1980, his time was largely spent in rebuilding his private finances[d], reacquiring in 1974 PPL (which he returned to private ownership) and rebuilding its core business of publishing scientific journals. PPL became of substantial importance in the development of RM's other companies as publishing scientific journals was a relatively straightforward business to run and produced a steady flow of cash and profits[e]; this came to be regarded by most of his associates and advisers as "the crown jewel" of his businesses.

The Maxwell Foundation

1.3 It is however necessary to go back to 1970 to explain the function of the Liechtenstein entities that played a role in the ownership of PPL and the subsequent development of RM's businesses. RM was always secretive about his businesses; he operated on a "need to know" basis that meant no one who worked within his businesses but himself was in a position to

---

a This company had been built up by RM primarily on the strength of the business of publishing scientific journals, had been floated on the stock market in 1964 and had been the subject of a take over by Leasco Inc which had led to the DTI enquiry.

b See paragraphs 340 to 343.

c We have summarised in Appendix 4 those findings of the 1971/73 Reports that are relevant to an understanding of his business methods.

d He did become involved in the workers' co-operative set up for the Scottish Daily News.

e Each year about £40m of cash was received between November and January when subscriptions were collected; expenditure was then spread over the year. RM was therefore able to use this cash flow to fund acquisitions and to take very substantial positions in gilts; he continued to do this throughout the 1980s. The business was also very profitable.

have a full picture of his various interests. This characteristic was particularly applied to everything that concerned the role of the Maxwell Foundation, one of these Liechtenstein entities.

1.4 RM's connections with Liechtenstein went back a long time. After the Second World War, RM met Dr Ludwig Gutstein, a Swiss lawyer practising in Zurich and from either the late 1940s or early 1950s RM had used Liechtenstein entities in connection with his business[a].

1.5 Liechtenstein had established in the 1920s certain distinctive types of entity; one of these was a Liechtenstein *Stiftung* or foundation. A Liechtenstein foundation was usually established on behalf of an individual, but had no owner, only beneficiaries. It could be used for family or charitable purposes or both; it could not itself engage in trade but could control trading companies. If a foundation was a "deposited" foundation, no information was publicly available about it. If it was registered, then very little information about it was publicly available; in particular its governing instruments (its statutes) were private documents.

1.6 In 1970 the Maxwell Foundation[b] was acquired or established on behalf of RM by Dr Gutstein as a deposited foundation through the General Trust Company of Liechtenstein[c].

1.7 Although the Maxwell Foundation had no owner, supreme power over the Maxwell Foundation was vested by its statutes in the holder of the "founder's rights". The founder of the Maxwell Foundation was the General Trust Company acting for Dr Gutstein whom it regarded as its mandator. Accordingly the founder's rights were passed by means of a blank transfer to Dr Gutstein[d]. These gave him the power to appoint the Director, to give him instructions, to appoint the beneficiaries and to change the purpose of the Maxwell Foundation and any other provision of its statutes. In the summer of 1987 Dr Werner Rechsteiner, a lawyer in Zurich, took over part of Dr Gutstein's practice and the founder's rights of the Maxwell Foundation were passed to him[e].

1.8 Dr Walter Keicher, a director of the General Trust Company was appointed by Dr Gutstein as the first Director of the Maxwell Foundation and the sole member of the board; he was, as far

---

a On 1 March 1954, Dr Gutstein had established International Trust Services for RM's sister, Brana.

b It was originally known as Swico Foundation, then changed its name to Pergamon Holdings Foundation in 1982, to Pergamon Foundation in November 1987 and to the Maxwell Foundation in February 1988.

c As explained at paragraph 3.24, Mr Haines was given information about the Maxwell Foundation in 1988 before finishing his biography of RM, "*Maxwell*". Mr Haines stated in this biography that the Maxwell Foundation was established because Dr Gutstein was concerned that RM and Mrs Maxwell were defendants in a large lawsuit brought by Leasco Inc.

d It is usual where a lawyer acts in this capacity that he does so for a client under a mandate that is either verbal or in writing. By using a Swiss lawyer, the client can claim that he does not hold the founder's rights and his identity is protected by Swiss secrecy laws.

e The transfer took place because Dr Gutstein was by then very old and it was anticipated that he might have to be cross examined in connection with litigation arising out of the Harcourt Brace Jovanovich Inc bid (see paragraph 3.20).

as the outside world was concerned, the person who controlled the Foundation. Dr Walter Keicher was succeeded by his son, Dr Werner Keicher in March 1986. In their capacity as directors, Drs Keicher had a fiduciary role to carry out the wishes of the founder; thus although they had all the legal powers, they had to exercise them in accordance with the will of the founder. As their relationship was with Dr Gutstein and then Dr Rechsteiner they would act on instructions from them, but they appreciated that in turn Dr Gutstein's and Dr Rechsteiner's client was RM who provided their instructions.

1.9 The beneficiaries of the Maxwell Foundation were not at first specified in its statutes; we were told this is not unusual in a family foundation as the lawyer will be given instructions as to who the beneficiaries are. The beneficiaries were in fact RM's family resident outside the US and the UK and charitable purposes[a]. In 1988 the beneficiaries were changed solely to charitable purposes in the circumstances described at paragraph 3.24.

1.10 In addition to the Maxwell Foundation, Dr Gutstein acquired for RM twelve other Liechtenstein entities in December 1984 and formed those that were not already foundations into foundations. We were told they were acquired for a specific purpose, but were not used and remained dormant until about 1989. Those included Akim Foundation, Alandra Foundation, Baccano Foundation, Corry Foundation, Jungo Foundation, Kiara Foundation and Nessi Foundation, all of which are mentioned in the following chapters. We were told that in 1988, RM gave to Dr Rechsteiner a list of which of his children were to be the beneficiary of each of these Foundations and that RM confirmed this to him in the summer of 1991 in the circumstances described in paragraph 21.4. KM told us that this was not correct and RM had given Dr Rechsteiner no such list and no such confirmation. After RM's death Dr Rechsteiner wrote to various of RM's children informing them of their respective interests, but they stated they knew nothing and renounced their interests.

1.11 The ultimate ownership of PPL was transferred to the Maxwell Foundation[b] by 1982.

1.12 Technically therefore all businesses owned by PPL were ultimately owned by and for the benefit of the Maxwell Foundation; however the Maxwell Foundation left the management of the companies to RM and acted on his instructions.

The acquisition of BPC

1.13 It was the acquisition by PPL in April 1981 of a controlling interest in British Printing Corporation (then known as BPC Ltd (BPC) and a publicly listed company) that was the most significant event in RM's re-establishment of his position after the earlier events relating to his

---

a This was also publicly asserted on 13 December 1984 during the course of a bid for John Waddington plc (see paragraph 3.12); the information was provided by Dr Keicher who obtained it from Dr Gutstein; RM gave similar information in the course of his bid for Extel Group plc in April 1987 (see paragraph 3.14).

b By 1982 the issued share capital of PPL was held through Pergamon Holdings Corporation (PHC) a US corporation owned by the Maxwell Foundation; a decision was made to transfer the ownership from the US for tax purposes, and those shares were passed by dividend to the direct ownership of the Maxwell Foundation by PHC pursuant to a resolution of its board dated 1 April 1983.

ownership of PPL. A chronology of the main acquisitions made by RM in 1980 – 1989 is set out in Appendix 5.

1.14 PPL commenced buying shares in BPC during 1980 and by 18 July 1980, after a dawn raid carried out through Grieveson, Grant & Co, PPL had acquired 29.4 per cent. of the company. Later in the year it was announced that PPL would be prepared to inject new capital into BPC and discussions were then held between National Westminster Bank plc (National Westminster) (who were BPC's Bankers), BPC and RM. On 16 February 1981 it was announced that RM would become Chief Executive and Deputy Chairman of the company and PPL would inject new capital conditional upon the trade unions agreeing to RM's "survival plan". On the acceptance by the unions of RM's survival plan, PPL injected £10m and took control of the company with a shareholding of 76.9 per cent.[a].

1.15 RM's appointment as Chief Executive of BPC and PPL's acquisition of control of BPC were particularly significant in the following respects:

- RM became a director of a publicly listed company despite the findings of the DTI Inspectors in 1971/73. In July 1977, some two months after the Solicitor General had announced that no prosecutions would be made as a result of the DTI Inquiry into PPL, RM approached the Stock Exchange to enquire what their attitude would be if he made a cash bid for a listed company; he told them that if they treated him unfairly, he would take them to court. The Stock Exchange concluded that it would not be right to place a bar on his appointment to the board of a listed company[b] although they would suggest to the sponsor of the company that some other person ought to act as independent Chairman as it was likely that RM would want to be the Managing Director of any company on whose board he sat. RM did not bid for a listed company in 1977, but when he did acquire a stake in BPC in July 1980, the Stock Exchange followed the view that it had formed in 1977. When RM became Chairman of BPC on 1 September 1981, the Stock Exchange took no action; the Stock Exchange told us it had no power to do so.
- The Bank of England was consulted in its traditional role as a "catalyst" between interested parties that were in financial difficulties. The Bank of England was unsure about the financial position of BPC and the quality of its management and Sir Henry Benson[c] considered that it would be better to have RM on the board where he would have to behave as a responsible director, though it was common ground he was

---

[a] The Stock Exchange was informed of this holding and took no objection in the light of the financial position of BPC, a dispensation granted by the Takeover Panel from the obligation to bid for the minority and the uncertainty at that time as to whether the condition applicable to listing (that 25 per cent. of a company had to remain in the hands of the public) was an enforceable continuing obligation.

[b] The reasons why the Stock Exchange reached this decision were: public criticism of the DTI Inspectors' conduct of their investigation, RM's re-establishment of his own business career, the Rehabilitation of Offenders Act 1974 (as an example in the relaxation of attitudes to hounding persons who had been convicted or criticised in public) and the fact that RM had not been prosecuted or convicted.

[c] Later Lord Benson. He was adviser to the Governor of the Bank of England on industrial matters from 1975 to 1983; he had been a partner of Coopers & Lybrand 1934-1975, but had severed all his links on appointment to the Bank of England.

unsuitable as a director. Sir Henry Benson maintained his views even though Hambros Bank Limited and Cazenove & Co also said they would resign as merchant bankers and brokers to BPC if RM joined the board[a]. He made clear to Lord Kearton on his appointment as Chairman of BPC that he would have the task of keeping RM under control[b].

- RM had the opportunity of turning around a business about which the circular to shareholders had stated that the only alternative to RM's plan was the appointment of a receiver. He took full advantage of this opportunity and within a year BPC was reporting profits.
- It strengthened RM's relationship with his bankers, particularly National Westminster[c]. His success re-established him in the eyes of bankers and ensured their support for his future expansion.

1.16 During 1982 and 1983 RM largely concerned himself with cost cutting and the development of the business at BPC. BPC subsequently changed its name and ultimately was known as Maxwell Communication Corporation plc (MCC)[d]. It is more convenient to call it "MCC" throughout the Report. Acquisitions were made of printing businesses. The acquisition of Odhams Printers Ltd, when merged with Sun Printers Ltd, permitted rationalisation and productivity gains such that, for the first time in many years, MCC's gravure business became profitable. MCC also in June 1983 made an unsuccessful bid for John Waddington plc, another company with a substantial printing and packaging business.

The acquisition of MGN

1.17 By the early 1980s MGN, as a subsidiary of Reed International plc (Reed), had acquired a number of newspapers. In England and Wales its principal newspapers were the *Daily Mirror* (which had been launched by Mr Alfred Harmsworth, later Lord Northcliffe, in 1903) and the *Sunday Mirror*. In Scotland its principal newspaper was the *Daily Record* which had been founded by Alfred Harmsworth's brother, Harold Harmsworth (later Lord Rothermere), in 1895. The *Daily Record* had a Sunday sister paper, the *Sunday Mail* and these were published

---

a Cazenove & Co resigned on RM's appointment to the board.

b Lord Kearton became Chairman on 18 February 1981; on 20 August 1981 he wrote to Sir Henry to tell him he felt his work was at an end and he was resigning as Chairman. His letter summarised what had been done at BPC, expressed the view that BPC would be profitable, and included the following passage:

> "It will be a most remarkable turnaround. If BPC had gone into receivership earlier this year, the equity shareholders would have got nothing, and nearly all the 10,500 jobs would have gone. Nat Wests' own losses would have been not far short of £20m.
> The credit for what has been achieved belongs to Robert Maxwell, who is a man of enterprise, resource, and vision. He is an outstanding negotiator, whether with the unions, the customers, the suppliers, or Nat West. He works long hours, extremely hard, and has great physical and mental robustness."

c RM had banked with National Westminster from at least the 1950s; they had considered whether they should continue to be his bank after the DTI Inquiry into PPL but as he had always honoured his commitments to the bank and had always behaved properly to them they allowed the relationship to continue with his then private companies.

d Its name was changed to The British Printing & Communication Corporation plc (BPCC) in March 1982 and was further changed to Maxwell Communication Corporation plc on 22 October 1987.

through a separate subsidiary, Scottish Daily Record and Sunday Mail Limited (SDR). MGN had also acquired *The People* and *The Sporting Life*.

1.18 In October 1983, Reed announced plans for a flotation of MGN as an independent company. Under the period of Reed's ownership the company had been run as a subsidiary with its own independent board, but with its banking and treasury operations controlled by the Reed central treasury. The plans for the flotation did not proceed smoothly partly because of the lack of investment available to renew MGN's plant, partly because of the lack of profitability of MGN, and partly because of stock market conditions.

1.19 RM announced in the course of the preparation for flotation that PPL was interested in bidding for MGN and, although Reed initially stated that they would not sell to him, on 12 July 1984 PPL's bid for the company at a price of £113.4m was accepted. RM gave various undertakings including one to make a partial flotation of MGN. Hill Samuel & Co Ltd[a] (Hill Samuel) acted for RM and PPL.

1.20 The bid was financed by two loans from National Westminster.

- A loan of £64m was provided on the basis it was to be repaid from the proceeds of the intended flotation[b].

- A loan of £23m was provided on the basis that it would be repaid from an intercompany debt of £23.3m that Reed owed to MGN and had agreed to repay to MGN as a term of the purchase agreement. To ensure that there was no infringement of legislation which prevented the assets of the company being used in the purchase of its own shares, it was agreed that the £23m that PPL needed to repay this bank loan would be paid by MGN to PPL in return for shares that PPL held in MCC; this was subsequently done in September 1984, as set out at paragraph 2.17.

We were told that the rest of the funds necessary for the purchase were provided from PPL's own resources.

1.21 On the evening that RM acquired MGN, he went straight to MGN's offices at the Mirror Building in Holborn, London and, although he arrived at about midnight, he immediately ordered that a board meeting be summoned. The board met at 2.45 am (when 9 directors including RM were present) and again later that same day at 2.45 pm (when 11 directors including RM were present). These board meetings are significant in that:

- They were the last formal board meetings held until 1991 at which matters of policy were raised. At the second meeting that day there was not an open discussion; for

---

a RM first consulted them on 2 July 1984 at a meeting attended by Sir Robert Clark (who became a non-executive director of MGN on its flotation in 1991) and Mr Leslie Goodman. Hill Samuel had first acted for RM in 1968 in connection with his attempt to acquire *The News of the World*.

b In fact this was subsequently extended and then refinanced through another facility.

example, when the way in which a threatened stoppage at SDR should be dealt with was raised, RM instructed how it was to be resolved.

- RM obtained from the board an amendment to the mandates relating to the bank accounts of MGN so that he had authority to sign cheques and make transfers from the accounts on his sole signature for any amount.

RM's full control over the management and finances of MGN obtained in this way was to remain an essential characteristic of his ownership of MGN thereafter.

2. 1984 - 1988: THE RESTORATION OF MGN TO PROFITABILITY

2.1 One year after RM's acquisition of MGN, steps were commenced to return MGN to profitability and by 1988, the major changes necessary to achieve this had taken place. During this period, RM as its proprietor transferred from MGN all its non-newspaper assets for use in his other businesses and began to use any surplus cash generated by MGN for the same purpose. However, from 1985, he also started to use the funds of the pension scheme in the furtherance of his other business interests. It is easiest to consider in this chapter what happened during this period under the following five headings:

(1) RM's control over
 (a) The management of MGN
 (b) SDR
(2) RM's control over the finances of MGN
(3) RM's use of MGN in connection with his other interests: the intercompany debt
(4) RM's control over the pension funds
(5) Steps taken to return MGN to profitability

A list of the directors of MGN and of some other of RM's companies is set out in Appendix 3.

(1) RM's control over the management

(a) MGN

2.2 During the period in which MGN was wholly owned by RM's private companies, MGN had numerous directors, but the board as such never met to run the company[a]; board meetings (generally of two directors) were held only for formal purposes, such as approving bank mandates, authorising dividends and making transfers of assets. Notice of such meetings was never given to the directors and minutes were never circulated. This was not unusual for some privately owned companies.

2.3 The fact that no notice was given of board meetings and no minutes circulated coincided with a change in the company secretary. On PPL's acquisition of MGN the company secretary had been Mr Hudgell. RM told Mr Hudgell shortly after the take over that he, Mr Hudgell, did not understand RM's ways. Accordingly on 13 September 1984, RM replaced him with Mr Alan Stephens who, as RM explained to Mr Hudgell, understood his management style. Mr Stephens was the secretary to RM's other private companies and understood that RM did not see any point in formal board meetings for his private companies and RM did not want notice given or minutes circulated[b].

---

a There is a minute that records a meeting on 6 March 1985 to pass concurrent powers of the board to a committee of four; its quorum was two, one of whom had to be RM. We were told this meeting lasted for five minutes. There was a minuted meeting on 23 July 1985 which initiated the bringing of proceedings against *Private Eye* but we were told that this was probably a discussion over one of the regular Tuesday lunches (see paragraph 2.7).

There is also a minute which records a meeting that took place in RM's sitting room in his flat at Maxwell House on 26 May 1989 (this is described at paragraph 4.30).

b We were told by Mr Hudgell that Mr Stephens explained to him his understanding of RM's style; "If the old man tells you to do something, you do it". Mr Stephens denied that he made such a remark. What Mr Hudgell

2.4 When operating companies were established within MGN in the circumstances described at paragraph 2.49, again their boards never met other than for a formal purpose.

2.5 Although RM effectively dominated the management of MGN[a] during the whole period of its private ownership and its board never met to run the company, there was a change in the way the management of the company was conducted between 1985 and 1988.

2.6 At first there had been a period of crisis management during which little was done to return MGN to profitability; RM was attracted by his personal involvement in the running of the newspapers and decisions were taken on an ad-hoc basis, generally at meetings between RM and 2 to 3 other people.

2.7 In October 1985, Mr Patrick Morrissey was appointed Senior Deputy Managing Director. His appointment coincided with the commencement of substantial reforms to labour practices and with the replanting of the printing business (described in paragraph 2.49). Mr Morrissey attempted to impose a management structure on MGN but did not mind that there were no board meetings as he considered RM to be a disruptive influence and found that better progress could be made without RM's presence at the meetings of the operational management because of the way RM behaved. Mr Morrissey also held meetings with the editorial staff each week. However despite this imposition of a management structure, RM continued to take important decisions himself convening meetings early in the mornings for this purpose and having so called "editorial lunches" each Tuesday, which the editors and the senior operational management were required to attend; he would often set management against the editorial staff at these lunches or pick on someone to bully. Indeed it was as a result of RM's bullying and humiliation of a colleague that one of MGN's directors, Sir Tom McCaffrey[b], resigned[c].

(b) SDR

2.8 Under the ownership of Reed, SDR had had its own board of directors (which reported generally to MGN in London), its own Chairman, Mr Webster, and its own Chief Executive, Mr Horwood. It also had one outside non-executive director, Sir Alwyn Williams[d]. The acquisition of MGN by RM had less impact on SDR than the impact on MGN in London.

---

described to us was precisely the way in which the company secretary of one of RM's companies had described his function to the Inspectors in 1971 as recorded at paragraph 256 of the 1971 Report; "To carry out Mr Maxwell's orders to the letter and to do nothing more".

a KM told us that RM always required reports and paper work to exercise control; he would always demand paper, but whether he actually read what he demanded was another matter.

b He was appointed by RM as director of public affairs in October 1984 and he resigned on 15 November 1985.

c We were told by IM he did not regard the manner in which RM treated the executive directors as being bullying. The meetings involved robust debate and a reasonable amount of give and take on all sides; RM was immensely inspirational and tough which was what was required to compete with Mr Rupert Murdoch's News Group Newspapers Limited.

d He had become a non-executive director prior to RM's take over; he had taken his duties seriously, reading books on the duties of non-executive directors and after RM's take over, reading the 1971/73 DTI Reports on PPL; he ceased to be a director in 1990 and was replaced by Sir Kenneth Alexander.

However the bank mandates were changed, Mr Horwood was relieved of his title of Chief Executive and made Managing Director and limits of authority on expenditure were imposed.

2.9 Although RM became a director of SDR on 17 September 1984 and Chairman on Mr Webster's retirement on 20 January 1986, the company continued to be managed by its board through regular monthly meetings, with agendas and papers being sent out beforehand and full minutes being taken. RM attended his first board meeting of SDR in Scotland in January 1986 and attended two further board meetings in Scotland that year. When Scottish Daily Record & Sunday Mail (1986) Limited became the operating company it was managed by its board in the same way that SDR had been managed; RM attended only one meeting a year and this took place in London. Those meetings which RM attended were modelled on the same lines as the monthly board meetings that took place in his absence, but discussion was substantially monopolised by RM and the operational directors did not question each other or discuss matters in the same way as they did when RM was not present.

(2) RM's control over the finances of MGN

2.10 Throughout the entire period of RM's control of MGN, there were two distinct departments that dealt with the finances of MGN, each with a separate location (see Plan 1).

- The finance department of MGN. This was located at Orbit House and was headed by Mr Lawrence Guest[a] who had been finance director of MGN since 1977. This department dealt with the operational activities of MGN.
- The central treasury. This was located at Maxwell House from 1987. When RM had acquired MCC it had had a treasury under the control of Mr Richard Baker[b], who in 1982 became finance director of MCC and one of RM's closest financial advisers. From 1984 the MCC treasury department became the treasury for all of RM's other companies. Thus when RM acquired MGN in 1984, the central treasury took on the role of a treasury department for MGN, dealing with all of MGN's relationships with banks and controlling the main non-newspaper assets of MGN, other than property.

2.11 This division of function meant that although the finance department of MGN collated together each day information on its bank balances and made cash transfers between SDR and MGN, its treasury function was limited to the issuing of low value cheques and obtaining RM's signature to high value cheques[c]. All other transfer of funds were carried out by the central treasury.

---

[a] He is a chartered accountant and worked in the publishing and newspaper industry from 1962. Mr Guest's office was in the Mirror Building.

[b] Mr Baker had been at the treasury of MCC since 1970; he was considered by many a very influential adviser of RM and an original thinker. He played a central role in many decisions until November 1990. The circumstances of his resignation are set out in the footnote to paragraph 9.10.

[c] The way in which RM exercised control over cheques is considered at paragraph 2.49.

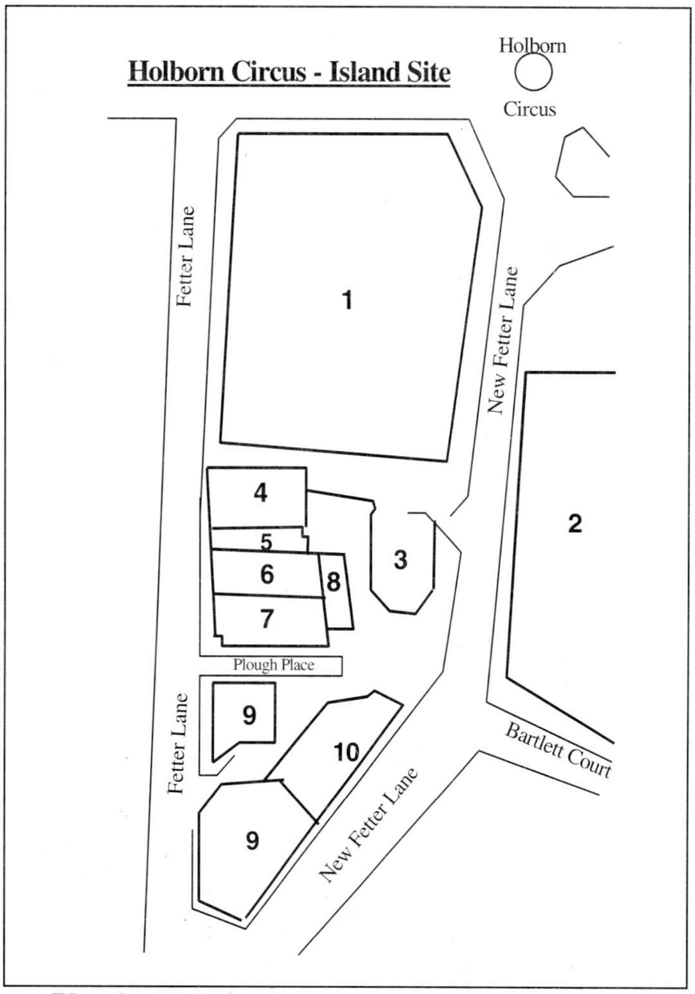

Key to Plan 1

1: Mirror Building, 33 Holborn Circus
2: Orbit House
3: Maxwell House (Strand House) including 8-10 New Fetter Lane
4: 54 Fetter Lane
5: 52-53 Fetter Lane
6: 50-51 Fetter Lane
7: Alliance House
8: 5 Plough Place
9: 43 Fetter Lane
10: 12-14 New Fetter Lane

Plan 1 – Holborn site

2.12 Consequently, it was the central treasury that controlled the major movements of cash from MGN's bank accounts to other companies owned or controlled by RM and to third parties. Not only did the central treasury report to RM, but RM himself played a significant role in its operations. He received daily cash reports and decided on the priorities for the use of that cash within all the companies he controlled. He initiated various substantial payments by direct instructions to the central treasury and in many such cases, particularly where the transfers were to or from companies under his ownership or control, no documentation would be provided to the MGN finance department to enable it to record properly the purpose for which the money had been expended or received. During the audits of MGN by Coopers & Lybrand Deloitte (CLD)[a], this information had to be obtained from the central treasury.

[a] The circumstances of their appointment are considered at paragraph 4.12; we refer to Coopers & Lybrand, Coopers & Lybrand Deloitte and their predecessor and successor firms as CLD.

2.13 Apart from this direct control over the central treasury, RM's financial power in all his companies (including MCC) was exemplified by the fact that he had sole signatory authority for an unlimited amount in respect of all the companies' bank accounts. He had had this in some of his companies in 1971 and it had been granted by the board of MCC[a], a listed company, in 1981 and introduced into MGN the day he took control as already explained at paragraph 1.21.

2.14 After one incident where funds were misappropriated from MGN by an employee in 1988, RM endeavoured to make sure that his staff and the auditors were vigilant to discover fraud; his concern was summarised in a paragraph by Mr Steere, the CLD audit partner at that time, in December 1990 in instructions to his audit staff:

> "The proprietor of Mirror Group plc is very sensitive to risk of loss through fraud. Once again we ask that audit staff be aware of the possibility of fraud and that any suspicious transactions are investigated by an appropriate level of [CLD] staff."

(3) RM's use of MGN in connection with his other interests: the intercompany debt

2.15 Following RM's acquisition of MGN in July 1984 it had, apart from its newspapers, a number of significant assets including approximately £37m in cash, a significant shareholding in Reuters Holdings plc (Reuters), and a long lease of the Mirror Building and interests in some other properties. In addition, MGN was a company with a strong cash flow.

2.16 From 1985 an intercompany account was used for the transfer of surplus cash and the non-newspaper assets from MGN to RM's other private companies; the intercompany account had two parts: a trading account and a "hard core account". In the case of almost every transfer of assets, no payment was made by the other private companies that received them, but the amount was charged to the hard core part of the intercompany account. It was never intended that this part of the intercompany account be repaid since it was regarded as a more efficient means of distributing assets and cash from MGN than by way of dividends.

2.17 To illustrate what happened, it is convenient to refer to the three main transfers:

- The £37m which MGN had in cash on RM's acquisition consisted of £23.3m from the intergroup debt that Reed had repaid to MGN[b], £11.4m from monies paid as a result of realisation of part of the investment in Reuters (which had occurred whilst MGN was owned by Reed) and other surplus cash. On 11 September 1984 in order to transfer this cash into PPL and to repay to National Westminster its loan to PPL referred to in paragraph 1.20, 20 million shares in MCC were transferred from PPL for £37.6m. The purchase of these shares was made by MGN's subsidiary, MGH Properties Limited. These MCC shares were subsequently sold on 29 December 1987

---

[a] They had been surprised at the request, but had agreed.

[b] This was a term of the purchase agreement - see paragraph 1.20.

to another of RM's private companies, Pergamon Group plc (PG) for £48m; this amount was not paid but charged to the intercompany account. The ownership of MGH Properties Limited was subsequently transferred to what became one of RM's main private side companies, Mirror Group plc (subsequently renamed Robert Maxwell Group plc (RMG)[a]) and the amount due to MGN remained outstanding.

- On 31 October 1985 the long lease of the Mirror Building was transferred to PPL for £10.9m (its net book value)[b]. This sum was never paid but charged to the intercompany account.

- The shareholding in Reuters comprised "A" and "B" shares. The Reuters B shares were, subject to an orderly marketing agreement[c], freely transferable. Between December 1985 and June 1986 the Reuters B shares were sold for a total consideration of £54m[d], and from the proceeds cash transfers were made to Pergamon Holdings Limited (PHL)[e].

2.18 MGN's cash flow was used to fund ventures such as the publication of the *London Daily News*[f] and the launch of *Mirror Colour Magazines* as well as satellite TV, software and other media interests. It was also used by RM for other deals and to acquire other investments in the stock market.

---

a It is convenient to refer to this company throughout as RMG.

b Although MGN continued to occupy it under an informal arrangement, it was leased by PPL to MCC in 1987 in connection with the financing referred to at paragraph 2.34. The informal arrangement continued with MGN's rent for its occupation being determined on a market basis.

c The majority of the sales were made in breach of the orderly marketing agreement and the sale in June 1986 was made during the closed period when RM should not have sold as he was a director of Reuters. When this sale was investigated by Reuters, despite the fact that RM attempted to blame Mr Baker, he was censured by the board of Reuters. However no further action was taken, though the apology RM made was reported in the press.

d The "B" shares were received by MGN and SDR at the time of the reorganisation and flotation of Reuters in 1984. They were not ascribed any value in the books of those companies. The interests of MGN and SDR in The Newspaper Publishers Association Limited and The Press Association, through which they were entitled to the "B" shares were held at a book value in MGN of £8,888 and at a book value in SDR of £1.

e The reasons for this company's formation are described at paragraph 3.7. This company was renamed in 1991 Headington Holdings Limited.

f Approximately £29.6m was used to fund the *London Daily News*.

2.19 The following table represents the major uses made of the assets and cash flow in the period to 1988, together with interest charged:

	Amounts transferred (£m)			Discharged by dividends (£m)[a]	Total left outstanding on the intercompany account (£m)	
	Assets	Cash	Interest		Per year	Cumulative[b]
1984	0	35[c]	0	0	35	35
1985	11[d]	26	6	(11)	32	67
1986	11[e]	78	6	(15)	80	147
1987	(2)[f]	26	18	(9)	33	180
1988	15[g]	1	23	(16)	23	203
Total	35	166	53	(51)	203	

Table 1 – Use of assets and cash flows 1984 to 1988

(4) RM's control over the pension funds

2.20 Until the contemplated flotation of MGN by Reed, the pension arrangements of MGN employees were within the Reed Publishing Pension Scheme. As part of the preparations for that flotation, a separate pension scheme, Mirror Group Pension Scheme (MGPS), was created for employees of MGN with a trustee company, Mirror Group Pension Trustees Limited (MGPT).

2.21 After the acquisition of MGN by PPL, RM attended a board meeting of the trustee company on 1 August 1984 and said he ought to be Chairman; he was therefore appointed a director and Chairman of MGPT. His attitude to the pension scheme is exemplified by an incident that we were told took place shortly after, when RM attended a meeting with the unions at which the question of pensions was discussed. He referred to the pension scheme as "his" fund and when a protest was made he asked Mr Hudgell to explain who owned the pension trustee company.

[a] In addition to the dividends which were paid by crediting them to the intercompany account with RM's private company that owned the shares in MGN, a dividend of £18m was paid in cash in 1986.

[b] The actual cumulative figures stated above are different from the notional dividends shown in the prospectus as described at paragraph 15.29.

[c] This is the net amount after a receipt of £2.875m from PPL.

[d] This represents the transfer of the Mirror Building.

[e] This represents part of the consideration for the sale of Reuters A shares to Funvale - see paragraph 2.39.

[f] This was achieved through the use of group tax relief.

[g] This represents the sale of the *Sporting Life* titles to Ivenham Limited (formerly Odhams Newspapers Limited).

When Mr Hudgell[a] explained that the pension trustee company was owned ultimately by PPL as the parent company of MGN, RM said "Exactly. So I own the pension scheme".

2.22 The board of MGPT was a board which generally stood up to RM; minutes were taken and circulated (even though often quite late). However, after an actuarial review made in September 1985[b] showed that the scheme had a substantial surplus, RM persuaded the trustees[c] in December 1985 to agree that enhanced benefits on pensions be part of the package enabling the survival plan for MGN (described at paragraph 2.49) to be put through. The trustees were independently advised by leading counsel that they had the power to do this and that it was proper to exercise that power in the way contemplated. RM also persuaded the trustees in July 1986 that MGPS should bear its administration expenses[d], which had previously been borne by MGN[e].

2.23 The administration of MGPS was carried out in conjunction with the administration of the schemes of other companies controlled by RM. Much of the work was concerned with the calculation and payment of benefits. Mr Cook, a qualified pensions administrator, was in charge of the administration[f]; he had no accounting or investment training and was not responsible for investment decisions in his capacity as an administrator.

2.24 What is significant, even from this period, is the way the investments of the pension scheme were made and how little was disclosed about this in the accounts.

2.25 It is important to recall that at the time "self-investment" was a normal part of a pension fund's investment. In 1985, there were no regulations imposing any limit on self-investment; these only came into effect in 1992. However the trustees of pension funds were under fiduciary duties and since November 1986 had a duty to disclose in pension fund accounts self-investment exceeding 5 per cent. of the total value of the net assets (see paragraph 2.40). KM told us that RM believed that the company had the obligation to support the pension fund but, equally, that the pension fund was an asset of the company. Investment in related companies,

---

a He was replaced as Secretary of MGPT by Mr Stephens in September 1985.

b Bacon & Woodrow, the consulting actuaries to MGPS, advised in September 1985 after an interim review that there was a substantial surplus; they confirmed this in their valuation on 28 April 1986.

c We refer throughout to the directors of MGPT and the other trustee companies as trustees of the pension schemes as this was their principal function.

d RM took the view that the surplus in the scheme should be used to benefit MGN and negotiated this as part of a package of other changes.

e The Report of the Pension Law Review Committee chaired by Professor Sir Roy Goode QC (Cm 2342-1 September 1993) recorded at Paragraph 3.1.33 that "most employers take on responsibility for the costs of administering their scheme".

f He first became employed by a company controlled by RM in January 1984; he was initially employed by MCC; between 1987 and April 1991 he was employed by PHL. In April 1991 he became an employee of MGN.

loans by the pension fund to the company and purchasing buildings occupied by the company were part of the connection which RM believed to exist; the pension fund was a strategic asset of the company and was critical to the view that RM would take of the value of any business. KM considered RM's approach to be normal for the time; what was different was the scale on which RM caused the pension funds to make related party investments.

2.26 By the spring of 1985[a] external fund managers, including Phillips & Drew Fund Management Limited (Phillips & Drew), Capel Cure Myers Capital Management Limited (CCM) and Montagu Investment Management Limited (MIM), had been appointed to manage most of MGPS's assets. It is necessary to explain a little about MIM, whose Chairman was Lord Stevens of Ludgate and which was at that time owned by Aetna Life & Casualty Company (Aetna).

2.27 In June 1984, PPL had acquired a 10.5 per cent. stake in Fleet Holdings plc (Fleet) from the Bell Group. This led to the first business meeting between RM and Lord Stevens, who was also chairman of United Newspapers plc (United Newspapers). In January 1985 RM sold PPL's stake in Fleet to United Newspapers. In September 1985 PPL bought another stake in Fleet[b] and in October 1985, United Newspapers were successful in their bid for Fleet. RM and Lord Stevens subsequently became interested in Extel Group plc (Extel) and Britannia Arrow Holdings plc (Britannia Arrow) which had been previously known as Slater, Walker Securities Limited. It is necessary to deal with Britannia Arrow now and more convenient to consider Extel later (see paragraphs 3.12 and 3.14). At the end of 1985 RM acquired a substantial stake in Britannia Arrow. Funds managed by MIM had also acquired a stake in Britannia Arrow. On 27 March 1986, Britannia Arrow announced its agreement to acquire MIM from Aetna. RM's private companies increased their stake to 48.4 million shares or 20.7 per cent. by April 1988. Britannia Arrow subsequently purchased Invesco Capital Management Inc. and changed its name to Invesco MIM plc (Invesco MIM) on 31 January 1990.

2.28 Within the investments that were managed by MIM for MGPS, there developed from 1986 what became known as the "special portfolio"; this was a series of holdings that was not traded, in companies such as MCC and United Newspapers connected with RM and Lord Stevens[c]. Lord Stevens told us that he did not recall a "special portfolio" but there were stocks such as Britannia Arrow and United Newspapers which were maintained on a separate list because MIM needed to identify these either as MIM had a director on the board or as there might be disclosure issues; the stocks had nothing to do with RM and were traded, but only after a check had been made with the company concerned. KM told us that RM hoped that by acting in these ways in relation to the transactions described in the preceding paragraphs he would be able to obtain institutional support for his own take over bids.

---

a The transfer of assets from the Reed Publishing Pension Scheme to MGPS did not take place until 21 May 1985.

b Lord Stevens told us he did not know that PPL had bought a stake in Fleet.

c Lord Stevens fell out with RM when he would not agree to having Express Newspapers printed by RM's companies on MGN's new plant (see paragraphs 2.49 and 4.26).

2.29 At first all the assets of MGPS (except for property and cash) were managed by these external fund managers, and overseen by an investment committee consisting of RM, Mr Guest, Mr Cook, Mr Bareau[a] and Mr Chapman[b]. However, from 1986 some assets began to be managed directly with investment decisions being made by RM[c].

2.30 It is in respect of the directly managed assets, including property and cash, that there were five significant matters.

(a) MCC shares

2.31 During 1985, MGPS acquired shares in MCC through the portfolio managed by MIM and by 5 April 1986 (the end of the accounting period for MGPS) MIM held 890,000 MCC shares; at the same date, the other external managers held 425,000 MCC shares between them. MGPS also started to build up a substantial stake in MCC as part of the assets managed directly. The first purchases were in December 1986, and at 5 April 1987, the holding was 800,000 shares; by 5 April 1988, this number had increased to 3.9 million shares[d]. Investment in MCC shares continued throughout the period of RM's control of MGPS[e].

(b) Maxwell House

2.32 The property assets passed by the Reed Publishing Pension Scheme to MGPS were managed by a property department under the direction of Mr Shaw[f]. In February 1986 MGPS[g] bought Strand House from the WH Smith Group for £17m and costs of £155,557, with funds realised through sales of other property; at the same time it was agreed to grant a 35 year lease to PPL together with an option to buy the property at market value at any time during the currency of the lease for as long as the lease was vested in PPL. As shown on Plan 1 at paragraph 2.10, Strand House was adjacent to the Mirror Building in Holborn and had been suggested to RM as an investment opportunity as it would form a key part of an "island" site for redevelopment in central London. RM told the investment committee of MGPS[h] that his companies would

---

a Mr Bareau was an economist who was a consultant to MGN and to certain fund managers.

b Mr Chapman had been a printers' reader and a union representative who stood up strongly against RM. In 1987 when he was made redundant, he was appointed General Manager of Pensions of PHL, but his function was essentially liaison with employees and pensioners; he had no financial background.

c His decisions generally had successful results and he gained much "kudos" for having made a recommendation prior to the October 1987 stock market "crash" that the managers liquidate part of their holdings.

d The value of the combined holding was £3.37m on 5 April 1986 (at a price of 256p per share) and on 5 April 1988 was £9.28m (at a price per share of 238p per share).

e KM told us that he had grown up with the concept that self investment was not only legally permitted but also a commercial reality due to the close link between the pension fund and the company.

f This department grew out of the property holdings that were owned by MCC; Mr Shaw was a chartered surveyor who had been a property consultant to MCC. Initially he reported to Lord Silkin of Dulwich QC, (see footnote to paragraph 3.13) but later to RM and KM; the department managed the property interests of companies controlled by RM.

g We were told that the purchase was agreed between RM and the Chairman of WH Smith Group.

h See paragraph 2.29.

take up occupation of part of the building and that he could interest Goldman Sachs[a] in the remainder; the investment committee agreed to its acquisition. At that time, RM had no firm commitment from Goldman Sachs but on 5 August 1986 an agreement was made between PHL and Goldman Sachs that they would take a 5 year lease and they occupied the building at about the same time[b].

2.33 After this agreement with Goldman Sachs, Strand House was sold in November 1986 by MGPS to Pergamon Holdings Limited (PHL) for a gross price of £18 m, or a net price of about £17.8m and thereafter renamed Maxwell House[c]. This price was the result of a financial calculation and no independent valuation was obtained, although Mr Shaw gave an informal confirmation of the price. Thereafter, Maxwell House was occupied partly by Goldman Sachs and partly by PHL, and the Mirror Building was sub-leased to MCC by PHL (to whom the long lease had been transferred from MGN as set out in paragraph 2.17).

2.34 On 25 June 1987, a £105m loan was obtained from a syndicate arranged by Goldman Sachs, in which seven other banks participated, secured on the Mirror Building, Maxwell House and other properties including State House, Kingsway, London. Lloyds Bank plc (Lloyds) were appointed as agents to the facility. For the purpose of this loan, Maxwell House (which had been sold by MGPS for £18m in November 1986) was valued by Savills in May 1987 at £36m (and in 1988 valued at £48.5m)[d].

2.35 Although MGPS made a small profit on this transaction, it did not obtain the large profit that should have been obtained; it is an inescapable inference that the pension fund was used to purchase the building for the ultimate benefit of RM's private companies which (we were told) did not have the resources available to pay for it in February 1986. The fact of the purchase and sale was disclosed in the MGPS accounts for the year ended 5 April 1986, but not the option granted on purchase to PPL nor the fact that it was sold to one of RM's private companies[e].

(c) Beecham shares

2.36 It was not until September 1986 that MGPS made its first significant direct equity investment. The circumstances in which this investment was made are significant because this type of transaction occurred many times thereafter.

---

a References in this Report to Goldman Sachs include all entities within the Goldman Sachs group save where otherwise stated.

b An arrangement was also made that PHL would sub-lease two floors from Goldman Sachs.

c A manuscript note records that the price was agreed by RM on 26 October 1986 in the presence of Mr Cook.

d The valuation was based in part on a 25 year lease of Maxwell House from PHL to MCC made in 1987 under which MCC was paying £3m a year in rent and in part on the sublease to Goldman Sachs.

e Questions about this transaction were raised by the Association of Mirror Pensioners in 1991, but RM would not allow the figures to be released to them.

2.37 On the acquisition of the Philip Hill Investment Trust plc by MCC (see paragraph 3.10), one of its substantial holdings that RM was reluctant to dispose of was a holding in Beecham Group plc (Beecham). Mr Baker told us he told RM it was not appropriate for MCC to carry this investment[a] and it was therefore decided that the pension funds of companies controlled by RM should acquire the holding of 12.46 million shares for £49.8m; MGPS, with the approval by the investment committee[b], acquired 7.92 million shares for £32.9m[c]. It was from the acquisition of this shareholding that there developed a portfolio of equity holdings which were selected by RM and held as directly managed investments of MGPS and not managed by the external fund managers; many of these directly managed assets, as can subsequently be seen, were acquired from companies owned or controlled by RM[d].

(d) Reuters A shares

2.38 A similar transaction involved MGN's holding of Reuters A shares. In view of its significance a more detailed account is set out in Appendix 6, but the following paragraphs contain a summary.

2.39 Unlike the Reuters B shares referred to in paragraph 2.17, Reuters A shares were not freely transferable. However, at the end of 1986 RM's private companies (of which MGN was one) needed cash, and it was considered that a sale of the Reuters A shares would satisfy this requirement. Both because of the restriction on transferability and because RM considered these were a good long term investment, he decided to transfer the shareholding to MGPS, but as title to the shares could not be transferred to MGPS a form of linked bond was devised: the shares were sold to a subsidiary of the pension trustee company, Funvale Limited (Funvale), for £33.5m[e] and Funvale received that sum from MGPS in return for a bond that was linked

---

a Lord Keith of Castleacre, then Chairman of Philip Hill Investment Trust plc and Chairman of Beecham, was concerned to see that this holding (and a large holding in another company) be placed in acceptable hands.

b See paragraph 2.29.

c After the purchase by the pension schemes, the following took place:

- The price on the sale to MGPS was 400p per share. No payment was made for the shares; in October 1986 MGPS acquired and paid for £10.2m of Austrian Bonds which it then transferred to MCC; this left a balance of £22m which was charged by MGPS to an intercompany account with MCC.
- On 15 December 1986, the entire holding was sold back to MCC at a price of 416p per share. This transaction was not settled in cash, but offset against the sum owing from the September purchase by MGPS and a debt due to PHL connected with the transfer to the pension funds of an interest in Reuters A shares - see paragraph 2.39.
- On 2 March 1987, MCC sold 2.368 million Beecham shares to MGPS for £13.5m (570p per share). This was settled by a cash payment to MCC.
- On 18 March 1987, MCC sold 1.828 million Beecham shares to MGPS for £9.99m (547p per share). This was settled by cash payments to MCC.

We have been unable to obtain a rational explanation for these further sales and purchases.

d There was a considerable advantage to RM in transferring profitable long term investments from MGN or his other private companies to MGPS, as he obtained immediately the cash he needed in MGN or for his other private companies, but was able to retain an asset for the benefit of MGN (and himself) in that if the value of the pension scheme appreciated, this could reduce the likelihood of MGN having to make contributions to MGPS.

e The price was calculated by using the market price of the B shares on 16 December 1986.

to the value of the Reuters B shares[a]. Mr Morgenstern of Nicholson Graham & Jones[b] devised this scheme. It was disclosed in the accounts of MGPS for the year ended 5 April 1987 as "Guaranteed Linked Bond - linked to Reuters shares".

2.40 After the coming into force of regulations[c] made under Section 56A of the Social Security Pensions Act 1975, added by the Social Security Act 1986, CLD (who were also the auditors to MGPS) became concerned in July 1988 as to whether this linked bond[d] should be disclosed in the MGPS accounts as "self-investment". Furthermore, in the autumn of 1988, discussions took place (of which RM was personally aware as a director of Reuters) concerning the plan to convert the A shares to B shares in the Spring of 1989; this was anticipated to be beneficial to the holders of A Shares. In these circumstances a decision was made by RM in March 1989 that the linked bond arrangement would be unscrambled. An agreement was made, signed by Mr Guest on behalf of MGN and by Mr Stephens on behalf of Funvale, under which the Reuters A shares were sold back to MGN for £27.6m. The price was fixed by reference to the market price of the Reuters B shares 21 days prior to the date that the agreement bears (30 December 1988) by an arrangement mirroring a provision of the linked bond. On that date (9 December 1988) the mid-market price of the Reuters B shares was 471p; by 30 December 1988 it had risen to 517p and continued to rise thereafter in January, February and March 1989 to a high point of 741p on 6 March 1989.

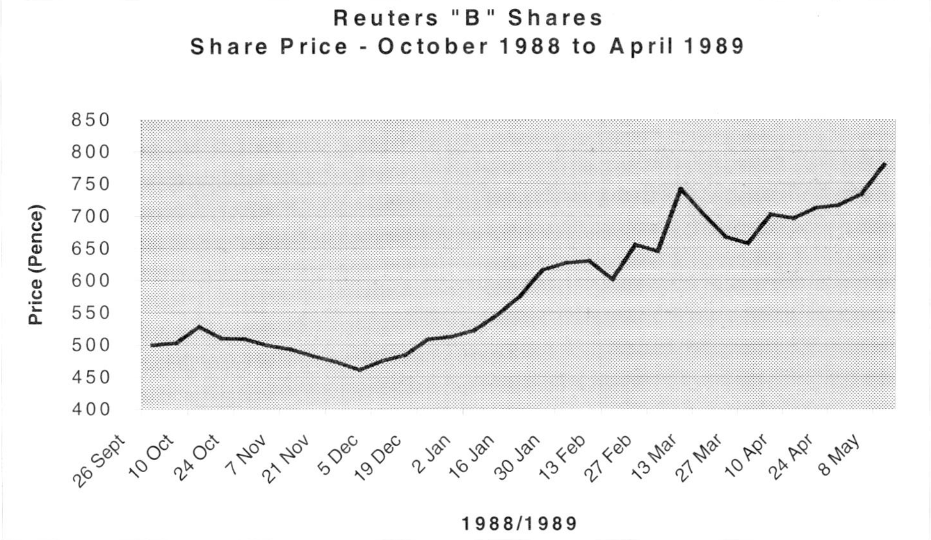

Graph 1

---

a Instructions were given to the external managers in mid December 1986 to sell equities to raise funds: MIM, CCM and Phillips & Drew each remitted approximately £10m to MGPS prior to 31 December 1986.

b They had been solicitors to MGN for many years and were appointed solicitors to the trustees of MGPS in April 1985. They also acted as solicitors to RM's private companies in other transactions and on some of the reorganisations of the ownership and structure of the companies.

c Occupational Pension Schemes (Disclosure of Information) Regulations 1986 (Disclosure Regulations), Schedule 3 paragraph 6. The regulations required the disclosure of all self-investment by a pension fund of more than 5 per cent of the total value of its net assets. They came into force on 1 November 1986 and applied to all accounts for all scheme years commencing on or after 1 November 1986.

d It had continued to be needed as permission was sought to transfer the shares in 1987, but refused.

2.41 The unscrambling of the transaction was effected in order to avoid disclosure of the transactions described above to the pensioners in the accounts of MGPS and in order to ensure that any benefit accrued to RM's private companies rather than MGPS; it resulted in a loss to MGPS of £5.9m over the initial investment and the lost opportunity of benefitting from any increase in the share price.

2.42 RM agreed in a letter dated 16 March 1989 that when the Reuters A shares were disposed of by MGN, MGN would remit to MGPS 50 per cent. of any profit made on the resale up to a value of £6m. On 31 March 1989 Reuters issued a circular announcing the conversion of the A shares into B shares, thereby making them freely transferable; the circular pointed out that this would benefit the A shareholders. The A shares, subsequently converted by Reuters into B shares, were (i) transferred by MGN to two of RM's other private companies, RMG and Mirror Group (Holdings) Limited in 1989, at book value and (ii) then transferred on 2 April 1990 to Pergamon Group Services Limited (PGS), another private company, and (iii) subsequently sold on the open market in May 1990 through Goldman Sachs for £60.4m. This last sale produced a profit of £32.8m. Despite the undertaking given by RM on behalf of MGN, no sum was paid to MGPS. No mention of the undertaking or the subsequent sales was made in any report or accounts of MGPS.

2.43 This is a significant transaction because:

- The unscrambling did not take place on 30 December 1988[a] and the documentation was backdated; this backdating enabled the price to be fixed by reference to the market price in December 1988[b] which was substantially below the market price at the actual date of the transaction which we are satisfied took place between 9 and 16 March 1989; that price of £27.6m (together with interest) was paid by MGN to Funvale on 13 March 1989. On that same day
  - Funvale paid the amount (£28.3m) to the pension funds.
  - £30m was transferred from the pension funds to PHL as explained at paragraph 5.25.
  - PHL paid £24m to MGN and £29m to MCC, having also received £14m from MCC.
- Apart from RM, Mr Guest and Mr Stephens, the trustees of MGPS were unaware of what had happened, other than the linked bond investment had been sold. The accounts of MGPS for the year ended 5 April 1988 did not disclose the circumstances in which the linked bond had been unscrambled, but merely stated:

  > "Since the year end the Guaranteed Bond linked to Reuters Shares has been repaid".

  Nothing was said in the accounts of MGPS for the year ended 5 April 1989 during which the unscrambling took place.
- What was done was for the benefit of the private companies and to the detriment of MGPS.

---

[a] The transaction was treated in the accounts of MGN as having occurred in December 1988.

[b] The linked bond provided for this to be fixed as described at paragraph 2.40.

2.44 KM told us that none of the professional advisers who worked on the Beecham and Reuters A shares transactions advised that the pension funds ought not to be used in such a way; rather, they worked to find a route by which the commercial objective (the generation of profit or cash) could be achieved[a].

(e) Use of cash and CLD's view on this during the 1988 audit.

2.45 Apart from these four significant transactions involving RM's companies, MGPS began from 1985 to lend pension scheme monies on an unsecured basis to MGN and other companies[b]. This type of transaction, which became of great significance later, began in 1985 with a short term loan of £20.7m by MGPS through MGN to PPL and MCC to assist in the purchase by MCC of the scientific journals business (described in paragraph 3.6). The document containing a summary of the main points arising on the audit for MGN for the year ended 31 December 1985 for the attention of the partner (CLD called these documents MAPs) stated:

> "**Pension Fund Loan of £20.706m**
> This loan was made from the MGN pension trustees and transferred via intercompany loan accounts to PPL (£12m) and [MCC] (£8.706m) in order to fund the purchase of PPL journals business by [MCC]. The loan has subsequently been repaid with interest of £7,000."

Mr Walsh[c], the audit partner, marked this "Noted".

2.46 However during 1986 and 1987 funds[d] were lent on a fairly regular basis by MGPS without any form of security being provided to MGPS for the loan of these trust monies. At each year end of MGPS, the balance was reduced to nil. CLD's knowledge of this at that time was as follows:

- The MAPs for the audit of MGN for the year ended 28 December 1986 stated:

> "It came to our attention on 25/6/87 that there had been a circular transaction to remove MGN's liability to the pension scheme just before the year end (and hence in the accounts) by replacing it with a liability to PHL; the amount involved was £5.5m. Subsequent to the balance sheet date the process was reversed (29/12/86). The effect in MGN's accounts was to decrease the balance owed by PHL on the intercompany accounts (part of debtors) and decrease the amount owed to other creditors - we understand from Robert Bunn that the reasoning is "political" (i.e. not to show borrowing from the pension scheme) even though the identity of the creditor does not need to be shown and the

---

a KM told us that RM's approach to advisers was "You are part of my problem, you are part of my solution". The approach was to solve problems, not to stand back and consider whether what was being done was correct.

b There was also an arrangement under which funds on deposit at the bank for the pension scheme were notionally aggregated with funds borrowed by other companies controlled by RM from the bank and interest was paid to the bank solely on the net balance. The monies saved by these companies through this arrangement were then paid over to MGPS. This was of benefit to MGPS as it received interest at the rate those companies paid to borrow and there was no mixing of the funds of the pension scheme with the funds of those companies in the bank accounts. This continued until August 1991.

c Mr Walsh had been a partner in CLD since 1970 and was the senior audit partner for RM's private companies after the retirement of Mr Corsan in 1986 (see paragraph 4.14).

d For example between 24 September 1986 and 29 October 1986 and between 22 December 1986 and 8 January 1987 over £20m was lent by MGPS to MGN; over the entire period 24 September 1986 to 5 February 1987, the amount lent remained in excess of £10m.

> pension fund receive a proper rate of interest. At our request the substance over form has prevailed and the transactions have not been recognised in the accounts (or indeed in group accounts)."

Mr Walsh marked this "good". He told us that this referred to the transaction not being recognised in the accounts.

- The MAPs for the audit of MGN for the year ended 27 December 1987 stated with respect to interest of £992,000:

  > " MGN "borrows" money from the pension scheme and pays out interest based on the market rates - prescribed by Pergamon. This has been a long standing arrangement."

  Mr Steere, the audit partner for MGN that year, marked this:

  > "This has been agreed".

  Mr Steere told us that he understood that there was an agreement between MGPS and MGN to borrow money on an arms-length basis and pay arms-length rates of interest.

- Although a small number of documents on the audit files for MGPS for the years ended 5 April 1986 and 5 April 1987 (the accounting year ends for MGPS) contain references to money being on deposit with MGN, it is uncertain whether the audit team for MGPS were aware that money was being lent to MGN; the audit partner for the years ended 5 April 1986 and 5 April 1987, Mr Glyn Thomas, told us he was not aware of money being lent.

2.47 During the MGPS financial year ended 5 April 1988 loans had at times exceeded £19m which represented the 5 per cent. limit for disclosure of "self-investment" (based on the net assets at the year end)[a]. During the audit of MGPS, for the year ended 5 April 1988, CLD considered whether they should require disclosure of these unsecured loans to be made in the MGPS accounts. This was resisted by Mr Bunn[b], at the instigation of RM; CLD accepted that, provided that at the year end there were no amounts outstanding, any loans during the course of the year did not have to be disclosed[c]. Although the pension scheme funds continued to be

---

[a] During the year the cash book had not been kept up-to-date and after the year end it was discovered that cash transactions in excess of £162m had not been recorded in the cash book. Entries were made in March 1989 to correct this.

[b] Mr Bunn was a finance director for the private side with responsibilities also at MCC.

[c] In April 1989 a draft management letter was prepared by CLD to be addressed to the directors of MGPT listing the weaknesses in controls and procedures discovered by them in the course of the audit of the MGPS accounts for the year ended 5 April 1988. The schedule to the letter drew attention to the loans under the following heading:

lent to the private companies on an unsecured basis throughout the period to 5 April 1990 and thereafter to November 1991, this fact was never disclosed in any of the pension scheme accounts[a], because we were told by CLD the loans were reduced to nil at the end of each year of the pension scheme accounts; nothing was said to the trustees of MGPS (other than RM) about the loans[b]. The use of pension fund assets for loans was thus concealed by "window dressing" the accounts. The independent members of the trustees of MGPS who were not told of these arrangements by the managers never learnt of them from the accounts.

2.48 RM always paid close attention to accounting dates in relation to the presentation of information, the notes to the financial statements and issues of disclosure, as Mr Bunn and CLD knew. KM told us that RM did that, in relation to the loans of cash to his private companies, not because he thought there was anything wrong in the loans but to avoid journalists writing about it, to avoid stirring the pension members' group into more action and to diminish self investment at the balance sheet date. He also stated that RM would avoid disclosure if he could, as it was a concept completely alien to him. That was part of his wish to present the best possible image at all times and never to show weakness about anything or any hint of a problem. RM's approach was to exploit the ability to present balance sheets in

---

Self-Investment

> "The SORP describes self investment as an investment in the business of the scheme employer and any connected companies and persons. At the year end if there is any self investment in excess of 5 per cent. of the value of the net assets of the scheme, then this should be disclosed in a note to the accounts. During our audit we noted that overnight deposits had been made with [MGN]; at times these exceeded £19m which represents 5 per cent. of the year end net assets."

Their draft recommendation read:

> "Whilst no disclosure is necessary for the 1988 accounts since the deposits were repaid before the year end, we recommend that the amounts of self investment are carefully monitored to ensure that there are no arrangements in place at the year end which would require disclosure. In addition the situation should be reviewed to consider whether the lack of disclosure is against the spirit of the SORP."

A manuscript note by Mr Cowling, the audit partner, against this passage reads "Reconsider" and against the first line . "Not sure whether on reflection want to say this" and against the last sentence "words". This letter was never sent.

Mr Cowling had joined CLD in 1977, qualifying as a chartered accountant in 1980. He was made a partner in the firm in October 1988 and became the audit partner for the Common Investment Fund, London & Bishopsgate International Investment Management plc, London & Bishopsgate Holdings plc and First Tokyo Index Trust plc as well as for MGPS and Maxwell Communication Works Pension Scheme.

The reference to the SORP is a reference to "Statement of Recommended Practice No 1 - Pension Scheme Accounts" issued by the Accounting Standards Committee in May 1986.

a The Disclosure Regulations were the Occupational Pension Schemes (Disclosure of Information) Regulations 1986 and required the accounts to "show a true and fair view of the financial transactions of the scheme during the scheme year and of the disposition, at the end of the scheme year, of the assets... and liabilities...." CLD first told us that they considered that a "financial transaction" means an item that alters the amount of the fund. They later submitted an opinion of leading counsel to the effect that the regulations only required a summary of the results of the transactions that had taken place during the year be shown. The opinion expressly mentioned the fact that it did not deal with the circumstances where self-investment in excess of 5 per cent. existed for a substantial part of the year, was eliminated before the year end and resumed shortly after the year end.

b Mr Guest told us he was unaware of these loans.

the best possible light; he would describe it as "managing his balance sheet" whereas others called it "window dressing".

(5) Steps taken to return MGN to profitability

2.49 A major transformation in the profitability of MGN was achieved in the period 1985 to 1988. There were three principal areas where changes were effected:

- The first (where RM made a substantial contribution himself) was the reduction in the labour force and the ending of the so called "Spanish customs"[a]. In late 1985 RM announced a survival plan which entailed cutting each department by a third (except Editorial[b]), and reducing the overall workforce by some 2,000 persons and transferring the printing and production workers to British Newspaper Printing Corporation plc (BNPC), a subsidiary of MCC which would print the newspapers owned by MGN[c]. Those that remained employed by MGN and SDR respectively were transferred to the employment of new operating companies, the most important of which were MGN (1986) Ltd and SDR (1986) Ltd[d].
- The second main respect in which RM achieved reform was the rigorous control of cost. He required all capital expenditure and most significant revenue expenditure to be authorised by him and he took it upon himself to sign most high value cheques; initially he signed all cheques over £7,500 but that level was gradually increased so that by 1991 he signed all cheques over £100,000.
- The third aspect was the replanting and the introduction of modern technology.
- The most important of these changes was the introduction of presses that could print colour; RM obtained the best quality presses and refused to allow any newspaper to be circulated in colour until the system was fully operational and of a quality acceptable to the editorial staff. The plant and premises were designed with capacity to print newspapers owned by companies other than MGN as RM hoped to obtain contracts for this. This replanting[e] was carried out by BNPC with the new plants coming on stream at new newspaper printing centres at:
    - Watford — the replanting began in 1986 and the new presses were installed by March 1988.

---

a These were restrictive practices. Examples of these were every employee was entitled to (and often took) 13 weeks' sick leave per year; employees claimed expenses on an almost fixed basis since amounts up to £150 per week would not be questioned; the despatch department had a staff of 48 but, during a 6 hour shift, only 24 would work at any one time.

b There were redundancies, but these were not as severe as in other departments.

c We were told that the principal reasons for this were to take advantage of the new Industrial Relations legislation and to use MCC to raise the necessary finance; it was also suggested that RM's motive was to boost MCC's profits.

d In the period between 1985 and 1990 the staff employed in both the publishing and printing divisions of MGN and SDR was reduced from 6,954 to 3,690.

e RM hoped to obtain contract printing for other newspapers and had planned a site at Birmingham; when these contracts did not materialise, the plans for a site at Birmingham were abandoned and Stamford Street was added as a site; this was needed because a number of different editions were printed.

- Stamford Street, London — the new presses were installed by the summer of 1988.
- Oldham — replanting was completed by December 1988.

Printing at the Mirror Building ceased in the summer of 1988 and at Withy Grove (the old printing facility for the north of England) in early 1989 as the new presses came into production.

2.50 MGN became a newspaper publishing company as the printing was (in consequence of the changes described) contracted out to BNPC, a wholly-owned subsidiary of the listed company, MCC. The new presses acquired by MCC's subsidiary, BNPC, were financed through leasing arrangements and the building works to house the presses were financed by an intercompany loan from MCC to BNPC. The price paid by MGN to MCC under the arrangement for the printing was calculated at MCC's cost of production plus a fee of £10m - £12m, even though MGN organised and financed the supply of the newsprint and provided some management. In 1988 this basis of charging was altered to a cost per copy basis with the price being fixed by RM to produce a return to MCC of 15 per cent. (before interest charges) on the capital employed at BNPC.

2.51 Two other important technological changes were the introduction of direct inputting equipment (enabling the editorial staff to create pages for printing in the Editorial Department and directly transmit them to the printing presses) and the introduction of inserting plant which enabled the paper to be expanded by the insertion of pre-printed pages and supplements.

2.52 Less needed to be done at SDR (which always made a profit during RM's ownership) as new plant had been introduced at Anderston Quay[a] in 1971 but RM did ensure that the labour force was reduced by 25 per cent. and did see to the removal of the "Spanish customs".

2.53 The effect of these changes was to improve greatly the profitability of MGN.

---

[a] See plan 3 in paragraph 6.73.

3. 1984 - 1988: THE EXPANSION AND OWNERSHIP OF RM'S OTHER COMPANIES

3.1 Although MGN was a separate company with a separate business, decisions made in respect of MGN and its pension schemes were significantly influenced by RM's actions in and the fortunes of the other companies controlled by RM[a].

3.2 The period from 1984 to 1988 (which we have just described so far as it relates to MGN) also saw the rapid expansion of RM's businesses through the other companies controlled by him, particularly MCC. As can be seen most easily from the chronology at Appendix 5, this was done at a frenetic pace. This chapter describes briefly that expansion and the changes made to the ownership structure to facilitate it.

3.3 It was during this period that KM[b] became an important member of the management of RM's businesses, but, he told us, always under his father's control. KM told us that his father remained throughout in control of everything from the highest level down to the minutiae and he liked the exercise of power. He wanted to know what was going on throughout his companies. RM could be described as "a control freak". RM also considered it vital to control information as this added to his power; illustrations of this were his "need to know" approach[c] and the collection of papers after board meetings. He never allowed his sons to work together. KM told us that when he and IM visited RM in August 1991 in Sardinia (as set out in paragraph 21.19), RM gave them the reason for this – his policy was one of "divide and rule". He was also exceptionally demanding of all who worked for him; he wanted perfection from them in all they did and could be very rude to anyone who did not match his expectations. KM told us he had a combative relationship with his father and they had rows[d], but he was persuadable; an illustration of this was that RM allowed him in 1990 to form committees to debate issues in a more structured manner so that better decisions could be made. KM had therefore formed finance, legal and property committees to provide a focus for these issues.

---

a The transfer of the printing of the MGN newspapers to MCC (see paragraph 2.50) and the acquisition of the Beecham shares by the MGPS (see paragraph 2.37) are examples of this.

b After leaving university in 1980 KM worked as a copy writer in the marketing and sales department of PPL. In 1983 he was sent by RM to the USA to launch a defence publishing business. After a year KM was effectively dismissed by RM and returned to be Managing Director of Waterlows Publishers. By 1988 KM was Chief Executive for Publishing for MCC and he was appointed Joint Managing Director of MCC in October 1988. In December 1988 KM was sent back to the USA to manage Macmillan as Vice Chairman and Deputy Chief Executive. In July 1989 KM returned to the UK.

c From the evidence we received KM developed an extensive knowledge of the interests controlled by RM. KM told us that he had the same knowledge as a small group of RM's closest advisers.

d KM told us that his father would in the end always tell him that it was his capital and he would make the decision.

The growth of RM's companies

3.4 At the time PPL acquired its stake in MGN, PPL was a direct subsidiary of the Maxwell Foundation. Until March 1986, all of the significant businesses in which RM was interested in the United Kingdom were owned through that one company; PPL operated the scientific journals business, it held all the shares of MGN and it held the substantial stake in MCC.

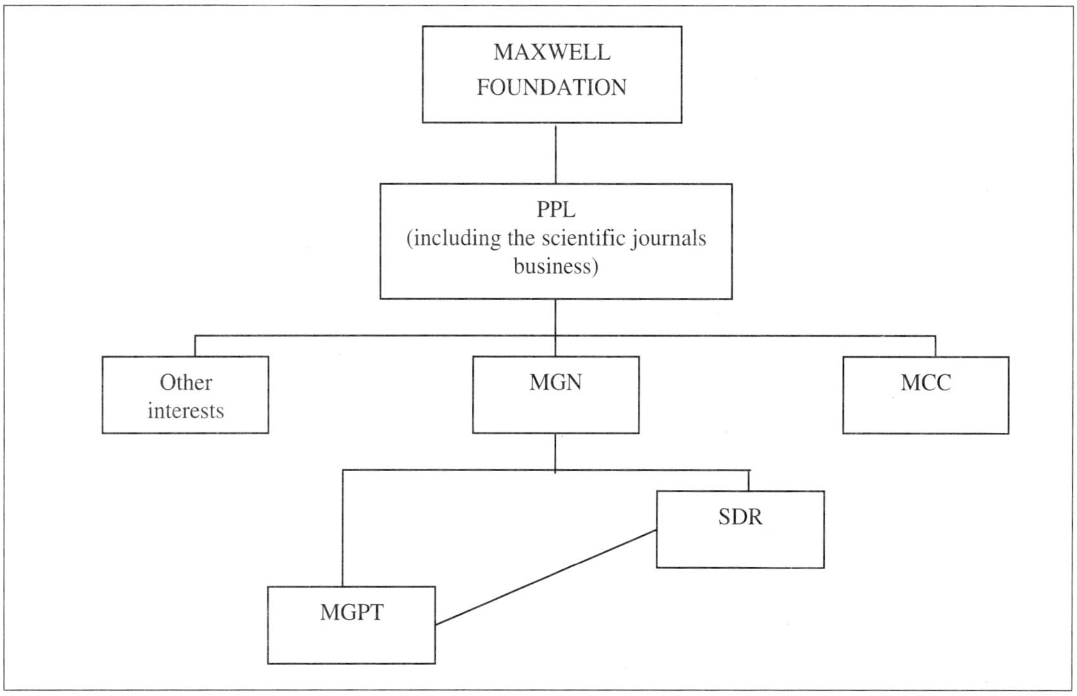

Figure 1 Ownership before March 1986
(main companies only)

3.5 The significant expansion of MCC took place from June 1984 (just prior to the time that PPL acquired MGN) with the acquisition of an investment trust, Bishopsgate Trust plc, which was paid for by a disguised rights issue through the issue of new MCC shares. The assets of this investment trust (approximately £47.9m in value) were liquidated and this enabled MCC to obtain a release from all existing fixed and floating charges on its business and assets. MCC was therefore placed in a position where RM could use it as a vehicle to expand his interests[a].

3.6 As already explained at paragraph 2.50, MCC had acquired at the beginning of 1986 the contract for the printing of MGN's titles[b]. This gave it a secure source of income. Of greater significance was MCC's acquisition from PPL of PPL's scientific journals business in March

a Various printing companies were acquired in 1985 and 1986. By taking advantage of the changes he had made by the implementation of his survival plan at MCC RM built a large printing business. At the same time, PPL acquired stakes in British Cable Services Ltd and Central TV, RM's first substantial television related assets.

b In connection with this MCC acquired Thompson Withy Grove Limited which owned the plant that had been used for printing northern editions of papers, including *The Daily Mirror*.

1986 at a cost of £238.7m satisfied through the issue of new shares in MCC[a]; the objective of this acquisition was to enable MCC to pursue its expansion through equity finance[b] and to provide it with another secure source of income[c].

The first reorganisation of ownership (1986): the private side

3.7 To facilitate the transfer of the scientific journals business to MCC and to enable the capital gain on this sale and on any future sale of MGN to be taken offshore, there was a reorganisation of the ownership structure within the UK principally devised by Mr Morgenstern and Mr Woods[d]. PPL was put into voluntary liquidation in March 1986, and its businesses apportioned between three companies; the scientific journals business was placed in Pergamon Journals Limited which was then sold to MCC (for the reasons described in the preceding paragraph), the shares in MGN were transferred to Mirror Holdings Limited, later renamed Robert Maxwell Holdings Limited (RMH) and the other interests, including interests in Hollis plc (Hollis)[e], were put into PHL.

3.8 After the sale of the scientific journals business to MCC, RM's business interests were treated by most who dealt with him, including the auditors and the banks as having a three-fold division:

- MCC
- MGN
- The "private side"; these were the other private companies which owned all his other interests including his majority stake in Hollis and his substantial investments in other

---

a 107.5 million new MCC shares were issued to the Maxwell Foundation; this took the Maxwell Foundation's stake in MCC (which was also held through subsidiaries in the UK and which had been reduced by the issue of shares on acquisitions) from 56.1 per cent to 74.9 per cent.

b MCC's capitalisation rose during 1986 from £290m to £900m by 1 December 1986; it became a FTSE 100 company on 1 July 1986.

c KM told us that when Mr Baker had persuaded RM to transfer PPL's scientific journals business into MCC from RM's private companies, it removed from RM's private companies a business which generated large cash flows.

d Mr Woods had worked for the Inland Revenue for four and a half years as an Inspector of Taxes; in 1969 he joined the BPC tax department and was working for it part time when RM acquired it. He then worked full time for RM both in tax and financial modelling in the acquisitions and disposals of companies. In 1987 he became a non-executive director of MCC and a director of many of RM's private companies.

e Hollis was a furniture manufacturer and timber importer with four factories in the north of England and Scotland in which RM took a stake and built up a majority holding in 1982. He developed Hollis so that it had services related divisions based around Oyez and the Solicitors Law Stationary Society plc and later AGB Research plc which became the main business Hollis retained; KM told us that Hollis was a classic example of RM's "on the hoof" decision making on the recommendation of a banker and of his control over a public company. In 1986 it was suggested to RM that a bid be made for AE plc (then a premier UK engineering company). Although Hollis was intended to be a professional services company, RM decided to launch a bid and, when it failed, announced that he was going to build up his own engineering business which he proceeded to do over the next 18 months. Details of some of the acquisitions by Hollis are set out in Appendix 5. Nobody on the board of Hollis (which included experienced public company directors) made any objection. Hollis was subsequently renamed Pergamon AGB plc as it had acquired in 1988 the market research company, AGB Research plc and eventually disposed of its main industrial businesses to Central & Sheerwood plc which was later renamed TransTec plc.

enterprises; the master company in the UK for holding the investments was PHL and later RMG.

All these shares were ultimately owned by the Maxwell Foundation at this time.

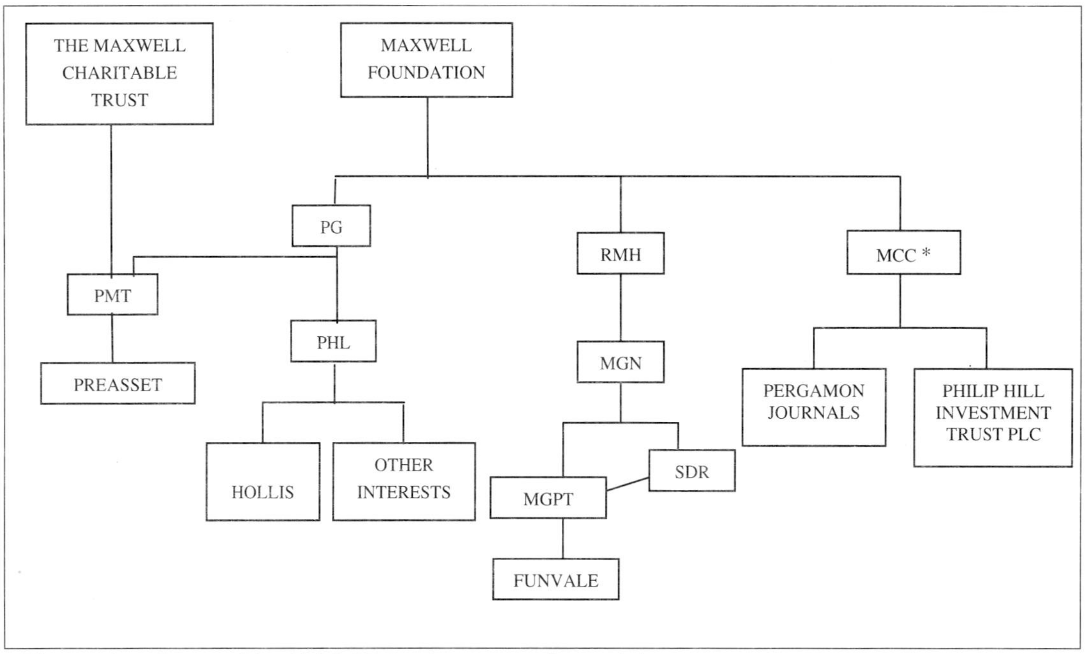

Figure 2 Ownership 1986-87 (main companies only)
* Part of the shareholding in MCC was held via subsidiaries of the Maxwell Foundation

MCC's acquisition of the Philip Hill Investment Trust PLC

3.9 With the two secure sources of income from the MGN printing contract and the scientific journals business, RM announced in April 1986 (when the revenues of MCC for the year ended 31 December 1985 had been £265m) that it was his stated aim to achieve through MCC a global communications and information company with revenues of £3 billion to £5 billion by the end of the 1980s. Mr Baker told us that as part of this plan it was RM's intention to transfer MGN into MCC once it had been returned to profitability.

3.10 To further this aim, RM strengthened MCC's finances in September 1986 by a second disguised rights issue through the acquisition of another investment trust, Philip Hill Investment Trust plc, which had net assets of £331.3m. Once more the consideration was satisfied by the issue of MCC shares[a]. This was the occasion when RM first dealt in shares with Goldman Sachs who purchased on a block trading basis the share portfolio of the investment trust when the offer had become unconditional. It was the start of a significant relationship. It was an

[a] The ultimate effect of this was to increase the share capital of MCC to 365 million shares and dilute the holding of RM, his family and the Maxwell Foundation to approximately 60 per cent at 31 December 1986; 29.8 per cent. was directly owned by the Foundation and 30.1 per cent held by UK subsidiaries and RM personally.

important and profitable piece of business for Goldman Sachs which, KM told us, they obtained due to their competitive price.

3.11 During the course of this acquisition of the investment trust, on 26 September 1986, RM purchased 19.3 million shares in MCC (7.65 per cent.) for £49.2m. He financed this purchase by a loan arranged in October 1986 by Henry Ansbacher & Co Limited (Ansbacher) from Paribas Suisse (Bahamas) Limited secured on the MCC shares purchased and on gilts. The reason for the acquisition of this holding was recorded[a] as follows:

> "We understand that these shares were purchased to support the [MCC] share price in September 1986"

In December 1986 RM stated he had acquired the shares for MGN (and not himself)[b] and at the same time the shares were transferred to Preasset Limited (Preasset) at a loss to MGN of £1.8m. This loss was charged by MGN to the intercompany account with PHL. Preasset Limited was a subsidiary of The Maxwell Charitable Trust[c].

The use of The Maxwell Charitable Trust

3.12 Bids had been made by MCC for John Waddington plc in 1983 and 1984 and in 1986 RM/PPL acquired a substantial stake in Extel[d]. While defending themselves from these moves, these companies made much of the fact that the ultimate owner of MCC and PPL was the Liechtenstein-based Maxwell Foundation, about which little information was available.

3.13 To overcome this difficulty, on 21 December 1986 an English charitable trust, known as The Maxwell Charitable Trust, was formed. The first trustees were IM[e], KM and RM,

---

[a] By CLD during the course of their 1986 audit.

[b] The shares were registered in a nominee name; MCC were notified that the beneficial owner between 26 September 1986 and 24 December 1986 was MGN.

[c] We have not been able to discover the reason for the transfer to Preasset other than a desire to have the control of the shares removed nominally from the Foundation for the reasons discussed in the following paragraphs. In April 1987, these 19.3 million shares were transferred to the Maxwell Foundation together with 10.7 million shares from PHL and placed in the market by Goldman Sachs and Smith New Court.

[d] The Takeover Panel ruled that RM was acting in concert with Demerger Corporation plc who were bidding for Extel.

[e] IM told us that he had no idea why he was appointed a trustee; he found himself appointed in similar manner to his appointment by RM as director of various companies. He had started working in RM's companies in 1978 at which time he had been given the choice by RM of starting at the bottom or starting at the top in RM's office. He chose to start at the bottom in order to see how the companies worked and also in order not to have RM "down his throat" every day. He started work as a sub-editor at PPL and, after time spent in France, went to the USA in 1980 to work for Pergamon Press Inc. where he became Vice-President for marketing. He moved back from the USA to France in 1983 and, in 1984, he worked as an adviser to the Prince's Trust. By 1985 he had been appointed to the board of MCC as group sales development director. In 1987 he returned once more to France, as chairman of a French newsagency; he described himself to us as, primarily, his father's 'gofer'. In late 1988 he returned to the UK as Chief Executive of Maxwell Macmillan Pergamon Publishing Corporation, a grouping of the European publishing operations of MCC. From the spring of 1990 he was involved in the launch of *The European* as right hand man to RM and then in the summer of 1990 took the post of Acting Managing Director of the company.

Lord Elwyn Jones[a] and Lord Silkin of Dulwich[b], the latter two being invited to become trustees of what appeared to be a charitable organisation. The Maxwell Charitable Trust was provided with 500,000 8.5 per cent. redeemable preference shares of £1 each in a new company, Pergamon Media Trust plc (PMT). These shares gave the trustees of the Maxwell Charitable Trust 70 per cent. of the voting power of PMT until 31 December 1989 when voting rights were to be reduced to 5 per cent.; in 1991 they were to be reduced to nil. The ordinary shares in PMT were held by PG, a subsidiary of the Maxwell Foundation. With this voting structure, it could properly be maintained that PMT was not controlled by the Maxwell Foundation although it retained the substantial economic interest and would within a short period obtain control. PMT was therefore in a position to be used by RM as a vehicle for the acquisition of companies without the danger of the "Liechtenstein connection" being used against him[c].

3.14 Once this structure was in place, the shares that RM/PHL had bought in Extel (with funds provided by Pergamon Press Inc (PP Inc)), together with a £24m loan from Ansbacher, were transferred to PMT[d]. Thus when RM signalled to Extel his intention to renew the bid[e] in March 1987, RM was able to maintain that the Maxwell Foundation did not control the stake held in Extel but that it was controlled by PMT.

3.15 On 16 April 1987, because PMT was not controlled by the Maxwell Foundation, it was used to acquire a stake in TF1 a French television station which was being privatised[f].

3.16 This role for The Maxwell Charitable Trust ceased in about June 1988 when arrangements were made to change the ownership of MCC so that it was no longer controlled by the Maxwell Foundation (as described at paragraph 3.27). However, The Maxwell Charitable Trust was used again when it became the owner of the shares in Bishopsgate Investment Management Limited which was appointed in 1988 to manage the Common Investment Fund of the pension scheme as described later at paragraph 5.6.

---

[a] He had been Attorney General and Lord Chancellor.

[b] He had acted for RM during the DTI Inspection in 1971 and became a director of MCC on 9 November 1981 and PPL on 25 February 1984. He played an active role in running the property portfolio of RM's companies until he was elevated to the peerage in 1985. He died in 1988 (see paragraph 5.6).

[c] A document prepared by CLD in 1987 recorded the following:

> "On 24 December [1986] it was decided that [PMT] would be the vehicle to own the Extel shares as its ownership was such that awkward questions about its owners could be answered without reference to the Liechtenstein foundation".

[d] On 27 December 1986 Extel were notified of the ownership of the shares by PMT and of the interest of The Maxwell Charitable Trust. They were subsequently provided with the names of the trustees.

[e] The bid was not pursued and the stake sold in April 1987 by a tender offer organised for PMT by N M Rothschild & Sons Ltd to United Newspapers plc who made a successful bid for the whole company.

[f] RM had had a publishing business in France since after the second World War. TF1 was his first successful large investment. It was acquired as part of a group of which the largest shareholder was M Bouyges and PMT the second largest; it was financed by a FF660m loan from Barclays Bank plc (Barclays); the loan and a further stake in TF1 are referred to in Chapter 5 in connection with the pension scheme in 1989 and 1990.

Expansion of MCC and the second reorganisation of ownership (1987-1988)

3.17 In October 1986 MCC began the acquisition of printing companies in the United States; it acquired the Webb Company and Providence Gravure in October and November 1986 respectively and in the first half of 1987, Diversified Printing Corporation. In addition to the acquisition of these printing companies MCC acquired in 1987 at a cost of Can $157m a 27 per cent. stake in Donohue Inc (Donohue), a pulp and paper products company which was being privatised by the Government of Quebec. This stake was acquired in conjunction with the acquisition of a stake in Donohue by Quebecor Inc. (Quebecor), a quoted Canadian paper and printing company.

3.18 Mr Baker explained to us that one of the reasons behind the acquisition of the stake in Donohue was RM's belief that the cycle of profit and loss in the pulp and paper industry could be used to the advantage of Donohue and MGN by the placing by MGN of a long term supply contract with Donohue. This was the primary motivation, rather than the interest in North American printing companies. The stake was therefore acquired, Mr Baker explained, in anticipation of the acquisition by MCC of MGN. Although this did not happen, the stake in Donohue and interests in the US printing companies acquired by MCC were included ultimately in the businesses forming part of the flotation of MGN. KM told us that he did not agree with Mr Baker's recollection which rather more reflected the view taken in 1990 when MGN acquired Quebecor Printing Inc. (QPI) a subsidiary of Quebecor and Donohue from MCC (see paragraph 6.51). The reasons in 1987 were, he recalled, two: first, MCC (through its subsidiaries Webb Company and Providence Gravure) was the second largest printer in North America, so needed large supplies of paper, and there was a long tradition of publishers and printers having interests in paper; secondly, the acquisitions of these Quebec companies were part of RM's wider policy of acquiring Francophone businesses described in the next paragraph.

3.19 In addition to his ambitions in North America, RM also wanted to develop interests in France. As described at paragraph 3.15 he had acquired a stake in TF1 in April 1987 and this was followed by further acquisitions made largely through MCC. These included interests in:

- Agence Havas: a stake in this leading advertising and communications company was acquired in the autumn of 1987.
- Marceau Investissements: the stake in this French investment trust was acquired by RM as a means of developing his investment profile in France.
- Société Générale: a French bank in which RM acquired a stake in the late summer of 1988 for £44.1m as part of an attempt led by Mr Georges Pebereau to take over this bank[a].
- Euris SA: a French investment trust of which RM became a director was acquired for the same reasons as the stake in Marceau Investissements.

These investments were subsequently transferred to the pension funds; the transfers and their subsequent history are described in relation to the use by RM of the pension funds.

---

[a] We were told by KM that RM bought the stake at the request of the French Government and, for similar reasons, retained the stake when others involved sold to realise the profits made.

3.20 The major acquisition attempted by MCC in 1987 was a bid for Harcourt Brace Jovanovich Inc, a leading US educational magazine and information publisher. The bid was not successful but was the cause of[a] a £630m 2 for 3 rights issue by MCC[b]. The rights issue was significant in two main respects:

- The first relates to the use made of the substantial funds raised by MCC. The cash raised was, effectively, used by RM (and RM alone with no involvement by the board of MCC[c]) in making various major acquisitions and entering into various substantial trades. RM liked to deal in stocks and shares every day; brokers had easier access to him than virtually anybody else. With cash from the rights issue RM took large stakes in[d]:
  - companies such as British Petroleum plc (£21m), J Sainsbury plc (£16.5m) and Storehouse plc (£53.4m) (primarily as trading stakes rather than strategic assets in companies related to MCC's business)[e], though in the case of some of these RM hoped to use the stock to influence the choice of printer.
  - Elsevier NV (Elsevier), Wolter Kluwer, Norton Opax plc (Norton Opax), De La Rue plc (De La Rue) and Bell Resources[f] (which could be viewed as strategic stakes for a future bid or to confuse the market as to a bid target).
  - various companies in the banking sector, such as Midland Bank plc (Midland) (£13.5m) on the basis that with MCC as a major shareholder in a bank, RM would be in a different position when he talked to the bank;
  - gilts.

  KM told us that when the stock market crashed in October 1987 MCC suffered an immediate paper loss, in excess of £350m, on the portfolio of investments which RM had acquired. Those losses were not then crystallised but when crystallised later totalled over £170m. Those losses were never revealed to the public and it was never disclosed that MCC had suffered such a substantial loss of capital. This lost capital came home, KM told us, in 1988 when repayments on facilities had to be made; MCC ought to have been able to make the payment with much greater ease than proved to be the case. We have been unable to confirm the extent of the crystallised loss from

---

a KM told us that Mr Baker explained to RM that the lesson to be learned from the failed bid was that you had to raise the money before you made the bid. The effect of the rights issue was to put the private side heavily into debt for the first time in order to take up the rights.

b An undertaking was given to Hill Samuel and Crédit Lyonnais Laing (MCC's brokers) that if within three years, MGN was disposed of, then MCC would have an option to acquire it, or if floated, then MCC shareholders would have preferential application rights.

c RM had been authorised in 1981 to exercise the power of the board as a committee of one (see paragraph 10.5).

d KM told us that the majority of these purchases were done in the name of Bishopsgate Investment Trust Limited, a nominee company whose function is described at paragraph 5.9. The stakes were then allocated to the private side or to MCC or split between them, sometimes contemporaneously and sometimes at the year end.

e In the case of Storehouse plc, RM believed that he might be able to obtain the printing contract for the Mothercare catalogue which had previously been printed within MCC and regarded as a "plum contract".

f In the case of Bell Resources, RM was extremely keen to acquire a major newspaper interest in Australia; we were told that he was motivated in this by his rivalry with Mr Rupert Murdoch.

the records available to us but the accounts of MCC for the year ended 31 December 1987 disclosed that the market value of investments was in the order of £50m less than their book value.

- The second significant point relates to the borrowing undertaken by the private side to finance its take up of the rights; at the time of the issue, the Maxwell Foundation owned (by itself and three subsidiaries) 51.2[a] per cent. of MCC. To pay for part of its subscription of £331.7m to this issue and to provide further funds, RM borrowed heavily:
  - the facility of £49.5m granted in October 1986 referred to at paragraph 3.11 was replaced by a £175m facility obtained from a syndicate of banks led by Paribas Suisse SA and arranged by Ansbacher.
  - in the same month, June 1987, Goldman Sachs also arranged the loan secured on the Holborn site as referred to at paragraph 2.34.
  - a further £100m was loaned by National Westminster on 30 June 1987[b].

3.21 The loan of £175m arranged by Ansbacher was significant in that it was largely secured on MCC[c] shares to a value of 200 per cent.[d] of the loan. This pattern of borrowing on the security of MCC shares[e] was followed on other loans; it was therefore of considerable importance to RM to maintain the value of the MCC share price as otherwise further shares had to be provided by way of security.

3.22 This very substantial increase in borrowing was one of the reasons for the second reorganisation of ownership that occurred between November 1987 and July 1988, but there were four other concerns that contributed to the need for further reorganisation:

- RM was advised that Liechtenstein ownership and control was a severe disadvantage in the expansion of MCC's media interests in France and elsewhere in Europe; much was also being made (in particular in the Harcourt Brace Jovanovich Inc. bid) of the "Liechtenstein connection"; it was therefore considered essential to end this control.

---

a The major reason for the reduction in the holding from that in December 1986 was a placing of 30 million shares in April 1987 at 305p per share producing a total of £91.5m for RM's interests; the source of these shares has been described in the footnote to paragraph 3.11.

b The loan was secured on gilts and made to a company known as Bishopsgate Investment Management Limited. The name of the company was changed to Bishopsgate Investment Holdings Limited in February 1988 when another company had its name changed to Bishopsgate Investment Management Limited and became the trustee of the common investment fund of the pension scheme (see paragraph 5.4).

c To enable the shares of MCC owned by the Maxwell Foundation to be charged to support this loan declarations of trust were executed.

d Together with the deposit of 9.5 million shares in Britannia Arrow; in September 1988 the security required was reduced to MCC shares to a value of 150 per cent. of the loan.

e RM had first used MCC shares as security for loans from National Westminster in September 1980 and he had used MCC shares to secure the loan made to PPL by National Westminster in connection with the acquisition of MGN; he had also used them for the loan in connection with the acquisition of Philip Hill Investment Trust plc referred to at paragraph 3.11.

- RM was advised in the later part of 1987 that under Liechtenstein law possession of founder's rights did not in fact give control over the Maxwell Foundation[a] and that therefore RM did not have the control he thought he had through the possession of the founder's rights by Dr Gutstein and Dr Rechsteiner. He was advised that in these circumstances he ought to specify the beneficiaries of the Maxwell Foundation and decide whether they were his family or charity.
- RM wanted to benefit his children (expressed in internal documents as a desire to "motivate them") although it was RM's stated position on many occasions that he intended to leave nothing to his family. KM told us that RM did not believe in inherited wealth and had made clear that he intended to leave nothing to his children; the reference in the internal documentation to motivation of the family was to give a credible reason for the reorganisation for banking and fiscal purposes.
- The interests of RM had become of such a size that it had become difficult to retain control of them outside the United Kingdom.

There were also fiscal considerations.

3.23 In the first stage of the reorganisation carried out in November and December 1987, a new company owned by RM and his family, Headington Investments Limited (HI), acquired a 25 per cent. interest in the main private side companies[b]. The Maxwell Foundation retained control and ownership of the two most valuable assets (the holding in MCC and the ownership of MGN) through an anstalt, another type of Liechtenstein entity[c], Pergamon Holding Anstalt (PHA) which was interposed at this time into the ownership structure[d]. PHA also acquired another US company, Pergamon Holdings US Inc (PHUSI)[e].

3.24 The next stage of the reorganisation was in February 1988 when the beneficiaries of the Maxwell Foundation were expressly set out in its statutes and specified to be charitable[f] with five particular objectives[g]. This was done just prior to the serialisation of the biography of RM

---

a Despite the provisions of the statutes of the Maxwell Foundation referred to at paragraph 1.7

b We were told that this was done at a cost of £22,000 as the net worth of the companies was so small.

c An anstalt is more like a company than a foundation; it can engage in trade and has an owner; that ownership is indivisible and controlled by the holder of the founder's rights of the anstalt. The founder's rights of PHA were on 12 November 1987 made the subject of an assignment in blank.

d PHA was a Liechtenstein anstalt and was interposed between the Maxwell Foundation and the UK companies because of concern that the Inland Revenue might not recognise a Liechtenstein foundation as a body corporate, but treat it as a discretionary trust with adverse fiscal consequences; at the same time the name of the Maxwell Foundation was changed to Pergamon Foundation. Dr Keicher was at first the sole director of PHA, but on 10 August 1989 Maître Raymond de Geouffre de la Pradelle de Leyrat and Mr Ellis Freedman were appointed to the board of PHA. PHA changed its name to Swico Anstalt in May 1991.

e This was described to us by Mr Ellis Freedman as "a very private, private company to handle financial matters".

f The concept is not the same as under English law.

g These were set out in various public documents including the prospectus of MGN; the charitable purposes included the support of scientific and medical research, the provision of financial assistance to the people of Israel, Jews and Arabs to contribute to establishing a lasting peace in the area and the encouragement of written by Mr Joe Haines; Mr Haines had insisted on describing the Maxwell Foundation and information had been provided to him about its origin and charitable purposes[a]. We were told that the founder's rights were passed to Dr Keicher as the sole member of the Maxwell Foundation board. Dr Rechsteiner was appointed the "Kollator" under the statutes of the Foundation; the functions of a Kollator appear to be unique to the law of Liechtenstein and he acts as a person to whom the board of the foundation can look for instructions and guidance and who will know the founder's wishes. There was also provision for the appointment of "Kontrollstelle", which have functions akin to an auditor. CLD had been approached in January 1988 by RM and were prepared to act as auditors[b] but they were not appointed.

3.25 These changes made no difference to the way in which the Maxwell Foundation acted. For the reasons set out in paragraph 1.8, Dr Keicher continued to look to Dr Rechsteiner for instructions which Dr Rechsteiner obtained in turn from RM. In accordance with his duties, Dr Keicher would carry out those instructions as they were the will of the founder.

3.26 The Maxwell Foundation did thereafter make some charitable donations, the principal ones being to the University of Leeds and to the Liechtenstein Institute. We were told that RM had intended the Maxwell Foundation to be used during his lifetime to build up his companies and thus the function of its holdings were to achieve this objective; after his death it was to be his monument and then engage in large scale charitable work.

3.27 The final stage of this reorganisation took place in the summer of 1988 with the stated aim of ensuring that MCC could no longer be said to be controlled from Liechtenstein[c]. To that end the family company, HI, acquired the 22 per cent. of MCC held by English subsidiaries of the Maxwell Foundation and valued at £260m[d]. Two further subsidiaries of HI, Visaford Limited and Magnacell Limited borrowed £170m from a syndicate of banks arranged by Lloyds in December 1988. The balance of the consideration of £260m due to the Maxwell Foundation[e] and its subsidiaries was satisfied by the transfer to the Maxwell Foundation of some loan stock in RMH (the company that held the shares in MGN which was by then a very valuable business), which had been granted to RM (personally) in March 1986; this was valued by CLD at a range the median of which was £90m. To mitigate stamp duty on this transaction a

---

young entrepreneurs. Despite this, RM refused to change the Maxwell Foundation from a deposited foundation to a registered foundation.

a The charitable purposes were set out at page 35 of Mr Haines' biography *"Maxwell"*. Mr Haines' role as a director of MGN is referred to at paragraph 10.25.

b RM approached Mr Brandon Gough (see paragraph 4.15) and Mr Gough discussed the proposed appointment in February 1988 with RM and Dr Rechsteiner. It was envisaged that the audit would be undertaken by the Swiss firm, Coopers & Lybrand A.G. However they were in the event not requested to carry out any work.

c This reorganisation had the additional benefit of enabling guarantees to be given in respect of the loan of £170 million to Visaford Limited and Magnacell Limited and of creating a group for capital gains tax purposes.

d PMT which had been controlled by the Maxwell Charitable Trust was also transferred to Pergamon Group plc (PG).

e Nothing was paid to the Maxwell Foundation but the funds were retained within the private side.

scheme was entered into involving a Gibraltar company called InterEuropean Trust and this company therefore held in consequence 51 per cent. of the shares of HI as a bare trustee for RM and his wife. Questions were raised by the media about this ownership in the autumn of 1991.

3.28 The £170m loan arranged by Lloyds was also secured on MCC shares to a value of 150 per cent. of the loan. Thus the two largest loans of the private side (arranged by Ansbacher for £173m and arranged by Lloyds for £170 m) totalling £343m[a] were largely secured on MCC shares.

3.29 At the end of the reorganisations (which were effected through schemes of great complexity designed to mitigate tax liabilities), the ultimate ownership was split between:

- the Maxwell Foundation, which retained its ownership of the newspaper interests (the most important of which was MGN) through RMG[b], a 31 per cent. stake in MCC and control of the other private side companies.
- HI which held for the family a 25 per cent. interest in the other private side companies and 22 per cent. of MCC.

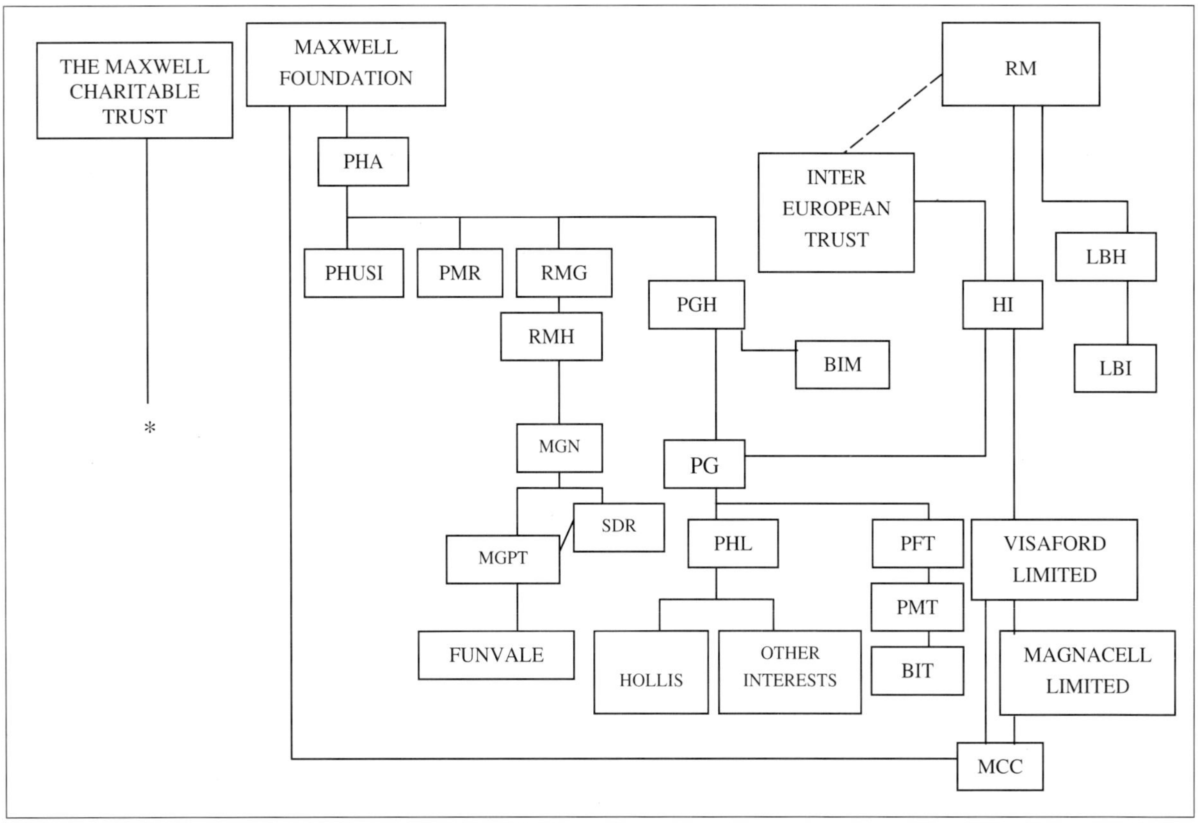

Figure 3 Ownership after the summer of 1988 (main companies)
* Holding in loan stock in PMT

[a] The loan arranged by Ansbacher was reduced to £173m in September 1988.

[b] This was a company incorporated on 21 October 1987 and acquired the shareholding in RMH which in consequence of the reorganisation in March 1986 had acquired the shareholding in MGN (as described at paragraph 3.7).

3.30 Instructions to leading tax counsel in February 1990 explained the rationale for the Maxwell Foundation retaining these holdings:

> "None of the Foundation shares in MCC (32 per cent.) nor the Anstalt's shares in [RMG] (probably the two most valuable assets) were transferred primarily to avoid their subsequent growth being brought into the ambit of UK tax. It was felt at the time that the benefit of owning those assets offshore outweighed the disadvantages of losing group relief between RMG and Pergamon Group and the inability to recover [advance corporation tax] on the MCC dividend flows in the event of the receiving company having surplus losses (which seemed unlikely at the time)."

4. 1988 - 1990: THE NEED FOR RM TO MAKE DISPOSALS

4.1 1988 was a turning point. Whereas that year saw the culmination of the changes in MGN and the major acquisition made by MCC, the assumption of the debt incurred by MCC and the private side brought about the need for the commencement of an asset disposal programme which had a significant impact on MGN and the pension funds. This chapter deals primarily with the impact of these events on MGN, particularly the work done in relation to a proposed flotation. The operation and use of the pension funds during this period is described in the following chapter.

Consideration of flotation in February 1988

4.2 By 1988 the savings in costs and the reduction in the workforce at MGN were beginning to take effect and the new printing facilities of BNPC were about to come on stream. Although RM had always said that he would float MGN, this was the first time that flotation could seriously be contemplated[a].

4.3 The first step to that end was the appointment of a merchant bank. RM approached S.G. Warburg & Co. Ltd and Barclays de Zoete Wedd Ltd (BZW). S.G. Warburg & Co Ltd refused to act as merchant bankers because of their view of RM as a man they would not act for[b]. BZW declined to act because they had another newspaper client. They told us that they would have declined even if they had not had that conflict of interest because they considered RM had not discharged the doubts they had arising out of the 1971/73 DTI Reports and in such circumstances would not be involved in the issue of securities by his companies to the public[c].

4.4 However, after RM had held discussions in February 1988 at a high level with the Midland Bank Group[d] and Midland Bank plc (Midland Bank) and with Samuel Montagu & Co Limited (Samuel Montagu) (the merchant banking arm of the Midland Bank Group), he appointed Samuel Montagu as advisers for a possible flotation of MGN. Although RM subsequently considered an alternative appointment, Samuel Montagu acted as the merchant bank and sponsor for MGN on its eventual flotation in April 1991.

4.5 The success of a flotation can very much depend on the perception by potential investors of the sponsors of the issue and thus the decision of Samuel Montagu, a leading merchant bank,

---

a RM had contemplated a separate flotation of SDR in the first half of 1985 and had retained Hill Samuel. Later in 1985 Hill Samuel were told this flotation was not going to proceed.

b The position of their subsidiary, Rowe & Pitman Limited, is considered at paragraph 4.21.

c As set out at paragraph 4.29, they did act on the transaction referred to in that paragraph.

d Midland Bank gave consideration to the 1971/73 DTI Reports when deciding whether or not to deal with RM. By this time it was some years after the Reports and Midland Bank perceived that RM had achieved much with his printing companies and MGN and also that other clearing banks and major international banks and investment houses had dealt with him. He was perceived as never having let a bank down and so someone with whom they could do extensive business. RM had first dealt with the Midland Bank in the early 1980s when acquiring Hollis and later acquiring Stothard & Pitt from receivers appointed by Midland Bank, although it had only been in 1986 that Midland Bank had begun marketing their services to MCC.

to act was very significant. That decision was made by the Corporate Finance Committee of the Corporate Finance Department of Samuel Montagu chaired by Mr Ian McIntosh, albeit that the decision was influenced by the fact that the Midland Bank Group at its highest level supported RM. Samuel Montagu felt that the DTI inquiry 17 years before had been overtaken by significant events since that time[a]; in the meantime RM had become chairman of a listed company, had been accepted by the Stock Exchange and had established a track record of achievements at MCC. They were also influenced by the strength of MGN's business, by the support major banks had given to RM, the fact that other merchant banks such as Hill Samuel had advised him, that the auditors to his companies had acted for him for a considerable number of years and that law firms of high repute such as Freshfields[b] had acted for some time on behalf of MCC.

4.6 Prior to that time Samuel Montagu had not acted for companies controlled by RM; subsequently they acted for MCC and Hollis in some transactions most notably in connection with the acquisition of Macmillan Inc. (Macmillan) and Official Airline Guides, Inc. (OAG) (see paragraph 4.8). Samuel Montagu told us that in acting on these transactions, they saw no hint of wrongdoing and they established a satisfactory relationship with RM; these two factors were the most important factors in Samuel Montagu's decision to act on the eventual flotation of MGN in 1991.

4.7 Some work was done by Samuel Montagu in the spring and early summer of 1988. They analysed MGN's figures and produced a draft report outlining issues that had to be dealt with in preparation for the flotation. This report identified the need to strengthen the management and the need to regulate the related party arrangements between MGN and other companies owned by the Maxwell Foundation. It also identified the difficulty that would be caused by the fact that critical to the profitability of MGN and MCC were the terms of the printing contract under which MCC's subsidiary, BNPC, printed MGN's newspapers; they appreciated that such a contract could be used to transfer profits between the two companies[c]. However after the completion of this report in July 1988, little happened until October 1988; RM was preoccupied with another venture - Macmillan.

The acquisition by MCC of Macmillan and OAG for over $3 billion

4.8 After the failure of the Harcourt Brace Jovanovich Inc. bid in 1987, MCC had continued to make further acquisitions. A great deal of effort went into identifying and examining various US companies that might be a target for a take over by MCC; this had been done in relation

---

a Samuel Montagu's view of the 1971/73 DTI Reports is considered in more detail at paragraph 10.10.

b Freshfields had been solicitors to MCC when RM acquired his controlling stake in MCC; they decided to continue as solicitors as they considered they owed a duty to all the shareholders and in particular to the minority. We were told they were conscious of the 1971/73 DTI Reports and always felt that RM had to be watched and that they had to be alert at all times. They refused to act for RM's private companies. The circumstances in which they ceased to act are described at the footnote to paragraph 6.17.

c In August 1988, RM told Mr Morrissey that he was to add mid year a further £2 million to the amount MGN paid MCC for the first half year. He protested in writing to RM who was very angry at this.

to R R Donnelly in 1987 and then IMS; in early 1988 much time was spent on looking at (and taking a stake in) Control Data but nothing came of the work. In the summer of 1988 RM began planning a major bid, the take over of Macmillan in the US. This was a bid where he faced severe competition from other bidders. He made the highest bid on 29 September 1988[a] and, after a court hearing, was successful on 2 November 1988; the cost was $2.6 billion[b]. OAG had also been acquired for MCC for $750m in October 1988[c]. Whereas the expansion of MCC into printing in 1986 and 1987 had been financed largely by equity, these key acquisitions into publishing were financed by borrowings of approximately $3 billion[d]; the borrowings were refinanced and in October 1989 the repayments were negotiated into the following tranches:

Tranche 1 $990m on or before 23 October 1990,
Tranche 2 $750m on or before 23 October 1992,
Tranche 3 $1,260m on or before 23 October 1994.
These borrowings were unsecured.

4.9 Although we have heard evidence that RM was probably right in buying the type of businesses owned by Macmillan and OAG, it is clear on the evidence that RM paid too much for them and that buying both companies at the same time overburdened MCC with debt[e]. We were told by Mr Woods that he resigned his role as the financial director of the private side companies at the end of 1988 because he was seriously concerned at their ability to survive, as RM had

---

a KM told us that Rothschild Inc., the investment bankers advising MCC, told RM that he could not be seen to fail in a second US take over bid (after his failure to take over Harcourt Brace Jovanovich Inc.) in the context of RM's known ambition to compete with Mr Rupert Murdoch's companies. In contrast, except for Mr Baker who was against the acquisitions, the board of MCC simply did not have the experience of dealing with deals of this size ($3.5billion was spent over the course of 10 weeks) to be able to withstand RM's strong desire to make a break through into the US that summer. Mr Pirie of Rothschild Inc. told us that his advice had been that if RM wished to achieve his stated goal of having $5billion of revenues in the USA he should give serious consideration to acquiring Macmillan; they did not say he could not be seen to have failed.

b Unless otherwise stated, $ are US$.

c KM told us that, the acquisition of OAG, in particular, reinforced KM's view of RM's standing. In order to get the deal through the vendors of OAG (Dunn & Bradstreet) insisted on a personal guarantee from RM for $250m and paid RM $5m to obtain it; that RM was thought by Dunn & Bradstreet to be good for that level of money impressed KM a great deal. KM told us that RM had before this always told him never to give a personal guarantee; Mr Pirie advised RM that on this occasion he had to do it. Mr Pirie told us that Rothschild Inc. gave no advice in this transaction and he made no such statement.

d These were financed through "off balance" sheet vehicles, Tendclass Investments (of which Mr Middleton and Mr Corsan – see paragraph 5.6 - were the shareholders), its subsidiary, Mills Acquisition Co and Keated Ltd (of which Mr Middleton and Mr Corsan were the shareholders). The use of these vehicles and their shareholding was fully disclosed in circulars issued by MCC. Short term financing for $1.16 billion was provided through a syndicate arranged by Samuel Montagu. One of the reasons for extending MCC's financial year to 31 March 1989 was to accommodate the subsequent incorporation of the off balance sheet vehicles into MCC's accounts.

e Mr Richard Baker opposed proceeding with the purchase of Macmillan at the price eventually agreed. Mr Woods, in private discussions with RM, gave RM projections which showed that if as a result of the acquisition of Macmillan the MCC share price dropped (as was likely as the earnings of Macmillan would not cover the cost of borrowing), there might be insufficient equity held by the private side to cover its borrowings. He also pointed out to RM that he was paying a premium price to acquire the whole of Macmillan, only to sell parts of it at a lower price, thus further affecting MCC's position. RM then asked him what earnings growth was needed to cover the debt; Mr Woods calculated this as 20 per cent and RM told him that was the rate they would have. He asked Mr Woods for all of the copies of the projections.

continued to acquire new business for the private side, including in October 1988 AGB Research plc for £134m[a].

4.10 One of the first steps[b] taken in the asset disposal programme[c] necessitated by these acquisitions was the disposal of MCC's UK printing operations (apart from BNPC's newspaper printing business) carried on in the name of BPCC; this was the subject of a management buyout led by BPCC's Chief Executive, Mr John Holloran, which was agreed in December 1988 at a price of £265m.

Further consideration of the flotation of MGN in October 1988: the role of CLD

4.11 In October 1988, a decision was made to press ahead with the flotation of MGN. To this end further advisers were appointed. CLD were appointed as reporting accountants; their role in reporting on the company is described at paragraph 7.6, but it is convenient to describe the origin of their relationship with RM, the circumstances of their appointment and the nature of their relationship with RM.

4.12 When RM regained control of PPL during the course of 1974, the auditors of PPL were Cooper Brothers, which eventually became the firm of CLD. They had been invited by the new board that had taken control of PPL from RM to replace the auditors who had acted during the period that was the subject of the DTI inquiry[d]. When RM re-acquired the company, CLD had been the auditors for four years. Although no one could provide to us any documents or recall precisely the circumstances in which CLD agreed to continue as auditors when PPL came under RM's control, we were told by CLD that they considered this carefully and decided that they, rather than anyone else, might as well act for a company controlled by RM since they were in a position to be able to stand up to him. They therefore agreed to remain the auditors to PPL and were thereafter appointed (except where previously appointed) as auditors to other companies subsequently acquired by RM. In the period to RM's death, they acted as auditors to all of RM's companies and their pension schemes within the United Kingdom[e] and most of

---

a This acquisition was financed by a bank loan of £125m.

b Apart from this and the subsequent disposal of BNPC (referred to at paragraph 4.25) major disposals included The Michie Company, Intertec Publishing Corp (see paragraph 5.29) and sales of large stakes in companies such as Société Générale (see paragraph 5.28) Norton Opax and Elsevier (see paragraph 5.29).

c Apart from the disposals, MCC continued to make acquisitions, albeit on a much smaller scale. The most significant of these was Merrill Publishing Co which was acquired in November 1989 and transferred into the joint venture with McGraw Hill referred to in paragraph 6.8.

d Cooper Brothers had provided consultancy services to one of RM's companies prior to 1970.

e CLD told us that in the year ended 30 April 1990, their UK firm earned fees from companies under RM's control of approximately £2.7m of which approximately £1m related to non-audit services. In the year ended 30 April 1991 the UK firm earned such fees of approximately £5m of which approximately £2.5m related to non-audit services. In both years these fees represented approximately 1% of the firm's total fees. We were told that the non-audit fees related primarily to due diligence and similar work; very little management consultancy or tax work was carried out.

the subsidiaries of MCC in the United States[a]. They did not act as auditors for his "offshore" entities (though as set out at paragraph 3.24, they were approached to act for the Maxwell Foundation) or the private side companies in the United States which were not subsidiaries of UK holding companies.

4.13 We were told that at first CLD watched RM "like a hawk" and they never treated him just like any other client as he was a proprietorial client and dominated the companies he controlled; there was a risk that "his dominance would lead to matters going awry" and that therefore they took this into account in their approach to their audits; that CLD were aware of the contents of the 1971/73 DTI Reports and RM was accordingly placed in the highest category of potentially difficult clients. Accordingly early audits were approached on the general assumption that he would be acting as he had acted in the past. As the years went by, however, there appeared to be no evidence that this assumption was fair and it was gradually replaced by an assumption that he was a client who needed careful watching because there might be mistakes in the accounts or misunderstandings regarding accounting principles.

4.14 Mr Corsan[b] was until his retirement in 1986 the auditor responsible for dealing with RM from the time he became their client in 1972 and was the partner responsible for the overall relationship between RM and CLD. He explained to us that it was not technically necessary (in his view) for one person to have an overview of what was happening within the three-fold division that made up RM's businesses[c] as described in paragraph 3.8. Each audit partner should have had a sufficient understanding of the assets within each group. He told us that it might have been desirable in the case of someone like RM (subject to any constraints of confidentiality) to have an overview particularly as regards business methods and the movement of assets between RM's various interests. Furthermore, when he had been with CLD, the firm had always operated on a two partner principle, so that a second partner would always review the work done on an audit, though it was up to each individual partner conducting the review to decide how best to do it.

4.15 On 16 December 1987, CLD had a client review meeting chaired by Mr Peter Smith and attended by Mr Walsh and Mr Taberner, the two most senior partners who dealt with the audits

---

a Mr Walsh, a senior partner of CLD, observed in an internal memorandum in June 1991:

> "It is of interest that, whereas RM has used almost every lawyer, every broker and every merchant bank in London, he has always been totally loyal to [CLD], and has never used another firm of accountants except in unusual circumstances. We believe that this is because we stood by him in the 1970s when everyone else avoided him (National Westminster Bank is in a similar position)."

CLD's strategy was described in the same memorandum as:

> "The first requirement is to continue to be at the beck and call of RM, his sons and his staff, appear when wanted and provide whatever is requested.
> The second requirement is for [CLD] to continue to avoid making errors in exceptionally difficult and exceptionally demanding circumstances."

b He was a trustee of The Maxwell Charitable Trust (see paragraph 5.6).

c He had himself had an overview for the purpose of advising RM.

of RM's companies after the retirement of Mr Corsan[a]. A note of the meeting records that it was vital for CLD to recognise the proprietorial nature of the group and respond to it; the roles of the various audits were discussed. The note of the meeting concluded:

> "..it was agreed that it would not be appropriate to introduce another senior partner to Bob Maxwell. The parallel and equivalent roles carried out by [Mr Taberner] and [Mr Walsh] in managing [CLD]'s relationship with Maxwell for MCC on the one hand and Hollis, Mirror and Pergamon on the other served to preserve the Chinese walls for the main listed company and provided sufficiently senior people with a well established relationship. [Mr Brandon Gough]'s involvement as overall director of our client service to Maxwell has also gradually increased and is likely to increase further..."

Mr Brandon Gough, the then Chairman of CLD, was sent a memorandum by Mr Walsh about the role he should play in RM's affairs in March 1988. Mr Gough replied in April 1988 stating his role was unresolved and leaving it to Mr Walsh and Mr Taberner to judge what sort of contact would be desirable and when. It is clear that Mr Gough did not therefore assume the role suggested in December 1987 and he was very much in the background of the relationship, but it is not clear what CLD did to replace the role performed by Mr Corsan.

4.16 KM told us that from 1990 onwards he had regular meetings with Mr Walsh[b] at which he kept Mr Walsh abreast of developments in the various companies; he considered that CLD had an overall view of RM's companies. In any case where RM and the relevant audit partner could not agree on an accounting treatment, RM would telephone Mr Gough, in order to have him sort the matter out[c]. Mr Gough told us that he had no recollection of being telephoned by RM to resolve accounting issues or being involved with his partners on accounting and auditing issues[d].

4.17 When CLD were appointed as reporting accountants in 1988, it was stipulated by Samuel Montagu that the partner in charge of the team to act as reporting accountants must not have been involved in the audit of MGN for the preceding five years[e]. The objective of this condition was to ensure that independent scrutiny was given to the accounts for that period and a fresh view taken of the company.

---

[a] A note of the meeting recorded that "a vital factor in [CLD]'s past relationship was the personal service provided by David Corsan and his willingness to give Maxwell top priority at all times as well as a longstanding personal relationship."

[b] There are notes of such a meeting on 17 January 1991.

[c] An instance of this was Mr Gough's intervention in relation to FTIT (see the footnote to paragraph 9.56).

[d] Once a year the various audit partners of the companies controlled by RM invited the senior management of MCC and the private side to a dinner where matters relating to the overall position of the companies would be discussed. KM told us that although RM would treat senior partners at CLD such as Mr Walsh and Mr Gough courteously, he fundamentally saw them as servants rather than independent auditors. As far as Mr Gough was concerned, he always considered he was treated by RM as a senior professional accountant.

[e] This was at a time when the Stock Exchange required the accounts of the company to be reviewed for a period of 5 years; by the time of the flotation, that period had been reduced to 3 years.

4.18 Linklaters & Paines were invited by Samuel Montagu to act as solicitors to the issue; Simmons & Simmons, Lovell White Durrant and Clifford Chance were approached to act as solicitors to the company and the last of these firms was appointed. The respective roles of the solicitors to the issue and the solicitors to the company are described at paragraph 7.6 but it is convenient to explain why these two firms agreed to act as it was the agreement of successive firms and banks of high reputation to act in connection with his businesses that continued RM's "rehabilitation" in the eyes of others. Both firms were appointed on the eventual flotation in April 1991 but their decisions to act on that occasion were based on the decisions that had been taken in 1988. Although the decision of legal advisers to act is not as important to the perception of a flotation as the decision of the sponsor to act, it nonetheless is helpful if the legal advisers are leading firms.

4.19 Mr Sheldon, the senior partner, made the decision for Linklaters & Paines; he was much influenced by the fact that his firm would be acting for Samuel Montagu and not RM; he considered in any event that the 1971/73 DTI Reports had been published some years before and RM now appeared to be running a successful company in MGN[a].

4.20 The decision that Clifford Chance should act in 1988 was made by Mr macLachlan, a senior partner, and other partners. He considered that the firm was acting for MGN and not RM[b]; that the 1971/73 DTI Reports had been 17 years before; that RM had become Chief Executive of MCC; and that the flotation was being sponsored by a top class bank. By the time of the flotation in 1991 Clifford Chance had also acted for The European Limited, one of the private side companies, and had advised London and Bishopsgate International Investment Management plc on two regulatory issues from 1989; their advice to this company is referred to at paragraph 9.57.

4.21 Six stockbrokers were approached to act as brokers on the flotation but all declined; those that gave reasons stated that they might have a conflict of interest[c]. BZW did so for the reasons set out at paragraph 4.3. Rowe & Pitman Limited (Rowe & Pitman) told us that they declined for the same reasons as their sister merchant bank S.G. Warburg & Co Limited had declined the request to act as merchant bankers, though they were prepared to execute share transactions for RM[d].

4.22 Nonetheless work proceeded. In November 1988 CLD produced a document identifying the issues that had to be dealt with and prepared a draft of a report which became available in January 1989.

---

a Mr Sheldon in a contemporary note observed that Samuel Montagu was aware "that they have something of a tiger by the tail and that difficult and delicate issues are going to crop up throughout the flotation exercise."

b Mr macLachlan had acted for PPL and Hill Samuel in advising PPL on its acquisition of MGN in 1984.

c We were told by Samuel Montagu that brokers were more reluctant by the late 1980s to act for companies controlled by RM because it had become more difficult to sell shares to UK institutional investors because of the high prices paid for acquisitions.

d See for example the purchase of the stake in FTIT described at paragraph 5.27.

4.23 In December 1988, however, work effectively came to a standstill. It is not apparent why this was the case although RM told Mr Morrissey that it was for reasons related to the Maxwell Foundation - in other words he would not explain why.

4.24 It is clear that there was one serious impediment to the proposed flotation - the fact that MGN's newspapers were printed by a subsidiary of MCC, BNPC. Consequently consideration was given to whether MGN should be transferred to MCC (as was part of the original plan to build up MCC described to us by Mr Baker (see paragraph 3.9)) or whether MGN should be floated separately with appropriate arrangements being made for the printing of its newspapers.

The sale of BNPC to MGN

4.25 RM made the decision that MCC would not acquire MGN and this was announced in April 1989; he had also decided by February 1989 that MGN would acquire BNPC and this was announced in May 1989. This was presented as the second stage of MCC's divestment of its printing business, the first stage having been the management buyout of BPCC, referred to at paragraph 4.10.

4.26 The only issue to be settled was the price to be paid by MGN. Replanting with new presses had been undertaken by BNPC not only with a view to being able to print the MGN titles but also to being able to do general contract printing for other newspapers (as described at paragraph 2.49). Outside contracts had not materialised, because other publishers were not prepared to entrust so essential a part of newspaper production to one of RM's companies. Therefore almost all the turnover of BNPC came from MGN.

4.27 The cost of the equipment leases had been financed by BNPC and the cost of building works had been financed by an intercompany loan from MCC (as set out at paragraph 2.50). Valuers, commissioned to value the site and plant on a going concern basis, produced a value of £281m. However these assets were carried in the books of BNPC at completion at £325m; this figure included commissioning and funding costs which had been capitalised.

4.28 Mr Baker told us that he and the other independent directors of MCC were determined that if BNPC was to be transferred to MGN, it had to be transferred at the cost reflected in the books of BNPC. He did not want it to be said that RM had used the resources of the listed company to re-equip MGN at a time when MGN did not have the resources to pay for it and that RM had then "warehoused" the new printing plants with MCC until MGN could acquire them. However the operational management of MGN considered that the book value was in excess of the market value and it would be disadvantageous to the future flotation of MGN if an unrealistic price was paid.

4.29 A meeting took place on Sunday 21 May 1989 at Headington Hill Hall, Oxford attended by representatives of the operational management of MGN, by different partners of CLD as accountants to both MGN and MCC, and by BZW[a] as financial advisers to MCC. The representatives of MGN told RM that the book value price required by MCC was too great by about £50m. On tendering this advice they were told by RM that they were no longer required to attend the meeting and RM thereafter agreed to the price that MCC wanted, although the price was reduced by an adjustment which took account of a deferred tax liability.

4.30 On 26 May 1989 RM summoned at short notice those directors of MGN who could be found, to a meeting in his flat in Maxwell House. Accounts of the meeting differ; the minutes signed by RM record it as a formal meeting and record Mr McIntosh of Samuel Montagu as having advised the meeting that the price payable to MCC was fair. It was not a formal meeting, but was merely an occasion used to obtain the appearance of consent from the other directors of MGN to the acquisition of BNPC. Mr McIntosh told us he did not advise on the fairness of the price, but merely that that part of the purchase price for BNPC to be satisfied by the issue of convertible loan stock to MCC should be arranged in such a way that if MGN was floated, that loan stock could be refinanced so MCC would not acquire a stake in MGN.

4.31 Agreements were thereafter signed under which BNPC was acquired by MGN. MGN paid £203m in cash in 1989; the balance of the consideration was payable in convertible loan stock of £62.5m. The total consideration was subject to adjustment.

4.32 Until this transaction MGN's only borrowings had been trading overdrafts, but to finance this purchase MGN made its first major borrowings. These borrowings totalling about £300m comprised equipment leases of about £150m and a £150m secured facility from a syndicate of banks led by the Toronto Dominion Bank (Toronto Dominion).

4.33 In connection with this acquisition and the facility led by Toronto Dominion, a number of non-newspaper subsidiaries of MGN some of which (including software companies) had been established and funded by MGN's cash flow were transferred from the ownership of MGN to the ownership of RMG (a private side company) at book value; the consideration was charged to the intercompany account as explained at paragraph 4.44, but no payment was made.

Further consideration of flotation in the autumn of 1989

4.34 Although there were one or two meetings about the possible flotation of MGN in the first half of 1989 nothing much happened until a meeting on 24 October 1989 between RM, Mr McIntosh, Mr Galloway[b] (both of Samuel Montagu) and Sir Michael Richardson[c] at which

---

[a] BZW acted on this transaction because Mr Leslie Goodwin (referred to in the footnote to paragraph 1.19) had joined BZW from Hill Samuel. Although BZW had declined to act on the issue of securities for MGN, they told us they were prepared to act as there was no issue of securities to the public and they were acting for the directors of MCC.

[b] He had been brought in to replace another director of Samuel Montagu whom RM had requested be replaced. Mr Galloway had day-to-day conduct on the flotation in 1991. He had worked for Samuel Montagu in corporate finance since 1979 and had been appointed an Assistant Director in 1987 and a Director in 1989. He had, on earlier transactions, been in day-to-day charge of matters without the supervision of a director.

[c] In 1964 Sir Michael Richardson had been a partner in Panmure Gordon and had thereafter dealt with RM until leaving Panmure Gordon in 1970. From 1970 to 1980 he had been a partner in Cazenove & Co; during that

it was agreed that work on flotation should be revived with the objective of flotation in April or May 1990. There was one further meeting in November 1989, but thereafter the work again petered out.

4.35 The consideration given in October 1989 to flotation is significant only because it marks the origin of Smith New Court's involvement in the flotation; they were the brokers to the eventual flotation in April 1991.

4.36 The involvement of Smith New Court came about through Sir Michael Richardson. The decision by Smith New Court to act for MGN and to act as brokers to MCC (to which position they were appointed in May 1990) was made by its Executive Committee. It was an important decision because the support of a leading broker is again perceived to be of considerable importance in the success of a flotation. Although Sir Michael was not a member of the committee which made the decision, the fact that RM was perceived to be his client was a factor that influenced the committee's decision. Both Sir Michael and the committee were influenced by the quality of the banks that supported RM; by the size of the loans made to MCC by other banks; the fact that leading houses, including Samuel Montagu and Goldman Sachs, dealt with him; and by the fact that RM had been permitted to become the Chairman of a listed company. There were doubts, but it had been 18 years since the DTI inquiry and MGN was perceived to be a profitable and successful newspaper business.

4.37 In January 1990 Smith New Court were invited by RM to examine the possibility of a private placement of MGN shares. It was quickly appreciated by the Smith New Court team that a private placement would involve almost as much work as a full flotation and would be difficult to achieve without a merchant bank. It was also apparent from their review of the work done by Samuel Montagu and CLD in 1988 that many matters needed to be dealt with before MGN could be floated, or a placement made. Work on the possible private placement lasted only three weeks and was suspended after a meeting on 25 January 1990.

The management of MGN after its return to profitability

4.38 In January 1990 Mr Morrissey, the Deputy Managing Director, left MGN. His influence at MGN had been substantially reduced since October 1988 when at a lunch meeting RM had announced that he would be assuming day-to-day control of MGN and that Mr Morrissey was to concentrate on the preparation of the flotation and other projects. RM had also indicated on that occasion that the editors of the MGN titles would be their own managing directors.

---

time he had no dealings with RM as Cazenove & Co did not deal with him. In 1980 he had become head of Corporate Finance at NM Rothschild & Sons Ltd who had only acted for RM in 1986-87 in connection with the RM's Extel stake and its sale to United Newspapers (see paragraphs 3.12 and following). Sir Michael had become a non-executive director of Smith New Court when NM Rothschild & Sons Ltd acquired a 40 per cent. stake in that company and it was in this capacity that he was asked by RM to attend the meeting in October 1989. He had, however, in the period since 1970 been invited to two of RM's birthday parties and had occasional meetings with RM in the period 1986-1989.

4.39 After that lunch meeting RM instituted regular meetings with the operational directors on Tuesdays and Fridays at 8.30am. These were often meetings at which RM would, depending on his mood, pick on someone to bully; some attended these meetings in fear. We were told by several operational directors that if a decision was wanted, it was best obtained on a one-to-one basis with RM.

4.40 After the institution of these meetings, Mr Morrissey was often by-passed and would learn of decisions later from those who were meant to report to him.

4.41 When flotation of MGN was being considered in the latter part of 1989 (as set out at paragraph 4.34) Mr Morrissey requested that RM agree to hold board meetings (as these would be required in a listed company) and also pressed for a proper management structure to be created. RM agreed that both would happen as from 1 January 1990 but when that date came he changed his mind and Mr Morrissey resigned.

4.42 After Mr Morrissey's departure, Mr Horwood was asked by RM to advise on the management procedures of the company. In a report produced on 25 January 1990, Mr Horwood recommended that RM appoint as Managing Director someone with an understanding of the editorial side of MGN's business in the hope that the operational and the editorial management would work more closely together. He also recommended the establishment of organised meetings at which directors would submit reports and planning forecasts and the establishment of an executive committee.

4.43 RM decided to appoint Mr Burrington as Managing Director; he had been editor of *The People* and on his relinquishment of that position in 1988 had been appointed Deputy Chairman of MGN and Assistant Publisher. He was not appointed because he had any corporate management experience but because of his editorial experience and knowledge. Mr Burrington attempted to have formal meetings of the directors each month with RM present, but these were abandoned very quickly as RM would not agree to them; RM wanted to continue to run the company through the meetings each Tuesday and Friday at 8.30am, without the formal meetings that Mr Morrissey had wanted, that Mr Horwood had recommended and that Mr Burrington had tried to achieve. Mr Burrington, could only therefore, continue the meetings of operational management that Mr Morrissey had instituted as referred to at paragraph 2.7.

Further support from MGN to the private companies

4.44 As has been explained at paragraph 2.16, most of the significant non-newspaper assets had been transferred from MGN in the period down to 1988; MGN had made its first borrowing in 1989 in consequence of the acquisition of BNPC. Furthermore MGN had a strong cash flow and this was used to support the private side. There were also transfers of some smaller assets to the private side companies, in addition to the transfers of the various companies which had been subsidiaries of MGN (referred to at paragraph 4.33).

4.45 One specific purpose for which the cash flow of MGN was used from 1988 onwards was the support of the development work on *The European* in the amount of £26m[a].

4.46 Throughout 1989 and 1990, the intercompany debt owed to MGN continued to grow and by the end of 1990 was approximately £334m.

	Amounts transferred (£m)			Discharged by dividends (£m)	Total left outstanding on the intercompany account (£m)	
	Assets	Cash	Interest		Per year	Cumulative[b]
1984-8	35	166	53	(51)	203	203
1989	38[c]	55	20	(7)	106	309
1990[d]	5	0	20	0	25	334
	78	221	93	(58)	334	

Table 2 – Use of assets and cash flow to December 1990

4.47 During the same period as the events described at MGN occurred, there were three other matters of significance to which it is necessary to refer:

- RM's dealings in MCC shares.
- The growth of the private side debt.
- The third reorganisation of ownership.

Secret purchases of MCC shares in 1989 through TIB and the Japanese placement

4.48 After the reorganisation in 1988, the holding of RM, his family, their companies and the Maxwell Foundation in MCC remained relatively stable at just over 50 per cent. in the early part of 1989, but a significant purchase was made in May 1989 using TIB. A detailed account of the dealings in MCC shares by RM in 1989 and thereafter is set out in Appendix 7. The following is a summary of two of the significant transactions in 1989.

---

a £11.7m was charged to the Mirror Colour Magazines intercompany account and £14.3m was charged to the European intercompany account.

b The actual cumulative figures stated above are different from the notional dividends shown in the prospectus as described at paragraph 15.29.

c The greater part of this represents the transfer of the Reuters A shares to the private side (see paragraph 2.42).

d The figure for 1990 is shown before the adjustments for commercial paper and group tax relief; these adjustments were used to reduce by £55m the intercompany account, as explained at paragraph 6.68.

4.49 The first was a purchase by TIB[a] a New York Corporation. Mr Ellis J Freedman[b], a lawyer who had acted for RM for many years and was then a partner in the New York firm of Whitman & Ransom, became its president. KM told us that instructions to form TIB were given by RM at a meeting attended by him and Dr Rechsteiner; he thought Mr Freedman was present by telephone, but Mr Freedman had no recollection of this meeting. TIB was to be a company able to deal in shares but which was to be owned by a foundation independent of the Maxwell Foundation. Mr Freedman told us that he understood subsequently from Dr Rechsteiner that TIB was acting as the nominee[c] of Akim Foundation which was one of the foundations acquired or founded for RM referred to at paragraph 1.10.

4.50 On 19 May 1989 Goldman Sachs sold to TIB 3.446 million MCC shares at a cost of \$11.2m[d]. As this was the first transaction by an offshore entity, it is necessary to refer briefly to the evidence we received:

- Mr Sheinberg[e] of Goldman Sachs told us that he was asked by RM to call Mr Freedman to see if he was interested in buying MCC shares. He did so and agreed the sale with Mr Freedman. He did not make any agreement with RM.
- Mr Freedman told us that these shares (and those purchased later) were purchased on the instructions of RM or KM, and that he did not learn of the transaction until after it had been agreed; he never negotiated any price with Mr Sheinberg.
- KM told us that RM and Mr Sheinberg did the deal and then notionally Mr Sheinberg re-did the deal with Mr Freedman.

TIB made further purchases of MCC shares and was used by RM in 1991 in the circumstances described at paragraph 20.50 for secret purchases of shares in MGN. The evidence of Mr Sheinberg, Mr Freedman and KM was similar as to each of the subsequent transactions involving TIB; we consider it more convenient to set out the evidence relating to all the purchases of MCC and MGN shares before stating our findings in relation to this conflict of evidence.

---

a TIB was originally called Torafugu Inspection Board Inc. and had been formed to import Torafugu into the United States; it was not required for that purpose and became a shelf company; shares in TIB were issued to Mr Ellis Freedman in 1990. Torafugu is a pufferfish found in sub-tropical and tropical waters; we understand it is poisonous unless cooked carefully.

b We were told that historically Dr Gutstein had paid some of Mr Freedman's fees and Dr Rechsteiner continued to do this in small amounts.

c The nominee status of TIB was formalised in 1990 by back dating a letter of instruction to 1989 as it was only then appreciated that the sale of the MCC shares by TIB described at paragraph 4.52 might give rise to a US tax liability.

d The cost of this - £6.95m - was paid out of the pension funds on 26 May 1989 and paid to TIB via Bishopsgate Investment Trust plc ; originally it was contemplated that these shares would be purchased by the pension funds - see paragraph 5.20.

e Mr Sheinberg had been a partner of Goldman Sachs & Co since 1970 and from late 1986 had been sole head of international equity trading. He told us that he knew RM was thought to be enormously wealthy and apparently dealt with virtually every major UK financial institution; he thought RM was controversial and he had heard of the 1971/73 DTI Reports, but from his knowledge of the other party to the dispute that had given rise to the Reports, he was inclined to think that RM would have behaved the better.

4.51 KM told Mr Sheinberg during 1989 there was no connection between the Maxwells and TIB. He did so because he understood that although TIB was owned by a Foundation which RM had asked Dr Rechsteiner to use for that purpose, it was not owned by the Maxwell Foundation or RM[a]. KM confirmed to Goldman Sachs in writing on 21 December 1989 that TIB was not controlled directly or indirectly by MCC or under common control or affiliated with MCC. KM told us that he did make these statements to Mr Sheinberg but that he did so believing them to be true, on the basis of that he believed that TIB had been set up as a vehicle owned by a Liechtenstein foundation other than the Maxwell Foundation.

4.52 Sometime between June and mid October 1989, RM decided to procure a placement of MCC shares in Japan through Nikko Securities Co (Nikko Securities)[b]. It was agreed eventually that the placing be for 30 million shares.

- On 18 October 1989 TIB[c] purchased from Goldman Sachs 15 million MCC shares at a cost of $47m (£29.4m)[d].
- 11.554 million MCC shares were transferred from the private side to International Bankers SA (IBI)[e]. This transfer was neither announced nor recorded in the private side's records, but 7.9 million of the shortfall so caused was made good by a purchase from the pension funds as described at paragraph 5.21[f] which similarly was neither announced nor recorded.
- The 11.554 million shares transferred to IBI, the 3.446 million shares purchased by TIB in May 1989 and the 15 million shares purchased by TIB in October 1989 were sold through Goldman Sachs to Nikko Securities who then placed them in Japan. The proceeds of the sales by IBI and TIB were paid by Goldman Sachs to IBI and TIB who paid them to the private side.

The transactions enabled RM to take the benefit of the placement in Japan without that fact being disclosed[g].

---

a KM told us that he saw TIB as being "unconnected" in the same way in which the vehicles used to acquire Macmillan and OAG were unconnected with MCC – see footnote to paragraph 4.8.

b On 16 March 1988 Nikko Capital Management (UK) Limited (Nikko Management) had been appointed at RM's behest as a sub-manager for part of the pension funds. RM had explained that Nikko Securities were the brokers MCC intended to use in the Japanese Market.

c The transaction took place during a closed period for dealings in MCC shares, when directors of MCC were not permitted to deal in the company's shares.

d The funds to settle the purchase were remitted on 6 November 1989 from PHUSI which had received $50m from LBI. LBI had raised $50m through financing from Lehman Brothers International Limited secured on pension fund assets by means of the arrangements described at paragraph 5.39.

e We refer to all the companies in the IBI group as IBI. Details about IBI are in the footnote to paragraph 5.21.

f The balance of the shortfall, 3.65 million shares, was not made good; when the Maxwell Foundation's holding was transferred to an English company as a consequence of the third reorganisation of ownership described at paragraph 4.6, 3.65 million shares remained recorded as being held by the Maxwell Foundation, but no share certificates could be found.

g The letter which KM signed on 21 December 1989 (referred to in paragraph 4.51) gave the same information in respect of IBI as it had in respect of TIB. KM was a director of IBI and the Common Investment Fund had a shareholding as set out in paragraph 5.21.

4.53 Although the effect of the transfer to IBI was to decrease the holding of RM's interests, the Maxwell Foundation and PHL had agreed to take dividends from MCC in shares instead of cash and this, together with some purchases, caused the disclosed holding in MCC to increase in the second half of 1989.

Bank lending and the private side debt

4.54 During the period of the expansion of RM's companies, banks including a number of major international banks[a], had lent very large sums of money to RM's companies. There were two basic reasons for this:

- RM had never defaulted on an obligation to his bankers; they believed that as he was dependent on them they would be the last persons to whom he would default.
- Dealing with RM was very profitable, not least because of the substantial fees that could be earned in arranging the borrowings.

4.55 Apart from the substantial debt of over $3 billion incurred by MCC in its acquisition of Macmillan and OAG, and the much smaller debt of £300m incurred by MGN in acquiring BNPC, the private side also had a very heavy debt burden arising from the substantial sums that the banks had lent. Although we have referred to some of the substantial borrowings made by the private side in describing the expansion of RM's businesses, as the burden of this debt played an increasingly important role, it is necessary to summarise the position.

4.56 By the beginning of 1990, the main components of the private side debt of just over £960m[b] were:

- Two facilities, one arranged by Ansbacher initially for £175m but which had been reduced in October 1989 to £100m and the other arranged by Lloyds for £170m. These were largely secured on MCC shares and had been provided in the circumstances described at paragraphs 3.20 and 3.27.
- A syndicated loan secured on property for £105m arranged by Goldman Sachs on the property in Holborn including the Mirror Building, Maxwell House and State House (as described at paragraph 2.34).
- A series of bilateral loans from various other banks including National Westminster[c], Barclays, Crédit Lyonnais, Bank of Nova Scotia, Bankers Trust[d], Société Générale,

---

[a] Of the many banks that lent to RM, we have mentioned two of the major clearing banks, National Westminster and Midland. Lloyds had also started to lend to RM, beginning in 1984. They had taken note of the 1971/73 Reports but had been impressed by what RM had done at MCC and that he had had the support of many other institutions. Barclays had also started to lend to RM at the same time and also took the view that RM had rehabilitated himself.

[b] These and subsequent figures for the private side bank debt include all UK borrowing and overseas borrowings as far as we have been able to determine.

[c] National Westminster had increased its loan to PHL in November 1989 to £150m (see paragraph 3.20).

[d] RM's companies became a client of Bankers Trust in about 1986; the relationship began in New York, but no information had been retained as to the factors considered when the relationship began.

Swiss Bank Corporation (SBC), Hill Samuel, Banque National de Paris (BNP) and Crédit Agricole secured on shares or other assets.

- Overdrafts from National Westminster and Barclays.
- Funds borrowed through two other private side companies, London & Bishopsgate International Investment Management plc and London & Bishopsgate Holdings plc[a]; these transactions are referred to at paragraph 5.39 and 5.40 below.

4.57 The complex structure of the private side, the different year ends[b] of the various companies which had large intercompany debts and the fairly frequent transfers of assets and of companies that were made between the various groups comprising the private side made it very difficult, if not impossible, for the banks to make an accurate assessment of the finances of the private side from the accounts of the various companies; these factors also made it difficult for the banks to compare one year to another and to carry out proper cash flow analysis[c]. One of the main bankers concluded in a report in November 1990 that in respect of the private side they had

> "a suspicion that the Group seeks to obfuscate".

In December 1990 another major bank took up RM's suggestion to send an employee on an attachment with the private side but his inability to obtain a proper understanding of the finances contributed to that bank's concern about lending to the private side.

4.58 For these reasons, all the facilities[d] granted to the private side were on a secured basis, the security in the main being shares[e].

4.59 Although the banks looked on RM's companies as comprising the three divisions referred to at paragraph 3.8 - MCC, MGN and the private side, it is important to appreciate that, when considering lending to all the companies in which RM was interested, the banks in assessing the overall strategy and exposure looked at the private side, MGN and MCC as one[f].

---

a The function and ownership of these companies is described at paragraph 5.14.

b These had arisen from purchases of companies with different year ends or because there were tax advantages. KM told us the banks had made him aware of the difficulties this caused in creating consolidated accounts for the purpose of decisions on loans. He had discussions in 1991 with Mr Walsh with a view to matching the year end dates of the private side companies.

c Because of these difficulties, each of the banks tried to pay regular visits to either KM or Mr Bunn to obtain up-to-date financial information on the position of RM's companies. As a result one bank visited the companies two to three times a week and thought that it had better information than anyone else; another bank regarded itself as "in a unique position, being the one with the least outstandings and the best security".

d Some of the overdrafts were not specifically secured.

e The central treasury controlled the collateral (for all loans other than those made through London & Bishopsgate International Investment Management plc- see paragraph 5.14) and computer schedules were used to monitor the position.

f Different banks favoured lending to different parts of RM's empire and in this they applied different criteria dependent on their assessment of the strength of each part. Those banks which carried out annual reviews of their lending to RM's companies carried out a review that extended across all the companies.

The third reorganisation of ownership (1990)

4.60 By the beginning of 1990 the pressure on the private side finances was such that there was a need to be able to present to banks a stronger balance sheet.

4.61 This pressure led to the third reorganisation of the companies within the private side. There were two specific concerns:

- The 31 per cent. shareholding in MCC owned by the Maxwell Foundation, although used for security in the UK, did not appear on any UK balance sheet, resulting in the UK balance sheets not looking as strong as they might.
- The private UK companies (including MGN) were fragmented into three groupings, namely PG, RMG and PMT, and this weakened the presentation of the private side's position (as shown in the diagram under paragraph 3.29).

It was therefore decided to strengthen the balance sheet by bringing into the ownership of an English company the 31 per cent. shareholding in MCC held by the Maxwell Foundation and by making the English companies subsidiaries of RMG[a]. A reorganisation along these lines also had fiscal advantages in the changed financial position of the private side, certain parts of which by now had losses[b].

4.62 As in the case of the second reorganisation that occurred in 1987/1988, a very complicated scheme was entered into in March 1990 to transfer assets around the empire. RMG acquired the UK holding companies of the private side and the Maxwell Foundation's 31 per cent. holding in MCC was acquired by PHA Investments Limited (PHAI) for £470m (which it settled by the issue of RMG convertible loan stock to the Maxwell Foundation)[c].

4.63 Although RMG remained a subsidiary of the Maxwell Foundation, to enable RMG to be a subsidiary of HI (RM's family company which had been established during the second

---

[a] The Maxwell Foundation retained on its books the 3.65 million shortfall in MCC shares brought about by the transfer to IBI as referred to at paragraph 4.52.

[b] These advantages included:

- Tax credits attaching to MCC dividends received by UK companies with trading losses would be recoverable, whereas they would be irrecoverable if the dividends were received by the Maxwell Foundation.
- It was necessary to deduct withholding tax on the interest payable by the companies within PG to the RMG companies as a group election was not possible; consolidation into a single group would eliminate this fiscal disadvantage.
- Because many of the PG companies had tax losses, it was desirable to be able to seek group relief for these losses against the profits being made, particularly by MGN, in the RMG Group.
- The benefits of taking offshore any capital gain made on the flotation of MGN had been diminished once RMG had been interposed between the company likely to be floated and the Maxwell Foundation.

[c] This was approved by a board meeting of PHA in Paris on 11 March 1990 attended by Maître de la Pradelle, Mr Freedman and Dr Keicher with Mr Woods and Dr Rechsteiner present. The minute records a report being presented by Mr Woods and the meeting lasting one hour. We were told that the Board considered this and the subsequent reorganisation from the standpoint of whether the interests of the Foundation were prejudiced. They left the detailed schemes to the advisers in London.

reorganisation as described at paragraph 3.23), control of the appointment of the board of RMG was passed to HI by an agreement dated 14 March 1990. Although this was not appreciated until the early part of 1991, RMG and all its subsidiaries had in effect two parent companies - the Maxwell Foundation and HI.

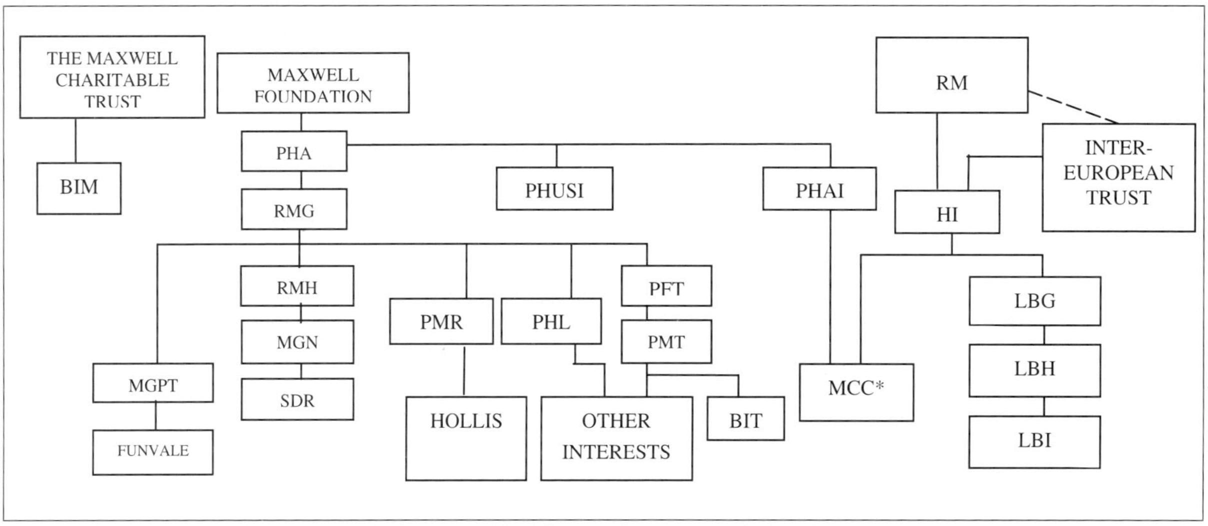

Figure 4 Ownership March 1990 to April 1991 (main companies only)
* MCC shareholding held via subsidiaries including Visaford and Magnacell

4.64 The reorganisation was completed in the autumn of 1990 when PHL ceased to be the main company for the private side and this role was transferred to RMG.

5. 1988-90: RM'S USE OF THE PENSION FUNDS

5.1 The fortunes of RM's businesses continued to have an impact on the pension funds, but as the need for cash became greater, so the pension funds developed as a source not only of cash but also of assets for use as collateral for bank loans. It is necessary first to refer to a change in legislation which gave RM the opportunity to obtain greater control over the assets of the pension schemes.

The transfer of the effective control over the pension funds to BIM

5.2 In 1988 the arrangements for the investment of the assets of MGPS and the pension schemes for other companies controlled by RM within the UK, including the Maxwell Communication Works Pension Scheme (MCWPS)[a], underwent a significant change. The management of those investments which had not been entrusted to external fund managers[b] passed into the effective control of RM, and even in respect of the assets managed externally, a greater influence was exercised by RM. This came about in the following circumstances.

5.3 One result of the Financial Services Act 1986 was that the trustees of MGPS were advised that it was not possible for them to take day-to-day investment decisions. This was of importance because by 5 April 1987 the assets administered directly by RM and the investment committee (as described at paragraph 2.29) comprised 31 per cent. of the assets of MGPS. As at 5 April 1987, the assets were as follows:

Investment	Directly managed £m	Externally managed £m	Total £m
UK Equities	74.00	176.40	250.40
Overseas Equities	8.60	55.50	64.10
Property	39.40	0.35	39.75
Cash	---	11.92	11.92
Other	1.20	30.60	31.80
TOTAL	123.20	274.77	397.97

Table 3 – Assets of MGPS at 5 April 1987

5.4 The trustees were advised by Nicholson Graham & Jones that an in-house investment company authorised by Investment Management Regulatory Organisation Limited (IMRO) could be

[a] The pension fund for the print workers at MCC; it was from this fund that a payment had subsequently to be made to a new pension fund established by BPCC after the buy-out referred to at paragraph 4.10. MGN became the principal employer of MCWPS following MGN's acquisition of BNPC referred to in paragraph 4.31.

[b] The use of these continued; however the continuation of the employment of specific managers did not always depend on their performance; for example Phillips & Drew had their contract terminated after an analyst at UBS Phillips & Drew Research Limited had written a circular critical of MCC.

incorporated to take day-to-day investment decisions. It was initially envisaged that the directors of this company would comprise RM, KM, Mr Stephens, Mr Cook, Mr Guest, Mr Chapman and Mr Talbot[a]. In the event however the directors of the company that was used, Bishopsgate Investment Management Limited (BIM) - KM[b], RM, IM[c], Mr Stephens, Mr Woods, Mr Bunn and Mr Cook - were all, apart from Mr Cook, closely involved in the running of RM's private companies. RM refused to allow the appointment of any other outside person, saying that the directors had to have appropriate financial or investment experience to be approved by IMRO and had to be available in London on a regular basis; there was not time, according to RM, to train anyone to meet the necessary requirements.

5.5 On 7 December 1987 the trustees of MGPS agreed to transfer all day-to-day decision making on investments to BIM. Under a Deed dated 31 March 1988 most of the assets[d] that had been directly managed for MGPS, for MCWPS and for other pension schemes of companies controlled by RM were transferred to a Common Investment Fund (CIF). This was a trust fund for the benefit of the participating schemes[e] and BIM acted as the trustee. The assets transferred were valued at £300m, over half of which came from MGPS. The assets that were managed by external fund managers (CCM, Phillips & Drew and MIM as referred to at paragraph 2.25) were not transferred to the CIF.

5.6 BIM was admitted to membership of IMRO[f] on 7 June 1988. At the meeting which approved the admission the Chairman, Mr Smethurst[g], recalled saying of RM something like that it was "a pity we can't exclude that crook". The information IMRO had was limited and they did not make further enquiries. At that time, BIM was ultimately owned by the Maxwell Foundation. On 17 April 1989 ownership of BIM was transferred to the Maxwell Charitable Trust (the

---

a He had been appointed a trustee of MCWPS on 24 May 1984.

b KM told us that he would have been appointed to the board of BIM in the same way that he was appointed to any other of RM's companies: he would have received the relevant form from Mr Stephens and be told that he had been appointed by RM.

c IM attended only two BIM board meetings in the period from his appointment to July 1991. He told us that, although he signed various documents in his capacity as director of BIM (for example, the "stock swap" between BIM and IBI and the share transfer forms relating to the provision by way of collateral of the MIM portfolio referred to in paragraphs 5.21 and 6.26 respectively), he had no recollection of the circumstances in which he signed those documents. He said he would normally, however, have relied on RM, KM or another person directly concerned in the transaction and checked that it was proper for him to sign.

d Certain shares remained in a portfolio directly held by the schemes and were not transferred.

e The participating schemes were pension schemes of companies controlled by RM and were MCWPS, MGPS and the Maxwell Communication Pension Plan. Subsequently Hollis plc Group Pension Scheme, Withy Grove Pension Fund and E.J. Arnold & Sons Limited 1978 Pension Schemes joined.

f Its membership was in the Occupational Pension Scheme (OPS) category, which meant that some of IMRO's rules disapplied. The most significant of these were those applicable to financial resources, accounting records, financial reporting and audit requirements. A detailed account of the admission of BIM is at Appendix 9.

g Mr Smethurst was a former adviser to H M Treasury (1969 - 71) and to the Prime Minister's policy unit (1975 - 76) and deputy chairman of the Monopolies & Mergers commission. Since 1991, he has been Provost of Worcester College, Oxford.

origin and original purpose of which is described at paragraph 3.13). In the latter part of 1988 Lord Elwyn Jones had asked[a] to retire as a trustee of the Maxwell Charitable Trust and in August 1988 Lord Silkin, the other independent trustee, had died. In their place, Mr Corsan (who, until his retirement in 1986, had been the audit partner at CLD responsible for the private side companies from the time RM became their audit client in 1974 and had been the partner responsible for the overall relationship between RM and CLD) and Mr Middleton (a retired partner in Clifford Chance) had been appointed by a Deed dated 5 January 1989. They agreed to be appointed on condition that there was a minimum income to The Maxwell Charitable Trust of £50,000 per year, that they were provided with a full indemnity by RM personally, that they could resign at any time and that they could never be outvoted by the Maxwells.

5.7 We asked Mr Corsan why he had received an indemnity and he replied "because I asked for an indemnity for everything I did for [RM]"[b]. He also told us that, when a partner in CLD, he was usually accompanied when he saw RM. Mr Corsan was informed that the purpose of transferring the ownership of BIM to The Maxwell Charitable Trust was to provide stability of ownership, but we were told by others that the real reason was that if ownership had remained with the Maxwell Foundation it was feared that it would have been necessary to provide the accounts and other information about the Maxwell Foundation to regulatory organisations.

5.8 Although the creation of a management company and a common investment fund was not unusual, there were a number of significant characteristics of the way in which the investment decisions for the CIF and pension schemes were made and reported:

- Investment decisions were, we were told, generally made by RM himself and later by KM[c]. Certain of the more significant investment decisions were subsequently ratified at board meetings, but we were told that the effective decision was always made by RM or KM. KM told us that he only spent about 30 minutes a week dealing with BIM matters. He did not make investment decisions but received instructions from RM as to particular investments that BIM was to make which he would relay to Mr Cook for implementation. RM took the investment decisions because he thought he knew best and, if he was wrong, then the company would stand in to make good any shortfall.
- The first that the pensions investment administration would hear of some investment decisions was when the contract note arrived, the decision having been made by RM without anyone in investment administration being informed.

---

a We were told he was being asked to sign commercial documents and was unhappy at this.

b Mr Corsan subsequently explained to us that he always asked for an indemnity in any situation when he acted in a personal capacity after his retirement (such as acting as a trustee or director) where he might have been exposed to personal liability; that the request was not made only because he was dealing with RM.

c In September 1990, KM replaced Mr Bunn as the senior person responsible for the CIF's investment administration. KM told us that he was not comfortable with the appointment as he was not a qualified accountant but his role was limited as Mr Cook supervised the preparation of all the necessary returns and brought them to him for signature.

5.8 continued

- Until the early part of 1990, Mr Highfield, the financial controller of the pension schemes and BIM was not allowed to know what investment decisions had been made or what the holdings were. This meant that in this period there was no effective monitoring by the financial controller over the expenditure of monies on investment, but this was justified by RM on the basis of a need to preserve confidentiality relating to investment decisions.
- Save for a brief period between November 1990 and February 1991 (after a visit by IMRO referred to at paragraph 13.29 below) the board of BIM never met to review investment strategy or its holdings[a].
- Although the external managers of the funds of the pension schemes reported regularly to the Investment Committee of MGPS[b], Mr Guest and Mr Chapman told us that in the case of BIM, RM refused to provide them with a schedule showing what investments had been made by the CIF[c]. Mr Cook told us that Mr Guest and Mr Chapman were shown detailed schedules and the transactions were explained to them each quarter. Mr Bunn told us that RM allowed them to see the schedules when they requested them, but did not allow them to retain copies[d].
- It was initially decided by BIM[e] and recorded in CLD's letter of engagement dated 4 August 1989 that the accounts of the CIF should be prepared on the basis that the SORP on Pension Scheme Accounts[f] be applied and that CLD were to report whether in their opinion:

> "the accounts show a true and fair view of the financial transactions of the [CIF] during the year and of the disposition at the end of the year of its assets and liabilities."[g]

In August 1989, Mr Highfield sent to Mr Cowling a draft format for accounts for the CIF for the year 5 April 1989 in which the accounting policies were described as being in accordance with the SORP and the Disclosure Regulations. However it appears that at the beginning of 1990, Mr Cook was given instructions that the SORP[h] was not to be applied; this was communicated to CLD, but it was intimated to them that the disclosures

---

a Mr Woods and Mr Stephens told us they had no clear idea what investments were being made by BIM or what investment strategy was being pursued.

b The trustees were provided with CAPS (Combined Actuarial Services Limited) reports on performance which compared the performance of the various parts of fund with the median performance of funds monitored by CAPS; the funds appeared on the basis of the reports to be doing quite well. These reports did not set out the actual investments of the funds.

c This position does not appear to have been reported to the other trustees of MGPS. We were told that if termination of BIM's appointment as manager had been proposed, "I would have kissed my job goodbye."

d Mr Cook also told us that the trustees of MCWPS were provided with detailed breakdowns of the holdings of the CIF managed directly by BIM. The evidence of the trustees is that this was never done save on one occasion when one trustee who specifically asked was shown a breakdown. The documents retained by the trustees is entirely consistent with their evidence.

e The CIF deed provided only for accounts to be produced without specifying their form.

f See footnote to paragraph 2.46.

g This was the same requirement as set out in the Occupational Pension Schemes (Disclosure of Information) Regulations 1986 referred to in the footnote to paragraph 2.46.

h See footnote to paragraph 2.47.

required by the SORP would be made in the pension scheme accounts. CLD agreed to this, but their letter of engagement was not amended[a]. However, there was no change to the requirement to report in the terms that we have set out and the auditors' reports on the accounts of the CIF used the words of the requirement. CLD's understanding of this was that it was not necessary for BIM to disclose in the accounts:

- the loans it made to the private side companies provided there was no balance outstanding at the year end; or
- the other dealings with related parties. However CLD told us that in accordance with accepted practice, they did carry out tests on related party transactions which they encountered with a view to checking that they had been carried out at a current market price.

- The certificates for the equity investments held directly by the CIF were handled as follows:
    - If the investments were registered in the name of BIM, the certificates were kept in a safe at Maxwell House, first in Mr Bunn's room and from about September 1990 in KM's room[b].
    - In the case of overseas investments, the certificates were generally held by an overseas bank.
    - If investments were acquired from a company owned or controlled by RM or the Maxwell Foundation, they were often held in the name of Bishopsgate Investment Trust plc (BIT) or they remained in the name of the original owner and the certificates were kept by the central treasury at Maxwell House.

5.9 BIT[c] was a nominee company used from 1987 to hold many of the investments of MCC, the private side, some of those of the pension funds and some of those controlled by RM[d]. We were told that it was set up because when RM bought shares it was not clear for whom he was buying them and it simplified matters if they could be put into the name of one nominee. Allocation of beneficial ownership was made then, later or at the year end. The use of BIT as a nominee also meant that those dealing with RM's interests did not necessarily know who owned the shares and the choice of name which was so similar to the names of BIM and other companies caused confusion. Although initially a register of the holder of the beneficial interests was kept by BIT, this was subsequently discontinued and after RM's death no register

---

[a] In a note the audit manager stated

> "Any deviation from these disclosures will require a supplementary letter to our letter of engagement which was originally signed by Mr Cook."

[b] KM's evidence was that two blue folders containing a number of CIF securities were placed into his safe, the key and the code to which was kept by his secretaries who would open the safe and retrieve documents when requested by RM, KM, Mr Cook or Mr Trachtenberg.

[c] The shares in which were allotted to PMT on 15 April 1987; it is probable that BIT had been owned by PMT since incorporation. An advertisement in the Financial Times of 12 January 1989 stated that BIT was a wholly-owned subsidiary of MCC (see the footnote to paragraph 5.29).

[d] As set out in Appendix 7, the accounts through which Goldman Sachs dealt with RM for the private side companies and the pension funds were all in the name of BIT.

could be found identifying the particular company or fund for which BIT held the shares. Transfers into the name of BIM from BIT, if they took place at all, took time.

5.10 The pensions administration was understaffed and always behind with its records. The pensions administration referred to at paragraph 2.23 was located at Dorrington Street (just north of the Holborn site), but until the early part of 1991 the department that administered the investments was located separately, first at Maxwell House and then at 50 Fetter Lane on the Holborn site.

5.11 Over the three year period between the creation of the CIF and the flotation of MGN in April 1991, there were only five full meetings of the trustees of MGPS[a]. The return on the investments and the information supplied to the trustees in the accounts of the CIF gave no indication that there was anything wrong with the way the CIF was being run.

5.12 In May 1988[b] Peat Marwick were instructed by PHL to conduct a review of the pensions department. They reported that it was evident that RM

> "had a profound influence on the management of the pension department. The Chairman's strong personality and high degree of energy and drive in his own management style was acknowledged frequently in the discussions that we held within the department. The Chairman had the reputation for demanding the highest quality of customer service, efficiency and cost saving."

The report did not deal with investments although those who ran the investment administration department were interviewed and it was made clear to Peat Marwick that RM controlled the investments. For example their note of an interview with Mr Stephens recorded that he had told them:

> "RM will control pensions until he dies"

Peat Marwick's note of a meeting with the trustees of MCWPS recorded what they were told by one of the trustees:

> "[RM] likes to have a large fund of pension scheme assets, part of which are under his direct control. [The trustee] went on to suggest that this could be very useful to a man of his financial acumen. He was clearly implying that the pension scheme assets were being used to assist [RM]'s business transactions, so I asked if the trustees were happy with such a situation. He replied that the trustees were happy to go along with this situation because the returns which have been achieved have been very good. He then said 'If the horse keeps winning, you don't break its leg'."

The report made no comment on these matters.

---

a These took place on 29 September 1988, 24 April 1989, 19 March 1990, 27 September 1990 and 25 March 1991. The board of MCWPS met more frequently, at first meeting in 1988 on 11 April, 19 May, 27 September, 21 November and 13 December; in 1989 on 23 February, 26 May, 9 October and 11 December. In 1990 the board of MCWPS only met on 1 March, 26 June and 27 September and did not meet again until 13 June 1991.

b Peat Marwick were also asked to review the internal controls on payments consequent on a fraud said to have been carried out by an employee.

5.13 RM had always regarded the pension funds as his, but the financial needs of his businesses made the use to which the pension funds might be put more important from 1988 onwards. Towards the end of 1989, RM told Mr Pittaway of Nicholson Graham & Jones, the solicitors to MGPS, that he wanted to remove funds from MGPS which had a substantial surplus. A conference was arranged with counsel (attended by Mr Woods and Mr Pittaway) for him to confirm the advice given by Mr Pittaway that the surplus could not be paid to MGN. Having received that advice, RM did not press the matter further. However, RM continued to use the pension funds as an adjunct to his other business interests as he had done earlier as described in Chapter 2; the creation of BIM made that use easier and the requirements of his private business interests made the need greater. It is convenient to refer first to another private side company that played a central role in that use of the pension funds.

LBI

5.14 In the same way that MGPS had appointed external fund managers, sub-managers were appointed by BIM for some of the CIF funds. The most significant appointment[a] was that of London & Bishopsgate International Investment Management plc (LBI), a company that had been acquired by KM in February 1988 and had applied for IMRO membership[b]. During the course of 1988 ownership of LBI was transferred to London & Bishopsgate Holdings plc (LBH), a company owned 75 per cent.[c] by RM[d], and 25 per cent. owned by the active senior

---

a The CIF also appointed as sub-managers Asset Managers plc, Duquesne Capital Management Limited and Nikko Management.

b LBI had been granted a licence under the Prevention of Fraud (Investments) Act by the DTI on 25 April 1988, 4 days before "A" day - the day on which LBI had to have interim authorisation from IMRO under the Financial Services Act. Mr Andrew Smith and Mr Trachtenberg were granted licences on 26 April 1988. LBI was admitted by IMRO at a meeting chaired by Mr Corsan on 13 July 1988. A detailed account of its admission is in Appendix 9.

c On 21 September 1990 RM transferred his 75 per cent holding in LBH to HI which then transferred them to a new wholly owned subsidiary London & Bishopsgate Group Ltd (LBG).

d In 1990, Mr Anselmini (whose primary role is dealt with at paragraph 6.58) was asked by RM to play a part in overseeing the management as a non-executive director. We were told that Mr Anselmini tried to recommend tighter management controls, but RM was not interested and Mr Anselmini tendered his resignation on 2 August 1990.

management of the company, Lord Donoughue of Ashton[a], Mr Andrew Smith[b] and Mr Trachtenberg[c].

5.15 On 21 June 1988, BIM appointed LBI to manage a minimum of £50m of the CIF and on 30 June 1988 implemented the decision by transferring to LBI a portfolio of "blue chip" UK and US stocks valued at £70m[d]. LBI sold the majority of the portfolio and reinvested the proceeds in a wide spread of shares and other securities, including US and Japanese shares, in accordance with the requirements of LBI's index-tracking programme. On 8 March 1989 it was decided that a further £30m of the CIF be transferred to the management of LBI[e]; this sum was paid on 13 March 1989 and immediately lent to the private side as set out at paragraph 5.25.

5.16 LBI had two main parts to its business - fund management[f] and proprietary trading (trading for its own account at its own risk in foreign exchange, bonds, derivatives and other markets). In the course of 1988 LBI acquired the management of:

- a fund of $50m from the Bulgarian Government

---

a Lord Donoughue was senior policy adviser to the Prime Minister from 1974 to 1979 and thereafter at The Economist Intelligence Unit and assistant editor at The Times from 1981-82. He joined Grieveson Grant & Co in 1983 and became a partner; he was in the Research Department considering global investment strategy. In 1988 he was invited to join LBI. Lord Donoughue became a director on 7 June 1988 and then became Executive Vice Chairman. He resigned as a director of LBI in 1991 in the circumstances described in Appendix 8.

b Mr Andrew Smith had been a research fellow at Wolfson College and taught at Keble College, Oxford. In 1985 he set up Global Analysis Systems with Mr Trachtenberg. He first met RM in 1987 and, following RM's acquisition of Global Analysis Systems, Mr Andrew Smith became a director of LBI on 22 February 1988. He moved to New York in 1990 to set up the US business of LBI but continued to play a role in the UK company. He resigned as a director of LBI on 9 February 1991.

c Mr Trachtenberg had been a full-time lecturer in the Department of International Relations at the London School of Economics from 1981-83 and had then moved to work for the University of Southern California. In early 1985 he was approached by Mr Andrew Smith and they set up an on-line information business, Global Analysis Systems, which was bought by RM in 1987 on terms that they formed together an index-tracking fund management business. LBI was then formed for that purpose. Mr Trachtenberg reluctantly became Compliance Officer at LBI without having had any training (as RM would not approve payment for this) and only after a proposal for third party back-office administration and a professional compliance officer had come to nought due to the cost. He told us that with hindsight he had carried out certain tasks half heartedly because he did not know any better.

d A minute of a board meeting attended by Mr Bunn and Mr Cook stated that this transfer was approved. Mr Trachtenberg told us that the proposal to RM by Mr Andrew Smith which led to the formation of LBI had been dependent upon LBI receiving substantial assets for management and, in June 1988, RM decided that LBI would receive an undefined amount of pension fund assets.

e A minute of a board meeting attended by KM and Mr Bunn stated that this transfer was approved and that the funds were to be managed on the same basis as the monies transferred on 30 June 1988.

f We were told that LBI was, in its fund management activities, technically ahead of much of the City and produced excellent results for its fund management customers.

- funds from Sun Alliance[a]
- two Macmillan pension funds[b]

In 1989, as set out at paragraph 5.27, it became the manager of an investment trust.

5.17 LBI also had a department which executed transactions. RM would give instructions direct to this department to execute transactions for the private side. These instructions would not necessarily involve the central treasury described in paragraph 2.10. These became significant in the second part of 1990 and in 1991.

The use of the Common Investment Fund (CIF)

5.18 The use RM made of the CIF can be conveniently considered under six headings:

(a) Investment in related companies.
(b) Loans of cash to the private side.
(c) FTIT.
(d) Acquisitions from related parties.
(e) Dealings for the benefit of MCC and the private side.
(f) Use of shares as collateral for loans for the benefit of the private side.

(a) Investment in related companies

5.19 Shortly before the establishment of the CIF, a formal resolution of the board of BIM recorded a decision to invest in MCC shares. On 6 April 1988 the holdings in MCC shares directly owned by MCWPS and MGPS (referred to at paragraph 2.31) were transferred to the CIF. By the 5 April 1989 year end, the number of MCC shares held by the CIF had increased from 9.9 million to 13.3 million valued at £27.4m (at a price per share of 206p).

5.20 In April and May 1989 immediately after the commencement of the new accounting year, there were very significant further purchases of MCC shares, details of which are set out in Appendix 7. One of the transactions is particularly significant.

- The sale of 3.446 million shares by Goldman Sachs to TIB, referred to at paragraph 4.49, appears initially to have been a sale to the CIF. The funds for that purchase were nonetheless provided by the CIF.
- The records of the CIF showed the purchase by them on 19 May 1989 of 3.446 million shares from Rowe & Pitman. No such purchase was ever made, but the shortfall was made good from purchases made in August 1990 in the name of BIT (see paragraph 6.17). At the scrip count for the audit of the CIF for the year ended 5 April 1990, CLD found that there were no share certificates for 3.446 million shares. KM provided a letter dated 16 November 1990 stating that BIT was holding 3.446 million MCC shares to the order of BIM.

By 30 September 1989 the CIF held according to its records 31.1 million MCC shares (valued at £1.3m at a price per share of 197p), but was in fact missing 3.446 million.

---

[a] LBI did not have custody of the Sun Alliance portfolio and acted on an advisory basis.

[b] These funds were acquired for management by LBI Inc. in New York but were managed on a shadow basis by LBI pending the setting up of offices in New York.

5.21 There were then two significant transactions:

- On 21 December 1989 BIM and BIT entered into an agreement with IBI[a] which resulted in a so-called "stock swap", through which IBI acquired 5.89 million MCC shares for $22.5m from BIM and BIM acquired 18,360 shares in IBI for $23 m, the difference being bridged by a promissory note. No cash changed hands but the agreement provided for the transactions to be reversed if notice were served by either party no later than 15 June 1990. In fact on 12 June 1990 the stocks were swapped back and a small financial adjustment made. We received no commercial explanation for this arrangement other than that it was an arrangement whereby MCC shares were "parked" during the year ends of MCC and the pension schemes so as to reduce the level of holding in MCC that had to be disclosed in MCC's annual report and the pension scheme accounts. However, we were told by KM and others that this transaction was a favour to Mr Lévêque of IBI who had been the principal backer of RM's expansion into France and a principal banker to RM's companies who had recommended Mr Anselmini[b] to RM. He was looking to place in friendly hands for a short period of time some shares previously held by a core Arab investor in IBI (the Baroom group) who had decided to dispose of the shares; the arrangement permitted IBI time to find another long term core investor. The reduction in the year end holding of MCC shares was, KM thought, merely an added benefit.
- On 26 March 1990 RM arranged for the transfer of 7.9 million MCC shares from the CIF to BIT through Goldman Sachs (New York) who did this as an agency transaction[c]; £13.5m of the purchase price of £14.3m that BIT had to pay Goldman Sachs was borrowed from the CIF on 30 March 1990 and repaid on 3 April 1990. The private side did not record this purchase in its share records, but the shares were used towards covering the shortfall brought about by the transfer of 11.554 million MCC shares to IBI in December 1989 in connection with the placing in the Japanese market as described at paragraph 4.48. A more detailed account of this transaction is set out in Appendix 7.

If these transactions had not been effected then the holding by the CIF in MCC at 5 April 1990 would, according to its records, have been 31.1 million shares (4.8 per cent. of MCC). The percentage of the net assets of MGPS invested in MCC would have been 7.66 per cent.[d] and the percentage of MCWPS would have been 9.05 per cent.[a].

---

[a] The IBI group of companies was established in Luxembourg with a subsidiary in Paris and was originally owned by a Curacao holding company. In 1988, Mr J.M. Lévêque (who had been Chairman of Crédit Commerciale de France and was later Chairman of Crédit Lyonnais) became chairman of the holding company and at about the same time the IBI group moved its headquarters to Paris. In the course of 1990 the group was reorganised with further shareholders becoming involved. Within the group, there were various companies including International Bankers SA and International Bankers France. Mr Lévêque asked RM to take a strategic stake in IBI as one of the core shareholders; consequently KM became a director and BIM invested $5m from the CIF in IBI shares.

[b] See paragraph 6.58.

[c] The fact that this transaction between two UK companies was carried out through Goldman Sachs & Co (New York) meant that it did not appear as a transaction on the screens of the London Stock Exchange.

[d] The disclosure made in the prospectus for the flotation of MGN in relation to the holding in MCC was what was actually held by the funds at 5 April 1990; in the case of MGPS this was disclosed as 4.7 per cent of the assets of the scheme and in the case of MCWPS as 5 per cent of the assets of the scheme; that disclosure did not in any way reflect the IBI transaction. The disclosure of the holdings were those at 5 April 1990 and the

5.22 Apart from these significant transactions in MCC shares, the CIF invested \$25m (£15.35m) in a \$300m issue of OAG stock made in March 1990. This issue was made by OAG to obtain funds which it could pass to MCC to repay part of the first tranche of the MCC \$3 billion debt referred to in paragraph 4.8.

(b) Loans of cash to the private side

5.23 In addition to the direct investment in MCC shares, cash from the CIF and pension schemes was lent to the private side companies. This was a continuation of the arrangement described at paragraph 2.45, under which MGPS had lent money to MGN. These loans were made in one of two ways:

- The CIF acted as "banker" to each of the pension schemes, and cash that a scheme held was passed to the CIF. Information about any cash held by the CIF was available not only to the pensions investment administration but also to the central treasury so that when cash was available, RM or KM instructed the pensions administration department to put in hand a transfer to the private side.
- Proceeds in respect of the sale of shares, particularly those that had been held in the name of BIT, were often remitted to BIT and "lent" to the private side.

Interest on money lent in either of these two ways was charged at the rate of one per cent. over base rate; regular payments were not usually made for interest on money lent, but the amount was added to the intercompany account. Until 5 April 1990, settlement of the intercompany account included the settlement of interest as well as capital. Although all bank lending to the private companies was on a secured basis[b], security was never given for the loans by BIM of the funds of the CIF or loans by the pension schemes. RM was therefore using the pension fund for risks the banks would not take.

5.24 During the first year of the operation of the CIF ended 5 April 1989, £25m was lent from the directly managed funds of the CIF to PHL on 28 December 1988 and a further £9.5m on 8 February 1989. Both sums were repaid by payments made on 31 March and 3 April 1989. As the loan balances had been cleared to zero by the year end, no disclosure of the loans during the year was made in the accounts of the CIF for the year ended 5 April 1989[c]. This was the consequence of the way (set out in paragraph 2.47) in which CLD interpreted the words of the Disclosure Regulations that were also used in their letter of engagement (set out at paragraph 5.8) and in their reports on the accounts of the CIF.

---

prospectus did not refer to the transactions that occurred after that date which are referred to at paragraph 6.17.

a This figure is after a reduction to reflect the liability of MCWPS to transfer funds to the BPCC scheme which transfer had not been effected at 5 April 1990.

b Except for negligible amounts - see paragraph 4.58.

c CLD knew of these loans and checked the interest calculations in the course of their audit of the CIF. The documents containing a summary of the main points arising on the audit for the attention of the partner, called by CLD "MAPs", also referred to the fact that amounts had been lent to MCC.

5.25 Cash was also lent through LBI in the years ended 5 April 1989 and 5 April 1990.

- Apart from the loans made through the transactions referred to at paragraph 5.33, LBI liquidated the portion of the CIF portfolio invested in Japanese securities to provide a loan of £27.5m to PHL over the year end at December 1988[a]. The fact that this loan was made in addition to the loan of £25m referred to in the preceding paragraph meant that at the end of December 1988, after other movements, £50.2m of the CIF's funds was lent on an unsecured basis to PHL.
- Between March 1989 and February 1990, £30m which had been passed by the CIF to LBI (as set out at paragraph 5.14) was lent to the private side by LBI[b].
  - The funds were paid to LBI on 13 March 1989 and on that day were paid to PHL. On that same day, as is set out at paragraph 2.43 in connection with the Reuters transaction, PHL paid £24m to MGN and £29m to MCC, and MGN paid £28.3m through Funvale to the CIF.
  - The fund of £30m was repaid by LBI to the CIF on 1 and 2 February 1990 and on the same days the CIF paid PHL £15m and £18.2m as referred to in the footnote to paragraph 5.28.

5.26 The CIF also made loans from its directly managed funds during the year ended 5 April 1990. On 12 April 1989, £5m was lent; further sums were then lent to a total of about £35m by 9 June 1989. The funds were all repaid by 30 June 1989. Loans were then regularly made and repaid in the succeeding months of the year, but the balance was cleared to zero by the year end and no disclosure of the loans was made in the accounts of the CIF.

(c) FTIT

5.27 In June 1988 LBH started to acquire, through Rowe & Pitman, shares in New Tokyo Investment Trust plc, then managed by Edinburgh Fund Managers plc. The stated objective

---

[a] The fact that this loan of £27.5m was made to the private side became known to CLD in the course of their audits of LBI for the year ended 31 December 1988; this was raised by CLD at an audit clearance meeting on 17 March 1989 attended by Mr Andrew Smith, Mr Trachtenberg and Lord Donoughue. CLD were told by LBI that the transaction was commercially beneficial to the CIF and the funds had remained in PHL's bank account. They were also told that Mr Bunn in his capacity as a pension fund trustee was aware of the use of the funds. Mr Bunn was a director of BIM and several private companies (see Appendix 3), although he was not a trustee of MGPS. Mr Andrew Smith told us that the decision to liquidate the portfolio was due to the economic climate at the time, that the money was lent because of the attractive rate of interest offered and that outside lawyers had advised that the deposits were proper. Mr Trachtenberg told us that he did not recall the meeting on 17 March 1989 but that a transaction of this sort would have been assessed by LBI according to its commercial benefit to the client, BIM, and its risk. Nobody ever questioned whether such a transaction was of itself wrong; he took comfort from the fact that CLD were aware of such transactions and assessed them in the same way as LBI. The accounts of LBI which were submitted to IMRO suggested that the sum of £27.5m was deposited in a client bank account, whereas in fact it had been loaned to PHL, as CLD had discovered during the audit of LBI's statutory accounts for that year. The description was inaccurate and misleading.

[b] In the audit of the CIF for the year ended 5 April 1989, CLD were provided with a schedule of the assets under the management of LBI which showed a cash amount of £30m; the signed accounts of the CIF were dated 27 February 1990. In the audit of LBI for the year ended 31 December 1989, the fact that £30m entrusted by the CIF to the management of LBI had been lent to the private side was drawn to the attention of the audit partner in the MAPs and considered by him on 21 March 1990. The accounts of LBI which were submitted to IMRO contained a description similar to that in respect of the loan made in December 1988.

of this acquisition was to secure the management of this investment trust for LBI. By November 1988 LBH had acquired a shareholding of 24.9 per cent. in New Tokyo Investment Trust plc at prices between 150p and 160p per share. On 28 November 1988 BIM agreed that the CIF would acquire LBH's shareholding in the investment trust if the shareholders of the trust accepted LBH's proposal to appoint LBI as manager of the trust for them to manage on an index-tracking basis. On 9 January 1989 the shareholders of the trust accepted the proposals of LBH and the trust was subsequently renamed First Tokyo Index Trust plc (FTIT). On 31 January 1989 the CIF acquired, through Rowe & Pitman acting as agents, LBH's 24.9 per cent. shareholding for a price of 165p per share or a total of £18.2 m[a]; this was paid for out of LBI's sub-managed part of the CIF portfolio[b]. Although LBH made a profit of over £900,000 on this sale, £1.1m was lost during the period of LBH's ownership of the stake in derivative transactions designed to hedge the investment. LBH contemplated transferring these losses to the CIF (whilst itself retaining the profit), but it appears that this did not happen.

(d) Acquisitions from related parties

5.28 In the same way that MGPS had been used as the "repository" for the Reuters A and the Beecham shares, the CIF was used on a much greater scale as a "repository" for investments that had been acquired by RM through MCC or a private side company which no longer served a strategic purpose, or for which by selling to the CIF he could raise cash and yet retain control. The driving force behind many of these acquisitions (mainly from MCC) was the need for MCC to raise cash in order to repay the short term financing organised by Samuel Montagu in connection with the acquisition of Macmillan and OAG (referred to in a footnote to paragraph 4.8). RM believed that these strategic stakes would be good long term investments and did not want to lose control over them. The most significant transactions were the following:

- **Agence Havas**. As set out in paragraph 3.19, MCC had acquired a shareholding in this company in 1987. Between June and December 1988 the CIF purchased 274,550 shares from MCC for a price of £18.1m[c]. These were held until June 1990 when they were sold through Goldman Sachs (at a profit of £28.1m to the CIF) and the funds used in the manner set out in paragraphs 6.5 and 6.16.
- **Société Générale**. As set out in paragraph 3.19, MCC had acquired a stake in this bank in August 1988 for £44.1m. On 10 November 1988 almost all these shares (1.1 million) were sold to the CIF for £54.9m[d] at a profit to MCC of £10m. Approximately one-third

---

[a] At the time of the acquisition of FTIT, it was thought that the index-tracking system developed by LBI offered an opportunity for successful investment and the subsequent record of FTIT confirmed this.

[b] This holding was not referred to in the 1989 accounts of MGPS (though it was one of the 20 largest investments) but is referred to in 1990 accounts of MGPS.

[c] The initial purchase in June 1988 for £10.9m was MCC's original holding. The shares purchased thereafter were bought by MCC for the CIF.

[d] On 7 November 1988, Mr Cook gave several of the external fund managers instructions to sell gilts held by them and remit the cash; the cash remitted included £18.8m from Phillips & Drew, £4.3m from London Life and £12.3m from MIM. Nikko Management were told on 7 November 1988 that a decision had been made to withdraw funds from the Japanese market and they were asked to return £10m to BIM as soon as possible. £11.6m was remitted from Nikko Management between 11 and 14 November 1990. £49.5m was paid to MCC on 3 November 1988 and £2.3m on 9 November 1988.

5.28 continued

of these shares were sold by the CIF in the following month for £20.2m through Goldman Sachs; the balance of the shares was sold in 1990 through Goldman Sachs. An overall profit of £6.5m was made by the CIF.

- **Invesco MIM loan stock**. PHL had acquired a parcel of 6.9 million nominal value unsecured loan stock in Invesco MIM[a]. This was sold to the CIF on 10 March 1989 for £8.2m, and subsequently sold by the CIF in the market in April 1990 for £9m.
- **"The October 1989" parcel**. By a document dated 2 October 1989 the CIF acquired largely from MCC the following parcel of shares for a total consideration of £77m[b].
  - **Euris SA**: 2.2 million shares (which had been bought by MCC and PMT in 1988/1989 as referred to in paragraph 3.19) were sold by MCC and PMT to the CIF for £32.6m.
  - **Marceau Investissements**: 1.2 million shares (bought by MCC for £11.9m in November 1987 as referred to in paragraph 3.19) were sold to the CIF for £13.6m.
  - **Banco Commercial Portugues**: 480,500 shares in this Portuguese bank (which had been bought by MCC for £7.5m in 1988/1989) were sold to the CIF for £11.4m[c].
  - **Quebecor Inc**: A holding of A and B shares in this company (which had a relationship with MCC through its interest in Donohue described at paragraph 3.17) had been bought by MCC for £7.6m in 1987 and 1988; the holding was sold to the CIF for £7.9m. The B shares were sold by the CIF on 3 April 1991 as part of a transaction involving 5 million MCC shares, referred to in a footnote to paragraph 9.8.
  - **TF1**: 127,000 shares in this French television station (in which PMT also had a stake as described at paragraph 3.15) had been bought by MCC in August 1989 for £5m and were sold to the CIF for £4.7m. They were sold by the CIF through Goldman Sachs at a loss of £841,000 in June 1990 and the funds used in the circumstances described at paragraph 6.16.

---

a This was in addition to the large holding of ordinary shares referred to in paragraph 2.27.

b This transaction was entered into the computer records of the CIF on 29 January 1990 and cash amounts transferred from the CIF totalling £63.2m on 30 January 1990 (£30m), 1 February 1990 (£15m) and 2 February 1990 (£18.2m); the amounts paid on 1 and 2 February 1990 were on the same days as LBI repaid £30m to the CIF as set out at paragraph 5.25. The transaction was posted to the intercompany account between MCC and the private side on 26 January 1990.
There are documents setting out cash transfers to the private side which show this transaction as having occurred on 2 October 1989. This date in October has apparent support from a letter signed on behalf of BIM dated 3 October 1989 which purports to confirm that the CIF had borrowed £54.5m in October 1989; if the transaction had taken place on 2 October 1989, this would have been the position and interest was in fact paid by the CIF on this basis. However the person who signed the letter was not employed in October 1989. Furthermore a board minute of BIM dated 18 October 1989 (attended by RM, KM, Mr Bunn and Mr Cook) recorded that instructions were to be given to fund managers to increase liquidity to a minimum of 20 per cent; Mr Cook was unable to explain how the purchase of shares to the value of £77m reconciled with this instruction or why the CIF would borrow to buy these shares. Furthermore an internal MCC memorandum dated 19 December 1989 shows that MCC considered they still owned the shares in Banco Commercial Portugues.

c We were told that RM made several investments in Portugal because it had a socialist government and he was very interested in investing in countries with a socialist government in power.

5.28 continued

- In addition to these significant interests the CIF also acquired a number of other holdings, including some shares in Harcourt Brace Jovanovich Inc.

None of these shares was transferred directly into the ownership of BIM, but all were the subject of declarations of trust in favour of BIM executed by MCC and PMT[a].

- **De La Rue**
  - In October and November 1987 RM had acquired a 14.9 per cent. stake (20.75 million shares)[b] in De La Rue. It was announced this had been acquired by MCC[c] but in fact the stake was held as to 40 per cent. by PHL and as to 60 per cent. by MCC.
  - The CIF had also itself bought small stakes of 400,000[d] and 250,000 shares in De La Rue in February and in May 1989.
  - In July 1989 a large stake of 8.85 million shares (6.1 per cent. of De La Rue) was purchased; this was done in the name of Scitex Corporation Ltd (Scitex) an Israeli company in which RM's private side companies had taken a stake and of which RM was Chairman[e]; an announcement was made to that effect. In fact Scitex had only acquired 4.425 million beneficially[f] and the other 4.425 million had been acquired for RMG. £17.25m of MGN's funds was used for the acquisition by RMG and this was charged to the intercompany account.
  - On 21 December 1989 the CIF bought for £14m the 4.425 million parcel acquired beneficially for Scitex.
  - As a result of these transactions MCC, the private side and the CIF together owned 30.45 million shares in De La Rue, a combined stake of 21.67 per cent.
  - This stake was sold as a block in October 1990 in the circumstances described at paragraph 6.56.

---

a On 5 April 1990 title to the significant holdings referred to had not been transferred; during the course of the audit of the CIF KM confirmed in December 1990 for the purposes of the audit that MCC held the shares to the order of BIM as at 5 April 1990, the year end; Mr Bunn confirmed on behalf of PMT that the shares in Euris SA were held to the order of BIM at 5 April 1990, free of any charge.

b This was one of the stakes acquired in the circumstances described at paragraph 3.20. The reasoning behind this acquisition, as explained to us, was that the printing companies which RM acquired had relatively low price earnings ratios and so could be used to sustain the growth into publishing where price earnings ratios were much greater.

c The announcement of this was made by Rowe & Pitman.

d This figure is that supplied by the broker and appears on the contract note; BIM's records show purchases of only 350,000 shares.

e We were told that this was with the objective of acquiring De La Rue's interest in Crossfield Limited which was in the same printing technology area in which Scitex specialised.

f This emerged in September 1989 when De La Rue served a notice on Scitex under section 212 of the Companies Act 1985.

- **The March 1990 parcel.** Under an agreement dated 29 March 1990 (just prior to MCC's year end) a parcel of shares held by MCC was transferred (as part of MCC's asset disposal programme) to the CIF for £25m, £20m of which was payable on account with the balance due after an independent valuation.[a] This parcel included holdings in The Lands Improvement Group Limited, Winglaw Group Limited[b], William Nash, SelecTV plc, W. Lucy & Co and The Daily Telegraph plc. All but SelecTV were unquoted and likely to remain so, except for the Daily Telegraph plc.

(e) Dealings for the benefit of MCC and the private side

5.29 Apart from the transactions that resulted in acquisitions from related parties, RM also entered into four significant transactions where the CIF was used for the benefit of MCC or the private side.

- **Cordmead Limited** ("Cordmead"). MCC needed £200m in cash in connection with the completion of the purchase of Macmillan and OAG[c] at the end of 1988; RM decided to sell the shareholding which MCC and the private side held in Norton Opax, Elsevier and De La Rue[d]. However, pending the sale he could not borrow on the security of the shares, as MCC's facilities contained a negative pledge. He therefore asked National Westminster to lend £200m to BIM for six months with the shares being transferred to BIM and being warehoused there pending sale. National Westminster agreed in principle and were made aware of BIM's role as manager of the CIF. A scheme was devised with the assistance of Mr Morgenstern under which the beneficial ownership in the shares was to be sold to Cordmead, a company whose shareholding was apparently beneficially owned by BIM[e]; Cordmead was then to borrow £200m from National Westminster which it was to pay to MCC for the shares which were then to be pledged to the bank as security[f]. It is clear to us that the documentation for the scheme was signed, £200m borrowed[g] and paid to MCC

---

a We were told by KM that these were transferred at above book value so as to raise cash for MCC and to ensure that the profit figure set had been achieved. Mr Bunn told us that RM put a director's valuation on them of £25m, but he refused to accept it. Although RM was angry at his refusal, RM agreed to the payment of £20m on account with the balance to be paid after a valuation. The payment of £20m was made on 29 March 1990 and the valuation was undertaken by Bankers Trust who valued the parcel at about £20m. RM would not accept this, but eventually by an agreement dated January 1991, the payment of £20m was treated as the full payment.

b RM had sold State House (referred to in paragraph 2.34) to a joint venture company in which the ordinary shares were owned by Winglaw Group Limited and the preference shares by PHL. As set out in paragraph 5.48, Winglaw Group Limited was one of the top 20 investments of the CIF at 5 April 1990.

c See paragraph 4.8.

d See paragraph 3.20.

e There were discussions about the capitalisation of Cordmead Limited, but we have found no evidence of its capitalisation.

f An internal note of the National Westminster which was sent to the Group Chief Executive noted the involvement of BIM as trustee and manager of the Mirror Group pension funds and recorded:

> "The transaction has been structured to ensure that the rights of the pension fund do not encroach on our security."

g National Westminster retained £30m of the facility to provide it with sufficient margin as the market price of the shares had fallen.

5.29 continued

and the shares pledged to National Westminster. RM provided a letter of comfort to National Westminster. We have seen no evidence of any transfer of the shares to Cordmead. The loan was repaid when the sales of the shares in Norton Opax[a] and Elsevier took place on 20 January 1989 and 16 February 1989 respectively; the balance of the loan was repaid with funds from MCC and LBI. The shares in De La Rue were not sold until October 1990 in the circumstance set out in paragraph 6.56. Mr Morgenstern's evidence was that there was an arrangement under which, if the profit exceeded a given amount, then Cordmead was entitled to it and, if there was a loss, that would be made good by MCC; there was a draft agreement to this effect, but no evidence of any signed agreement[b].

- **Robert Fraser Group**. The CIF made two loans to Robert Fraser Group Limited (Robert Fraser) in which RM had taken a stake[c] and of which KM was a director.
    - £5m was lent in December 1988 to assist in an attempt to sell the financial service companies of Robert Fraser to Dewey Warren plc in which Robert Fraser had taken a 29 per cent. stake. This loan was repaid with interest in February 1989. A further £5m was lent in June 1989 to assist Robert Fraser with its liquidity margins after the failure of Robert Fraser's attempt to complete the transaction with Dewey Warren plc. Interest was not paid but rolled up; this loan together with the amount due for unpaid interest was transferred to the private side by documents dated 29 June 1990 at the time RM attempted to gain control of Robert Fraser in the summer of 1990 in the circumstances described at paragraph 6.41.
    - $5m was lent in July 1989: a scheme to mitigate the tax arising on the sale of Intertec Publishing Corp (a subsidiary of Macmillan) in 1988 had involved an intermediate sale to IWC[d], a company financed by Rothschild Inc, Euris SA and a client of Robert Fraser who contributed $5m. When Robert Fraser's client wanted to terminate his involvement in July 1989, $5m was lent from the CIF to make good that contribution. This was repaid in November 1990 with an exchange loss to the CIF of £500,000.
- **Paramount Communications Inc**. A stake costing $11.5m and call options costing $2.5m were purchased through Goldman Sachs in June 1989 during the bid by Paramount Communications Inc (Paramount) for Time Inc. We were told that the call options were purchased to give RM the opportunity to acquire more shares without putting up cash. KM

---

a The shares remained registered in the name of BIT. On 12 January 1989 an advertisement for an offer for the shares in Norton Opax was published in the Financial Times. It stated that the shares were being offered for sale by BIT which was described as a wholly-owned subsidiary of MCC. If there had been a transfer to Cordmead, this would have been untrue.

b There was an apparent profit of about £1m between the apparent value of the transfer to Cordmead and the sale to the third party purchasers. However, this does not take into account the interest on the loan.

c We were told by KM that RM had acquired this stake because of the introduction through Lord Rippon of Hexham QC who was a director of MCC and of Robert Fraser.

d The shareholdings of Rothschild Inc. and Euris SA were bought out and IWC subsequently lent to PHL $119m of the aggregate amount owing to MCC under the instalment sale. $25m was repaid in September 1990, but the balance remained outstanding.

told us RM was considering mounting a take over of Paramount himself and attempting to raise funds through The Chase Manhattan Bank N.A. (Chase) and Bankers Trust; RM had finance offers for all but a part, which it was agreed could be financed on a bridging basis with all of the assets of the private side as security. The bid did not proceed due to difficulties in fitting the financing structures together[a]. The options expired without being taken up. RM also approached Crédit Lyonnais for a $250m facility to buy a 10 to 15 per cent. stake in Paramount[b] which was explained as part of his strategy of creating a world wide film and TV company. The stake costing $11.5m was sold through Goldman Sachs in May 1990.

- **Really Useful Group plc**. RM used the CIF to acquire a stake of 14.4 per cent. on 4 August 1989 for £10.9m. When he negotiated for the sale of this stake to enable Sir Andrew Lloyd Webber to complete his management buy-out RM tried to extract conditions in relation to Mr Bower's biography of RM which had been published by Aurum Press Limited, a company the Really Useful Group plc had acquired. RM wanted Sir Andrew Lloyd Webber to withdraw support for the litigation RM was engaged in with Aurum Press Limited and Mr Bower, but this was refused. The stake was sold for £11.184m, less commission.

(f) Use of shares as collateral for loans for the benefit of the private side

5.30 In addition to borrowing money from the CIF and the pension schemes, the private side began from the autumn of 1988 to use the shares of the CIF as collateral for bank loans. The use of the shares of the CIF by the private side in this way has been described as "stocklending". This is to misunderstand the nature of what was done. Stocklending in the conventional sense is a necessary part of ordinary market making activity: a market maker "borrows" stock through a money broker from institutions or fund managers in order to meet his commitments to deliver stock to a purchaser from him when he does not have sufficient stock on his own books to meet the commitment and would otherwise have to purchase stock in the market. Security is given by the market maker who later returns replacement stock through the money broker; the institution lending the stock earns a fee[c] and therefore enhances the overall return on the portfolio being managed.

5.31 The shares of the CIF were not lent to market makers in this conventional way, but used as collateral against which to borrow money from banks for the benefit of the private side. This was at times described as "stocklending"; such a description of the transaction would have made it appear to be the type of conventional activity described in the preceding paragraph. KM told us that RM saw the use of the shares (an idea introduced to him by Mr Andrew Smith of LBI) as being a way of leveraging assets owned by the pension fund and as being a standard

---

a KM told us that the fact that RM had contemplated the deal was evidence of his primary weakness, which was to be seen as the competitor to Mr Rupert Murdoch and which bankers were not slow to nurture.

b A commitment for the facility was made to PHL on 19 October 1989 and $30m was drawn down on 2 November 1989 and repaid by 22 December 1989; part of the collateral was the CIF's holding in Paramount.

c This is a regulated activity to which the Inland Revenue allows special tax treatment.

part of the market. RM saw the payment of fees "without the pension funds doing anything" as a benefit for the funds and also saw his use of the stocks as being part of the connection between the fund and his companies and being an additional way of supporting his companies.

5.32 The use of the CIF's shares as collateral for loans for the benefit of the private side began in the autumn of 1988 with the use of the portfolio entrusted to LBI as sub-managers as described at paragraph 5.14[a]. It happened as follows.

5.33 In June 1988, Morgan Stanley Trust Company (MSTC) were appointed custodians by LBI[b]; they entered into agreements with LBI and subsequently with BIM. MSTC told us that the CIF portfolio managed by LBI was placed in a separately designated account that was operated under the agreement with LBI and not BIM[c]. Mr Cook told us that he considered that MSTC acted as custodians under the agreement between MSTC and BIM. Mr Trachtenberg told us that in 1988 MSTC had only just set up offices in London and were unsure what documentation was required; accordingly, they wanted an agreement not only with LBI as the fund manager but also with BIM as the client[d].

- Under the system operated by MSTC the shares in the portfolio managed by LBI were delivered to MSTC which held some of the shares through sub-custodians. MSTC provided to LBI a computer terminal through which LBI could direct delivery and settle transactions in respect of the shares as well as carry out other transactions such as foreign exchange. In essence the system was one directed at ease of settlements and was one where MSTC had to act solely on LBI's instructions; therefore MSTC maintained they owed no obligation to anyone other than LBI[e]. MSTC accepted that under this type of custodianship the shares were only as secure as they would have been in LBI's safe.

---

a Sometime between 20 September and 15 November 1988 a provision permitting stocklending was added to the agreement between BIM and LBI under which LBI managed part of the portfolio. This agreement also permitted LBI to enter into transactions with related parties if the terms were those that would have been obtained at arms length in the market. Mr Trachtenberg told us that he thought that such a clause had always been in the agreement between BIM and LBI ever since the BIM portfolio had been transferred in June 1988.

b We were told by Morgan Stanley that they knew that RM had a link with LBI but they did not perceive any reputational risk in providing these services to LBI as he was said to be a passive investor and LBI was said to be independent of him; they did not want to act for RM as he was perceived to be a predator. Mr Trachtenberg told us that he recalled a meeting with MSTC in New York when it was clearly explained to them what RM's role was in LBI.

c Mr Trachtenberg told us that the appointment of MSTC was made in anticipation of the receipt by LBI of the pension fund assets; LBI did not have the necessary administration to hold the securities itself.

d We were told by MSTC that the agreement with BIM never became effective; BIM however paid the fees for MSTC's custodianship of the LBI portfolio and MSTC provided BIM with a computer terminal at their premises through which BIM could examine all transactions carried out by LBI. MSTC told us that this was done under the agreement with LBI. Another of the staff at BIM, Mr Abrahart, told us that he believed that no shares were held by MSTC to BIM's order. Morgan Stanley knew of and referred to the CIF portfolio as the "BIM account".

e We were told on the hypothesis that MSTC knew that LBI were using the pension funds for LBI's sole benefit (which given the limited nature of MSTC's service they were highly unlikely to know), they were not under any obligation to report this to BIM. If they had become aware of fraud, they would have taken appropriate steps in conjunction with relevant authorities.

- MSTC's system provided a facility for conventional stocklending either by MSTC arranging the stocklending to market makers or by LBI itself using the system for such a purpose.

5.34 In November 1988, another company within the Morgan Stanley Group, Morgan Stanley International (MSI)[a] agreed to lend LBI $30m on the basis that collateral be provided to the value of 200 per cent. of the loan[b]. LBI provided this collateral by pledging the CIF portfolio under its management which was held at MSTC.

- The MSTC stocklending system was used to record this pledging of the CIF's shares, though as explained above, pledging shares as collateral for a loan is quite different to conventional stocklending.
- In the loan agreement with MSI, LBI warranted that it was the beneficial owner of the shares pledged[c]. A copy of this was provided to MSTC, but was not read and MSTC told us that they did not realise that a warranty had been given; MSTC knew that the shares were beneficially owned by the CIF and formed part of the pension funds, but they told us that there was a "Chinese wall" between them and other Morgan Stanley companies so that information could not be passed without the consent of the client.

The funds lent to LBI were not used for any purpose but held by LBI in their bank account[d] for 10 days before being repaid[e].

5.35 Apart from this, LBI also used the CIF portfolio during 1988 and 1989 to provide collateral to MSI to cover margins on LBI trading account. We were told by MSTC that they believed

---

[a] Morgan Stanley Group had no investment banking relationship with RM as they did not want him as a client because he was viewed as a predator. MSI made it a condition of each loan that the funds were not to be used for a take over.

[b] Mr Trachtenberg told us that he simply handled the mechanics for loans such as these, the structure of which would most often have already been worked out between RM and Mr Andrew Smith.

[c] The loan agreement was signed by Mr Andrew Smith for LBI. He told us that the loan and similar loans were used to get a better income for the portfolio and funds were usually put with the central treasury to get a better rate. Mr Trachtenberg told us that the loans were part of a plan to leverage the portfolio in order to improve investment performance and also produced fee income for LBI. Mr Andrew Smith told us that he did not read the agreement and did not know of the warranty on beneficial ownership. He also told us that he was told that outside lawyers had checked the documents. Mr Trachtenberg told us that he was advised (although he could not recall by whom) that the clause in the investment management agreement between LBI and BIM relating to stocklending permitted transactions such as this and permitted LBI to describe itself as the beneficial owner.

[d] Further payments of $17m and $1.9m were received into the same bank account at about the same time which the bank statements showed as coming from Morgan Stanley; these amounts were repaid at the same time as $30m loan. We have not been able to establish the source or use of these additional funds.

[e] CLD were told in the course of their audit of LBI for the year ended 31 December 1988 that this loan was negotiated for PHL at the time of the acquisition of AGB Research plc (see paragraph 4.9), but was not to be used for acquisition purposes. They were told by Mr Trachtenberg that the funds were not in fact used and they confirmed this from an examination of the account into which the funds were paid. CLD did not know that the CIF portfolio was used as collateral. Although CLD were supplied with a list of holdings annotated with various letters including "L" (which in fact stood for "loan"), CLD did not enquire into the meaning of the annotations. Mr Trachtenberg told us that he could not recall how he knew that the funds had not been used nor could he recall knowing why PHL wanted the funds.

that LBI was trading for the account of the CIF but in fact[a] a number of the transactions were for LBI's own proprietary trading account[b].

5.36 Further loans were made by MSI to LBI in 1989 with security again being provided from the CIF portfolio held at MSTC. In those loan agreements with MSI, LBI did not warrant that they were owners of the shares but that they held them as managers for the CIF under a discretionary management agreement and that they had authority to pledge them[c].

- $50m was lent between 28 March and 6 April 1989; this was converted into sterling and lent to PHL[d] by LBI on an unsecured basis[e]. PHL passed the funds to MCC.
- $10m was lent from June to December 1989[f]; it is uncertain what use was made of this sum.

5.37 We were told by MSTC that they did not act as custodians for the Macmillan pension schemes after March 1990 because they were unable to provide the type of service - involving monitoring of compliance with the pension plan trust deed and detailed reporting of transactions - that was required by US Department of Labor regulations, under the Employee Retirement Income Security Act of 1974 ("ERISA"). We were provided with a detailed memorandum on this legislation which required persons who had direct or indirect authority and control over the management and disposition of plan assets to act in accordance with strict fiduciary standards[g] and administer the plan exclusively for the benefit of participating employees and their beneficiaries.

5.38 In late 1989, LBI started to use the MSTC stocklending system that had been used to pledge the CIF portfolio to MSI to pledge that portfolio for loans by other banks. LBI did this through

---

a The records at LBI have not enabled us to determine the extent with any certainty.

b LBI was initially capitalised with £1.1m in 1988 to satisfy the IMRO requirements; £20m was provided to LBH by way of loan; LBH sustained trading losses in the course of 1989 and 1990 and this loan had to be capitalised to cover the losses. Mr Andrew Smith told us that he was told that counter security was provided for the shares used as collateral.

c MSI required a legal opinion on LBI's right to pledge the shares; Titmuss Sainer & Webb provided an opinion in support of this. Titmuss Sainer & Webb had doubts about the authority of LBI to pledge the shares of the CIF under the discretionary management agreement and their opinion was only provided after receipt of a letter on BIM note paper dated 23 March 1989 signed by KM and Mr Bunn giving express authority from BIM for the transaction. Mr Trachtenberg told us that the funds borrowed from Morgan Stanley would be lent on to the private side at a 2 per cent. or 2½ per cent. higher interest rate than that payable to Morgan Stanley.

d Vinelott J commented in a judgment given on 25 February 1994 in the MCC administration proceedings that this loan was a breach of trust.

e The agreement was signed by Mr Trachtenberg for LBI; the minute of a board meeting on 25 March 1989 attended by KM, Mr Andrew Smith and Mr Trachtenberg records approval of this loan. As set out in Appendix 12, the LBI audit team were aware of this transaction but did not know that the funds were lent to MCC.

f A minute of a board meeting attended by Lord Donoughue, Mr Andrew Smith and Mr Trachtenberg records the approval of this loan. The agreement was signed by Mr Andrew Smith. None of Lord Donoughue, Mr Andrew Smith or Mr Trachtenberg could recall much about this or whether such a board meeting had taken place. Lord Donoughue was told that loans made to the central treasury were made to secure a turn on the higher interest rate.

g These standards included extensive prohibitions on related party dealings described as transactions with "parties in interest". Parties in interest included the fiduciaries of the plan. Custodians, depending on the nature of the services provided, might or might not be fiduciaries.

the computer terminal in their office since an instruction could be given that the securities be pledged without any involvement by MSTC, although certain banks required confirmation from MSTC or physical delivery of the shares. However, it was possible for LBI during the term of the bank loan to use the system to delete any record of the pledge of the shares securing that loan and either sell the shares or pledge them to another bank. This in fact happened[a].

5.39 In addition to this use of the LBI portfolio of the CIF, the directly managed shares of the CIF were used from the autumn of 1989 as collateral for loans for the benefit of the private side. The significant transactions involving both the LBI and directly managed portfolios in the latter part of 1989 were the following:

- From late October 1989, shares of the CIF were deposited with BNP in connection with a £50m facility granted to PHL in July 1989. No security interest was created, but shares of the CIF were included amongst the shares deposited with BNP as a sign of goodwill and proof of the wealth of the private side; there was also a negative pledge.
- On 6 November 1989 Lehman Brothers International Limited (Lehmans)[b] provided finance of $50m[c] on the security of shares provided from the CIF portfolio managed by LBI and from the CIF itself[d]. This transaction is explained more fully in Appendix 8, but a short summary is required. Agreements were entered into between Lehmans and BIM for this transaction. The funds were remitted to LBI (as BIM's agent) and LBI remitted them to PHUSI. On the same day PHUSI provided $47m which was paid to Goldman Sachs for the purchase of 15 million MCC shares by TIB that had been made on 18 October 1989 for the purposes described at paragraph 4.52[e]. This financing was increased in the circumstances described at paragraph 6.26. The original financing

---

a Mr Trachtenberg told us that he did not use the MSTC system as he had agreed with Miss Bonita Baker (see footnote to paragraph 5.45) that he would not be involved in back office administration. He could not recall any such occurrence and could not understand how the system would have permitted it to happen.

b We refer to all companies that are subsidiaries of Shearson Lehman Brothers Holdings Inc as Lehmans. Lehmans viewed this financing as fully collateralised and some of those operating it understood that for this reason they need not concern themselves about RM's reputation. Lehmans did not have regard to the findings of the 1971/73 DTI Reports in the context of their dealings with RM and companies associated with him and they did not perceive anything in the reputation of RM or the structure of the financing that caused them concern. As set out in the footnote to paragraph 21.73 Lehmans acted in 1991 as lead investment banker for the sale of a holding in Scitex. We were told that although the investment banking side of Lehmans were aware that RM was a controversial figure, they were not aware of any question marks over the conduct or reputation of RM which suggested that Lehmans should not have conducted business with companies associated with him.

c The transaction was structured as a loan by Lehmans to BIM of US Treasury Bills against the security of shares, and the sale of those Treasury Bills to Lehmans to provide the cash to be paid to LBI. The obligation of the borrower was to return US Treasury Bills of the same denomination and not cash. It was suggested to us that this form of financing (as opposed to an ordinary loan of cash) might have certain advantages including smaller collateral requirements and a lower effective rate of interest. It was nonetheless a financing transaction very similar to a loan of cash.

d Several Lehmans personnel knew of BIM, but not of the CIF.

e Mr Trachtenberg told us that he heard a year or two after the Lehmans transaction that the funds from Lehmans were used (in part) to capitalise LBI Inc in New York; he understood that, within a few weeks of the Lehmans transaction, $25m of capital had been provided to LBI Inc. and LBI Inc. had begun operating as a broker/dealer and fund management house.

transaction was considered during the audit of the CIF for the year ending 5 April 1990 (see paragraph 9.38).

- In the period from November 1989 to March 1990, shares from the LBI part of the CIF portfolio and the directly managed portfolio of the CIF itself were used as collateral for a facility of £150m made by National Westminster to PHL[a].
- In November and December 1989, shares in Paramount (part of the directly managed portfolio of the CIF) were used as collateral for a loan from Crédit Lyonnais as referred to at paragraph 5.29.

5.40 When LBI acquired the management of FTIT (as set out at paragraph 5.27), LBI had placed the FTIT portfolio under the custodianship of MSTC under the agreement made between LBI and MSTC, but in a separate account; the board of FTIT in March 1989 authorised conventional stocking lending to improve the income of the investment trust. However LBI[b] began using the MSTC stocklending system in the spring of 1989 to pledge the portfolio of "blue chip" Japanese shares that comprised the FTIT portfolio as collateral for loans made by banks to LBH/LBI which were used for their proprietary trading activities and for lending to other private side companies[c]. By July 1989 shares in the FTIT portfolio to the value of £55.6m were being used as collateral for bank loans. The most significant loans obtained in this way were:

- loans from Nomura Bank International plc (Nomura) of Yen 2 billion in May 1989 which was increased to £30m between June and September 1989[d] (which LBI lent on to PHL on an unsecured basis) and of Yen 3 billion from October 1989 to January 1991.
- a loan of Yen 2 billion from Nikko Bank (UK) plc between September 1989 and January 1991[e].

5.41 During the course of the audits of LBI, LBH and FTIT for the year ended 30 December 1989, CLD[f] became aware that

- the shares of the CIF were used as collateral for the loan by MSI in March/April 1989 referred to at paragraph 5.36;

---

[a] This transaction is explained in paragraph 1.23 in Appendix 8. The shares were released from charge on 27 March 1990 and cash collateral substituted. On 11 April 1990 after the year end of the CIF, most of the shares were placed again as collateral with National Westminster and the cash collateral released.

[b] An account of the dispute that arose out of this is set out at paragraphs 9.45 to 9.56.

[c] Mr Trachtenberg told us that this was another of Mr Andrew Smith's portfolio leveraging exercises which was designed to produce income as Japanese stocks paid so little by way of dividend.

[d] Mr Trachtenberg signed a Memorandum of Acceptance for the facility on 16 May 1989. No board minute can be found.

[e] There is a minute of a board meeting attended by Lord Donoughue, KM, Mr Andrew Smith and Mr Trachtenberg which records the approval of this agreement. The agreement was signed by Mr Trachtenberg. Mr Andrew Smith told us that he left it to Mr Trachtenberg to find the security. Mr Trachtenberg agreed that one of his roles was administering the provision of security for transactions already agreed by Mr Andrew Smith. Lord Donoughue could not recall much about the board meeting or whether it had taken place, but told us that he was told by Mr Andrew Smith and Mr Trachtenberg that the loan was for proprietary trading. Collateral was initially provided from shares held by MSTC for LBI in its proprietary trading account (57), but these were substituted by shares from the FTIT (56) account in October 1989.

[f] Further details of this are set out in Appendix 10.

- the shares in the FTIT portfolio were used as collateral for the loan by Nomura in June 1989 referred to in paragraph 5.40;
- the sums borrowed by LBI in this way were loaned on to other private side companies on an unsecured basis.

Mr Cowling, the audit partner responsible for these audits of LBI, LBH and FTIT and the audits of the CIF and the pension schemes from 1988, told us he did not consider whether the activity carried on by LBI could properly be described as "stocklending". The distinction between conventional stocklending and the use of shares as collateral was not "a question that I was asking myself at the time".

5.42 Mr Cowling told us that no specific training was given at CLD on fiduciary duties and that an auditor did not set out to identify breaches of fiduciary duty. If he did come across breaches of fiduciary duties, that would be reported to the directors or to the regulators; had he been satisfied that the use being made of the shares of the CIF or FTIT was a breach of fiduciary duties, he would have reported this to the regulators and to the boards of the CIF and FTIT.

5.43 CLD subsequently told us that it was not an auditor's function to act as a compliance officer for the entity whose accounts he audited; his role was to report on the truth and fairness of the accounts. However if the auditor came across circumstances where he believed that the entity or its officers had not complied with their obligations, then if either the matter might have an impact upon the truth and fairness of the accounts or serious issues of impropriety arose, the auditor would enquire further. The nature of such enquiries would depend upon the circumstances, but would in most cases involve a discussion with management. When an issue involving serious impropriety appeared to arise, the auditor would take into account professional guidance[a] which appeared to indicate that the circumstances in which a report was appropriate were confined to those cases where the auditor considered that investors were at significant risk of incurring material loss as a result of persons carrying on business in a manner which was not fit and proper or that was in breach of the regulations. There was no requirement to report breaches of fiduciary duty and the focus was on investors incurring a significant risk of material loss.

5.44 The private side[b] needed to use the shares of the CIF and FTIT as collateral because the shares held by the private side by the latter part of 1989 were not attractive to the banks as security because they were either not readily marketable or were shares in MCC. There was an increasing degree of reluctance on the part of banks to lend on the security of MCC shares because they would in effect be taking for a loan to one group of companies controlled by RM,

---

[a] Auditing Guidelines: Communications between auditors and Regulators under section 109 and 180(1)(q) of the Financial Services Act 1986, issued July 1990. We were told by IMRO that section 109 was not seen as effective; no reports were made to IMRO and few, if any, to other regulators; auditors were not the agents of the regulators and did not want to be seen as such, as they did not want to damage the trust on which the working relationship with their client was founded.

[b] LBI and LBH also needed to use the shares entrusted to their management as collateral for margins or for loans for their proprietary trading as they did not have sufficient capital to support their activities.

collateral from another company controlled by him[a]. In contrast, the FTIT and CIF portfolios comprised a large number of readily marketable securities.

5.45 In return for the use of the shares in the portfolios of FTIT and the CIF as collateral for the loans by banks to the private side, there was meant to be counter security provided by the private side to FTIT and the CIF. As at 5 April 1990 (the year end for the CIF) there was said[b] to be in place counter security provided by the private side companies in respect of the "lending" of readily marketable UK, US and Japanese shares from both the CIF and FTIT portfolios managed by LBI. This counter security was said to be pooled and consisted of shares in the following:

Ansbacher
Central & Sheerwood
Guinness Peat Group
Agence Havas
Paramount
SelecTV
MCC

We have seen no register or other records of the counter security available.

5.46 We received the following evidence of the existence of counter security:

- Mr Ford told the counsel to the Accountants' Joint Disciplinary Scheme that it had been made clear to him that no counter security had been in place in respect of FTIT's lending to LBH for the year ended 31 December 1989, but claimed that thereafter arrangements for counter security had been in place. He told us that when employed by CLD he had checked the counter security in 1990 during the course of the audits of FTIT and LBI for the year ended 31 December 1989, and had been shown some certificates in a safe[c]. In a letter to the Chairman of FTIT on 12 April 1991, when he was the Finance Director of LBI, he stated:

> "I personally was one of the [CLD] officers auditing the accounts of LBI, LBH and [FTIT] during the whole period of 1989 and can confirm that this question of [counter security] was regularly pursued, and that Mr Trachtenberg showed me on several occasions the certificates held by the manager as [counter security], and that the value of these certificates exceeded the value of stocks lent."

---

a Some bankers call this market practice "pig on pork".

b This information was provided to CLD in the circumstances described in paragraph 9.40 by Mr Ford, a former employee of CLD who had been employed on the audit of FTIT and LBI for the year ended 31 December 1989 carried out in 1990 and became LBI's Finance Director in January 1991 Although CLD carried out an audit of LBI for the year ending 30 December 1990, which was completed in April 1991, and knew stocks were being used as collateral for loans to RM's private companies, they took no steps to ascertain whether there was any counter security. At a meeting on 8 May 1991, Mr Cowling was recorded as saying that the programme may have been fully collateralised, but the evidence to support this was not in place; the schedules of counter security CLD had seen were less liquid than normal UK marketable equities.

c Mr Ford told us that he did not believe his evidence to us and his evidence to the Accountants' Joint Disciplinary Scheme were inconsistent as the audits for the year ended 31 December 1989 had taken place during the early part of 1990.

In relation to this letter, Mr Ford told the counsel to the Accountants' Joint Disciplinary Scheme that he could not justify the statement that, whilst at CLD, he had been shown counter security on several occasions. He said he had only been shown counter security on one occasion whilst at CLD, which was during the course of the LBH audit for the year ended 31 December 1989, in about mid-1990.

- Mr Carson, the legal counsel and assistant compliance officer of LBI, told us he had been shown a share certificate by Mr Trachtenberg who then wrote him a memorandum on 10 January 1991 confirming that LBI held on behalf of FTIT counter security totalling over $98m (£52m) as security for the "stocklending" between FTIT and the private side. Mr Carson later became LBI's compliance officer.
- Mr Trachtenberg told us that there was and had been counter security since the beginning of January 1989 when, after he had expressed concern to KM that LBI needed counter security for the loans to the private side, RM had given him share certificates and blank transfer forms for a basket of blue chip UK shares (including Central TV, Invesco MIM, Singer & Friedlander). The value of those shares was in excess of £50m, in accordance with the agreement between RM and Mr Trachtenberg that cover of 150 per cent. would be required at all times. The share certificates were in the names of private side entities and Mr Trachtenberg was assured by RM and, later, by Mr Bunn that they were private side assets. Mr Trachtenberg discussed the counter security with Mr Andrew Smith who told him that the stakes had not themselves been pledged as security for loans as they were large strategic stakes which RM wanted to retain and not to make public. Mr Trachtenberg placed these share certificates in a safe specially installed in his office for the purpose (RM had refused to let him place them in custody at MSTC) and he kept a schedule of the shares on his own computer, having been told by RM that nobody (other than KM) was to know of the shares. In fact, however, Mr Trachtenberg told us that (in addition to Mr Andrew Smith and Lord Donoughue) Mr Carson, Mr Ford and Miss Bonita Baker were all aware of the existence of the shares – Miss Baker helped on occasions to value the shares for security purposes[a]. Mr Trachtenberg told us that there were numerous occasions on which requests were made (usually by Mr Bunn) for shares held as counter security to be returned, with other shares being provided in their stead. Mr Trachtenberg told us that during office moves at the beginning of 1991, his desktop computer became corrupted and everything on the computer was lost; the back ups were not recoverable either. Mr Trachtenberg said that some paper records were held but most was on the computer because of a need to maintain confidentiality on the issue. It was for these reasons that no records were available. Mr Trachtenberg told us that the share certificates were returned to RM in June 1991.

5.47 However, in June 1991, Arthur Andersen, who had been retained by the independent directors of FTIT as a result of the dispute described in chapter 9, reported that they had seen no evidence to support the oral representations that counter security was available or that it was

---

[a] However, Miss Baker who was the portfolio administration manager in charge of administration, reporting and the computer records said that she knew of no counter security held at LBI to cover the use of the FTIT or CIF shares.

actually pledged to FTIT as security, or that its valuation was properly monitored during the period. CLD also considered at the same time whether it was possible to confirm counter security had been provided to FTIT; CLD concluded that it would be very difficult to look at RM's safe and decide which particular shares were counter security for the FTIT stocks which had been used; trying to do that over the previous 18 months would have been very difficult. They decided not to proceed. It is quite clear that the conclusion of Arthur Andersen was correct as to the lack of records. Even if counter security had been given, it is clear that the recording system was wholly inadequate.

The position of the CIF at 5 April 1990

5.48 As a result of the transactions referred to earlier in this chapter, the top 20 investments of the CIF directly managed by BIM at the end of its financial year on 5 April 1990 had the following related party aspects:

		Number of Shares	Value (£m)	Related party aspect
1	Agence Havas	274,550	46.6	acquired from MCC
2	Lazard Property UT	14,300	42.9	
3	MCC[a]	17,325,420	36.1	self-investment
4	Euris SA	2,228,479	33.9	acquired from MCC/PMT
5	Teva[b]	50,329,456	28.1	
6	IBI	22,360	16.7	related party aspects
7	OAG	250	15.2	self-investment
8	Marceau Investissements	1,200,000	14.9	acquired from MCC
9	Banco Commercial Portugues	1,016,850	12.8	acquired from MCC
10	De La Rue	5,025,000	12.0	related party aspects
11	Invesco MIM loan stock	6,608,141	7.9	acquired from PHL
12	EMAP[c]	3,769,656	7.4	
13	Land Improvement	6,475,051	7.3	acquired from MCC
14	Property at Stevenage[d]		6.3	acquired from Hollis
15	Property at Swindon		6.0	
16	Quebecor A	820,100	5.7	acquired from MCC
17	Paramount	200,000	5.5	related party aspects
18	Winglaw	252,000	5.3	partly acquired from MCC
19	Property at Ipswich		5.0	acquired from Hollis
20	TF1	127,000	4.6	acquired from MCC

Table 4 – Top 20 investments of the CIF directly managed by BIM at 5 April 1990

[a] This includes the 3.446 million MCC shares referred to at paragraph 5.20.

[b] This holding in Teva Pharmaceutical Industries Limited (Teva) was purchased by an agreement dated 3 May 1989 for £18m from Bank Leumi Le-Israel B.M. and Bank Hapoalim B.M.

[c] This was bought on 31 January 1989 and sold on 9 May 1990.

[d] Fairview Road, Stevenage and Waterside Works, Ipswich were both acquired from Hollis in June 1988 for a total price of £9.45 million; they were both old factory sites with development potential. These were the major related party property dealings.

In addition there was the holding in FTIT itself valued at £11.5m at this date which was held in the portfolio of the CIF managed by LBI; it had been acquired from LBH as set out at paragraph 5.27.

5.49 Although the self-investment in MCC and OAG was disclosed in the report and accounts of the pension schemes, the related party deals were not.

6. 1990: CIRCUMSTANCES LEADING TO THE DECISION TO FLOAT MGN

6.1 Although as set out in paragraph 4.9 Mr Woods had relinquished his principal position on the private side because of his concern at its ability to survive, he remained a director of MCC and a tax adviser. He had continued to maintain financial models as he needed an overview of RM's companies partly for tax planning and partly because he was concerned about the impact of the private side debt on MCC[a]; he felt that the MCC share price would have to fall (because of the negative impact on earnings caused by the acquisition of Macmillan and OAG) and the private side would have insufficient collateral to cover its debt. In the summer or autumn of 1990 Mr Woods made a presentation to KM and RM which showed that within two years the interest burden arising from the private side debt would swallow the private side assets. This analysis spurred RM into the decision that an asset disposal programme would have to be set in train – the flotation of MGN and the sale of the scientific journals business of MCC[b] were to be two of the principal assets in the programme. Both MGN and the scientific journal business produced a strong cash flow. Mr Woods presented to RM and KM probably in the early autumn of 1990, a projection that showed the benefits of floating MGN[c]. Calculations were also done as to the price that would have to be realised to compensate for the lack of cash flow. If a sufficient price was not obtained for MGN, RM determined he would have to ensure that there was access to its cash flow as the other companies were dependent on it.

6.2 KM told us that the need to float MGN became a particular necessity as soon as MGN had acquired QPI and Donohue from MCC (as set out in paragraph 6.51). RM had wanted to obtain the necessary capital to pay for the acquisition by floating MGN but there was not time: a £360m facility was, accordingly, taken on by MGN pending a flotation. IM told us that RM was reluctant to float MGN, although he had made a commitment to do so in 1984, because it was not really in his nature – he was a buyer rather than a seller.

6.3 It is necessary therefore to consider the events in the summer of 1990 which had a marked effect not only on the timing of the decision to go ahead with the flotation, and on the assets that were to be included in that flotation, but also on the pension funds. This chapter covers those events:

(1) the substantial borrowings from the pension funds and the even greater use of the shares as collateral resulting from pressure on the finances of the private side. (This chapter

---

[a] Mr Woods told us that he based his models on the information he had available to him when he had a significant role in the finances of the private side; after he had relinquished that role, he updated them from information provided by Mr Bunn.

[b] KM told us that he opposed the sale and had rows with his father about it; RM decided that it had to be sold as he saw his future in newspaper and the US assets. Mr Woods told us that he did not believe the flotation of MGN was considered as part of the programme until November 1990.

[c] Mr Woods told us he put forward three advantages – the cash raised would reduce the private side debt, quoted shares would be available as security for that debt and, if the MCC share price dropped (as Mr Woods believed was inevitable), RM could substitute MGN shares as security for the private side debt and, if need be, issue more shares to enable MGN to take over MCC. At this time, Mr Woods was told that the value of MGN was about £1 billion; he considered floating 25 per cent. of MGN would be sufficient, though extant working papers show calculations were also done on the basis of floating 40 per cent.

contains a summary, but a detailed account of the use RM made of the funds of the CIF and pension schemes from this period until 30 April 1991 is set out in Appendix 8);

(2) MCC's need to dispose of sufficient assets in a more difficult economic climate so as to repay on 23 October 1990 $415m[a] of the $3 billion facility and the purchases of MCC shares by RM to support the MCC share price. (We set out a summary of the transactions in MCC shares in this chapter, but a more detailed account of all these transactions is set out in Appendix 7);

(3) the further problems of the private side - the need for further funds, the use of pension fund assets and the attempt to acquire Robert Fraser;

(4) the events of the autumn of 1990 - the transfer of the interests in QPI and Donohue to MGN and MGN's borrowing of £360m;

(5) the decision to proceed with the flotation of MGN.

(1) Borrowings by the private side from the CIF in May and June 1990

6.4 In May and June 1990, pressure on the private side finances arose from a number of factors including the need to repay the £150m facility from the National Westminster[b].

6.5 To assist it in meeting these pressures, the private side began borrowing again from the CIF on 20 May 1990 and by 29 June 1990 approximately £100m had been borrowed. This was comprised of the transfer of cash (some of which was obtained from the external fund managers through BIM) and the proceeds of sale of investments held by the CIF[c]. In order to discharge that debt prior to the year end of PHL on 30 June 1990[d], agreements dated 29 June 1990 were made to transfer the two most valuable blocks of shares owned by the private side (apart from the holding of MCC and the interest in TF1) at their market value to the CIF.

- **A holding in Scitex.** In January 1989 RMG had invested $39m in Scitex, the Israeli company referred to at paragraph 5.28 . In May 1990 Mr Bunn was told by RM that the CIF was to acquire this investment which had, by the end of May 1990, risen in value to £104.3m. KM's evidence was that the decision to make the sale was RM's. The whole investment was not transferred partly because it was considered by Mr Cook to be too large a concentration of investment for the CIF and partly because it might have been difficult to shelter the capital gain made by RMG on the sale. In the event, therefore,

---

[a] The amount due in respect of the first tranche of $990m had been reduced by payments on 30 January 1990 ($115m), 20 March 1990 ($50m), 31 March 1990 ($300m - largely from the proceeds of the OAG loan stock) and on 11 June 1990 ($110m). Under the terms of the facility MCC was obliged to apply 85 per cent of the proceeds of the disposals to repay the first tranche of the loan.

[b] National Westminster agreed to make a further loan in June 1990 but reduced the amount from £150m to £75m because of the concern about the level of borrowings by RM's companies.

[c] Sales included the greater part of the holding in Agence Havas (£31.4m). The main explanation given for the sale of the investments of the CIF was the need to build up funds to make the transfer payment due to the new pension scheme of BPCC. The cash was then "deposited" with the private side. The explanation given by RM was that the private side had assumed the obligation to meet the transfer payment to the new BPCC pension scheme.

[d] PHL remained at that time the main investment holding company for the private side and the CIF lent all funds to the private side through it.

Scitex shares to the value £57.7m (at a market price per share of $37.25) were covered by the agreement to transfer to the CIF[a]. KM's evidence was that the sale to the CIF was of beneficial but not legal ownership which was retained by RMG.

- **The holding in Invesco MIM** To make up the balance of the assets needed to be transferred in order to discharge the debt owed to the CIF, an agreement was made to transfer the private side's 20.7 per cent. stake in Invesco MIM[b] to the CIF for £61.9m (being a market price of 128p per share). No notification of the sale was made to Invesco MIM and the holding remained registered in the name of PHL.

6.6 At the time of the agreement, the shares in both Invesco MIM and Scitex were pledged by the private side as collateral for bank loans.

- The Invesco MIM shares were pledged to Barclays for the FF660m loan that had been granted to PMT to buy an interest in TF1 (see paragraph 3.15) and they remained so pledged until January 1991 when they were redelivered to the central treasury and used as collateral for other private side loans. The holding in Invesco MIM was sold in March 1991 as described at paragraph 9.25.
- The Scitex shares were pledged either to National Westminster or to Bankers Trust[c] and remained pledged with these banks until they were used as collateral for loans with other banks[d].

The shares were never delivered to the CIF or re-registered.

6.7 RM was therefore able to continue to use these two large holdings as part of the collateral to support the private side borrowings (which at the end of June 1990 were just over £970 m) despite the agreement to transfer them to the CIF to discharge the debt in respect of cash borrowed from it.

(2) The difficulties faced by MCC

(a) The continuation of MCC's asset disposal programme

6.8 MCC continued with its asset disposal programme, but it also had made some further acquisitions, including The Prentice Hall Information Services and businesses from the private side company, Pergamon AGB plc, and had entered into a joint venture with McGraw Hill.

6.9 A further significant disposal took place on 28 February 1990, when MCC concluded an agreement to sell the various printing interests that it had acquired in the United States[e] (see paragraph 3.17) to QPI, a subsidiary of Quebecor, which had interests in printing and related

---

[a] 2.7 million shares were transferred to the CIF and the private side retained 2.096 million. In August 1990, there was a one for one bonus issue; after that the private side held 4,192,762 and BIM held 5.4 million.

[b] This had been acquired by the private side in the circumstances set out in paragraph 2.27.

[c] It is not possible to tell which, as the entire holding remained registered in the name of RMG.

[d] The Scitex shares were sold in October 1991 - see paragraph 21.73.

[e] The Webb Company, Providence Gravure Inc. and the printing assets of Diversified Printing Corporation which had subsequently been formed into Maxwell Graphics Inc.

services. Those interests were sold to QPI for $510 m, $410m of which was paid in cash and $100m of which was attributed to the issue to MCC of a 25.8 per cent. stake in QPI. This stake was transferred to MGN in October 1990 as set out in paragraph 6.51 and formed part of the assets of MGN on flotation.

6.10 After this disposal, difficult economic conditions were said to make further disposals less easy to achieve. Since, however, on 23 October 1990 $415m of the first tranche of the facility taken out in connection with the acquisition by MCC of Macmillan and OAG was due to be repaid, it was vital that disposals be made[a].

6.11 By August 1990 prospective purchasers sensed that it was essential that MCC made disposals. It became apparent to MCC that sales to outside parties could only be achieved at "fire sale" prices; this problem was solved largely by the sale of the interests in QPI and Donohue to MGN in October 1990 as described at paragraph 6.51. However the perception about MCC also caused the price of MCC shares to decline[b].

Market price of MCC shares : July 1990 to December 1990

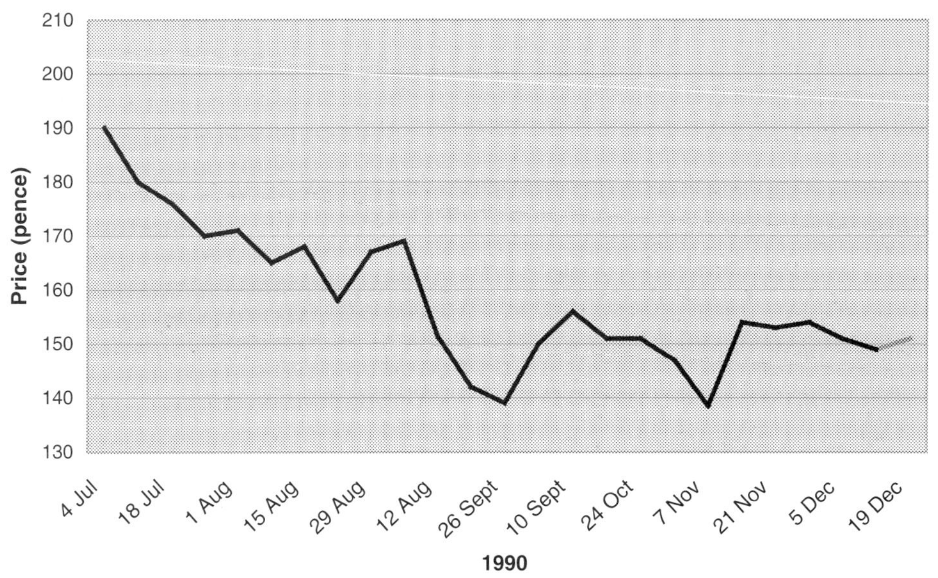

6.12 It is convenient first to consider the attempts to remedy this decline in the share price; two methods were employed, the second of which was of greater significance:

- RM planned that MCC should acquire Scottish Investment Trust plc[c]; by offering to pay for it through the issue of MCC shares, he sought to increase MCC's capitalisation through

---

[a] Prices obtainable on sales of assets were lower than they had been save for publishing assets of the highest quality such as the scientific journals business acquired by MCC in 1986 (as set out in paragraph 3.7).

[b] The market was well aware of MCC's debt repayment deadlines and, accordingly, buyers sought to take advantage by stalling negotiations. This resulted in delays such as those that occurred in the disposal of the Panini and Collier Encyclopedia businesses (see paragraph 6.57).

[c] Shares in Scottish Investment Trust plc were first purchased in December 1989 and during 1990 a holding of 3.5 million was built up. The purchases were in the name of a nominee company controlled by LBG,

the same means employed on the acquisition of Philip Hill Investment Trust plc (see paragraph 3.9); this project was abandoned in early September 1990.

- Purchases of MCC shares were made on a substantial scale before and after this projected acquisition.

(b) The purchase by RM's interests of MCC shares

6.13 The dealings by RM during 1989 in MCC shares have been described at paragraphs 4.48 to 4.53. At the beginning of 1990, the shareholding of RM, his family, their companies and the Maxwell Foundation was approximately 54 per cent. of MCC. During the course of 1990, that holding rose to 64.2 per cent. and approximately £130m was spent on these purchases[a]. In addition as described below purchases were also made by RM on behalf of the pension funds.

6.14 In March 1990, Mr Sheinberg spoke to RM about the inflow to the London Market of shares from the Japanese Market that had been placed in the circumstances described at paragraph 4.52; this put the share price under pressure. Mr Sheinberg told us that he saw a trading opportunity as RM would not want to see the price decline because of his ego and the position of MCC in the FTSE 100. He believed RM would buy or introduce someone to buy any large block of shares Goldman Sachs wished to sell; he believed RM had a fixation about the price of MCC shares. He told RM that Goldman Sachs would maintain a market in MCC shares but their resources were not unlimited and he wished to make a sale of shares he had purchased. Mr Sheinberg told us that RM and KM suggested the use of a share option.

6.15 Accordingly, on 30 March 1990, Goldman Sachs entered into an "option" contract with BIT. This gave RM (for a premium of 24p per share)[b] the right to acquire from Goldman Sachs 10 million MCC shares at a price of 189p on 29 June 1990. The intention behind this was to ensure RM bought any shares that Goldman Sachs might acquire in the market, but the form of the option contract used, a call option, did not reflect the underlying intention since the exercise of the option lay with RM. The acquisition of the option was announced on 10 April 1990 as HI acquiring an interest in 10 million MCC shares on 30 March 1990.

6.16 On 29 June 1990, when the market price of the shares was 189p, RM exercised the option on behalf of BIT at a cost of £18.99m. On 19 June 1990 the larger part of the CIF's shareholding in Agence Havas and TF1 (see paragraph 5.28) had been sold through Goldman Sachs and the remaining part was sold on 28 June 1990[c]. To meet the cost of exercising the option, the

---

Quotescreen Limited, but Scottish Investment Trust plc were told, in an answer to their enquiry, that the beneficial owner was LBH; the shares were recorded in the accounts of LBH at 31 December 1990 as the only substantial asset in the strategic corporate account of LBH; the shares were sold in March 1991.

a This figure includes the purchase of 10 million shares made on 2 August 1990, but does not include the cost of purchases made by Mr Aboff (see paragraph 6.19).

b As explained in Appendix 7 this was negotiated. The fair value of such a premium if calculated by an expert derivatives dealer for a traded option would have been in the order of 10p.

c Mr Sheinberg told us that the TF1 transaction was significant for Goldman Sachs as it helped establish their block-trading presence in France.

proceeds of the sale on 28 June 1990 of shares in Agence Havas and TF1 were transferred from BIM's account for the CIF at Goldman Sachs to the account of BIT pursuant to an authority signed by Mr Bunn[a] and used to settle the cost of the MCC shares.

6.17 In July and August 1990 a number of very substantial purchases of MCC shares were made and a second "option" agreement was entered into with Goldman Sachs.

- Mr Sheinberg told us that sometime prior to 2 August 1990 he told RM that he had built up a substantial position in MCC shares which he wanted to reduce; that either KM or RM then spoke to him and suggested that International Bankers France (IBF) (a company within the IBI group which is described in the footnote to paragraph 5.21) might purchase shares; that on 2 August 1990 he spoke to IBF and sold 10 million MCC shares to them at 182p, a total cost of £18.2m. KM told us that Mr Sheinberg initiated the transaction and that RM negotiated and agreed the price with Mr Sheinberg, as RM would not let anyone else negotiate the price; IBF would have then been told the price and asked to implement the deal. Mr Sheinberg's evidence was that he negotiated the price with Mr. Mantelet at IBF. We received other evidence that Mr Mantelet was asked to carry out this transaction whilst a colleague was on holiday and to implement what had been agreed between RM and Mr Lévêque[b] as a *portage*[c] for RM's companies; the price was fixed by Goldman Sachs without any negotiation with him; Mr Mantelet did not speak with Mr Sheinberg but with Mrs Jennie Gomez, Mr Sheinberg's secretary[d]. A draft agreement between BIT and IBF evidenced by a letter dated 3 August 1990 was drawn up for this purchase under which BIT would pay for the cost of the shares and interest at 1 per cent., but this agreement was never completed by BIT[e]. In the event settlement of the purchase in the sum of £18.2m was made by BIT to whom the shares were delivered by Goldman Sachs[f]. They were recorded in the private side's records as a purchase by BIT.

---

a The amount paid by the CIF in this way was added to the debt owed by the private side to the CIF which was intended to be discharged by the agreement to transfer of the Scitex and Invesco MIM shares as described at paragraph 6.5.

b He was the founder of the IBI group; see the footnote to paragraph 5.21. Mr Mantelet was one of the Managing Directors of IBF.

c A "*convention de portage*" is an arrangement in which a financial institution agrees to subscribe for or purchase shares on behalf of another party with the obligation on that party to buy them after a pre determined period and at a price agreed in advance.

d Mr Sheinberg was on holiday on the day the trade was booked. Goldman Sachs told us that no secretary would be responsible for establishing the terms of a trade with a counterparty and that Mrs Gomez was not responsible for doing so in this case; those terms were established between Mr Sheinberg and Mr Mantelet.

e An internal memorandum of IBF stated that the shares were to be purchased through them by BIT because MCC did not want Goldman Sachs to know who was the final purchaser. However, by two faxes subsequently sent to Goldman Sachs, IBF confirmed that Goldman Sachs were to hold the MCC shares to the order of BIT and BIT was to pay for them directly in place of IBF.

f The acquisition by BIT of 10m shares was announced on 29 August 1990.

6.17 continued

- BIT on behalf of RM, his family, their companies and the Maxwell Foundation also bought in July and August 1990 MCC shares from Astaire & Co (Astaire) (1.15 million shares for £1.9m), Smith New Court (5.3 million shares for £9.2m), Rowe & Pitman (250,000 shares for £420,427), and on 24 August 5.779 million shares from Goldman Sachs[a] for £9.6m[b].

- Notification of these purchases by BIT to MCC was short by 3.446 million shares. These were recorded in BIT's records as being for the account of the CIF and it is to be inferred that they were put into the CIF to make good the shortfall that had arisen when TIB acquired in May 1989 3.446 million shares which the CIF records showed as having been purchased by the CIF, as explained at paragraph 5.20.

- By 13 August 1990, Goldman Sachs had accumulated 15 million MCC shares; Mr Sheinberg told us he asked RM if he wished to purchase them[c]. On 14 August 1990 RM entered into a second "option" contract with Goldman Sachs, but on this occasion the form of the option, a put option, was more apposite in that Goldman Sachs acquired the right to require BIT to buy up to[d] 15.65 million MCC shares on 30 November 1990 at a price of 203.55p per share, a total cost of up to £31.85m. The premium paid by Goldman Sachs to BIT for this contract was 5p per share[e], when the market price of MCC shares stood on 14 August 1990 at 170p. The option was in effect a deferred sale by Goldman Sachs. RM maintained initially that the existence of the option did not have to be disclosed, but the transaction was first announced on 23 August 1990 by MCC as the acquisition by RM and his companies of "an interest" in 15.65 million shares[f].

---

a Announced as 5,388,000 on 31 August 1990.

b LBI purchased 144,500 MCC shares on 21 August 1990 for £243,007.

c We were told by KM that Mr Sheinberg pressed RM to buy the block he had built up.

d The agreement specified that the option was exercisable in whole or in part.

e The premium paid cannot be explained on the basis of ordinary option pricing as the premium bears no relation to what would be charged by an expert derivatives dealer for a traded option which would have been in the order of 28p. If such a premium had not been charged, a profit would have been almost guaranteed simply by buying shares at the current market price of 170p and requiring BIT to buy them at the exercise price of 203.55p in November 1990. The exercise price was explained to us by Mr Sheinberg as being the market price on August 14 1990 plus the cost of carrying the shares until 30 November 1990, repayment of the premium and profit. As it was clear the option would very likely be exercised, this was in effect a deferred sale by Goldman Sachs and the price was in effect calculated on this basis. Mr Sheinberg did not accept this in his evidence to us, though in his evidence to the US Securities & Exchange Commission (SEC) he accepted that in retrospect it was a delayed purchase.

f In a return to the Stock Exchange which MCC claimed it made it was described as "put option against acquirer" but the Stock Exchange say this was not received by them until later in the year. On 15 August 1990 Goldman Sachs made dislcosure of the details of the option to The Securities Association including the exercise price of 203.55p.

- On 30 August 1990 RM was advised by Freshfields[a] and Smith New Court (who had been retained to advise on the bid for Scottish Investment Trust plc) that neither he nor interests connected with him (including the pension schemes) could any longer acquire shares in MCC whilst this bid was under consideration[b]; he was advised to report his recent purchases to the Takeover Panel. A contemporaneous note of a meeting with the executive of the Takeover Panel on 30 August 1990 records that KM explained that the purchases had been made "in order to keep the show on the road"; KM told us that he did not recall using these words, but would have said the purchases were being made as a show of continued support by RM and his family to MCC. Neither Smith New Court nor Freshfields nor the executive of the Takeover Panel were told at that meeting of the second "option" contract with Goldman Sachs; KM told us the transaction was known about (because of the announcement on 23 August 1990 of the acquisition of an "interest" in 15.65 million shares) and discussed at the meeting, although the fact that it was an option and the pricing of the option was not known. When Freshfields were told of it after the meeting, they advised on 31 August 1990 and again on 4 September 1990 in strong terms that there had to be disclosure of the price paid. A further announcement by MCC about the "option" was then made on 6 September 1990 that the exercise date was 30 November 1990 and the strike price was 185p[c]. The announcements made by MCC were misleading as they concealed from the market:
  - the true price to be paid for the shares.
  - the fact that RM was paying a high price which he would have found difficult to explain.
  - the true nature of the agreement reached was not an option but a method of enabling RM to defer payment until November 1990.

The "option" was exercised on 30 November 1990 and £31.85m paid for the shares[d].

6.18 On 14 September 1990 a further meeting took place between Freshfields and RM. Freshfields were told that the bid for Scottish Investment Trust plc was not proceeding and RM considered that he and the interests connected with him were free to buy more MCC shares in the short time before the closed period for MCC began on 29 September 1990. The following purchases were then made:

---

a We were told by Mr Richards, the partner at Freshfields primarily concerned, that he had given this advice after being told by Smith New Court that RM had told them that Freshfields had advised that he was free to buy shares. Freshfields had given no such advice and Mr Richards considered that RM had lied to Smith New Court, but he did not suggest that at the time. At the conclusion of the transaction, Freshfields decided that they would accept no further instructions from MCC. They had not received payment of substantial fees charged to MCC and so did not inform MCC of their decision until the fees were paid in the summer of 1991.

b RM told Freshfields that he had bought the MCC shares after unfavourable press comment "to stop a run on the shares which may eventually have forced MCC out of business".

c Some confusion arose as a result of the use of the terms "strike price" and "exercise price". They are, however, synonymous and the announcement of a strike price of 185p was untrue. RM had insisted this price be used and had explained the difference to his advisers as being commission paid to Goldman Sachs.

d The payment was made out of funds borrowed from Chase and Bankers Trust in the circumstances set out in paragraph 6.67.

- Substantial purchases were made on behalf of the pension funds.

Date - 1990	Quantity	Total value in £	Broker
17 September	50,000	84,588	Astaire
18 September	600,000	1,009,024	Smith New Court
20 September	10,000,000	17,000,000	Goldman Sachs[a]
25 September	2,700,000	4,219,492	Smith New Court
27 September	500,000	780,433	Kleinwort Benson
27 September	100,000	152,133	Crédit Lyonnais Laing
27 September	250,000	381,478	Astaire
28 September	1,000,000	1,480,305	Hoare Govett

Table 5 – Substantial purchases of MCC shares in September 1990 for the pension funds

All these purchases were made for the CIF save for 2.6 million of the 10 million shares purchased on 20 September 1990 which were passed to the directly held portfolio of MCWPS. These purchases took the holdings of MCC shares recorded by BIM to be under their control to 41 million or some 6 per cent. of MCC[b].

- BIT also bought from Smith New Court 450,000 shares for £760,000.
- After the sale of 10 million MCC shares to the pension funds on 20 September 1990 (as set out in the table above), Goldman Sachs still held over 14 million MCC shares and continued to purchase. By 28 September 1990, their holding was over 28 million MCC shares. On 28 September 1990 20 million[c] shares were purchased at a price of 158p per share from Goldman Sachs by RM and the Maxwell Foundation for £31.6m[d].
- A total of 2.285 million shares were bought during September and October 1990 by Jupiter Participations SA (Jupiter Participations), a French company owned by IBF, part of the IBI group. They were sold in the circumstances described in paragraph 9.8 in January 1991. Jupiter Participations purchased MGN shares in 1991 in the circumstances described at paragraph 20.50.

6.19 Mr Aboff, a senior employee of RM's companies in the USA, bought on behalf of RM, during periods when RM could not purchase shares himself or through his companies:

- in early September 1990 1.075 million shares for about £1.8m
- in early October 1990 1.8 million share for about £2.6m

---

a The settlement was to be made on 15 October 1990 and the price reflected the delayed settlement.

b This was based on the figure of 41.03 million shares which the records of the CIF at that time identified BIM as controlling; this figure appears to have included a parcel of 3.446 million shares which the CIF had paid for in May 1989 but which instead of being sold to the CIF were sold to TIB. As set out at paragraph 5.20, the records of the CIF showed this as a purchase from Rowe & Pitman.

c The consent of the Takeover Panel to this was obtained by representing to it that part of this purchase was conditional on their approval whereas in truth there was no such condition (see Appendix 7).

d Settlement was to be made on 12 November 1990; the price reflected this delayed settlement.

He sold some of these in November and December 1990. Further details are set out in Appendix 7. Mr Aboff purchased MGN shares in 1991 in the circumstances described at paragraph 20.56.

(c) The failure to disclose the extent of BIM's holding

6.20 Miss Debbie Maxwell[a], a solicitor employed as legal adviser to all RM's companies but no relation to RM, had discussed with Titmuss Sainer & Webb earlier in 1990 the disclosure of the substantial shareholding BIM had acquired in MCC. On 26 September 1990 she sought formal advice on behalf of BIM. On 3 October 1990 Titmuss Sainer & Webb advised that the holding of shares by BIM (and not the proportions attributable to each pension scheme) should be counted as one holding for disclosure if the level of 3 per cent.[b] was reached. KM told us that RM forcefully disagreed with the advice and said disclosure was not going to be made. He telephoned Mr Morgenstern of Nicholson Graham & Jones[c] to seek a second opinion and also spoke of seeking a second opinion from counsel, but, as far as we have been able to ascertain, none was ever obtained[d].

6.21 Disclosure of holdings of MCC shares in excess of 3 per cent. was required in the circular to MCC shareholders relating to the disposal of MCC's interests in QPI and Donohue to MGN (referred to at paragraph 6.54). By 11 October 1990, Miss Maxwell had been told that the CIF held 6 per cent. of MCC and she understood that no disclosure of this was to be made in the circular as RM refused to permit this. The circular stated:

> "Save as disclosed above, the Directors are not aware of any person whose interest represents 3 per cent or more of [MCC]'s issued share capital."

As no disclosure was made of the shares controlled by BIM, this statement was untrue. The independent directors were not informed of this at the board meeting of MCC on 11 October 1990 which was called to consider the transaction and the circular; nor were Freshfields who were verifying the circular.

---

a She was not a Compliance Officer within the meaning of the Financial Services Act 1986, but she did have a role (as part of her job as legal adviser to MCC) in ensuring compliance with obligations under the Companies Act 1985, Stock Exchange regulations and the Takeover Panel Code. We were told by Mr Vogel of Titmuss Sainer & Webb and Miss Roberts (see paragraph 20.27) that they thought that Miss Maxwell performed the role of Compliance Officer for the Maxwell "Group". She signed a few letters as "Compliance Officer"; as to one of these she told us that this was typed in RM's office and was an error.

b That threshold level for disclosure is set by section 199(2) of the Companies Act 1985. The previous threshold of 5 per cent was altered by the Companies Act 1989 as from 31 May 1990 to 3 per cent.

c Mr Morgenstern had no recollection of such a call and thought it was most unlikely that any such call was made.

d KM told us that RM would keep on going until he obtained an opinion that he agreed with. If he persistently got advice he did not like from a lawyer, then he would fire the lawyer.

6.22 On 24 October 1990, an article appeared in *The Daily Mail* pointing to the size of the self-investment by the pension funds in MCC (and other companies connected with RM) on the basis of published information. This was prompted by certain pensioners who were concerned at RM's failure to increase their pensions. When RM read the article he was extremely angry but equally relieved when he learnt that the real interest of the pensioners was an increase in their pensions.

6.23 Draft letters[a] to make disclosure of a 6 per cent. holding were prepared by Miss Maxwell on 30 October 1990 but were never sent as RM refused to allow this to be done. Largely because of this Miss Maxwell resigned as group legal adviser. KM told us that he had a high professional regard for Miss Maxwell, he did not want her to resign, and she did not really want to leave but could not stand RM not following her advice; so KM suggested to her that she remain but work on the MGN flotation[b]. Shortly after she was re-employed as a consultant to MGN on its flotation[c]. During the flotation Miss Maxwell did not bring either the accumulation of MCC shares or the concealment by RM of the holding to the attention of any adviser or director. Mr Cook never mentioned this either. Mr Cook had given an undertaking to Bacon & Woodrow as actuaries to MGPS to notify them of changes in self-investment, but he never advised them of this increase in self-investment[d].

(d) Explanation for the purchases of MCC shares

6.24 RM stated at the time that he had made share purchases to take advantage of the weak price of the shares, the price had been under pressure because of concern at the ability to repay a $415m tranche of the $3 billion loan. The evidence set out above and in Appendix 7 establishes that there was substantial support for the share price at this time. We set out at paragraph 22.82 our views as to what was in fact happening.

---

a Titmuss Sainer & Webb also raised the issue as to whether KM, RM and IM as trustees of BIM would have to disclose their own holdings as well.

b KM told us that RM was profoundly irritated by Miss Maxwell's decision to resign and regarded it as a sign of disloyalty as he considered she had no right to resign. He subsequently agreed that co-ordination of the MGN flotation was an important job that she should do.

c RM circulated an announcement on 1 February 1991 that Miss Maxwell would be working full time on the flotation of MGN and relinquishing her other responsibilities to achieve this. It said nothing about her resignation. She sent a copy of the announcement to Goldman Sachs adding in the covering letter of 28 January 1991 "I attach a copy of [RM]'s announcement from which you will see that I am moving to the Mirror Group where I will be engaged full time on the impending flotation".

d Mr Simon of Bacon & Woodrow spoke to Mr Cook on 24 October 1990 to seek an explanation as to why investment by MGPS in MCC was not self-investment for the purposes of pension regulations made by the Occupational Pensions Board under the Social Security Act 1975 as amended, the definition of which included investment in a company directly or indirectly controlled by the same person who controlled the employer company. Mr Cook told Mr Simon there was no self-investment as MGN was not controlled by RM but from Liechtenstein. Mr Cook told us he did this in reliance on advice from Nicholson Graham & Jones. He had been relaxed about this at the time, but had since become unhappy about what he had said. Nicholson Graham & Jones told us that they had not given such advice. However Mr Cook signed a return to the Occupational Pensions Board on 16 July 1990 which included a statement that at 5 April 1990 self-investment did not exceed 10 per cent of the fund.

(3) The problems of the private side

(a) The use of the CIF and pension schemes for cash and collateral

6.25 The private side finances were significantly affected both by the need to fund these purchases of MCC shares and by the movement in the price of the MCC shares. MCC shares collateralised the two largest private side loans (as referred to at paragraphs 3.28 and 4.56) and were used in part as collateral for other loans; a decline in the share price necessitated the deposit of more collateral. The detailed position of the finances of the private side is very complex but the overall position can be summarised as follows:

- the level of the bank borrowing of the private side had increased from just over £970m at the end of June 1990 to just over £1,060m at the end of September 1990 and was £1,045m at the end of November 1990. New banks (including Swiss Volksbank, Bayerische Vereinsbank and Crédit Suisse) entered into new bilateral loans and other banks made available from time to time increased facilities.
- for the reasons explained at paragraph 4.57 each of the bank loans had to be collateralised. Further collateral was needed in this period largely because of the decline[a] in the MCC share price, the increase in the borrowings and the sale of the holdings in De La Rue in October 1990 (described at paragraph 6.56); the private side had not only used its own stake[b] in De La Rue as collateral but also that belonging to the CIF and MCC.

6.26 For these reasons the CIF and FTIT continued to be used to provide further cash and further collateral. In October 1990, the need for collateral became so pressing that shares from the externally managed portfolios began to be used. Details of the transactions are set out in Appendix 8 but can be summarised as follows:

- A formal agreement which bears the date of 25 July 1990 was entered into between LBI (as managers of FTIT) and RMG under which FTIT shares could be "lent" to RMG[c].
- Collateral continued to be made available from the CIF and FTIT portfolios managed by LBI and from the directly managed assets of the CIF.
- There were two important transfers of shares from the CIF to the private side so they could be used as collateral.
    - On 3 September 1990, KM informed Euris SA that almost all the CIF's shareholding in Euris SA had been transferred to PHL[d]; the shares were then charged to BNP to

---

[a] On about 6 August 1990, the decline in the MCC share price meant that two of the principal private side loans secured on MCC shares (the facility arranged by Lloyds and one from SBC) were insufficiently collateralised; the position worsened as the MCC share price declined further and was only remedied in late October 1990.

[b] The stakes are described at paragraph 5.28.

[c] Mr Trachtenberg told us that the need for an agreement was brought up by Mr Carson who had, on his appointment as Compliance Officer in January 1991, undertaken a survey of all LBI's transactions.

[d] KM's evidence was that he recalled RM telling him that the asset had been sold and he assumed that he was dealing with an asset of PHL.

6.26 continued

secure a £18.2m loan to PHL. Nothing was paid to the CIF and no entries were made in the books of the CIF.

- On 27 September 1990, the shareholding of the CIF in Marceau Investissements was sold to PHL at a price to be fixed by valuation; the shares were subsequently pledged to Crédit Commercial de France for a loan of £8m. The agreement for the sale was amended in February 1991 and a price fixed at £17.9m (inclusive of interest); this amount was not paid by the private side to the CIF but added to the debt owed by the private side to the CIF.

- A decision was taken on about 5 October 1990 that the shares of the externally managed portfolios be used as collateral[a].
  - On 9 October 1990 part of the portfolio of MGPS managed by CCM (valued at about £40m) was delivered to Lehmans and used as collateral for an increase of $28.9m to $82.4m of the financing under the arrangements with Lehmans described at paragraph 5.39. The amount of the financing was further increased by $28.4m to over $100m on 31 December 1990.
  - On 19 October 1990 MIM delivered part of the portfolio it managed for MGPS (valued at £22.5m) to Mr Trachtenberg who provided it to Crédit Suisse as collateral to enable a further £22m of a £50m facility to the private side to be drawn down; the facility had up to that time been secured with shares belonging to FTIT and the CIF.

- The loans of cash continued and by 31 December 1990 the amount owned by the private side to the CIF was in the order of £100m. Cash had been obtained largely from the sales of various investments[b] and transfers of cash from the external fund managers.

- In addition to this support to the private side, MGPS lent to MCC about £15m from July 1990 by buying MCC commercial paper[c].

---

a A board minute of BIM dated 5 October 1990 at which RM, KM, Mr Stephens and Mr Cook are recorded as being present purported to give authority for the MIM and CCM portfolios to be entered into "stocklending arrangements", with Mr Trachtenberg as the adviser to the programme. Mr Stephens told us he was certain he was not at the meeting and knew nothing of the arrangements. Mr Cook was told that stocklending would give the pension fund more income and that these particular portfolios were needed as they contained the right type of shares for lending. KM's evidence was that he was aware at the time of the board meeting that both managers had been visited by either Mr Trachtenberg or Mr Cook and had agreed to take part in the programme. His role was limited to being co-signer of letters to the managers; he did not recall speaking to anyone at CCM and, whilst he did speak to some officers at MIM, those conversations would not have included the use to which the stocks were being put. A formal agreement based on the draft for the FTIT "stocklending" was entered into between BIM and RMG sometime after 26 November 1990, but backdated to 1 October 1990.

b These sales included all the shares (except those in MCC) in the "special portfolio" which had been redelivered by MIM in July 1990 to MGPS, the sale of some Lazard property units for £8m in July 1990, the sale of a portfolio valued at £15.8m through Goldman Sachs in August 1990 and the sale of De La Rue shares in October 1990.

c For the purchase by MGN of MCC commercial paper - see paragraph 6.68.

6.27 In addition to this use that was made of the CIF and pension funds, from 8 November 1990, the private side began to utilise part of the substantial shareholding of MCC in Berlitz (valued at over $156.35m at that time) as collateral.

(b) Unauthorised overdrafts at 31 December 1990

6.28 Although during December 1990 the private side had obtained new loans, the private side had to repay over £105m at the year end. These repayments were covered by overdrafts obtained through LBI[a] in the manner set out in the next paragraphs. At the year end the total private side bank borrowings (including the overdrafts) had risen to about £1,105m and at the end of January 1991 they had only reduced slightly to about £1,075m.

6.29 The largest overdraft was obtained though MSTC's custodianship and settlement system (described at paragraph 5.33) which was used by LBI for the FTIT and CIF portfolios and its own proprietary trading[b]; this system was utilised by LBI to borrow $135m (£74.4m) in various currencies without MSTC's authority[c]. A detailed account of the circumstances in which the overdraft was obtained and repaid is contained in Appendix 8, but it is necessary to set out a summary here.

6.30 LBI obtained the overdraft by entering into MSTC's system instructions for the receipt of funds[d] and instructions for a corresponding payment out to be made prior to that receipt; in such circumstances MSTC's system would make the payment out before the receipt of matching funds. By a series of such instructions, LBI procured by the end of December 1990 the payment by MSTC of over $135m for which MSTC did not receive funds and thus achieved unauthorised overdrafts of this amount over the year end; of this sum, $56.7m was overdrawn on the CIF account[e].

6.31 LBI initially explained this to MSTC as a series of mistakes, but the Morgan Stanley Group became very concerned when the sums remained outstanding[f]. By mid January 1991[g] they started to apply considerable pressure to obtain repayment which they achieved in stages with the overdraft finally being repaid on 19 February 1991. MSTC did not notify BIM of this unauthorised overdraft nor did it notify any regulator nor any one else, because they told us

---

a We were told by Mr Ford that he understood (after his appointment as finance director of LBI in January 1991) that the purpose of the overdrafts had been to put money into the holding companies over the year end.

b LBH had opened its own separate account with MSTC in March 1989 for the proprietary trading activities of itself and LBI.

c MSTC was not allowed under its charter to lend funds.

d We were told that LBI "made up"some of the banks from which funds were going to come.

e The proprietary trading account was overdrawn in the sum of $76.3m.

f MSI had also lent LBI $28m in January 1991; we were told they did not know of the unauthorised overdraft when they made the loan.

g Mr Trachtenberg provided Morgan Stanley with 7.6 million Berlitz shares as a sign of good faith and also offered them the prospect of their being appointed custodian for all the pension funds' assets.

that it did not occur to them to do so as they said they believed the overdraft was "accidental" or due to "operational difficulties"; in any event they said they had no obligation to do so.

6.32 The private side also used LBI and LBH's accounts at Lloyds for a few days over the year end to obtain overdrafts totalling £52.8m[a]. Payments were made by Lloyds on the basis that they would be covered by inwards payments which did not materialise. The funds were repaid in early January 1991[b]. The overdrafts were explained as due to inadequacies in the administration. After these incidents Lloyds did not make payments out until funds arrived; at the end of March 1991, there were further occasions when Lloyds were asked to make payments on the basis that funds would be expected. When the expected funds did not arrive, although Lloyds had not made any payments out, they requested LBI to close all their accounts. KM told us that he first got an explanation of the overdraft after the event during his preparations for meetings with Lloyds concerning the closure of LBI's accounts. Lloyds, KM recalled, regarded the issue as being overtrading of the accounts by LBI which KM accepted.

6.33 We were told by Mr Trachtenberg and KM that there were tremendous strains over the year end. RM told Mr Trachtenberg he could not take a planned holiday. Instructions were relayed to effect the transactions that created the overdrafts either directly by RM (who was on his yacht in the Caribbean) or on his behalf. These unauthorised overdrafts are of considerable significance as without them, it is unlikely that the private side companies could have survived the year end.

(c) The Worship Street premises and Robert Fraser

6.34 The private side's finances were also assisted by the transfer to MGN of the tenancy of premises at 74 Worship Street under a 25 year lease; this was included on the flotation of MGN as one of its liabilities.

---

[a] They were in different accounts in the following amounts: $24.275m, $40m, £13.14m and £5.96m. There was also another overdraft of FF10.5m as a result of a transaction effect by the Treasury Department of Lloyds. Mr Trachtenberg told us that he could not recall whether he was involved in the administration of these payments but that they would have been made on the instructions of the central treasury.

[b] The overdraft of $24.275m was on an account designated by Lloyds as "LBI client a/c"; there had been overdrafts on other client accounts of LBI and there had been discussion within Lloyds as to whether this was permissible. Advice was taken from Cameron Markby Hewitt but we have not been provided with a copy of that advice as legal professional privilege has been claimed for it. We were nonetheless told by Lloyds that had not this overdraft been repaid by 4 January 1991 and an apparently plausible explanation been given, they would have investigated the cause of the overdraft themselves and satisfied themselves that LBI actually had authority from the client to overdraw the account.

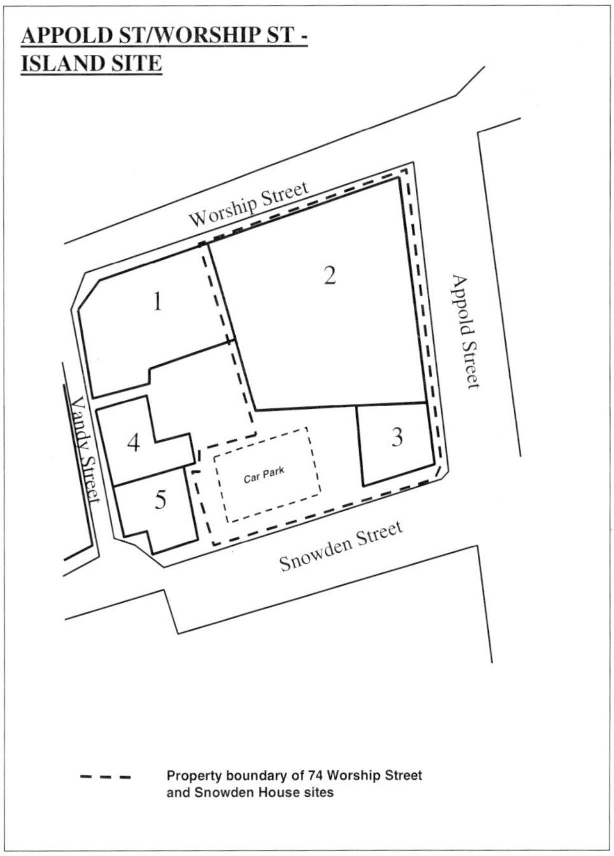

Key to Plan 2

1: 66 – 70 Worship Street
2: 74 Worship Street
3: Snowden House
4: 14 Vandy Street
5: 12 Vandy Street

Plan 2 – Worship Street

6.35 In order to understand the significance of this transaction it is necessary to explain its origin. MCC had had a printing works at 74 Worship Street, a site adjacent to developments that have subsequently taken place near Liverpool Street Station, London. At the time of RM's acquisition of MCC in April 1981 he had moved his headquarters to part of these premises and renamed that part "Maxwell House" and acquired another site (66-70 Worship Street) thereafter with a view to securing another "island" similar to that acquired at Holborn (see paragraph 2.32). After the acquisition of MGN, RM had moved his office to the Mirror Building and had started to plan the development of the Worship Street site. He negotiated an agreement for a 25 year lease with the Property Services Agency for HM Customs & Excise[a].

6.36 In December 1987, 74 Worship Street[b] was sold by MCC with the benefit of the agreement for a lease to the Property Services Agency to two companies comprising the Worship Street Partnership for £28.15m with completion to take place two years later; the agreement was varied in September 1989 to defer completion for a further year, to increase the price to £33.15m and to defer to December 1994 £14.25m of the payment due on completion. The

---

a Customs and Excise had been tenants of RM's interests at 12-14 New Fetter Lane (part of the Holborn site) and as the lease there was about to expire he offered them the premises at Worship Street. Customs and Excise decided in 1988 that they did not wish to take the lease and were released from the obligation on the payment of a reverse premium to MCC of £6.9 million in April 1990. This transaction was the subject of a National Audit Office Report printed on 10 December 1990.

b As well as that part of the site known as "Snowden House".

partnership was a joint venture between Robert Fraser Estates Limited[a] and one of their clients, Blackford Holdings Corporation. By a further agreement made in December 1987 the partnership agreed to reimburse MCC on completion for the sums (about £19 m) which MCC was bound to spend under the lease in improving the premises.

6.37 We were told that in the spring of 1990, RM had become concerned at the ability of Robert Fraser Estates Limited to raise the necessary finance to complete the transaction as Robert Fraser was facing financial pressures for the reasons set out at paragraph 5.29. RM "introduced" Corry Foundation, (one of the Liechtenstein foundations acquired as described at paragraph 1.10[b]), to Robert Fraser as a purchaser. On 8 May 1990 Corry Foundation acquired the companies comprising the Worship Street partnerships and at the same time MCC became tenant of 74 Worship Street under a 25 year lease on terms similar to those which had been agreed with the Property Services Agency for HM Customs & Excise who had withdrawn from their arrangement in April 1990.

6.38 By late September 1990 it was decided that:

- Corry Foundation would sell the companies comprising the Worship Street partnership which owned 74 Worship Street, to PHA Finance Ltd (PHAF), a subsidiary of PHA.
- MGN would take a lease of the premises at 74 Worship Street for 25 years on the same terms as the leases to the Customs & Excise and MCC[c].
- MCC would be released from the terms of the lease and completion of the sale of the premises by MCC (agreed in 1987) would be brought forward to 16 October 1990 from December 1990.
- The premises with the benefit of the lease would be used to raise finance.

6.39 BNP[d] were approached on 26 September 1990 for a loan on the basis of a mortgage of the premises at 74 Worship Street and on being provided with a valuation of £55m for the property with the benefit of the lease to MGN agreed to loan £36m[e].

---

a A company within Robert Fraser Group. Adjoining premises at 66/70 Worship Street were sold in June 1988 for a price (as varied) of £15.7m to a second partnership (The Second Worship Street Partnership) with a completion date (as varied) in June 1991. Several other premises were subject to similar agreements.

b Dr Rechsteiner was given all the instructions and he relayed them to General Trust Company who also administered this foundation and provided its directors; those directors gave instructions to Titmuss Sainer & Webb who acted on behalf of Corry.

c The agreed rent was varied to a fixed initial figure of just over £5m with similar provisions for increases.

d They had declined to make a further loan on the basis of the security of the shares in Marceau Investissements referred to at paragraph 6.26.

e The purpose of the loan was said to be for general corporate purposes, possibly including the reduction in the MCC facility and RM's recent share support operations. KM told us that Mr Anselmini was ultimately responsible for this loan since he had the contacts at BNP, as with the other French banks.

6.40 On 16 October 1990

- MGN acting by Mr Guest signed the lease of those premises. He was told that it had been decided that MGN would move to Worship Street when the Mirror Building complex at Holborn was redeveloped. However, it was decided during the preparation for the flotation in the circumstances explained at paragraph 14.14. that this site would not be used by MGN.
- MCC were released from the lease under which they had agreed in May 1990 to become the tenant.
- £36m was lent by BNP and a mortgage given in respect of 74 Worship Street[a].
- The private side paid Corry £4.5m for the companies comprising the Worship Street Partnerships; £4m of this was immediately returned through PHUSI to the private side.
- Completion of the sale by MCC to the companies comprising the Worship Street Partnership took place and the amounts due to MCC on completion (£35.56m) were credited to the private side's intercompany account with MCC.

Although there was a need for MGN to have alternative premises during the redevelopment, the predominant purpose of MGN taking the long lease was to enable the loan from BNP to be obtained on the strength of MGN's cash flow.

(d) The Bank of England's involvement in RM's attempt to acquire Robert Fraser and in answering an enquiry from the Bank of Israel

6.41 RM was able to take advantage of the financial pressures on Robert Fraser to attempt to gain control of this group (with its merchant bank) using the fact that Robert Fraser owed funds to RM's interests (as described at paragraph 5.29) as well as a smaller amount to Ansbacher.

6.42 On 6 July 1990, Ansbacher as advisers to Robert Fraser[b] saw the Bank of England. The Bank of England indicated it would have to consider the fitness and properness of RM and to look back to past events at PPL. They indicated RM was not to influence the day-to-day affairs of the merchant bank which would need robust independent management, a strong board independent of the majority shareholders, including quality non-executives. Further discussions followed in July 1990 in which the Bank of England were assured:

- RM would not be on the board;
- there would be an independent chief executive;
- there would be three non-executive directors of repute to ensure robust independent management;
- a "ring fence"[c] would be put round Robert Fraser to stop business being done with RM's companies;

---

a The funds were paid to RMG which had paid £35m to PHL on 15 October 1990; PHL had paid £17.5m on 15 October 1990 to BIT which used the funds to pay for share purchases, including the 10 million MCC shares purchased for the CIF and pension schemes on 20 September 1990 as referred to at paragraph 6.18.

b Ansbacher tendered their resignation as advisers to Robert Fraser on 20 July 1990. In September 1990 they acted only for RM's interests, with the assent of Robert Fraser.

c The meaning of this term is considered at paragraph 12.14.

- the controlling interest acquired by RM would go into a trust held for the commercial benefit of RM's companies, but RM would have no voting control[a].

6.43 On 6 July 1990 the Bank of England told a meeting of the College of Regulators[b] called by the Bank of England and attended by representatives from the Securities and Investments Board (SIB), The Securities Association (TSA) and IMRO about the plans RM had and their views. Subsequent to that IMRO (which had regulatory responsibility for the fund management company within Robert Fraser) was kept informed of the progress; on 20 July 1990, the Bank of England in the course of updating IMRO told them:

> "A rescue package has been put together by Robert Maxwell. The Bank of England is of the view that the package is "just about workable", although there would still remain a net asset deficiency. The benefit of the proposal is that it would provide time for asset disposals within the group. The bank considered that Robert Maxwell is probably not fit and proper. They have therefore made a proposal to Ansbacher (acting on behalf of Maxwell) that a trust should be set up. Maxwell would be a beneficiary of the trust but would not be a trustee. The trustees would be those deemed suitable by the bank. Maxwell would have no voting control."

6.44 We were told that it was perceived that the attitude of the Bank of England was one of disquiet, but they might have been prepared to let RM acquire Robert Fraser on the terms proposed. We were told by IMRO that the Bank of England had no new information other than that known to them in 1988 on the admission of LBI and BIM as members.

6.45 Robert Fraser managed to raise funds to pay off the loans to RM's interests and Ansbacher in August 1990 and the attempted take over did not proceed in the form envisaged. Negotiations between Robert Fraser and RM's interests continued.

6.46 At about the same time, the Bank of England had to consider another question about RM. On 13 July 1990, the Supervisor of Banks at the Bank of Israel spoke to Mr Quinn, an Executive Director of the Bank of England, and told him that RM wanted to buy one of the four largest banks in Israel which was up for sale. Under Israeli law, a person proposing to acquire over 10 per cent. of the means of control had to satisfy various requirements, including not only his financial soundness but also his personal and commercial integrity. Mr Quinn asked the Supervisor of Banks at the Bank of Israel to write formally but referred him to the 1971/73 Reports of the Inspectors to which, despite their age, the Bank would have to give due consideration. The Bank of Israel formally wrote on 18 July 1990 seeking from the Bank of England any information on RM which might influence their decision.

---

[a] If this structure had been used, then the issue of RM's fitness and properness might not have arisen, as he might not have been a controller under the provisions of the Banking Act 1987.

[b] The College of Regulators was not a formal body but a term applied to meetings between different regulatory bodies which supervised the financial service and banking activities of companies within the same group; each group was assigned a "lead" regulator based on the dominant activity of the group and it was responsible for calling meetings with other regulators concerned with the group if a need arose. The Stock Exchange was not part of this system as it was not a regulatory body dealing with financial services and banking. In November 1992 a structured information exchanging network was established amongst regulators with a wider composition than the College of Regulators including such bodies as the Stock Exchange.

6.47 The Bank of England formally responded on 30 August 1990; they set out details of the shareholdings that RM had in various banks (including Robert Fraser), but pointed out they had not had to consider RM's position as a controller under the UK Banking Act as his shareholding was under 15 per cent. They added:

> "[RM] has given us no grounds for complaints or criticisms in our dealings with him.
> Finally, as part of the background of [RM] I should draw your attention to a report written in 1971 by Inspectors appointed on behalf of the UK's Department of Trade and Industry. This Report... contained criticisms of [RM] and I would suggest that you obtain and read a copy of the Inspectors' Report.
> It is only fair to point out that [RM] disputed the findings of this Report and took legal action against the Inspectors. This action was eventually dismissed by the Court of Appeal".

There was a further telephone conversation after this, but the position was left that they would talk further if RM proceeded. He did not.

6.48 On 4 September 1990, Ansbacher was informed by KM that RM was again considering with Robert Fraser acquiring control of the group[a]. At the end of September 1990, the Bank of England were informed that RM's private side companies intended to seek full control of Robert Fraser as it was not intended to rescue Robert Fraser without such control[b]. The matter was reported to the Deputy Governor of the Bank of England in an internal note that indicated a slight inclination to allow things to go ahead. The note observed:

> "There are questions about [RM's] empire's financial strength (prob not crucial). The issue is more his reliability as an owner and avoiding some kind of shenanigans later. 1969 is a long time ago. But eyebrows would be raised nevertheless."

6.49 In subsequent discussions the Bank of England[c] said that they would have to be satisfied as to "fitness and properness" and they would consider the 1971/73 DTI Reports on PPL as part of

---

a A note of a meeting records

> "KM stated that 'he was afraid of what might come out if the Bank [Robert Fraser's merchant bank] goes under'. He was not specific but appeared concerned that at a critical time for MCC there might be adverse publicity".

KM told us that this was in fact a reference to his concern that the various property transactions entered into by MCC with Robert Fraser might not proceed and this might have an effect on MCC as the profits had been brought into account. He was subsequently advised by Mr Shaw (see paragraph 2.32) that it did not matter as the deposits had been received and they would be able to keep the properties, though others at MCC were in favour of supporting Robert Fraser. Ansbacher thought that this referred to the involvement of Robert Fraser in IWC (see paragraph 5.29); Ansbacher had come across IWC in the course of their work. At a meeting on 11 September 1990 Ansbacher strongly advised RM not to proceed.

b If this route was followed, then it was necessary for the Bank of England to consider whether RM was a fit and proper person to be the controller of a bank under the Banking Act 1987.

c A Bank of England memorandum recorded that in a meeting on 4 October 1990:

> "KM admitted that the banking business was not a key part to his plans but it was complementary to the fund management business, providing the capability of doing fx. It is intended to inject new capital into [Robert Fraser] and introduce banking executives to run the bank. David Corsan (IMRO and ex Coopers & Lybrand) has already been approached to be a non-executive director and Ansbachers are willing to provide staff until qualified personnel are recruited; CLD are ready to examine the systems and replace Peats as auditors. No banking business with other Maxwell group companies would be done and such undertakings would be given."

Mr Corsan told us that he had been approached but was unaware of the identity of the company and had not agreed to any provisional appointments.

this and be "intrusive" into RM's business affairs[a]. RM did not proceed with the acquisition after his advisers expressed concern about possible significant financial uncertainties within Robert Fraser. The Bank of England was informed of this on 7 December 1990.

6.50 At a further meeting of the College of Regulators[b] on 28 December 1990, the Bank of England reported that they would have had difficulty in finding RM "fit and proper".

(4) The events of the autumn of 1990

(a) The transfer to MGN of the interests in QPI and Donohue

6.51 Because of the difficulty MCC was having in the late summer of 1990 with the asset disposal programme necessary to raise funds to repay $415m on 23 October 1990 (as set out at paragraph 6.11), it was suggested by Mr Baker that the interests of MCC in Donohue and QPI (which MCC had acquired in the circumstances described at paragraph 3.17 and 6.9 respectively) be transferred to MGN. These interests were included in the flotation of MGN. There were a number of reasons why this proposal was attractive to MCC, RM and the banks:

- MCC had disposed of most of its interests in printing and these two interests were not a part of MCC's core business of publishing; their disposal would mean that core assets did not have to be disposed at "fire sale" prices.
- MGN would be able to borrow sufficient funds to acquire the interests in these companies at the price at which MCC had acquired them and at which they were carried in the MCC books[c]; it was thought at the time to be essential that MCC did not make a loss on the sale so as to ensure that the profits of MCC were not affected and so that the private side were not seen to be benefiting at the expense of the public shareholders of MCC.
- MGN was perceived by the banks as having a strong cash flow and thus able to support the borrowing necessary to enable it to acquire and finance these interests on those terms.
- If the interests were to be retained within a company owned by RM, Donohue fitted more logically into MGN than MCC as it was a newsprint supplier and, as the stake in QPI had its origins in the relationship with Quebecor, it could be said that it too more logically fitted into MGN rather than MCC.

6.52 In addition to this proposal, it was also decided that MGN would repay early the £62.5m of loan stock which it had issued to MCC in part payment for the acquisition of BNPC, the re-planted printing operation that MGN had acquired in May 1989 as referred to at paragraph 4.31. As no final price adjustment (as required by the terms of the sale agreement between MCC and MGN) had been carried out, this was immediately effected and further loan stock of £9.6m was issued to MCC on 8 October 1990. The interest accrued on the stock was then calculated to be £13.1m, so that a total payment of £85.2m was needed to redeem it.

---

a The Bank of England had to consider the application fairly; information about HI (the parent company of that part of the private side that it was envisaged would hold the shares in Robert Fraser) was submitted to the Bank of England and detailed questions asked including questions on the financial strength of MCC as shares in MCC were the largest asset of HI.

b Attended by representatives of TSA, FIMBRA, LAUTRO and IMRO.

c In addition, in the case of QPI, MGN was also to pay the carrying costs from February 1990.

6.53 In order to redeem the loan stock and to acquire the stakes in QPI and Donohue MGN needed:

- £85m
- £71m for the stake in Donohue
- £58m being the cost attributed to the acquisition of the interest in QPI and the cost of carrying that interest from February 1990.

To finance these payments, MGN was required to make substantial new borrowings. Before describing the borrowing arrangements that were made for MGN, it is convenient to complete the account of the solution of MCC's immediate debt repayment problem although the payments by MGN had almost achieved this.

6.54 On 2 October 1990 the acquisition by MGN of MCC's stakes in Donohue and QPI was announced by RM. On the same day Bankers Trust were commissioned on behalf of MCC to provide an independent opinion to the shareholders of MCC on the sale. Bankers Trust visited both QPI and Donohue and provided a report by Friday 5 October 1990[a]. The report concluded that the price being paid by MGN for the stake in Donohue was at a 65 per cent. premium to the market price[b], but stated that the market price did not reflect the long term value of the shares due to the cyclical nature of the industry or the strategic value of the stake. In respect of the stake in QPI (which was not a quoted company) Bankers Trust concluded that QPI had somewhat higher trading multiples than those of comparable companies. This was, however, not a valuation by Bankers Trust, but just a report to the shareholders of MCC that it was a fair and reasonable transaction from their stand point. On 11 October 1990 a board meeting of MCC approved the sale and the circular to shareholders was issued on 18 October 1990. The sale was approved at an EGM of MCC on 5 November 1990.

6.55 MGN formally approved the purchase at a board meeting on 16 October 1990 attended only by RM, KM and IM. The operational management of MGN (who were also directors of the company) played no part in the acquisition of the interests in QPI and Donohue and were given no opportunity to discuss their value or the strategic reasoning behind their acquisition[c]. IM told us that he did not recall this board meeting but he did recall that Donohue was regarded as being a good commercial investment for a newspaper group and that QPI was regarded as, generally, being a good investment. However, it was a decision made by RM principally to solve MCC's immediate debt repayment problem. KM told us that once the decision had been made by RM, the owner of MGN, then nothing further was required; none of the operational directors of MGN could have had any say in the matter, just like they had had no say in the

---

[a] Their fee was £300,000. KM told us that Bankers Trust always performed to a tight timetable and were paid accordingly; also after seeing fees of many millions paid to the unsuccessful party on the acquisition of Macmillan, RM would have regarded fees such as this as being comparatively small.

[b] The 65 per cent. premium to the market price was based on the information available to Bankers Trust in early October 1990 when they carried out their work. At the date of the sale to MGN later in October 1990, the price paid had become a premium of 77 per cent. to the then market price.

[c] Titmuss Sainer & Webb who had been retained to act for MGN advised KM on 4 October 1990 that the "independent directors" of MGN would need to have sufficient information to decide to proceed at prices they considered in excess of the market prices; no meeting of the "independent directors" was in fact held, though the in-house legal adviser was present at the meeting approving the purchase.

decision by RM to spend £600m moving *The Mirror* into colour printing (although they were involved in implementing that decision). Nonetheless, the view (which was, KM thought, correct) was that Donohue was a good investment to acquire at a time when the paper market cycle was at a low. A complex scheme was then devised to give effect to the transfer from MCC to MGN which included a loan by RMG of Can $35m to MCC companies, of the same amount by MCC companies to MGN companies and of the same amount by MGN to RMG[a].

(b) The sale of the stake in De La Rue and the repayment by MCC of bank debt of $415m

6.56 Apart from these transactions involving MGN, only one other significant disposal was achieved by MCC prior to the due date for repayment of its debt of $415m on 23 October 1990. That was the disposal of the combined stake of MCC, the private side and the CIF in De La Rue (the origins of which are described at paragraph 5.28) which was sold for £72.4m through Smith New Court on 9 October 1990[b]. The amount that the CIF obtained from this sale was £10.75m and this was accounted for[c] in the intercompany accounts towards payment for the 10 million MCC shares that RM had bought on behalf of the CIF and MCWPS on 20 September 1990 (see paragraph 6.18).

6.57 Other sales, including the sale of the Panini and the Collier Encyclopaedia businesses, were being negotiated by MCC but neither sale had been completed by the time the debt of $415m became repayable on 23 October 1990[d]. However, by that time MCC and MGN had bridging facilities of $290m and £85m in place (in respect of the sale of the stakes in QPI and Donohue and the repayment of the loan stock) enabling MCC's debt of $415m to be repaid.

6.58 In reality, as was perceived by some of MCC's bankers at the time, MGN's acquisition of the interests in QPI and Donohue amounted to the refinancing of MCC's debt by MGN. The perceptions of the bankers were aided by a change of policy by RM. KM told us that prior to the end of 1990 RM's companies had provided banks with minimum information only. During 1990, however, RM accepted advice from Mr Anselmini[e] that in order to obtain fast and positive responses from banks in relation to applications for credit the banks would require

---

[a] The scheme was designed to comply with a covenant in a bank loan to MCC (so that it did not have to be refinanced) and to mitigate tax liabilities in Canada. Its treatment during the flotation is considered at paragraph 15.25.

[b] The stake had cost the various interests associated with RM about £119m to purchase and the loss on the sale was about £48m.

[c] It was in fact paid to the private side and debited in the CIF's books to the loan account between the private side and CIF. It was from this account that on 15 October 1990 there was credited £17m to pay for the MCC shares acquired on 20 September 1990.

[d] These two sales were mentioned in the circular sent to MCC shareholders; during the verification of the circular, Freshfields were provided with letters of intent for both sales; the letter in respect of Panini was signed by Schroder Venture Advisers and that for Collier Encyclopedia signed by Brockhaus AG.

[e] Mr Anselmini had been a banker with Crédit Lyonnais until 1988 when he had been appointed Deputy Chairman of MCC. His principal role was dealing with banks not only for MCC, but also for the private side. He assisted in the introduction of continental European banks. We were told that he was an influential adviser to RM on all banking matters, particularly in the second half of 1990 and the early part of 1991; that he regarded himself as constructively dismissed in March 1991 when he was not provided with information about what was happening in MCC.

better information concerning the companies. As a result, more information was volunteered to banks; presentations were made and visits arranged to the operating companies.

(c) MGN's new borrowing - £360m facility – and the use of MGN's cash flow

6.59 Lloyds and Crédit Lyonnais were approached to arrange the new borrowing that MGN required for the repayment of the loan stock and for the acquisition of the interests in QPI and Donohue. As there was to be a new borrowing, it was easier to have one facility; accordingly it was decided to repay the £150m facility that had been arranged by Toronto Dominion (see paragraph 4.32) and to seek a new secured facility for £360m. By 25 October 1990 that new facility had been underwritten by Lloyds, Crédit Lyonnais, Midland Bank, The Bank of Nova Scotia, Societé Générale, BNP, SBC and The Long Term Credit Bank of Japan. Other banks were then invited to participate in the loan.

6.60 Apart from concerns that the banks had about the strategy behind MGN's acquisition of the interests in QPI and Donohue and the price being paid, two other matters concerned them:

- that the money provided under the facility should be used by MGN and not "leaked" to other businesses controlled by RM;
- that there be a proper programme for repayment by MGN.

6.61 The first of these concerns is common when a bank wishes to lend to one part of a group that it considers provides much better security for its loan than any other part of the group and it makes appropriate arrangements to ensure that money is not passed on to those other parts of the group. Arrangements that are so designed are sometimes referred to as "ring fencing". One of the banks involved in the MGN facility took the view that the complexity of the company structure would make it extremely difficult for a "ring fence" to be created around MGN. However, it was decided to insert into the loan documentation a series of covenants intended to prevent the funds of MGN being used by other parts of RM's private side. The banks appreciated that such covenants could be broken but, as in the past RM had always honoured commitments to his bankers and had "seen them right", they thought that such covenants would be complied with. KM told us that during the negotiation of this facility careful attention was paid to the wording of the exceptions so that they could be utilised to maintain the transfer of MGN's cash flow to other companies controlled by RM[a]. RM would not have permitted the facility to be signed unless he believed he could continue to make use of MGN's cash flow in this way[b].

6.62 Allied to the banks' concern to see that funds were not passed from MGN to RM's private side companies was the concern for a programme of repayment. The figures prepared for the banks (and analysed by them) showed that the cash flow of MGN alone was insufficient to repay the loan to the banks; even were MGN to dispose of some of its assets, it would be necessary for

---

a The same happened when a new facility was negotiated at the time of the flotation (see paragraphs 12.14 and 15.35).

b We were told by KM that RM had discussions about raising the price of *The Mirror* by 1p to produce additional cash flow. This would have produced in 1991 a gross annual revenue increase of £8.9m and a net annual revenue (allowing for lost sales and retail and wholesale margins) increase of £5.9m.

other companies on the private side[a] to dispose of assets and pay the proceeds to MGN to enable it to repay the facility; the payment of the proceeds to MGN would have the effect of reducing the intercompany account. KM told us that this was, therefore, viewed as a hybrid loan with MGN's cash flow as the primary source of repayment and MGN's assets such as the titles and QPI/Donohue (which were security for the facility) the secondary source. Allied to those sources the banks were all aware that it was intended to float MGN but none were happy to rely on the flotation as a source of repayment to cover the shortfall on MGN's cash flow, since market conditions might not permit this. Accordingly, Mr Anselmini came up with the idea of not pledging further private side assets but of drawing up an asset disposal programme details of which were set out in an information memorandum produced in October 1990 for the banks invited to participate. It contained the following table.

Number	Investment	Per cent. owned	Date to be disposed	Amount (£)[b]
1	Central TV	20	January 1991	30,000,000
2	MTV Europe	50	January 1991	40,000,000
3	British Cable Service	100	January 1991	10,000,000
4	*The Sporting Life*	100	October 1991/ June 1992	25,000,000
5	*The People*	100	October 1991/ June 1992	50,000,000
6	QPI	25	October 1992/ June 1993	50,000,000
7	SDR	100	By June 1995	50,000,000

Table 6 – Asset disposal programme at October 1990

The first three investments, Central TV, MTV Europe and British Cable Service were owned by RMG/PHL. The terms of the facility agreement required RMG and PHL to apply the proceeds of the sale of these companies to the repayment to MGN of the intercompany debt.

6.63 It was, however, not anticipated that any of these three companies would be disposed of prior to January 1991. Therefore, in the financial projections that the banks were given, the level of the intercompany debt due from PHL was projected to be at 31 December 1990 exactly the same as it had been as at 31 December 1989[c]. The balance from the other private side companies was projected to reduce from £86.8m at 31 December 1989 to £81.7m by 31 December 1990.

a Which in fact owed MGN approximately £334m at 31 December 1990 on its intercompany account (as set out at paragraph 4.46).

b Some of the amounts were based on earlier valuations performed by Bankers Trust in connection with RM's attempts of acquiring Paramount (see paragraph 5.29) and then updated.

c The intercompany debt due from PHL was stated to be £176.1 million at both dates and was said to bear interest at 1 per cent. over base and to have arisen on the transfer to the private side of non-newspaper assets and surplus cash.

(d) Subscription to the facility and the two payments of £30m

6.64 Although the facility had been underwritten by 25 October 1990, the facility agreement was not signed until 23 November 1990. Attempts were then made by the lead banks to complete subscriptions from other banks to the facility. This did not prove to be an easy task[a].

6.65 A meeting was arranged on 6 December 1990 to try and encourage other banks to participate in the facility; KM who had been responsible with Mr Bunn and Mr Anselmini for negotiating the facility said at that meeting[b]:

> "I think one additional important point which is not reflected in the information memorandum is that, since that date, we have repaid £60 million of intercompany debt between Pergamon and *The Mirror*. This anticipated the disposal inflows of Central Television and MTV Europe so that we, as a borrower, have made good on £60 million of the £80 million that we had indicated we would do so during the course of 1991. That is a very positive improvement from *The Mirror's* point of view".

6.66 Shortly after that meeting Lloyds (who had been present at the meeting) asked for confirmation in writing of what KM had said. Confirmation was not provided until 22 February 1991 when Mr Bunn wrote to Lloyds to tell them that £60m of the intercompany debt owed to MGN has been repaid. In March 1991 Lloyds received from MGN a further letter signed by KM and dated 12 December 1990 which stated that MGN had received[c]:

> "Monies in repayment of the intercompany loans made to [RMG] or [PHL] in two amounts of £30m each on 30 November 1990 and 3 December 1990. This being an amount equal to the proceeds of the sale of MTV/Central TV."

KM told us that he had no specific memory of signing the letter and, if it had been brought to him by Mr Bunn (who prepared it), he may well have just signed it; it was not his custom and practice to read everything carefully or ask questions. Lloyds told us that none of the banks present at the meeting subscribed to the facility.

6.67 In fact, shortly prior to 29 November 1990 Chase had been told that in order to get the £360m facility fully syndicated by other banks, a loan of £30m was required to PHL, it being intended that the loan would be applied to reduce the amount of the intercompany debt owing to MGN and to bridge the receipt by PHL of the proceeds of the expected sale of Central TV. Bankers Trust similarly was told shortly before 3 December 1990 that a loan of £30m was required to reduce the intercompany debt owing to MGN by bridging the receipt of sale proceeds from the expected disposal of MTV. Both Chase and Bankers Trust each agreed to provide loans of £30m and these were drawn down and applied as follows:

---

a National Westminster, Bankers Trust and Sumitomo Trust and Banking Co. Ltd. had subscribed by 23 November 1990 and they were followed by The First National Bank of Chicago, Barclays and Crédit National.

b KM told us that he recalled the origin of the idea being Mr Anselmini, who thought that a positive announcement would help assist in the syndication.

c A similar confirmation was given to Bankers Trust.

- £30m was drawn down from Chase on 29 November 1990 and PHL paid £30m on 30 November 1990 into MGN's account at National Westminster; however it was paid out by MGN on the same day to another private side company, RMH which paid £30m to PHL.[a]
- £30m was drawn down from Bankers Trust on 3 December 1990 and paid into a bank account of PHL[b], but nothing was paid into any MGN account on or about that day in discharge of all or part of the intercompany debt.

KM told us that he had no specific recollection of the events of 6 December 1990 set out in paragraph 6.65 but that there must have been some movement on the intercompany account for him to have said what is recorded above[c]. KM told us that no one would have stood in front of a meeting of bankers and told a bare faced lie. In any event, however, the statement about repaying the debt owed by PHL to MGN was correct; it fitted with the approach of RM at the time that you would not go on to make full disclosure and say that the total overall intercompany debt had remained the same. You would not be telling a lie by not providing all the information – it is being "economical with the information".

(e) Draft accounts of MGN at 31 December 1990: MCC commercial paper and other matters

6.68 Under the terms of the facility agreement, consolidated accounts of MGN for the year ended 31 December 1990 were required to be presented to the banks participating in the facility. Draft unaudited accounts sent to Lloyds in April 1991[d] showed:

(1) The amount due from PHL[e] was shown as having been reduced by £61m, in line with the £60m reduction that the banks had been told by KM in December 1990 had been repaid. This had been achieved in the following way: £30m of the reduction was achieved through the payment to MGN of £30m from the loan from Chase referred to in paragraph 6.67, but which was paid out the same day by MGN to RMH and then back to PHL. However, after accounting for payments between MGN and PHL during the year, interest charges made by MGN and other adjustments the balance was not the £60m less that the bankers had been led to expect but about £70m less; an adjustment of £9m was

---

a KM told us that he did not doubt that the money had gone round in a circle but that he had no specific recollection of the payments; it was, he thought, an example of crisis management. The route would have been decided on by RM in accordance with his view of what was permissible by the letter (although not the spirit) of the covenants in the £360m facility.

b The £60m borrowed from Chase and Bankers Trust was used in part to repay the loan by BNP to PHL referred to at paragraph 5.39, in part towards payments for the 15.65 million MCC shares payable under the second "option" agreed between RM and Goldman Sachs in August 1990 (see paragraph 6.17) and in part for other purposes of the private side.

c KM also told us that he would have expected Mr Guest who was present to have seen there was no such movement and commented. However, as the funds would merely have passed through the accounts, it is highly unlikely that Mr Guest would have been alert to the movement and said anything.

d By the time these draft accounts were provided to Lloyds, it had been agreed to replace the £360m facility with a £150m facility as explained at paragraph 15.34; the draft accounts were prepared with the £360m facility in mind and sent to Lloyds who were one of the arrangers under both facilities. They were only circulated to the banks who were invited to participate in the £150m facility.

e This was shown in the draft accounts sent to Lloyds as "debtors- amounts due after one year: due from related parties"; from the information supplied to the banks in October 1990, this would have been understood to refer to the debt due from PHL.

made to increase the amount due from PHL and reduce that due from RMG so that the reduction in the amount due by PHL was about £61m[a].

(2) Even though the debt due from PHL was shown as having been reduced, the overall amount of the intercompany debt due to MGN was shown as having increased by £7.7m above the projected figure given to the banks in October 1990. This had been achieved in the following way: the increase had in fact been much greater as the net amount due from private side companies other than PHL (and its subsidiaries) had increased by £118.9m[b]. In the draft accounts a reduction in this part of the intercompany debt was achieved through:

- a credit item of £25m being in payment for group tax relief to which RMG was entitled;
- a transaction involving £30m nominal value of MCC commercial paper.

The MCC commercial paper[c] was recorded as having been acquired by RMG[d] on behalf of MGN at a cost of £29.6m on 27 December 1990 and was subsequently credited to the RMG intercompany account in MGN's books; MGN did not make any payment and therefore this acquisition had the effect of reducing the intercompany debt owed by RMG and its subsidiaries.

(3) The acquisition of the MCC commercial paper provided another benefit, in terms of the ability to present figures in the draft accounts in line with the projections given to the banks. It was included in the draft accounts as a "current asset investment"; by offsetting against unsecured bank overdrafts of £18.1m the MCC commercial paper (valued at its cost of £29.6m) and by including the small amount of cash in hand (£185,000), the cash position of MGN could be viewed as being in line with the projected figure of £11.8m given to the banks in October 1990.

KM told us that the primary motive for investing in MCC commercial paper would have been that MCC needed the cash, the secondary motive would have been that using commercial paper was thought to be an exception to the ring fence in the £360m facility. After the transaction had been carried out, accounting ingenuity would have been employed to derive the best possible accounting presentation for the transaction.

Effect was also given to these adjustments and transactions in MGN's statutory accounts.

---

a KM told us that this sort of accounting adjustment would not have been unusual. There was an occasion in 1991 that the MCC/private side intercompany debt had been £180m ahead of figures prepared for banks; a cheque from the private side for £180m was provided to MCC and kept in the safe over the relevant date in order to square with what the banks had been told.

b As set out at paragraph 6.63 the bankers had been told in October 1990 that the projected debt from the private side other than PHL and its subsidiaries would be reduced to £81.7m, but it had increased to £205.6m, before the adjustments for group tax relief and commercial paper.

c Commercial paper is a means by which companies can borrow money on an unsecured basis if they have sufficient credit standing to enable loan notes for a fixed term to be sold by banks as principals on their behalf.

d This was effected through LBI. It was documented as one month commercial paper maturing on 28 January 1991.

6.69 The acquisition of the commercial paper was considered in the course of the audit of MGN for the year ended 31 December 1990 and the preparation for the flotation; CLD were told that it represented the investment derived from part of MGN's surplus funds which had been passed to the private side over the years. The documentation provided in respect of the commercial paper is more conveniently described at paragraph 11.6 below.

6.70 CLD told us that the adjustment of £9m referred to in subparagraph (1) of paragraph 6.68 and an adjustment for interest[a] were drawn to their attention and explained initially to one of their junior staff as being necessary to bring the accounts into line with what the banks participating in the £360m facility had been told. Subsequently Mr Steere, the audit partner, was told that this was not the reason for the adjustments as the adjustments had been made to rationalise the structure of the indebtedness with the private side and to apply appropriate interest to the indebtedness of RMG. CLD told us that they understood that although there was a restriction imposed on MGN under the terms of the £360m facility which prevented MGN passing its surplus cash to PHL, there was no restriction on MGN transferring money to reduce borrowings; and that surplus cash had been passed to RMG's subsidiary, RMH, for this purpose[b]. CLD were later provided with letters of agreement signed on behalf of the private side companies confirming the position.

6.71 Mr Steere told us that he considered that there was nothing improper on its face in reducing the overall debt owed by PHL by £61m and increasing that owed by RMG (or decreasing that owed by RMH) accordingly, and CLD had received reasonable explanations for what had been done. He told us that the adjustments were in any event immaterial to MGN's accounts and did not affect the truth and fairness of the accounts on which CLD were reporting; it was not CLD's concern to verify information provided to bankers[c].

(f) Consideration of a separate flotation for SDR

6.72 Among the businesses that the banks were informed would be disposed of by MGN in connection with the £360m facility (see paragraph 6.62), were three businesses that were ultimately floated with MGN - *The Sporting Life*, *The People* and SDR. Of these, a separate

---

a Interest had not been charged on the intercompany debt due from RMG in earlier years. A further adjustment had been made to the accounts to charge interest of £3.3m to RMG on the intercompany debt; this was calculated at a rate of 15 per cent and applied to the net increase in the balance due from RMG and RMH to MGN during 1990.

b The state of the intercompany accounts was such that at 31 December 1989 a net amount of about £59m was due to RMH from MGN, though on the overall state of the private side accounts (which took into account this figure) the amount owed to MGN was £309m (see paragraph 4.46). During 1990, net cash payments of £45m had been made to RMH by MGN and after taking into account some smaller items, the balance due from MGN to RMH at 31 December 1990 was £13m.

c It was agreed (as set at paragraph 15.34) that this facility was in any event to be repaid and by the time the accounts of MGN were signed Mr Steere knew this.

flotation of SDR was seriously considered in the autumn of 1990[a], and one of the banks was advised that a placement of part of SDR would serve to underpin the value of MGN. Steps were taken in September 1990 to commence work on a flotation of SDR and on 4 October 1990 CLD's Glasgow office sent draft terms of appointment for the production by them of a report on SDR. The first draft of this report was available by 29 October 1990.

6.73 As referred to at paragraph 2.52, the SDR plant had been modernised in 1971. Nevertheless from about 1989 Mr Horwood had had discussions with RM about replanting SDR. RM was attracted to the idea of using the SDR site at Anderston Quay for redevelopment and to moving SDR to a greenfield site, but the board of SDR was against this. Whilst discussions on this were still continuing the following had happened:

- As part of his plans in 1987 and 1988 to expand his interests in France (see paragraph 3.19) RM had ordered six new Koenig and Bauer presses. The venture for which these presses had been acquired did not prove practicable and SDR was asked early in 1989 if they would like the presses; it was agreed they would have five and finance was arranged in early 1990 for these presses with a plan to install them in 1991.

- SDR had started to acquire land around Anderston Quay; it acquired the premises at 44 Warroch Street (adjacent to Anderston Quay) and the freehold of 38 Anderston Quay in May 1990. It also started negotiating to acquire a cooperage belonging to the Distillers Company plc situated at 64 Warroch Street and acquired it in November 1990.

It became apparent, however, that a separate placement or flotation of SDR would not be practicable in view of the anticipated cost of the replanting and the development of a site, whether at Anderston Quay or elsewhere, and the separate flotation was abandoned.

---

a A separate flotation had also been considered in 1985 as mentioned in the footnote to paragraph 4.2.

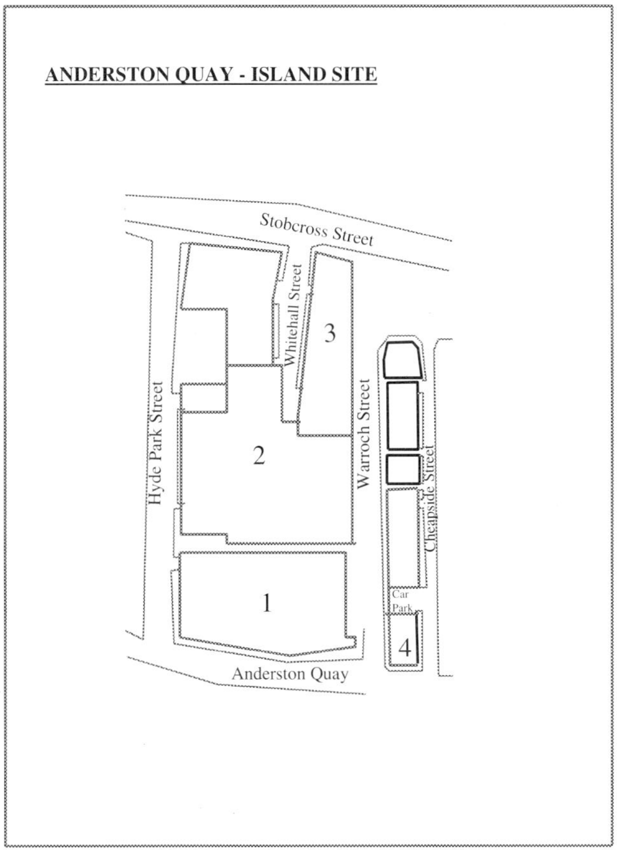

Key to Plan 3

1: 40 Anderston Quay, SDR's premises
2: 64 Warroch Street (Distillers Cooperage; land intended to be developed by SDR to house the new press hall)
3: 44 Warroch Street (Magic Bus Depot)
4: 38 Anderston Quay

Plan 3 – Anderston Quay

(5) The decision to float MGN in November 1990

6.74 In about the middle of November 1990, RM decided that he would proceed with the flotation of MGN[a]. The flotation was undoubtedly needed then because:

- the overall indebtedness of RM's companies needed to be reduced and the £360m facility repaid.
- collateral in the form of quoted MGN shares was needed by the private side which was using significant quantities of shares from the CIF, the pension schemes, FTIT and MCC as collateral[b].

KM told us that another important factor for RM in floating MGN (rather than selling a participation in it to a group of private investors)[c] was to reward staff who had been through the reorganisation of the business by allowing them to have a stake in the company as an investment – RM had always been keen on employee incentives such as ESOP schemes and the flotation was the result of the same thinking on his part.

[a] RM had publicly announced on 2 October 1990 that he expected to float MGN in the second half of 1991.

[b] KM told us that whilst it later became apparent that MGN shares would be useful collateral for private side loans (in the Spring of 1991 the tenor of bank negotiations changed so that collateral other than MCC shares became important), at the time of the decision to float that point had not been identified and was not a motivating factor.

[c] KM said they considered with Bankers Trust the issue of convertible bonds which would have enabled RM to raise capital without diluting the equity.

6.75 KM gave us two contemporaneous reasons for the timing of the flotation - the desire to repay the £360m facility[a] and that the recent resignation of the then Prime Minister which was likely to provide a window for the flotation. He told us that these were the market and macro-economic reasons that favoured a float at that time.

6.76 However, RM's other companies were dependent on the cash flow produced by MGN. RM was not in a position to relinquish access to that cash flow unless a sufficient price was obtained for MGN to compensate for the loss of that cash flow and there was a very substantial reduction in its overall debt. We were told by KM that RM could never have permitted the flotation to proceed if access to MGN's cash flow was to be ended.

---

[a] The timing was further explained to a meeting of MGN staff by Sir Michael Richardson in January 1991 on the basis of his perception of market conditions.

PART TWO
THE FLOTATION

7. THE ROLES AND DUTIES OF THE DIRECTORS AND ADVISERS ON THE FLOTATION

The duties of the directors and due diligence

7.1 Underlying the whole process of bringing a private company to the stock market for the public to invest in there are two principal obligations:

- The provision of a prospectus that must contain not only what is required by the regulations of the UK Listing Authority but also all information that investors and their professional advisers would reasonably require, and reasonably expect to find, for the purpose of making an informed assessment of the assets and liabilities, financial position, profits and losses and prospects of the company; in determining what information is to be included in the prospectus, regard must be had to the type of person likely to consider buying shares.[a] Each director is under an obligation to ensure that all matters in the prospectus of which he has direct knowledge are accurate and to use reasonable care to see that proper enquiries are made to ensure that the remainder of the prospectus is accurate and complete.
- The use of due diligence[b] to prepare the company so that it is one that is suitable for public listing. This is a duty owed by the directors and the sponsors[c].

7.2 This second obligation[d] was emphasised in the Stock Exchange Yellow Book extant in 1991 at Section 1, Chapter 1, paragraph 5:

---

[a] Financial Services Act 1986, Section 146.

[b] It was suggested to us that "due diligence" was an American concept but the evidence is that the term "due diligence" was in common use in the City to describe part of the obligation on a flotation; in any event the term "due diligence" has a long English usage being used from the nineteenth century onwards in statutes and cases.

[c] It is a point of uncertainty whether the duty that rests on the sponsors to ensure that the company is suitable for listing is a duty owed only to the UK Listing Authority or is a duty owed to investors who subscribe for the shares; it can be argued that the only duty owed to those who subscribe is one in respect of the accuracy and completeness of the prospectus and not a duty to prepare the company so that it is suitable for listing.

[d] We were told that this obligation was recognised long before it was expressly set out in the Yellow Book in 1985. In February 1975 the Stock Exchange raised with the Institute of Chartered Accountants the concern it felt about the number of cases in which it had been evident that the accounting records and financial controls of companies that had recently achieved a listing on the Stock Exchange were shown to be inadequate. In 1978 the Council for the Securities Industry initiated a proposal for a Code of Conduct in relation to flotations and other new issues, many of the suggestions coming from Sir Henry Benson; the reason for the proposed Code were concerns expressed in DTI enquiries in the 1960s and 1970s particularly Rolls Razor Limited, Blanes Limited and Ralph Instone Transport Services Limited. These concerns were summarised as follows:

> "there should be a general requirement that those sponsoring public issues should form an overall opinion whether those running a private company are fit to run a public company. A prospectus may contain no mis-statements and may yet give a wrong general impression. An entrepreneur may run a

"...the Council attach particular importance to the sponsors' role in preparing the company for listing. That role involves satisfying themselves, on the basis of all available information, that the company is suitable to be listed. Sponsors should pay particular attention to the composition of the board of the applicant and to whether the range of skills and experience necessary to the board is available. Some of these may well, with advantage, be provided through the appointment of non-executive directors.

In particular, therefore, the sponsors should satisfy themselves that the directors:-

(a) can be expected to prepare and publish all information necessary for an informed market to take place in the company's securities;

(b) appreciate the nature of the responsibilities they will be undertaking as directors of a listed company; and

(c) can be expected to honour their obligations both in relation to shareholders and to creditors."

7.3 Although traditionally emphasis has been placed on the first of these obligations as a matter of law, City practice has long recognised the second obligation.[a]

The duties of the advisers

7.4 Advisers were chosen who were of high reputation and calibre. Their decision to act was critical to the success of the flotation as each lent their name and reputation to its credibility and success. It is doubtful whether without advisers of such high reputation and calibre it would have been possible for the flotation to have gone ahead successfully.

7.5 There was virtually no published material which delineated the duties of the advisers on a flotation; consequently this was a matter on which we sought and received a large amount of evidence. In the circumstances we have included in Appendix 10 a detailed analysis of the functions and duties of the advisers on the flotation in 1991.

7.6 However to understand what happened it is necessary to set out a brief summary of the duties of each of the advisers.

---

private company very successfully as a one-man show, but be unwilling or unable to submit to the disciplines, in regard to accounts, board meetings etc required in a public company"

The principal purpose of the Code was to ensure that there was a proper determination by the sponsor of whether those who had managed a private company were likely to be able to manage a listed company; it emphasised the responsibility of the sponsor to satisfy itself of the fitness of the management. Consultation was sought upon the Code from leading houses, lawyers and accountants. The Code met with powerful and effective opposition in the City; for example, one leading house described it as "an admirable instruction manual for junior employees of merchant banks and other sponsoring bodies". As a result of this opposition, it was agreed in May 1980 that in place of a Code the Stock Exchange would insert into the Yellow book a statement of the basic principles underlying a sponsor's responsibilities.

[a] A number of witnesses emphasised to us that the public very much relied on the professional advisers preparing the company so that it is suitable to invest in, as it may not be realistic today to expect potential private investors to read the prospectus in detail.

- **Samuel Montagu**. They were appointed as "sponsors" since on a large flotation a merchant bank was generally needed. Their primary responsibility was to co-ordinate the work that needed doing during the process leading to flotation and to see that the other advisers were properly instructed to carry out their responsibilities. They also had to satisfy themselves that, on the basis of the information available to them, the company was suitable for listing.
- **Smith New Court**. They were appointed as brokers to the issue. Although they had with the merchant bank a joint responsibility to prepare the company so that it was suitable for listing, in practice where (as here) a merchant bank acted as a sponsor that duty was primarily assumed by the merchant bank. The broker's principal functions, therefore, were to act as a liaison with the Stock Exchange (as it was the practice in 1991 for the Stock Exchange to channel all documents through the broker and generally to deal with the broker rather than the merchant bank or other advisers)[a] and to price and market the issue.
- **CLD**. They were appointed as reporting accountants. Their first task was to prepare an independent report known as a "long form report" addressed to the directors of the company and to the sponsor which was intended to provide a complete and wide-ranging review of all matters material to the company and its business. The report had in particular to draw attention to any matters which were required to be dealt with prior to the flotation of the company. It was the practice for such reports to be provided in draft and for the sponsor to review such reports carefully with the reporting accountants to ensure that all matters raised were dealt with. The reporting accountants also produced a separate report known as a "short form report" which was included in the prospectus and dealt with the financial information provided by the company in accordance with the requirements of the Stock Exchange Yellow Book.
- **Clifford Chance**. They were appointed to act as solicitors to the company. Their principal function, apart from advising on legal matters arising out of the flotation, was to ensure that the Articles of the company were appropriate for a listed company, to advise and assist in the drafting of the prospectus, to carry out certain investigative work without duplicating the work of the reporting accountants and to carry out the task of verifying what was contained in the prospectus.
- **Linklaters & Paines**. They were appointed solicitors to the issue. They advised the sponsoring bank and prepared the legal documentation that had to be agreed between the sponsoring bank and the company and its directors. They also had to satisfy themselves on behalf of the sponsor that matters within the responsibility of the solicitors to the company were being properly performed. Because a leading firm had been appointed as solicitors to the company, Linklaters & Paines were specifically instructed by Samuel Montagu not to duplicate their work.

---

[a] In July 1988, the Stock Exchange modified its former rule that all dealings had to be through the broker; it decided to allow meetings with other advisers without the broker being present, but on a flotation required the broker to lodge all the documents and obtain the approval of the prospectus. At the end of 1993, the Stock Exchange introduced a system of approved sponsors which included persons other than brokers.

- **Dewe Rogerson**[a]. Dewe Rogerson had not been involved in earlier consideration of the flotation of MGN. They were selected on 18 January 1991 as marketing and communication advisers for the MGN share offer. Their responsibilities were to organise market research, advise on advertising and deal with the media.

The overseas offer - the role of SBIL

7.7 Shortly after the decision to proceed with the flotation, RM accepted advice that it would be desirable to make a simultaneous offering to professional investors in Europe, the Far East and North America. Salomon Brothers International Limited (SBIL)[b], a company within the global business of Salomon Brothers Group of Companies, were appointed at the end of February 1991 for this purpose. During the course of 1990 SBIL had had some dealings with RM in some foreign exchange transactions but they had never acted for him. In deciding to act for MGN, they were aware of the 1971/73 DTI Reports and the fact that RM was very controversial, but they considered that the Reports had been 18 years before, that RM was the chairman of a listed company, that MGN and RM had leading firms as advisers and that major banks and institutions including Lehmans, Goldman Sachs and Bankers Trust dealt with RM. SBIL were also enthusiastic to act as they anticipated that the continuation of the asset disposal programme of MCC and of the private side would result in further work.

7.8 SBIL's responsibility was solely in respect of the overseas offering. It was decided that in respect of the offering to be made in the USA this would be done by means of an offer to professional investors under Rule 144A[c] and not by means of an offer to the general public. This meant that registration of the offer document with the SEC was not required and the UK prospectus could be used (with a suitable addendum known as a "wraparound") and the offer aimed solely at professional investors in compliance with US regulations. This considerably reduced the expense of complying with regulatory requirements but meant that the shares could not be marketed in the US either on the offer or subsequently to anyone other than professional investors[d].

---

[a] They decided carefully whether they should act and did so mainly because the other advisers were well known to them and because they were only being appointed in respect of the offer for sale and not as general PR advisers.

[b] Consideration was also given to appointing SBC or Merrill Lynch Europe Limited; Merrill Lynch Europe Limited had been asked to act in the placing of MCC shares in the summer of 1990 in connection with the planned acquisition of Scottish Investment Trust plc (see paragraph 6.12) and were involved in subsequent discussions about placing MCC shares. SBC were told that they were not being appointed because a US house was needed because of the interest of the US market.

[c] This was adopted on 19 April 1990 in respect of the Securities Act of 1933.

[d] The professional investors were denominated as "qualified institutional buyers" under Rule 144A which was promulgated by the SEC in 1990. It had been used on one or two occasions prior to the MGN flotation. Prior to the promulgation of Rule 144A, it had been possible for foreign securities to be offered to "accredited investors", without registration of the prospectus for such securities with the SEC on condition that there be no public offering in the USA and that all subsequent dealings in the shares be offshore.

7.9 The fact that the offer was to be made under Rule 144A did not affect the duties of either MGN and its directors or SBIL to ensure that the prospectus was accurate and complete and their obligation to exercise due diligence[a]. For this reason and because SBIL were marketing the issue, SBIL were concerned to exercise due diligence appropriate to their role; this included considering the drafts of the long form reports, satisfying themselves as to the management of MGN and attending prospectus drafting meetings.

7.10 The marketing in Europe and in the Far East was made only to professional investors and on the basis of the prospectus used in the UK, again with a suitable "wraparound".

Taking special care because of RM

7.11 Although many of the financial institutions knew of the 1971/73 DTI Reports and the well-known conclusion set out at paragraph 1.1 above, fewer recalled by 1991 the description of RM's business methods set out in the Reports. A number of people felt that the Reports were "history"; some considered that the DTI Inspection procedures had been unfair and that the Reports' conclusions were open to question as no action had been taken as a result of them; others felt that with the passing of time, the Reports could be forgotten either because RM had learnt his lesson or because his success showed that he had changed. The fact that he took every opportunity presented to meet leading statesmen and was treated by them with apparent respect was seen by some as showing how he was accepted[b].

7.12 There were some, however, who would not have any dealings with RM either because they had some direct experience of his unscrupulous behaviour when they had had dealings with him or because they considered the 1971/73 DTI Reports had accurately concluded he was untrustworthy. We were told that it was easy by asking questions in the City to learn first hand of examples of such unscrupulous behaviour. Others perceived there was a reputational risk, either because RM had a "hidden agenda", or because of his "need to know" attitude[c], or because he would not heed advice; acting for him on that basis was unacceptable because, if there were problems, the adviser's reputation was tarnished through no fault of his own[d].

7.13 Although there were these different views (some of which were known to the relevant advisers), there were undoubtedly a number of special factors that the advisers on the flotation

---

a Technically under US law due diligence is a defence to issuing an inaccurate or incomplete prospectus, but SBIL in their contemporary documents and in their evidence to us referred to their carrying out extensive due diligence. A decision of the US Supreme Court in February 1995 made it clear that in a private placement such as one made under Rule 144A, a claimant had to prove the seller had *scienter* or acted recklessly and that the claimant relied on the misstatement or omission.

b Some of those who gave evidence to us reminded us of the favourable statements made about RM by senior politicians and other leading figures immediately after his death.

c Described at paragraph 1.3.

d Some such as Rowe & Pitman and BZW who held these views would transact share dealings for RM's companies as they did not perceive that executing share purchases and sales on the Stock Market posed any reputational risk.

of MGN felt that they had to take into account when considering arrangements that were designed to make the company one suitable for listing.

7.14 The perception of many professional investors as to the way in which RM's major listed company, MCC, had been operated was one such special factor; it was suggested to us that account had to be taken of each of these factors as follows:

- MCC's board was perceived to be weak and thus MGN required a strong board.
- MCC was perceived as having no management other than RM and KM. It was necessary to demonstrate the strength of the operational management of MGN.
- MCC was perceived to be a business without a consistent strategy and prone to a significant amount of "wheeler dealing". It was necessary, therefore, to emphasise that MGN had only one core business which was strong.
- MCC was perceived to be debt laden. It was necessary to ensure that this did not happen to MGN.
- Assets were perceived to have been moved between the private side and MCC. It was necessary to ensure that all trading and other relationships between MGN and the private side were strictly controlled.
- There was no stability in the shareholding of MCC held by the interests associated with RM. It was necessary to ensure that similar instability did not affect MGN.

The market perception of MCC was not generally favourable, though some were attracted by its high dividend yield. It was necessary to make MGN be seen as an entirely separate business.

7.15 There was also the view held by a number of professional investors that RM was not a man to be trusted, particularly where the interests of the other shareholders were involved. That is not to say that there was a perception (save perhaps on the part of a very few) that RM was dishonest or a "thief" or a man "likely to put his hand in the till", but rather that he was someone who would, by any means, seek to achieve what he wanted[a].

7.16 Despite this perception of RM and despite the Report of DTI Inspectors in 1971, Mr McIntosh of Samuel Montagu took the view that no special degree of care beyond the high degree of care normally taken by them was required on this flotation[b]. That was also the view of Clifford Chance and CLD as the reporting accountants[c]. SBIL summarised its position:

---

a The term "The Maxwell Factor" or "The Max Factor" had been coined by the financial institutions and press to describe both RM's methods of doing business and the discount attributable to the shares or value of any business which RM controlled (although the reasons behind such a discount differed according to the different perceptions of RM and the different attitudes towards him).

b Mr Clarke of Samuel Montagu told us he thought that Samuel Montagu were more alert than usual because of RM; Samuel Montagu also stated that it took actions it would not have taken in other circumstances, including the greater involvement of Mr McIntosh, the size of their team and the extent of due diligence.

c Linklaters & Paines told us that they considered that the duty was to take reasonable care in all the circumstances which in the case of MGN involved doing more in a number of areas than would normally be done on a more straightforward flotation.

"With such an entrepreneurial client, there is a need to exercise especially close care and diligence in any activities undertaken by Salomon".

The duties of the Stock Exchange

Four duties of the Stock Exchange

7.17 The Stock Exchange had at least four duties that were relevant to the flotation of MGN:

(1) **Forming an opinion as to the accuracy and completeness of the prospectus**

This is a difficult issue as the Stock Exchange altered its understanding as to the extent of its responsibility imposed under the Listing Particulars Directive[a] which required the Stock Exchange only to approve the publication of a prospectus if it was of the opinion that the prospectus satisfied all the requirements set out in the Directive[b]. It altered its understanding following the advice of leading counsel given the day after the prospectus for MGN was published and set out its new understanding in a memorandum in early 1992 to H M Treasury:

- We were told that the Stock Exchange considered at the time of the flotation of MGN that it was its function (1) to review the prospectus so that it could form an opinion that the prospectus properly covered the specific requirements set out in the Yellow Book and the Listing Particulars Directive and (2) to read the prospectus critically with a view to seeing if anything arising from the prospectus needed clarifying, developing or putting right. It considered it had no responsibility in respect of, nor did it have to form an opinion about, the overall completeness or accuracy of the prospectus; that was a matter solely for the directors and sponsor.
- On 1 May 1991, the Stock Exchange was advised by leading counsel that the opinion that the Stock Exchange was required to form under the Directive was an opinion arrived at on a reasonable basis[c].
- In early 1992 the Stock Exchange told HM Treasury that it accepted that it had a duty to form an opinion as to the accuracy and completeness of the prospectus and that that opinion had to be:
  - (a) that there was a high probability that the prospectus was accurate and complete; and
  - (b) that the opinion was formed on reasonable grounds.

The Stock Exchange told us that the change in its view made no practical difference to what it in fact did or ought to have done. The Stock Exchange said that its 1992 view of its duty conformed with the practice of most other exchanges within the European Community. On the basis of that view, the Stock Exchange considered that it was

---

[a] Directive 80/390 of 7 March 1980.

[b] Article 18.3.

[c] Leading counsel confirmed that it was not necessary for the Stock Exchange to participate personally in verification procedures; that, subject to a system of monitoring, the Stock Exchange might rely on assurances by sponsors and others as to the adequacy of verification and due diligence procedures applied in the preparation of the prospectus; he advised that the Stock Exchange should continue to check that each and every item set out in the Yellow Book as requiring to be disclosed had been included.

entitled to rely on the performance of due diligence by the sponsors and other advisers, provided it critically examined and gave detailed consideration to the prospectus.

(2) **Forming an opinion on the directors**

Although the sponsor bore the responsibility to ensure that the directors were suitable for the company[a], the Stock Exchange also had to decide, on the basis of information available to it, whether a person was suitable to discharge the functions of a director[b] in terms of integrity rather than in terms of skill. The Stock Exchange required directors to submit information which was then checked by the TSA; it considered what information it held as to any untoward history and if, because of that information, it considered a person was not suitable, it would raise that issue with the sponsor. However it rarely refused to accept a person put forward by a sponsor, as the Stock Exchange have told us that their only power was to refuse to admit the company to the list[c].

(3) **Consideration of the articles of association of the company**

The Stock Exchange had in its opinion a duty to verify that the Articles of the company complied with the requirements of the Yellow Book.

(4) **Consideration of the accountant's report**

The Stock Exchange was obliged to consider the accountants' report[d].

Suitability for listing

7.18 In April 1991 it was not the practice of the Stock Exchange to consider whether the company was suitable for listing; its view for many years had been that it was the responsibility of the sponsor to prepare the company for listing and satisfy itself that it was suitable. The Stock Exchange told us that in 1993 its view of its obligation as to suitability was essentially the same: although it had a discretion to refuse to admit the company to listing on the basis of an overall view as to the unsuitability of the company on the grounds that admission would be detrimental to investors, there was no duty on the company to satisfy the Stock Exchange that it was suitable for listing and therefore no onus on the Stock Exchange to adjudicate on such suitability. It accepted that it had to be alert to any sign of a threat to the interests of investors that might be posed by the admission of a company to listing.

7.19 Although, therefore, the Stock Exchange accepted that it had in 1991 a duty to form an opinion on the accuracy and completeness of the prospectus, it told us in 1993 that it never had, and

---

a See Yellow Book Section 1 Chapter 1 Paragraph 5.

b In a memorandum written in November 1973 commenting on the 1971/73 DTI Reports on PPL, the Stock Exchange noted that the Stock Exchange did not (as paragraph 1213 of the 1973 Report had stated) leave it to the sponsor to make an evaluation of a director.

c The Stock Exchange relied on Article 9(3) of the Admission Directive which they said gave it power only to refuse to allow an applicant to be admitted to the list (where the requirements of the Listing Rules had been met in all other respects) if "the issuer's situation is such that an admission would be detrimental to investors' interests".

d Article 19 of the Listing Particulars Directive.

did not have, a responsibility in respect of the obligation of the sponsor and the directors, as to suitability for listing.

The procedures of the Stock Exchange

7.20 Even on as significant a flotation as MGN (which involved a controversial figure like RM), the primary responsibility for the review of the prospectus fell upon two readers who were comparatively inexperienced individuals. The selection of these readers was as follows: the first reader of the MGN prospectus took the prospectus from the pile of documents which had come into the Stock Exchange as she wanted to deal with it and her manager concurred in the absence of a more senior and experienced reader being available and because of her past experience in dealing with MCC; the second reader was allocated to the task as being the only available qualified accountant within the two Listing Groups at that time. Without receiving a background briefing or reviewing any files that the Stock Exchange kept relating to RM, they read and annotated the prospectus; they were not given and did not themselves make a written analysis of the important issues that might arise. The review of the prospectus by the two readers was supplemented by a review of some of the drafts by a more senior member of the Stock Exchange[a] but he had neither the time nor the resources to be able to carry out any detailed review himself. The reading of the prospectus was also supplemented by the reference of any difficult points raised by the readers to the "Listing Advisory Group", a committee of senior officers of the Primary Markets Division of the Stock Exchange. A more detailed description of the way in which the Stock Exchange operated is set out in Appendix 11.

---

[a] He also considered the related party arrangements - see for example paragraph 12.12.

8. ORGANISATION AND TIMETABLE OF THE FLOTATION

Organisation

8.1 The first meetings to discuss the issues that arose on the intended flotation and its planning took place on 28 November and 11 December 1990. Thereafter the work necessary for the flotation process was carried forward through regular meetings of a Co-ordinating Committee chaired by RM when he was present in the UK, and in his absence at first by KM and later by IM or by Mr McIntosh of Samuel Montagu. All the principal advisers, except Linklaters & Paines, were regularly present at these meetings which provided a forum for discussion and decision-making[a]. All major decisions were taken ultimately by RM; even when decisions were apparently taken by KM, it was the perception of everyone that he already had, or would afterwards obtain, his father's agreement. KM told us that during the period of the float RM was extremely busy, spending a lot of time in New York in relation to the *New York Daily News* and, therefore, he needed somebody who would execute his instructions and represent him; that was KM's role from December 1990 until around March or April 1991 when the flotation had almost acquired a life of its own and did not need constant attention. KM, although only 31, had by 1990 some years of experience of corporate finance in substantial transactions whereas IM had none. He therefore took on the role of dealing with banks, the City, finding non-executive directors and deciding on what was to be included in MGN when floated. He also played a role in the relationships with the advisers and in discussions as to the decisions to be made when RM was not in London. His evidence to us was that he did this as RM's representative and all his actions were carried out in that capacity.

8.2 On 20 December 1990 it was agreed that an April 1991 date for the flotation would be sought from the Stock Exchange as RM wanted the flotation to proceed as rapidly as possible and this would fit in with the likely timetable for other flotations. In early January 1991, a day in the week of 15 April 1991 was agreed as the date for the publication of the prospectus ("impact day"). This was subsequently put back to 30 April 1991. The reason for this slippage was almost entirely due to the fact that RM insisted on approving personally the business plan for MGN as is described at paragraphs 8.3 and 15.43, but he was preoccupied with other activities, particularly the acquisition during February and early March 1991 of the *New York Daily News*.

Timetable

8.3 A chronological summary of the sequence of events that led up to impact day can be briefly given:

(1) **Initial work**

Although there were some meetings in December 1990, the intensive work on the project began in January 1991.

---

[a] There were other committees that dealt with legal matters and marketing.

(2) **Preliminary report**

CLD were asked by Samuel Montagu to produce at the earliest opportunity a report on:

> "The matters which in your view need to be actioned or otherwise resolved in relation to the offer for sale, including the identification of businesses not to be included in the flotation, the identification of all principal intragroup trading and other relationships, the current management structure of the Group, any tax matters and clearances required and any other key issues which the directors, together with ourselves, should be aware in completing our due diligence and otherwise preparing MGN for flotation."

CLD provided their report entitled "Desktop Review" on 17 January 1991. This was in draft, but treated as a final document.

(3) **Announcement to the management**

Although there had been press reports in early January 1991 about the probability of flotation[a],the operational management were informed of the decision to float MGN at a meeting on 24 January 1991. This enabled more intensive work involving the staff to begin.

(4) **Long form report**

Whilst issues raised by the desktop review were being considered, CLD proceeded to commence work on their long form reports relating to the businesses that were to be included in the flotation of MGN. As mentioned at paragraph 6.72, a long form report had already been prepared on SDR which was intended to be used as a model for all other reports. The first draft of the report on the main business of MGN was available on 11 February 1991.[b] First drafts were subsequently produced on the other businesses to be included in the flotation; after a detailed review by Samuel Montagu of the drafts; successive drafts were produced thereafter and final drafts were available on all aspects of the business, save pensions, by early April 1991. The first draft of the report on pensions was not available for circulation until after 2 April 1991 and the final draft not available until 26 April 1991.

(5) **The audit of MGN**

Simultaneously with the work on the long form report, a separate team from CLD was carrying out the audit of MGN for the year ended 31 December 1990.

(6) **The business plan**

Figures for a business plan were provided by Mr Guest to Mr Michael Stoney (an accountant who was the Finance Director of one of RM's main private side companies).

---

[a] Mr Burrington, the Manager Director of MGN, first learnt of the decision to float when he read of it whilst on holiday in January. Neither he nor any of the other senior management of MGN had been informed of or involved in the discussions that had taken place in December 1990.

[b] A report (known as the Farringdon Report) which had been prepared when a float of MGN was considered in 1988/1989 was used as a basic draft.

The figures were available for RM in January but were not approved by him, and therefore not formally presented, until 12 March 1991.

(7) **The short form report**
The first draft of this was prepared on 6 March 1991.

(8) **The prospectus**
The first draft of this was available on 11/12 March 1991, after drafts of the long form report became available[a].

(9) **Verification**
This was begun on 1 April 1991 and substantially completed by 16 April 1991 although important aspects were only finalised later.

(10) **Marketing**
Although there was the usual pre-marketing publicity, marketing to the institutions in the City began on 15 April 1991; on 17 April 1991 there was a formal marketing launch with the publication of a Pathfinder Prospectus.

(11) **Sale of the shares**
The prospectus was published and the offer period began on 30 April 1991. During the offer period there were "road shows" (overseas visits to promote the sale of the shares). The offer period closed on 9 May 1991 and dealing began at 2.30 pm on Friday 17 May 1991.

8.4 This was undoubtedly a very tight timetable, but we were told that, although this had necessitated long hours of work, there had been enough time to deal with matters properly.

The main issues that arose on the flotation

8.5 Much time was spent by the advisers in assessing and describing the business of MGN and SDR, but as is referred to in Chapter 14 below, it is our view that the main businesses of MGN were correctly described and it is unnecessary to deal with this aspect at length. There were a number of other issues that were material to the flotation, both in terms of their treatment in the prospectus and in terms of the exercise of due diligence to make the company suitable for public listing; it is convenient to consider these topic by topic, each of which is dealt with in following chapters:

(1) Control over the management of the company (Chapter 10)
(2) Control over the finances of the company (Chapter 11)
(3) Control over the relationship with the majority shareholder at flotation (Chapter 12)
(4) The adequacy of the arrangements for the pension schemes at flotation (Chapter 13)

---

[a] The prospectus drafting committee was established as a result of a decision of the Co-ordinating Committee on 28 February 1991.

(5) The businesses and other assets included in the flotation (Chapter 14)
(6) Other financial information relevant to the prospectus (Chapter 15)
(7) Comfort on the private side finances at flotation (Chapter 16)
(8) The marketing of the shares in April and May 1991 (Chapter 17)
(9) The success of the offer (Chapter 18)
(10) Those who benefited from the proceeds of the flotation (Chapter 19)

But before doing so, it is necessary to summarise the events happening at the same time elsewhere in RM's businesses that had a material effect on MGN and its flotation.

9. JANUARY TO APRIL 1991: EVENTS CONCERNING RM'S OTHER INTERESTS

Summary of the position of RM's interests at the end of December 1990

9.1 By the end of December 1990, the position of RM's interests can be summarised as follows:

- **MCC** Although MCC had repaid the first tranche under its main borrowing facility, it still had a substantial debt and its share price was weak. There was perceived to be a need to make further disposals and to reduce the debt. Because of prevailing trading conditions there was also concern about MCC's operating profitability, but MCC still retained the strong cash flow of the scientific journals business although attempts were being made to sell that business.

- **The private side** This held a number of different businesses, some property, a 64.2 per cent. stake in MCC and some other quoted holdings[a], but carried a debt burden which was £1,105m[b] at the end of December 1990 and about £1,075m[c] at the end of January 1991. In addition the private side had extensive undisclosed borrowings and liabilities in respect of the cash borrowed from the pension funds and in respect of FTIT and pension fund shares being used as collateral for loans from banks.

- **MGN** Its business had been modernised, it was profitable and was producing a strong cash flow that was still being used to help the private side. However it had assumed a heavy debt burden through the £360m facility in addition to the equipment leases of £150m.

9.2 The events of early 1991 can be grouped under four topics:

(1) The dealings by RM in MCC shares and the MCC share price

(2) The private side debt, its asset disposals and need for collateral

(3) The audit of the CIF

(4) Events at FTIT.

---

[a] The most significant of these were that part of the holding in Scitex the private side had retained (4.192 million shares valued at $63.42m (or £32.86m), together with Central TV and TF1.

[b] Including the overdraft of $135m (£74.4m) from MSTC referred to at paragraph 6.29 and borrowings from Lloyds of £52.8m through LBI and LBH's accounts referred to at paragraph 6.32 which had been passed to other private side companies.

[c] The private side had repaid the Lloyds overdrafts and a significant part of the MSTC overdrafts, but had obtained new loans.

(1) The dealings by RM in MCC shares and the share price

9.3 It is necessary to refer briefly to the market in MCC shares and the MCC share price primarily because:

- The performance of its share price was perceived to be important to the ability to market MGN shares.
- The level of that price and the ability of RM to sell MCC shares was also critical to the review of the finances of the private side undertaken by CLD and described in Chapter 16.
- RM expended a further £105m[a] to purchase MCC shares in the period to 30 April 1991 both openly through BIT and secretly through other entities; three of these entities were used to purchase MGN shares after the flotation. In consequence at 30 April 1991 the disclosed holding of RM, his family, their companies and the Maxwell Foundation in MCC rose to 68 per cent.; RM also had acquired through the other entities and Mr Aboff a further 8 per cent.[b] and thus controlled some 76 per cent. of MCC. The expenditure on these purchases placed a considerable strain on the finances of the private side which was attempting to reduce its debt burden by the sale of its other assets.
- The sale by MCC of the scientific journals business announced in March 1991 was significant as it was MCC's main cash generative business in the same way as MGN was the main cash generative business of the private side.

Further details about the transactions in MCC shares and the market in 1991 are set out in Appendix 7, but the main events can be briefly summarised.

9.4 As referred to at paragraphs 6.17 and following, RM's interests had acquired a substantial number of MCC shares in the autumn of 1990.

9.5 On 30 November 1990, after the delivery of the shares under the second "option" referred to in paragraph 6.17, Goldman Sachs still held on their books 28.6 million MCC shares; because of this and other significant exposures to RM and his companies amounting to $160m, Mr Sheinberg was asked by the Management Committee of Goldman Sachs to reduce the exposure. Mr Sheinberg told us that the MCC shareholding was the only item within the exposure which was readily marketable; he therefore told RM Goldman Sachs wanted to sell its MCC shareholding. On 4 January 1991 RM (through BIT) entered into a third "option" contract with Goldman Sachs in the form of a put option under which Goldman Sachs could require BIT to purchase a further 30 million MCC shares on 15 February 1991 at a price of 162.105p per share; it was exercisable in whole or in part. The "option" was notified by MCC to the Stock Exchange immediately though the price announced was 152p[c]. The premium paid

---

[a] This sum excludes the purchases from the pension funds on 26 April 1991 referred to at paragraph 9.8. The settlement of some of the purchases in the period to 30 April 1991 took place in May 1991.

[b] In addition BIM held on 30 April 1991 2.3 per cent.; the reduction from 6 per cent. referred to in paragraphs 6.18 to 6.23 was in consequence of the transactions on 26 April 1991 referred to in paragraph 9.8.

[c] The price notified to the TSA by Goldman Sachs was a strike price of 152p and an exercise price of 162.105p. These terms are synonymous to any person active in the market. The Stock Exchange was initially only notified of the strike price of 152p and that is what was announced but were subsequently supplied with a

by Goldman Sachs to BIT was 4p per share at a time when the market price was around 150p[a]. The announcement made by MCC was misleading as it concealed from the market:

- the true price paid for the shares.
- the fact that RM was paying a somewhat higher price than the conventional pricing of an option would justify and a price that was higher than he might have found it convenient to explain.
- the true nature of the agreement reached was not an option, but a method of enabling RM to defer payment until February1991.

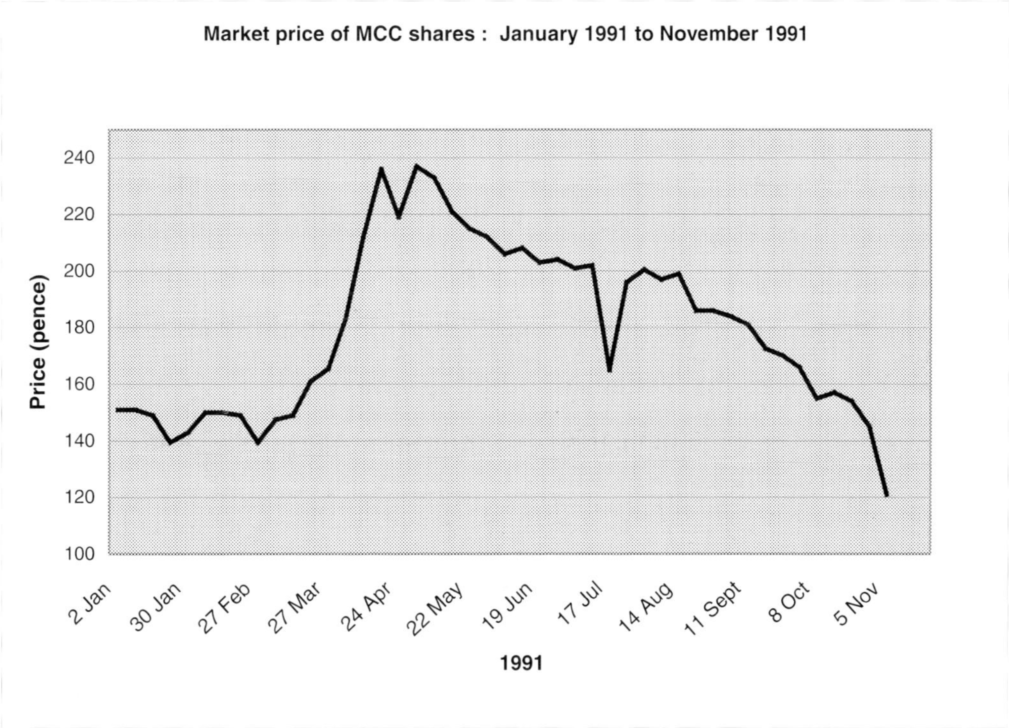

Graph 3

9.6 The "option" was exercised by Goldman Sachs and 30 million shares acquired by BIT at a cost of £48.6m on 19 February 1991. Goldman Sachs borrowed some shares to settle this transaction. It was announced that the effect of the exercise of the option took the shareholding of the Maxwell Foundation to 38.14 per cent. of MCC. This took the combined holding of RM, his family, their companies and the Maxwell Foundation to 68 per cent. During

---

copy of the contract that gave the exercise price of 162.105p. As explained in Appendix 7, the records of the Stock Exchange do not record, and no one involved can recall, what consideration was given to the price differential.

a The premium paid cannot be explained on the basis of ordinary option pricing which would have required a premium in the order of 12p. The price of 162.105p at which RM was to buy the shares was calculated in a similar way to the price calculated for the second option - the market price plus the cost of carrying the shares until 15 February 1991, repayment of the premium and profit (on this occasion the profit was much smaller). As it was clear that the option would be exercised, this was again in effect a deferred sale; indeed, a term of the agreement indicated such, as there was to be an adjustment in the price if the shares were paid for earlier by BIT. In effect the price would be reduced to reflect the lower carrying cost on a pro rata basis (see Appendix 7 – paragraph 11.7).

December 1990 and from January to March 1991 the share price of MCC had remained relatively depressed as the graph above and that in paragraph 6.11 show.

9.7 In the period between January and 30 April 1991 Goldman Sachs was involved in two types of sales of MCC shares

- sales where it acted on an agency basis; and
- sales, from its books, of shares purchased in the market by Mr Sheinberg who continued to buy shares, particularly in late March and in April 1991.

The sales of shares by Goldman Sachs to the entities set out in the following paragraphs were sales to entities who in fact acted for RM. We were told by KM that the deals and prices were all negotiated and agreed between Mr Sheinberg and RM as part of a strategy described in paragraph 9.14; that RM believed that the use of the entities was sufficient to make it legal.

9.8 The main transactions were the following:

- On 11 January 1991 Goldman Sachs carried out on an agency basis the sale of 2.285 million MCC shares from IBF (whose subsidiary Jupiter Participations had bought the shares in September and October 1990 through a French broker as referred to at paragraph 6.18) and the purchase of those shares by Dr Rechsteiner for £3.4m. This was the first of several occasions on which Mr Sheinberg dealt with Dr Rechsteiner. Dr Rechsteiner was acting for Corry Foundation at the request of RM.
    - Mr Sheinberg told us that when Dr Rechsteiner was suggested as a purchaser he did not think that RM would introduce him to someone who was not legitimate or good for the money. However to exercise due diligence he enquired of RM whether anything was reportable and was told there was nothing[a]. Dr Rechsteiner was expecting the call. Mr Sheinberg told him how many shares he had for sale and what the price was. Dr Rechsteiner agreed to this purchase. Mr Sheinberg did not make any agreement with RM.
    - KM told us that this transaction and the subsequent transactions involving Dr Rechsteiner were dealt with in the same way as the sales to TIB and IBI. RM and Mr Sheinberg would do the deal and then arrangements would be made for it to be effected through Dr Rechsteiner.
- On 8 February 1991 Goldman Sachs sold 2 million MCC shares from its books to Jupiter Participations for £3m.
- On 9 April 1991 Goldman Sachs purchased 2 million MCC shares from Jupiter Participations for £3.72m and sold that stake to Lakeport Nominees Ltd for £3.8m. Lakeport Nominees Ltd were a nominee company of Coutts & Co (Lausanne) SA who

---

[a] The confirmation of the transaction with Dr Rechsteiner who was buying the shares said he had to provide only £128,723. The confirmation sent to the seller (IBI/Jupiter Participations) said they were to "deliver to Barclays Bank ... for the a/c of Goldman Sachs - N.Y. .. for the a/c of Werner A. Rechsteiner the sum of £3,293,750 pounds sterling for value January 14, 1991". It would have been difficult to explain why IBI/Jupiter Participations, as the seller, was passing £3.293m to Goldman Sachs for the account of Dr Rechsteiner unless IBI/Jupiter Participations were making a loan to Dr Rechsteiner. The sum of £3.293m was in fact paid by PHL to IBI who then paid Goldman Sachs.

9.8 continued

were acting for Blackmore Trust on the instructions of Mr Emson[a]. Mr Emson told us he had been asked by RM to buy the shares for the benefit of a trust and, as the transaction was said to be urgent, he agreed to use Blackmore Trust pending the transfer to another trust. The shares were paid for by PHL who transferred the funds to Robert Fraser Group which then remitted them to Lakeport Nominees Ltd. The evidence of Mr Mitchell of Coutts & Co was that Mr Emson asked him to buy the shares and that the price would be 190p. Thereafter Mr Sheinberg rang him and told him that he understood he was interested in purchasing MCC shares at 190p and the trade was agreed[b].

- After selling 5 million MCC shares from its books to TIB on 26 February 1991[c] and then repurchasing that stake onto its books on 3 April 1991[d], Goldman Sachs sold 5 million shares from its books to TIB on 17 April 1991 for $21.1m. TIB is the company referred to at paragraph 4.49 and the shares were purchased on the instruction of RM or KM and paid for by funds remitted to Dr Rechsteiner largely from RMG[e].
- On 24 April 1991 Goldman Sachs sold from its books 14 million MCC shares to TIB at a price of £30.95m and 3 million MCC shares to Servex AG (Servex) for £6.63m.
    - Mr Sheinberg's evidence was that he had accumulated a position of 20 million MCC shares by mid-April 1991 and told RM he wanted to sell; RM at first declined to buy. KM told us that RM's companies were in a period of extreme illiquidity as they were awaiting the proceeds of the sale of the scientific journals business of MCC (referred to in paragraph 9.10); however, Mr Sheinberg would have made it clear that he had to reduce his position and that, if RM could not find a friend to buy at a price that would not rock the market, then he would have to find a buyer at a price that did and put the share price under pressure.
    - Mr Sheinberg told us that he never made any such statement, but that later, on 24 April 1991, RM and KM telephoned him and asked if he was interested in selling and that he had said that he would sell. KM's evidence was that RM would not have telephoned, but Mr Sheinberg would have kept up the pressure to buy; in conversations such as this, Mr Sheinberg would have asked RM whether he was

---

a Mr Emson was the Chief Executive of Robert Fraser.

b Mr Mitchell's evidence was that Mr Sheinberg had telephoned again on 16 April 1991 and asked if he was interested in buying a further 5 million shares. He refused, but soon after Mr Emson rang to ask him to make the purchase; Mr Mitchell again refused. Mr Mitchell's evidence was that he considered Mr Sheinberg was premature in his telephone call and was supposed to have called after Mr Emson had arranged the transaction. Mr Sheinberg said that he had spoken to Mr Mitchell only once and that was on the occasion of the purchase by Lakeport Nominees Limited of 2 million MCC shares. He denied making any second or other call to Mr Mitchell.

c This sale was re-booked as a sale on 15 March 1991 at a slightly increased price but with an extended settlement date.

d This purchase was part of a series of sales by BIT of other shares including parcels of Scitex and Quebecor (beneficially owned by the CIF); Mr Sheinberg told us he believed BIT was the seller of the MCC shares but the documentation reflects a sale by TIB.

e Funds were also derived from a sum of £2m that PHL had transferred to Dr Rechsteiner on 12 October 1990.

9.8 continued

taking up the shares or whether they were being taken up by the "man in the mountains", a reference to Dr Rechsteiner[a].

- Subsequent to the telephone conversations between RM, KM and Mr Sheinberg, Mr Freedman[b] acting on the instructions of RM called Mr Sheinberg who made the sale to TIB of 14 million shares. This sale took TIB's holding to 19 million shares, just below the 3 per cent. at which disclosure would have been required; Mr Sheinberg told us that he might, as a matter of good customer relations, have mentioned to Mr Freedman that if TIB's holding went over 19 million TIB might have to report it.
- Mr Sheinberg told us he then had a further conversation with RM and KM and at their suggestion spoke to Dr Rechsteiner and sold 3 million MCC shares to him on behalf of Servex[c].
- As explained at paragraph 20.20, £11m of MGN monies were used after the flotation in part payment for these shares[d].

- On 26 April 1991 Goldman Sachs carried out on an agency basis the sale by MGPS and MCWPS of 12.5 million MCC shares each and the purchase of 16 million shares by Servex (for £35.4m). The purchase by Servex took its holding to 19 million MCC shares, again, as in the case of the purchases by TIB a few days earlier, to just below the 3 per cent. at which the holding would have been reportable. The balance of 9 million shares was purchased by Yakosa Finanzierungs AG (Yakosa)[e] (for £19.92m). The reasons for this transaction and the disposition of the proceeds are dealt with in paragraph 13.15; it was carried out to reduce the holding of the pension funds to avoid disclosure during the flotation of MGN. Because the transaction was effected as an agency transaction through Goldman Sachs, New York, the transaction was not reported on the screens of the Stock Exchange (just as had been done in the sale by the CIF of MCC shares in March 1990 as set out in paragraph 5.20) or otherwise disclosable[f]. Mr Sheinberg told us he chose to do it as an agency transaction in New York to avoid undue publicity for Goldman Sachs consistent with his trading philosophy; on an agency transaction there was no market disclosure as there was no market trade. Dr Rechsteiner was acting on the

---

a Mr Sheinberg denied he ever used this phrase and told us it was ridiculous to think that he would have referred to a peson he knew only as a lawyer in Zurich who acted for UBS or the Swiss Central Bank as "the man in the mountains".

b As explained at paragraph 4.49 he was a lawyer who had acted for RM for many years.

c Dr Rechsteiner was acting for Akim Foundation on the instructios of RM. Akim Foundation was one of the Foundations acquired or founded for RM as set out at paragraph 1.10; the circumstances in which TIB was said to be the nominee of Akim in connection with the purchases by TIB in 1989 are set out at paragraph 4.49.

d The balance of £26.59m was provided from RMG.

e Yakosa was owned by PHA, which is another Liechtenstein entity referred to at paragraph 3.23.

f Mr Sheinberg checked with his compliance department about the reportability by Goldman Sachs of such a trade; he was told that as the trade involved more than 3 per cent. of MCC it would be reportable if done with Goldman Sachs as a principal, but not as an agent. That was because as an agent Goldman Sachs would not become the owner of the shares.

instructions of RM; the shares bought by Servex were acquired for Akim Foundation and those by Yakosa for Nessi Foundation, one of the foundations acquired or founded for RM as set out at paragraph 1.10.

9.9 There were other relevant transactions in MCC shares in the period January to 30 April 1991:

- During January 1991 Mr Aboff[a] purchased for RM 550,000 MCC shares at a cost of £796,704 but sold 540,000 for £770,259. He purchased a further 100,000 MCC shares on 1 March 1991 for £142,067. Further disposals totalling 100,000 MCC shares were made at the end of April 1991.
- Between 17 and 26 April 1991 Mr Emson sold in the market on behalf of a client 500,000 MCC shares, part of that client's holding. RM was not pleased and told Mr Emson that in future he (RM) would find a purchaser for any MCC shares that his client might want to sell. This happened in July 1991 as set out at paragraph 21.4.

9.10 There were two announcements on 28 March 1991 of events[b] that significantly affected MCC:

- RM would be resigning as Chairman and Chief Executive of MCC as from 1 July 1991 and Mr Peter Walker would take over as Non-Executive Chairman[c], with KM as Chief Executive. KM told us that the origin of the idea of RM resigning as Chairman of MCC was to be found in Sir Michael Richardson's advice that, for marketing reasons concerning the MGN flotation, RM ought not to be Chairman of both MGN and MCC[d].
- MCC had agreed to sell its scientific journals business to Elsevier . Discussions with Elsevier had been taking place during the second half of 1990 and a price of £440m (subject to adjustments) was agreed. The sale was explained in a circular to MCC shareholders as having been made because an attractive price had been offered and because there was difficulty in the then economic climate of achieving satisfactory prices on the disposal of non-core businesses[e]. The banks were told, and this was the understanding of the directors of MCC, that the proceeds would be used to repay early the next tranche of the $3 billion facility that MCC had taken out in order to acquire Macmillan and OAG and would be used to reduce MCC's overdrafts[f].

9.11 Those who considered the sale had different views as to its significance and what it meant to the future of MCC; some thought that it showed a determination on RM's part to solve the debt

---

a He had purchased a substantial number of shares in the autumn of 1990 as explained at paragraph 6.19.

b On 19 February 1991 it was announced that Mr Baker had taken early retirement. This was not noted to be an event of significance at the time. His retirement came about because in November 1990 he had had a serious disagreement with RM over RM's unsuccessful attempt to "improve" MCC's interim statement after it had been approved by the board; as a result RM required him to retire or resign.

c Mr Peter Walker had insisted on freedom to choose the board but had agreed that RM and KM could sit on the board to represent the family's interest.

d See paragraph 11.26.

e RM told Sir Michael Richardson that the disposal was part of a plan to concentrate on MCC's operations in the US.

f A significant part of proceeds of sale were used by the private side in the summer of 1991 as set out at paragraph 21.4.

problems of MCC; others considered that if he had to sell the business upon which his success had been built, MCC was in a difficult financial position. The development of the scientific journals business had been achieved by RM organically (rather than through acquisition) by the creation and development over time of new scientific titles; it had been very profitable. The cash flow from those titles had been used by RM to fund his various acquisitions but that cash flow had been lost to the private side when Mr Baker had convinced RM to transfer this business to MCC[a]. Although the sale to Elsevier provided a large cash sum to MCC, it deprived MCC of significant cash flow[b]. KM worked extensively on the negotiations for the sale of this business; but it was RM who agreed the price with the Chairman of Elsevier[c].

9.12 From about 1 March 1991, when the MCC share price stood at 140p, the price rose to 174p at the end of March 1991, to 185p on 9 April 1991 and to a closing peak of 239p on 15 April 1991. Although this rise in the share price is of specific relevance to the review of the private side finances in connection with the flotation described in Chapter 16, it was generally seen by the market as being "helpful" to the prospects of a successful flotation of MGN. Many in the market considered that the price was rising because Goldman Sachs were buyers and wondered why.

9.13 When RM was asked why the MCC share price was rising he said that he was much admired in the United States where bankers and institutions were buying shares. This was accepted as a plausible explanation, given that Goldman Sachs were seen in the market to be the principal buyers.

9.14 KM told us that:

- RM was obsessed with the share price.

- During 1990 and 1991 RM and Mr Sheinberg would speak daily, whether RM was in London, New York or on his yacht[d]. Mr Sheinberg told RM that he would mop up shares in the market, enforce physical delivery by short sellers and so cause the price to rise. This would get rid of the bears and, in Mr Sheinberg's phrase "reduce the liquidity of the stock in the market", thus improving the share price. They agreed on this strategy and, if RM

---

a As set out at paragraph 3.6.

b The sale of the scientific journals business and the flotation of MGN (which were the core cash generative businesses of RM's entire interests) were very significant events as they had been significant cash sources for MCC and the private side respectively.

c IM told us that RM put KM in charge of the sale because he (RM) could not bring himself to be involved in the disposal of "his real baby". However, the price being offered from a major competitor was astonishingly high and, despite his reservations, RM would not allow there to be any sacred cows.

d KM told us that RM did not have time for many friends as his lifestyle and his addiction to his business did not give him time; however, within the context of RM's relations with bankers, he was very close to Mr Sheinberg and they had drinks together – RM did not have drinks with everybody. Mr Sheinberg told us that his only relationship with RM was their trading relationship; he had drinks with RM on perhaps three occasions between 1986 and 1991.

heard there was a bear raid on MCC shares, he would at once telephone Mr Sheinberg. KM recalled conversations between RM and Mr Sheinberg when the talk was of driving the share price up to £4, £5, even £10.

- RM believed Mr Sheinberg when he said he would do this as he believed Mr Sheinberg was assisting him as his client. When KM questioned this, RM told him he knew nothing and that "the great Mr Sheinberg knew everything" as was his belief from the many deals done since 1986. RM did not regard this to be a wrongful manipulation of the market but, rather, using a market maker to counteract those who were manipulating the price of MCC share downwards.

9.15 KM also told us that RM had understood that if he was paying cash for shares, then all those shares were to be bought in the market and there was a commitment to that effect. Mr Sheinberg never told him he was borrowing stock to settle transactions[a]. If RM had known that Mr Sheinberg had met his delivery obligations under sales agreed with RM (even if carried out by entities connected with RM) by borrowing shares[b] and not by buying them in the market, contrary to the strategy that he had agreed with RM, he (RM) would, KM told us, have "shot him" and ended the relationship.

9.16 Mr Sheinberg said that this was wholly untrue.

- He explained to us that he believed that there were short positions on MCC shares in the market (which he had also believed was the case in October 1990)[c] and he could make a substantial profit by acquiring MCC shares and "squeezing" those who held a short position. He thus was an active purchaser of shares and the price rose in consequence.
- There never was any agreement with RM to cause the price to rise.
- He always followed his own trading strategy and never described it to RM.
- It would have been irrational for him to commit himself to a fixed trading strategy.
- He may have spoken to RM about the share price going to £4, £5 or even £10, but that was in the context of what might possibly happen if there was a large short position.
- He did not speak daily to RM.

9.17 We have carefully examined the evidence in relation to short positions and have set it out in Appendix 7. Although there were in October 1990 rumours of a "bear" raid on MCC for which there was some substance, the short positions in the market were not material. We are satisfied from our enquiries that in the period between January and April 1991 there was no evidence of a bear raid or any material short positions. Therefore, in the period during which the MCC price rose prior to the flotation of MGN, there was no basis in fact for

---

a See for example, the settlement of the third option referred to in paragraph 9.6.

b Goldman Sachs accepted that some of the shares were borrowed. Furthermore, some of the shares which they delivered in settlement of the Baccano purchase of MCC shares (see paragraph 21.4) were shares pledged to them by BIT as collateral for a margin loan (see the footnote to paragraph 21.11).

c A prosecution was brought against Mr Peter Marks of Branston & Gothard for making a false statement about MCC to Goldman Sachs on 12 October 1990 but this was unsuccessful (see Appendix 7 paragraph 9.8).

Mr Sheinberg's evidence that he could make substantial profits from those who held a short position.

9.18 We set out at paragraph 22.82 (after we have considered the further transactions in MCC and MGN shares), our views as to what in fact was happening and the way in which the market was being misled and manipulated.

9.19 As set out in Appendix 7, the Stock Exchange did try and investigate the second and third options between December 1990 and July 1991[a], but it did not discover the wider picture of the market in MCC shares.

(2) The private side debt, its asset disposals and its need for collateral

9.20 By the end of 1990 the banks were becoming concerned about their exposure to RM's companies and in particular the private side. In December 1990 KM[b] raised with both National Westminster and Midland Bank a proposal for a "jumbo" facility for the private side companies. The objective of this proposal was to persuade the banks who were lending to the private side on a bilateral basis to join into one overall facility with pooled security; the only assets to be left out of this arrangement were the newspapers and the Holborn site. That facility was then to be repaid by an orderly asset disposal programme, the advantages to the private side companies being that all the banks would have to act together (thereby removing the risk that one bank which had strong security would interfere with the orderly disposal programme by seeking to enforce its security) and that there would be time to sell the assets and not face the risk of "fire sale" prices. KM told us that the idea for a jumbo facility came from Mr Anselmini who had pointed out that various of the private side facilities had surplus collateral and that it would be sensible to spread the collateral evenly among all lenders. The asset disposal programme included a proposed disposal of MCC shares targeted to raise, during the course of 1991, £200m[c].

9.21 The proposals for a jumbo facility were further developed in January 1991, but there was a reluctance on the part of those banks which had strong security to participate and little progress was made; the proposal had been abandoned by March 1991.

9.22 During the period in which work was progressing on the flotation, the general perception amongst the bankers to RM's companies remained that it was essential for the asset disposal programme of the private companies to continue and the debt to be reduced, but that banks would continue to renew their facilities whilst this happened. This, generally, proved to be the case and it was the exception for banks to refuse to renew or rollover facilities. There was,

---

a A further enquiry was undertaken in 1992 as set out in Appendix 7, paragraph 19.4.

b KM chaired two committees - one for the RMG group and one for MCC that managed the disposal programme and the borrowings.

c IM told us that KM came increasingly, more particularly from 1991 onwards, to play a role in the disposals programme and also in relation to debt management.

however, one significant facility that required renewal in June 1991 which was not straightforward. This was the facility referred to at paragraph 2.34 which was secured on the Holborn site and for which the agent was Lloyds. The renewal is considered at paragraph 21.30.

9.23 Although an asset disposal programme was in progress, RM nonetheless continued to acquire other interests. In March 1991 RM acquired, through RMG's subsidiary Maxwell Newspapers Inc, control of the *New York Daily News*[a]. Although a substantial payment was made to the private side on this acquisition, it was appreciated that the business could not be "turned round" without the injection of further funds. KM told us that RM seriously considered whether the *New York Daily News* should be included in the flotation as he was very confident that it would be turned around during 1991 and it would provide MGN with an international dimension.

9.24 The private side had continued with its asset disposal programme, disposing during January and February 1991 of its 10 per cent. stake in TF1[b] for £62m and its stake in Central TV for £24.6m. The bank borrowings of the private side had decreased from about £1,105m[c] at the end of December 1990 to about £1,075m at the end of January 1991 and then decreased to about £1,050m at the end of February.

9.25 On 25 March 1991, the private side raised further funds by selling the 20.7 per cent. stake in Invesco MIM which it had agreed to transfer to the CIF by documents dated 29 June 1990 (see paragraph 6.5) but which had continued to be used as collateral by the private side[d]. The shares were sold by Goldman Sachs under a profit sharing agreement and realised a total of £35m; £33.87m was paid to the CIF and on the same day as this was received, £35m was paid by the CIF to RMG and debited to the intercompany account. The shares had declined in value by £27m over the period they had been transferred into the CIF. The disposal of this holding was notified to Invesco MIM as a disposal by BIT of the shareholding of PHL[e].

---

a IM told us that, although questioned in some quarters at the time, this was an astute investment that served to give RM a tremendously positive profile in the USA which helped in the marketing of the MGN float.

b The stake was sold partly as the result of a breakdown of relations within TF1 between RM and Mr Bouyges and partly to realise the investment. IM told us that RM was more comfortable with newspapers than television. The sale was effected through Goldman Sachs.

c Including the overdraft from MSTC and other borrowings from Lloyds on LBI's proprietary trading account.

d KM had a meeting in March or April 1991 with Mr Johnson and Mr Engineer of Invesco MIM in connection with this sale; they did not know and were not told that the shares had been sold to the CIF in June 1990. They were told by KM that the holding was being sold as it was peripheral to their strategy as a media group and they were disposing of all such holdings. KM introduced them to Mr Sheinberg as the person who was handling the sale.

e This was reported in the press as a sale by RM's private companies.

9.26 Although by the end of March 1991, the bank debt of the private side had been reduced to about £990m[a], it rose during April and by 30 April 1991 it was about £1,030m. The shares[b] owned by the private side that could be used as collateral were:

- the 68 per cent.[c] stake in MCC (worth at 185p per share £814m and at 239p per share, £1,052m)
- the Scitex holding (valued at £43m)
- the holdings in Ansbacher (£5.7m)
  Central & Sheerwood (£3.6m)
  Guinness Mahon (£2.5m)
  Singer & Friedlander (£7.4m)
  and other small holdings (£15.6m).

As some banks would not take MCC shares, the fact that the private side had only comparatively small holdings of other assets in comparison to its debts, necessitated continued use of shares from the CIF and pension funds; by 30 April 1991 shares to the value of approximately £270m were being so used. In addition cash continued to be borrowed from the CIF and the amount remained in the order of £100m[d].

(3) The audit of the CIF

9.27 The position of the private side was exacerbated by the discovery by the independent directors of FTIT of the use being made by LBI of the shares in the FTIT portfolio. Before outlining what happened and its specific relationship to the flotation of MGN, it is necessary to refer to the audit of the CIF for the year ended 5 April 1990.

(a) Related party connections in the investments

9.28 In the course of the audit, the following investments of the CIF were identified as Maxwell-related in the document containing a summary of the main points arising on the audit for the attention of the partner (MAPs). It was noted that the investments amounted in value to £100m.

- MCC
- IBI KM a director (see the footnote to paragraph 5.21)

---

a Over this period bank loans were rearranged and some bank borrowings repaid; the net reduction appears to have been covered by obtaining the release of £10m cash collateral and replacing it with shares and through borrowings from the CIF and MCC.

b Three loans included in the private side debt were secured on property.

c This excludes the purchases made by the offshore entities.

d The payment of £35m made by the CIF to the private side on the day of the receipt of the proceeds of the sale of Invesco MIM shares is included in the figure of £100m. The amount of £100m is however exclusive of the debt of £108m which was meant to have been discharged by the agreement to transfer the shares in Invesco MIM and Scitex by documents dated 29 June 1990 but which were never delivered to the CIF or re-registered, though the value of the Scitex shares (£75m) is included within the figure of £270m in respect of the value of the shares being used as collateral.

- Euris SA RM a director (see paragraph 3.19 and paragraph 5.28)
- OAG subsidiary of MCC

Mr Cowling (the partner in charge of the audits of all the Maxwell pension funds, the CIF, LBI and FTIT) annotated the MAPs with the comment:

> " Forward to scheme accounts. Disclosure" "20 per cent. of funds"
>
> "NB above does not include normal working capital balances with employer companies".

Mr Cowling has told us that this reference to disclosure was a reference to disclosure in the scheme accounts as opposed to the CIF accounts.

9.29 Mr Cowling told us that disclosure was discussed with Mr Cook and that he was told that unless there was legislation which required disclosure, there was to be no disclosure[a]. Mr Cook did not recall such a conversation but told us that it might well have taken place as Mr Cowling's recollection accurately reflected the general policy on disclosure imposed by RM. Mr Cowling annotated the MAPs:

> "No requirement to do so in these accounts, but will be done in participating schemes. I have told them of our views but cannot force disclosure".

This was in fact done and the investments were listed in the investment report included within the report and accounts of the participating schemes, but without reference to the related party connections, as it was CLD's view that the SORP and Disclosure Regulations did not require such disclosure.

(b) Loans of cash

9.30 The loans of cash[b] by the CIF to the private side companies (referred to at paragraph 5.26) were considered during the audit and noted in the MAPs.

9.31 We were told that CLD examined the loans made by the CIF to the private side and that they ensured that all movements in the bank statements were picked up and that interest had been paid; they verified that all loans had been repaid by 5 April 1990. The MAPs noted that £937,000 interest had been earned.

9.32 Papers provided to CLD showed that a further £20m had been paid to the private side on 20 May 1990 (as in fact had happened - see paragraph 6.5), but we were told by CLD that at the time they did not appreciate that there had been a further loan so soon after the year end. They also read the board minutes that recorded the purchases of the Scitex and Invesco MIM shares,

---

[a] Mr Cowling told us that if there was something which he really felt ought to be disclosed, he would have pressed until he achieved it.

[b] These were referred to as "deposits" in the MAPs.

but we were told that this was considered as a transaction that would be accounted for in the next accounting period[a].

9.33 The MAPs also noted an adjustment that had been made to the accounts because LBH had borrowed cash from the CIF portfolio in 1989 to pay for a large stock purchase, the funds had been placed on deposit overnight, and the interest received on this deposit had not been credited or paid over to the CIF portfolio. Mr Cowling annotated the MAPs:

> "LBH is another client of the fund manager in this sense. The transactions were designed to be arms length at commercial rates - hence the above adjustments."

(c) Related party dealings

9.34 The purchases of shares by the CIF during the year ended 5 April 1990 from related parties were noted in the review of investments on the MAPs:

- The October 1989 parcel (see paragraph 5.28)
- The March 1990 parcel (see paragraph 5.28)

The MAPs also referred to[b]:

- The arrangement with IBI entered into on 21 December 1989 (see paragraph 5.21)
- The sale of the shares in Marceau Investissements to PHL in September 1990 (see paragraph 6.26)

9.35 Mr Cowling told us that the fact there were related party dealings between the CIF and RM's companies was not something that had to be reported on; that he was concerned as an auditor to see that the transactions were at an appropriate price and were of a normal nature[c]; that the disclosure requirements had been specifically drawn up and did not require disclosure of the sources from which investments had been acquired.

9.36 CLD considered whether the transaction with IBI was an attempt to reduce the holdings for the purposes of disclosure of BIM's holdings in MCC in MCC's accounts for the year ended 31 March 1990. The CIF audit team was told by the MCC audit team that the reduction did not have a material effect on the disclosure in MCC's accounts. CLD also noted in the MAPs the disposal of 7.9 million MCC shares on 26 March 1990 (referred to at paragraph 5.21).

9.37 In their management letter on matters arising from the audit which was drafted (and provided to BIM in draft) in February 1991, CLD commented that shares purchased from MCC and

---

[a] The minutes only referred to the quantities of shares and not their value; they did not identify the party from whom the shares had been acquired.

[b] The sale of the shares in Marceau Investissements was in the valuation section of the MAPs. CLD also noted in the MAPs the sterling and dollar loans to Robert Fraser (see paragraph 5.29) and noted in other audit papers that the sterling loan note had been sold to PHL on 29 June 1990 and the proceeds had been debited to the intercompany account with PHL.

[c] See also paragraph 5.8.

PMT had not been registered in the name of BIM; they recommended that this be done as soon as possible[a]. We were told they were given no explanation as to why this had not been done.

(d) Use of shares by the private side as collateral

9.38 In view of the important consequences to MGN and its pension schemes resulting from the use of the shares as collateral, a detailed account of this aspect of the audit is set out in Appendix 12, but a summary is necessary here. CLD's knowledge of the use being made of the shares of the CIF and of FTIT that they had acquired during the audit of LBI, LBH and FTIT for the year ended 30 December 1989 has been summarised at paragraph 5.41. During the course of the audit of the CIF to 5 April 1990 (which took place between September 1990 and February 1991) it came to the attention of CLD that BIM had earned income categorised as "stocklending fees". This was examined and, in response to an inquiry from CLD, a letter dated 9 January 1991 was sent to CLD by Lehmans (who had provided the financing described at paragraph 5.39 on the basis of collateral provided through LBI). The letter attached what was in fact a list of shares from the CIF portfolio valued at $76.9m[b] entitled:

> "Outstanding loan detail report - collateral"

and a portfolio of US Treasury Bills to the value of $51.9m entitled:

> "Outstanding loan detail report - bonds".

Lehmans said in the letter

> "At the request of [BIM] we write to confirm as per the attached statements those outstanding positions as at 5 April 1990.
>
> We have held these securities as collateral or loaned them in connection with the stocklending arrangement made between [BIM] and [Lehmans] using [LBI] as its agent.
>
> As at 5 April 1990, we held no other certificates, cash or any other assets for [BIM]".

This letter was sent by Mr Haas of Lehmans who amended a draft response prepared by BIM[c].

9.39 An explanation of this letter was sought by CLD from BIM and LBI; CLD were told that there was an arrangement under which the Treasury Bills were lent by Lehmans to RMG and were used by RMG to raise finance whilst the shares provided by BIM were held by Lehmans as collateral for the Treasury Bills; BIM received a fee for providing its shares as collateral. The

---

a The letter was sent on 20 June 1991.

b These were relatively small parcels of readily marketable "blue chip" US securities, such as shares in AT & T and Boeing, (comprising half the value of the portfolio) and a block of MCC shares (comprising the other half).

c A detailed account is given at paragraphs 5.8 to 5.10 of Appendix 12.

rationale for the transaction was recorded in the MAPs[a] in the following terms:

> "The reason for this route is that [RMG] only has three large investments and Lehman have a maximum of any one stock that can be given as collateral. Therefore BIM's portfolio was used."

CLD had identified what in fact were the essential features of the arrangement involving Lehmans through which the shares of the pension schemes had been used as collateral for financing for the benefit of the private side.

9.40 CLD made inquiries of LBI as to what counter security RMG had provided and were given by LBI a list of that counter security as set out at paragraph 5.45.

9.41 Mr Cowling[b] was concerned about this transaction. He first consulted more senior partners at CLD, Mr Walsh and Mr Lamb. Mr Lamb told the counsel to the Accountants' Joint Disciplinary Scheme that he had only the vaguest recollection of the meeting[c], but thought his advice would have been that Mr Cowling should find out the facts and ensure that there was disclosure in the accounts. Mr Cowling then telephoned Mr Cook on 4 February 1991 and his note of the conversation records the following:

> "I said that I was concerned over the quality of the collateral and whether the arrangement represented in effect, a loan of pension fund assets to [RMG] as the treasury bills which were subsequently obtained from [Lehmans] by [RMG] were discounted for cash."

9.42 Mr Cowling told us that he then attended a meeting with Mr Cook during the course of which Mr Trachtenberg, who was responsible for organising the programme at LBI, was asked over the telephone to give an explanation. He did so and subsequently confirmed this in writing by a letter dated 15 February 1991. This letter said that the explanation previously given of the Lehmans transaction had been an error, that Lehmans held the CIF's shares and the Treasury Bills for BIM and that the list of the counter security provided to CLD was being used for entirely different purposes. The letter did not make commercial sense and was in fact untrue[d]. The Treasury Bills had in fact been sold for cash which was used by the private side.

---

a The MAPs described the transaction in these terms:
> "Lehman Brothers 'lent' USD Treasury bills to [RMG]. [RMG] used these bonds to raise finance. Value of bonds $51.8 million.
> The collateral for this arrangement with Lehman Brothers is part of BIM's LBI portfolio and 12 million MCC shares held by BIM centrally. Value as confirmed by Lehman Bros at 5/4/90 $76.9 million.
> [RMG] have lodged collateral with LBI (now held by Morgan Stanley) for the stock provided as collateral to Lehman Brothers.
> LBI confirmed that, at 5/4/90, the value of collateral held by them on BIM's behalf was in excess of $100 million.
> In terms of the above arrangements BIM receive "stocklending" fees from [RMG] on the value of stock provided to Lehman Brothers as collateral".

b He had known from his work as audit partner for FTIT, LBI and LBH for the year ended 31 December 1989 that the shares of the CIF and FTIT had been used as collateral for loans to LBI and the funds had been loaned to the private side as referred to at paragraph 5.41.

c By the time of his interview with us, some four years later, he had no recollection of the meeting on that day.

d Millett J described the letter in his judgment in *Macmillan v. BIT* (10 December 1993) as "a masterpiece of ambiguity and *suggestio falsi*". Neither Mr Trachtenberg nor KM gave evidence at the trial in that case.

9.43 Mr Trachtenberg accepted in his evidence to us that the letter was untrue. He told us that, in the light of his explanations to CLD of the true position in relation to the use of pension fund stock as collateral for loans to the private side (as set out in paragraph 9.39) CLD had raised concerns with the fact that pension fund stocks were being used in this way. He thought that the letter had been written by him after further discussion with CLD and Mr Cook in an attempt to explain the transactions in a way which would enable the arrangements with Lehmans to continue. He was fairly certain that the text of the letter would have been discussed in draft with CLD and Mr Cook, as the letter was intended to meet a requirement that the transactions be disclosed separately. He had no doubt that CLD fully understood the Lehmans transactions[a] and the letter merely restated the position for the purposes of the audit.

9.44 Mr Cowling told us that he understood from Mr Trachtenberg's explanation and this letter that the Treasury Bills had not been passed to RMG but that Lehmans held not only the CIF shares but also the Treasury Bills. He required written confirmation from BIM (which he subsequently received in a letter prepared by CLD but signed by Mr Cook and KM) that the transaction between BIM and Lehmans had involved no third parties. He was told that the fee income (which could only have arisen if the securities had been "lent" to third parties) was also an error that should be reversed. On the basis of these explanations and without further enquiry, Mr Cowling told us he was satisfied that as at 5 April 1990 there had been no use of pension fund shares for the benefit of the private side and he signed the audit report on the CIF accounts[b] on that basis. As explained at paragraph 5.39, this was not in fact the case.

(4) Events at FTIT

9.45 At the same time as the audit of the CIF was being conducted, CLD were also conducting the audit of FTIT for the year ended 31 December 1990[c]. As described at paragraph 5.40, LBI had been using the shares in the FTIT portfolio in exactly the same way as it had been using the shares of the CIF as collateral for loans; an explanation was provided to a member of CLD's staff (recorded in a note dated 7 February 1991[d]) that shares were "lent" from the FTIT

---

a After the death of RM, Mr Trachtenberg gave a similar account of the rationale for the transaction, as set out in paragraph 9.39 to a team from CLD appointed to investigate.

b A note to the accounts drafted by Mr Highfield described the transaction as follows:
"**Collateral Swap Programme**
During the year, [LBI], as manager of part of the Fund's investments, entered into a Collateral Swap agreement with [Lehmans], on the Fund's behalf. Under this arrangement, securities are deposited with the money broker in exchange for (in this case) US Treasury Bills. These bills can either be lent onwards, sold and the cash placed on deposit, or used as collateral for other transactions. In this way, an additional margin can be made while retaining full rights and entitlements (including dividends) relating to the securities deposited. As at 5 April 1990, securities to a market value of £46,825,000 were held on deposit by [Lehmans], and Treasury Bills to the value of £31,600,000 had been issued in exchange."

c During this phase of the audit, no attempt was made by CLD to carry out any work on counter security or to verify independently that it existed.

d The text of the note (which Mr Cowling told us he did not see) reads as follows:

> "FTIT lend stock to LBI and the Mirror who use the stock as collateral for various loans taken out with brokers (Nomura, Crédit Suisse, Morgan Stanley, etc).
> In order not to be exposed to the risk of default on these loans LBI and Mirror also place collateral with FTIT, greater than the value of the stock lent by FTIT. This collateral usually takes the form of shares in group companies such as MCC.

portfolio to provide the private side with collateral for its bank loans; this explanation was essentially the same as the first explanation provided to CLD on the audit of the CIF. CLD had identified again in early 1991 what were in fact the essential features of LBI's similar arrangement to use the shares in the FTIT portfolio under its management as collateral for loans for the benefit of the private side.

9.46 At the same time as the audit of FTIT was being conducted, the level of its income from "stocklending" came to the attention of Mr Woolland of Rowe & Pitman who were the brokers to FTIT. He examined the draft accounts in relation to special liquidation provisions and became concerned that the level of "stocklending" income might jeopardise the tax status of FTIT. Legal advice was then sought from Ashurst Morris Crisp and leading counsel. On around 20 February 1991, in the course of obtaining that advice it was discovered by both Rowe & Pitman and Ashurst Morris Crisp that the "lending" of FTIT's shares was not conventional stocklending but the "lending" of shares to LBH and RMG. Ashurst Morris Crisp and Rowe & Pitman immediately became concerned about the propriety of this "stocklending"[a] and among those informed was one of the directors of FTIT, Mr Willett[b] who had not known of this prior to that time but was at once very concerned as he understood the implications. KM's evidence to us was that he first learned of a potential problem at FTIT from Mr Tapley[c] in early 1991; he was extremely annoyed to be told of the problem after it had arisen. RM felt extremely let down by the LBI management[d]. Mr Tapley's evidence was that he had not been involved in the use made of shares in the FTIT portfolio and had not withheld information from RM or KM but had tried to deal with the issues[e]. At about the time of the FTIT board meeting on 26 February 1991 KM had a meeting with RM and Lord Donoughue at which it was agreed that FTIT would be offered an indemnity in relation to tax, as something for the board to fall back on[f]. At the board meeting on 26 February 1991 discussion concentrated on the legal advice concerning the possible effect on the tax status of FTIT. KM recalled that many directors wanted the "stocklending" programme to continue. However, the

---

> The whole exercise is necessary because the outside brokers usually require a diversified portfolio of share certificates as collateral (which FTIT has) rather than one big holding in a Maxwell Company."

In addition in a document for the attention of Mr Cowling dated 12 February 1991, it was stated

> "In order to finance their activities, LBH have historically borrowed share certificates from FTIT to use as collateral in securing funds provided by their brokers".

a They were also concerned that the transaction would be within the Stock Exchange's "Class 4" rules with respect to related parties.

b He was a former partner in Grieveson, Grant & Co and employed by RM as a financial consultant on a part-time basis.

c Mr Tapley had joined LBI as managing director in 1990; his previous experience had been in fund management.

d Since the autumn of 1990 there had been serious differences at LBI between Lord Donoughue and Mr Tapley on the one hand and Mr Trachtenberg on the other. These are outlined in Appendix 8.

e For an example of the action taken by Mr Tapley see Appendix 8 paragraph 8.8.

f KM was of the view that the indemnity offered was more for PR purposes than because it was likely to have any financial value. KM told us that Mr Tapley was present at the meeting but Mr Tapley denied this.

board of FTIT resolved that the programme be terminated but it appeared that not all the members of the board were then aware of the "lending" to LBH and RMG.

9.47 By the beginning of April 1991, the shares used as collateral for loans for the benefit of the private side were returned from the banks and this source of collateral ceased to be available. KM's evidence was that he had discussions with MSTC concerning the return of the stock and also personally intervened in the process of the stock being returned to ensure this was done promptly. One of the consequences of this was that replacement collateral was needed for a Yen loan amounting to £9m from Daiwa Europe Bank plc which had been made to LBI on 11 March 1991; £4.225m was taken from the LBI managed portfolio of the CIF to provide cash collateral for this loan.

9.48 In early March 1991, IMRO were contacted by Mr Carson in relation to stocklending. The issues raised by Mr Carson and discussed with IMRO at a meeting on 11 March 1991 were very general questions about IMRO rules, as reflected in the exchange of letters between Mr Carson and IMRO[a]. IMRO were first told something about an issue arising out of the relationship between FTIT and LBI in July 1991.

9.49 Ashurst Morris Crisp were instructed to carry out an investigation which revealed that a very high proportion of FTIT's shares had been "lent" for the benefit of LBI, LBH and RMG. The directors of FTIT not connected with RM or his companies and Mr Willett[b] maintained that they had only authorised conventional stocklending of the type described by us at paragraph 5.30 (which was to be through Morgan Stanley as brokers) and not "lending" to LBI, LBH and RMG, but KM told us RM disputed this[c]. Further investigations and inquiries had been carried out by 24 April 1991[d] by which time the independent directors, Mr Willett, Rowe & Pitman and Ashurst Morris Crisp were concerned that there might be a need to make an announcement to the Stock Exchange, in particular if the board were to require the resignation of LBI[e] or describe what had happened at FTIT.

---

a Mr Carson explained in a letter to IMRO that investments were deposited with LBI's eligible custodian and lent only in return for counter security.

b KM told us that Mr Willett had been extremely unhappy at what had gone on. He had expressed concerns to KM about the events of FTIT and had used the analogy of someone taking a car without the owner's consent and then returning it undamaged; it was still taking something that did not belong to you.

c Mr Trachtenberg (who had been the Company Secretary at FTIT) told us that he was certain that the whole of the FTIT board (Lord Donoughue in particular) was aware of the lending to the private side companies – the directors had been told about it in writing (most notably in the form of schedules which showed who the borrower was) and orally on several occasions. Lord Donoughue has always denied this and the documentation supports his evidence that he did not know of lending to the private side until January 1991. Mr Willett and the other independent directors have always denied they knew of lending to the private side and the documentation supports their evidence. KM told us that it was his view and RM's at the time that what had happened had been authorised.

d By April 1991, Mr Trachtenberg had been suspended from LBI; on 19 April 1991, Lord Donoughue wrote to KM pressing for Mr Trachtenberg to be suspended from all positions in LBH until the dispute with FTIT was resolved. On 23 April 1991, Lord Donoughue also sought the resignation of Mr Andrew Smith.

e Their concern was heightened by the fact that the results of FTIT for the year end had normally been announced at the end of February and Rowe & Pitman was receiving inquiries as to the position.

9.50 The advisers to FTIT and its independent directors were also aware that the flotation of MGN was imminent and that were any announcement to be made or were LBI to be dismissed as managers to FTIT, this might adversely affect the flotation[a]. It was therefore decided at a meeting on 24 April 1991 that Rowe & Pitman and Ashurst Morris Crisp should visit the Stock Exchange.

9.51 Accordingly on 25 April 1991 a meeting was arranged with Mr Fryer and Mr Miller, senior officers of the Stock Exchange. Ashurst Morris Crisp and Rowe & Pitman took with them a file containing the reports that had been made available to the board of FTIT and other information relating to the "loan" by LBI of FTIT's shares to LBH and RMG. They explained to the Stock Exchange that LBI had been engaged in unauthorised "lending" of FTIT's securities and provided them with a schedule showing the significant amounts involved; the values varied over the period but for example, over £50m was shown as "lent" in June/July 1989 and £37m - £38m was "lent" in the last three months of 1990. The Stock Exchange were also told that the shares had been "lent" to "Mirror Group". Mirror Group plc was the name by which RMG was known at this time, but the Stock Exchange understood this to be a reference to MGN.

9.52 The file of reports was offered to the Stock Exchange but was declined. There is a difference in recollection as to why this occurred[b]. After Rowe & Pitman and Ashurst Morris Crisp left, Mr Fryer asked Mr Miller to look through the latest draft of the MGN prospectus to see if it contained anything concerning the matters about which they had been told. The draft prospectus was examined and nothing found. The group of persons at the Stock Exchange who were examining the MGN prospectus were not informed of any of this and nothing was said by the Stock Exchange to any of the advisers concerned on the MGN flotation. Thereafter, Rowe & Pitman kept the Stock Exchange informed of events concerning FTIT but nothing further was asked by the Stock Exchange or said by Rowe & Pitman in relation to the impact these events might have upon the flotation of MGN.

---

a Mr Russell of Titmuss Sainer & Webb who were acting for LBI had advised RM that the actual use made of FTIT's shares had not been authorised by the independent directors of FTIT; although they had authorised "stocklending", they had not known that the shares had been "lent" to RM's companies and had they known they would not have approved of this, certainly not without proper counter security arrangements. RM's principal concern, Mr Russell believed, was to avoid a scandal that might affect the flotation of MGN. Titmuss Sainer & Webb in fact prepared a draft disclosure document to give Samuel Montagu notice of the dispute between LBI and the board of FTIT; it drew attention to the fact that LBI was the manager of a part of the CIF. Mr Russell told us that he had no recollection as to what was done with this document.

b Mr Woolland of Rowe & Pitman told us that Mr Fryer had asked if they were making a formal complaint about "Mirror Group" and asked whether Rowe & Pitman would authorise them to speak to the advisers to MGN about what they had told the Stock Exchange in confidence. Mr Woolland told us that he replied that they were not in a position to give that authority but were there to speak about FTIT. Mr Fryer told us that he had asked whether the matter in any way concerned the MGN flotation and that he was told that the matter was quite separate and had nothing to do with the flotation and the papers were not complete. He therefore declined to take the papers. Mr Sparrow of Ashurst Morris Crisp told us that they had concluded prior to the meeting, that they had insufficient information to make a formal complaint but felt the Stock Exchange should be made aware of the position; accordingly they replied to a question from Mr Fryer as to what their purpose was in coming to see the Stock Exchange, by saying simply that the Board of FTIT was concerned that the Stock Exchange should be made aware of the problems at FTIT.

9.53 KM told us that the visit to the Stock Exchange was evidence of the very serious deterioration that had occurred during March and April 1991 in the relationship between FTIT and LBI. RM considered that there was a vendetta against him by Ashurst Morris Crisp[a] as FTIT's professional advisers, though we are satisfied that there was no such vendetta. RM's reaction was to fight as he was not at all embarrassed about what had happened at FTIT; his view was that either the board of FTIT accepted that LBI had had back office problems or made an allegation of fraud. KM tried to find a middle course, which led to rows with RM, but Ashurst Morris Crisp would not consider an approach to IMRO as a means of resolving the dispute.

9.54 The independent directors of FTIT and Mr Willett resolved at a board meeting on 30 April 1991 (the day of the publication of the MGN prospectus) that LBI should resign immediately and that this should be announced. The board meeting then adjourned and when it reconvened later that day the board was informed that one of RM's private companies had appointed a merchant bank and intended to make a bid for FTIT at its full asset value. The board were requested not to make an announcement nor force the resignation of LBI[b]. The board suspended the resolution for 24 hours to allow the offer to be prepared. KM told us that the bid was his idea[c]; he thought that it might at least buy some time and would lessen the impact on the MGN flotation. RM was, however, very much against it in spite of the imminence of the MGN flotation and took some time to agree; he only finally agreed during the adjournment of the board meeting.

9.55 The Board met again on 1 May 1991 and resolved to recommend the offer in principle. The board did so as the proposed offer was attractive and in the best interests of the shareholders of FTIT; an announcement was made on 1 May 1991 that an offer was to be made on the basis of the full asset value of FTIT. It was not however until the bid documents for FTIT were published on 4 July 1991 that any of the advisers to MGN (other than CLD) or the general public became aware that LBI had been involved in the "lending" of FTIT's portfolio of securities and that there were allegations that this had not been properly authorised[d]. Mr Willett, as a director of FTIT, was aware from 21 February 1991 of the "lending" of the shares

---

a The origins of the antagonism between RM and Ashurst Morris Crisp we are told related to matters connected with affairs which had given rise to the DTI Reports of 1971/73 when there had been a confrontation between a partner in the firm who was acting for Rothschild and RM.

b RM had made it clear to Mr Trachtenberg that he would be made the scapegoat in respect of FTIT as he wanted to protect himself and the flotation.

c Mr Russell of Titmuss Sainer & Webb told us he had discussed a bid with KM on 29 April 1991.

d The disclosure made on the bid was expressly approved by leading counsel (instructed on behalf of the independent directors) in terms which it was felt sufficiently disclosed the transactions but which did not discourage RM and his private companies from proceeding with the bid. A note to the accounts stated:

> "During the year ended 31 December 1900 and except to a small degree during the year ended 31 December 1989 the Company's programme of securities lending was conducted by LBI with its holding company, London & Bishopsgate Holdings plc, and with an associated company although the manner and terms of the securities lending programme should have been approved by a resolution of the Board."

Leading Counsel advised that, if this disclosure was made, the independent directors of FTIT could not be criticised for not having given the full facts or for not having informed the regulatory authorities or the press. An article in the *Daily Mail* on 6 July 1991 observed:

> "The First Tokyo Index Trust bid was originally announced on 2 May as the [MGN] flotation was in full swing. What a tangle there would have been if these details had emerged then."

of FTIT to LBH and RMG, the fact it had not been authorised and subsequently of the reason why the bid was being made; he appreciated the impact that these facts would have on the flotation of MGN. Although he was a member of the MGN prospectus drafting committee (referred to in the footnote to paragraph 8.3), Mr Willett considered that the information he had was confidential to him in his capacity as a director of FTIT and that there was nothing to suggest to him that similar unauthorised activities were occurring in relation to the CIF; it was also in the interests of the shareholders of FTIT that the matter be resolved without the publicity that would have arisen from a dispute at that time, so he considered he should say nothing about it to those concerned with the flotation of MGN. KM (who was present at the Board meeting on 30 April 1991) told us that despite the fact that the FTIT board had been extremely hostile they had nonetheless accepted the position.

9.56 Mr Cowling was also involved in further investigations into the use of FTIT's shares after most of the audit work had been completed:

- On 10 April 1991 Mr Cowling wrote a letter to the board of LBI setting out the information that CLD had concerning stocklending transactions relating to FTIT; the letter included the following:

  > "On various occasions during the last two years we have had discussions with LBI senior management concerning the collateral associated with the stock lending transactions and the arms-length nature of the transactions. In particular we received oral representations from Mr Trachtenberg, a director of LBI and former Compliance Officer of the company for regulatory purposes, that all stock lending was fully collateralised and that the fees arising had been negotiated at normal commercial rates. We have obviously no reason to doubt assurances from such an individual. . . .
  > [The contents of this letter are] based on information contained in our files and from discussions with staff involved."

  In fact the files contained a statement in the 1989 MAPs "Lending to LBH, no collateral given" and a note of a meeting on 20 February 1990 which recorded information then given by Mr Trachtenberg that "LBH does not necessarily provide collateral". Mr Cowling's explanation was that he prepared the letter in a few hours in a rush because of other commitments and it was not possible for him to review the files in the time available.

- On 22 April 1991, Mr Cowling met with KM. They discussed the counter security available in respect of the loan of stocks by FTIT; Mr Cowling's note of the meeting records that:

  > "[KM] acknowledged that the directors were uncomfortable about the evidence to support the collateral position and that in future they would still wish to pursue stocklending activities, provided this was supported by proper systems."

- On 25 April 1991 Mr Cowling consulted Mr Lamb (whom he had earlier consulted about the transaction involving Lehmans as set out at paragraph 9.41) about information provided by Ashurst Morris Crisp about the use of FTIT's stocks by LBI and the accounting treatment of the income derived from that use. He reported Mr Lamb's views to Mr Walsh, as he considered that the potential problems could give rise to "some flack" from RM; Mr Walsh needed to be aware of this, as it potentially affected the relationship between CLD and RM. Mr Walsh recalled little of this matter. Although Mr Cowling had been aware since the audit of LBI and FTIT for the year ended 31 December 1989 (as set out at paragraph 5.41) that the shares had been used by private side companies as collateral for loans, he told us that he was unaware until 13 May 1991 of the fact that this was alleged to be unauthorised[a].

9.57 Clifford Chance had been asked to advise LBI from 1989 on certain specific points.

- Mr Trachtenberg sought advice from Clifford Chance in September 1989 about regulatory requirements in the course of which stocklending was mentioned as an activity of LBI[b].
- On 3 November 1989[c], Mr Trachtenberg sought specific advice from an assistant solicitor at Clifford Chance, Mr Osborne, on lending the stock of a client and depositing the counter security for the stocks lent with an associated company of the client. Mr Trachtenberg told us that he telephoned Clifford Chance specifically in order to seek advice about the Lehmans transaction, of which he had only just learned (see paragraph 5.38). Clifford Chance advised that provided the agreement was wide enough and the stocks were deposited with an eligible custodian, this was permissible and that they were:

  > "not aware of any IMRO requirements restricting the [counter security] for the stocks loaned from being put on deposit with an associated company of the client, when it is at the request of the client and the expected yield on that deposited will be greater than that obtainable in the market place."

- Further details of two types of transaction were explained to Mr Osborne between 3 and 22 November 1989 - what he understood to be conventional stocklending and an arrangement whereby the counter security for the stocks lent was subject to a "repo" agreement[d]. On the latter, Mr Trachtenberg appears to have told Mr Osborne that the counter security would be a Treasury Bond. Mr Osborne advised that for the use of the counter security for a "repo" transaction:
  - the investment management agreement had to cover the "repo" and the IMRO client money regulations had to be disapplied or otherwise the cash received for the counter security would be deemed client money and subject to segregation.

---

a Mr Cowling continued to be involved. On 6 June 1991 he had a meeting with Mr Trachtenberg to discuss what counter security there had been. Mr Trachtenberg told him counter security had been provided by way of shares owned by the private side which he had kept in a fire proof cabinet; that he had monitored it on a spreadsheet, but had overwritten it as the position had changed. After that meeting RM complained to Mr Brandon Gough who asked Mr Walsh to deal with it. Mr Walsh reported to Mr Gough that RM had believed Mr Cowling was using as a basis for his meeting with Mr Trachtenberg questions prepared by Ashurst Morris Crisp who were conducting a vendetta against him.

b Mr Trachtenberg told us that this advice was sought primarily on behalf of Mr Andrew Smith who wanted to set up an LBI Inc entity in London approved by the TSA.

c This was at the time the financing with Lehmans referred to at paragraph 5.39 was being negotiated by LBI with Lehmans.

d A "repo" is a form of financing transaction; it generally involves the sale of securities (such as Treasury Bills) with an agreement to repurchase securities of the same type at an agreed price at a future date.

- title in the counter security had to pass to the client so that he could execute the "repo" and the stocklending agreement had to provide for this and the return of comparable securities or cash.
- that the cash or replacement counter security obtained through the "repo" had to be separately identifiable as forming part of the client's funds under management as it remained the client's security for the stocklending.

Mr Osborne's evidence was that the party to the stocklending agreement was never identified, but he understood it to be a client of LBI. Neither the borrower nor the associated company of the client was ever identified.

9.58 In June and July 1990, LBI sought further advice from Mr Osborne and a tax specialist at Clifford Chance in connection with regulatory requirements for stocklending and on the tax position. We were told by Mr Carson that Clifford Chance prepared a draft for a stocklending agreement between LBI as managers of FTIT and RMG (referred to at paragraph 6.26) and provided tax advice; he was certain that Mr Osborne must have known that the stocklending was with RMG[a]. Mr Osborne's evidence was that, although he and the specialist in tax advised LBI in June and July 1990, he did not draft the agreement and was unaware of the party to whom the stock was lent[b].

9.59 On 25 March 1991, Mr Barlow, a partner at Clifford Chance (not on the flotation team) was asked to advise LBI. On being given to understand that the stocklending agreement between FTIT and LBH contained customary market terms for stocklending agreements between parties operating at arm's length[c], he advised that LBI was permitted to enter into it under the terms of its agreement with FTIT.

---

a We were told by Miss Maxwell that she recalled being told by Mr Carson in 1990 that the agreement had been drafted by Clifford Chance; this evidence shows that Mr Carson had made this point long before the discoveries consequent upon RM's death in November 1991.

b We were told by Clifford Chance that the agreement did not conform to their standard form and contained terms as to the retention by the lender of title to the shares and the distribution of dividends which they would not have inserted into a stocklending agreement as it would have meant that the agreement was not an arrangement that the Inland Revenue would have accepted for tax purposes under section 129 of Income and Corporation Taxes Act 1988. We enquired whether there was a fee note which covered this period; we were provided with a fee note that was expressed to cover the period between 11 May 1991 and 19 November 1991, but that the analysis of the bill showed it covered the work done in June and July 1990 though it did not describe it. No copy of the draft of this agreement exists, but the signed agreement bears the reference "SCC/LBI"; Mr Carson told us that the final version of that document was produced by him, albeit on the basis of a Clifford Chance precedent; the agreement contained references to the management agreement between FTIT and LBI and to board resolutions which Clifford Chance have told us they did not see. Mr Trachtenberg told us that his recollection was that Clifford Chance produced a draft agreement which Mr Carson then had typed on his own word processor so that he could make various amendments.

c Mr Carson told us that he thought that Clifford Chance had a copy of the stocklending agreement, but the only stocklending agreement we have seen is the one between LBI as managers for FTIT and RMG.

9.60 In the course of the work done by Clifford Chance on the flotation, Mr Barlow was asked to look at the terms of the revised management agreement between LBI and BIM which had taken effect on 1 January 1991. Nothing was brought to his attention that indicated the shares of the CIF had been used in a similar manner to those of FTIT. However he did notice that the agreement between LBI and BIM expressly disapplied the client money rules. He raised the question as to whether this was permissible, but he did not know of the earlier discussion between Mr Trachtenberg and Mr Osborne when disapplying the client money rules had been raised.

10. THE FLOTATION: CONTROL OVER THE MANAGEMENT OF THE COMPANY

10.1 It was essential, when MGN became a listed company, that effective control of the management of the company be passed from RM to a board of directors and that RM cease to be entitled to exercise the same control as when the business had been a private company. This chapter examines this issue by considering the main aspects of what was then known about RM and the way he ran his companies and what was done to achieve the objective of passing control to the board.

Sources of information of the way RM operated

10.2 In preparing for the flotation it was necessary to know how RM had run his companies so as to know what needed to be done to pass control to the board. There were three principal sources of information available on the way RM ran his companies.

10.3 The first, and the most important was to ascertain the way RM had run MGN as described in paragraphs 1.21, 2.2 and 4.41. This can be summarised by saying that MGN had not been run by a board; RM had resisted attempts to get him to attend meetings run along the lines of a board meeting; he had preferred to run the company by means of morning meetings; he had bullied[a] some of the senior management although others had stood up to him; he had on occasions given direct instructions to less senior management, thereby by-passing reporting structures. Although SDR had been run in an entirely different manner, the way in which RM ran MGN was characteristic of the way he ran his other private companies based in London.

10.4 The second source of information was the three Reports of the DTI Inspectors published in 1971/73. The facts set out in those Reports showed that:

- RM had held board meetings without giving notice to other directors in order to clothe his own decisions with formality[b].

- RM had taken decisions that should have been made by the board without reference to the board[c].

- RM had carried out transactions of which other directors and the board had been unaware, particularly transactions with family companies[d].

---

[a] Anxiety about RM was not confined to those who worked for him. We were told that some analysts were reluctant to express publicly their real views of RM because they were concerned that pressure might be put on their employer to secure their dismissal; some journalists had a similar reluctance because of their fear of being sued by RM.

[b] 1971 Report, paragraphs 180 - 191.

[c] 1971 Report, paragraph 231.

[d] 1971 Report, paragraphs 278, 280; 1972 Report, paragraph 371; 1973 Report, paragraph 773, 784, 809, 818, 1115 - 1119.

- The function of the Company Secretary of a company run by RM had been described as:

  "To carry out Mr Maxwell's orders to the letter and to do nothing more."[a]

- RM had expected his executives to carry out his instructions to the letter which sometimes placed management in a position where they had to do what they were told or resign[b].

10.5 Whether RM operated within a listed company in the same manner as would have been evident from both of the above could have been examined by reference to the way RM had run MCC[c]. There were two significant features of the way in which the board of that company operated:

- In November 1981 at RM's request, the board of MCC had delegated to him, as a committee of one, the entire powers of the board. It had been explained to the board that this was necessary to enable RM, if abroad or if circumstances required, to sanction on his own any transaction[d]. This delegation remained in force at RM's death in November 1991. The power was used by RM but we were told by Mr Woods and Mr Baker that, as far as they were aware, the power had not been abused[e].

- Board meetings were often called at short notice; papers for the meetings were generally provided to directors only half an hour prior to the commencement of the meeting. After the conclusion of a board meeting the directors were requested to return the papers, although some did keep them.

The information considered

10.6 It was appreciated by Samuel Montagu that steps had to be taken to ensure that the management of MGN was placed under the control of the board rather than RM; this was because there was a controlling shareholder and not because the controlling shareholder was RM. However in order to ascertain the steps that would be required to achieve this objective, Samuel Montagu, as a sponsor to the issue, would require adequate information. Ordinarily a sponsor would expect to obtain such information from the long form report on the company.

---

a 1971 Report, paragraph 256.

b 1972 Report, paragraph 425.

c We were told by Lord Williams of Elvel (who acted as the representative of PHL on the board of Hollis when it was a public company) that the board of Hollis was run in a proper manner, as papers were circulated in advance and departmental heads gave a detailed report; Sir Bernard Audley was the chairman and the secretary was variously Mr Rowe, Mr Stephens and Mr Hanton. In March 1990, RM had acquired all the shares in Hollis and board meetings had ceased. (The business of Hollis is summarised in the footnote to paragraph 3.7). MCC was a far larger, listed company and the only listed company controlled by RM in 1991 prior to the flotation of MGN.

d The resolution permitted the power to be exercised in RM's absence by Mr Stephens and another director; KM was substituted for Mr Stephens by an amendment made in June 1986 at a meeting at which Lord Silkin QC took the chair.

e However, he had used it to trade in shares and gilts, see paragraph 3.20.

10.7 Both the audit and reporting accountant teams of CLD were aware of the way in which RM had run MGN. Documentary assessments of MGN made by their staff in connection with various MGN audits contained comments such as:

> "Maxwell totally dominant."
> "Senior Management answers to Robert Maxwell. If he wants a particular treatment, then senior management comply."
> "[The board] do what the publisher tells them."

Mr Steere, the audit partner, told us that he agreed with most of the remarks but he commented that the second remark we have quoted was flippant because it did not reflect his experience. Those members of the audit staff whom we interviewed said the comments were seriously meant. In a draft management letter prepared in connection with the audit for the year ended 30 December 1990 a member of the CLD staff with some experience of previous audits included a paragraph (subsequently deleted by the audit partner Mr Steere[a]) that stated the position:

> "In the past board meetings have been used as a rubber stamping exercise. In addition during 1990 there was one example when a key company decision did not appear to be approved by the board since there was no record of [it in] the minutes. This particular example occurred when the company acquired a £29.7 million investment in MCC commercial paper."[b]

10.8 In the desktop review[c], CLD had advised that it would be necessary to appoint a management team, including a board of directors, that would be suitable for a listed company and would fairly represent the minority shareholders, and to provide strong executive and non-executive direction to the company. CLD had also advised that non-executive directors would be needed and that the board of MGN had to be seen to be independent of MCC. In the long form report, although the functions of the existing operational management were described, nothing was said about the way in which MGN had been run, or about RM's role save for a single sentence paragraph:

> "The publisher has significant influence over the control of the operations of the business."[d]

10.9 CLD explained that their reason for not including in their long form report the information known to them about the way in which MGN had actually been run was because they thought that Samuel Montagu and the other advisers were aware of those facts and of RM's dominance,

---

a His explanation of this was that it was no longer appropriate as MGN was a listed company; the board structure had been altered and past practices such as rubber stamping no longer applied. This passage was in a draft of the letter dated 30 May 1991 and the management letter with the passage deleted was sent on 26 June 1991.

b The reason for the acquisition of commercial paper has been referred to at paragraph 6.68.

c See paragraph 8.3.

d The report on SDR described the way that company had been run and its board had operated as referred to at paragraph 2.9.

that CLD had pointed out in their desktop review[a] that a change in management was required, and that if Samuel Montagu had wanted to know more, they would only have had to ask and more information would have been provided. CLD did not consider providing information concerning MCC since what the CLD audit team for MCC[b] knew was confidential to them in their capacity as auditors to MCC and because they considered that Samuel Montagu was aware of how MCC was run. They were never asked to comment on MCC.

10.10 The position of Samuel Montagu can be summarised as follows:

- In fact, although Samuel Montagu appreciated in general terms the dominant influence of RM, they did not know about the way in which MGN[c] had actually been run.
- They knew, however, that nothing was contained in the long form report and they did not ask for more information; we were told by Mr Galloway that Samuel Montagu did not regard what had happened in the past and the way in which MGN had been run by RM as relevant. As Mr Galloway put it: "the past could not be taken as a guide to the future"..." the change is thus effected on the flotation and flotation is the catalyst for that change". Samuel Montagu therefore did not seek more information from CLD.
- No one from Samuel Montagu considered in any detail the 1971/73 DTI Reports. These were regarded as relating to events more than 20 years before (in respect of which no action had been taken against RM) and they had been challenged in the courts[d]; they were not regarded by Samuel Montagu as a reliable source of information. Since that time RM had achieved much; instead they had regard to the matters we have already summarised at paragraph 4.5 which they had taken into account when they agreed to act and their subsequent experience summarised at paragraph 4.6.
- No information was sought about MCC[e]. They considered it was a separate organisation and would only have taken the step of seeking information if they had strong cause to doubt the suitability of RM to be chairman of a listed company.
- They relied on their judgment that the company would be run through a board comprised of persons who in their judgment were capable of running MGN in a manner appropriate to a listed company; those persons gave no indication that the new arrangements would not work.

---

a Linklaters & Paines (who were in fact unaware of those matters) told us that the comments made in the desk top review could be applied to almost any private company that intended coming to the stock market.

b Mr Taberner, the audit partner for MCC, told us he did not know of the delegation resolution or the way board meetings were arranged and conducted.

c Samuel Montagu did know about Mr Morrissey's attempts to establish a management structure (referred to at paragraph 2.7) but had understood that senior management refused to accept it.

d See *re: Pergamon Press* [1971] Ch 388 and *Maxwell v DTI* [1974] 1QB 523. The challenges were unsuccessful and the procedures of the Inspectors approved.

e We were told by Mr Clive Chalk, the director at Samuel Montagu principally responsible for dealing with MCC, that he had seen little of the internal workings of MCC, but from the few board meetings he had attended, and his dealings with the senior executives, he did not consider there was anything that caused him to be concerned about RM's fitness to have stewardship of a listed company.

SBIL told us they never saw the desk top review and expected that the long form reports would cover all relevant information.

10.11 Lord Williams of Elvel had asked KM in November 1990 to call regular board meetings of the companies of which he was a director. KM told us that he recalled Lord Williams' request and that there had been a board meeting of PHL at which documentation had been presented, approved and signed ratifying previous decisions. KM also recalled Lord Williams asking for a board meeting of MGN. Lord Williams wrote to KM on 14 December 1990 asking for quarterly board meetings of the companies of which he was a non-executive director which included MGN. No action resulted so Lord Williams contacted Miss Maxwell in February 1991; subsequently in March 1991 he spoke to Mr Galloway about the fact that no board meeting of MGN had been held and that the board had not been asked to approve the accounts[a]. Mr Galloway asked Linklaters & Paines to enquire whether the accounts had been approved by the board; they, in turn, asked Clifford Chance to confirm they had inspected the minute books of MGN to ensure that the accounts had been approved and filed with the Registrar of Companies. Clifford Chance did not check the minute books but looked at Companies' House records and documents supplied by Mr Stephens that showed that the accounts had been approved and filed; the junior assistant concerned explained to her senior that she did not have time to look at the minute books; we were told by Clifford Chance that there was no point in checking the minute books as the search at Companies House provided the definitive means of confirming that the accounts had been filed.

The steps taken in respect of the corporate governance of MGN

10.12 A number of steps were taken with the objective of ensuring control of the management of MGN passed to its board. It is easiest to consider the matters by reference to a number of individual topics, albeit that it is the collective effect that is ultimately significant.

(a) The role of RM as Executive Chairman

10.13 The appointment of a new Chief Executive was mooted during the course of the flotation and RM said he had made an approach. KM told us that Sir Michael Richardson was pushing for RM to agree to the appointment of a Chief Executive. In fact two approaches were made[b] but,

[a] Mr Galloway's recollection was that the failure of the MGN board to approve the accounts had been mentioned in the course of a conversation about several matters; Lord Williams had said that he was not sure whether the MGN board had met to approve the accounts. Accordingly in the instructions to Linklaters & Paines Mr Galloway had emphasised checking whether the accounts had been approved by the board, not the general issue as to whether there had been board meetings, as he had not considered this was an issue.

[b] Mr Andrew Neil had been approached at the end of January 1991 to be managing editor and editor-in-chief of MGN, *The European* and the *New York Daily News*; he felt RM was a dubious character and thought that the papers would end up with two editors in chief - himself and RM; he therefore set conditions which RM considered but which he thought RM would never accept; it is clear that RM would never have accepted them. IM told us that he discussed the appointment of Mr Neil with RM as RM wanted a big name Editor to support the float and did not have much confidence in the existing editors. IM advised against it, as he considered that Mr Neil was too right-wing for *The Mirror* and that the editorial staff would not accept him. More fundamentally, he thought that RM and Mr Neil would never be able to work together. KM told us that Mr Andrew Neil was not offered the job since RM did not consider him to be a sufficiently tough controller of the editorial budget. The other person approached was Mr David Montgomery. He told us that he was offered the job of Editor in November 1990 with a substantial increase in salary and complete editorial freedom; he did not take up the post.

when in March 1991 RM announced that the person he had approached had declined there was no time to seek another person; it was decided that a new Chief Executive was not essential as there were the senior executives who had been managing the English and Scottish newspaper businesses.

10.14 The prospectus described RM as "Executive Chairman"[a]; he was described as such because it was appreciated by Samuel Montagu and SBIL that he would take a significant executive role in the management of MGN and this was the most accurate description.

10.15 Samuel Montagu told us that they were "perfectly happy" for RM to be Executive Chairman of MGN, subject to the appointment of a suitable board of executive and non-executive directors and to the other arrangements made by them as described by us in the following paragraphs. They took this view because:

- MGN had performed strongly in the three years prior to the flotation and had the highest operating profit margin in the industry.
- RM was regarded at the time of the flotation by the financial community as running successful companies, particularly MCC; the huge financing of the major acquisitions made - Macmillan and OAG - demonstrated the degree of acceptance of RM by the banking community.
- RM had acquired the *New York Daily News* (referred to at paragraph 9.23) and had been acclaimed in the US for saving that paper; he had also started *The European*.
- If RM had had any other role, it would not have reflected the reality of what was going to happen and would have been seriously misleading to prospective investors.

10.16 Nonetheless, it was necessary to see that RM acted as Executive Chairman under the direction and control of the board.

(b) The executive directors

10.17 Samuel Montagu took the view that when MGN had been a private company there were too many directors and that the board of the listed company should comprise a smaller number of directors. It was eventually agreed that there should be nine executive directors, apart from RM:

IM:	He was appointed Deputy Chairman although he had very little prior involvement in the management of MGN. He was 35 years old[b].
Ernest Burrington:	He was appointed Joint Managing Director with responsibility for the English companies. He was a newspaper man with little corporate financial experience.
Victor Horwood:	He was appointed Joint Managing Director with responsibility for SDR.
Roger Eastoe:	His responsibility was marketing and the sale of advertising which he had previously run with little interference from RM.

[a] The Stock Exchange had questioned the role of RM as Executive Chairman in a comment on an early draft of the prospectus; they believed this was sufficient to draw the point to Smith New Court's attention.

[b] IM's involvement in RM's companies is set out in a footnote to paragraph 3.13.

John Ferguson:	He was responsible for the printing of the English newspapers, but the management structure of the companies that did the printing in England did not give him full control and enabled RM to by-pass him.
Endell Laird:	He had had a career in journalism as an editor and was one of the last appointments to the board. He represented the editors of the Scottish newspapers.
Charles Wilson:	He had only been employed within RM's companies since December 1990 when he was appointed Editor-in-Chief of the *Sporting Life*, but had been used in the meantime by RM on various projects including the temporary editorship of *The Daily Mirror* and the acquisition of the *New York Daily News*. He was to be responsible for editorial policy for the English titles, but had little involvement in the flotation.
Lawrence Guest:	He was appointed the finance director } Their position is considered
Michael Stoney:	He was appointed a director } in Chapter 11.

10.18 Samuel Montagu told us that they were impressed with a number of key individuals among the directors who stood their ground with RM, whom RM respected and who were experienced and competent; that impression was derived from their experience during the flotation.

10.19 All of these were very competent and experienced as managers of a national newspaper business. However, Mr Burrington and Mr Eastoe had no experience of a company being managed through a board and Mr Wilson's experience was limited[a]; all the executive directors of MGN based in London (other than Mr Wilson) had been accustomed for some years to running the company under the management of RM, rather than themselves managing the company.

(c) The appointment of non-executive directors

10.20 The appointment of non-executive directors was generally perceived to be of central importance in seeing that RM acted under the direction and control of the board and that the board had proper charge of the running of MGN; however Samuel Montagu considered that the purpose of appointing non-executive directors was to supplement the board so that it was appropriate for a listed company, rather than to enable the board to control RM. The appointment of the non-executive directors was heavily emphasised in the marketing of the issue.

10.21 RM had not reacted favourably in 1988 when he had been told that non-executive directors had to be appointed, but had eventually agreed that it was essential. However, KM told us that RM was quite happy to have non-executives on the board; he had had a policy of having "luminaries" on boards for some years. He had given jobs to former ministers, politicians and officials, as he had seen this as a way of exercising power in the Labour Party and helping friends who had lost office. RM also saw them as lending their name to the company just as

[a] He had been on the board of George Outram Ltd (a Lonrho plc subsidiary) and Editor of the *Glasgow Evening Times*, *Glasgow Herald* and *Scottish Sunday Standard* (1976-82) and had attended informal gatherings of the board of Times Newspapers plc when editor of *The Times*.

distinguished scientists lent their name to his scientific journals by becoming members of the editorial boards of the journals. However, beyond that, non-executive directors had no function in RM's world.

10.22 Possible names were discussed in January 1991[a] and an approach was made in February 1991 by KM to Mr Alan Clements[b] (who had retired as Finance Director of ICI in 1990) and in March 1991 by RM to Sir Robert Clark[c] (then Deputy Chairman of TSB Group plc). Mr Clements had had no material dealings with RM or his companies prior to this approach[d] but Sir Robert Clark had dealt with RM on a number of previous occasions. He had dealt with him first in 1968 in connection with RM's attempt to acquire control of the *News of the World* and Hill Samuel had thereafter acted as one of RM's merchant banks. When he became Chairman of Hill Samuel Group in 1980, he told us he had ceased to have day-to-day dealings with RM[e].

10.23 Mr Clements and Sir Robert Clark became involved in the work on the flotation at the end of March 1991 when they were sent a copy of the draft prospectus. They were later supplied with one of the long form reports that dealt with MGN as a whole, further drafts of the prospectus and each was given a briefing at a separate meeting on 11 and 12 April 1991[f]. Mr Clements

---

a Samuel Montagu produced a list of possible non-executive directors which included the name of Sir Bernard Ingham the former Chief Press Secretary to Lady Thatcher when Prime Minister. RM exploded when he saw the name of a person regarded as a supporter of the Conservative Party on the list as a suggested non-executive director of the only newspaper group that supported the Labour Party. He swore that Samuel Montagu were hopelessly incompetent and that they were not to have anything further to do with the selection of non-executive directors, though this view was not conveyed to Samuel Montagu and they continued to be involved in the final selection.

b He had had a long career at ICI becoming Treasurer and then, in 1979, Finance Director. He was a founder member of the Association of Corporate Treasurers and a lay member of the Council of the Stock Exchange. Since 1980 he had held a number of non-executive directorships.

c Sir Robert had qualified as a solicitor and had become a partner in Slaughter & May. In 1962 he had left and become Head of Corporate Finance at Hill Samuel Bank Limited. He subsequently became Chief Executive of Hill Samuel Group and from 1980 to 1988 he was Chairman of Hill Samuel Group. He had held since the 1950s a number of non-executive directorships, a number of government appointments and had served on the Court of Directors of the Bank of England between 1976 and 1985.

d He had met KM, a fellow non-executive director of Guinness Mahon, and had been asked by him in the autumn of 1990 to become a member of the investment advisory board of a proposed new investment fund for Eastern Europe to be entitled "Maxwell Central & East European Partners". That proposal had not been proceeded with. Mr Clements told us he made discreet enquiries about MGN before deciding to accept.

e Sir Robert told us that he recalled little involvement in the transactions on which Hill Samuel had acted for RM and companies controlled by him during the 1980s. He told us he did not believe he was personally involved in handling the transaction in which Hill Samuel acted for PPL in the take over of MGN, but that he was kept informed of developments; such documents as Hill Samuel retain show that he attended an initial meeting with RM and had a preliminary exchange with National Westminster but that he had no greater involvement. Others recalled that Sir Robert was involved in RM's acquisition of MGN and until 1987 was one of the few advisers in the City to whom RM would listen. We were told he was a regular visitor to RM in 1986 and 1987. Sir Robert did not accept this.

f All the executive and non-executive directors were supplied with a memorandum prepared by Clifford Chance on the liabilities of directors for listing particulars and the other duties of directors of a listed company. The emphasis was on the technical duties of a director under legislation and City codes. It did not (and was not intended to) deal with corporate governance.

was told by Samuel Montagu that the matters dealt with in the 1971/73 DTI Reports were in the past, and he should look at the business of MGN. It was pointed out by Samuel Montagu to Mr Clements that, if you let him, RM would "proceed all over you" and Sir Robert Clark was told that MGN was run dictatorially.

10.24 Apart from a brief visit to the Watford plant and the Mirror Building and their attendance at two formal board meetings on 16 and 29 April 1991 (at which the board was concerned formally to approve the flotation arrangements and the prospectus), Mr Clements and Sir Robert Clark did not take the opportunity to get to know any of the executive directors of MGN nor to attend any meetings concerned with the business or management of MGN until after the flotation[a].

10.25 The other two non-executive directors were Lord Williams of Elvel and Mr Haines. Mr Haines[b] had been a key adviser on political and labour matters for RM but had never served on a board that managed a company and had little financial experience[c]. He was given no briefing on his duties and responsibilities as a non-executive director. Lord Williams had worked in an executive capacity for RM for five months in 1985; since that time (although he had been a director of several companies controlled by RM) he had played no executive role at all and his only active function was to represent RM's interests on the board of Hollis when it was a listed company controlled by RM. KM told us that Lord Williams' appointment was made by RM because of his links with the Labour party, the fact that he was a peer and that it was thought (from previous experience) that he would not "rock the boat". Samuel Montagu told us that they gave Lord Williams a briefing on 15 April 1991 at their offices. Lord Williams told us he returned from Wales during that morning and was in the House of Lords that afternoon; he had no meeting with Samuel Montagu, and he did not recall ever attending a meeting at Samuel Montagu's offices.

(d) The Articles

10.26 The Articles of MGN were brought into line with what the Stock Exchange required for a listed company and were duly approved by the Stock Exchange. Two significant special provisions were made in the Articles[d]; one of these was a provision that required that transactions with "related parties" be approved by "independent directors". The companies which were owned or controlled by the Maxwell Foundation, RM or his family were the identified related parties; independent directors were those who had no interests in the ownership of RM's companies

---

a In contrast, Mr Peter Walker visited three of the UK companies and travelled to New York and Chicago to learn about US companies when invited to become Chairman of MCC.

b Mr Haines had been involved with the newspaper industry all his life apart from his tenure in the office of Press Secretary to Harold Wilson, when he was Prime Minister. He had joined the *Daily Mirror* in 1977 and held senior positions on the editorial side until he retired in July 1990. He had been a director of MGN from 1 October 1985 and of MGN (1986) Limited from 1986.

c KM told us that Mr Haines was an important link to the Labour party and to the unions; his appointment had nothing to do with management of the company through the board.

d There was also a special provision dealing with borrowing powers.

or those who were not employed by or were directors of those companies - that is all the directors except RM, IM and Mr Stoney. This provision is considered further in Chapter 12[a].

10.27 No consideration was given to limiting the power of the board to delegate its powers or to requiring independent directors to form a quorum of the board for the purposes of all meetings. The advisers were unaware of the delegation of the board's power at MCC and of a similar resolution at MGN which was not revoked[b]; the view was also taken that the independence of the directors was relevant only to related party dealings and not to the control of RM in other matters; Clifford Chance told us that power to delegate was entirely normal (as this was contained in the articles in Table A to the Companies Acts and in the standard Stock Exchange approved articles) and they expected it to be exercised responsibly; they thought that adequate and proper notice of all board meetings would be given to the directors so that they would know of all board meetings.

(e) Creation of operating companies

10.28 There was a determination on the part of SDR not to become subject to the control of a board that had operational responsibility for the English newspapers. SDR wanted a structure where there would be a group board with two operating companies, one for England and one for Scotland[c]. This was what was put in place on flotation.

10.29 Little was required to be done in respect of the board of SDR as it was used to operating in a conventional manner, but the business of the English newspapers had never been run by a board. Nonetheless, RM was made Chairman of the English operating company, MGN Limited, whose board was intended to meet regularly and report to the main group board.

10.30 The business of MGN was only transferred to MGN Limited on 19 April 1991 (in the manner described at paragraph 15.9). The board of MGN Limited never met prior to the flotation other than for formal purposes; no structure or other organisational plans (apart from the work done by Mr McNab referred to at paragraph 11.27) were made for its board to meet or to report to the main MGN board.

---

a It was in fact very simple to change status to an independent director; all that had to be done was to resign employment or a directorship with the related party. Lord Williams did this in April 1991 and, as explained in paragraph 21.56, Mr Stoney did this in October 1991.

b On 6 March 1985 (as referred to in the footnote to paragraph 2.2), the board of MGN had established a committee with concurrent powers with the board; the composition of the committee had been altered on 9 October 1990 when its composition had been reduced to two, one of which was to be RM or KM.

c The directors of SDR at the time of the flotation were RM, IM, Mr Horwood, Mr Laird, Mr Haines, Mr John Anderson, Mr Derick Henry, Mrs Helen Liddell, Mr Colin McClatchie, Mr Kevin McMahon, Mr Gordon Terris and Sir Kenneth Alexander.

(f) The audit committee

10.31 At the board meeting of MGN on 16 April 1991 it was resolved to establish audit and remuneration committees of the board. The minute stated that the audit committee would be:

> "Responsible for reviewing the Company's statutory accounts and interim statements and for liaising with the auditors."

It was not envisaged that this committee would review matters that had arisen during the 1990 audit as it was anticipated that any matters that had already come to the attention of the auditors would be remedied in the performance of the due diligence obligation on flotation.

10.32 The audit committee was regarded as important and its existence referred to in the prospectus:

> "The board of the Company has two principal committees, Audit and Remuneration. These committees which comprise non-executive Directors of the Company, are respectively responsible for reviewing the Group's statutory accounts and interim statements and liaising with the auditors; and for determining the remuneration of the executive Directors."

However, no chairman was appointed[a], no terms of reference were set and no arrangements were made for the organisation of meetings. It first met nearly a year later.

(g) Company Secretary

10.33 A Company Secretary is recognised as having a key role in ensuring that board procedures are followed including the timely giving of notice of meetings to the directors, the preparation of papers in sufficient time for the board to consider them properly and the keeping of proper minutes of board meetings.

10.34 The Company Secretary of MCC and of RM's private companies was Mr Alan Stephens whose appointment as Secretary to MGN has been described at paragraph 2.3. Consideration was given during the course of the flotation to whether the secretarial department could continue to provide services to MGN and MCC, but a decision was reached on 25 March 1991 that MGN should have its own secretary. It was initially proposed that Mr Stephens' deputy, Mr Codrington, should be Company Secretary to MGN but that decision was changed and it was decided that Mr Codrington would be appointed Company Secretary to MCC and Mr Stephens remain Company Secretary to MGN. KM told us that the driving force behind the separation of the MCC and MGN secretarial departments was not the flotation of MGN but, rather, the impending appointment of Mr Peter Walker as Chairman of MCC.[b] Mr Peter Walker did not

---

a Lord Williams told us that as a result of a consultation with RM he thought Mr Clements was going to chair the Committee; Mr Clements told us he had never been asked and, if asked, would have refused because he had made up his mind that he would not do so because of his other commitments.

b As set out at paragraph 9.10.

want Mr Stephens as Company Secretary at MCC but wanted a fresh start[a]. To that end, it was proposed that Mr Stephens deal with MGN and that Mr Codrington take over at MCC[b].

10.35 Although it was decided that MGN and MCC should have separate company secretaries, the decision was never implemented. Mr Stephens remained the Company Secretary of MGN and MCC until after RM's death and the secretarial department continued to be run as one department. Nothing changed, save that the registered office of MGN was moved to the Mirror Building and the statutory books brought to London. KM told us that the separation never happened because Mr Peter Walker never took up his post at MCC as explained at paragraph 21.3.

10.36 No one considered with Mr Stephens how the MGN secretarial department should be operated and thus nothing was done to prevent the continuation by Mr Stephens of his practice at MCC of not circulating board papers until half an hour prior to the commencement of a board meeting[c]. Nothing was done to see that the company secretarial department operated independently of RM and that procedures were put in place for the proper operation of the board.

---

a Mr Peter Walker had been critical of board meetings being summoned without proper notice and without proper papers being available.

b It appears that RM wanted Mr Stephens to remain the secretary of MGN as RM was to retire from involvement in MCC and Mr Stephens "knew his ways".

c Mr Brookes as the newly appointed finance director at MCC was trying to remedy this at MCC. Mr Stephens told us that he did not withhold the documents - they were not made available to him.

11. THE FLOTATION: CONTROL OVER THE FINANCES OF THE COMPANY

11.1 One of the requirements of the change from a private company controlled by its proprietor into a listed company controlled by a board is the transfer of control over the finances to the board. Although it is necessary in the case of a proprietorial company to distinguish between the finances of the company and those of its proprietor, it is not unusual for the proprietor of a private company to exercise a dominant control over its finances. It is not, however, acceptable for anyone to exercise such control in a listed company.

Sources of information about RM's control over finances

11.2 The first step in order to determine what had to be done was to find out about RM's control over the finances of MGN as described at paragraphs 2.10 to 2.13. In summary RM was in a position to exercise complete control of the finances in such a manner that the finance department of MGN were unable to document some transactions or understand why some funds had been transferred. The information known to CLD about this is considered at paragraph 11.6.

11.3 The second source of information was the 1971/73 DTI Reports. These Reports had identified the following defects in financial control:

- The ability of RM to transfer monies from an account under his sole signature without the knowledge of other directors.
- The use made by RM of the funds of listed companies to discharge an indemnity given by him in his personal capacity. This had been regarded by the Inspectors as:

> "An instance of the intermingling of public and private companies' funds."[a]

11.4 Whether RM had the same degree of control (evident from both of the above) over the finances of a listed company could have been examined by reference to MCC where, although it was a listed company, he had sole signatory authority over its bank accounts for an unlimited amount. In addition, at MCC the treasury reported directly to RM and not to Mr Basil Brookes who had been appointed Acting Finance Director of MCC in August 1990 and Finance Director in November 1990. Mr Brookes was not provided with information on foreign exchange transactions or on the purchases of investments carried out by the central treasury as that department reported to RM either directly or through KM.

The information considered

11.5 Samuel Montagu appreciated that the finances of MGN had to be operated entirely independently from the finances of MCC and of the private side, and under the control of the board of MGN.

[a] 1973 DTI Report, paragraphs 838-867.

11.6 However an understanding of what needed to be done required knowledge of the way in which some treasury transactions had been carried out on the instructions of RM without the provision of documentation to the MGN finance department and also of the fact that RM had sole signatory authority over all of the accounts of his listed and private companies. CLD were aware of both these matters.

- Mr Steere (the partner in charge of the audit of MGN for the year ended 30 December 1990) and his audit managers were aware of RM's sole signatory authority at MGN, but those who comprised the reporting accountants' team were not informed of this by the audit team nor did the team discover it from their own investigations. Mr Wootten assumed that RM had sole signatory authority over the bank accounts of the private side companies, including MGN. Mr Walsh told us that he knew RM had sole signatory authority for his other private companies, but he was not sure whether he considered this in relation to the flotation; but if he had done so, he would have assumed RM did and would not have been concerned, as this was not unusual in a proprietorial company.
- In the management letter sent by CLD on 25 June 1990 reporting on matters that had come to their attention as a result of their audit of MGN for the year ended 30 December 1989 two substantial transactions[a] were identified as having been initiated by RM through the central treasury but for which no documentation was available in the MGN finance department.

  During the course of the audit of MGN for the year ended 30 December 1990 which was taking place at the same time as the work on the flotation, two further significant transactions were identified that fell into the same category of large transactions carried out through the central treasury for which there was no documentation as explained below.

  - **The purchase of MCC commercial paper in December 1990**

    A purchase of £30m nominal value MCC commercial paper for £29.6m (the reasons for which have been described at paragraph 6.68) was recorded as having been carried out through LBI or the central treasury, but only notified to the MGN finance department sometime in the course of January 1991[b]. No documentation was provided to the MGN finance department until 26 February 1991 even though the commercial paper had matured on 28 January 1991. Although a sum of £33m was paid to MGN by RMH on 12 April 1991[c], and this was subsequently said to be a sum

---

[a] One involving a foreign currency purchase of DM50m and SF50m and the other involving a loan of £35m from the National Westminster.

[b] The accounts published in the prospectus contained a reference to the commercial paper acquired in December 1990, but it was not referred to as MCC commercial paper; we were told that the omission of the reference to MCC was because the commercial paper had been repaid. KM told us that this was the type of note to accounts that RM would have been interested in and probably the type of note in respect of which RM would have demanded from CLD some flexibility.

[c] On 12 April 1991, RMG borrowed £30m from National Westminster for the period Friday 12 to Monday 15 April 1991; this sum was paid by RMG to an account at National Westminster in the name of MGN Re [RMH]; on instructions from Mr Bunn and IM (on behalf of RMH) this sum was paid to MGN from that account. IM could not recall this payment but thought that it might have formed part of the preparation of MGN's finances for the flotation. This eliminated an overdraft on an MGN bank account of £16m and produced a credit balance of £15m on the same account (after other transactions). On Monday 15 April 1991,

11.6 continued

that included the proceeds of the redemption of the commercial paper and interest thereon, no documentation was (or has since been) produced which in any way explained or evidenced that payment[a]. KM told us that he recalled Samuel Montagu expressing a preference (but no more than that) that the commercial paper not be an investment held by MGN as at flotation; Samuel Montagu strongly disagreed with this evidence. Although KM could not recall exactly, his instinct was that the repayment of the commercial paper would have been included in the £33m payment made on 12 April 1991; the only reason for the private side to make payments to MGN prior to the flotation was to establish whatever intercompany balance was required for the flotation. In relation to commercial paper the required balance had been zero at that date.

- **Interest rate cap and collar contracts**[b]

  In March 1990 the central treasury had, on the instructions of RM, entered into five contracts covering £300m of exposure to protect MGN against any rise in interest rates under the £150m facility arranged by the Toronto Dominion (see paragraph 4.33) and the equipment finance leases which had variable interest rates. These particular contracts came to the attention of CLD's audit team at the latest by 26 February 1991 when it again became apparent that these were transactions carried out on the instructions of the central treasury in respect of which the MGN finance department did not have any adequate documentation[c].

£28m was paid by MGN to RMH which RMH then paid to RMG which then repaid £30m to National Westminster. The statement of indebtedness set out in the prospectus was calculated at the close of business on 12 April 1991 and the effect of the transfer was to reduce the amount of indebtedness by £16m to £583.7m (see paragraph 15.30).

a One of the consequences of this was that it was stated in the accounts for the year ended 30 December 1990 that the commercial paper was readily convertible into cash, and in the accountants' report in the prospectus that the commercial paper had been disposed of since 30 December 1990. Mr Steere understood it had been repaid and the reporting accountants' team had been shown the bank statement which recorded the payment of £33m which CLD were told included the repayment of the sum due for the commercial paper. But on the settlement of the intercompany debt which took place on 19 April 1991 it was not treated as paid (see paragraph 15.24); this was noticed by CLD during their work on the interim results for 6 months ended 30 June 1991 (see paragraph 20.71).

b This is a transaction in which the seller makes a payment to the buyer if interest rates rise above a specified rate, the payment being calculated by reference to an agreed notional principal sum. In return the buyer pays the seller a fee for entering into the transaction. The transactions are used to enable the buyer to insure against the consequences of interest rates rising above the specified rate.

c KM told us that there was no way that documentation relating to a transaction of this scale in the ordinary course of MGN's business would not have been passed to MGN except by oversight. It was not until March 1991 that the formal documentation was provided for two of these; at 30 April 1991, the formal documentation for the other three had not been completed. These contracts are considered further at paragraph 16.23 as they were subsequently the subject of an indemnity given by the private side.

The management letter covering the audit for the year ended 30 December 1990 (subsequently sent to MGN on 26 June 1991) stated:

> "As in previous years there were a number of significant transactions affecting MGN which originated in other areas of the Maxwell organisation. In some of these cases, the documentation to support these transactions was not available within MGN."

The two examples of such transactions in 1990 cited by CLD in that letter were the acquisition of commercial paper and the cap and collar contracts to which we have referred.

KM told us that the fact there was often a lack of documentation available to MGN relating to transactions undertaken by the central treasury for MGN had been evident for years; it had also been the case for many years that reconciliation of the intercompany accounts was extremely difficult.

11.7 There is no reference in either the desktop review or the long form reports to the fact that RM had sole signatory authority over MGN's bank accounts. CLD explained to us that it was not necessary for them to draw this to the attention of Samuel Montagu since in their opinion it was not an internal control weakness and, as Samuel Montagu would (in any event) be considering the future of the treasury, bank mandates would be dealt with by Samuel Montagu and remedied through their work on the treasury. Samuel Montagu told us that they would not review bank mandates when considering the future of the treasury.

11.8 The long form report also stated:

> "The accounting systems of MGN are regularly updated and produce timely management accounts. From our review, which included reviewing recent years' audit files, no major points of weakness were identified and we are satisfied that in overall terms the financial records and accounting systems are adequate and effective."

11.9 There is no reference in either the desktop review or the long form reports to the way in which RM and the central treasury were able to initiate transactions nor to the fact that the MGN finance department did not receive adequate documentation relating to some such transactions[a]. CLD explained to us that they had sent the 1988 and 1989 management letters to Samuel Montagu (probably under cover of a compliments slip) and these letters did identify the problem[b]; but in any event, as a new treasury system was to be put into place, CLD considered that what had happened in the past was not relevant; control of transactions with related parties would be dealt with under the new arrangements. Moreover, the fact that RM initiated such

---

[a] The member of CLD's staff who drafted this explained to us that he understood that, as this was sensitive information critical of the client whom he thought was RM, it was not appropriate to include any reference to the deficiencies in the long form report, but he drew the matter to the attention of his manager to deal with in another way.

[b] Mr Steere told us that he had told Samuel Montagu (at a meeting between mid December 1990 and mid-January 1991) that the most significant difficulty with the audits of MGN was caused by the late adjustments to the accounts as a result of details of related party transactions not being relayed to MGN's management promptly. Mr Galloway had no recollection of this.

transactions personally was merely, according to CLD, an aspect of his dominant character. CLD did not consider providing information concerning MCC since what the CLD audit team for MCC[a] knew was confidential to them in their capacity as auditors to MCC and they were never asked to comment on MCC.

11.10 Samuel Montagu denied receiving either of the management letters and said they had no knowledge of RM's sole signatory authority nor of the manner in which treasury transactions were initiated by RM without documentation being passed to the MGN finance department; they expected CLD to have drawn these matters to their attention.

Steps taken in relation to MGN's control over its own finances

11.11 Only one significant decision was taken to ensure that MGN had control over its own finances - MGN was to have its own separate treasury or its own separate treasurer. Even that decision was not implemented. Accordingly the board of MGN did not have control over the disposition of MGN's funds when the flotation occurred and, as is explained in Chapters 20 and 21, they did not obtain control thereafter. So far as we have been able to discover, no one actually told RM that he should relinquish the control which he exercised over cash movements and which (after flotation) enabled him to continue to use MGN's cash flow as if nothing had changed[b]; it was assumed he would relinquish control. RM, however, always intended to go on using its cash flow, as that was essential for the needs of his other businesses in 1991, once it became clear that the price obtained on flotation was insufficient to make dependence on that cash flow unnecessary.

(a) A treasury for MGN

11.12 In 1988 the need for MGN, if it were to become a listed company, to have a separate treasury and to be in control of its own finances had been identified in a draft report produced by CLD as a key issue in the following terms:

> "As a minimum with regard to the treasury function, it seems wholly inappropriate for a quoted company not to have control over its own cash."

This issue was again identified by CLD in the desktop review as a basic issue. However during the Co-ordinating Committee meetings in January and February 1991 RM resisted the creation of a separate treasury. He told the committee that it would be administratively impossible to separate the functions carried out by the central treasury, and that to do so would be to the disadvantage of MGN and would only "satisfy the bureaucrats in the City". Consideration was therefore given to allowing a central treasury to continue to operate over MGN, but with a structure to ensure that there was no intermingling of MGN's cash with that of RM's other companies. By February 1991 Samuel Montagu had, however, come to the view that MGN should have its own treasury and by March 1991 this was accepted by RM.

---

a Mr Taberner knew of the sole signatory authority, but it had not to his knowledge been abused.

b Samuel Montagu told us that it was unnecessary to tell RM that he should relinquish control as it would have been extraordinary for RM to assume that he could continue to exercise control over cash movements.

It was their evidence that the establishment of a separate treasury for MGN was for them a *"sine qua non"* for the flotation to proceed.

11.13 KM told us that the treasury was treated no differently by the advisers from any other common service; no-one "banged the table" in relation to the issue and it was not mentioned by Samuel Montagu or CLD as being vital[a]. Towards the end of the preparations for the flotation there was a view that MGN was going to have a separate treasury but that idea was ended when RM finally focused on the point; RM, who had very strong views about the control of cash (which was one of his primary tools for operation and control of the businesses), decided that MGN would have a separate treasurer but not a separate treasury[b]. In other words, whilst MGN's existing accounting function would be enhanced by the appointment of an experienced treasurer, control of cash and use of surplus cash, including MGN's cash, was to remain under common control by the central treasury. The motivation behind that decision was, KM thought, simply that RM was going to remain 51 per cent. owner of MGN and ought therefore to retain control over its cash; in reality control over surplus cash was something that RM was never going to give up as he needed access to it for use across his companies. The way RM had operated his companies was going to continue[c].

11.14 Although RM was, according to KM, prepared to appoint a separate treasurer[d], nothing had been done either to appoint a separate treasurer or, if that was to be done, to separate the treasury by the time the prospectus was published. The treasury remained under the direct personal control of RM and not under the control of the MGN finance department or the board. Mr Galloway told us that it was not the responsibility of Samuel Montagu to see the decision had been implemented; that was a matter solely for the directors of MGN. KM told us that RM simply took a long time to settle on who the treasurer was going to be. In the end the decision was not made until after the flotation, (see paragraph 20.25).

(b) The sole signatory authority

11.15 The evidence we received from the four major clearing banks was that, whilst it was not unusual in a private company for the Chairman to have sole signatory authority for an unlimited amount, in a listed company it would be highly unusual for anyone to have such power. Although each bank was aware of the fact that RM had such power over MCC's accounts and MGN's accounts (after it had become a listed company), they have told us that as this was mandated by the board of each company, there was nothing they could have done about it.

---

a One of the lawyers said his perception of the attitude of Samuel Montagu was that the separation of the treasury was not an issue "for which they would die".

b Samuel Montagu were not told of this nor did they become aware of it.

c KM told us that the arrangements were to be as they had been for MCC for some ten years, where MCC had a Finance Director but its cash was controlled by the central treasury. These arrangements had never been the subject of adverse comment.

d The appointment of a treasurer had been discussed at co-ordinating committee meetings and Mr Craggs (a member of MGN's finance department) had been suggested. Mr Guest sent a memorandum to RM asking him to confirm the appointment of Mr Craggs on 25 April 1991.

11.16 In March 1991 the MGN finance department raised with Mr Guest the question of whether it was appropriate for RM to retain sole signatory authority once MGN became a listed company. Mr Guest decided, after speaking to Mr Basil Brooks at MCC and discovering from him that RM had sole signatory authority in that company, that it was not practicable for him to ask RM to agree to a change since to do so would be to question his honesty. He never raised the issue with the outside advisers or the non-executive directors. No other director who knew of RM's sole signatory authority took any action.

11.17 In the result RM's sole signatory authority on MGN's accounts continued[a].

(c) RM's continued ability to initiate treasury transactions without proper documentation

11.18 Nothing effective was done to curtail RM's ability to initiate treasury transactions and to transfer funds from MGN, though a small step was taken by MGN's finance department. At the end of April 1991, MGN's cashier (who had been used to funds being transferred to or from the private side in respect of which the only documentation he would receive would be a transfer authority) was instructed by Mr Hemple, MGN's deputy finance director, to record on a schedule any transaction that occurred for which proper documentation evidencing its purpose was unavailable. The cashier monitored the daily cash balances on MGN's accounts and was therefore aware when any monies were transferred to or from MGN's accounts. However, whilst this schedule made it easier to identify transactions by which moneys were transferred in or out of MGN's accounts without adequate explanation[b], nothing was done by the directors or anyone else to address the real problem of obtaining adequate documentation and preventing such transfers.

11.19 The fact that nothing was done to remedy the ability of the central treasury to transfer MGN's funds is exemplified in the days immediately prior to the flotation not only by the payment to MGN on 12 April 1991 of £33m which was attributed (without the provision of documentation) to the repayment of £29.6m commercial paper purchased in December 1990 (as referred to in paragraph 11.6), but also by the following transactions:

- 15 April 1991 payment by MGN of £28m to RMH;
- 29 April 1991 payment by MGN of £5m to National Westminster Capital Markets Ltd;
- 30 April 1991 payment by MGN of £24.8m to National Westminster Capital Markets Ltd.

No documentation was provided to the MGN finance department in support of these three significant payments. We have been unable to ascertain any specific reason for the payment of £28m unless it was to repay the National Westminster facility for £30m made available between 12 and 15 April 1991 (referred to in the footnote to paragraph 11.6) or as part of the general need of the private side for cash as described in chapter 9. The two payments made

---

a MGN Limited, as the new operating company, took over the accounts of MGN.

b Explanations were obtained for some transactions, but as set out in chapters 20 and 21 there were transactions that remained unexplained or undocumented.

on 29 and 30 April 1991 were explained to the MGN finance department in late May 1991 as having been made to acquire MCC commercial paper[a]. No documentation in support of this explanation was produced to MGN until after RM's death[b]; we have satisfied ourselves from documentation provided by National Westminster that the funds were indeed used for that purpose. KM told us that this transaction probably occurred because MCC needed the money in the period prior to the anticipated receipt of the proceeds of the sale of the scientific journals business in mid-May (see paragraph 9.10)[c]. These payments did not come to the attention of CLD, in their work as reporting accountants; the payments were not reported to Samuel Montagu.

11.20 The fact that these substantial sums of money were transferred in this way, the last transfer being made on the day of the publication of the prospectus, exemplifies the absence of independent control over the finances of MGN by its board and finance director at the moment of flotation and the complete control RM exercised[d].

11.21 Not only was the lack of documentation a problem in the control of transfers of sums of money out of MGN but also in the explanation of sums transferred to MGN. The transfer of £33m into MGN on 12 April 1991 is one example of this. On 29 and 30 April 1991 £8m and £7.5m were transferred by RMH into MGN. Again there was no documentation provided to the MGN finance department which explained these payments and we have been unable to discover any specific reason for the payments on 29 and 30 April 1991 other than the possibility that it was an attempt to try and balance the account between MGN and other private side companies.

(d) The restricted role of the finance director

11.22 Mr Guest's experience throughout his career had been restricted to the financial aspects of the operational side of MGN's business; he had had virtually no dealings with the banks, external finances having been dealt with by the central treasury[e]. Whether or not it was appropriate to appoint Mr Guest Finance Director of MGN as a listed company had been considered in 1988 and was again considered during 1991. KM was very keen that Mr Stoney be appointed Finance Director since he was a very competent accountant, got on well with auditors, was extremely interested in management information systems, and was a very competent presenter

---

a This was repaid on 21 May 1991 as mentioned at paragraph 20.19 below.

b The payment of £24.8m on 30 April 1991 was made on the signatures of IM and Mr Bunn. IM could not recall this payment and could not recall having been told that it was for the purchase of MCC commercial paper.

c RM would have viewed the use of commercial paper as a permitted route for intercompany movement of funds (see paragraphs 6.61 and 15.36).

d KM told us that he agreed with this conclusion but that RM would not have thought these payments to be wrong at the time; MCC was due to receive shortly a large sum from the sale of the scientific journals business and so would be in a position to repay the commercial paper.

e Samuel Montagu considered that this would not make any difference as he was to be the finance director of a pure newspaper business; as MGN had the new £150m facility (as described at paragraph 15.34), it was not anticipated that MGN would be engaged in negotiations with financial institutions for the foreseeable future. KM told us that it was clear that MGN would have new deals, bond issues and the like after the float and that Mr Guest would not be equipped to manage them; Samuel Montagu did not accept this.

to analysts and financial institutions; he had, in KM's view, a range of skills that Mr Guest could not match. KM sought the support of Samuel Montagu for the appointment of Mr Stoney as the senior financial director[a], whilst leaving Mr Guest to continue with his responsibilities in the operational role, but did not receive it. The view taken was that the Finance Director should be someone with experience of running newspapers. RM decided that Mr Guest be appointed Finance Director and he was so described in the prospectus[b]. It was mooted that Mr Stoney be given the title Deputy Managing Director (Finance) which was a title used within RM's companies for a very senior director (senior to any Finance Director) who dealt with what can be described as corporate finance activities in contrast to operational accounting activities[c]. However, Samuel Montagu said that the title would be confusing and it was not used.

11.23 This left the role of Mr Stoney undefined as he was not appointed to any specific position. A large number of those who worked as advisers on the flotation told us how impressed they were with his command of financial information and his ability to present it. He was thought to be more adept at presentations to the investment community and to banks than Mr Guest (despite Mr Guest's substantial knowledge of the operational finances of the business) and it was therefore decided that in presentations to potential institutional investors both in the UK and overseas Mr Stoney would represent the company rather than Mr Guest. On these occasions he was described as "commercial director".

11.24 As set out at paragraph 6.65 the £360m facility obtained for MGN in October 1990 had been negotiated principally by KM with the assistance of Mr Bunn. During the flotation when a new £150m facility for MGN was negotiated (as described at paragraph 15.34) it was Mr Stoney rather than Mr Guest who assisted KM and Mr Bunn in the work.

11.25 Consequently at the time of flotation Mr Stoney understood that he would continue to deal with corporate finance matters, the banks and the analysts[d]. Although this position was not formalised by RM until 20 May 1991 (in the circumstances described at paragraph 20.22), at the date of the publication of the prospectus the real position was that Mr Guest would not fulfil the usual role of a Finance Director and Mr Stoney, although a director of several private side companies, had taken on a significant role in MGN's finances.

---

a He did this at a meeting as early as 28 November 1990 attended by Mr McIntosh and Mr Galloway.

b KM told us that RM was much influenced by the management of MGN who did not want an outsider as Finance Director. This was important to RM, as Mr Guest had skillfully managed the relationship with the editorial staff for a number of years. KM told RM at the time that having both Mr Guest and Mr Stoney on the board dealing with finance matters would lead to turf wars and that proved to be the case (see paragraph 20.21).

c Mr Stoney was appointed by RM to this position on 21 October 1991 as described at paragraph 21.56 below.

d KM told us that dealing with analysts was part of the constant task of trying to build an audience for a public company's shares so that there was an available market (for example, for a rights issue) when necessary. Similarly, dealing with the banks was a regular activity as RM had accepted in the summer of 1990 the need to keep the banks informed on a regular basis even if there was no specific transaction in mind.

(e) The role of KM

11.26 It was the clear intention that after flotation there be a complete separation between MGN and MCC. To this end it was decided that KM could not be a director of MGN nor have any responsibilities or authority at MGN since he was to be Chief Executive of MCC. He was removed from MGN's bank mandates. KM told us that the emphasis in relation to his role was always one of being able to market the issue and not one of proper corporate governance; there had to be a clearly drawn line between MGN and MCC[a]. Samuel Montagu told us that this was not the case and there were good reasons why KM was not to be a director of MGN[b]. As explained at paragraph 4.59, the banks had generally regarded RM's companies as one exposure when considering their overall position, but this approach of the banks does not seem to have been appreciated by those advising[c] on the flotation nor by any of the independent directors of MGN. Thus during the days immediately prior to the flotation (and thereafter as set out at paragraph 20.29) the banks continued to deal with KM concerning the strategy of MGN's borrowings. For example, it was KM who negotiated the £15m facility for MGN with Barclays in April 1991 (referred to at paragraph 15.40) and it was KM who gave an assurance on behalf of MGN that it was unlikely to be drawn down. KM told us that there was no change in his role. Prior to the float he had dealt with MGN matters as the representative of the family and, in particular, RM; he had no executive responsibility. Similarly, after the flotation (although he was no longer a director of MGN) he still acted as RM's emissary, acting on his instructions and on his behalf. It was in this capacity he had dealt with the banks and continued to do so.

(f) The reporting system

11.27 One small step was taken by Samuel Montagu, but it proved in practice irrelevant to the issue of control. Samuel Montagu were keen to ensure that there be an adequate financial reporting system for MGN and raised this matter with CLD. Accordingly Mr McNab, a partner in CLD with considerable experience in management accounting was retained to provide a preliminary report on management reporting systems. On 9 April 1991 he produced a report on a format for monthly reports to the MGN board. Mr Stoney told us that he worked on this project and

---

[a] Part of that process of separation, KM told us, was a push made in February 1991 by Sir Michael Richardson for RM not to be the Chairman of both MCC and MGN. When it was clear that RM would not give up the chairmanship of MGN, Sir Michael Richardson proposed that RM should not be Chairman of MCC and that some other candidate (he suggested Mr Peter Walker and others) ought to be appointed (see paragraph 9.10). Sir Michael Richardson told us that RM emphasised on a number of occasions that he was most anxious to keep MGN entirely independent of his other interests after the flotation. Sir Michael Richardson had no idea that KM would have any responsibility for MGN's banking relationships after the flotation.

[b] (1) As the chief executive officer of MCC, he would spend the vast majority of his time at MCC; (2) he had no operational involvement in MGN; (3) he would not have been an independent director for the purposes of related party dealings; (4) the interests of the family were adequately represented.

[c] Mr Kheraj of SBIL did appreciate this although he considered that the banks would treat their individual exposure to MGN differently to their exposure to MCC or the private side. Whilst he thought that RM would not have any day-to-day responsibility for the banking relationships of MGN, Mr Kheraj expected KM to play a role as the representative of the majority shareholder and give assistance (together with RM) in respect of the broader relationships between the banks and companies controlled by RM.

was in favour of it[a] but there was resistance to change from some within the MGN finance department and Mr McNab was not retained to complete his work. Nonetheless, the finance department made improvements to the management accounts that it produced.

11.28 Although the improvements to the reports meant that better information was available to the board about the business, the improvements did not in any way address the deficiencies to which we have referred in the preceding paragraphs, as the system reported only what was known by the finance department.

---

[a] KM told us that he was informed by Mr Stoney that the information systems at MGN were not adequate by the standards of the rest of RM's companies and KM told RM that better quality information was required.

12. CONTROL OVER THE RELATIONSHIP WITH THE MAJORITY SHAREHOLDER AT FLOTATION

12.1 The need to ensure that the relations between MGN and other Maxwell interests were properly regulated was raised when considering the proposed flotation in 1988 (as described at paragraph 4.7). This was an area also identified in the desktop review of January 1991 and there was a consensus among those concerned on the flotation as to the necessity for appropriate arrangements to be made.

12.2 Indeed, more detailed attention was given to this particular aspect of control by the independent directors, than to the more general issues of control over management and financial controls discussed in the two preceding chapters. The reason behind this was that Samuel Montagu were well aware that there would be no prospect of MGN being floated successfully if such arrangements were not put in place, since it was a requirement of the Stock Exchange (and the perception of others) that there must be proper arrangements to ensure fair treatment of the minority shareholders in MGN.

12.3 There were two quite separate questions to be addressed:

(1) The need to control trading relationships and any other dealings between MGN and MCC and the private side companies.

(2) The need to establish proper arrangements to regulate the use that might be made of RM's majority control.

(1) Control over dealings with related parties

12.4 There were three significant areas to be considered - the provision of group services, commercial trading relationships and the problem of competition.

(a) Group services

12.5 When RM's companies had comprised only one major listed company and a number of different private side companies, various arrangements had developed under which MCC provided certain of its services on a group basis to the private side and under which the private side provided services to MCC. Examples of these group services were the central treasury and the common company secretariat already referred to but other instances included car fleet services, insurance and property management. CLD were commissioned to carry out a review of all of these services and to advise which services it would be appropriate for MGN to be provided with on a group basis and to recommend in such cases the terms on which services should be provided. CLD's report was reviewed and considered by some of the operational directors of MGN, by KM and Mr Stoney on behalf of the private side and by Mr Basil Brookes for MCC; agreements between MGN, the private side and MCC for the provision of such services were then drafted by Clifford Chance and Titmuss Sainer & Webb. It was agreed that the costs of the services would be reviewed annually by the auditors and they would provide an opinion as to whether the costs were fair and reasonable.

12.6 A sentence was inserted into the prospectus stating that any variation of these agreements had to be approved by a majority of the independent directors of MGN and this commitment was approved by the MGN board on 16 April 1991.

12.7 Apart from the fact that one joint project between MGN, MCC and the private side (known as project DIMPE)[a] was omitted, the agreements were to give rise to no problems after flotation.

(b) Trading relations

12.8 The principal trading relationship outside group services was between a subsidiary of MGN and The European Limited relating to the printing of *The European*; a contract was drawn up to regulate that relationship after the flotation.

12.9 The special provision in MGN's Articles (to which we referred at paragraph 10.26) disentitled RM, IM and Mr Stoney (because of their position as employees of, or shareholders in, related parties) from voting on any resolution of the board concerning any contract with a related party[b]. It was the intention of Samuel Montagu that all such dealings be subject to the control of the independent directors of MGN, but, although related party issues were raised with the directors, no procedures were put in place to ensure that transactions with related parties were brought to the attention of the board. It may have been anticipated that the relevant director would report the matter to the board but nothing appears to have been done by Samuel Montagu to ensure that there were procedures within MGN (such as a requirement that accounting and other staff identify and report any such transaction) to enable this to happen; Samuel Montagu told us they did not regard this as their responsibility. Although in principle the terms of the arrangements seemed entirely appropriate, there were in fact no procedures to ensure that the board controlled what happened[c].

12.10 The position was made more difficult to control by the way in which the intercompany debt between MGN and MCC and the private side was settled as part of the arrangements made on flotation. The intercompany loan account through which all transactions between MGN and the private side were processed had two constituent elements (see paragraph 2.16)

- The hard core account to which the asset transfers and surplus cash were charged on the basis that they would never be repaid.

---

[a] This was a project with the European Commission to develop multi-media publishing; it was noted by the reporting accountants' team but not mentioned in the long form report by name; nor did the long form report refer to the involvement of MCC in the project which entailed estimated charges by MCC to MGN of £693,000 in 1991. This possible contravention of the ring fence was never brought to the attention of IM, whom RM had given the role of chairing the project.

[b] A provision of the non-competition agreement between RM, the private side and Samuel Montagu prevented this article being altered; the effect was to prevent alteration of the group service agreement and to prevent trading with the private side without the consent of the independent directors.

[c] An example of this relates to Project DIMPE. In July 1991 after the flotation, advice was sought by the MCC legal department on behalf of MGN from Clifford Chance about Project DIMPE. Clifford Chance advised that the agreements should be submitted to the independent directors for approval, but this was not done.

- The trading accounts which were settled between the companies from time to time on normal trading terms.

12.11 When the intercompany debt was settled by means of the payment of a dividend by MGN as described at paragraph 15.13, the hard core account was settled but the trading accounts were not. Accordingly when MGN changed from being one of several companies that was wholly owned by RM's interests, to being a listed company where trading relationships with the other private companies were strictly regulated, no line was drawn on the intercompany account to separate what had been past transactions between private companies from what were to be future trading transactions subject to the strict control of the independent directors of MGN. As there was no clean break and no agreement on the composition of the balances prior to the publication of the prospectus on 30 April 1991, the balances had to be sorted out thereafter. Because the documentation and records in respect of the intercompany balances were not always adequate (as the transaction involving commercial paper exemplifies), the opportunity was provided for funds to be moved between MGN and the private side under the guise of adjustments to the balances. Instances of what took place in April 1991 have been referred to at paragraphs 11.19 to 11.21.

(c) Competition

12.12 RM held through his private side companies various competing newspaper interests. An agreement was made giving the right of first refusal to MGN to purchase *The European* and certain other newspaper interests upon any disposal by the private side. At the instigation of the Stock Exchange, HI undertook not to compete in the newspaper business for a period of five years.

12.13 No material issues arise out of this restriction.

The "ring fence"

12.14 The term "ring fence" is commonly used to describe a structure created around a subsidiary company to prohibit its assets being transferred to another part of a group or to a parent company, or as Mr Kheraj of SBIL said:

> "it means that everything that is inside it, you keep inside it"

It is, therefore, hardly surprising that many understood that term at the time[a] (and most have understood it subsequently) as referring to the imposition of controls over RM to prevent him misusing the assets of MGN. KM told us that he agreed with Mr Kheraj's view of the term "ring fence"; it was a banking term referring to the bankers' aim to keep a company's cash flow within the company. However, at the time of the flotation of MGN, it was KM's view that the term was not used to describe anything other than the banking covenants in the £150m

[a] Samuel Montagu and most of the other advisers did not think this term was used until the autumn of 1991, but we received substantial evidence that it was used during the flotation.

facility[a] – it was never perceived by him that the advisers on the flotation or the banks thought that controls had to be put in place to prevent RM misusing assets.

12.15 Samuel Montagu also told us that they never believed such controls to be necessary to prevent RM misusing the assets of MGN, as they never thought RM would misuse the assets of MGN. They considered that the imposition of the related party arrangements described in this chapter, the appointment of a board including non-executive directors and the establishment of an audit committee would be sufficient (as described in chapter 10). Samuel Montagu told us that when the term came subsequently to be used in relation to MGN in the autumn of 1991, they understood it as a colloquial expression for the controls that they had put in place to deal with related party transactions described in this chapter.

(2) Proper exercise of majority control

12.16 When drafting of the prospectus began, it was the general assumption of all involved that the Maxwell Foundation exercised control over MGN's parent company, RMG, and so would ultimately control the majority shareholding in MGN. However, in late March 1991, it came to light that the Maxwell Foundation had passed to HI the ability to control the composition of the board of RMG (in circumstances set out at paragraph 4.63) and it became necessary for the advisers to consider whether MGN in fact had two parent companies - the Maxwell Foundation and HI - and, if so, how this should be dealt with in the prospectus. Because arrangements for the proper exercise of majority control would be required, it was important to identify who controlled MGN.

(a) The fourth reorganisation of ownership

12.17 Samuel Montagu requested sight of the agreement by which HI had been given control of RMG but RM declined to provide it, just as he declined to provide documents relating to the Maxwell Foundation[b]. Mr Woods was then asked by RM to consider whether or not the companies could be reorganised so as to eliminate control of RMG by the Maxwell Foundation. By 13 April 1991 Mr Woods had prepared a scheme to put to the board of PHA that met in Zurich[c]. A complicated scheme was carried out, the effect of which was to pass a controlling shareholding in RMG from the Maxwell Foundation to HI in return for the issue to the Maxwell Foundation of loan stock in HI which was immediately converted into preference shares. This reorganisation was effected on 15 April 1991 and full control of RMG, and hence MGN, was passed to HI.

---

a These covenants, which are referred to at paragraph 15.35, were derived from the covenants in the £360m facility set out in paragraph 6.61.

b Mr Morgenstern told us that this refusal was an example of RM's "need to know philosophy" - RM did not like lawyers and accountants knowing things. A legal opinion by Meier & Wolf (counsel to the Maxwell Foundation and lawyers in Vaduz, Liechtenstein) setting out the status and objectives of the Maxwell Foundation was provided to the advisers.

c Amongst the reasons recorded in the minutes of PHA for their agreement to the change was the desire to have an investment in a more conservative form guaranteeing a regular income and the need to give the Maxwell family "real incentive to continue to build for the future".

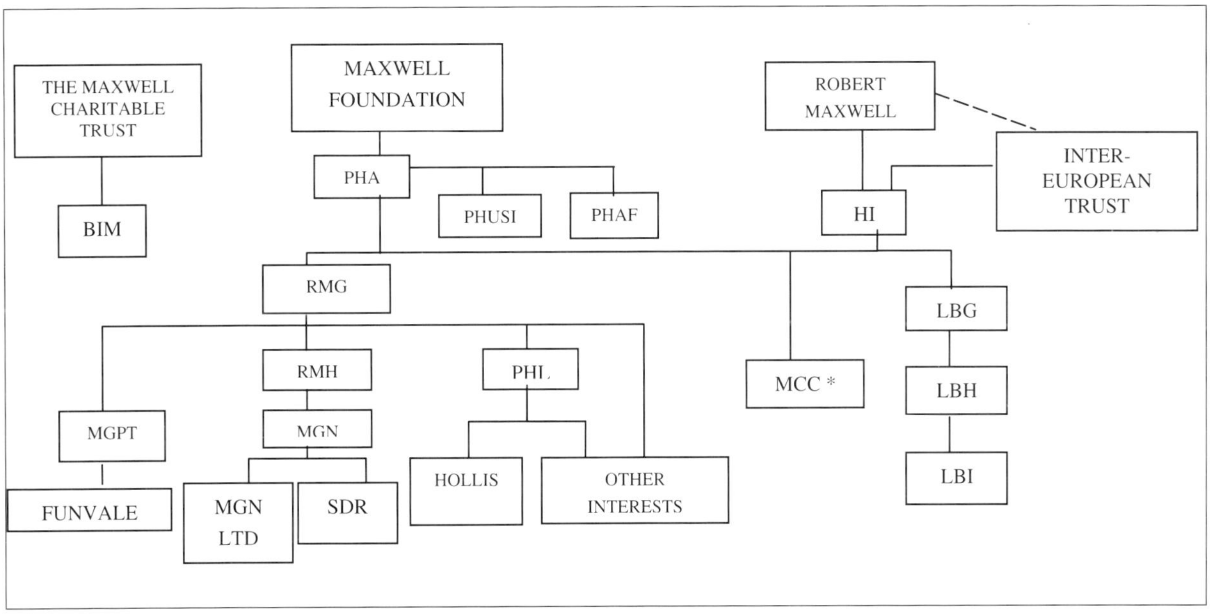

Figure 5 Ownership after 15 April 1991 (main companies only)
* MCC shareholding partly held through subsidiaries including Visford, Magnacell and PHAI.

12.18 Accordingly, for the purpose of making disclosure in the prospectus the advisers decided that it was sufficient to make disclosure in respect of HI only and to state that HI was controlled by RM and his family. Although InterEuropean Trust did own 51 per cent. of the shares in HI, it did so for the sole beneficial interest of RM and his family; its role in this respect (as explained in paragraph 3.27) had been solely to give effect of a stamp duty saving scheme. It was not considered necessary to disclose this interest.

12.19 It was also decided that it was not necessary to make extensive disclosure[a] in respect of the Maxwell Foundation because, after the fourth reorganisation of ownership, it had no form of control over, but only an economic interest in, MGN.

(b) The undertakings given

12.20 The change in the ultimate ownership of MGN from the Maxwell Foundation to HI considerably simplified the giving of the necessary undertakings for the proper exercise of majority control, as these could now be given by a company known to be controlled by RM and his family. Accordingly, an undertaking was given that the voting rights of the shares controlled by RM and his family would be exercised so as to maintain a majority of independent directors on the board of MGN and to ensure that there be at least two non-executive directors on that board. HI gave a separate undertaking that it would ensure that its relationship with MGN would not result in any conflict of interest for MGN between its obligation to HI and its duty to the general body of its shareholders.

12.21 No material issue arose from these arrangements.

---

[a] The prospectus referred to its status as a Foundation and to its charitable objectives on the basis of the legal opinion provided.

(c) Arrangements to maintain stability in the shareholding

12.22 Because of the market's perception of the way in which dealings in MCC shares had occurred[a] and because the banks had insisted on a covenant being inserted into the £150m loan facility to the effect that RM and his interests would maintain a 51 per cent. shareholding in MGN, an agreement was made under which RM and his interests agreed neither to acquire nor to dispose of MGN shares without the consent of Samuel Montagu until after publication of the interim statement of MGN for the six months ending 30 June 1992.

12.23 There was discussion as to whether RM and his interests would be entitled to pledge the shares comprised in their 51 per cent. shareholding in MGN. KM told us that it had originally been suggested by Samuel Montagu that pledging would not be permitted but that RM had reacted against that view and insisted on retaining the ability to pledge. Samuel Montagu agreed that it would be unreasonable to prevent RM from being able to make such use of valuable assets and the right to pledge was specifically referred to in the agreements restricting sale or acquisition of shares; the description of the agreement in the prospectus did not refer to the right of pledge but only to restrictions on disposal, sale and transfer. It was considered that the restriction on sale or purchase was sufficient for the purposes of flotation, though inherent in any pledge was the right of the bank to enforce its security and sell the shares and so put MGN in breach of the terms of its main borrowing facility[b].

---

a See paragraph 7.14.

b KM told us that he did not regard the covenant to maintain a 51 per cent. shareholding as being of great importance; it was a requirement that was not set in stone. So, at the end of September 1991, the syndicate of banks within the £150m loan facility, after a request by KM, indicated their agreement to the deletion of the covenant (see the footnote to paragraph 21.73).

13. THE ADEQUACY OF THE ARRANGEMENTS FOR THE PENSION SCHEMES AT FLOTATION

The scope of work required on the flotation

13.1 To ensure that proper disclosure was made and that due diligence had been exercised[a], it was appreciated by the advisers that it was necessary to investigate the pension arrangements of MGN; this was done against the background that the flotation was not a flotation of the pension schemes and the importance of the pension funds to the flotation was the impact that the fortunes of the funds might have on the company. It was appreciated that this was particularly important in the case of MGN because of the contribution of the pension fund surplus to the profit projections of MGN.

13.2 There were two separate but uncoordinated investigations into the pension schemes:

- CLD provided a long form report on the pension schemes[b];
- Clifford Chance and Linklaters & Paines also obtained a lot of detailed factual information about the pension schemes.

The respective functions of CLD, Clifford Chance and Linklaters & Paines in the investigations are set out in Appendix 10. Apart from one meeting on 5 April 1991 which the solicitors and CLD both attended in conjunction with the other advisers, the investigations were entirely separate. CLD do not appear to have been made aware of what the solicitors were doing and the solicitors were not provided with a draft of the long form report until after their work had been completed and the prospectus finalised.

The way in which the funds had been operated

13.3 The way in which the pension funds had been operated has been referred to at paragraphs 2.20 to 2.48, 5.1 to 5.49, 6.4 to 6.7, 6.18 to 6.31 and 9.25 to 9.44. It is sufficient here to summarise five respects in which the operation of the pension funds were (and would have been regarded at the time as) material to the flotation:

(a) Investment in related companies

As described at paragraphs 5.19 and 6.18, the CIF had made significant purchases of MCC shares from 1988 onwards with substantial purchases being made in September 1990. In addition MGPS had made what in effect were loans to MCC through the

---

[a] When considering what was required to be done on the flotation of MGN in respect of the pension scheme it is of particular importance to ensure that hindsight is not used to judge what in fact was done. Nevertheless the fact that there was a contemporary perception in 1991 of the need to investigate and make disclosure about the arrangements for the pension schemes is demonstrated by:

(1) The fact that the surplus in MGPS meant that MGN was not projected to make any contributions to the scheme for some years and this fact was taken into account in profit projections for the company.

(2) The fact that the prospectus contained more than a half page description of the pension arrangements which set out the investments made by the schemes in related party controlled companies and the related party aspects of the management of the pension schemes' investments.

[b] This took the form of one of the supplements to the summary long form report on MGN. We refer to it is as the long form report on pensions.

13.3 continued

purchase of MCC commercial paper from July 1990 onwards as referred to at paragraph 6.26. For some time prior to and at 30 April 1991, the amount lent in this way was £15m.

(b) Loans of cash to the private side

By April 1991 the amount owed by the private side companies (principally RMG) to the CIF was about £100m. This figure is exclusive of the £108m[a] which was meant to have been discharged by the agreement to transfer the shares in Invesco MIM and Scitex by documents dated 29 June 1990[b] but which were never delivered to the CIF or re-registered. Borrowing from the pension funds had originated in 1985 in the way described in paragraphs 2.45 and 5.23.

(c) Related party dealings

There had been for a period a significant number of transactions, primarily between the CIF and the private side and MCC, which had resulted in the pension schemes and CIF becoming a repository for many of the investments that had had to be disposed of by the private side/MCC in order to raise cash. Examples (apart from the transfer of the shares in Scitex and Invesco MIM referred to in the preceding paragraph) included:

- the transfer to the pension scheme in 1986 of an interest in Reuters A shares for £33.5m and the retransfer in 1989 for £27.6m;
- the transfer of shares to the value of £54.9m in Société Générale in November 1988;
- the transfer by documents dated 2 October 1989 of shares to the value of £77m in Euris SA, Marceau Investissements, Quebecor, Banco Commercial Portugues and other companies;
- the transfer for £20m from MCC by agreements dated 29 March 1990 of a parcel of shares which were largely unquoted.

Although the transactions appear to have been at arms length prices, these transactions had not been subject to any scrutiny by the independent trustees of MGPS.

RM had also used the pension funds for the purposes of his other interests. Examples include:

- The purchase of Strand House (Maxwell House) in New Fetter Lane in 1986.
- Loans to Robert Fraser Group.

---

a The Invesco MIM shares were sold in March 1991 (as set out at paragraph 9.25) and £33.87m was paid to the CIF. On the same day that £33.87m was received by the CIF, £35m was paid by the CIF to RMG. The payment of £35m is included within the figure of £100m owed by the private side to the CIF in April 1991.

b See paragraph 6.5

(d) Use of shares by the private side as collateral

This had begun in 1988

- In the year to 5 April 1990 shares from the CIF had been used as collateral for loans to the private side from National Westminster, Morgan Stanley and Crédit Lyonnais, but no shares remained pledged to these banks at 5 April 1990.
- As at 5 April 1990 shares[a] from the directly managed portfolio of the CIF and the portfolio managed by LBI were pledged to Lehmans to secure financing of approximately $50m under the arrangements made in November 1989 (see paragraph 5.39).
- After 5 April 1990, shares from the CIF were used as collateral for loans to the private side from a number of banks. From October 1990 the shares in the MGPS portfolios managed by CCM and MIM were also used as collateral for such loans, including the increase in the financing provided by Lehmans, as set out in paragraph 6.26.

At 30 April 1991 the shares of the CIF, MGPS and MCWPS being used by the private side as collateral for loans amounted to a value of about £270m[b].

(e) The way the CIF was managed and its domination by RM

There were the serious deficiencies in both the internal controls and administration of BIM and over its investment policy outlined at paragraph 5.8 to paragraph 0.

The accounts of the pension schemes and the CIF which were subject to audit

13.4 Although the Stock Exchange would not normally be prepared to admit a company to listing where the latest financial period reported on ended more than 6 months before the date of flotation, there was no such policy in respect of the accounts of the pension fund of the company. Indeed, sometimes the audit of a pension fund had a low priority; whereas the audited accounts of a listed company were required to be issued within seven months of the year end, the accounts of a pension fund were sometimes produced twelve months or more after the year end. In the case of MGPS and the CIF, work on the audit for the year ended 5 April 1990 had (as described at paragraph 9.38) commenced in the autumn of 1990[c] and much work was still being performed on that audit in December 1990 and January 1991. The accounts of the CIF for the year ended 5 April 1990 were only signed on 1 March 1991, the accounts of MGPS for the year ended 5 April 1990 were not signed until 4 April 1991 and those of the MCWPS were still in draft at the date of the flotation.

---

a Some shares owned by the CIF were also deposited with BNP under the arrangements described at paragraph 5.39.

b This figure includes the Scitex shares (then worth £75m) which it had been agreed were to be transferred to the CIF by documents dated 29 June 1990, but which had not been delivered to the CIF or re-registered.

c Apart from a scrip count of the central assets of the CIF held at Maxwell House that had taken place at Maxwell House on 5 April 1990.

13.5 No accounts of the CIF or the pension schemes were produced for the year ended 5 April 1991 because the trustees of MGPS agreed to extend the financial year of the scheme at a meeting on 26 March 1991[a]. We were told that the suggestion was made by RM or KM that the accounting date of the scheme should be changed to be the same date as that of MGN and, as the trustees were advised that the legislation did not permit the shortening of the financial year to a nine month period, the accounting period was extended to a 21 month period ending on 31 December 1991[b]. KM told us that, with hindsight, this had to do with RM postponing the need to put the balance sheet back into whatever shape was required or desired. Because of the decision to extend the accounting period, a scrip count[c] of the assets of the pension schemes and the CIF did not take place on 5 April 1991. As explained at paragraph 13.34, a special financial review at 31 December 1990 was undertaken, but this proceeded on the basis that the assets were assumed to exist. No check on the existence of the assets was made.

The information considered by the advisers on the flotation

13.6 Before we set out the information actually considered by the advisers on the flotation in relation to the matters to which we have referred at paragraph 13.3 (in the light of which they made the disclosure in the prospectus and embarked upon the performance of their due diligence obligations), it is necessary to refer to the position of CLD as reporting accountants. The letter of instructions from Samuel Montagu specified:

> "Your long form report should cover the matters set out in the attached Appendix, together with such further matters as appear appropriate in the course of your work."

The Appendix included:

> "2(h) Details of pension arrangements, including details of latest actuarial valuations."

> "9(h) An analysis of the current funding position on MGN's pension scheme, with particular reference to the company's accounting treatment of pension costs."

13.7 The reporting accountants' team took three views of their instructions that are of considerable significance:

- They considered that their obligation in respect of details of pension arrangements was limited to such matters as the fund name and type, details of membership and contribution rates; it was not their function to report on matters such as the management of the pension scheme.

---

a The board of MCWPS approved the change of the accounting period on 13 June 1991; there is no board minute of BIM approving any such change for the CIF.

b Mr Guest questioned the wisdom of this as he did not see how the audit of the pension scheme, which had always taken a year, would ever be ready within the period within which MGN as a listed company would be expected to announce its preliminary results after its year end or the 7 months for the audited accounts. He was, however, told by Mr Cook that the backlog within the pensions administration department would be cleared and that the audit could be carried out in a short period.

c Documents of title to investments (such as share certificates) were physically examined and compared to the books and records.

- They considered that it was their obligation as reporting accountants only to report in the long form report on the pension scheme up to the date of the latest audited accounts (5 April 1990).
- They did not consider that they had to examine any of the MAPs relating to the CIF- the documents containing a summary of the main points arising on the CIF audit work for the attention of the partner - or any of the detailed audit papers, whether of the CIF or of the pension schemes.

This meant that CLD as reporting accountants did very little to examine what had happened in relation to MGPS or MCWPS in the year that had elapsed since 5 April 1990 and did nothing to examine the CIF where over half MGPS's assets were administered "in house" by a company controlled by RM, save to look at the accounts. They told us Samuel Montagu knew that over half of the assets were managed in the CIF, but Samuel Montagu never instructed CLD to investigate the CIF.

13.8 Samuel Montagu told us that they disagreed strongly with the views of CLD in relation to their duties and did not understand why CLD adopted these views and did not check Samuel Montagu's acceptance of them. Samuel Montagu told us that the reporting accountants' role on pensions was in their view essentially no different to their role on other aspects of the flotation; they considered that to obtain a proper appreciation of the assets of MGPS, it was necessary for the reporting accountants to consider the assets of the CIF which could easily have been done by looking at the MAPs relating to the CIF.

13.9 Mr Cowling was provided with a preliminary draft of the long form report on pensions on 24 March 1991. In a short note[a] annotated on that draft he drew specific attention to what were in fact the issues of self-investment (including the arrangement between the CIF and IBI) and the use of CIF shares as collateral; he also briefly explained his observations to the senior manager in the reporting accountants' team. After these matters had been drawn to their attention, the senior manager in the reporting accountants' team

- decided to make enquiries about all the matters to which Mr Cowling had referred and in respect of two of them (items 3 and 4 - see the footnote below) in so far as there had been any material developments after 5 April 1990. We were told that they did this because they regarded the matters as falling within the general words of their instructions set out in paragraph 13.6 above. Apart from that, the long form report did not deal with any matters that had occurred after 5 April 1990[b].

---

a His note read:

"1. List of top twenty investments will flag the related parties
2. Also watch the cash balance and any interest offset arrangements
3. IBI arrangement
4. Collateral swap post year end but prefloat?"

By item 1, Mr Cowling told us he was referring to self-investment. His reference to the collateral swap is further explained at paragraph 13.25.

b The covering letter to that report stated that they had examined the audited accounts and unaudited management information to 31 December 1990, but we were told this was an error as it replicated the covering letters for the reports on MGN where the passage in the letter correctly described the position. Mr Kheraj told us that SBIL relied on the date of 31 December 1990.

- did not carry out any review of the CIF. The team made no comments on the operation of the CIF, other than to describe the ownership of BIM and the members of its board.

13.10 No written instructions were given to Clifford Chance or Linklaters & Paines; they did what they understood solicitors instructed on a flotation normally do (see Appendix 10). They dealt with matters for the purposes of their investigation and drafted the prospectus by reference to the position at 5 April 1990; they obtained from Mr Cook, as part of the verification of the prospectus, an assurance that there had been no material change after that date[a].

(a) Investment in related companies

13.11 The long form report specifically identified those investments that were self-investment as at 5 April 1990 and also the IBI transaction (referred to at paragraph 5.21) which was described thus:

> "At 5 April 1990 there was an outstanding stock swap option with IBI Holdings. CIF agreed to purchase shares of IBI Holdings who in turn agreed to purchase shares in [MCC]. Since 5 April 1990, both parties have exercised the option on these shares."

The paragraph did not refer to the size of the transaction nor did the long form report refer to the sale by RM on behalf of the CIF on 26 March 1990 of 7.9 million shares in MCC to BIT (see paragraph 5.21), as the reporting accountants' team did not know of it.

13.12 The impact of the IBI transaction in reducing the self-investment at 5 April 1990 was not apparent to those who read the long form report; furthermore the meaning of this paragraph in the report was not clear and the significance of the transaction in demonstrating how RM was using the pension funds could only have been understood if further information had been provided.

13.13 No reference was made in the long form report to the very substantial purchases of MCC shares made in September 1990 by the CIF and MCWPS in the circumstances described at paragraph 6.18, which had taken the holding controlled by BIM to more than 6 per cent. of MCC[b]. This was because the reporting accountants' team did not know about these matters, as they took the view they were not required to report on anything relating to the pension schemes that occurred after 5 April 1990.

13.14 Clifford Chance and Linklaters & Paines also sought information about self-investment. First Clifford Chance met Miss Maxwell. As set out at paragraph 6.23, Miss Maxwell had been

---

[a] In fact the way the pension funds had operated before 5 April 1990 and the nature of the use that had been made of the funds had both continued thereafter, although the loans of cash and the use of shares as collateral materially increased.

[b] This was based on the figure of 41.03 million shares which the records of the CIF at that time identified BIM as controlling; as explained in the footnote on page 104, this figure appears to have included a parcel of 3.446 million shares which the CIF had paid for in May 1989 but which instead of being sold to the CIF were sold to TIB.

aware by October 1990 that the holding of BIM in MCC had increased to 6 per cent., but, probably before her employment as a consultant to MGN, she had enquired of RM as to what had been done and had been told by him that the holding had been reduced below 3 per cent. The size of the holding in MCC was discussed at a meeting with Miss Maxwell and Mr Cook on 21 February 1991, but nothing was said about what had happened in October 1990 or what Miss Maxwell had subsequently been told by RM. The solicitors then asked further questions of Mr Cook. They were concerned that the information derived from the accounts at 5 April 1990 was, by April 1991, one year out of date. They were told by Mr Cook:

> "As far as self investment is concerned, unfortunately, the only information which we have available which is auditable and therefore is perhaps the best data to release, is that as at 5 April 1990. Information at 31 December 1990 is not readily available, and of course, would not be auditable."

Detailed records were in fact kept and Mr Cook knew of the substantial increases in the holding of MCC shares.

13.15 Although the firms of solicitors asked about this on a number of occasions, they decided, in conjunction with Mr Stewart of Samuel Montagu (who had been asked by Mr Galloway to deal with pensions), to accept this position on assurances from Mr Cook there had been no material changes after 5 April 1990[a]. This was confirmed in writing by Mr Cook only after a substantial transaction had been carried out to reduce the holding of MCC shares. What actually happened was as follows:

- On 2 April 1991 the CIF sold 25 million MCC shares in two equal parcels to MGPS and MCWPS. This was done in consequence of the advice received in October 1990 from Titmuss Sainer & Webb (referred to at paragraph 6.20) that the MCC shares held by the CIF were one holding for the purposes of disclosure under the Companies Act. It was subsequently decided that if a large number of MCC shares were passed to the two pension schemes, the holding by the CIF could be brought down to a level at which it would not have to be disclosed, as the holding would have been divided amongst three different beneficial interests.
- This transaction did not alter the fact that the holding of both MGPS and MCWPS in MCC was materially greater than it had been as at 5 April 1990. On 16 April 1991, as part of the verification carried out on pensions, Mr Cook was asked by Clifford Chance to confirm that the investments of the pension funds would be substantially the same as at 30 April 1991 as had been the case at 5 April 1990. Mr Cook told us that although he had been told by RM that it was intended to reduce the MCC holdings, that had not been done. He, therefore, declined to give the confirmation required by Clifford Chance until the shares had been sold, although he did not inform Clifford Chance of the reasons for the delay in replying.
- The 25 million shares were sold through Goldman Sachs to Servex and Yakosa by the transaction referred to at paragraph 9.8. The contract note is dated 26 April 1991. The

---

[a] Mr Kheraj told us that Mr Cook had given him a similar assurance at the meeting on 5 April 1991 referred to in Appendix 12.

market price that day was 235p per share as against the 220p[a] paid by Servex and Yakosa, but the deal might have been agreed on 25 April 1991 when the market price was about 220p. Mr Sheinberg told us the price should have been a market price. He also told us the sale was done as an agency transaction as the size of the shareholding was such that it would have required disclosure by Goldman Sachs (New York) if they had acted as principal.

- Because of the rise in share price during April 1991, the sale of the shares should have resulted in payment to MGPS and MCWPS of £54.9m but this was not due under the terms of the sale until 28 May 1991[b]. This date was put back to 31 May 1991 when the sale price of £55.3m was paid by BIT on behalf of Servex and Yakosa (as buyers) to Goldman Sachs and Goldman Sachs paid £54.9m to BIT on behalf of MGPS and MCWPS (as sellers). Instructions had been given by Mr Cook to pay MGPS and MCWPS but these were amended by KM in instructions sent to Mr Wood, the operations manager for equities at Goldman Sachs in London, to request payment to BIT. Goldman Sachs complied with this and BIT never paid MGPS or MCWPS. KM's evidence was that he gave the instruction for the payment to be made to BIT on the instructions of RM who told him that the amount would be added to the BIM/RMG intercompany account; at the time KM did not focus on the fact that the sellers of the shares were the underlying schemes, MGPS and MCWPS, rather than BIM.

13.16 During April 1991 MGPS also held about £15m of MCC commercial paper, but this was not made known by MGPS to Clifford Chance or Linklaters & Paines and the holding was not mentioned in the long form report as the reporting accountants' team did not know about it. Consequently no disclosure of this was made in the prospectus.

(b) Loans of cash to the private side

13.17 The long form report on pensions did not refer to any of the loans that had been made by the pension funds to the private side.

13.18 The loans did not come to the attention of the reporting accountants' team because they looked at the year end audited accounts of the pension schemes which revealed nothing[c] about the loans since CLD (as auditors) had taken the view in respect of the accounts of MGPS for the year ended 5 April 1988 and thereafter that such lending did not have to be disclosed if there was no amount outstanding at the year end (see paragraph 2.47). The continuation of these loans during the year ended 5 April 1990 was known to Mr Cowling (as they were referred to

---

a This price in the contract note was 221.32 pence per share but this included commission and stamp duty.

b Settlement of the transaction for the other purchases by Servex and TIB made on 24 April 1991 (when Goldman Sachs acted as principal and sold from its books) also occurred at this time - see paragraph 20.20.

c As is referred to in Appendix 12 it does not appear that the CIF audit papers were looked at. An employee of CLD only looked at the MAPs and at the audit files of MGPS and MCWPS; he did not look at any CIF audit papers; there seems to have been no one else whose task it would have been to look these documents in the course of CLD's work as reporting accountants.

in the MAPs prepared for him during the audit of the CIF for the year ended 5 April 1990). Again, the audit of PHL for the 18 months ended 30 June 1990 had revealed a debt by PHL to the pension fund of £43m. For the reasons set out at paragraph 13.22, Mr Wootten was unaware of this.

(c) Related party dealings

13.19 The fact that a substantial proportion of the CIF's investments had been acquired in the circumstances already described from related parties was not identified by the reporting accountants and not included in the long form report nor was it known to the solicitors. The long form report and the work carried out by the solicitors merely identified that over 50 per cent. of MGPS was managed by BIM and part of that managed by LBI; the prospectus disclosed that fact but said nothing about what had happened to those investments whilst under BIM's management.

13.20 Although a term of the instructions from Samuel Montagu required the reporting accountants' team to examine related party transactions[a], we were told by Mr Wootten that CLD did not interpret this term as requiring them to report on related party transactions involving the pension funds[b]. Mr Galloway told us he agreed with this, but considered CLD had a general duty to draw material matters involving the pension funds to Samuel Montagu's attention.

13.21 The work that had been done by CLD during the audit of the CIF for the year ended 5 April 1990 identified (in the MAPs produced for Mr Cowling as set out at paragraphs 9.28 and 9.34) a number of the significant transactions with related parties but these were not mentioned in the CIF accounts; the audit team also identified some of the transactions after 5 April 1990 to which we have referred[c]. However the reporting accountants' team, because of the general view taken by them of their instructions set out in paragraph 13.7 and the specific view of Mr Wootten referred to at paragraph 13.20, did not deal with related party transactions at all. It would have been a relatively straightforward matter to have reviewed how the major investments of the CIF had been acquired (by, for example, discussing these with Mr Cowling or Mr Cook, or looking at the MAPs of the CIF or the investment records or the board minutes of BIM) and therefore to have discovered the related party dealings both up to 5 April 1990 and thereafter, but this task was not attempted.

13.22 There was another way in which such transactions might have come to the attention of the reporting accountants' team. Mr Wootten, the second partner on that team, was the audit partner of PHL (then a main private side company) for the 18 month period ended 30 June

---

[a] "Full details of relationships with MCC and other companies which may be related either through common shareholders, directors, trading relationships or in other ways. This should include details of the terms and comment as to the arms length nature or otherwise of such relationships."

[b] An early draft of a section of the long form report dealing with common services stressed the need for the management of the pension funds to be and to be seen to be free from undue influence from related parties and mentioned the possibility of reducing the proportion of self-investment.

[c] The sale of the holding in Marceau Investissements and the transfer back of the shares swapped with IBI.

1990. That audit took place at the end of 1990 and during January 1991, during which time Mr Wootten was also working on the flotation. The audit staff working on PHL were aware of the sale of the holding in Invesco MIM shares worth £61.9m to the CIF (as described at paragraph 6.5). Although it was the largest sale of investments by PHL that year and the amount involved significant, Mr Wootten told us that he was unaware that it was a sale to the CIF. He explained to us that it was the practice of a partner in CLD acting on an audit, apart from a very brief review of the files, only to consider the MAPs, unless he wished to clarify a particular point. If he wished to clarify a point, he would then undertake a detailed review of the relevant part of the file or discuss the point with the manager. A review of the PHL audit papers in relation to this large transaction would have shown the fact that it was a sale to the CIF and that the shares remained pledged[a] but Mr Wootten (as the partner in charge) never became aware of it. Mr Cowling was aware that the investments purchased by the CIF as part of the £77m transaction (where the documents are dated October 1989 - see paragraph 5.28) had been purchased from related parties, but he did not draw this to Mr Wootten's attention as he assumed that Mr Wootten, as the partner responsible for the audit of PMT (which held part of one of the blocks of shares transferred) would be aware of the facts.

13.23 We were told by CLD that Mr Walsh was the review partner for the audit of PHL for the 18 months ending 30 June 1990. Mr Wootten told us that he believed he discussed with Mr Walsh the question of how to account for the disposal of the Invesco MIM shares, but as he (Mr Wootten) did not know that they had been transferred to the CIF, Mr Walsh was not made aware of this.

(d) The use of shares by the private side as collateral

13.24 The long form report on pensions contained the following paragraph:

> "Since 5 April 1990 MGPS have entered into a collateral swap arrangement whereby they have lodged certain securities with [Lehmans] and [RMG] and these parties have lodged other securities with MGPS. MGPS earns a fee on the collateral lodged with the third parties. We understand there have been no material developments on this arrangement."

This was the only information[b] relating to the use of the shares of the pension funds as collateral by the private side which was made available to the directors of MGN (other than RM) and to those working on the flotation. Although Mr Willett was aware of transactions

---

[a] A letter from Barclays to CLD dated 13 July 1990 stated that the shares were pledged on 30 June 1990. A member of CLD's staff accepted the explanation given by the private side for this, namely that "the intercompany" agreement to sell the shares had been made on Friday 29 June 1990 and that Barclays was not informed until July 1990.

[b] This referred to MGPS. The only arrangements with Lehmans to which Mr Cowling had drawn attention had been carried out through the CIF as that was the only arrangement he knew of; it would appear that CLD's reporting accountants' team did not appreciate from the conversation with Mr Cowling that the CIF was involved in the transaction but thought MGPS was. In the conversation between the reporting accountants' team and Mr Cook on 28 March 1991 (referred to in Appendix 12), a member of the reporting accountants' team understood Mr Cook to refer to MGPS being involved in the arrangements with Lehmans. This had happened in fact only in October 1990 when the CCM portfolio was delivered to Lehmans as set out in paragraph 6.26.

concerning the share portfolio of FTIT as referred to at paragraph 9.55, he told us he was not aware that similar use was being made of pension fund shares and was not aware of the long form report.

13.25 Mr Cowling had a feeling (gained during the course of the 1990 audit of the CIF referred to at paragraph 9.41) that the transaction with Lehmans might in fact have taken place after 5 April 1990 in the way which had originally been described to his audit staff. Consequently, he drew to the attention of the reporting accountants' team both the original and the revised explanation so that they might consider the matter. In view of the importance of this issue, we have set out the sequence of inquiries and events as part of Appendix 12. As is explained in that Appendix, no more information was obtained by the reporting accountants' team other than that set out in the paragraph of the long form report on pensions which we have quoted at paragraph 13.24. This paragraph was inaccurate and incomplete.

(e) The way BIM was managed and its domination by RM

13.26 CLD had reviewed BIM's procedures in the course of their audits and in relation to a routine visit to BIM made by IMRO in November 1990.

13.27 CLD, as auditors, were aware of most of the matters concerning the operation of BIM highlighted at paragraphs 5.8[a].

- They had identified the risks associated with RM's position as regards the pension funds in 1987. In one of the assessments for the pensions audits for the year ended 5 April 1987, a member of CLD's audit staff had made the following comments:

> "Q: Does it appear that there is a dominant personality amongst shareholders, directors or senior management who may wish to and who is in a position to influence the preparation of the accounts, including items that ought to be disclosed in the notes to the accounts?
>
> A: The Chairman of the Trustees [RM] is in such a position, although there is no evidence of him using this influence to date.
>
> ...
>
> Q: Are there other factors which are relevant to the assessment of the risk of deliberate misstatement of the accounts by owners or senior management?
>
> A: [MCC] may wish to borrow liquid assets of the pension funds for their own activities.
>
> **Audit Strategy Implications**
> The main point of the above comments [which included other comments] is to be aware of the possibilities of interference by the trustees, in particular that the pension funds may be forced to carry out transactions in the interests of the [MCC] group, not their own interests. Transactions with [MCC] and decisions of the trustees should be thoroughly reviewed."

---

[a] CLD were not aware of the limited involvement of Mr Stephens or Mr Woods or of the fact that the full board meetings that had been commenced in November 1990 had been abandoned in February 1991.

- On 24 July 1987, members of CLD's staff discussed this issue with the chief accountant of the pension schemes. The note of the meeting recorded the following:

  "[CLD's staff] voiced concern as to whether [RM] should be taking the investment decisions. Conflicts of interest could arise, mainly because investments could be made for the interests of [MCC] rather than the pension scheme members, particularly in the absence of a formal investment strategy. It had been noted during the scrip count that [MGPS] had purchased shares in [MCC], in which [RM] has a personal interest. In this position as trustee, [RM] had a duty to ensure that such conflicts could not arise, [The Chief Accountant] said that [RM] would argue that the investments are made in [MCC]'s interests, but that the interests of the group are coincident with the interests of pension scheme members."

- In one of the assessments for the audit of the CIF for the year to 5 April 1989 a member of CLD's audit staff had made the following comments in his assessments of the controls:

  "The overall organisation is controlled by RM, the control systems are not good.

  Conclusions: A high risk company easily influenced by senior management, without the procedures/controls to influence these extraneous pressures.

  Apparent weaknesses: No evidence of deliberate misstatements, however pressure may be applied to influence [investment] decisions."

  CLD told us that they took these matters into account during the audits for 1989[a] and 1990, although in 1990 the assessment was not updated. Mr Cowling added that had these matters not been taken into account "we would have been grossly over auditing" the CIF.

13.28 However, no reference was made in the long form report to any of the internal control weaknesses at BIM or to the domination of its investment decisions by RM, because the reporting accountants' team did not know about these matters and considered that their instructions did not require them to investigate.

13.29 IMRO visited BIM in November 1990 for a day. They notified BIM about 6 weeks in advance. RM personally supervised the very considerable preparation undertaken by Mr Cook; he made Mr Cook take him through all the files that were to be provided to IMRO.

13.30 Those from IMRO that conducted the visit were not aware of the 1971/73 DTI Reports on PPL and were not made aware of the views expressed by the Bank of England about RM referred to at paragraph 6.42. They saw KM and Mr Cook and reviewed files:

- They told us they were told by Mr Cook that CLD were making monthly visits to monitor compliance and recorded this contemporaneously. Mr Cook was certain he had not told them this, as such visits had ceased.

---

[a] In a memorandum issued by CLD to plan the work to be done on the audit for the year ended 5 April 1989 (called an audit strategy memorandum) it was noted that the "The Chairman could exert pressure on individuals to reflect his own designs".

- They told us they were told by Mr Cook and recorded on their notes that all assets were held in the name of BIM. Mr Cook told us he could not have told them this as it was not the case.
- They were told by Mr Cook (and he agreed) that he reviewed all transactions with Maxwell companies for compliance and suitability and these were reported to the trustees of the schemes each quarter; Mr Cook meant, in the case of MGPS, the investment committee which included Mr Guest and Mr Chapman.
- They recorded that they were told by KM that when the CIF decided to buy a Maxwell owned stock, an independent body was used to value the stock. KM told us that he did say that assets were transferred and that valuations were obtained and he showed them a Bankers Trust valuation.
- They were shown a list of the CIF portfolio at 31 October 1990, but not being experienced in fund management did not appreciate the fact that 76 per cent. of the portfolio managed by BIM directly was comprised in 9 holdings and that the holding in MCC was over 10 percent of the value of the entire CIF.
- They were told nothing of the loans of cash to the private side or the use of shares as collateral.

This visit is dealt with in greater detail in Appendix 9.

13.31 Clifford Chance and Linklaters & Paines were made aware by Mr Cook of the IMRO visit in November 1990 and IMRO's overall conclusion which was:

> "As an Occupational Pension Scheme member many of the IMRO rules are disapplied. However it was noted that the Member had incorporated into its compliance programme many of these rule requirements as a matter of best practice. It is also clear that considerable resources have been applied in order to ensure strong systems are in place. Based on the above it is our opinion that the member is conducting its permitted business in a satisfactory manner and that no matters have come to our attention which might affect the fit and proper status of your Membership."

The advisers were provided with the correspondence with IMRO relating to the report on the visit; they told us that they took a degree of assurance from IMRO's conclusions and proceeded with their work on the flotation with this comfort.

The steps taken in relation to the pension schemes during the flotation

(a) Control over related party dealings

13.32 Arrangements for the control of related party dealings between MGN and the private side were provided for as part of the work on the flotation (as set out in Chapter 12), but no steps were taken to put in place any similar system of controls in relation to the pension schemes or BIM which carried out the investment of over half the schemes' assets. The only step taken[a] was to require KM to resign as a trustee of MGPS and to appoint in his place Mr Clements and Mr

[a] The ownership of MGPT had been transferred to RMG from MGN and SDR in August 1989. The advisers asked that the ownership be transferred back, but RM refused. We have not been able to discover any explanation that was given for that refusal, and the only reason which those concerned have been able to proffer is that ownership of MGPT by the private side companies gave RM control over the appointment of the directors of MGPT, who were the trustees of MGPS. The advisers accepted RM's refusal because they considered the appointment of Mr Clements and Mr Burrington to be sufficient. Mrs Cox of Clifford Chance did not know the reason why MGPT had not been transferred back and did not know of RM's refusal.

Burrington[a]. However, KM was not required to resign from BIM which continued to have a board, with the exception of Mr Cook, wholly comprised of directors of private side companies. KM told us that nobody ever suggested that he resign as a director of BIM.

13.33 Mr McIntosh told us that Samuel Montagu were unaware of the transactions involving MCC shares (such as the disposal of 7.9 million shares in March 1990 and the purchases in September 1990), the loans of cash to the private companies, the related party dealings, the use of shares as collateral and the way BIM was managed and dominated by RM. They assumed that it was a conventionally run pension scheme, albeit that it invested in somewhat unusual investments. If they had been made aware of the facts, they would have taken action and it is probable the flotation would not have proceeded on the planned date and possible that it might not have proceeded at all.

(b) The special financial review

13.34 Because of the significance of the actuarial surplus in MGPS, it was decided to obtain a special financial review of MGPS as at 31 December 1990. This involved much of the work required for an actuarial valuation[b]. To carry out this review, the actuaries were provided with a balance sheet for MGPS as at 31 December 1990[c]. However, that balance sheet was not audited largely because the audit for the year ended 5 April 1990 had not been completed (as the general state of the administration of the pension fund did not make this an easy task) and neither the actuaries nor anyone else pressed for an audited balance sheet. Furthermore, the balance sheet did not give details of the investments of the scheme or their disposition and so did not disclose what had happened since 5 April 1990.

(c) The disclosure in the prospectus

13.35 During the course of investigations, Mrs Cox of Clifford Chance told Samuel Montagu on 9 April 1991 of the sense of unease concerning the related party arrangements which she and Mr Thurnham of Linklaters & Paines shared: her note of the telephone conversation recorded her telling Samuel Montagu of:

> "[Mr Thurnham's] and my general unease re incestuous relationships of companies especially investment management and presence of Maxwells as directors and mix of Maxwells and surplus. Agreed all we can do is disclose and leave punters to form view."

---

a He was appointed to this position without being consulted; he attended only one board meeting which took place in June 1991.

b It was not formally entitled an actuarial valuation because some of the necessary formalities had not been complied with: an actuarial valuation would have had to have been done on a prescribed basis under the Finance Acts and would have had to have been circulated to all the members of the scheme.

c The review was carried out on the basis that the assets were assumed by the actuaries to exist and valued on the basis of the "discounted value of projected future income assuming existing assets notionally invested in a portfolio comprising the constituents of the FT actuaries All Share index with allowance for future dividend growth of 5 per cent. p.a.". Bacon & Woodrow told us that valuations by actuaries were carried out on the basis that the assets were assumed to exist; they told us that they expected the auditors to verify the existence of assets in the course of their audits.

13.36 As foreshadowed by that note, it is clear that Clifford Chance and Linklaters & Paines carried out their work (which did not include reviewing investments or financial information), with the objective of making the section of the prospectus covering pensions as full as possible as regards related party arrangements.

13.37 No disclosure was made of the five matters to which we have referred earlier in this chapter nor were any of them rectified.

(d) Action in respect of the concerns of the Association of Mirror Pensioners

13.38 The Association of Mirror Pensioners had been formed in January 1991. Its members' principal concern was the failure to increase pensions but they also had other concerns: the use that had been made of the pension scheme to assist MGN in its survival plan; the transfer of the administration expenses to the scheme (referred to in paragraph 2.22); the nature of some of the investments of the scheme; and the purchase by the scheme of Strand House (Maxwell House). They attempted to obtain information from the pensions administration department but did not (in their view) make satisfactory progress[a]. Accordingly, they saw the flotation of MGN as an opportunity to try and force the trustees to deal with their concerns. At the beginning of April 1991, therefore, they raised their concerns and attracted some publicity. The concerns expressed were almost exclusively directed at the failure to increase pensions and not at the state of investments of the scheme because (as was explained to us) they did not have sufficient information concerning investments[b] to support any complaint. The concerns of the pensioners about pension increases were considered by the advisers to MGN. Clifford Chance and Linklaters & Paines advised Samuel Montagu that they did not consider the claim supportable in the light of existing authority and on that basis it was concluded that nothing had been raised that affected the flotation.

The transfer of MCWPS

13.39 It had been agreed in principle that after the transfer of a large number of the employees under MCWPS to the new BPCC pension scheme in March 1990, the members who had become employees of MGN after its acquisition of BNPC would be transferred to MGPS[c]. It was apparent in September 1990 that once this had been done, MCWPS would only have very few active members and would not be viable as a scheme; consideration was then given as to

---

[a] It was, for example, the policy of the pension administration department to charge the Association for copies of some documents they requested.

[b] Mr Boram told us that the Association appreciated that investment was a sensitive issue. In October 1990 (faced with little progress) he had supplied certain information which enabled the *Daily Mail* on 24 October 1990 to write an article raising the issue of self-investment to which we referred at paragraph 6.22. Before Mr Boram had seen the article that morning Mr Guest had been on the telephone to him to say that RM was very angry. RM subsequently contacted Mr Boram and asked him whether he was concerned about the investments or only the lack of pension increases. Mr Boram told RM that if the investments were legal he was not concerned, but that his real concern was to secure an increase in pensions. RM said that he would do something about it. This resulted in the announcement of an increase.

[c] They remained employees of BNPC, but on its acquisition by MGN were employed by the MGN group. It is convenient to refer them as employees of MGN, though they remained employees of one of MGN's subsidiaries.

whether the active members could be transferred to other schemes and whether the position of the pensioners and deferred pensioners be covered by the purchase of annuities from an insurer. On 6 January 1991, the members of MCWPS who were employed by MGN became members of MGPS, but at 30 April 1991 no transfer of assets had taken place. Nothing was done to expedite this during preparation of MGN for listing, although the position as to the transfer of the employees of MGN was correctly described in the prospectus. It appears that no solution to the position of the remaining active members of MCWPS, the pensioners and deferred pensioners, was reached until June 1991 when the trustees of the two schemes agreed in principle to the merger of the schemes and the transfer of most of the active members to another scheme, subject to the fulfilment of certain conditions. The necessary documentation had not been signed nor the transfer of assets made by the time of RM's death.

14. THE BUSINESSES AND OTHER ASSETS INCLUDED IN THE FLOTATION

14.1 In the period during which RM controlled MGN, RM had returned it to profitability as described at paragraph 2.49. He had as owner transferred its non-newspaper assets to other private side companies and used its cash resources for those other interests. The total benefit derived amounted to over £300m which had been charged to the intercompany account. MGN had borrowed in June 1989 £150m from banks in connection with the acquisition of BNPC from MCC as well as taking on finance leases for new equipment. In the autumn of 1990 MGN had borrowed further funds to transfer from MCC the interests in QPI and Donohue for £129m and a further £85m to pay MCC for the redemption of loan stock and interest (as adjusted) due in respect of the purchase of BNPC.

14.2 On flotation MGN's main assets were therefore the newspaper businesses and the interests in QPI and Donohue. This chapter deals with the businesses and other assets included in the flotation and some other assets MGN had but which were transferred out immediately prior to the flotation[a]. Chapter 15 deals with the way in which the debt of over £300m owed to MGN by the private side companies was discharged, MGN's banking facilities and other financial information.

The newspaper businesses

14.3 The principal businesses were the newspaper publishing and printing businesses of MGN - the *Daily Mirror,* the *Sunday Mirror* and *The People*, the newspaper businesses of SDR - the *Daily Record* and the *Sunday Mail* - and the business of *The Sporting Life.* It is unnecessary for us to deal at any length with any of these businesses for, after the return to profitability of MGN[b] during the period of RM's ownership, they were generally regarded as sound, cash generative businesses[c].

14.4 As mentioned at paragraph 6.62 a separate sale of *The People* was one of the disposals notified to the banks for the purpose of the £360m facility obtained in the autumn of 1990; this was

---

a The only assets which were transferred out which were important to MGN's business were the properties described below. Some other properties were transferred out together with some companies that were irrelevant to MGN's business such as British International Helicopters Ltd.

b SDR had always returned a profit.

c There was a more substantial debate as to whether the company that printed the magazines, Mirror Colour Magazines Ltd (which had been entirely funded by MGN's cash flow) should be included. The magazines were at that stage loss making and it was proposed that they be printed and produced by a private side company under a contract with MGN. The effect of this would have been to increase the earnings of MGN and, as it was contemplated that the shares would be priced on an earnings or yield basis, this would have enhanced the price obtained on flotation. Samuel Montagu and Smith New Court considered that would attract substantial criticism and after some debate it was abandoned. KM told us that this was one of the few areas where a potential conflict of interest between MGN and the private side was identified by Samuel Montagu (being the possibility of the private side through Mirror Colour Magazines Ltd printing publications that competed with MGN); that it was dealt with by Samuel Montagu and KM working together to lobby RM until he agreed to including the printing of the magazines in the flotation. Samuel Montagu told us they had identified many areas with a potential for conflict – the treasury, the secretarial department and the areas identified in the non-competition agreement.

based upon an approach that Mr Richard Stott had made to RM to lead a management buyout of that paper. The negotiations had not proceeded far by October 1990 and although an attempt was made to progress these negotiations in the period of the flotation, RM decided to include *The People* in the businesses offered for sale[a].

14.5 The *Sporting Life* was also included in the businesses floated and the proposal for a separate sale was abandoned. The business of the *Sporting Life* included plans to launch the *Racing Times* in the United States.

14.6 We have found nothing of material significance relevant to the description of the businesses in the prospectus which it is necessary to mention[b]. It has been pointed out to us that the strength of the businesses has been demonstrated by their ability to survive events that occurred after the flotation.

Property

14.7 A review of the property owned by MGN was carried out as part of the work on the flotation and consideration given to the Mirror Building and the properties regarded as an alternative location in the event of the Mirror Building being redeveloped (Worship Street or Great Dover Street).

14.8 It was decided to transfer to the private side all the properties that were not immediately necessary for the operation of the newspaper business. Accordingly there were transferred out various properties, the most significant of which were those at Killick Street (near Kings Cross in London), Craigie/Miller Street (Manchester) and various properties owned by SDR. These were transferred out at market value in April 1991, but the sums due from the private side companies to which they were transferred were charged to the intercompany account prior to its discharge by means of the very substantial dividend paid by MGN in the manner described at paragraph 15.9.

(a) SDR properties

14.9 The only properties of operational significance were those contiguous to the SDR premises at 40 Anderston Quay, Glasgow - a site used for the SDR car park and the two properties which had been purchased with a view to the replanting of Anderston Quay (as set out at paragraph

---

a During the period of the flotation, Mr Roy Greenslade resigned as Editor of the *Daily Mirror*. He was replaced for a short time by Mr Charles Wilson and thereafter, on RM's decision to include *The People* in the flotation of MGN, Mr Richard Stott became again the Editor of the *Daily Mirror*.

b The prospectus did not draw attention to the fact that the replanting had been carried out with a view to obtaining other contract printing (which had not materialised for the reasons set out at paragraph 4.26). The prospectus did disclose that contract printing was undertaken; it stated "within the constraints of printing [MGN]'s newspaper titles, there is still printing capacity available" and it stated that the directors believed that MGN was well placed to attract further contract printing. Fuller disclosure would probably have made no material difference to those intending to purchase shares. Stamford Street was subsequently closed because of overcapacity and the reduction in the number of different editions produced.

6.73). RM insisted[a] that these properties be transferred out of SDR, including the premises at 44 Warroch Street where the new presses for SDR had been stored. He did agree, however, to grant SDR a five year option to buy back at market value 2.5 acres of the former cooperage premises at 64 Warroch Street.

14.10 At page 8 of the prospectus disclosure was made in respect of the new capital investment to be made by SDR in the following terms:

> "SDR is making a major capital investment in four new Koenig & Bauer Commander web offset colour printing presses to replace the existing plant which is now 20 years old. The new equipment is expected to be fully operational in 1994 and together with its infrastructure, it is expected to cost approximately £83m (of which £37m has already been spent)."

14.11 The prospectus said nothing about the transfer out of the property that had been purchased adjacent to Anderston Quay[b] nor of the option to reacquire it, nor was the anticipated cost of the property to be acquired under the option[c] included in the figure of £83m disclosed. Although the figure is immaterial in the overall context, what RM had done provided an insight into the way RM operated. Furthermore, no firm decision had been made by RM to proceed with a redevelopment since no final decision had been taken by him whether the development would proceed at Anderston Quay or on a greenfield site[d].

(b) The Mirror Building and Orbit House

14.12 The Mirror Building had been occupied by MGN under an informal arrangement with MCC[e], but the flotation meant a formal lease was required. To assist the refinancing of the loan secured on the Holborn site (see paragraph 9.22) the private side initially wanted MGN to take a 20 year sub-lease from MCC with an option to determine at any time. The objective of the private side was to have as long a lease as possible to secure the financing but with a break clause to enable them to redevelop the site. There were extensive negotiations on this and it

---

[a] These properties had been offered to Barclays in January 1991 as security for a loan made by Barclays to PHL Estates Limited (PHLE); their security over these properties was perfected on 12 April 1991.

[b] The list in the prospectus of the property MGN owned and leased included for Scotland only 40 Anderston Quay.

[c] The price was to be a market price; after RM's death the site was purchased by SDR for £1.67m.

[d] After the flotation the private companies tried to charge SDR a rent for the premises at which the presses were stored and for their car park. Mr Horwood continued to press RM to make a decision and shortly before his death, after receipt of a report from Mr Horwood and Mr Shaw, it was finally decided to carry out the redevelopment at Anderston Quay. Negotiations were also put in hand in the late autumn of 1991 to secure additional finance to pay for this development.

[e] The property had been leased by MCC from a private side company which in turn held it under a long lease (which had been transferred from MGN as described at paragraph 2.17). On 29 March 1990 another private side company, Logocourt Limited, entered into an agreement with MCC to acquire MCC's leasehold interest in the Mirror Building and other properties in Holborn for £20m with completion to be on 29 March 1992. Logocourt Limited's obligations were guaranteed by RMG. We understand that MCC took credit for £20m from this transaction into their profit and loss account for the year ended 31 March 1990. On 26 April 1991, Logocourt Limited consented to MCC granting an underlease of the Mirror Building to MGN and the completion date for the acquisition of the lease from MCC was further deferred.

was eventually agreed that MCC would grant MGN a sub-lease for a term of 3 years at a rent of £7m a year.

14.13 Orbit House, a property connected to the Mirror Building by a bridge, (see the plan at page 20) had also been occupied by MGN under an informal arrangement and used by the finance department. The premises had been held on a long lease from 1986 by PHL and MGN had been the sub-lessee between 1979 and 1987 when the sub-lease was assigned to MCC.

(c) Worship Street

14.14 MGN had taken the leases of two other premises - Great Dover Street[a] near the Elephant & Castle in London and, in the circumstances referred to at paragraph 6.34, the former Maxwell House at 74 Worship Street. Mr Burrington was given the task of deciding which of these two properties was more advantageous for any relocation of MGN. He decided upon Great Dover Street and thus the property at Worship Street, the lease of which had only been agreed to in October 1990 became surplus to MGN's requirements.

14.15 RM decided that the new tenant of Worship Street should be PHL, one of the private side companies, but since the lease for the premises had been taken from another private side company (PHAF) the question was raised as to whether MGN's liability under the terms of the lease should be terminated by the grant of a new lease to PHL or whether MGN's liability to the other private side company should be released. We were told by Clifford Chance and Linklaters & Paines that they understood that this had been raised with BNP (who had made available a loan of £36m to PHAF on the strength of the lease as set out at paragraph 6.39) and they refused to allow MGN to be released; however BNP told us that they had no record of such a request having been made to them[b]. We were told that Lewis Silkin, the solicitors acting on the property transfers, made no approach to BNP. KM told us that BNP had been approached to agree to release MGN but had refused since MGN was a better covenant; he also recalled that the question of releasing MGN had been raised after the flotation during a meeting in Paris attended by himself, Mr Anselmini and Mr Thomazeau of BNP.

14.16 Neither Clifford Chance nor Linklaters & Paines thought that a refusal on BNP's part to release MGN to be significant as they considered that the bank was merely being prudent. When the lease was assigned by MGN to PHL, an indemnity in respect of MGN's obligations under the

---

[a] A lease of this had been taken in June 1989 as an alternative relocation site for MGN at a cost of £3m. It was valued on 17 April 1991, as at 30 December 1990 by Conrad Ritblat at £575,000. Mr Stoney investigated this decline in value and recommended that the loss be transferred back to the private side. RM blamed the property department for this purchase (although Mr Shaw told us he had advised against its acquisition) and said MGN's loss should be claimed from them. The sum of £2.5m was therefore charged by MGN to PHLE and this sum was included in the settlement of the intercompany accounts described at paragraph 15.16. We were told by Mr Guest he was unaware of this claim.

[b] BNP's consent to the assignment was required under the terms of the mortgage; they took the view that MGN's credit rating was superior to that of PHL and therefore wanted to retain the commercial benefit of MGN remaining liable. They were advised to record on the letter consenting to the assignment a statement that MGN continued to remain liable; BNP refused Mr Bunn's request that this reference to MGN be removed.

lease to PHAF was therefore provided to MGN by the main private side companies. The prospectus[a] disclosed the arrangements in the following paragraph:

> "Agreement dated 29 April, 1991 between Headington Investments, RM Group and RM Holdings ("the Covenantors") and the Company under which the Covenantors agreed to indemnify the Company, inter alia, against all liabilities in respect of 74 Worship Street London EC2 and Snowdon House, Appold Street, London EC2, of which the Company was the original tenant under leases dated 16 October 1990, which have been assigned to PHL."

It was not disclosed that 74 Worship Street had been leased from another private side company as none of the advisers considered this material. Comfort had been obtained on the private side finances as set out at paragraphs 16.2 to 16.20. Subsequent to the death of RM and the insolvency of the private side companies, MGN was exposed to substantial liabilities under this 25 year lease. The annual rent was £5.75m increasing to £7.75m by June 1995, thereafter subject to upward only reviews which over the period would have resulted in total rent of approximately £176m, though the actual loss suffered by MGN could have been mitigated.

The interests in Donohue and QPI

14.17 The circumstances in which the interests in Donohue and QPI had been acquired by MGN have been described at paragraph 6.51. There was a long debate between RM and the advisers as to whether these two investments should be included in the group to be floated. Samuel Montagu and Smith New Court took the view that it was preferable that they not be included. Their main reason was that on the flotation a better price could be obtained for the shares in MGN because of the effect on the earnings of MGN (as the interest cost exceeded the share of the profits) and because the value of these stakes would be discounted and not reflected in the price; Samuel Montagu also considered that their inclusion also would highlight in the minds of investors the "shuffling" of assets which had been perceived to be a weakness at MCC. Quite independently of Samuel Montagu, CLD also advised they should not be included, though for different reasons.

14.18 However, RM decided that they should be included[b]. KM told us that RM wanted MGN to have its own mergers and acquisitions strategy after the flotation. To avoid issuing more shares and diluting control, such a strategy would require MGN to have assets that could be sold in order to produce acquisition finance. QPI and Donohue were such assets as they were not strategic. Donohue was particularly suitable since (in accordance with the newsprint cycle) it would be likely to be worth more within 18 to 24 months after the flotation. Samuel Montagu told us that none of this was mentioned to them and they acted on their own views as set out in paragraph 14.17. Consideration was then given to a rationale by which their inclusion could be explained. In the case of Donohue, its position as a producer of newsprint and supplier to MGN was put forward, but no satisfactory rationale for the inclusion of QPI, other than that it was a good investment, could be found. Nothing was therefore put into the prospectus as a rationale for QPI's inclusion; it was simply described as an investment.

---

[a] This indemnity was disclosed as a material contract at page 27 (xiv) of the prospectus.

[b] An alternative considered at the time by RM and KM was to realise the value of the investment in Donohue by proposals such as a private placement of a convertible bond; KM continued the discussion of the convertible bond in respect of Donohue until June 1991.

14.19 Their inclusion however was questioned by professional investors at meetings[a] both in the UK and overseas and it was an issue that concerned a number of journalists. Concern was expressed as to whether they had been acquired by MGN on an arm's length basis and as to why they had been included. In a note written in November 1991 an analyst at Smith New Court commented:

> "The lack of obvious synergy between MGN and QPI was a controversial element during the MGN float - the real rationale of the deal was that MCC needed the cash and as MGN was then a private company RM was able to force the deal through (it was obviously to MCC's advantage)."

It can be seen from the facts outlined at paragraph 6.51, this was the real rationale and that this might have been a material consideration to a potential investor in MGN because it highlighted a significant aspect of RM's methods of doing business.

14.20 The stakes in both these companies were accounted for in the financial information provided in the accountants' short form report as associated companies at the value for which they had been acquired; a more detailed consideration of this is set out in Appendix 13. The issues raised by this accounting treatment are not of significance because, for the reasons explained in the next paragraph, MGN was valued on a yield and earnings basis; therefore the price at which the two interests were included in the accounts were not of material significance to potential investors.

Valuation of the floated business and the titles

14.21 The price of 125p fixed on 29 April 1991 for the shares was aimed to provide a yield of 7 per cent. and a price/earnings ratio of 10. Although the price was reached after much detailed consideration, the advisers were concerned to value the business for the purpose of its flotation on the basis of yield and its price/earnings ratio. The only substantial areas of debate were the applicable multiple and the level of discount required because of the "Maxwell Factor". RM, his family and the Maxwell Foundation were advised by Bankers Trust to seek a high multiple because of the strength of the business in comparison to similar businesses; because Bankers Trust did not consider that the "Maxwell Factor" was a discounting factor, they put forward a price/earnings ratio of between 11 and 12. SBIL took a less optimistic view advocating a price/earnings ratio between 9.5 and 11.5 and a yield between 5.8 and 7.1 per cent. Smith New Court and Samuel Montagu put their views at the lower end of the price/earnings ratio scale and, after much argument, finally prevailed.

14.22 Included in the financial information provided was a valuation of the titles of the newspapers[b]. This was carried out by the business valuation unit of CLD under Miss Maggie Mullen and Mrs Caroline Woodward. A detailed account of the valuations, the circumstances of the

---

[a] These were organised for RM and some of the other directors of MGN to make presentations to professional investors - see paragraph 17.19.

[b] As explained in more detail in Appendix 14, what was valued was the "title" itself (defined to us as "the name associated with a particular style, format, content and readership demographic appeal of a newspaper") without any of the other assets of a newspaper publishing business.

approval by the directors of the valuation and its inclusion in the accounts published in the prospectus is contained in Appendix 14; a summary is sufficient here.

14.23 CLD's business valuation unit had been commissioned to value the titles in April 1990 and had provided by the autumn of 1990 a valuation for all the titles in the range of £557m to £669m. This valuation was used in connection with the obtaining of the £360m facility and when the accounts for MGN's main parent in the UK, RMG, at 31 December 1989 were produced in December 1990, RM decided that the appropriate value within this range was £625m; this was considered acceptable by Mr Steere, the audit partner.

14.24 Samuel Montagu decided at CLD's suggestion that it would be appropriate for a further valuation at 31 December 1990 be made for the purposes of the flotation and it was agreed that this should be done by Miss Mullen and Mrs Woodward.[a] They concluded that the valuation of £625m was still appropriate.

14.25 Although that valuation was important for the purposes of the reorganisation described in the next chapter, and although without it the balance sheet of MGN included in the consolidated accounts would only have shown assets of £7m, it has been put to us that it was of little importance to any investor and did not affect the basis on which MGN was valued for the purposes of the flotation. The evidence that we received was unanimous that all professional investors ignored valuations of newspaper titles for a number of different reasons[b]. Rating agencies took very much the same view.

---

a There was some debate as to whether the business valuation unit was independent given CLD's position as auditor, but Samuel Montagu concluded after meeting Miss Mullen and Mrs Woodward that they were independent.

b These include the fact that although apparently objective, valuations were based on discounted cash flows which could be substantially influenced by subjective factors: the fact that some leading companies did not carry such valuations; the fact that valuations were treated differently by the accounting standards in different countries; the fact that some countries did not permit the inclusion in balance sheets of intangible assets that had been developed rather than acquired.

15. OTHER FINANCIAL INFORMATION RELEVANT TO THE PROSPECTUS

15.1 Apart from the consideration given to the businesses and assets to be included, it was considered necessary prior to the flotation to deal with the amount of over £300m owed by the private side to MGN. This chapter describes what was done in relation to that debt owed to MGN, the bank borrowings made by MGN and its business plan.

The advice given on flotation about the debt owed by the private side

15.2 As set out at paragraphs 2.19 and 4.46, the hard core element of the amount that the private side owed to MGN had grown in each year from 1984 up to the end of 1990 when it was approximately £334m. It grew further in 1991 as explained at paragraph 15.18.

15.3 It was decided (on the advice of Samuel Montagu and Smith New Court) that the amount due to MGN from the private side had to be settled prior to the flotation, as MGN would not be attractive to outside investors if it was owed such a substantial sum of money by the private side companies. The general reasons behind the growth of the debt were well understood by Samuel Montagu. It was made clear by them that if the debt was not totally extinguished, then the prospectus would probably have to disclose both the history of MGN's funding of other of RM's companies and the lack of an asset appropriate to MGN's business that could be transferred by the companies to extinguish that debt, as this would be necessary to explain the security which Samuel Montagu would have required for any outstanding balance.

15.4 The settlement of this hard core debt was achieved through the utilisation of a dividend paid to the private side companies which was made possible only by means of an elaborate reorganisation scheme, described below.

15.5 Because of the settlement, nothing was said in the prospectus about the history of the funding by MGN of RM's private side companies, though it was clear from the accountants' short form report in the prospectus that the substantial debt owed by the private side had been discharged.

The scheme to enable a dividend to be paid

15.6 Consideration was first given to repaying the debt or replacing it with assets. Since most of the assets of the private side were charged (such as the properties in Worship Street), the transfer of those would not have solved the problem. Samuel Montagu and Smith New Court did not want part of the private side's major asset - the shareholding in MCC - to be transferred into MGN, since such a transfer would have created a link between MGN and MCC that would have made the flotation much less attractive to potential investors. In any event, such assets would have had to be transferred into MGN at full market value and that value was likely to be discounted once those assets were included within the whole business of MGN that was to be offered for sale on the flotation.

15.7 Consequently, consideration was given to a scheme that involved MGN paying a dividend to the private side which the private side could then use to extinguish the debt owed to MGN. In the accounts of MGN as they initially stood, a maximum dividend of only £190m was considered feasible, with the balance to be left outstanding in the form of a loan note. However when the size of the intercompany debt was more precisely examined, it was realised that it was in the order of £310m after taking into account the two credits referred to at paragraph 15.17 (rather than the £250m that had been supposed during earlier discussions). It was proposed therefore that in addition to the dividend and the loan note, the freehold of the properties at Great Dover Street[a] and Worship Street would also be transferred to MGN, but this was not attractive for the reasons given in the preceding paragraph.

15.8 Mr Woods then developed a scheme, the objective of which was to create reserves in the accounts of MGN from which a dividend of sufficient size could be paid. Companies are not entitled to pay dividends that are not derived from "realised profits"[b] and the scheme was therefore designed to create such profits.

15.9 Mr Woods' idea was taken up by the advisers and a very substantial amount of work done on it by the advisers in consultation with leading tax and company counsel. The details of the scheme are set out in Appendix 15 but in essence it involved:

- The sale by MGN of its English newspaper publishing business (the main asset of which was the newspaper titles valued at £585m) to a new company that was outside the MGN group but was owned by a holding company controlled by RM.
- That sale would produce a "realised" profit within MGN which could then be utilised to pay the dividend.
- The shares in the company to which the business of MGN had been transferred would then be acquired by MGN and renamed MGN Limited as the operating company to which we referred at paragraph 10.30.

15.10 In reality no profit would be (or was) made by MGN as a result of the scheme because the business of the group would be (or was) the same before and after reorganisation. The effect of the scheme was merely to transfer the business of MGN to a subsidiary company, albeit that this was done in the manner in which (as a matter of company law) there was produced a "realised profit".

15.11 Before the scheme was carried out, it was explained by Smith New Court to one of the two readers at the Stock Exchange considering the prospectus. A report was made by the reader to the Listing Advisory Group who decided to seek on a "no names" basis the advice of a partner at Peat Marwick whom they used regularly as a consultant. He is recorded as having expressed the view that the scheme was legal but that his firm would resist any client of theirs adopting such a scheme. After further discussion within the Stock Exchange, the Accounting Standards Board was consulted, again on a no names basis. They advised that they might look at the issues raised, but could do nothing until a document was published. On learning this,

---

a RM was negotiating to buy the freehold.

b Section 263 of the Companies Act 1985.

the Stock Exchange decided that Smith New Court should be informed that the Stock Exchange might refer the matter to the Financial Reporting Council or to the Accounting Standards Board. Smith New Court were told this on 17 April 1991, the day of the publication of the Pathfinder Prospectus but before the reorganisation was carried out.

15.12 The Stock Exchange's concern was relayed to Mr Walsh at CLD, but as the advice of leading counsel had been taken and the matter considered at a high level by partners within CLD not involved in the flotation, he was not concerned at this. No further action was taken by the Stock Exchange prior to the publication of the prospectus, save to obtain confirmation from CLD that MGN had sufficient distributable reserves to pay the dividend.

15.13 Accordingly, on 19 April 1991, the reorganisation was carried out and a dividend was paid by MGN to the private companies who used the funds paid to discharge the hard core intercompany debt[a].

15.14 The steps taken to reorganise the companies in order to enable payment of the dividend were set out in the prospectus. Although the advisers had been concerned that there might be adverse comment that the scheme was a "cash stripping exercise", there was little comment on it either from the press or from institutional investors.

15.15 After the publication of the prospectus, the Stock Exchange in May 1991 referred the matter to the Financial Reporting Council which decided that it had no jurisdiction as the reorganisation scheme was included in an accountants' report in a prospectus and not in a set of statutory accounts. After further consideration the Stock Exchange decided that they ought to take the matter further and in August 1991 submitted to the DTI a short paper that questioned the implications of the scheme which had enabled a dividend to be paid to discharge the intercompany debt owed to MGN[b].

The settlement of the hard core intercompany debt

15.16 The settlement of the hard core intercompany account was effected on 19 April 1991.

15.17 The amount due from the private side companies at 31 December 1990 had been reduced by two credit items amounting to approximately £55m, as described at paragraph 6.68:

- £25m in payment for group tax relief to which RMG were entitled.
- The MCC commercial paper purchased on behalf of MGN for £29.6m.

15.18 In the period from 31 December 1990 to 19 April 1991 the intercompany debt, as recorded in the books of MGN, increased by £26m.

---

a Approval of the reorganisation had to be obtained from the banks that had lent money to MGN. They again took steps to satisfy themselves of the legality of what was proposed.

b The paper submitted by the Stock Exchange to the DTI in August 1991 was considered by the DTI and advice was sought. The DTI concluded that as the reorganisation scheme was disclosed in the prospectus no further action was necessary.

- net cash amounts of £8.8m were passed to the private side[a];
- £9.28m was charged to the intercompany account in consequence of the property transferred out of MGN and SDR referred to at paragraph 14.8[b];
- £8m was charged to the intercompany account for interest.

The books held by the MGN finance department had not recorded by 19 April 1991 the large payments made on 12 and 15 April 1991, as documentation had not been provided to them for the reasons explained at paragraph 11.19; nor had entries been made to reflect the maturity of the commercial paper which was said to have occurred on 28 January 1991. Accordingly as set out at paragraph 15.24, these sums were not included in the intercompany settlement.

15.19 To effect the settlement of the hard core debt, a novation agreement was drawn up which transferred the various debts to RMH so that there could be a direct settlement between RMH (which was to receive the dividend under the reorganisation scheme) and MGN. The figures on this agreement had to be "adjusted" so that they did not show the growth recorded in MGN's books in the intercompany debt due from PHL during 1991 and particularly the cash payments to PHL, for the reasons explained in connection with the £360m facility[c].

15.20 The novation agreement was drafted by Titmuss Sainer & Webb. The balances shown in the agreement were not made subject to audit or review by CLD.

Items left out of the settlement

15.21 Four items were not included in the settlement of the intercompany indebtedness.

(a) The trading accounts

15.22 Whilst the hard core intercompany debt was settled on 19 April 1991 in this way, the trading accounts that existed between MGN and the other private companies were not (as has been explained at paragraph 12.11). For example, cash sums that had been transferred from MGN to fund the development of *The European* were repaid as part of the settlement of the hard core intercompany debt, but sums owed to MGN for printing *The European* were not settled since these formed part of the trading accounts. The amounts in themselves were immaterial, but the omission to deal with the trading accounts was significant in the period after the flotation.

---

a There were cash transfers to PHL of £17.7m, though there were net payments in MGN's favour of £9m on the account with RMG.

b This was the net amount after charging the sum of £2.5m claimed from PHLE in respect of Dover Street as explained in the footnote to paragraph 14.14.

c See paragraph 6.65.

(b) The amount due on the maturity of the MCC commercial paper

15.23 The settlement did not take into account the amount due to MGN on the maturity of the MCC commercial paper on 28 January 1991 (£30m) or interest due (£825,000) on this amount from that date.

(c) The cash payments on 12 and 15 April 1991

15.24 The settlement did not take into account the three payments totalling £39.5m made by the private side to MGN on 12 April 1991[a] or the payment of £28m by MGN to the private side on 15 April 1991. The net effect of these transactions together with the amount due on the maturity of the MCC commercial paper was to leave a balance due from the private side to MGN of £19.325m.

(d) The Can$35m loans

15.25 As explained at paragraph 6.55, MGN had become involved in a scheme that involved it being lent Can$35m by an MCC company and lending the same amount to RMG. The long form report drew attention to this scheme and MGN's part in it and it was considered in the audit of MGN for the year ended 31 December 1990. However it was not mentioned as a material contract in the prospectus and no settlement was made of the obligations. Mr Galloway told us that it was included in the figures in the accountants' report in the prospectus and the transaction was not viewed as material. Mr Guest had no recollection as to why no specific reference was made in the prospectus.

15.26 Subsequent to the death of RM, when MGN's interest in QPI was sold, the loan by the MCC company had to be repaid to MCC, but MGN was unable to make a recovery of its loan to RMG because of the insolvency of the private side.

The three year record

15.27 The scheme that was carried out in order to eliminate the intercompany debt created a difficulty in presenting fairly to potential investors the history of the profits of MGN over the three year period required by the Stock Exchange. If the financial information had been presented on the basis of the actual position prior to the scheme, then the earnings per share would have been more favourable than if the information were presented on an adjusted basis that took into account the effect of the scheme and assumed that the amounts charged to the intercompany account had been distributed by way of dividend.

15.28 The Stock Exchange considered whether figures should be included in the prospectus which took into account the adjustments required for the scheme and the financial effect of the amount that would be raised by the flotation. After some discussion the Stock Exchange agreed that the financial information should be provided both on the adjusted basis (which took into account the effect of the scheme) and a *pro forma* basis which separately identified the effect of the amount that would be raised by the flotation. Both were included in the prospectus.

---

[a] It was claimed later in April 1991 that the largest of the payments on 12 April 1991 (£33m) was in settlement of the MCC commercial paper (as explained at paragraph 11.6).

15.29 CLD prepared the adjusted and *pro forma* figures. They prepared the adjusted figures by allocating the dividend retrospectively[a] and by removing the interest receivable on the intercompany debt; in doing so, they showed a track record of earnings per share as if the amounts that had been charged to the intercompany account had been distributed by way of dividend.

The statement of indebtedness

15.30 The statement of indebtedness was calculated at the close of business on 12 April 1991. MGN was described in the prospectus as having:

"Bank loans - secured	£360,790,933
Bank loans- unsecured	£15,159,922
Bank overdrafts - unsecured	£19,994,433
Finance lease commitments	£187,788,059
Gross indebtedness	**£583,733,347**"

15.31 On 12 April 1991, there were three payments from the private side to MGN:

- £33m This payment has been described at paragraph 11.6. Its effect was to reduce the amount of the overdraft on an MGN account at National Westminster by £15.96m and leave a credit balance on the account.
- £5.5m Its effect was to reduce the overdraft on the MGN account at Lloyds by £5.5m.
- £1m Its effect was to reduce the overdraft on the MGN account at Midland Bank by £1m.

Each of these overdrafts was unsecured.

15.32 The combined effect of these payments was to reduce the indebtedness by £22.5m. In the context of the overall indebtedness of £583.7m its effect was immaterial. It was material, however, in the context of the unsecured bank overdrafts disclosed in the statement of indebtedness. On 15 April 1991, £28m was repaid to the private side; we were told that this represented MGN's surplus cash.

15.33 We received two explanations for the payment of £33m - one that it was for the payment of the sum due in respect of the MCC commercial paper[b] and the other, from Mr Woods, that it was part of a tax scheme[c]. We have been unable to conclude that either of these is the correct explanation.

---

a They allocated £170.3m to the period prior to 1 January 1988 on the basis that that amount of the intercompany hard core debt had accrued in that period and then allocated the balance to the years 1988 and 1989 which absorbed the remainder of the notional dividend.

b see paragraph 11.6.

c Interest charged on the balances on the intercompany account with the private side companies was for tax purposes dealt with on a receipts basis. Accordingly, it was necessary for interest to be paid by the private side in order to bring it into charge to tax. It was important for this to occur in the accounting period which effectively terminated with the transfer of titles and business to MGN Limited as part of the reorganisation scheme in order to provide taxable income to be covered by group relief from private side companies where

MGN's borrowing facilities in 1991

15.34 It was decided that £210m of the proceeds anticipated from the flotation would be used to reduce the amount borrowed by MGN under the £360m facility. This facility was however secured on the assets of MGN and, although the borrowings in the private side companies were secured on assets, the major borrowings that MCC had made were unsecured. Since RM was adamant that MGN be treated in the same way as MCC, it was decided that a facility would be sought for £150m on an unsecured basis. A number of banks were invited to tender to lead that new facility and four banks became the lead arrangers: Barclays (who had the most important role), Lloyds, Crédit Lyonnais and Midland Bank. Some banks were reluctant to agree that the facility be unsecured, but eventually all agreed because they regarded MGN as a robust business that would be further reinforced when it was a listed company run by a board and listed on the Stock Exchange.

15.35 The banks, nonetheless, insisted on the inclusion within the facility of specific covenants, relating particularly to acquisitions[a] (which were limited to a specified level) and intercompany transactions (all loans and guarantees of RM's private interests were prohibited). As with the £360m facility, some bankers attached the term "ring fencing" to these covenants[b]. KM told us that the covenants in the £150m facility were derived from the ring fence covenants in the earlier £360m facility (described at paragraph 6.59) and were required by the banks simply because this was to be a loan based on cash flow rather than on security. Those covenants were not extraordinary in any way; RM would never have agreed to any terms that could be seen to be "Maxwell" terms as he did not want to be perceived as any different to any other Chairman of a FTSE company. Clifford Chance advised that the covenants in the £150m facility were normal.

15.36 As far as RM was concerned the discussions relating to the exceptions in the loan documentation permitting other companies to use MGN cash (such as loans to authorised institutions, foreign exchange transactions and extension of credit for a period not exceeding 60 days) were vital just as they had been in the £360m facility. He would not have permitted the facility to be signed if he had felt he could not continue to use the cash flow by taking advantage of these exceptions as a justification[c]. Further, KM had no doubt that the lending

---

it was perceived there would be surplus tax losses. National Westminster told us that they had been told in 1991 that the loan of £30m (which they made to the private side between 12 and 15 April 1991 that was used to fund this payment as referred to in the footnote to paragraph 11.6) was needed for a tax scheme.

a KM told us that the banks were very concerned that RM would immediately start buying companies; they did not want him to transfer the *New York Daily News* to MGN.

b These were parallel arrangements to those put in place by Samuel Montagu (outlined at paragraphs 12.4 to 12.11) which were also described as "a ring fence".

c KM told us that the use of such exceptions (for example, treating BIM and LBI as authorised institutions and buying commercial paper) which he now accepted were not in accordance with the spirit of the agreement and did not seek to justify, were then thought to be within its letter and, therefore, that RM was confident that such use of MGN cash flow would be permitted. We were told that when payments were made to BIM in August 1991 (as set out in paragraph 21.22) they were not considered by KM or Mr Stoney to be a breach of the ring fence provisions.

banks were aware from the past history of the use made by RM's other companies of MGN's cash flow and that such use was likely to continue after the float, since that was the only way the other companies controlled by RM could be supported.

15.37 Apart from the "ring fencing" covenants, the banks required a covenant that 51 per cent. of the shareholding be maintained in the ultimate ownership of RM, his family or the Maxwell Foundation. This had been a standard requirement of the banks for some years in all of the major facilities granted to RM's companies[a]; it was explained to us that the purpose of this covenant was to give the banks some say in any change of control over any of RM's companies but it was perceived by some others as being a measure of the confidence the banks had in RM.

15.38 Because of the attractiveness of MGN's business, the facility was oversubscribed with offers of participation of £230m for the £150m required.

15.39 Apart from this major facility, the adequacy of the other facilities and overdrafts that MGN and SDR had were reviewed by CLD when considering MGN's business plan and working capital requirements. As a result of that review, it was decided that a further facility was needed and this was obtained from Barclays for £15m[b].

15.40 The £150m facility and the £15m facility from Barclays were negotiated primarily by KM and Mr Bunn with assistance from Mr Stoney. When Barclays were asked to provide the £15m facility, it was KM who gave them an assurance that it was a stand-by facility (as was the case) and unlikely ever to be drawn down[c]. Although Mr Guest was Finance Director of MGN and had for example suggested the need for the further £15m facility, neither he nor anyone else in the MGN finance department played any real part in any of the negotiations. As the finance department of MGN was not involved, it did not develop its own independent relationship with the banks.

---

a KM told us that RM was proud of the requirement that he retain 51 per cent. ownership. KM and Mr Woods disagreed and thought it would be helpful if ownership could go below 51 per cent. because, although a substantial minority shareholder could still block a bid, the possibility of a bid would cause the share price to rise. RM violently disagreed with some suggestions they made for a placing and nothing ever came of their idea.

b One of the reasons why the Barclays facility was required was that SDR had obtained from Kansallis-Osake-Pankki (KOP) a £15m facility. The designated purpose of the facility was assisting in the costs associated with the building and equipping of a new press hall for SDR. Representatives of KOP had visited SDR and were prepared to lend to it for this specific purpose. Despite the fact that the loan was intended for this specific purpose and no decision had been reached as to where to build the press hall (as explained at paragraph 14.11) let alone any works having been commenced, the full facility of £15m had been drawn down and transferred to MGN on 8 March 1991. When it was appreciated by the advisers that this had happened, it was realised that a more general facility was needed in its place, but no question was raised about the propriety of drawing down the KOP loan in the circumstances described.

c KM agreed that he would probably have given the assurance but thought that it would have been asked for by the bank officers in order to get the loan approved by the credit committee; certainly none of the lending bankers to RM's companies would have expected such a standby facility not to be used, as there was no history of not using facilities.

15.41 The role of KM in the relations with the banks during the period leading up to 30 April 1991 was not perceived, at least by SBIL[a], to be unacceptable because they appreciated that the banks looked at all of the companies controlled by RM's interests as one for the purpose of borrowing limits and because they saw KM (as a representative of the majority shareholder of MGN) as having, both during the flotation and afterwards, a role to play in the relationships with banks. KM told us that when dealing with the banks in relation to MGN he was acting as the representative of the family and, in particular, RM as the Executive Chairman of MGN. That said, however, he accepted that MGN was still treated for banking purposes as part of the whole empire; he thought that the advisers were aware of that at the time and nobody suggested that there was anything peculiar about it. As far as he was concerned, the advisers fully expected him to continue in his same role after the flotation, though Samuel Montagu told us emphatically that this was not their view.

15.42 As MGN's banking relationships were conducted at the time of flotation (and thereafter) as part of an overall relationship with RM's companies, with negotiations being controlled by KM, this meant MGN was not an entirely stand alone company in respect of its banking relationships.

The business plan and working capital report

15.43 The production of the business plan was substantially delayed because RM wanted to consider it and he was preoccupied on other matters (as explained at paragraph 8.2). When he had done so, he made various suggestions in an attempt to improve the profit projections of MGN, including cutting out the entire promotion budget. Some marginal changes were made but the more extreme suggestions (such as the elimination of the promotion budget) of RM were not put into effect.

15.44 A report on the business plan was produced by CLD and they subsequently provided a comfort letter covering MGN's working capital requirements to Samuel Montagu who in turn provided the customary comfort letter to the Stock Exchange.

---

[a] SBIL expected him to have a role after flotation as a representative of the majority shareholders, but this would be very different to his role prior to the flotation.

16. COMFORT ON THE PRIVATE SIDE FINANCES AT FLOTATION

16.1 During the course of the flotation Samuel Montagu concluded that "comfort" was required in relation to the state of the finances of the private side. They obtained this from CLD, but no mention of their enquiry or its result was made to the independent directors of MGN or in the prospectus. A more detailed analysis of the request to CLD and the work done by CLD is set out at Appendix 16, but a summary is set out in this chapter.

The decision to seek comfort on the finances of RM's private companies

16.2 KM told us that the financial position of the private side companies higher up in the company structure through which MGN was owned had been raised at an early stage of the preparation for the flotation but that, once the flotation was agreed as an issue of new shares rather than a sale of existing shares, Samuel Montagu lost any interest in the point. Samuel Montagu did not accept this. They had, they said, always been interested in the private side finances, but did not issue any instructions for any review to be carried out until, at a late stage in the preparation for flotation, they realised that any reduction in RM's shareholding in MGN below 51 per cent. could result in a breach of covenant under the £150m facility to maintain a 51 per cent. shareholding in MGN (referred to at paragraph 15.37). Such a sale would also be in breach of the agreement to maintain the stability of the shareholding (see paragraph 12.22). They realised therefore that it was necessary, by commissioning a review to look into the private side finances (which they knew were not in robust financial health), to obtain comfort that there would be no need for RM to sell shares in MGN. Prior to that time, Samuel Montagu had looked at the £150m facility simply from the point of view of assessing whether or not MGN would have sufficient working capital once floated. However, by that time in the flotation process, it was simply not possible to produce a full long form report on the point, though, as we explain, CLD provided the comfort requested by Samuel Montagu.

16.3 On about 21 March 1991, CLD were approached to see whether they would be prepared to provide "comfort" on the financial position of the private side companies. Mr Walsh agreed that CLD might be able to give some comfort, because CLD had, in the ordinary course of their duty as auditors of the private side and MGN, to be satisfied as to the recoverability of the intercompany debts owing between the various companies.

16.4 Samuel Montagu provided to CLD prior to CLD commencing their work a draft of the type of comfort letter that they were seeking. After discussion on the scope of the work to be carried out and after material redrafting, the letter to be provided was in a form acceptable to CLD, Samuel Montagu and SBIL.

The work carried out by CLD

16.5 Work was commenced by CLD on 9 April 1991 and was completed by 15 April 1991 when Mr Walsh and Mr Wootten had a meeting with KM to go through what had been done. Their work was not in the nature of an audit and was expressly limited in its scope.

16.6 In April 1991

- the private side companies did not have cash flow projections and budgets for 1991;
- draft accounts in the form of consolidation spreadsheets at 31 December 1990 for RMG and its subsidiaries had been prepared; although the books of the trading companies were up to date, the books of the holding companies, RMG and PHL, had not been written up since 31 December 1990;
- draft balance sheets for the other principal private side companies were available.
- the latest audited accounts of the private side companies were either those at 31 December 1989 or 30 June 1990.
- CLD had a draft of a management letter referring to matters arising from their most recent audits which pointed out that the quality of accounting systems, management information, and statutory accounts fell well below the level considered adequate.
    - The non-coterminous year ends of private side companies led to significant problems with agreement of intercompany balances.
    - Many books of account were not written up on a regular basis. Transactions were often recorded several months and sometimes more than one year after the event.
    - There were many instances where basic accounting controls were not evident or poorly applied.
    - A consolidated view was produced from *pro forma* consolidations based on latest audited accounts adjusted for known significant transactions.
    - There was no control over the completeness and accuracy of private company transactions in the accounting records.
    - Certain issues relating to significant transactions were not addressed by the accounting departments because they never knew of their existence.

16.7 CLD considered that a more conventional analysis was not possible[a] and therefore the review was based upon a schedule produced by Mr Bunn which set out the investment assets and the external liabilities of the private side companies as at 8 April 1991 and projected asset disposals and loan repayments . CLD reconciled this schedule to the draft accounts and draft balance sheets at 31 December 1990 and the net assets in those accounts to the latest audited accounts; they also reviewed the schedule itself.

16.8 The schedule showed that there was a surplus of investment assets over external liabilities of £952m. By far the largest asset was a holding of MCC shares valued at £811m using a price of 185p which was the market price on 9 April 1991.

16.9 The conclusion drawn by CLD from their review was that the private side would not have to dispose of any shares in MGN provided that it was able to roll over its loans and its asset disposal programme could proceed in a timely manner. A further analysis was therefore carried out by CLD to ensure that if the loans were not rolled over then sufficient assets could

---

a KM told us that he did not recall CLD stating that such an analysis was precluded by the state of the accounting records. His recollection was that CLD complained that there was insufficient time to carry out a proper in depth review and that it would be a rushed, rough and ready exercise.

be sold to meet commitments to the banks without the forced sale of any of the shares in MGN. This analysis showed that it might be necessary to secure the disposal of a significant number of MCC shares to the value of £200m in the event that loans were not rolled over or cash was needed for other reasons.

16.10 Having reached these conclusions from these analyses of the schedule and a reconciliation to the draft accounts at 31 December 1990, Mr Walsh and Mr Wootten discussed with KM and Mr Bunn the ability of the private side to rollover its loans and to achieve its asset disposal programme.

16.11 As a result of the analysis carried out and of that meeting, CLD felt able to provide to Samuel Montagu and SBIL the following assurance;

> "On the basis of the work described above and given the alternative courses of action open to the private interests if intended roll-over arrangements and asset disposal programmes are not implemented, we report that nothing has come to our attention which would suggest that:- (a) the private interests will not be able to meet their liabilities as and when they fall due; or (b) the present financial commitments of the private interests would require them to realise any of the Ordinary Shares of [MGN] held by [RMH]; or (c) would make it inappropriate for the private interests to undertake obligations under the above warranties and indemnities."[a]

The letter containing the assurance drew express attention to the fact that the accounts of many of the principal private side companies for the year ended 31 December 1990 had not been audited and to the limited scope of CLD's work. Apart from this, the letter did not draw attention to the quality of the accounting systems and records. Samuel Montagu told us that they were not made aware of matters affecting the quality of the accounting systems and records (and in particular the significant problems with the agreement of the intercompany balances) or that many of the books of account of the private side companies were not written up on a regular basis. If they had been made aware by CLD, it would have caused them to enquire of CLD as to the efficacy of their review and how CLD were able to form a meaningful view of the financial standing of the private side.

The completeness of the information provided to CLD

16.12 The draft accounts at 31 December 1990 provided to CLD for this review:

- did not include £132.5m of the liabilities of the private side to banks within the figure of £785m for bank loans and overdrafts[b];
- did not include the debt of RMG to the CIF of £46.9m.

---

a This was a reference to the various indemnities considered at paragraph 16.23.

b They were included within the category "other creditors"; the amount omitted from its proper category represented a substantial part of the liabilities of LBH and LBI to Lehmans, MSTC and Lloyds (see paragraphs 6.26, 6.29 and 6.32). KM told us that there would have been no reason to leave out these borrowings (particularly from Lehmans) since CLD was in the process of carrying out the audits of LBH and LBI and the omission would, he thought, have been spotted in due course.

Some adjustments were not made when aggregating the accounts[a] and this resulted in an overstatement of the current assets of the private side by approximately £91.2m[b]. None of these matters were considered by CLD in the course of their work.

16.13 The schedule of the liabilities of the private side in April 1991 provided by Mr Bunn to CLD omitted five substantial borrowings by the private side, even though CLD were told it was complete[c].

- The liability amounting to £57m to Lehmans in respect of financing through the arrangements involving the pledge of the shares of the CIF and pension schemes against the loan of Treasury Bills described at paragraph 5.39 and 6.26.
- A margin loan of £25m made by Goldman Sachs in March 1991.
- A loan from Bankers Trust which in March 1991 had been £7m but from 4 April 1991 had been £10m.
- A loan from Daiwa Europe Bank plc to LBI of £9m
- Net overdrafts provided by National Westminster totalling £31.7m

These were not considered by CLD in the course of their work. We were told by KM that the omission of the liability to Lehmans and the Daiwa loan probably occurred because the internal schedules from which Mr Bunn probably prepared the schedule given to CLD did not contain the borrowings made by LBI and LBH[d].

16.14 The schedule also omitted any reference to the amount owed to the pension funds which by April 1991 was about £100m (as set out at paragraph 13.3) and the use by the private side of the shares of the pension funds to a value of about £270m as collateral for loans. KM told us that the borrowings from the pension funds were always treated as intercompany borrowings and not as external liabilities which is what Mr Bunn's schedule showed. He thought that CLD were in any event aware of the borrowings from the pension funds and that they were treated in the accounts on an intercompany basis.

Other factors

16.15 Apart from the matters referred to in the preceding paragraphs which did not come to the attention of CLD, there were two other important issues.

---

a Such adjustments are made to eliminate balances between companies.

b CLD have suggested (on the basis of information on their files) that there was also an overstatement of liabilities of £80m (including £25m said to be owed to subsidiaries). We have been unable to establish whether there was such an overstatement because of the state of the available records and the retrospective nature of the exercise carried out without the benefit of the contemporaneous accounting records.

c Some of the borrowings and facilities included in the draft accounts at 31 December 1990 had been repaid and there had been significant new borrowings.

d We received other evidence that showed Mr Bunn treated borrowings from LBI and LBH as intercompany borrowings.

(a) The cash flow of the private side

16.16 No information on cash flow or the trading performance of the private side companies was available for the period after 31 December 1990; there were three major changes to the private side in 1991 - the loss of MGN's cash flow consequent upon its flotation, the need for capital for the relaunch of *The European* and the acquisitions made by RM in 1991 (mentioned at paragraph 9.23) which included the *New York Daily News* and other newspapers. CLD did not consider it necessary to examine trading performance because of the significant surplus shown in the schedule provided to them by Mr Bunn.

(b) The ability to dispose of the MCC shares

16.17 The schedule provided to CLD had included the MCC shares at a valuation of 185p (the price on 9 April 1991), but as described at paragraph 9.12 the share price was rising. By 11 April 1991 when CLD were carrying out their analysis, it had risen to 212p. In their analysis CLD considered that not only was it right to use a market price of 185p in valuing this holding (particularly as Mr Bunn had produced his schedule on the basis of a lower price than that pertaining at the time of their work), but also that it would be possible to dispose of blocks of the shareholding at this price level to meet any shortfall in cash requirements of the private side as referred to in paragraph 16.9. They did not analyse or seek independent information[a] on the ability of the Maxwell interests to make disposals in the market:

- without undermining the share price and
- at the times required to meet the private side's possible shortfall in their cash requirements, taking into account the two month closed periods preceding the announcements of MCC's results.

16.18 At a meeting on 11 December 1990, KM had told Mr Steere (who was considering the overall solvency of the private side companies for the purpose of approving the accounts of RMG for 31 December 1989 that were being finalised at that time) that he intended to dispose of 15 per cent. of MCC. This did not happen. RM had on occasions told Sir Michael Richardson that he wanted to reduce his shareholding in MCC but Sir Michael had told him that it would be impossible to place the shares in London. The only substantial buyer at the time was Goldman Sachs. KM told us there were discussions with investment banks and brokers for a non-UK placing of MCC shares and other schemes were being worked on to monetise the value of the MCC shares.

16.19 Sir Michael Richardson told us that a sale by RM of a substantial block of MCC shares would have had to have been as one placing and not in the series of sales contemplated in the schedule provided to CLD. Sir Michael told us that he believed it could not have been done at all in London and Mr Sheinberg said that a sale of any substantial size by RM might have required due diligence on MCC to be performed.

---

[a] KM told CLD at the meeting on 15 April 1991 that there were substantial holdings in MCC shares that were not pledged and although there might be some delay in ensuring an orderly market, there were no long term problems in selling MCC shares.

16.20 Although CLD were not permitted by RM to show Samuel Montagu the schedule of the assets and liabilities of the private side companies provided to them by Mr Bunn, Samuel Montagu were told by CLD that the value of the MCC shares at a price of 187p[a] exceeded the total borrowings of the private interests by 15 per cent. before taking into account other private side assets and that this contrasted with the current market value on 18 April 1991 of 237p. Samuel Montagu told us that they were not told and did not know that it might be necessary to dispose of a significant number of MCC shares; CLD told us that they thought that this was well known and had told Samuel Montagu.

Overall effect

16.21 The true state of the private side finances was not identified. The private side was dependent on the support of its bankers; had the bankers been aware in April 1991 of the debt of £100m to the pension funds and the use of the shares of the pension funds as collateral for private side loans, the collapse that occurred in November 1991 would have occurred in April 1991[b].

Consideration of the finances by the banks

16.22 As referred to at paragraph 4.57 the main banks who lent to RM's companies visited the companies at frequent intervals to try to ensure that they had an understanding of the finances. Each of the banks prepared their own internal reviews of the finances of the private companies for the purpose of reviewing their exposures. Three major banks carried out internal reviews for the purpose of their lending to the private companies in May 1991 and each concluded that, although the support of the banks was needed to enable the businesses to be rationalised and to enable the debt to be reduced by an asset disposal programme, disposals could be made at attractive prices and the support of the banks would be maintained whilst this was done. It was not until the events at the end of June and early July 1991, that the attitude of the banks started to change for the reasons explained at paragraph 21.4.

The indemnities given

16.23 Although assurance was originally sought in respect of the financial position of the private side to ensure RM's interests did not have to dispose of their 51 per cent. shareholding, that assurance also became necessary in order to have comfort on the strength of various indemnities that had to given to MGN by the private side companies on flotation. We have already referred to two of the more important of these, namely that in respect of the Worship Street lease (see paragraph 14.16) and that in respect of the group tax relief (see paragraph 15.17) but there was a third significant indemnity that had to be given. This was in relation to

---

a This was the price Samuel Montagu recorded in their note of the meeting; CLD had used Mr Bunn's price of 185p.

b KM told us that this is an accurate view of any banker after the collapse of RM's companies but did not represent accurately what banks (and in particular National Westminster) did at the time when armed with knowledge. He considered that a refinancing would have been feasible at this stage as MCC had received the cash from the sale of the scientific journals business and the flotation of MGN had reduced the size of the private side debt. Sir Robert Clark told us that, whilst it was impossible to say with any certainty what would have happened, it was entirely conceivable that if RM's "depredations" had come to light whilst RM was alive, RM would have persuaded the banks to mount some sort of rescue package, if only to save face on their part.

the interest rate cap and collar contracts to which we have already briefly referred at paragraph 11.6.

The interest rate cap and collar contracts

16.24 No documentation or other information had drawn the existence of cap and collar contracts to the attention of Samuel Montagu prior to a telephone conversation on 15 April 1991 when Mr Wootten informed Mr Galloway of the existence of these contracts[a]. Although the contracts had been of advantage to MGN in the period following their inception in March 1990[b] the level of interest rates was such that by April 1991 consideration was given to making a provision for prospective liabilities to the banks under these contracts.

16.25 Samuel Montagu decided that it was essential that those prospective liabilities be removed from MGN. Samuel Montagu told us that KM agreed to this. KM accepted this but told us that he could not see at the time why these contracts – which were commercial transactions hedging the cost of MGN's borrowing – had to be removed from MGN. The potential exposure of MGN was thought at the time to be relatively small. However, once it was decided it was necessary for the liabilities to be removed from MGN, no real thought was given to what this meant for the private side as the concentration was on their removal as an imperative in relation to the flotation.

16.26 KM agreed that an immediate approach would be made to the five banks concerned (National Westminster, Toronto Dominion, SBC, Chase, and Société Générale) to seek their consent to the assignment of the contracts to the private side. KM told us that he did not remember this being an issue which would cause the flotation to be postponed; he also thought that the banks would consent to the private side taking over the liability (which was not seen as a great risk).

16.27 As the Pathfinder Prospectus was due to be published, KM agreed to provide a letter of comfort to Samuel Montagu to the effect that steps would be taken to assign the contracts to the private side companies before 30 April 1991, and in the meantime that the private side would hold MGN harmless from any liability that might arise under the contracts[c].

16.28 An approach was made to National Westminster (who in May 1991 formally agreed to the proposed assignment). We were told by Mrs Raperport (who worked on a part-time basis in the central treasury department and had been given the responsibility for finalising the

---

[a] These contracts had been brought to the attention of the reporting accountants' team (working under Mr Wootten) by the audit team (working under Mr Steere) at the end of February 1991. Passing on this information to Samuel Montagu appears to have been overlooked despite the fact that the contracts were relevant not only as important financial commitments of MGN but also because they represented a clear example (to which we referred at paragraph 11.6) of how treasury transactions were carried out without the involvement of the MGN finance department.

[b] As payments had been made under them to MGN.

[c] A note on the existence of the contingent liabilities under these contracts had been drafted for the accounts of MGN for the year ended 31 December 1990 , but it was deleted from the draft accounts when an assurance had been received that the contracts would be assigned.

documentation in respect of these contracts) that she contacted each of the banks, but that (apart from National Westminster) they all declined to assent to the proposed assignment. However, two of the other banks have told us that no approach was made[a]. After she had reported the attitude of the banks to Mr Fuller[b] she was told either by him or by KM not to pursue the assignment further. KM told us that after the flotation of MGN no one was told not to pursue the question of assignment. He recalled raising the issue with Société Générale during a meeting in Paris where he was accompanied by Mr Anselmini; it was certainly he thought on the agenda with banks after the flotation. Whichever of these versions is correct, the true position was that four of the banks had not by 25 or 30 April 1991 agreed, either in principle or otherwise, to the assignment.

16.29 Samuel Montagu considered that it was important to resolve the position regarding these contracts, particularly as no mention of them had been made in the Pathfinder Prospectus. They therefore continued to press for the matter to be dealt with. Eventually the position was explained to them in a further comfort letter that was signed by KM on RMG notepaper on 25 April 1991. This stated (in its material section):

> "We have spoken with the five bank counterparts to these contracts and they have agreed in principle to the assignment of these contracts to ourselves, but it will not be possible to complete the documentation for the assignment prior to the marketing launch for the proposed flotation of the Company. We will however, use our best endeavours to achieve such assignment prior to the proposed Impact Date for the flotation, 30 April 1991."

The letter went on to provide an indemnity to MGN from RMG in respect of any liability that might arise under the contracts.

16.30 KM told us that there was no reason why the banks would not have been approached. He did not recall signing the letter of comfort but, since it had been prepared by Mr Stoney and it was only a letter of comfort (and not a guarantee), he may not have read it before signing. He was left with a memory of a couple of the banks being worried about swapping the MGN covenant for the private side covenant and that, as an alternative, they suggested that the contracts simply be bought out.

16.31 During the course of 26 April 1991, Mr Galloway was informed that documentation could not be agreed with the banks prior to impact day and so instructions were given to enter into a formal indemnity agreement. This was done: the agreement provided for RMG to use its best endeavours to secure an assignment of the contracts and in the meantime to indemnify MGN against any liabilities that might be incurred[c]. KM told us that the fact that the formal

---

[a] The other two banks accepted that they were approached; Toronto Dominion told us that an approach was made but they refused to consent to the assignment. Société Générale told us that Mr Anselmini asked if they would agree to an assignment but they refused. KM told us that he had raised the question of an assignment with SBC by raising it with the group's senior account officer in London, Mr Paul Bowen.

[b] He was the Group Treasurer and a qualified accountant who had been employed by BPC when it was taken over by RM.

[c] The existence of this arrangement and the other indemnities were referred to in the prospectus.

indemnity agreement had been signed by Mr Woods (who was always very careful) and that Mr Woods had not raised any issue with him, showed that at the time of the float the contracts were not seen as a significant liability.

16.32 No steps were subsequently taken to procure the assignment of the contracts with those four banks and in respect of the National Westminster (which formally agreed in principle in May 1991) no assignment was in fact executed[a]. KM told us that he thought it had been intended to follow the course of buying out the contracts but, after the flotation, things might have slipped and there might have been difficulties in the private side actually getting together the money to get the banks to agree to the assignment. Also, there was no one who saw it as their job to push for the assignments and so they did not happen. On the insolvency of the private side companies following the death of RM, the indemnity provided by RMG proved worthless and MGN had to seek a release from these contracts on payment of a total of £22m[b].

---

a The securing of the assignment became the responsibility of Mr Stoney and Mr Griffiths. As set out at paragraphs 20.22 and 20.26, Mr Stoney was given board responsibility for the Treasury and Mr Griffiths made Treasurer.

b KM told us that the scale of potential loss had been seriously underestimated by him at the time of the flotation.

17. THE MARKETING OF THE SHARES IN APRIL AND MAY 1991

The marketing strategy

17.1 Once it had been decided to make an offer to overseas professional investors in addition to UK investors, there were three main markets to which the offer was to be directed.

- The UK institutions
- The general public in the UK, particularly the readers of newspapers published by MGN
- Overseas professional investors

Prior to the privatisation issues of the 1980s, the price of an issue in the UK had generally been fixed by the sponsoring bank and broker in consultation with the company and its shareholders; the issue of the shares at that agreed price had then been underwritten by the sponsor and sub-underwritten by institutions in the market. However, because of concern that the early privatisation issues had been underpriced, what was known as a "book building" exercise had been used in later privatisations based upon the way in which new issues of securities were made in the United States. In a book building exercise, the broker sought to make a firm placing of a proportion of the issue with institutional investors so that the level of demand for the shares could be gauged and the price that the institutions were prepared to pay could be ascertained. The objective was to seek to exploit what were described to us as the competitive tensions in the market in order to increase the price where there was an excess of institutional demand for the number of shares likely to be available.

17.2 Smith New Court considered that this was an appropriate strategy to adopt for the flotation of MGN because (although they knew of a significant body of institutions in the City that would not buy shares in any company connected with RM) they estimated that there would be sufficient demand from institutions to make book building an appropriate route. After extensive discussions with both RM and Samuel Montagu, this strategy was approved. The marketing to overseas investors was left to SBIL; they considered that because media companies were more highly valued in the United States than in the UK, and because the perception of RM in the US was favorably influenced by his acquisition of the *New York Daily News* and his entrepreneurial style, there would be strong demand in the United States at the price that the shares were likely to be offered. This thinking proved correct.

The marketing to the public

17.3 Marketing to the public (which RM was keen to provide)[a] was an essential part of the marketing strategy. Attempts were made to persuade the Stock Exchange to agree to preferential rights of subscription for Reed shareholders[b], for MCC shareholders and

---

[a] At one of the first meetings to deal with the flotation he had been inclined to market only to the public and to entrust the writing of the prospectus to Mr Haines.

[b] PPL had given an undertaking to Reed on the acquisition of MGN in 1984 that Reed shareholders would be given preferential rights of subscription on a flotation of MGN.

subsequently for all readers of the MGN newspapers[a]. The Stock Exchange refused to allow any such preferences, much to RM's displeasure.

17.4 In order to gauge the interest of the public a market survey was conducted between 21 and 22 March 1991 which led Dewe Rogerson to conclude that it was a flotation about which the public was generally unaware, but for which there was considerable potential demand. As a result of this research, it was decided that the issue was not of such a size that it would be worthwhile spending the large sums of money necessary to advertise it widely, but marketing should be concentrated on the readership of the newspapers published by MGN and the "Andy Capp" image should be used.

17.5 Before this decision was made there had been considerable discussion as to whether the MGN newspapers should merely report the publication of the prospectus, include the prospectus in a copy of the newspaper and say no more, or whether the newspapers should be used to promote an awareness of the flotation[b]. After discussion it was decided that it was appropriate for MGN to communicate with its readership through its newspapers, but that all such articles would be carefully reviewed by Clifford Chance and Samuel Montagu for conformity with the Financial Services Act.

17.6 An insert describing the flotation was distributed with MGN's main newspapers on 3 and 5 May 1991 and several articles were also published. Considerable steps[c] were taken to ensure that they were confined to factual reporting and that there was no attempt to persuade the readers to buy shares[d]. However it was accepted that it was very difficult to present a factual story (particularly given the pressures from RM[e]) that was uninfluenced by enthusiasm for the success of the issue.

17.7 The view was expressed to us that on any future flotation of shares in a company that owns or publishes a newspaper, that newspaper ought only carry advertisements for the issue and ought not to be able to report on it.

---

a The Stock Exchange refused to grant this on the basis that there was not an identifiable class of persons to be benefitted.

b This is an issue that has been addressed on overseas flotations of other newspaper publishing companies.

c On 26 April 1991 RM wrote to the Chairman of The Securities & Investment Board (SIB) for guidance on the reporting of the flotation in MGN newspapers. The SIB advised that there should be no difficulty about "straightforward factual reporting", but there should be no question of including anything that could be interpreted as a recommendation to buy.

d There were only two occasions when the advisers were concerned about what had been published and both seem to have arisen from a misunderstanding rather than from any attempt to evade the stringent scrutiny of the advisers.

e On 29 April 1991 RM instructed his editors that the flotation should be treated as a "story of worldwide interest". What was written in accordance with that edict was, however, substantially modified by the lawyers and Samuel Montagu.

The provision of information on RM's background

17.8 The description of RM in the prospectus merely referred to his other directorships. It did not mention the 1971/73 DTI Reports.

17.9 We were told that some of the institutional investors, when considering the flotation of MGN, had the conclusions set out in the 1971/73 DTI Reports in their minds; in addition they had some (or all) of the perceptions of MCC to which we referred at paragraph 7.14.

17.10 However it is doubtful whether the readers of the newspapers published by MGN (to whom the issue of new shares was specifically directed) knew much about any of these aspects of RM's background. We received evidence that overseas professional investors held a different perception of RM to that held by many UK professional investors[a].

17.11 Mr Hannam, who had considerable responsibility at SBIL for marketing the issue overseas, was aware of the 1971/73 DTI Reports and that RM had been criticised but was unaware until after the offer had closed of the conclusion reached about RM's fitness to have stewardship of a publicly quoted company. No questions were asked by overseas investors about the 1971/73 DTI Reports, or about RM's background or about the way in which MCC had been run; as far as Mr Hannam was concerned, what they were selling was a newspaper business and RM's past was irrelevant to that, particularly as he understood that RM would be stepping down within a year.

17.12 Nonetheless, within the UK, the coverage of the flotation in competing newspapers did not hesitate to remind the readers of those papers about RM's background and the well known conclusion of the 1971/73 DTI Reports. To the extent that any reader of the MGN newspapers read other newspapers, he would have been aware that there was controversy surrounding RM.

17.13 We were told by Samuel Montagu that they gave some thought to including in the prospectus a reference to the 1971/73 DTI Reports. They concluded that the Reports had been overtaken by RM's subsequent rehabilitation (as exemplified, in their view, by the Stock Exchange's acceptance of him as chairman of MCC); to have included both a reference to the past and to that rehabilitation would have been confusing to potential investors. If, as Mr McIntosh put it, a "health warning" had to be given, then the conclusion was that the company was probably not suitable for listing.

17.14 If RM's past had been considered material, we were told, MGN's readership probably would have learnt of it from the coverage in other newspapers to which we have referred. Consideration of this issue of disclosure does not appear to have been raised with the directors of MGN.

---

[a] SBIL told us that they did consider whether any mention should be made of RM's past, but noted that nothing had been said in the prospectus for a rights issue by MCC in 1986 or in the prospectus issued for the listing of shares in Berlitz on the New York Stock Exchange in 1989.

The marketing launch

17.15 Approaches to the institutional market in the UK began on 15 April 1991 and a lack of enthusiasm was encountered. The institutions raised questions on the 1971/73 DTI Reports, on how QPI and Donohue had come to be included within MGN, on the strength of the board and on the protection against RM dealing with his private side companies. In contrast considerable interest was shown when the approach was made to the overseas markets between 16 and 25 April 1991; there was a desire for more information about certain aspects of the business and a desire to meet the management of MGN.

17.16 On Thursday 25 April 1991, Smith New Court began to see if they could build a book. It became apparent very quickly that there was little demand amongst the UK institutions for a firm subscription to the shares, although there were offers to sub-underwrite the issue in the traditional way. Smith New Court found it hard to persuade the institutions to overcome the initial hurdle of looking beyond RM and considering the merits of the business of MGN. Smith New Court told us that they had underestimated the hostility of the institutional market to RM which arose partly from a lack of trust of RM, partly from the dislike of his business methods and partly as a result of his rudeness to institutional managers and analysts[a].

17.17 It was therefore decided to abandon book building and to proceed in the traditional manner with Samuel Montagu underwriting the offer and Smith New Court seeking sub-underwriting participation[b]. It was also decided to increase the proportion of the offer available to the overseas markets and to seek SBIL's assistance in the sub-underwriting and selling within the UK.

17.18 By 30 April 1991 the issue had been fully sub-underwritten, although those that had declined to sub-underwrite included many of the leading institutions. Many simply wanted to have nothing to do with MGN[c], even on a sub-underwriting basis.

17.19 Between 2 and 8 May 1991, to ensure the success of the overseas part of the issue, "roadshows" were organised in Paris, Toronto, Boston, New York and Zurich[d]. These were successful and stimulated a demand in each of those centres. RM attended all of them and we were told appeared to some as a very charismatic figure.

---

a KM told us that, whilst RM was impatient with and rude to institutional investors who often took some time to catch up with his business ideas, he got on well with many analysts.

b Sir Robert Clark and Mr Clements were not made aware of this.

c The list of those who declined to participate was described to us as reading "like Debrett's, ... a pretty impressive list in terms of calibre. In fact I would say it is the best list you can possibly look at from a sub-underwriting point of view."

d Institutional presentations were made in the UK. IM told us that, whilst doing these, RM was called away. Against the protestations of various advisers, RM left the presentation to IM who performed creditably. IM also attended the overseas roadshows except those in Boston and Zurich.

17.20 In the UK, although a number of analysts thought that the issue would go to a premium, UBS Phillips & Drew Research Limited (UBS Phillips & Drew) put out a circular (entitled "Can't Recommend A Purchase") which was very critical of the issue[a].

---

[a] RM was very angry at this and he went to considerable lengths to bring pressure to bear on UBS Phillips & Drew who later issued a paper on MGN, the terms of which arose out of a substantial discussion between UBS Phillips & Drew and the Maxwells. KM told us that RM telephoned the Chairman of the bank; RM told the Chairman that if the analyst was not fired immediately he would terminate relations between the group and the bank. RM visited UBS' offices. The analyst left the employment of UBS Phillips & Drew in July 1991 to take up an alternative position at Kleinwort Benson.

18. THE SUCCESS OF THE OFFER

The closure of the lists

18.1 Under the terms of the offer, applications had to be received by 10.00 am on 9 May 1991 and the lists could close at any time thereafter; normally lists close just after the latest time by which applications have to be made. Shortly before 10.00 am on 9 May 1991, reports from the receiving bank indicated that it might be a "close run thing" to get the issue fully subscribed and that it might be slightly short; with a 95 per cent. subscription, the undersubscribed shares would then have had to be spread amongst the many sub-underwriters. We have been told by the receiving bankers that the state of the lists was not known at 10.00 am and that applications came in thereafter.

18.2 When Samuel Montagu learnt it might be undersubscribed, Mr McIntosh considered with Sir Michael Richardson what could be done. Sir Michael said that Smith New Court would be happy to subscribe but would want to ensure that there was proper disclosure. Both Smith New Court and Samuel Montagu took legal advice on this point and were told that if Smith New Court applied in such circumstances, then the application would have to be disclosed and an announcement made about the circumstances in which it had been made.

18.3 Whilst this advice was being taken, Mr Galloway and Mr McIntosh had a conversation with RM; it was clear that RM also knew that it was not certain that the issue had been fully subscribed. Samuel Montagu then learnt either from RM or through Smith New Court that Goldman Sachs were going to make an application; Samuel Montagu received the impression that Goldman Sachs had been encouraged to do this by RM, who, we were told by KM, considered MGN to have been undervalued by the market; RM was very disappointed and he saw the same pressures at play as he believed had affected the MCC share price and thought that people were shorting the market. The bookbuilding had not gone as well as the primary underwriters wanted and there was some surprise that Goldman Sachs had not participated. KM told us that, at a meeting over a drink between RM, KM and Mr Sheinberg, Mr Sheinberg promised RM that he would subscribe for 5 million MGN shares and that he would keep them. Mr Sheinberg told us that there was no such meeting and no such agreement. He would never have made any agreement that restricted his ability to trade. In any event, he had to undergo surgery in New York on 2 May 1991 and did not visit London between mid-April and mid-June 1991. He had only subscribed for shares because of the conversation referred to in the next paragraph.

18.4 Very early on that morning of 9 May 1991 New York time, Mr Sheinberg was telephoned by KM. Mr Sheinberg told us that KM said he was relaying a message from RM:

> "Would we subscribe for 5 million shares of [MGN] ?"

Mr Sheinberg thought there was little risk in this and they might even make some money. KM thought that this telephone conversation was probably KM chasing him up following the meeting to make sure that Mr Sheinberg did in fact subscribe. Mr Sheinberg therefore decided to subscribe for the sake of good customer relations. He instructed his London office accordingly. At some time between 12.00 noon and 12.30 pm an application for 5 million shares was received from Goldman Sachs and shortly thereafter at about 1 pm the lists were closed[a].

Those who bought the shares

18.5 Later on 9 May 1991, it was announced that the offer had closed oversubscribed with 100,000 applications from the general public. The following day Samuel Montagu announced that a subscription had been received for 121.92 million shares out of the 114 million shares on offer in the UK. The basis of allocation[b] was announced and it was stated that it was anticipated that dealings would begin at 2.30pm on Friday 17 May 1991[c].

18.6 The subscription to the offer[d] was approximately the following:

(1) United Kingdom offer: About 2,000 applications came from MGN employees and about 102,000 from others. Of these applications

- SBIL applied for 33 million shares[e]
- Goldman Sachs applied for 5 million shares
- 5 other offers were of 1 million shares and over
- 16 offers were of between 200,000 shares and 1 million shares
- 95,000 applications were for 1000 shares or less and of these 41,000 were for the minimum allocation of 200 shares. It was assumed that these were largely from the readership of the MGN newspapers.

---

a Goldman Sachs received 4.5 million shares because of scaling down.

b Applications for up to 1500 shares were met in full; applications for more than 1500 shares were met as to 90 per cent of the amount applied for.

c There was some controversy about the timing of the commencement of dealing. SBIL wanted it brought forward as it was their view the period between the close of the offer and the commencement of dealing could lead to nervousness; they also wanted the dealing to start at 2.30pm as this was much easier for New York. The controversy that arose was largely due to a failure in communication between Smith New Court, Samuel Montagu and the Stock Exchange; although it caused some acrimony and complaints at the time, we are satisfied that what happened was as a result of misunderstanding and confusion.

d The combined offer was for 192.5 million shares; the UK offer was for 114 million shares and the overseas offer for 78.5 million shares.

e For placing with mainly overseas clients in addition to the 78.5 million shares forming part of the overseas offer; SBIL were allocated 29.7 million shares in respect of the 33 million shares applied for.

(2) Overseas professional investors: The overseas offer comprised approximately 40 per cent. of the issue; SBIL sold over 70 per cent. of the overseas offer and of this offer and the 29.7 million shares allocated to them from the UK offer, 64 per cent. was sold in the US, 24 per cent. in Europe, 12 per cent. in the Far East.

19. THOSE WHO BENEFITED FROM THE PROCEEDS OF THE FLOTATION

The destination of the proceeds of the flotation

19.1 The total amount raised from the flotation after the payment of expenses and commissions on the overseas offering was £238.4m. This sum was applied as follows:

- £210m Replacement of £360m facility by £150m facility
- £18m Payment to RMH[a]
- £2.9m UK offer commissions
- £7.5m Balance left for MGN

19.2 It had been anticipated at an earlier stage that very much more than £18m would be raised for the private side; it was only of this small order because the shares had been floated at a much lower price than RM had anticipated. However Smith New Court told us that the reaction of the market (as described in the preceding chapter) indicated that the price obtained was at the higher end of what could have been obtained.

19.3 The fees paid to the advisers[b] amounted to £8.95m:

Samuel Montagu	£ 3.5m
Smith New Court	£ 0.75m
SBIL	£ 1m
CLD	£ 1.48m
Clifford Chance	£ 1.2m
Linklaters & Paines	£ 0.48m
Dewe Rogerson	£ 0.54m

Table 7 – Fees paid to advisers on the flotation

The benefits of the flotation to RM's interests

19.4 The principal benefits obtained by the flotation for RM's interests were the reduction of the overall debt owed to the banks and the ability to use MGN shares as collateral for the private side's borrowing requirements.

19.5 There was one potentially very substantial disadvantage. MGN had been a substantial provider of cash to the private companies and the effect of the flotation should have been to cut off this source of cash, except in the form of dividends. However, for the reasons given, RM's use of the cash flow was in fact going to continue as before.

19.6 When referring to the benefits of the flotation, we have referred to that benefit as accruing to RM's interests. By the time of the flotation, control of all the UK companies had passed to

[a] A scheme was arranged involving a dividend payment and a loan to make this payment "more tax efficient".

[b] Excluding underwriting commission.

RM's family company, HI, and the Maxwell Foundation had merely an economic interest in those companies. However, in earlier years the Maxwell Foundation had enjoyed the complete economic interest in and control of MGN and the other companies the Maxwell Foundation owned and controlled had benefited from the use of MGN's assets and cash flow; as set out in Chapters 1 and 3, the Maxwell Foundation followed RM's instructions and had been used very largely for RM's own advantages[a].

19.7 As described in the previous chapters of this Report, whenever adverse publicity or an impediment to expansion arose from the fact of Liechtenstein control and when there ceased to be any fiscal advantages in Liechtenstein ownership or control, control or ownership from Liechtenstein was removed, albeit that this was done carefully so as to avoid exposing the reality of the previous position.

The reasons for the flotation

19.8 The prospectus set out what was aptly described to us by a member of the Stock Exchange's staff as the conventional reasons for a flotation - the reduction of MGN's debt, the advantage from listing of access to capital markets and the ability to give further incentive to staff by offering share options and employee share schemes.

19.9 At an early stage in the drafting of the section of the prospectus that set out the reasons for the flotation, consideration was given to including a passage on the need to reduce the indebtedness of RM's companies. Such a passage was drafted by Mr Willett who considered that the reason why the company was being floated at that time was that RM wanted to reduce the indebtedness of the private side companies and a flotation was part of the overall programme to reduce the indebtedness of the private side companies[b].

19.10 Mr Willett's perception was largely correct; there were two reasons why the flotation took place when it did and both related to the private side:

- the need to reduce the overall indebtedness of RM's companies;
- the need to have additional collateral available in the form of marketable shares to collateralise the debt incurred or to be incurred by the private side[c].

No mention was made in the prospectus of either of these reasons[d]. Technically, the issue was an offer for the sale of new shares and it might be said that it was not a primary function to

---

a An example of another advantage was that he could claim that where control of a company lay with the Maxwell Foundation he did not control that company; this was used as the reason by Mr Cook for not relaying to Bacon & Woodrow the increase in self-investment in October 1990 (see paragraph 6.23).

b RM required Mr Willett to take him through parts of the prospectus line by line, particularly those sections where RM had a special interest, including the historical perspective and reasons for transactions. Mr Willett told us RM's attitude to the topics upon which he focused was co-operative and painstaking.

c As set out in a footnote to paragraph 6.74, KM told us this reason only became apparent in the Spring of 1991.

d Mr Galloway could not recall why the paragraph drafted by Mr Willett was deleted but thought that it might have been included in an early draft of the prospectus and have reflected a proposal that RMH would sell some of its MGN shares and apply the proceeds in repaying the balance of the private side's debt to MGN.

reduce the debts of the private side. However, that was not the reality.There was given in the prospectus as one of the reasons the reduction in the bank debt of MGN. KM told us that the need of the private side to reduce debt was well known in the market at the time but that the prospectus had been drafted by the professionals involved.

19.11 Nothing was said in the prospectus about the financial state of the private side as the majority shareholder in MGN. Samuel Montagu and SBIL did consider the financial position of the private side as material in so far as it related to the issues identified at paragraph 16.23; Samuel Montagu had asked CLD to carry out a review of the private side finances (which we have described) as part of their due diligence procedures and had kept SBIL informed of the results. However, Samuel Montagu did not give consideration as to whether anything should be said in the prospectus about the state of the private side finances. We were told by Samuel Montagu that prior to the flotation of The Telegraph plc in 1992 (which took place with the benefit of the knowledge of what had happened to MGN) disclosure had not been made about the finances of any majority shareholder and the Stock Exchange had not required it. SBIL told us that they did consider whether something should be said, but decided, in the light of the letter from CLD and the fact that the intercompany debt had been eliminated, that nothing need be said.

Samuel Montagu told us that a reader of the prospectus taking account of various paragraphs in the accountants' report would have been aware that one of the reasons for the flotation was to reduce private side debts; they accepted it was not spelt out as a reason.

PART THREE
THE EVENTS AFTER THE FLOTATION

20. MAY TO JULY 1991

20.1 The two chapters forming this part of this Report set out the circumstances in which MGN was run and its assets dealt with in the period between the publication of the prospectus and the death of RM on 5 November 1991[a]. What happened to the pension fund after 30 April 1991 has been outside the scope of our enquiry.

20.2 It is convenient to consider first what happened up to the time the interim results of MGN were announced at the end of July 1991 and to do this under four main headings:

(1) Control over the management of MGN
(2) Control over the finances of MGN in May and June 1991
(3) The market in MGN shares and the secret purchases of MGN shares by RM
(4) The interim results

(1) Control over the management of the company

20.3 The flotation made little difference to the way SDR operated; it continued to be managed through its board in Scotland.

20.4 The English operating company, MGN Limited, did not have meetings of its board. Mr Burrington, however, held regular meetings of the operational directors which were minuted but which RM refused to attend; IM went along occasionally on his own initiative, primarily as an observer, since he wanted to have a general view of what was happening in the company, which he could not get at formal board meetings[b]. These meetings, although not formal board meetings, were considered by most of the operational directors to be as good as board meetings. Nevertheless RM continued the 8.30am meetings through which he had run the business prior to the flotation (as referred to at paragraph 4.43) and important operational decisions continued to be referred to him rather than taken at board meetings.

20.5 The board of MGN[c], the listed holding company, met for its first monthly board meeting on 11 June 1991[d]. No agenda had been sent out as RM had not approved it and papers were only

---

[a] We were told by several witnesses that in their view RM was not as well in 1991 as he had been and was not as alert; he would fall asleep in meetings. IM and KM, in particular, told us that RM was not in the same physical condition that he had previously enjoyed, that his attention-span and temper had got shorter and that he was much more tired.

[b] IM also instigated lunchtime meetings with Mr Burrington in his office where they would discuss operational matters in some detail.

[c] IM told us that the new non-executive directors did not help overcome the management problems because they did not take any initiative to make contact with the other directors: they merely turned up at board meetings.

[d] Mr Ferguson and Lord Williams were not present.

provided to those who attended when they arrived for the meeting. They were kept waiting by RM whilst he agreed the agenda with Mr Stephens.

20.6 It is necessary to describe this meeting in a little detail in relation to three significant matters.

(a) Approval of the bank mandate

20.7 The first item on the agenda was the approval of previous board minutes. There were undoubtedly a number of minutes in the papers that were in the folders provided to the directors for them to read when they arrived. These included minutes for the board meetings that had taken place on 16 and 29 April 1991 in connection with the flotation and meetings of some committees of the board that had dealt with various share option schemes. There had, however, been a meeting of the board attended only by RM and Mr Stoney on 20 May 1991 when a bank mandate had been approved for a new bank account for MGN at the National Westminster. The mandate had been drafted to give RM sole signatory authority for an unlimited amount, in accordance with the standard practice for RM's companies and was authorised by the board meeting attended by RM and Mr Stoney on those terms.

20.8 After the death of RM there was considerable controversy as to whether the non-executive directors and certain of the executive directors of MGN had known that RM had sole signatory authority for an unlimited amount and whether they had approved a mandate for MGN in that form[a]. We are satisfied that amongst the minutes of previous board meetings that were before the directors of MGN at their first full board meeting on 11 June 1991 was the minute of the meeting on 20 May 1991 at which RM and Mr Stoney had approved the mandate with RM's sole signatory authority. However, as the papers were only provided to the directors as they arrived and they therefore did not have a proper opportunity of reading them prior to this item of the agenda being reached, they appear to have approved the minutes of previous meetings, including the meeting of 20 May 1991 approving the bank mandate, without appreciating that they were sanctioning RM's sole signatory authority on that mandate. At the conclusion of the meeting, Mr Stephens, in accordance with the practice that was followed at MCC, collected up the papers from the directors who were present, unless any director wanted to keep any particular papers. Some did, but others handed their papers back.

(b) Delegation of the board's powers

20.9 Shortly before the meeting RM had asked Mr Stephens to send to him the text of the resolution of the board of MCC that had delegated to him as a committee of one all the power of the board (to which we referred at paragraph 10.5)[b]. This was sent together with a draft resolution providing for delegation of the whole of the powers of the board to RM as a committee of one and, in his absence, to a committee of two (one of whom was to be IM) to deal with formal matters.

---

a None of the payments to which we refer subsequently that were made from MGN were made using this account.

b The resolution of MGN's board in October 1990 giving concurrent power to a committee comprising RM or KM and one other referred to at paragraph 10.27, had not been revoked.

20.10 At the meeting on 11 June 1991, RM told the board that certain decisions would have to be taken rapidly and he suggested the appointment of a committee of the board with himself as one of the members. He told them that any such decisions would be reported to the whole board at the next meeting so they could ratify them. Some of those present understood that this was to deal with formal matters, but all those present approved the delegation in principle and the preparation of the resolution was left to Mr Stephens. A resolution was subsequently prepared, but for reasons that we have been unable to determine, it did not (like the MCC resolution) delegate the whole of the powers of the board to RM alone, but delegated them to a committee of two, one of whom was to be RM; in RM's absence, a committee of two, one of whom was to be IM was to be entitled to deal with formal matters. This resolution continued in full force and effect until after RM's death, although it was amended (for the reasons explained in paragraph 21.33 below) at the board meeting on 12 September 1991.

(c) Other matters

20.11 Reports on the operations of the business were then presented and management accounts made available to the board. There was then discussion of some policy issues. Sir Robert Clark asked if, in future, financial reports could be provided prior to the meeting and RM readily agreed that they should be provided two days ahead of time[a]. Nothing was said about the payments in April and May 1991 between MGN and the private side or the payment to Goldman Sachs (described at paragraphs 20.18 and following); nothing was reported about the division of responsibility between Mr Guest and Mr Stoney which RM had formally implemented on 20 May 1991 (as described at paragraph 20.22).

20.12 Although there was not a great deal of discussion at the meeting, we were told that RM was courteous and treated with a degree of deference the views expressed by Sir Robert Clark and Mr Clements.

20.13 There was then a separate meeting of the board to consider the sub-letting of part of the Great Dover Street premises to MCC and the offer of an interest in *The European*. Although the meeting was chaired by Sir Robert Clark, RM remained present, but neither of the two matters discussed is material.

20.14 There was also a further meeting on 11 June 1991 which was unknown, at that time, to the other members of the board. The minute of this meeting records that it was attended by RM and IM[b] and a resolution was passed ratifying the cap and collar contract with SBC which it had been agreed in April 1991 would be assigned to RMG. In the documentation sent to SBC consequent upon that meeting, nothing was said about the intended assignment[c].

[a] Mr Stephens submitted a minute of the meeting of 11 June 1991 which contained a full discussion of the meeting. RM deleted most of it as he wanted only the main points recorded and it was this version that was put before the directors at the next meeting.

[b] IM told us that he knew nothing about any cap and collar contracts at that time and, therefore, that he doubted whether he had in fact attended this board meeting.

[c] Titmuss Sainer & Webb gave an opinion letter dated 12 June 1991 to SBC on the validity of the contract and the authority to execute it. They obtained their instructions from Mr Fuller and Mrs Raperport as they were unaware that there had been any separation of the treasury and were also unaware of the agreement to use best endeavours to procure an assignment.

(2) Control over the finances of the company in May and June 1991

(a) Information available to the MGN finance department

20.15 During the period to the death of RM in November 1991[a], there were a number of payments made between MGN and the private side, between MGN and US investment banks and between MGN and BIM. Although the MGN finance department knew within a day that payments had been made[b] and knew to whom they had been made or from whom they had been received, no documentation showing the purpose of a significant number of substantial payments was ever provided.

20.16 The cashier within the MGN finance department received daily statements of the account from the banks and, in respect of a transaction for which no documentation was available, recorded it on a schedule in accordance with the instructions given by the deputy finance director in April 1991 to which we have referred at paragraph 11.18. That schedule contained, apart from the transactions to which we will refer, a number of other transactions for which documentation subsequently became available. It is important to appreciate that the whole position was then not as clear to those in the finance department of MGN, as it became following investigations after RM's death. Nonetheless, the size of the transactions and the fact that many of them remained undocumented for so long was undoubtedly apparent at the time.

(b) Transactions in May 1991

20.17 There are set out in Appendix 17, details of the transactions between MGN, the private side and certain banks between April 1991 and 16 July 1991. It is necessary only to deal with the more significant transactions in the body of this Report.

20.18 There were three significant transactions in May 1991. On 21 May 1991 under an authority signed by RM, £20m was transferred to RMH. No documentation to explain the transfer was ever provided to the MGN finance department. Enquiries have established that it was used (together with funds from MCC and LBG) towards repayment of loans made by Barclays and Bank of Nova Scotia to the private side.

20.19 On 21 May 1991 £30m was transferred into MGN. No documentation was ever provided to the MGN finance department that properly explained this transfer, but they were subsequently told that these funds were the proceeds of the redemption of the MCC commercial paper purchased on 29 and 30 April 1991 as set out at paragraph 11.19. Evidence from National Westminster confirms that this was in fact a correct explanation.

20.20 On 29 May 1991, £11m was transferred to Goldman Sachs under the sole authority of RM.

---

[a] There were in fact some smaller payments after his death arising out of the transactions that had occurred prior to then.

[b] Except in the case of the loan from Bankers Trust made in October 1991 which is referred to at paragraph 21.58.

- RM explained this payment to Mr Stoney as being a deposit with a US investment house in order to show the financial strength of MGN in connection with a proposed placement of MGN's shares in the United States and this explanation was passed on to the finance department. At this time (as referred to at paragraph 22.63), consideration was in fact being given to obtaining a credit rating for MGN from Moody's and Standard & Poor's for this purpose and work was actively in hand to produce a preliminary information memorandum for them.
- The payment had in fact been made towards settling the amounts due to Goldman Sachs in respect of the purchase of 3 million MCC shares by Servex on 24 April 1991 and 14 million shares by TIB on the same day (as referred to at paragraph 9.8).
- KM requested Mr Wood at Goldman Sachs to write to Mr Stoney acknowledging the payment[a]. Mr Wood did so in the following terms:

  > "This is to confirm that value date 29 May 1991 Goldman Sachs & Co received £11,000,000 from [MGN]."

  This letter was not of the kind and did not set out the usual information that would be supplied when funds are deposited with an investment house. The letter did not provide details of the account into which the funds had been deposited or the investments which would be made with the funds. It was simply a receipt.
- KM told us that he recalled asking Goldman Sachs for a receipt. Normally such a request would have been made by the treasury department so it was unusual for KM to have been making the call. He said that he thought he made the call as the result of being asked to do so by Mr Stoney.
- The real purpose behind the payment of this amount to Goldman Sachs was unknown to the MGN finance department save for the oral explanation that it had been made as a deposit. No further documentation was provided to the finance department or to Mr Stoney[b].

(c) RM's decision in relation to the roles of Mr Guest and Mr Stoney on 20 May 1991

20.21 Mr Stoney had spent a very substantial amount of time working on the flotation of MGN, but he had no clearly defined role within MGN apart from his understanding that he would continue to deal with corporate finance matters, the banks and probably the analysts (as referred to at paragraph 11.25). He was concerned about his position and raised it with KM on several occasions.

---

a Mr Stoney told us that he had pressed KM for this letter; when he received it, he told KM that this did not provide the information he would need to satisfy the auditors.

b KM told us that he did not recall Mr Stoney telling him this.

20.22 On 25 April 1991 Mr Guest had written a memorandum to RM seeking the appointment of a treasurer[a]. Nothing had happened and so on 16 May 1991 he sent a similar memorandum. This time there was a response; RM summoned him and Mr Stoney to a meeting on 20 May 1991[b]. Although recollections of what transpired at that meeting differ, the result of the meeting was a memorandum laying down their respective functions, which RM required both Mr Stoney and Mr Guest to sign.

- Mr Stoney was to be answerable to RM and solely responsible for the bank relations, the treasury function[c], investor relations and relationships with the auditors, including accounting policies;
- Mr Guest was to be answerable to RM and solely responsible for the finance functions within MGN and SDR, preparation of the monthly management accounts and compliance with group internal control systems.
- A joint area of responsibility was defined to include the setting up of a standardised form of management accounts and reporting system, the provision of information to the audit committee and the preparation of the statutory accounts.

The important effect of the memorandum was to confirm the curtailment of Mr Guest's functions effectively to being that of the Chief Accountant responsible for the internal aspects of MGN's financing and the position of Mr Stoney as responsible for dealing with the external aspects of MGN's finances. It varied the responsibilities set out in the prospectus within days of listing and left Mr Stoney, who was not an independent director, in charge of the treasury where he was in a position of conflict of interest[d].

20.23 Mr Guest accepted this position because he considered Mr Stoney had experience in dealing with the matters assigned to him and, had he not accepted the position laid down by RM, he would have had to resign. This division of responsibilities was never formally reported to the board but it was not kept confidential. For example, in the information memorandum subsequently prepared for the credit rating agencies, this division of responsibility was clearly set out[e]. Mr Horwood was told privately by Mr Guest of RM's decision and Mr Burrington had learnt of it by August 1991.

---

a KM told us that the memo (see footnote to paragraph 11.14) from Mr Guest was part of a "turf war" between MGN and the other parts of the empire and had nothing to do with proper corporate governance; Mr Guest shared the attitude common among MGN executives of seeming to look down on the other parts of the empire as lacking the glamour of newspaper publishing and was simply anxious to keep MGN a separate group.

b KM told us that there had been conflicts between Mr Guest and Mr Stoney as to their areas of responsibility and Mr Guest had taken up some of KM's time asking questions about wider corporate finance points. KM told RM that things had to change and that there must be a separation out of operational finance which Mr Guest should deal with, Mr Stoney dealing with the rest.

c Mr Stoney told us that he spoke to KM regularly on MGN's cash flow requirements as he regarded him as having a position where he had an overview of what was happening in all the Maxwell companies; for example on 21 June 1991, he sent a memorandum to KM setting out MGN's funding requirements, because he wanted KM to supervise this whilst he was on holiday. He told us he continued to do this until September 1991 when he was told by RM to cease consulting KM. KM agreed with this evidence.

d KM told us that he could not recall any concern being raised by anyone about Mr Stoney not being an independent director.

e This was supplied to many of the directors, but it was generally not read in detail.

20.24 The non-executive directors were unaware of the decision and it appears that, although some of the other executive directors knew that Mr Stoney was playing a greater role in the financial affairs of MGN, they did not know what RM had formally decided. KM told us that the decision was not kept secret from them or anyone else[a].

(d) RM's appointment of a treasurer on 5 June 1991

20.25 A concern that arose from the discussions that had taken place with Standard & Poor's and Moody's (during their initial review to enable them to give an indication of a credit rating) was the degree of segregation of MGN from the rest of the private side companies and the adequacy of the ring fence (to which we refer at paragraph 22.63). One of the specific concerns that the rating agencies raised and which Mr Stoney conveyed to RM, was related to the treasury. On 31 May 1991 Mr Stoney sent a memorandum to KM which informed him that Standard & Poor's and Moody's would be focusing on the following points in relation to the treasury function:

> " (1) Details of this operation
> (2) Treasury policy
> (3) Staff levels
> (4) Treasurer's name
>
> I have made it quite clear to Salomon Brothers and CLD in our discussions that the Treasury function within MGN comes within my areas of responsibility, and advised them that this is in the process of being separated.
>
> I would be grateful if I could discuss with you, as a matter of urgency, the exact mechanisms and timings of this."[b]

20.26 On 5 June 1991, RM appointed as treasurer of MGN, on the recommendation of Mr Fuller, Mr Simon Griffiths who had worked in the central treasury department since February 1990. His appointment was made without consultation with Mr Guest who first met him on 6 June 1991. Mr Griffiths was told to report to Mr Stoney and not to the finance department of MGN, because RM had given Mr Stoney the responsibility for the treasury.

20.27 Mr Griffiths continued to share the same office and secretary as when he had worked in the central treasury[c] and he continued to do work for MCC after his appointment as treasurer of MGN, particularly during July 1991 and into early August 1991[d]. Mr Griffiths remained in

---

a He recalled speaking to Mr Clements about the split in responsibilities between Mr Stoney and Mr Guest. Mr Clements had no recollection of being told and was very surprised when he learnt of this from Mr Guest in October 1991.

b The member of CLD's staff who was dealing with a report on MGN for the credit rating agencies agreed that he had been told what Mr Stoney said in the memorandum; Mr Stoney said he told Mr Corbett of SBIL this; Mr Corbett has since died.

c His appointment was not announced until 29 July 1991.

d Miss Roberts, who also worked in the central treasury said the separation of the treasury into three parts - MGN, MCC and private side - did not take place until early August 1991 when she was appointed Treasurer of the private side. Her evidence is probably accurate as the separation appears to have resulted from the discovery of the matters at MCC set out at paragraph 21.4 and was one of the steps taken consequent upon that discovery at the insistence of the independent directors of MCC.

this office until September 1991 when a separate office for himself and Mr Stoney was provided on a different floor of Maxwell House. Arrangements were also made by the MGN finance department for Mr Griffiths to have an office within the department (which was at Orbit House) but he never moved to that office.

20.28 Mr Griffiths told us that during the period to 5 November 1991, he received some instructions from Mr Stoney, some from Mr Fuller, some from KM and some from RM. Therefore, although from 5 June 1991, MGN had its own treasurer, his office was always in a different building to the MGN finance department, he reported not to the finance department of MGN but to Mr Stoney and took his instructions not from the finance department but from RM and occasionally from KM and from the two other persons who were primarily associated with MCC and the private companies. He was not in any sense the treasurer independent of RM's other interests.

(e) Dealing with the banks

20.29 Although dealing with the banks was the responsibility of Mr Stoney, KM's role in dealing with the banks on behalf of the private companies and MCC, as well as MGN, continued after the flotation. When the banks had their meetings with KM, they continued to discuss with him questions relating to borrowing by MGN. All the clearing banks did this, as did Midland Montagu[a], a related company of Samuel Montagu. Midland Montagu had been told by RM that KM was not to be a director of MGN as Samuel Montagu had advised that this was not appropriate, though they had understood from RM that he had not wanted this to happen. They nonetheless continued to discuss with KM the affairs of all RM's companies (including MGN); they had become used to talking to KM[b] as the most important person to deal with in relation to the empire and RM remained, through his private side companies, the majority shareholder in MGN[c]. KM told us that his meetings with bankers was as a representative of the 51 per cent. shareholder in MGN, in particular RM, as the banks needed to deal with the companies as if one. But the dealings with the banks went further than that, KM recalled; for example, Barclays continued to deal with the treasurers and finance directors of all companies as still being part of one team. Those dealings were not consistent with MGN being an independent entity, but KM told us that he did not perceive that to be a requirement at the time.

20.30 Although most of the dealings with the banks were simply discussions on various proposals which were never implemented, Lloyds discussed with KM two matters relating to MGN which were carried through in August and October 1991, as described at paragraph 21.44 below.

---

a This was the name of the investment banking division of the Midland Bank Group.

b One banker told us that he had only had one discussion with IM and that was in relation to the seating plan for the annual award luncheon of "Banking World", the journal of the Chartered Institute of Bankers, the publication of which IM oversaw.

c Mr Clements told us he did not become aware of KM's role until after RM's death when he attended a meeting at Lloyds with Mr Guest; he was surprised that KM insisted on attending and behaved as if he was still in charge of the MGN finances.

(f) The position of the private side finances: the use of MGN shares as collateral

20.31 At the end of May 1991 the private side's debt to the banks was approximately £980m but it also had significant borrowings from MCC and the pension funds.

20.32 In consequence of the flotation, the private side had MGN shares available to it for use as collateral and the shares were so used. One significant use of MGN shares as collateral was that in connection with financing from Lehmans. In order for LBG to raise finance of $41m (using an arrangement involving US Treasury Bills identical to that used for the financing that had originated in November 1989 - see paragraph 5.39), 45 million MGN shares were pledged as collateral. These were pledged on 13 June 1991, but when it was appreciated at Lehmans that the size of the stake (which was about 11.25 per cent. of MGN) meant the interest would have to be announced, Lehmans immediately agreed with LBG that MCC shares be substituted for 33 million of the MGN shares so the stake would be brought below the notifiable 3 per cent.[a].

20.33 During the period up to RM's death shares in MGN were pledged to secure private side loans from a number of banks including Midland Bank, National Westminster[b], Lloyds, and Goldman Sachs[c]. Morgan Stanley took 28 million MGN shares as security for a loan to RMH for 7 days in June 1991; they did not appreciate that this interest had to be disclosed until August 1991 when they read the announcement by Goldman Sachs referred to at paragraph 21.16; the Stock Exchange and then H.M. Treasury were advised of the position. The Stock Exchange at first decided that no disclosure needed to be made, but later changed their mind and required disclosure. Details of the pledges are set out in Appendix 18.

(g) Transactions with the private side in June 1991

20.34 Although there were undocumented transactions during June 1991, there were no significant net payments from MGN's accounts. On the contrary, there were three significant receipts from the private side companies in June 1991:

- 14 June £4 m
- 25 June $19m (£11.7m)
- 28 June £8m

---

[a] The interest of Lehmans in the shares was notified to MGN on 17 June 1991 as having been acquired on 14 June 1991, the date the financing was made available; informal notification had been given by telephone on Friday 14 June 1991; Smith New Court were notified by MGN on 19 June 1991. No announcement was made to the public of this interest. The Stock Exchange were consulted but as both they and Smith New Court understood that the stake had been held for two days, nothing was announced and MGN were told not to act in this way again. In fact Lehmans did not return 33 million MGN shares until 25 June 1991 but Lehmans have told us that they ceased to regard themselves as interested on receipt of the MCC shares on 19 June 1991. The 33 million shares were re-registered in the name of RMH on 27 June 1991; when Lehmans received the MCC shares they held as collateral for this financing, as they already held MCC shares as collateral for the financing originally arranged by LBI as referred to at paragraph 5.39 , their holding of MCC shares as collateral was over 4 per cent of the share capital of MCC, but Lehmans did not appreciate this.

[b] see further paragraph 21.8

[c] The circumstances of the pledge to Goldman Sachs are set out at paragraph 21.11

No documentation to explain these payments was ever provided either to Mr Griffiths as treasurer or to the finance department of MGN. The only logical explanation of these payments is that they represented transfers to MGN of funds to reduce, prior to the end of MGN's half year on 28 June 1991, the balance on the intercompany account that had arisen as a result of the payments made from MGN in April and May 1991, details of which are set out in Appendix 17.

(h) The foreign exchange dealings

20.35 In addition to these three receipts there were two other significant pairs of transactions which represented unauthorised foreign exchange dealings carried out by the central treasury. There is no supporting documentation that explains the purposes of these transactions but they form part of a series of foreign exchange transactions carried out with numerous banks.

20.36 From about June 1991 each of RM's main bankers had experienced for the first time in their history of dealing with RM, the failure by one of his companies to honour a commitment. These had all occurred in the context of foreign exchange deals. Although the failures were explained to the banks as having been caused by errors in the "back room", the banks became concerned, albeit that they did not appreciate that:

- each of the other main banks had experienced similar problems;
- the "failures" on the transactions involving the private side were used as a means of very short term borrowings to assist the private side in its increasingly difficult financial position. KM told us that, with hindsight, he agreed that the failures had created short term liquidity.

20.37 In the second half of June 1991, the first of the foreign exchange transactions for MGN was carried out by Mr Griffiths on the instructions of Mr Fuller:

- On 21 June 1991, \$17.9m was sold for £11m which was credited to MGN's National Westminster account. The authority for this transaction was signed by RM.
- On 24 June 1991, \$17.9m was purchased from Goldman Sachs. Settlement of this was effected by a sterling payment of £11m from MGN's National Westminster bank account. The authority to effect the sterling payment was signed by Mr Burrington and KM. Mr Burrington told us he was requested to sign the authority by KM who told him that no other signatories were available and that the funds were urgently needed for a foreign exchange deal; Mr Burrington thought KM was acting at the behest of RM (who was in Moscow) although he knew KM was Chief Executive of MCC and not a director or officer of MGN. Mr Burrington did not consider the transaction to be unusual as MGN had dollar commitments[a]. KM thought it likely that Mr Burrington would have received the authority and then called him for confirmation that it was in order for him to sign; KM

[a] Mr Burrington told us that he subsequently made enquiries of Mr Guest about this transaction and that Mr Guest had told him, possibly in August 1991, that he had checked this out and that it was a proper transaction. Mr Burrington also told us he was told by Mr Craggs that the auditors had seen nothing wrong with the transaction. Enquiries were also made by Mr Burrington of Mr Hemple and Mr Craggs after RM's death. Mr Guest told us that he could not recall Mr Burrington mentioning this and he did not think he knew that Mr Burrington and KM had authorised the payment until after RM's death.

would have told him that it was, based on RM's instruction that the trade should be effected.

There was a loss on this foreign exchange transaction of £32,000 and this was charged to RMH on the intercompany account.

20.38 A similar foreign exchange transaction was also carried out on 24/25 June 1991:

- On 24 June 1991, Mr Griffiths sold $17.3m for £10.6m and the sterling proceeds were remitted to MGN's bank account at the National Westminster. The authority for this transaction was signed by RM and KM.
- On 25 June $17.3m to pay for this transaction (which had been effected through Lloyds) was transferred to Lloyds from MGN's dollar account under an authority signed by KM and Mr Bunn.

This transaction resulted in a profit to MGN of £81,000.

20.39 Neither KM (who was a signatory for three of these transfers) nor Mr Bunn was at the time an authorised signatory on any of MGN's bank accounts. Nevertheless, National Westminster consider that they may have had sufficient authority to make the payments and that MGN suffered no overall loss.

(i) Position on the intercompany account at 28 June 1991

20.40 In order to produce half year accounts as at 28 June 1991, the MGN finance department attempted to achieve a reconciliation of the position involving the transactions that had occurred in April, May and June 1991. They were told that the payments out on the 29 and 30 April 1991 matched the repayment on 21 May 1991 of £30m and were referable to MCC commercial paper, that the foreign exchange transactions were to be left out of account and that the £11m payment to Goldman Sachs on 29 May 1991 was to be treated as a deposit. This meant, because there had been substantial repayments in June 1991 and the payment of £11m to Goldman Sachs was treated as a deposit, there was only a balance of £175,000 arising from the payments and receipts that could not be explained; their calculations showed, however, a debt of £25.8m was owed by the private side to MGN at 28 June 1991[a]. This comprised:

- £20.7m due from RMG in respect of the principal and interest due on the loan made by MGN to RMG of Can $35m which MCC had loaned to MGN in connection with the acquisition of the interests in QPI and Donohue as referred to at paragraphs 6.55 and 15.25;
- £5.1m on the intercompany accounts; a significant part of this related to trading under the common services agreement, but part of it related to other transactions with the private side.

---

[a] Mr Guest told us that he had an awareness that some payments had been made between MGN and the private side in May and June 1991, but he thought they were to do with the flotation; he was shocked to learn of their extent after RM's death.

(3) The market in MGN shares and the secret purchases by RM

(a) The share price

20.41 Shortly after dealing commenced in MGN shares, the MGN share price began to decline and this continued in May and June 1991 as set out in the graph.

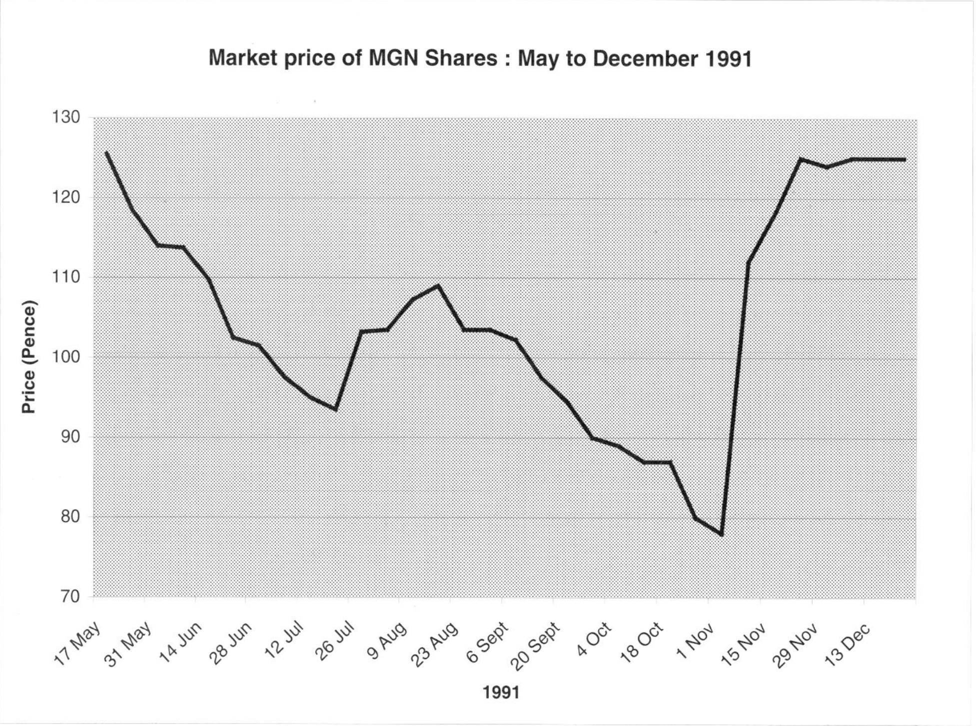

Graph 4

(b) Request by RM that shares be bought after the commencement of dealing

20.42 Before dealing started, Samuel Montagu took advice from Linklaters & Paines as to whether the pension funds could buy shares; they were advised that the terms of the agreements to maintain the stability of the shareholding (referred to at paragraph 12.22) prevented this without the consent of Samuel Montagu[a]. Probably as a result of a request from RM, SBIL made a similar request to Linklaters & Paines and were given similar advice.

20.43 On 17 May 1991 Mr Galloway took advice from Linklaters & Paines as to whether Samuel Montagu could buy shares in the market as it was anticipated that RM would ask them to do so when dealings commenced, although RM never in fact did. Linklaters & Paines advised Samuel Montagu that this would give difficulties because of their possession of price sensitive information and other Financial Services Act considerations.

(c) The dealings by the Salomon Brothers Group of Companies on 17 and 21 May 1991

20.44 The Salomon Brothers Group of Companies operated as an integrated house; its market-making activities in the UK were carried out by Salomon Brothers UK Equity Limited (SBUKE), a separate company from SBIL. After the close of the offer Mr Hannam (who had been

[a] In the case of MGPS, this was because MGPT, the corporate trustee of MGPS, was a subsidiary of RMG; in the case of the CIF this was because BIM was controlled (for the purposes of the agreement) by RM as he was the settlor and a trustee of The Maxwell Charitable Trust which owned BIM.

responsible for organising the sale of MGN shares during the offer in the overseas market) was put in charge in the UK of market-making responsibilities for MGN shares, reporting to those in New York with ultimate responsibility for the market-making activities of the Salomon Brothers Group of Companies.

20.45 On 16 May 1991 SBIL had sold all of the shares that were subject to the overseas offer and the subscription they had made to the UK offer, except for 5.6 million shares which they had that day sold to the market-making book of SBUKE.

20.46 During the period between the close of the offer and the commencement of dealings on 17 May 1991 Salomon Brothers Inc perceived a marked change of attitude from US investors who had received some of the circulars that were critical of the offer (in particular that written by UBS Phillips & Drew). When dealing started, the price opened marginally above the offer price of 125p but there was a substantial amount of selling. Within an hour, SBUKE decided to purchase up to 25 million shares. Their motivation (they explained to us) was that they thought that the shares had a true value of between 140p and 160p and that the price would soon move to this level. By the close of trading on 17 May 1991 SBUKE's holding amounted to 4.35 per cent. of MGN; when trading commenced again on Monday 20 May 1991 their purchases took their holding to 6.23 per cent. of MGN.

20.47 On 17 May 1991 RM had spoken to SBIL and encouraged them to buy. In the week of 20 May 1991 he telephoned again on a daily basis to find out how shares were trading and to encourage Mr Hannam to buy. We were told by Mr Hannam that these conversations with RM played no part in SBUKE's decision to increase its stake and by SBUKE that it was not uncommon for the market-making division of Salomons to take positions in shares of the size taken in respect of MGN.

20.48 A holding of 5 to 6 per cent. was maintained by SBUKE throughout the summer and early autumn of 1991.

(d) Secret purchases by RM on 22 May 1991

20.49 On the first day of dealing, Mr Sheinberg started to sell the 4.5 million shareholding which Goldman Sachs had obtained as a result of the subscription described in paragraphs 18.3 and 18.4 and by the end of the day he had reduced his position to 2.7 million shares. KM told us that RM would have been extremely angry if he had known that Mr Sheinberg had so rapidly sold these shares as he had made a "gentleman's agreement" to keep them, (as described in paragraph 18.3). On the next two trading days Goldman Sachs, which was a market maker in MGN shares, purchased shares. Mr Sheinberg denied that there had been any such agreement; he told us that on 21 May 1991 RM telephoned him and he suggested to RM that RM should buy MGN shares, but RM told him he was not allowed to do so under the terms of the underwriting agreements. He told RM that Goldman Sachs would make a market in MGN shares, but said to RM (as he had said in respect of MCC shares) that Goldman Sachs did not have unlimited funds.

20.50 Mr Sheinberg told us that RM later telephoned him to suggest he speak to Mr Freedman at TIB and also to IBI about a purchase of MGN shares and Mr Sheinberg did so. On 22 May 1991, Mr Sheinberg (who had by then acquired a position of 7.2 million MGN shares) sold 10 million MGN shares to TIB and 3 million MGN shares to Jupiter Participations[a]. If the 13 million shares had been bought by one person, then the holding by that person would have exceeded 3 per cent. and been disclosable. These entities had dealt in significant quantities of MCC shares as referred to at paragraph 9.8. Mr Sheinberg's evidence was that he had dealt at Jupiter Participations with Mr Field and there was some negotiation over the price to be paid. We received other evidence that Mr Field was only executing with Goldman Sachs decisions made by Mr Lévêque[b] and Mr de Brem; he had been told by Mr Lévêque on the first occasion when he had purchased MCC shares that the arrangement was a *portage*[c] agreed with RM. There was nothing to negotiate between Mr Field and Mr Sheinberg about these purchases. KM told us that the manner of dealing in MGN shares was the same as it had been for MCC, namely RM and Mr Sheinberg would agree the deal and the price before any contact was made by Mr Sheinberg with any offshore entity or person. The only exception, KM thought, might have been Mr Aboff where RM may have trusted him to do a deal "at best". The funds of $21.4m to pay for the shares purchased by TIB came from RMG. More about these transactions and the other transactions in MGN shares is set out in paragraphs 15.1 to 15.20 in Appendix 7.

20.51 On 22 May 1991 RM telephoned Mr Emson[d] of Robert Fraser and asked him to buy 400,000 MGN shares which he did through Peel Hunt. The funds of £471,000 to purchase these were provided to Robert Fraser by PHUSI which obtained them from PHL. RM also made purchases of 360,000 MGN shares through Mr Aboff on 17 and 22 May 1991. The funds were provided partly by RMG.

(e) Secret purchases by RM on 21 June 1991

20.52 During May and June 1991 RM rang Mr Galloway on several occasions to ask him if he, RM, could buy MGN shares which he thought to be good value. On 17 June 1991, there was a discussion between Sir Michael Richardson and Mr Galloway about the possibility of RM being released from the covenants not to buy MGN shares. After the matter had been discussed with Mr McIntosh, Samuel Montagu stated they would not release RM from his covenants as the flotation had proceeded on that basis and there had been no unforeseen event or change in circumstances which could justify a release from the restrictions.

---

[a] KM told us that IBI had bought the shares on the same basis as they had bought the MCC shares, namely they would only hold them for 3 months and would then expect to be paid.

[b] He was the founder of the IBI group; see the footnote to paragraph 5.21. Mr de Brem was the Chairman and Director General of IBF.

[c] This arrangement is described in a footnote to paragraph 6.17.

[d] Mr Emson told us he was told by RM that the purchases were on behalf of trusts and when the funds were provided by PHUSI, he was told by KM that PHUSI was not within any Maxwell beneficial ownership. PHUSI was in fact owned by PHA. KM told us that he did not recall the transaction or this conversation but that, as there had been other transactions between Robert Fraser and PHUSI earlier in 1991 he thought it unlikely that Mr Emson would have asked for such a confirmation at this time.

20.53 After the sales to Jupiter Participations and TIB, Goldman Sachs held a short position of 5.75 million shares; Mr Sheinberg was content to do this as he thought the market would decline. It did and he gradually bought shares. His position on 13 June 1991 was 14,200 shares and by 21 June 1991 he had accumulated 8.038 million shares.

20.54 Mr Sheinberg told us that RM telephoned him and told him that Dr Rechsteiner was interested in buying MGN shares. He then spoke on 21 June 1991 to Dr Rechsteiner and sold Servex 10 million MGN shares. This purchase was paid for on 26 July 1991 with funds from RMG; RMG had obtained £35.2m on 24 July 1991 from the proceeds of the sale of the LBI managed portfolio of the CIF[a].

20.55 Mr Sheinberg told us that he looked at TIB, Jupiter Participations and Servex as parties friendly to MGN management and that he had relied upon the statements that had been made to him earlier to the effect that these entities were separate from RM and his companies. He did not consider that RM was buying these shares as he had said he could not. He agreed with each of the entities the terms of those sales and had binding contracts with each of them.

20.56 RM also made purchases of 250,000 MGN shares through Mr Aboff on 4 June 1991 and a further 100,000 MGN shares on 9 July 1991. Part of the funds was provided by RMG.

(4) The interim results

(a) Decision to bring forward announcement of the interim results

20.57 Because of the decline in the price of MGN shares, RM decided to bring forward the announcement of the interim results which some of the directors had anticipated would be announced in August or September 1991. The MGN finance department therefore put in hand work to ensure that the financial information was available to them as soon as possible. Mr Guest had arranged his holiday for the second half of July 1991; he offered to cancel it, but RM told him that he should go.

(b) Further transactions to benefit the private side between 1 and 17 July 1991

20.58 £38.1m of MGN's funds was used on 4 and 5 July 1991 to meet commitments of the private side under further foreign exchange transactions which were part of the series carried out in the summer of 1991 in the circumstances described at paragraph 20.36[b]:

- On 4 July 1991 RM signed an authority requesting National Westminster to provide a banker's draft for £20m in favour of Salomon Brothers Inc London. This was done and the draft delivered to SBIL; the use of a banker's draft to effect this payment meant that SBIL did not know that the money had come from MGN. The money was needed to settle a foreign exchange transaction on which BIT had not performed.

---

a A letter dated 19 August 1991 from Mr Trachtenberg to Mr Cook records that this was the proceeds of £36.27m of the first stage of the liquidation of the LBI managed portfolio of the CIF which had been liquidated on 24 July 1991 and the proceeds placed on deposit with RMG at LIBOR plus 1.25 per cent.

b These transactions appear to have been made to assist in covering a shortfall that arose between the repayment by the private side of a facility of £105m to National Westminster at the end of June 1991 and the grant by National Westminster to the private side of a new facility for £75m some days later.

- On 5 July 1991 there was transferred to Goldman Sachs[a] £18.1 m, the transfer being effected on the sole authority of RM. This was in settlement of a foreign exchange transaction undertaken by LBI.

20.59 A further payment was made from MGN of £4m to RMG on 8 July 1991, the transfer being made on RM's sole authority. An amount equivalent to this was repaid by RMG on 12 July 1991 on the authority of IM and KM, but we have been unable to ascertain a specific reason for the transfer or the repayment.

20.60 There were, however, transfers back to MGN on 4 and 5 July 1991 of three payments totalling £16.4m and between 9 and 16 July 1991 further payments totalling £26.8m made by the private side to MGN[b].

20.61 In the period 1 to 17 July 1991 the payments out almost balanced the payments in; in addition, there were a series of foreign exchange transactions involving MGN.

- On 5 and 8 July 1991, MGN received in settlement of foreign exchange transactions a total of £31.875m from Fuji Bank, Crédit Suisse and BNP in respect of which it should have delivered to these banks $51.2m on the same days. $51.2m was not delivered to these banks until 9 July 1991, with interest being paid for the delay. MGN made good its dollar funds by purchasing $50m from National Westminster on 11 July 1991 for £30.86m.
- On 8 July 1991, MGN entered into further foreign transactions with Crédit Suisse and Crédit Lyonnais[c], purchasing Swiss and French Francs for a total cost of £4.453m. On 15 July 1991, MGN sold a similar amount of Swiss and French Francs as they had purchased.

We have been unable to determine any ordinary commercial rationale for these transactions, except that they were used as a means of short term borrowing or currency speculation.

20.62 The transactions with the private side then ceased in the period 17 July to 1 August 1991.

(c) Meeting between Mr Stoney and CLD

20.63 On 17 July 1991 Mr Stoney arranged a meeting with Mr Walsh and Mr Wootten. The accounts of that meeting differ. Mr Stoney told us that when he had returned from holiday on 9 July 1991, he had learnt from Mr Griffiths of transactions that had taken place between 24 June 1991 and that time, including the two payments to Goldman Sachs referred to at paragraphs 20.20 and 20.37 and the payment to SBIL (referred to at paragraph 20.58). He understood that

---

[a] The person who primarily dealt with KM on this was Mr Lawrence Wood, the operations manager at Goldman Sachs, London who had dealt with the settlement of almost all the MGN and MCC share trades with RM and entities to which we have referred. He was not a foreign exchange dealer. He consulted foreign exchange personnel about the terms, entry and processing of the transaction.

[b] One payment was of £5.5 million from RMG made on 16 July 1991 on the authority of IM and Mr Woods. IM told us that he had no recollection of signing the documentation relating to this payment nor the earlier payment on 12 July 1991.

[c] RMG made the payment of £1.1m to Crédit Lyonnais on 8 July 1991 and MGN reimbursed RMG for this payment on 9 July 1991 under RM's sole signature.

CLD were going to review the interim results and was concerned to seek the advice of Mr Walsh and Mr Wootten whom he knew better than the audit partner, Mr Steere. He told us that he explained to Mr Walsh and Mr Wootten in general terms that there had been three transfers totalling £50m, although the money had come back over a period and that the net balance was at the time about £1m, though the gross amounts had been much larger. He told us that he got the impression from Mr Walsh and Mr Wootten that CLD would not look at the existence of a net balance of between £1m and £2m as being a breach of the "ring fence" provisions.

20.64 Mr Walsh and Mr Wootten's account of the meeting was different in significant respects. They said that Mr Stoney only mentioned that there had been one payment made by MGN to the private companies after the flotation but before the separate MGN treasury department had been established; that this had been possible under the group treasury arrangements then in force and had been a mistake; but the money had been repaid with interest. Mr Wootten recalled that the amount was £20m; Mr Walsh could not recall whether it was £20m or £29m. Mr Stoney had assured them that this would not happen again and that he had made it clear to KM that he would resign if it did. They told us that they did not do or say anything to convey the impression that transactions with the private side were permissible provided the net balance remained at £1m to £2m; they were not asked about this and had they been, they would have said that any such transaction would not have been permissible unless the transactions were approved by the independent directors; the net position was irrelevant.

20.65 Although the account of that part of the meeting differs, all agreed that Mr Stoney had asked whether this would be discussed with the audit committee and Mr Walsh and Mr Wootten had said that they could not prejudge what the audit partner, Mr Steere, would do but the audit committee would be bound to ask if the affairs of MGN were being kept separate from those of the private side and in those circumstances Mr Steere was bound to refer to the transaction, even if he had not done so on his own initiative.

20.66 That same day or the following day, Mr Walsh and Mr Wootten told Mr Steere of what Mr Stoney had told them[a]. It was agreed that if the matter came up at the audit committee, the audit committee would need to be told. No note of any of these meetings was made by any of Mr Steere, Mr Walsh[b], Mr Wootten or Mr Stoney.

20.67 As explained at paragraph 20.72, the audit committee, though it should have met to consider the interim results, never did. Mr Steere never brought to the attention of any of the other directors of MGN the conversation that Mr Stoney had had with Mr Walsh and Mr Wootten, even though that conversation had made it clear there had been a significant breach of the "ring fence" provisions. Mr Steere's explanation was that he understood that the breach had been immediately detected by senior management and corrective action taken.

---

a According to Mr Steere, this information was imparted to him in reassuring terms by Mr Walsh; he gained the impression that Mr Stoney had been given to understand by Mr Walsh that this was not a matter on which CLD needed to take proactive action.

b Mr Walsh made a note nearly six months later on 3 January 1992.

20.68 When Mr Stoney reported his conversation with CLD to RM, RM was angry that he had not spoken to him first, but became less angry when it was reported to him that CLD were not unduly concerned.

(d) The consideration by CLD of the interim results

20.69 By about 15 July 1991, MGN's finance department had done sufficient work to enable CLD to commence their review of the interim results. As the decision had been made to bring forward the timing of the work on results, MGN and CLD had not agreed on the scope of CLD's work. CLD decided to review the figures for reasonableness and the programme CLD decided to follow for their work was based on that used for another substantial listed company client. They were not carrying out work in the nature of an audit or verifying any of the figures.

20.70 During the course of their work, CLD reviewed the results; they also reviewed the board minutes, but only to see what transactions had taken place. Although the programme provided for a confirmation from the management that all internal control procedures were operating properly and no significant weaknesses had been identified, CLD told us that the purpose of this procedure was to look at the reconciliations and ask the management questions rather than to review the internal control mechanisms. A more detailed review might have identified the effecting of transactions without the provision of proper documentation and the use made by RM of his sole signatory authority, but this was not requested.

20.71 A number of material items were drawn to the attention of Mr Steere by his staff and these were reviewed at a meeting on 19 July 1991 between Mr Steere and the audit manager, Mr Merry, Mr Stoney and Mr Craggs. Among the many points raised were four which are relevant:

(i) **The payment of £11m to Goldman Sachs**. There had been two payments to Goldman Sachs of about £11m on 29 May 1991 (see paragraph 20.20) and 24 June 1991 (see paragraph 20.37). In accordance with what the MGN finance department had been told, the first of these was recorded as a deposit and CLD's staff were told that there were no documents in respect of the transaction. The transaction was drawn to Mr Steere's attention for him to ask questions, but Mr Steere told us that he was not advised of the lack of documentation. No questions were asked by CLD as to why no documentation was available as CLD have told us that this was not an aspect they had to pursue on the type of review they had undertaken. The note of the meeting records that Mr Stoney said that it was a foreign currency transaction which involved no disclosable commitments or unusual items. Mr Stoney explained to us that had he been asked about the payment of £11m to Goldman Sachs, he might have thought about the second payment of £11m made on 24 June 1991 that related to a foreign currency transaction and given this explanation.

(ii) **Balances with the private side**. Mr Merry, as manager, had been made aware of the conversation between Mr Stoney and Mr Walsh and Mr Wootten. At the meeting therefore a question was asked about the balances with the private side; CLD's note records that Mr Stoney said they were trading balances and they were not large. Nothing more seems to have been asked about them.

(iii) **Commercial paper**. The finance department of MGN gave to CLD a schedule[a] showing that the commercial paper acquired by MGN in December 1990 had been repaid with interest on 12 April 1991 and that a further amount of MCC commercial paper had been acquired on 29 and 30 April 1991 and redeemed on 21 May 1991. The staff of CLD immediately appreciated that if the commercial paper purchased by MGN in December 1990 had in fact been repaid on 12 April 1991, then there had been an error in the calculation of the gain made on the transfer of the business to MGN Limited as part of the scheme described in Chapter 15; this would have arisen because the MGN finance department, not knowing of the payment on 12 April 1991, had not taken this into account when dealing with the transactions necessary to bring about that scheme. Instead of an extraordinary gain of £50m, the extraordinary gain to MGN would have been £80m. This point was therefore raised with Mr Stoney at the meeting on 19 July 1991. CLD's note records that Mr Stoney said that the commercial paper had not been liquidated prior to the transfer of the business to MGN (on 19 April 1991); Mr Stoney explained to us that he could not understand how this answer had been recorded as he had been certain that the commercial paper had been repaid on 12 April 1991[b].

(iv) **The interest rate cap and collar contracts**. During the course of their work, a member of CLD's staff had been told that the contracts had not yet been assigned but that RMG had provided a guarantee. This matter was raised at the meeting with Mr Stoney. CLD's note merely records

> "Gone".

It was thought Mr Stoney had said the liability had gone and it was therefore concluded that the member of CLD's staff had been given incorrect information.

(e) Failure of the audit committee to meet

20.72 Although the prospectus had stated that the interim results would be reviewed by the audit committee, that committee never met for this or any other purpose until after RM's death. The non-executive directors inadvertently overlooked the fact that this commitment had been made; Mr Guest was on holiday; Mr Stephens said that he had no authority to convene a meeting unless RM requested it; and Mr Stoney did not see it as being his responsibility to convene a meeting of the audit committee.

---

[a] But no accompanying documents as there were none.

[b] In the accounts for MGN for the year ending 31 December 1991 the payment on 12 April 1991 was treated as substantially referable to the repayment of the commercial paper acquired in December 1990. We were told that this was done on the basis of advice by counsel, but that the only evidence on which his advice was based was Mr Stoney's statement repeated to CLD in January 1992 that this was what the payment of £33m made on 12 April 1991 substantially represented.

20.73 CLD were told that the date of the board meeting to approve the interim results had been changed at short notice and that the members of the audit committee had not been available but were told that the audit committee would meet shortly. Mr Steere did not consider it necessary to ask for a meeting of the audit committee to consider the payment that he had been told had been made from MGN as, taking account of his understanding of Mr Walsh's view, he felt that this represented an isolated breach of control which had immediately been detected and corrected by senior management; he expected, however, to meet the audit committee in due course to discuss the planning of the next audit.

(f) The board meeting on 23 July 1991

20.74 After CLD's review of the interim figures, RM had meetings with Samuel Montagu, SBIL and Smith New Court. No particular points on the results emerged from those meetings[a]. There was no discussion of the results with any of the directors of MGN not even with Mr Burrington, who was the Managing Director. He only learnt of the results on Friday 19 July 1991 or on Monday 22 July 1991, the day before the board meeting.

20.75 A board meeting had been scheduled for 31 July 1991 but was moved earlier in July 1991 to 24 July 1991 and then to 2.30pm on 23 July 1991 to fit in with RM's movements. As a consequence a number of the directors were not present at this meeting:

- Mr Clements: He had planned a holiday for the end of July 1991 as he had not anticipated the interim results would be available so soon after the half year end. He only read the agenda for the board meeting (which showed that the meeting would consider the interim results) whilst he was on holiday and only shortly before the meeting was to take place[b].
- Sir Robert Clark: The change in the date of the meeting meant that he was unable to attend because he was in the United States. The papers were not ready for him to consider before he left.
- Lord Williams: Because he only learnt of the change of the board meeting from 24 July 1991 to 23 July 1991 at very short notice, he could not attend because of a commitment in the House of Lords.
- Mr Guest: He was on holiday. He offered to return, but RM said that this was not necessary.
- Mr Laird: } Because of the very late change in the time of the meeting, } they were unable to get down from Glasgow in time.
- Mr Horwood: }

a Although RM appears to have shown SBIL the draft of both the results and the Chairman's statement, he did not show the statement to Samuel Montagu and Smith New Court.

b He probably received the agenda on 19 July 1991 and took it with him together with the other papers he was taking on holiday.

20.76 Although the meeting was called in order to consider the interim results, no papers were made available to the directors until very shortly before commencement of the meeting. Arrangements were made for Sir Robert Clark and Mr Clements to listen to and participate in the board meeting by telephone[a]. The results were explained to them over the telephone as these had not been sent to them. RM told the board meeting that either he or Mr Stoney had been through the figures and the draft statement with SBIL, Samuel Montagu, Smith New Court and CLD. The discussion of the results was brief and the results and statement were approved. There was no detailed consideration of any of the figures. None of the directors present objected to the way in which the meeting had been arranged[b] and conducted[c].

20.77 As at the board meeting held on 11 June 1991, the minutes of the previous full board meeting and of any board meeting that had occurred after that meeting were in the papers that were put before the directors as they attended at the meeting. We are satisfied that amongst the papers before the board was the minute of the further meeting on 11 June 1991 (referred to at paragraph 20.14) attended by RM and IM who had ratified the cap and collar contract with SBC. Again it appears that none of the directors noticed this minute. Even if it had come to the attention of those present, it is unlikely that it would have been seen as of significance by anyone apart from RM or Mr Stoney as the directors had virtually no awareness of the agreement that had been made to assign the liabilities under these contracts.

20.78 The interim results were announced on 24 July 1991.

---

a The minute records that Lord Williams was present by telephone; this is an error as he was on the floor of the House of Lords at the time.

b Mr Clements did not realise in advance of the meeting that virtually every board member with financial experience was going to be absent.

c Mr Ferguson told us that he and Mr Eastoe complained to Mr Burrington after the meeting. Mr Burrington had no recollection of this, but he told us that, had they done so, he would have told them that they had as much right as anyone else to complain at the meeting.

21. AUGUST TO 5 NOVEMBER 1991

21.1 The period from the beginning of August 1991 to the death of RM on 5 November 1991 saw a resumption of payments out of MGN. From mid August 1991 Mr Guest started to become concerned about the payments and at the end of September 1991 he and Mr Burrington notified Samuel Montagu of their concerns. By the end of October 1991 RM had agreed to a meeting of the audit committee, but he died before it met. The material events in this period are therefore dominated by the payments out of MGN but there was also one other significant transaction involving the Mirror Building.

21.2 The events of this period are more complex than those of the preceding three months but it is necessary to explain them in a little detail to gain an understanding as to how it was that such substantial sums of money were taken from a listed company to support the finances of the majority shareholder.

The position of MCC and the private side as at August 1991

(a) MCC

21.3 On 16 July 1991 *The Independent* had printed a report that Mr Peter Walker was not to become Chairman of MCC as had been announced in March 1991 (see paragraph 9.10). The report had mistakenly stated that this decision had followed from an internal review of MCC's finances that had suggested that MCC was in a difficult financial position[a]. This report had a significant impact on RM's relationship with his banks and upon the MCC share price and was followed by a formal announcement that Mr Walker was not going to become chairman of MCC.

21.4 Unknown to the public, (or to the directors of MGN or to CLD), there had occurred two events of substantial significance involving MCC of which it is necessary to provide a brief summary:

(1) **Further MCC share purchases**

A more detailed account of these transactions and events is set out in Appendix 7.

- Goldman Sachs had during the period after the sales on 24 April 1991 to TIB and Servex (referred to at paragraph 9.8) been steadily buying MCC shares. Mr Sheinberg told us that after initially failing to persuade RM to buy them, he was telephoned on 3 July 1991 by RM who, after ascertaining that Mr Sheinberg wished to sell, suggested Mr Sheinberg telephone Dr Rechsteiner. He did and sold him 10 million MCC shares at a cost of £21.6m to Alandra Foundation, another Liechtenstein foundation controlled by Dr Rechsteiner as set out in paragraph 1.10.
- As set out in paragraph 9.9, RM had told Mr Emson that if his client wanted to sell more shares[b], then RM would find a buyer; on 3 July 1991, Mr Emson sold on behalf

[a] Mr Peter Walker told us that in his view the key business of MCC was in the US, following the sale of the scientific journals business and that it should be run from the US. RM had agreed with this advice. KM told us that RM simply changed his mind about appointing Mr Peter Walker; Mr Peter Walker had no shares in MCC and RM was simply not willing to give up control.

[b] Mr Emson told us that RM told him that the funding was not coming from the Maxwell interests.

21.4 continued

of his client to a trust established at RM's request 1.3 million MCC shares; funds were provided by RMG to finance this purchase.

- On the morning of 16 July when the story in *The Independent* was published, Mr Sheinberg told us that he was telephoned by RM and told that there was a further bear raid on MCC shares. He told us that he told RM that, although Goldman Sachs would maintain a market in MCC shares, they would not hold such large positions as in the past; that Goldman Sachs were not going to be a bushel for him or anyone else and if Goldman Sachs did not sell the shares to RM or someone to whom RM introduced them, they would sell to someone else. Mr Sheinberg said he saw a market opportunity for Goldman Sachs and started to buy more MCC shares. Thereafter following further conversations with RM, he made the sales set out below of MCC shares to Dr Rechsteiner who was acting for Liechtenstein foundations acquired or founded for RM as explained at paragraph 1.10.

18 July 1991	10 million	for Jungo and Kiara Foundations
23 July 1991	10 million	for Baccano Foundation
5 August 1991	5 million	for Alandra Foundation

The total cost of these further purchases was £49.8m[a].

Dr Keicher, the director of the Maxwell Foundation[b] told us that in the summer of 1991 he had been told by Dr Rechsteiner that MCC shares had been acquired in the following circumstances. Dr Rechsteiner had been telephoned by Mr Sheinberg and been told that he (Dr Rechsteiner) had bought MCC shares for RM personally who had donated them to the Foundation on condition they could be used as security. Dr Rechsteiner told Dr Keicher that he (Dr Rechsteiner) had not been involved in negotiating the purchases and that when Mr Sheinberg rang him to deal with the shares, the purchases had already been executed.

The way in which the purchases by Jungo and Kiara were settled led to concern on the part of Goldman Sachs as to whether the purchases were reportable. On 27 August 1991, after the ending of the trading relationship between Mr Sheinberg and RM for the reasons explained at paragraph 21.16, Mr Robert Katz, the General Counsel of Goldman Sachs, wrote to enquire of Dr Rechsteiner whether these purchases by these Foundations should be aggregated for reporting purposes. Before their enquiry was answered, RM confirmed to Dr Rechsteiner that the beneficiaries of these Foundations were different members of his family. Dr Rechsteiner wrote to Goldman Sachs that the entities who had purchased MCC shares from Goldman Sachs were beneficially owned by individual third parties and therefore their holdings were not aggregable for reporting purposes. KM told us that RM had not given Dr Rechsteiner any confirmation that the beneficiaries of these Foundations were different members of his family.

---

a Part of the sums required to settle the Jungo, Kiara and Baccano purchases were derived from sums paid by MGN through BIM to LBG in the series of payments described at paragraph 21.22 and detailed in Appendix 17.

b See paragraph 1.8.

(2) **Payments from MCC to the private side**

- In early July 1991 Mr Basil Brookes, the finance director of MCC, had discovered that £180m had been lent by MCC to RM's private companies as at 30 June 1991[a] and that on 4/5 July 1991 a further £75m had been paid to the private side companies[b]. Mr Basil Brookes could not obtain satisfactory information relating to these payments and consequently obtained legal advice[c] as to his position as Finance Director. He was advised to require a meeting of the MCC board be called and to inform the other directors of his concerns. This he did and a board meeting was eventually arranged for 6 August 1991. By the time the board met the amounts owing by the private side to MCC had been reduced to about £150m.
- At the board meeting on 6 August 1991 the independent directors insisted that the funds be repaid and that new procedures be implemented to try and prevent payments to the private companies[d]. We were told that no one outside the board of MCC was made aware of this decision as the directors were advised that they owed a duty to the shareholders to try to recover the assets for MCC and that recovery of those assets would be jeopardised if what had happened at MCC became public knowledge.

(b) The financial position of the private side

21.5 On 23 July 1991, the board of RMG had had to consider whether the accounts for the year ended 31 December 1990 could be prepared on a going concern basis and whether the private side could pay their debts as they fell due. They took advice from Titmuss Sainer & Webb and CLD[e] and, on the basis of documents provided by Mr Bunn and statements from KM and RM, decided that the company was solvent and the accounts could be prepared on a going concern basis. KM's evidence was that the issue of going concern had been raised with him by

---

a It was at this time that the cheque referred to in the footnote to paragraph 6.68 was provided to MCC.

b These funds had been obtained from the cash received by MCC for the sale of the journals business referred to at paragraph 9.10.

c From Lovell White Durrant; subsequently he and other independent members of the board took advice from Macfarlanes.

d These were implemented at a meeting on 21 August 1991 and included a requirement that all intercompany transactions be approved by independent directors; the finance committee was to approve all foreign exchange transactions and monitor the intercompany position. The sole signatory authority of RM over MCC's bank accounts was not removed nor was the delegation resolution revoked.

e Mr Walsh recorded in a note that it was reasonable to draw up the accounts of RMG on a going concern basis in that:

- there was no reason to expect the MCC share price to fall substantially given its resilience in the previous very difficult week;
- in the absence of a serious problem with the MCC share price, there was no obvious reason for the banks to refuse to rollover their loans or grant new facilities;
- there were substantial assets in addition to MCC shares (MGN and the properties) so the private interests were not wholly dependent on the price of MCC shares;
- At the prices used for MGN and MCC shares, the private side's assets exceeded their liabilities by over £25m and were expected to do so in the foreseeable future;
- Previous rollovers forecast by KM had happened.

This conclusion was reached on the basis of the information provided to CLD which omitted a number of liabilities including those to MCC and the CIF.

Mr Bunn in his role as Finance Director based on his concern that the income being generated by the private side was insufficient to meet the interest payments falling due, unless assets were disposed of or loans rolled over. KM told Mr Bunn that the issue had to be addressed immediately, so it was arranged for the board meeting. KM had never considered the question of going concern before (save on an extremely formal basis) so he sought guidance from Mr Walsh and Mr Wootten in advance of the meeting as to what was expected, what preparations and documents would be required. Mr Walsh told him that an update of the work done in April 1991 on the flotation of MGN would be sufficient and that was done. The meeting itself, KM considered, was necessary but not serious.

21.6 In fact, the private side was under extreme financial pressure as a result of a number of factors, but particularly the attitude of RM's bankers in consequence of the failed foreign exchange transactions referred to at paragraph 20.36 and the need to reduce the intercompany debt to MCC prior to the MCC board meeting that was held on 6 August 1991. Furthermore, the asset disposal programme was not proceeding as quickly as had been anticipated, as the planned disposals of the holdings in Scitex, MTV Europe and Thomas Cook Travel Inc had not taken place.

21.7 KM told us that this was a period of crisis management; there was a very acute liquidity crisis and it was getting worse. KM and RM would have a meeting or conversation early each morning at which RM (who would have been provided with the daily banking position sheets or information drawn from them) would give instructions to KM as to the scheme of payments to banks or operating companies to be made that day for onward transmission to the various treasurers. KM said he found it complicated since RM was the only person with a total picture of the transactions. At the same time as cash was being moved in this way, there were the pressures of asset disposals, demands from banks and the needs of the operating companies for cash.

The need to pledge the whole of the MGN shareholding

21.8 At the beginning of August 1991, this financial pressure made it necessary for RM to pledge all the MGN shares owned by the private side and the 20 million shares he had purchased secretly through TIB and Servex as described at paragraphs 20.50 and 20.54. This occurred in the following circumstances[a].

21.9 By 1 August 1991, RMG's account with National Westminster (on which the overdraft limit was £23m) was overdrawn by £92m and MCC's (which had a limit of £35m) was overdrawn by £51m. RMG's overdraft had occurred largely because a promised receipt of funds against which National Westminster had agreed to allow RMG to pay £50m to MCC had not been received and substantial funds had been paid out by MCC. In addition there were three outstanding foreign exchange transactions for a total value of $105m which MCC had not honoured[b].

---

[a] Details of all the pledges are in Appendix 18.

[b] For $30m with Westpac Banking Corporation, for $35m with Chase and for $40m with Bank of America.

21.10 At a meeting with KM on Friday 2 August 1991, it was agreed all but £15m of MCC's overdraft be transferred to RMG as that account was secured. As this took RMG's overdraft to £130m, National Westminster asked KM for additional security to cover this in the form of MGN rather than MCC shares. KM promised to provide 40 million MGN shares over the weekend. National Westminster also insisted that CLD be used to carry out a reconciliation in relation to MCC and RMG's accounts. KM's evidence was that at the meeting neither he nor National Westminster were very clear what the position was; KM had difficulties reading the documents provided to him by the treasury and National Westminster had at first calculated the excess at a substantially lower level than it appeared to be. It was agreed that CLD should come in over the weekend to help reconcile the books of account so that, by Monday morning, everyone would be certain what the true position was.

21.11 Over the weekend of 3 and 4 August 1991

- CLD carried out a reconciliation between MCC's and RMG's books and the bank statements; National Westminster had separate meetings with RM, KM, Mr Stoney and Mr Basil Brookes.
- RM and KM telephoned Mr Sheinberg and asked him if Goldman Sachs[a] would lend BIT $35m for seven days against collateral of MCC shares; Mr Sheinberg rejected MCC shares and asked that 40 million MGN shares be lodged as further collateral. Under the relevant loan documentation, this loan and an earlier loan would be cross collateralised. RM agreed to provide MGN shares and gave his word that this new loan would be repaid in seven days. KM told us that RM was very upset that Mr Sheinberg would not accept MCC shares; he regarded it as being a betrayal of their relationship. Mr Sheinberg was categoric, in telling us, that RM did not react in this way. He said that RM had merely asked "what do you want?" to which he (Mr Sheinberg) responded "MGN shares" and then they negotiated the pledge of the MGN shares.
- The MGN shares promised to National Westminster were not delivered to them.

21.12 On Monday 5 August 1991

- Dr Rechsteiner gave Goldman Sachs instructions to deliver the 10 million MGN shares purchased by him for Servex to a Miss Morgan; Miss Morgan, who was not known to Goldman Sachs (but was Mr Bunn's secretary), collected the 10 million MGN shares[b].
- 37.4 million MGN shares were delivered by RMG to Goldman Sachs as collateral for the loan of $35m. On checking the shares, Mr Wood of Goldman Sachs noticed that the shares delivered as collateral included the 10 million shares which had been handed to Miss Morgan. KM then telephoned and said there had been a mistake and sent other MGN shares in their place together with additional shares to provide the full collateral required. KM told us that he could not recall such a conversation with Mr Wood, but it may have had something to do with the promise he had made on 2 August 1991 to National

---

a Goldman Sachs had made a loan to RM's private side companies on 25 March 1991 for £25m (secured on MCC shares) which was still outstanding and a short term loan in July 1991 which had been repaid.

b The 10 million shares purchased by TIB had been delivered by Goldman Sachs to Mr Gould on 16 July 1991 on the instructions of Mr Freedman. Mr Gould was in fact Group Financial Controller of HI.

Westminster to provide 40 million MGN shares as security; KM recalled that National Westminster might have been given the share certificate numbers (perhaps copies of the share certificates) and that those shares had been sent to Goldman Sachs in error. Goldman Sachs then made the loan of $35m. The loan was used to settle the failed foreign exchange transaction between Chase and MCC[a].

- National Westminster were offered MCC shares. They rejected these and had further meetings with KM who told them RM had agreed to pledge the MGN shares elsewhere. KM asked if National Westminster would help him meet liabilities under the three foreign exchange transactions totalling $105m. KM's evidence was that RM had told him to offer group security to National Westminster and that he had taken that to include MGN shares, which he then offered to the bank. RM later told KM that he had not meant to include MGN shares; there was a standing rule that any pledge of MGN shares had to have RM's personal approval and his signature on a form and none of that had been done. Nonetheless the attitude of National Westminster in this period was genuinely supportive and (on 7 August 1991) they advanced the $40m needed to settle one of the failed foreign exchange deals.
- 17.5 million MGN shares were delivered later that day to National Westminster as collateral for the overdraft.

21.13 The following day, 6 August 1991, senior officers of National Westminster met KM and RM. RM told them that KM had had no authority to offer 40 million MGN shares as security to National Westminster and he had himself offered the shares to Goldman Sachs on 5 August 1991. National Westminster however refused to make an advance needed to settle one of the foreign exchange transactions until MGN shares were delivered as security. A further 20 million MGN shares were delivered on 7 August 1991 and funds then advanced taking RMG's overdraft to £156m[b]. The remaining failed foreign exchange transactions (between MCC and Bank of America and Westpac Banking Corporation) were then honoured.

21.14 RM had mentioned to the National Westminster on the weekend of 3/4 August 1991 that he was considering going to the Bank of England to discuss the liquidity of his companies. National Westminster had itself considered the possibility of involving the Bank of England at this time, but although they regarded the situation as extremely serious, they did not consider anything had happened that would require notification to the appropriate authorities. Neither RM nor National Westminster brought the subject up at the meeting on 6 August 1991 and the Bank of England does not appear to have been involved until later. KM told us that RM's attitude was that he should go to the Bank of England because of the scale of short term funds that the companies required; he thought it would lead to a club-type approach. National Westminster advised strongly against it and insisted that their package of security be put in place before any such step be taken. RM raised the point again, KM told us, on 12/13 August

---

a The use made of the loan was not known to Goldman Sachs.

b By 12 August 1991 National Westminster held 103.2 million MCC shares, 94.4m MGN shares, 5.1 million Scitex shares and 8.2 million shares in Ansbacher. The overdraft was slowly reduced and after the sale of the Scitex shares in October 1991 (as set out at paragraph 21.73) reduced to £28m.

1991 during the visit to RM's yacht in Sardinia[a]; it was decided to see how things went, but RM was still minded to go to the Bank.

21.15 We were told by National Westminster that following what they had learnt over this period in August 1991, they concluded that the foreign exchange transactions had been used to borrow funds by delaying settlements[b] and they became concerned about KM and RM's probity and integrity in the sense that they had not dealt fully and frankly with the bank; they also felt that RM was becoming unpredictable.

21.16 On 12 August 1991, RM telephoned Mr Sheinberg and told him that the loan of $35m due for repayment that day would not be repaid. Mr Sheinberg told us that this was the first time RM had reneged on a deal and that it represented the end of their business relationship. From that time on Goldman Sachs' efforts were directed to obtaining repayment of the loans they had made and settlement of the outstanding transactions[c]. RM continued to purchase MCC shares secretly using Mr Aboff; in the period between 14 August 1991 and 4 November 1991 RM spent £9.7m on purchases through Mr Aboff[d]. On 12 August 1991 Goldman Sachs notified MGN and MCC of their interests in MGN and MCC shares and an announcement was made on 13 August 1991 that the private side companies had pledged shares amounting to 10 per cent. of MGN and 4.8 per cent of MCC. This announcement received a good deal of publicity. Goldman Sachs have said that the delay in notification was an inadvertent error on their part[e].

21.17 The announcement caused Samuel Montagu to check what the position would be if the pledged MGN shares were to be sold; pledging of MGN shares was permitted under the arrangements made on flotation (as referred to at paragraph 12.23) and they were advised that if the pledges were enforced, a sale probably could not be prevented[f].

21.18 As by August 1991 the whole of the private side's shareholding in MGN had been pledged in the circumstances described above, the control of MGN through its shareholding and

---

a See paragraph 21.19.

b This method of short term borrowing has been described at paragraph 20.36.

c The details are set out in Appendix 7.

d Details are set out in paragraph 18.1 of Appendix 7.

e They said that they had conducted a review of their exposure and had asked their solicitors for advice as to whether the security interest had to be disclosed on 9 August 1991; when the solicitors had advised that the interests had to be disclosed, they did so at once. They added that the mistake had arisen because the loan had been made by a Goldman Sachs company that was not exempt from disclosure and had they intended not to disclose their interest they could have made the loan through a company that was exempted from disclosure. This explanation was confirmed to us by Mr Katz, the General Counsel to Goldman Sachs. National Westminster did not have to disclose their interest as they were a banking company and the security interest was taken in the ordinary course of their business (see the then section 209 (1) (g), (5) of the Companies Act 1985).

f SBIL ascertained from KM at the same time that the shares were pledged to support margin loans for the private side; they took the view that this was entirely consistent with the financial structure of the private side where all loans were secured.

compliance with its banking covenants was to a large extent dependent on the state of the private side's finances.

Payments for the benefit of the private side August to 7 October 1991

21.19 This financial pressure on the private side also brought about a resumption of the payments from MGN on 5 August 1991. In the period to 7 October 1991 there were three distinct ways in which the funds were paid out, details of which are set out in Appendix 19. We were told by the cash office manager at MGN that a number of these transfers were preceded by a telephone call from either KM or Mr Stoney to ascertain what MGN's cash position was; if he told them there was an unutilised part of MGN's overdraft, then there would on occasions follow a request to make one of the types of transfer referred to below. IM told us that, at the beginning of August 1991, he had a meeting with RM (also attended by Mr Alan Thompson who had recently been appointed Managing Director of *The European*) during which RM gave him a dressing down and told him in the clearest of terms that all transfers of money would have to be approved by RM. Thereafter, on every occasion that he signed an authorisation, IM did so only with his father's approval which he would usually have obtained in person or on the telephone, or (if RM was not available) after the event. KM told us that he recalled a conversation with RM and IM around 12/13 August 1991 held on RM's yacht in Sardinia when RM sought to re-establish the rules of conduct, namely that he (KM) was not to make any transfers without RM's authority. KM told us that these payments were made as part of the crisis management described in paragraph 21.7 and arranged in the same way as all other cash movements between the companies.

(a) Payments to US investment banks

21.20 Beginning on Monday 5 August 1991 a series of payments was made to Lehmans and Morgan Stanley totalling £14.2m.

- **payments to Lehmans of**
  - £1m on 5 August 1991
  - £5.2m on 7 August 1991
  - £3m on 2 September 1991

  The first sum was used to collateralise the financing to LBG through the use of US Treasury Bills (referred to at paragraph 20.32); the second sum was used as collateral for Japanese equity purchases by RMG; the third payment was made to settle an advance made to LBG by Lehmans on 30 August 1991 until 2 September 1991, pending the delivery of Japanese securities that LBG had purchased from Lehmans and paid for.
- **a payment to MSTC of**
  - £5m on 12 August 1991.

  This was made to LBI's own account, converted into dollars and on LBI's instructions paid on to RMG.

21.21 Although the payments were made by the MGN treasury, neither the treasury nor the MGN finance department received any documentation from Lehmans or Morgan Stanley or anyone else acknowledging receipt of the funds or explaining the purpose for which the sums had been paid. They were told by Mr Stoney that he had been told by RM that the funds had been placed on deposit with these investment houses in order to demonstrate the financial strength of MGN in connection with the credit rating application being considered by Standard & Poor's. Mr Guest, when he asked RM about these sums, received the same explanation. IM told us that these payments were explained to him as being deposits of some sort. No documentation was ever provided; nor could documentation showing the sums had been deposited ever have been provided, given the purpose for which the payments were actually made.

(b) Payments to and receipts from BIM

21.22 Commencing on 20 August 1991 a series of payments was made to BIM[a] and, on occasions, monies were paid back. The payments to BIM immediately came to the attention of the MGN finance department. Mr Stoney told us these payments were explained to him by either KM or RM on the grounds that MGN was falling behind budget and it was suggested that surplus cash be placed on deposit with the pension fund in order to earn interest[b]. This explanation was passed on to the MGN finance department and Mr Guest received, in due course, a similar explanation for these payments from RM. KM told us that he did not recall giving any such explanation and he thought it unlikely that he would have done as he would not have known, due to his distance from MGN, what MGN's trading performance was like at the time. It should be noted that:

- MGN did not have any surplus cash. The sums that were being placed on deposit were monies borrowed under MGN's overdraft and other facilities. This was appreciated by Mr Guest and he enquired as to the rate of interest that would be paid by BIM; Mr Stoney told us that it was agreed that deposits with BIM would earn 1.25 per cent. over base rate, a small margin over the 1 per cent. over base rate that MGN was paying to borrow the money. KM told us that this was seen as a normal activity at the time.
- Any additional sum of money earned at this marginal rate on the amounts placed with BIM (which at the maximum did not exceed £25 m) was very small and could not have made any realistic contribution to MGN's profitability.
- BIM was owned by The Maxwell Charitable Trust and hence it could be contended (as it was subsequently) that, since it was not a related party, the placing of funds on deposit with BIM would not amount to an infringement of the "ring fencing" provisions put in

---

[a] Some of the payments that were claimed to be "deposits" with BIM were in fact payments to LBG. We were told that the explanation given for that was that KM sometimes requested that the transfer be made to LBG as a matter of convenience. We were told by Mr Ford that LBG was being used by the other private side companies for payments and receipts to avoid any receipts being offset against bank overdrafts of the other private side companies.

[b] Mr Stoney told us that sometime in September 1991 he spoke to RM about the amount of money on deposit with the pension fund. RM said that he had not been aware of the size of the deposits and asked Mr Stoney who had authorised the transfers. Mr Stoney told RM that the instructions had mainly come from KM and that IM had signed most of the authorisations. RM then called KM into his office and, in his presence, told Mr Stoney not to take any further instructions from KM to transfer funds. RM then called IM on the telephone and told him not to sign any more authorisations without RM's approval. IM told us that he could not recall such a telephone conversation; he had already been told by RM at the beginning of August 1991 not to sign authorisations without his approval, as set out in paragraph 21.19.

place on flotation[a]. KM and Mr Stoney told us that the ownership of BIM was seen contemporaneously as an exemption to the ring fencing provisions of the facility.

21.23 Documentation was ultimately provided in respect of these transactions. Mr Abrahart, who was in charge of the investment administration at BIM, produced "certificates" for these deposits and took them to Mr Stoney for counter-signature. He told us that Mr Stoney declined to sign them. Mr Stoney told us that this did not happen until after RM's death when he was asked to work out the loan position; he felt unable to sign them because of what he then knew.

21.24 Mr Abrahart told us that on receipt of the funds paid by MGN, he would generally be asked by KM to transfer the funds to the private side. He would then prepare the necessary payment instructions to effect the transfer to the private side and on the signature of these documents the monies would be paid over. KM told us that the funds were moved in a planned sequence as a result of the daily instructions given by RM as described in paragraph 21.7. Instructions would be given simultaneously for all the sequential payments as the ultimate destination of the funds was pre-planned. When funds were in fact returned to MGN, the process was sometimes reversed. All the funds were returned on 7 October 1991 in the circumstances set out at paragraph 21.45.

(c) Transactions with the private side companies

21.25 Transactions with the private side companies continued in August and September 1991. There were both payments to and from the private side, but during these months direct payments to the private side were generally made to LBG[b].

Action taken by the executive directors of MGN

21.26 Just before Mr Guest was due to go on holiday on 16 July 1991, his attention had been drawn to a number of payments, including some of those made after 1 July 1991 referred to at paragraph 20.58. He spoke to Mr Hemple during his outward journey and was told by Mr Hemple that he had sent a memorandum to Mr Griffiths and would take up the further payments that had been drawn to Mr Guest's attention. On his return from holiday Mr Guest was told by Mr Stoney that the intercompany transfers had stopped and that the money had been returned; however no documentation had been provided, even for the payment of £11m to Goldman Sachs on 29 May 1991 described as a "deposit".

21.27 On 15 August 1991 Mr Guest became aware of the payments to the US investment banks and on 20 August 1991 of the payments to BIM. Shortly thereafter he mentioned these payments in very general terms to Mr Burrington, but did not say anything in detail until they had a conversation on 29 August 1991 during the course of a function for the sports awards

---

[a] As set out in paragraph 15.36 KM told us that RM had ensured that these exceptions were carefully drawn to permit the private side to continue to use MGN's cash flow.

[b] Mr Trachtenberg told us that at this time LBG was used by RM to make payments to and receive payments from MCC, other parts of the private side, Pergamon AGB plc and the pension funds. The payments were administered by Mr Ford; Mr Trachtenberg would sign as second signatory on the authorisations.

promoted by *The People*. At about the same time Mr Guest telephoned Mr Horwood and told him of his concerns. Mr Horwood, who knew that RM was looking for an excuse to replace Mr Guest with Mr Stoney as the finance director of MGN, advised caution as he did not believe that Mr Guest had sufficient evidence to challenge RM.

21.28 On Mr Burrington's advice, Mr Guest wrote a memorandum to Mr Stoney on 3 September 1991 about the payments. Following this memorandum RM spoke to Mr Guest and repeated the explanations for the deposits with BIM and the US investment banks set out above. Mr Stoney, after initially stating that he wished that nothing had been put in writing, discussed the memorandum with Mr Guest and agreed to try and obtain documentation and to arrange for Mr Griffiths and Mr Craggs to go through the payments. Mr Guest also spoke to Mr Cook, the manager of the pension funds, and Mr Cook explained to Mr Guest that BIM was investing the money short term and that these were not related party transactions as BIM's position (as a subsidiary of The Maxwell Charitable Trust) meant that it was not a related party[a]. The results of these inquiries temporarily satisfied Mr Guest.

21.29 The making of further substantial "deposits" with BIM on 16 and 18 September 1991 (when reported to Mr Guest on 20 September 1991) however caused him renewed concern. He was thereafter in frequent contact with either Mr Stoney or RM and was told that the money would be returned and documentation provided. Nothing happened as a result of these promises and therefore Mr Burrington and Mr Guest decided to mention the payments to Samuel Montagu which Mr Burrington was able to do at a meeting on 26 September 1991 in connection with another transaction. It is convenient now to deal with that other transaction before explaining the action taken by Samuel Montagu after being notified by Mr Burrington of the concerns that he and Mr Guest shared about the payments from MGN.

A new lease for the Mirror Building and other events

(a) The need to renegotiate the lease of the Mirror Building

21.30 At the time of the flotation of MGN a sub-lease by MCC to MGN of the Mirror Building was negotiated (as set out at paragraph 14.12) and that sub-lease was used in connection with the refinancing of the private side's loan secured on the Holborn site (referred to at paragraph 9.22). By 10 July 1991 terms for a loan for £90m (in place of the previous amount of £105 m) had been agreed and invitations were circulated by the leaders, Lloyds, Barclays and Sumitomo for participation in a syndication. A few days later Mr Peter Walker's decision not to become Chairman of MCC was reported and this had a serious effect on confidence and it became necessary to renegotiate the terms of the facility. The banks decided they required

---

[a] Mr Cook told us that he was told that the payments were advances on pension contributions or made in error; that he received subsequently a memorandum from Mr Abrahart dated 16 September 1991 that covered several matters at BIM that had given Mr Abrahart cause for concern, including the "deposits" placed with BIM by MGN; that he passed this to KM under cover of a memorandum in which he (Mr Cook), besides dealing with the other concerns raised by Mr Abrahart, stated that he could not throw any light on payments from MGN, that BIM was not a deposit-taker and if payments had been made by mistake, they should be paid out; he had asked Mr Abrahart to treat them as an advance on contributions. KM signed this memorandum "agreed". However this evidence must be contrasted with what Mr Cook told Mr Guest (as set out above and recorded in a contemporary note on 5 September 1991) and the fact that Mr Cook signed, as set out in Appendix 19, three instructions for payments to MGN for sums totalling £0.8m.

better security and made it clear that a new seven year lease from MGN was essential[a] and that they might not be able to lend as much as £90m.

21.31 On 7 August 1991 there took place a series of telephone conversations between Mr Guest, Mr Horwood and RM which were subsequently minuted as a meeting of a committee of the board of MGN. During the course of these conversations, RM proposed that MGN's lease of the Mirror Building be extended to seven years at a yearly rent of £7m and that in return RMG would pay MGN £4m and acquire the lease of Great Dover Street at its book value of £650,000. Mr Guest and Mr Horwood favoured this arrangement as they thought that it would give MGN greater security of occupation at the Mirror Building; they only discovered later that the new lease contained a clause enabling MCC to give notice to determine if the private side wanted to redevelop the site. The minute of the "meeting" recorded that the committee of the board had approved the transaction subject to ratification by the full board of MGN.

21.32 Advice was taken from Titmuss Sainer & Webb on behalf of MGN; they advised that the transaction would require approval by the company in general meeting[b]. They had also pointed out that the resolution of the board delegating all its power to a committee was unusual and could not in any event be used for this transaction since the delegation resolution required RM or IM to be a member of any committee, but the Articles of MGN prevented RM or IM from being a member of a committee resolving to enter into a transaction with a related party (see paragraph 10.26). However, the letter giving this advice was sent to Mr Stoney and not passed on to other members of the board; he told us that he believed the advice was passed to the company secretary, but Mr Stephens denied having received this.

21.33 The obtaining of this advice delayed the transaction, but when the next meeting of the board was held on 12 September 1991, the opportunity was taken to amend the delegation resolution so as to remove the requirement that RM or IM be a member of that committee of the board when related party transactions were being considered.

(b) The board meeting on 12 September 1991

21.34 Apart from amending the delegation resolution, the board considered the management accounts for the period to 28 July 1991 which were circulated in advance of the meeting. There was nothing in these management accounts to bring to the attention of the board any of the transactions that occurred in the period to 28 July 1991[c] to which we have referred in

---

[a] The sub-lease to MGN had been important to MCC as the income from the Holborn site was falling because other sub-leases (including that to Goldman Sachs) had come or were coming to an end. The sub-lease to MGN became more important after the announcement in July 1991 about Mr Peter Walker because the banks became concerned about the strength of MCC's ability to perform its obligations under the lease to the private side.

[b] Approval of the Company in general meeting is required under section 320 of the Companies Act for substantial property transactions with related parties and the Stock Exchange generally requires non-revenue transactions with related parties to be notified to shareholders and approved in general meetings under its "class 4" rules.

[c] It appears that they were contained in the figure for bank balances and deposits.

Chapter 20. Neither Mr Guest, Mr Stoney, Mr Burrington nor Mr Horwood mentioned any of these transactions to the board. Mr Guest explained to us that if he had mentioned to the board the concerns that he had about the payments to the US investment banks and to BIM that would have amounted to a direct challenge to RM; he had no proof of his suspicions and he had little doubt that at the meeting RM would have given the impression that all was well and would afterwards have arranged Mr Guest's dismissal. Mr Burrington told us much the same.

21.35 No other matters of significance were raised at the meeting.

(c) Samuel Montagu's involvement in the Mirror Building lease

21.36 At some time during September 1991, RM spoke to Mr McIntosh about the Mirror Building lease. He advised RM that the transaction was unusual since it envisaged a payment being made by MCC and further pointed out that the transaction would be a transaction requiring approval of MGN's shareholders. On about 17 September 1991 Samuel Montagu became more closely involved and started to prepare a circular to the shareholders. Their view was that shareholder sentiment would be negative as the transaction was being effected in order to facilitate the funding of a private side loan. In the course of their discussions, Samuel Montagu appreciated that Mr Burrington was strongly opposed to the proposal.

21.37 However, at the beginning of October 1991 Samuel Montagu ceased to be involved and the transaction was restructured so that shareholder approval was not necessary. Titmuss Sainer & Webb had taken the advice of leading counsel who advised that approval of MGN in general meeting would not be required if the transaction was effected by extending the period of the lease and by reducing the rent to the then open market rent. This alteration enabled Smith New Court to obtain the Stock Exchange's consent that the transaction did not have to go to the MGN shareholders for approval; it appears that this consent was given on 21 October 1991. This was also acceptable to the banks providing the refinancing; documentation was therefore negotiated and finalised on this basis. The lease had to be approved by the board of MGN and pressure from the banks to finalise the transaction made this urgent.

21.38 A meeting of the board of MGN was held at about 1 p.m. on 24 October 1991. Notice of this meeting was only given shortly before the meeting took place. This was because KM had wanted the transaction approved by a committee of the board of MGN (subject to ratification by the full board later), but Titmuss Sainer & Webb had advised KM on that morning (24 October 1991) that this was not possible and that it was necessary for the full board to be given notice of a board meeting and to approve it at such a meeting.

21.39 The directors present[a] agreed to the new lease with an extended term of seven years (from three) and a reduced rent of £6.2m (from £7m); MCC retained the right of determination on 18 months notice. The directors agreed because they thought it was in MGN's interests[b] to have

[a] The directors present were Mr Stoney (who chaired the meeting), Mr Eastoe, Mr Wilson, Mr Tominey (subsequently appointed Commercial Director) and Mr Haines; IM was present but did not vote. Mr Horwood and Mr Laird were present by phone. RM telephoned during the course of the meeting.

[b] Independent advice had been sought from Conrad Ritblat and Savills.

a longer term at a reduced rent and so obviate the need to move[a] to Great Dover Street[b]. Mr Stoney thought that those present were aware of the connection between the extension of the lease and the refinancing for the private side[c]. The other directors present could not recall this being discussed; the only explanation of the urgency of the meeting they could recall was that it was said to be the only time RM was available to speak to them from New York. However even if the real need for the urgency - the pressure from the banks to complete the refinancing for the private side - had been explained, it is likely that the directors would still have agreed to the new terms for the lease, though they may have discussed matters more widely[d] and asked for an adjournment to enable the non-executive directors[e] (who apart from Mr Haines were not present) to attend.

21.40 On the basis of this new lease the private side were able to obtain the refinancing by a loan of £80m which was the amount that the banks were by then prepared to lend.

The intervention of Samuel Montagu

21.41 A meeting in connection with the lease of the Mirror Building enabled Mr Burrington to tell Samuel Montagu of the concerns that Mr Guest and he had about the payments that had been made from MGN[f]. He did this on Thursday 26 September 1991 and during the first three days

---

a A committee of the staff had strongly recommended against the move to Great Dover Street.

b Mr Burrington did not attend the meeting. He had taken steps to call a board meeting of MGN earlier in October 1991, but RM had persuaded him not to hold it on the assurance that the lease would be discussed by the full board of MGN. Mr Burrington told us that he was on his way to a luncheon meeting when he was told of the meeting and decided to go ahead with his luncheon as he did not believe that Mr Stoney was empowered to call a meeting nor would be able to obtain a quorum, nor that RM would be "present" when in New York, nor did he know what the business of the meeting would be. He had circulated a note prepared by an in-house lawyer on the issue of the lease. Others viewed his absence as "diplomatic".

c Titmuss, Sainer & Webb were present at the meeting and prepared minutes which did not refer to the financing for the private side; these were signed. Further minutes were also prepared which referred to the financing for the private side as these were to be used for that financing. These were also signed.

d Mr Horwood asked for MGN to have a similar right of determination to that accorded to MCC. This was discussed, but the transaction agreed without it. In fact, as the terms of the lease had been agreed with the banks providing the financing to the private side and the loan documentation finalised on this basis, negotiation of such a term would not have been possible within the time available, if at all.

e Sir Robert Clark, Lord Williams and Mr Clements each recalled being telephoned by Mr Stoney and being told that all of the other directors were in favour and on that basis gave their approval. None was told of the opposition of Mr Burrington. Mr Stoney accepted he had not told them about Mr Burrington's position, but he had taken this course as Mr Burrington had not attended the board meeting and if he had been strongly opposed he should have done so.

Lord Williams told us that he had discussed with Sir Robert Clark and Mr Clements after a meeting in April 1991 working together as a group of non-executive directors; underlying his remark to them was his thought that cultural changes in the way MGN was run would be difficult to effect and it might take two to three years to bring these about. He had attended the board meeting on 12 September 1991, but not those on 11 June 1991 or 23 July 1991; after the call from Mr Stoney about the Holborn lease he felt uneasy and tried to contact Sir Robert Clark and Mr Clements, but without success.

f In addition to contacting Samuel Montagu, both Mr Burrington and Mr Guest continued to press Mr Stoney for further information and documentation in relation to the deposits. Mr Stoney told them that the moneys would be returned. Mr Stoney explained to us that by this time he felt that he was not in a happy position;

of the following week, Mr Galloway[a] (who dealt with this matter in close conjunction with Mr McIntosh) obtained from Mr Guest further details of what had happened. Samuel Montagu advised Mr Guest to speak to Mr Clements whom Mr Guest and Mr Burrington anticipated they would meet at the traditional *Mirror* cocktail party during the Labour Party Conference at Brighton.

21.42 Mr Burrington, Mr Guest and Mr Horwood went to Brighton on 2 October 1991, but Mr Clements did not attend and the opportunity of speaking to him was missed. However a meeting between RM and Mr Burrington took place at Brighton at which RM asked Mr Burrington why he was questioning the extension of the lease of the Mirror Building and "having trouble" with Mr Stoney. Mr Burrington expressed his views on the Mirror Building and said he was questioning Mr Stoney because of the lack of documentation. Having been told this, RM informed Mr Burrington that his duties were to be restricted to the internal operations of MGN. Mr Burrington told RM that if that was the position, he could not discharge his duties as he saw them and would resign as soon as this could be arranged. RM agreed to this. Although some of the directors were told of Mr Burrington's intention to resign, no steps had been taken to implement his resignation before RM's death[b].

21.43 Contact had not been made with Mr Clements and Samuel Montagu decided to raise the issue of the payments from MGN directly with RM; they took advantage of a meeting that had been arranged for 4 October 1991 to discuss the *Panorama* Programme which had been broadcast on 23 September 1991[c]. After the meeting concerning the *Panorama* Programme, Mr Galloway and Mr McIntosh spoke to RM. They told him that in their review in relation to the extension of the lease of the Mirror Building, they had come across deposits with US Investment Banks and with "Bishopsgate". RM expressed surprise that there had been deposits with BIM; there was a "ring fence" and he could not see how it had happened. Mr McIntosh told RM that deposits of spare cash should be with UK banks and also complained about Mr Stoney having control over MGN's cash. RM agreed to look into matters and to get back to Samuel Montagu.

The repayment of the BIM "deposits" and "the purchase of gilts"

21.44 During the course of September 1991 a concerted attempt had been made to raise further bank loans for MGN. This had been largely unsuccessful but there were two significant further facilities which KM persuaded each of the banks to grant by telling them that if the bank made

---

he was unable to get documentation from RM yet the other directors were blaming him for this and were treating him with suspicion.

a Mr Galloway also took advice from Linklaters & Paines.

b There was a delay over his pension arrangements.

c RM was incensed by the programme and wanted to bring proceedings for criminal libel; advice was given subsequently that the claim in respect of the competitions (including "Spot the Ball") would fail and create a negative view of RM.

available to MGN the facility that they had made available to the private side, that would enable him to persuade another bank to transfer a facility from MGN to the private side[a]:

- On 30 September 1991 following negotiations between KM and Lloyds, Lloyds agreed to increase their overdraft facility to MGN by £10m[b].
- A new facility for £20m was granted to MGN by Crédit Lyonnais. Crédit Lyonnais had had a facility with RMG since April 1991 and were asked by KM if they would lend £20m to MGN[c] in place of the facility to RMG. The facility to MGN for £20m was approved by a meeting of the committee of the board of MGN attended by RM, IM and Mr Stoney on 7 October 1991. KM told us that although Crédit Lyonnais was not happy to renew its lending to RMG, it was perfectly happy to substitute a loan to MGN. KM had told Crédit Lyonnais that the only way RMG was going to be able to repay its loan was if a loan was made to another of RM's companies; Crédit Lyonnais agreed to make the loan to MGN.

21.45 Mr Guest and Mr Burrington had on 3 October 1991 prepared a further memorandum to Mr Stoney which was sent out under Mr Guest's name with a copy to RM, Mr Horwood and Mr Burrington. The memorandum set out their concern at what they had been given to understand were the short term deposits with BIM and the US investment banks and asked for documentation to be supplied. A reply to this was drafted by Mr Stoney on Friday 4 October 1991 and shown to RM on Saturday. RM then redrafted the entire memorandum making it very much more threatening towards Mr Guest, telling him that he was to do nothing without first clearing it with Mr Stoney. The draft was given to Mr Stoney, but he re-amended it to something closer to his own original version. This was handed to Mr Guest on Monday 7 October 1991 and contained the explanations for the payments to which we have referred[d]; it stated that the monies would be returned from BIM.

21.46 On the same day, Monday 7 October 1991, £22.8m was repaid by BIM to MGN. This represented the balance of the money that had been paid to BIM together with interest as calculated by Mr Griffiths. KM told us that there had been concerted pressure from Mr Guest to have the monies returned, primarily due to operational reasons and also the size of the sums involved.

---

a KM told us that he was using the stronger credit of MGN in order to raise money, the bank being happier with the MGN covenant. He accepted that this was not consistent with MGN acting independently, but he did not perceive that to be a requirement at the time and the banks were well aware of the connections between the entities.

b KM had originally proposed a short term loan for RMG to provide bridging facilities pending asset disposals. This was granted for a short time. Thereafter KM persuaded Lloyds to make the advance to MGN on the basis that if MGN were lent money by Lloyds another lender to MGN would be prepared to lend to RMG if their facilities to MGN could be reduced. Lloyds had also effected a foreign exchange contract in August 1991 to hedge the investments in QPI and Donohue.

c KM had said this would allow him to replace a loan from another bank which would then lend to other companies controlled by RM.

d The memorandum also stated that payments to BIM were not a breach of the "ring fencing " provisions as it was not a related party as BIM was owned by The Maxwell Charitable Trust and not by the private side and was managed by "Independent Directors". Mr Stoney told us that RM added this and he left it in.

21.47 After receipt of the funds from BIM and from the Crédit Lyonnais facility, on 7 and 8 October 1991 £38.8m was paid out of MGN to LBG. These payments were arranged by Mr Stoney on the instructions of RM. It was explained to us by Mr Stoney that he had been told that RM had decided to invest in gilt edged securities and that these were to be purchased by Mr Trachtenberg of LBG. Prior to making these payments, Mr Stoney had discussed the making of this investment in gilts with Mr Trachtenberg and he had been provided with faxes from Rowe & Pitman[a] and SBIL[b] about a programme for the purchase of gilts. Documentation was promised relating to these purchases[c]. Mr Trachtenberg told us that he was called by RM in October 1991 and told that RM wanted to invest in gilts; RM asked him to find out what gilts to invest in. He did so only to find that, over the next few weeks, Mr Stoney and Mr Guest would phone him to ask if he made an investment in gilts; he said he had not and that he had only been asked to find out information.

21.48 No documentation was ever provided in relation to the purchase of gilts; on the contrary (after receipt of a further £14m from MCC) LBG paid out on 7 and 8 October 1991:

- £27.3m towards settlement of the liability to the BPCC pension fund in respect of the transfer payment due[d].
- £20m due to Crédit Lyonnais to repay the loan to RMG[e].
- £3.1m due for purchases of MGN and MCC shares made by Mr Aboff[f].
- £2.2m due to Peel Hunt for the purchase of 1.3 million MCC shares by Jupiter Participations[g].

---

a Mr Trachtenberg had spoken to Rowe & Pitman and sought from them their research papers on gilts.

b KM telephoned Mr McVeigh at SBIL on 7 October 1991 and asked for advice on gilts; Mr McVeigh asked one of their traders to speak to KM and that trader subsequently sent the fax referred to. Nothing further was heard. KM told us that he asked for the information on instructions from RM and handed the information received to RM or Mr Stoney; that was his entire involvement.

c Mr Stoney told us that he had obtained the impression at a meeting attended by Mr Guest, Mr Burrington and Mr Horwood subsequent to the purchases that RM had discussed the principles of the purchase with them prior to the purchases being made. Mr Burrington, Mr Horwood and Mr Guest told us they had no knowledge of the purchase of gilts until after the purchases had been made.

d This was in respect of the liability following the buyout of BPCC referred to at paragraph 4.12; there was tremendous pressure to settle this liability. KM told us that, in this period, of all the issues to be dealt with, RM regarded the settlement of the liability to the BPCC pension fund as being the top priority, partly due to the pressure being applied by the management of BPCC but mainly because it was a contractual and moral obligation that he felt he should meet.

e Crédit Lyonnais had made sure that the facility to RMG had been repaid on that day before they allowed drawdown of the loan to MGN.

f Mr Aboff had purchased in the period 14 August to 26 September 1991 2.4 million MCC shares on RM's instructions. He also purchased 860,000 MGN shares between 14 August and 24 September 1991. He made further purchases of MCC and MGN shares in October and November 1991.

g These shares had been held by a client of Robert Fraser. Mr Emson told RM he wanted to sell and RM had asked for the name of Robert Fraser's broker so that he could put a purchaser in touch with those brokers. The shares were then sold on 20 September 1991 through Peel Hunt to Jupiter Participations and paid for by the private side; they were registered in the name of Quotescreen Ltd, a nominee company controlled by LBG.

21.49 Between 9 and 15 October 1991 there had been 3 payments totalling approximately £9.5m to MGN which were described as the repayment of the deposits placed with Morgan Stanley and Lehmans; two of the payments were said to have been from Morgan Stanley and one from Lehmans. Some semblance for this was provided by the fact that one payment of £2.1m was made to MGN from MSTC. It was in fact made on LBI's instructions from one of their accounts under their control. The other monies came directly from LBG[a].

The involvement of the non-executive directors

21.50 As RM had not got back to Samuel Montagu after their meeting on Friday 4 October 1991, on Wednesday 9 October 1991 Mr McIntosh and Mr Galloway again spoke to RM. RM said that the deposits with BIM had been repaid but was dismissive about the deposits with the US investment banks. RM also told them that Mr Stoney was to resign his private side directorships and become an independent director. After this conversation Mr McIntosh and Mr Galloway appreciated that the inquiries they had made were not making much progress and so they decided to speak to Mr Clements.

21.51 The following day Mr Galloway spoke to Mr Clements and summarised the position (as Samuel Montagu understood it) to him[b]. It is not clear what Mr Clements did following this conversation; his recollection was that he spoke to Mr Guest but Mr Guest had no recollection of this and a contemporaneous note made by Mr Galloway of a further conversation with Mr Clements on 22 October 1991 records Mr Clements as having told him then that he had not yet contacted Mr Guest. In any event, whether he contacted Mr Guest or not, no other action was taken by Mr Clements[c], in part because between 16 and 22 October 1991 he had been confined to bed with a slipped disc and his office was under instructions not to refer calls to his home.

21.52 Some time between 21 and 24 October 1991 Mr Clements contacted Sir Robert Clark and they both agreed, having obtained information on the up-to-date position, that they would see RM after a board meeting that was scheduled for the following week (Tuesday 29 October 1991); they decided that they would not tell the other non-executive directors - Lord Williams and Mr Haines. Mr Clements told us he had not appreciated how worried Mr Guest was (about the gilts and deposits) until he had lunch with him on 29 October 1991; Mr Guest's hands were

---

[a] Mr Guest obtained a giro slip for the other payment which was said to have come from Morgan Stanley (£2,998,542). The giro slip showed that the funds in fact came from LBG; he asked Mr Stoney about this and he was told it was a mistake. Mr Stoney told us he asked LBG who said the slip was in error and the funds had come from Morgan Stanley. LBG obtained the funds from several sources, but we have seen no evidence that they came from Morgan Stanley.

[b] Mr Clements asked to be reminded of any particular duties of a non-executive director; on 11 October 1991, Mr Galloway wrote to him reminding him of his duties as a member of the audit committee, remuneration committee and as an independent director in related party transactions.

[c] Mr Stoney told us that Mr Clements spoke to him by telephone about investments in gilts; that he told Mr Clements that £38.5m had been invested in gilts, but he had no documentation and RM was dealing with it. Mr Clements told us there was no such conversation and could only recall one telephone conversation with Mr Stoney during this period which related to the Holborn lease . (This conversation is referred to in the footnote to paragraph 21.39.) Mr Stoney's personal assistant told us she recalled Mr Clements telephoning to speak to Mr Stoney on a number of occasions when Mr Stoney was unavailable and these were probably in October 1991, but she did not know if Mr Stoney had returned the calls. Mr Stoney was adamant that he did.

shaking, he hardly touched his food and he smoked continuously. Before this meeting with RM on 29 October 1991 there were significant events to which we must refer, but it is first convenient to mention a discussion between Mr Guest and Mr Craggs and CLD.

The meetings with CLD

21.53 On 10 October 1991 there was a meeting between Mr Steere and Mr Merry, Mr Mellett (another member of CLD's staff), Mr Guest and Mr Craggs to discuss the programme for the 1991 audit. At the conclusion of the meeting, Mr Guest asked Mr Steere to stay behind. There is a difference of recollection as to what then occurred. Mr Guest told us that he told Mr Steere about the deposits and the cash movements that were taking place. Mr Steere told us that Mr Guest merely asked whether CLD would, when they did the audit work, look at the intercompany accounts, but Mr Guest gave no explanation of why he had made the request[a]. There was also a conversation between Mr Craggs and Mr Mellett. Mr Craggs' recollection was that that occurred immediately after the meeting and that he had told Mr Mellett about the transactions that had been effected through the treasury for which MGN had not received supporting documentation. Mr Mellett did not recall such a conversation that day but he did recall a discussion with Mr Craggs shortly afterwards in which Mr Craggs had mentioned that there had been certain transactions effected by the treasury for which MGN did not have full details. Mr Mellett then spoke to Mr Merry about examining the treasury functions to see what the transactions were and a member of CLD's staff with treasury experience was asked to look at the treasury during the week commencing 28 October 1991. This work was then postponed because Mr Griffiths was on holiday.

21.54 Some other audit work at MGN in the nature of planning and information gathering was done by CLD's staff (although not connected with examining the transactions about which Mr Guest and Mr Craggs told us they had spoken to CLD), but this work was terminated after Mr Stoney relayed to Mr Steere a request from RM that the team be pulled out[b]. The team ceased work thereafter.

---

a Mr Steere subsequently discussed this with Mr Walsh, Mr Wootten and Mr Merry. They concluded that it was unlikely that any transfers to the private side similar to that which Mr Stoney had reported on 17 July 1991 had taken place, because Mr Stoney had given an assurance that this would not happen and, if it had, Mr Guest would have mentioned it explicitly. They speculated that Mr Guest's concern might have related to a charge under the agreement relating to the provision of group common services between MGN, the private side and MCC (referred to at paragraph 12.5), but that this would be dealt with in the forthcoming audit. No reference was made by Mr Guest to the deposits and cash movements in a letter he wrote to Mr Steere on 1 November 1991 with his comments on the management letter sent by CLD to MGN on 26 June 1991 (referred to in the footnote to paragraph 10.7) although the letter had referred to transactions with other Maxwell companies.

b Mr Stoney told us that the reason why RM wanted the team pulled out was to ensure that the finance department concentrated upon finalising the 1992 budgets. CLD told us that this reason was not given to them and they would not have accepted it, as those working on the budget were not those who would be affected by the audit work. Mr Stoney told us that the presence of auditors was viewed as an excuse for not getting things done and that he was told by CLD that stopping the work would have no effect on the audit timetable; they did not express to him any concerns.

Events between 10 October and 29 October 1991

21.55 Between the time of the conversations with both CLD and Mr Clements about the payments out of MGN and the meeting of the board on 29 October 1991 three significant events occurred - the promotion of Mr Stoney to the position of Deputy Managing Director (Finance) of MGN; the making of a loan by Bankers Trust to MGN for £50m; and the signing of a new lease of the Mirror Building in the circumstances that we have already described at paragraph 21.38. In addition, there was a further settlement of the intercompany accounts which resulted in further payments out of MGN to the private side.

The appointment of Mr Stoney as Deputy Managing Director (Finance)

21.56 On 3/4 October 1991 Mr Stoney had resigned his directorships of various of RM's private companies with the intention of becoming an "independent" director of MGN[a] for the purposes of the company's Articles (described at paragraph 10.26). On Monday 21 October 1991 RM announced the appointment of Mr Stoney as Deputy Managing Director (Finance) of MGN[b]; there had been no consultation with any other member of the MGN board, although RM had told Mr Horwood that he might do this and Mr Horwood tried to persuade him not to do so. A press announcement of the appointment was made, and the company secretarial department learnt of Mr Stoney's appointment from the press notice; it was from this that they prepared a board minute for the appointment of Mr Stoney (and that of Mr Tominey as Commercial Director[c]) after finding out from Mr Stoney who had been present when RM had made the decision[d]. This, we were told, by Mr Stephens, was the way directors in RM's companies were often appointed[e]. In consequence of this appointment, Mr Stoney's seniority in the management of MGN was formalised.

The loan of £50m from Bankers Trust

21.57 Bankers Trust had made short term secured loans to the private side since 1987 (see paragraph 4.56) and were participants for £20m in the £170m syndicated loan arranged by Lloyds (referred to at paragraph 3.27)[f]. On 31 May 1991 they had lent RMG £50m until 30 September 1991 secured on MGN and MCC shares and this loan was to be repaid from private side

---

[a] He had not resigned from FTIT or AGB Pension Trustees Ltd. Mr Stoney told us that this was an administrative error and he had intended to resign from these but the administrative procedures had not been carried out.

[b] This was a position contemplated for Mr Stoney during the flotation (see paragraph 11.22).

[c] Mr Ferguson had been suspended by RM in September 1991 and had left MGN on 10 October 1991; the acceptance of his resignation was recorded in a minute of a board meeting said to have been attended only by RM, IM and Mr Stoney on 11 October 1991.

[d] The minute then recorded that RM, IM and Mr Stoney were present. IM told us that he did not recall attending any such meeting and that he always referred to Mr Stoney as the Commercial Director.

[e] This was not the only type of matter that was dealt with in this way. It was decided that an account should be opened for MGN with the Royal Bank of Scotland; a bank mandate (which included RM's sole signatory authority) and a minute of a board meeting attended by RM, IM and Mr Stoney on 18 October 1991 were prepared and signed approving the mandate, even though Mr Stoney was in the Far East that day.

[f] They also had smaller exposures on loans to MCC.

disposals[a], including the holding in Scitex. On 21 June 1991 Bankers Trust had been supplied by KM with a package of information about the private side. This was reviewed by Bankers Trust and a memorandum was sent by Mr Michael Moore, a managing director of Bankers Trust, to other officers of Bankers Trust on 28 August 1991. The memorandum reviewed the private side companies including the loss-making companies that owned *The European* and the *New York Daily News*; it concluded that the Maxwell companies were able to service the interest on their loans but were reliant on the disposal programme and that the credit risk in the various borrowing companies to which Bankers Trust were exposed was reasonable. The memorandum contained an analysis of the cash flow of RMG (which included as two of the items, £100m as operating profit from MGN and a deduction of £12m as dividends to MGN investors) and stated:

> "The estimated cash flow for RMG in 1991 is comprised of income from MGN (less dividends payable to shareholders), property income and MCC dividend income, set off against losses in the Daily News and the European."
>
> ...
>
> "The cash flow of MGN should provide sufficient support for future cash requirements in the Daily News and the European."

Although this memorandum referred to cash flow from MGN (in contra distinction to RMG's dividend income from MCC), we were told by Mr Moore that Bankers Trust understood that the private side's only source of income from MGN was dividend income. The credit department's copy of this memorandum contained the annotation against the figure for cash flow from MGN:

> "Not available to RMG."

21.58 In early September 1991, the loan to RMG was rolled over to 31 October 1991 or the date of the receipt of the proceeds of the sale of the Scitex shares[b], whichever was the earlier. Some time between the end of August and 17 September 1991, the report prepared on MGN for the credit rating agencies was provided to Bankers Trust. On 17 September 1991, Mr Moore submitted a new proposal in respect of Bankers Trust's exposure. This stated that the Maxwells had originally requested that a further loan be extended to RMG repayable from asset sales other than the Scitex disposal but proposed:

> "In order to manage down our overall exposure in an orderly manner while the asset disposals already fully documented occur and to have more than one clearly identifiable source of repayment it is proposed that
>
> 1. MGN borrows £50m from [Bankers Trust] for up to six months.
> Reason: the clearing Banks ([National Westminster], Barclays, Lloyds/ Midland) have overdraft facilities in MGN which it is proposed replace the current RMG loan of [Bankers Trust], i.e. no-one increases or decreases exposure but (a) [Bankers Trust] achieves its desire to see more than one exit and (b) the clearers are prepared to accept the RMG asset disposal time frame that we are probably not.

---

a Bankers Trust had an investment banking relationship with RM's companies and during the summer of 1991 were retained by the private side in connection with the disposals of the Pergamon AGB plc companies and Thomas Cook Travel Inc.

b This transaction is referred to at paragraph 21.73; there had been a delay in the sale.

2. Additionally, and contingent on the £50m, [Bankers Trust] gets its Visaford exposure reduced from £20m to £10m by way of Maxwell arranging a purchase by another bank of half our position.

Rationale
1. [Bankers Trust]'s net exposure falls by £10m.
2. The riskiest exposure falls by 50 per cent..
3. We are lending to an asset owning, cashflow producing, well covenanted Company ringfenced from the rest of the Group."

The reference to Visaford was a reference to the syndicated loan for £170m arranged by Lloyds.

Mr Moore told us that he had been told by KM that the clearing banks were prepared to switch their facilities to MGN across to RMG[a]. He told us that the repayment of the loan by RMG to Bankers Trust was not dependant on the loan to MGN; Bankers Trust were prepared to lend to MGN because of their assessment of it as a company. KM's evidence was that Mr Moore was under pressure from his credit officers to demonstrate that the loan to RMG was not permanent and, therefore, to have a period of time when the loan was not outstanding. Then Mr Moore told KM that the loan would have to be repaid. KM was not prepared to accept that and asked Mr Moore to maintain a level of lending to RM's companies on the basis that he could more or less choose where he would prefer to lend. Mr Moore chose to lend to MGN but KM made it clear to him that he would not be in a position to repay the RMG loan unless Bankers Trust made the loan to MGN.

21.59 The proposals put forward by Mr Moore were communicated to Mr Moore's seniors in London and New York. On 14 October 1991 Mr Moore had a meeting with KM at which KM stated that he wanted to enter into the MGN loan as soon as possible. On 16 October 1991 Mr Moore had a further meeting with KM and took with him a draft loan agreement and other documents. Bankers Trust proposed that they would only lend £30m to MGN until £10m of their exposure on the syndicated loan arranged by Lloyds could be removed. KM requested that Bankers Trust lend £10m to RMG with collateral in the form of MGN shares but Mr Moore said he would not recommend this. Mr Moore's report of the meeting included the following paragraph:

"I did some calculations based on the information we have and told him that as far as we could see he had sufficient liquidity with our [£30m] to see him thru at least until [1 November]. This is based on proceeds of sales to date and executed in the private side and the maturity schedule given to us yesterday. He agreed but said it was too tight to enable him to sleep. Hence the request to come... ."

KM subsequently spoke to Mr Ralph MacDonald, Mr Moore's senior in New York, and told him that an overall reduction in the liquidity of the Maxwell companies brought about by the repayment of £50m would be awkward. KM asked if a loan could be made to MGN. Mr MacDonald had understood from a conversation with RM that the purpose of a loan to MGN would be to permit repayment of MGN's clearing bank overdraft facilities.

---

[a] In fact this was very much the same as had been said to Crédit Lyonnais and Lloyds.

21.60 We were told that Bankers Trust were therefore persuaded to lend to MGN having been told by KM that the clearing banks would in such circumstances transfer the equivalent facility from MGN and make it available to the private side. They were, however, not prepared to lend to MGN until the RMG loan was repaid, as they did not want to increase their overall exposure by both loans being outstanding at the same time. Mr MacDonald was satisfied from what RM and KM had said that the MGN loan was an entirely separate transaction from the RMG loan repayment.

21.61 Accordingly, on 17 October 1991 Bankers Trust agreed to a proposal under which Bankers Trust would be repaid £50m by RMG, MGN would be lent £50m and that within three weeks their exposure under the syndicated facility arranged by Lloyds would be removed and £10m repaid by MGN. On 17 or 18 October 1991 KM told Mr Moore that the Scitex shares had been sold and had asked if he could repay the loan to RMG in US dollars. On 21 October 1991 Mr Bunn[a] wrote to Bankers Trust to inform them that RMG had given instructions to Chase to pay to Bankers Trust $86.78m in discharge of their £50m loan and interest.

21.62 The documentation for the loan to MGN by Bankers Trust was signed on 21 October 1991; the terms of the loan required a number of documents to be signed not only by MGN but also by its various subsidiaries. There is some dispute as to what happened, but Mr Stoney told us that he had been summoned back from the Far East and was persuaded by RM and KM on the morning he had returned to sign the documentation. Although he had been against taking the loan as it was of so short a duration[b] (as he had made clear in a memorandum to KM of 16 October 1991), RM had explained to him that it would be used to buy US Treasury Bills.

21.63 KM's evidence was that prior to October 1991 RM had started to develop a plan (together with Mr Morgenstern of Nicholson Graham & Jones) for capitalising on the *New York Daily News* as an asset. At that time it was a subsidiary of Maxwell Newspapers Inc and, ultimately, of RMG. RM wanted to place the *New York Daily News* into a stand-alone vehicle not connected with RMG in order to be better able to raise capital and finance independently of his existing companies; an English company called DuoCrown Limited had been incorporated to be that vehicle[c]. When KM had told RM that Bankers Trust wished to transfer their lending to MGN from RMG and started discussions as to which of the other bankers would be asked to extend their lending to RMG, RM told him that that would take too long. RM said that he had decided that he would sell the *New York Daily News* to MGN and the £50m from Bankers Trust should be as a first payment on an option for that purchase. KM told us that he thought that the option decided upon by RM had its origins in RM's earlier consideration of including the *New York Daily News* in the flotation of MGN (see paragraph 9.23).

---

a A draft of the letter was prepared by Mr Moore at Mr Bunn's request; Mr Moore explained to us that this letter was needed to cover the fact the repayment was to be in US dollars rather than in sterling.

b £10m was repayable on 31 October 1991 and £40m on 20 December 1991.

c DuoCrown Limited was acquired by Nicholson Graham & Jones as an off the shelf company to perform a role in the efficient disposal of the *New York Daily News*. It was Mr Morgenstern's recollection that the objective was never progressed as no directors were appointed, shares issued, the company reorganised or any business transacted.

21.64 The documentation for the Bankers Trust loan that was signed by RM and Mr Stoney included minutes of board meetings for several companies of which neither RM nor Mr Stoney were directors. Mr Stoney told us that he knew when he signed these documents that he was not a director of those companies, but that he had signed them in reliance on an assurance by RM that the position would be regularised by his subsequent appointment as a director of those companies. He appreciated, however, that the appointments could not be backdated to the time at which he had signed the documents in order to validate retrospectively his signature. A member of the company secretarial department was asked to put in hand the procedures necessary to appoint RM and Mr Stoney as directors of these companies; we have received no evidence that Mr Stoney was ever appointed a director of these companies.

21.65 Mr Stephens, as Company Secretary, was summoned to assist; he told us that he only saw Mr Stoney and that the minutes and loan documentation had already been signed when he arrived. Mr Stephens certified a copy of some of the board minutes. After the loan documentation and the minutes had been signed, one copy was retained by Bankers Trust and the other by RM.

21.66 Instructions were then given on 21 October 1991 in two letters signed by RM and Mr Stoney that the facility be drawn down and payment be made to Citibank for the account of Lehmans. A foreign exchange deal had been agreed by KM with Lehmans to convert £50m into $86.1m which was then remitted to Maxwell Newspapers Inc in New York. The dollar funds were used to make the payment of $86.7m that RMG had said it would make to discharge the £50m loan by Bankers Trust to RMG[a].

21.67 KM's evidence was that the loan was drawn down and remitted to Maxwell Newspapers Inc (as the parent of the *New York Daily News*) and that thereafter the private side (on the instructions of RM) used those funds over a number of days to repay the RMG loan to Bankers Trust. After thc loan was drawn down KM asked RM whether the issue of the purchase of the *New York Daily News* by MGN would be brought up at the next board meeting since it was a substantial transaction and would require a Class 4 circular and shareholder approval. RM told him that he would bring it up at the next board meeting, fixed for 29 October 1991. In the last conversation KM had with RM on 30 October 1991, KM asked whether the issue had been raised at the MGN board meeting. After RM's death, KM discussed the transaction with Mr Stoney[b] and they were confused as to what RM had done; they decided that it would be best to reverse the transaction.

21.68 As the payment under the Bankers Trust loan to MGN was made directly to Lehmans, it did not, therefore, go through any of MGN's bank accounts in England, and was unknown to the MGN finance department or to Mr Griffiths as treasurer and nothing was recorded in the books of account. Furthermore, because RM retained all the documentation, the various board

---

a The amount was remitted by Chase in 4 payments made between 21 and 24 October 1991 from the account of Maxwell Newspapers Inc.

b Mr Stoney's evidence was that he was not aware of the existence of DuoCrown Limited nor of the discussions concerning it and the *New York Daily News*.

minutes of MGN and its subsidiaries were not passed to the company secretarial department to be included with the papers for the board meeting that was held on 29 October 1991. As a result none of the directors of MGN (other than RM and Mr Stoney) knew of this loan until sometime after RM's death. Mr Stoney told us that after RM's death he was persuaded by KM not to tell the other directors of the loan whilst refinancing was being negotiated.

The October 1991 settlement of the intercompany accounts

21.69 The MGN finance department had produced a schedule of the position of the intercompany accounts as at 29 September 1991. A decision was made by Mr Stoney, in consultation with RM, that there should be a settlement of the balances due on those accounts. The accounts showed balances due to the private side companies of £1.1m and to MCC of £1.7m and these two sums were settled by way of transfers from MGN on 23 October 1991.

The meetings on 29 October 1991

21.70 The board meeting that took place on 29 October 1991 was uneventful. For the reasons already given at paragraph 21.68, no papers relating to the Bankers Trust loan were placed before the board and the board was not informed of it by RM or Mr Stoney during the meeting. Although the board was supplied with a financial report for the period to 29 September 1991, the amounts that had been paid to the US investment banks and to BIM in that period were not identified as such. The phrase[a]

> "deposits and equivalent net of overdraft"

was used in the accounts in order to achieve a net figure of £5.1m. Mr Stoney had suggested to Mr Craggs that the deposits should not be shown separately and it was agreed this phrase be used. The effect of its use was to prevent monies paid to the US investment banks and for the "purchase of gilts" being shown separately in the accounts; had separate figures been given overdrafts of £39.7m and "deposits" of £44.8m would have been disclosed.

21.71 Nothing was said at the board meeting about these payments by Mr Clements and Sir Robert Clark as they had agreed to see RM afterwards[b]. We were told that RM was totally charming during the separate meeting with Mr Clements and Sir Robert and explained to them that the appointment of Mr Stoney had been made because he was very good with the City and because Mr Guest, although a good figures man, had not been up to being finance director. They both told RM that this was a matter for the audit committee. They then raised with him the money paid out for the purchase of gilts and RM explained that this was a one-off transaction and that these would be repaid shortly. They asked if the audit committee could be convened and RM agreed to this. Mr Clements said he would draft the terms of reference. RM then brought the

---

[a] This phrase had been used in the management accounts for the preceding month but these were not put before the board.

[b] Mr Guest, Mr Horwood and Mr Burrington knew this. Mr Clements had had lunch with Mr Guest prior to the meeting and had for the first time learnt how concerned Mr Guest was; he spoke to Sir Robert Clark after the lunch and agreed with him the course of action to follow. IM was not aware of this meeting. He told us that no one approached him concerning the payments out of MGN that had been made. If he had been approached, IM would have passed any concerns on to RM and would have relayed RM's views.

meeting to a close by saying that he was late for an appointment and would explain what had happened in more detail the following week.

21.72 Later that afternoon RM telephoned Mr Stoney and told him to draft terms of reference for the audit committee and then telephoned Mr Clements to tell him that Mr Stoney would be drafting the terms of reference; Mr Clements told RM that he would continue drafting his own terms of reference. Mr Stoney subsequently raised the content of his terms of reference at a meeting with Mr Steere and Mr Merry on 31 October 1991 at which it was also agreed that no audit work would be done until after the meeting with the audit committee.

1 to 5 November 1991

21.73 On 17 October 1991, the Scitex shares owned by RMG and the CIF[a] were sold realising £139m; the proceeds were paid to National Westminster[b] who used them to discharge RMG's overdraft referred to at paragraph 21.13 and to make a payment of £30m to another bank. When Goldman Sachs learnt of this sale, they correctly appreciated RM had no substantial assets left, apart from the holdings in MGN[c] and MCC[d].

21.74 At a meeting in New York on 22 October 1991 between RM and Goldman Sachs, RM paid the remaining balance outstanding on the MCC shares purchased by the foundations in July and August 1991, referred to in paragraph 21.4. Goldman Sachs told RM on Wednesday 30 October 1991 after giving RM warnings on several occasions to the similar effect, that they would begin realising security for the two loans $35m and £25m[e] made by them if no repayment was made. Goldman Sachs began to sell their holding of MCC shares on 31 October 1991[f]. KM told us he requested Goldman Sachs not to do this. Goldman Sachs told us that KM made no request in relation to selling the shares until he wrote on 4 November 1991[g].

---

a The way in which the shares in Scitex has been divided between RMG and the CIF was described in paragraph 6.5; the CIF had by an agreement dated 4 July 1991 sold its holding to RMG, but retained beneficial ownership until payment. Lehmans acted as the lead investment banker for the sale.

b We were told by National Westminster that they refused to release the Scitex share certificates held as collateral by them; they sent one of their senior employees to New York with the share certificates for hand delivery at the time of the sale.

c SBIL had been working on a proposal to raise finance for RMG through a bond convertible, subject to the right to redeem for cash, into MGN shares. This could have meant RM losing control. Enquiries were made of the banks that had provided the £150m facility and they indicated they would consent to the deletion of the covenant (described at paragraph 15.37) requiring RM, his family and the Maxwell Foundation to keep 51 per cent. ownership.

d The private side had some property, but this was largely mortgaged as security for loans, and the disposal of the interest in Thomas Cook Travel Inc had not taken place.

e See paragraph 21.11.

f On 31 October 1991, Goldman Sachs sold 2.2 million MCC shares. On 31 October 1991 and 1 November 1991, RM purchased 2.05 million MCC shares through Mr Aboff.

g KM told us he asked Mr Katz, the General Counsel to Goldman Sachs, how their actions were compatible with the fact that Mr Sheinberg had advised the strategy and provided the margin loans that had led to this disaster. Mr Katz told him: "We have to look after our own; that is history"; Mr Katz had no recollection of any such conversation and told us that he believed he first spoke to KM on 7 November 1991, a conversation that he

21.75 On Thursday, 31 October 1991 RM left London for his yacht.

21.76 The same day Mr Stoney agreed that MGN would make two payments on behalf of RMG (to Citibank NA and Société Générale) totalling £2.7m out of an amount of £3.5m that had been paid to MGN for RMG. The payment to MGN appears to have been done so as to avoid the funds passing through the accounts of the private side where they would have been used by the bank concerned to reduce its overdraft. KM told us that he was a little puzzled by this motivation since there were other accounts (not at National Westminster) that the private side could have used to receive the payment. This transaction , however, did not result in any net outflow from MGN. On either 30 or 31 October 1991, National Westminster told KM that the bank would not pay cheques totalling £6.5m presented to them for payment.

21.77 On the morning of 5 November 1991, further amounts totalling £6.6m were paid to MGN which were said to have come from Lehmans and Goldman Sachs in apparent repayment of the "deposits". In fact, the funds came from LBG who had obtained them through a failed foreign exchange transaction involving Swiss Volksbank.

21.78 On Monday 4 November 1991:

- Mr Eugene Fife of Goldman Sachs in London telephoned Mr Eddie George, Deputy Governor of the Bank of England, to tell him that there would be an announcement the following day the effect of which would be that it would become known that Goldman Sachs would be selling the MCC shares it held as collateral for loans to RM's companies[a].
- Citibank NA, in confirming the receipt of a £2.3m payment referred to in paragraph 21.76, informed KM that they would also begin realising the security they held[b].
- Lehmans, that evening, served recall notices[c] the effect of which was to entitle Lehmans to terminate the financing through the use of US Treasury Bills that had originated in 1989. KM's evidence was that it was simply not possible to comply with the notices (i.e. to repay $80 million within 24 hours). Lehmans had agreed that they would withdraw the earlier recall notices served on 29 October 1991 and withdraw from the "stocklending" programme in an orderly fashion so as not to disrupt RM's companies but had gone ahead and served the notice nonetheless. He was extremely angry with Lehmans for taking this unilateral action, particularly since they were, as he recalled, over collateralised at the time.

21.79 *The Financial Times* had been investigating the debt burden of RM's companies and had

---

recollected as having begun with his expression of condolences on the death of RM. A more detailed account of these events is given in Appendix 7.

a A note made by the Bank of England recorded that Goldman Sachs had said it had got tired of waiting, particularly given that RM appeared to have sold a number of entities recently but had not distributed any of the proceeds to them.

b They held this as security for a foreign exchange transaction from the time it went into default.

c Recall notices had been served on 29 October 1991 but no further action had been taken as further collateral was promised.

compiled a structure chart of his companies. On the morning of 5 November 1991, they had a meeting with KM[a] to go through the chart with him.

21.80 On the afternoon of Tuesday 5 November 1991 the board of MGN was told that RM had fallen overboard from his yacht. On the advice of Samuel Montagu the board of MGN decided to seek a suspension of the shares and the board of MCC did exactly the same.

21.81 The death of RM was announced on 6 November 1991.

a Referred to in *The Financial Times* on 6 November 1991 when the structure chart was published.

PART FOUR
CONCLUSIONS, RECOMMENDATIONS AND LESSONS FROM THE EVENTS

22. CONCLUSIONS

22.1 In this chapter we summarise our conclusions in four sections:

	Paragraphs
(1) What was appreciated about RM and the pension funds by the beginning of 1991?	22.2 –22.12
(2) Was MGN suitable for listing?	22.13 – 22.66
(3) What had changed at MGN after the flotation?	22.67 – 22.81
(4) How did the market in MCC and MGN shares operate?	22.82 – 22.92

The approach we have adopted in arriving at our conclusions, as explained more fully in the Preface on pages 1 to 7, is:

- to investigate so as to ascertain and record facts and not to make legal determinations on any issue.
- not to call the acquittals of the defendants to the criminal proceedings into question or cast doubt on the conclusions of the jury on the honesty of the defendants as regards their course of conduct.
- to produce a candid report setting out the facts, our views of the respective responsibility and, as conduct can be blameworthy without being criminal, our criticisms where we considered them to be justified.

Where therefore we attribute responsibility, we do so in that context and in terms of blame.

The following has happened to certain of those we criticise[a]:

- KM, IM, Mr Bunn and Mr Trachtenberg faced a criminal trial and KM was bankrupted.
- Mr Stoney, apart from facing criminal charges, was expelled from membership of the Institute of Chartered Accountants in England and Wales.
- CLD and some of their partners were disciplined by the Accountants' Joint Disciplinary Tribunal.
- Goldman Sachs were disciplined by their self-regulatory organisation (SFA).
- CCM, Lehmans and MIM were disciplined by their self-regulatory organisations (SFA and IMRO).

We set out in Appendix 20 details of the disciplinary action taken. In addition, many have been subject to much adverse publicity.

It is important to remember that as a result of the events we describe, many pensioners suffered anxiety and loss in relation to their pensions and that employees of RM's companies suffered from uncertainty and in some cases redundancy.

---

[a] CLD, Goldman Sachs and Lehmans were contributors to a substantial settlement with the pension schemes and BIM, without admission of liability.

<u>Section 1: What was appreciated about RM and the pension funds by the beginning of 1991?</u>

22.2 In this section we summarise:

(1) the characteristics of the way RM operated

(2) the abuses of the pension funds

which are identified in the first part of this Report. We also explain why the abuses of the pension funds (which had such a significant impact on MGN and which played a significant part in the collapse of RM's companies in November 1991) had not been stopped before work started on the flotation. We also attribute responsibility for this failure.

(1) The characteristics of the way RM operated

22.3 It was clear to many who dealt with RM that:

- he operated on the basis of "need to know";
- he was a bully and a domineering personality, but could be charming on occasions;
- he was very astute and clever in achieving his purposes.

However it was not universally appreciated that there was a clear and unmistakable warning about the consequences of these characteristics in the 1971/73 DTI Reports[a].

22.4 In the period after 1981, banks and other professionals of the highest reputation dealt with RM, leading politicians were entertained by him and entertained him. RM had been adept at exploiting this. Whereas banks and advisers were often attracted to deal with RM by the high level of fees that RM's businesses generated, RM benefited from the advantage he could derive in terms of rehabilitation and acceptance from the fact that they dealt with him and that leading politicians received him. Many banks and professionals took comfort from RM's dealings with other banks and professionals of the highest reputation, but in the light of the way in which RM operated, this should in fact have told them nothing positive about RM's stewardship of a listed company.

22.5 Many of the banks and other professionals thought that, because RM had been successful, he had changed and that the well known conclusion of the 1971/73 DTI Reports was no longer applicable. He also appeared to rely on and follow their advice. In the judgment of many he had by 1984 been very successful at MCC and by 1988 also at MGN.

22.6 We have discovered no evidence which showed that he had "changed his spots" as regards his stewardship of a public company; this is not the judgement of hindsight for the reasons we have explained at page 7 of the Preface. There was moreover no objective evidence on which anyone should have been justified in acting towards RM and his companies without a high

---

[a] RM considered the *Panorama* programme (see paragraph 21.43) had revived the principal criticisms of these Reports which he recorded as follows in a note prepared in connection with possible criminal libel proceedings:

"(1) That I set out to establish an artificially high value for shares.

(2) That I made exaggerated claims.

(3) That I over-stated profits.

(4) That transactions between Pergamon and family Private Companies were a means to that end."

degree of circumspection and care[a]; for example it was clear that his "need to know" approach and the structure of his companies made it very difficult to obtain an accurate picture of the financial position. In short, the characteristics we have summarised were employed to conceal the abuses of the pension funds.

(2) The abuses of the pension funds

22.7 RM bears the primary responsibility for the abuse of the pension funds of MGN which had begun in 1985. As the need for cash became greater due to financial pressures on RM's companies, this abuse became more extensive and easier to achieve given the control he exercised over BIM and the CIF. The practice of being economical with information which would have alerted bankers or regulators to the full extent of reliance on borrowing from the pension funds helped RM's abuses of those funds to continue unchecked. The abuses were all breaches of RM's fiduciary duties to the pensions schemes and the CIF. The major abuses were[b]:

- **Investment in related companies**
  The pension funds had been used to purchase significant quantities of MCC shares, particularly in the spring of 1989[c] and the autumn of 1990[d], but the extent of the purchases had been concealed from the majority of the trustees and from members of the pension schemes. OAG loan stock[e] and MCC commercial paper[f] had been also purchased.

- **Loans of cash**
  RM's private companies had began borrowing cash in late 1985 on an unsecured basis; by June 1990 the amounts being borrowed exceeded £100m and there was a similar amount borrowed by the end of December 1990[g]; the practice of borrowing had been concealed from the majority of the trustees and from members of the pension schemes. The accounts were window dressed by ensuring that no sums were borrowed over the year ends of the pension schemes and the CIF[h].

---

a See the contemporaneous evidence of the approach of the Bank of England described at paragraphs 6.43 and 6.48 to 6.50 (in relation to Robert Fraser) and 6.46 to 6.47 (in relation to the Bank of Israel); see also the views of IMRO at paragraph 3.3 of Appendix 9.

b A provision of the Rules of MGPS stated:

> "No decision of or exercise of a power or discretion by the Trustees shall be invalidated or questioned on the ground that the Trustees or any of them or any director or officer of a Trustee had a direct or other personal interest in the mode or result of such decision or of exercising such power or discretion."

This is, we understand, a common provision in pension fund rules, but it cannot in any way justify the abuses we have identified.

c see paragraph 5.20.

d see paragraph 6.18.

e see paragraph 5.22.

f see paragraph 6.26.

g see paragraphs 6.5 and 6.26.

h see paragraph 5.26.

- **Related Party dealings**
The first major related party dealings where the pension funds were used to benefit RM's other companies often to the detriment of the pension schemes were the transactions in the Beecham and Reuters shares[a]. The true purpose of these transactions had been concealed from the majority of the trustees and from members of the pension schemes. When the CIF was established, similar transactions continued with significant instances being the Société Générale shares, the Agence Havas shares, the holding in FTIT, "the October 1989" parcel and the March 1990 parcel[b].

- **Use of the funds for the benefit of MCC and the private side**
The first transaction where the pension fund was used solely for the benefit of RM's private companies was the purchase for RM's private companies of Strand/Maxwell House in 1986[c] through MGPS and this was followed, after the creation of the CIF by the loans to Robert Fraser, the purchase of shares and options in shares of Paramount Communications Inc and the purchase of the stake in the Really Useful Group plc[d].

- **Use of the shares as collateral for loans to the private side**
The use of shares as collateral began in November 1988 and by the end of 1989 a number of the loans to the private side were dependent on the use of the shares of the pension funds as collateral; by the end of December 1990, the total value of the shares being so used was about £206m[e].

The lending of cash on an unsecured basis to his companies and the use of shares as collateral for loans for the benefit of the private side were flagrant breaches by RM of his fiduciary duty.

22.8 The first question that needs to be considered is who bears the responsibility for carrying out the decisions made by RM:

- **KM**

KM gave very substantial assistance to RM[f] and bears a heavy responsibility.

  - We accept that he was brought up to believe that self-investment by the pensions funds was usual and that there was a close relationship between the funds and the companies. However, as he accepted, he did not put the interests of the pension funds before the needs of the private side.

---

a see paragraphs 2.36 to 2.44.

b see paragraph 5.28.

c see paragraph 2.32.

d see paragraph 5.29.

e see paragraphs 5.30 to 5.40 and Appendix 7 paragraph 6.25.

f see paragraphs 5.8, 5.23 and Appendix 8.

22.8 continued

- KM knew:
  - of the substantial scale of the investments in related companies, the practice of loans of cash on an unsecured basis, the considerable number of related party dealings, the instances where pensions funds had been used for the benefit of MCC and the private side and the use of shares as collateral.
  - that these matters were not disclosed in the reports submitted to the trustees, but he did not take steps to bring the matters to their attention.
  - that disclosures to bankers, regulators and others lacked frankness[a]. When representatives of IMRO visited BIM in November 1990 they were inexperienced; he confined his answers to questions they specifically asked and sought, in accordance with RM's wishes, to present everything in a favourable light[b].
  - that by the end of 1990 there were tremendous strains on the finances of the private side companies which were borrowing on a substantial scale from the pension funds.
  - that the use of CIF's assets as collateral for loans for the benefit of the private side could not be described as normal stocklending.

In our view, in light of this knowledge, KM's conduct was inexcusable.

- **Mr Bunn**

It is our view that, although not an originator of the abuses, he gave substantial assistance to RM and bears a significant responsibility[c]. The views we express about his conduct must, however, be understood in the light of the following facts. Mr Bunn was taken ill during the course of the criminal trial and it was not possible to interview him further[d]. Passages from our draft report and our provisional conclusions about his conduct were provided to his legal advisers but, on medical advice, these were not put to him. In consequence we have not been able to ascertain from him what facts, he says, were within his knowledge or whether he accepts those facts to be correct nor whether he has any explanation or defence for his conduct nor to get his response to our provisional conclusions about his conduct. Accordingly we have had to rely on documents and the evidence of others some of whom had a conflict of interest with Mr Bunn.

- **Mr Andrew Smith**

Mr Andrew Smith was the originator of the plan to use the shares in the portfolio of FTIT and the CIF as collateral. He bears a significant responsibility for this.

---

[a] see paragraph 6.67. KM told us "if the question is, "has the inter-company between Pergamon and Mirror been reduced" and it has, then you can say that. What you don't go on to then say is that the total inter-company remains the same. So it is being economical with the information. It was not anybody's habit, ... not mine, ... to tell a banker an outright lie, particularly when there was not the need to."

[b] see Appendix 9 paragraph 5.13.

[c] See paragraphs 5.28, 6.5 and 6.26 and Appendix 8.

[d] One interview with Mr Bunn was undertaken prior to the criminal trial.

- **Mr Trachtenberg**

Although we accept he had little experience of business when he joined LBI and therefore knew only the culture of RM's companies, he played a significant role in the arrangements for the use of the shares in the portfolios of FTIT and the CIF as collateral and with Mr Smith bears a significant responsibility for this. He accepted that the letter he signed about the Lehmans transaction for the purposes of the audit was untrue. Although at an earlier stage he had explained the true nature of the transaction his signature of the letter was inexcusable.

- **Mr Cook**

He bears a significant responsibility as the manager of the pension schemes and a director of BIM; he assisted in effecting the transactions and did not protest at RM's management of the assets of the CIF and facilitated some of the transactions. He did not report to the trustees of the schemes, the investment committee of MGPS or to IMRO what was happening.

- **IM**

IM signed many documents without considering their implications and failed to carry out all the duties he had undertaken as a director of BIM.

22.9 The second question that needs to be considered is who bears the responsibility for the fact that these abuses were not brought to light and stopped; in our judgment each of the following bears a measure of responsibility.

- **CLD**

CLD[a] bear a major responsibility for failing to report to the trustees of the pension schemes the abuses set out below. We are satisfied that they accepted a presentation of the accounts which had the effect that the interests of RM were preferred to those of the trustees and beneficiaries, thus failing in their duties as independent auditors. Mr Cowling accepted[b] that breaches of fiduciary duty of this nature and extent ought to have been reported, but he did not in fact appreciate that what RM was doing constituted serious breaches of fiduciary duty. CLD's principal failures were in respect of:

Loans of cash

- CLD as auditors of MGPS knew from at least the time of the audit for the year ended 5 April 1988 that monies were being lent to the private side and during that audit considered whether this should be disclosed[c].
- They decided that disclosure was not necessary. They did this on the basis that the loans were reduced to nil at the end of each year of the pension scheme accounts even though this reduction to nil was the means by which the accounts were window dressed. They also adopted an interpretation of the Disclosure Regulations which we

---

[a] Although Mr Walsh gave factual evidence to us, he died on 7 November 1996, after a long illness; the criticisms sent to CLD in May 1996 were not, in these circumstances, made known to him. In our criticisms of CLD we have had very close regard to this.

[b] see paragraph 5.42.

[c] see paragraphs 2.46 and 2.47.

22.9 continued

consider was mistaken[a] but that mistaken view did not justify the accounting treatment given the fact that the balances were reduced to nil at the year end and lending commenced again in the new financial year. Whatever their view of the regulations they should not have acquiesced in RM's window dressing of the accounts in this way.

- Although there was, in any event, an obvious conflict between RM's wishes and the interests of the trustees and members of the pension schemes, CLD acted on their interpretation and acquiesced in RM's insistence that there be no disclosure, without bringing the loans to the attention of the trustees of the pension schemes and discussing with them the interpretation of the Disclosure Regulations.
- Their decision facilitated the borrowing of large sums on an unsecured basis from the pension funds without any disclosure being made. By 31 December 1990 about £100m was owed by the private side to the pension funds.
- There was nothing to alert those who examined the accounts of MGPS (as another team from CLD were to do in preparation for the flotation) or of the CIF about the practice[b].
- CLD were also aware that LBI was lending cash to RM's private companies from the CIF portfolio managed by LBI, but failed to make enquiries about this when conducting audits of the CIF[c].
- The accounts of LBI for the year ended 31 December 1988 which were submitted to IMRO suggested that the sum of £27.5m was deposited in a client bank account[d], whereas in fact it had been loaned to PHL as CLD had discovered during the audit of LBI's statutory accounts for that year.

Use of shares as collateral

- From the audit work he carried out at LBI and LBH for the year ended 31 December 1989, Mr Cowling knew[e] of the use that had been made of the shares in the portfolio of the CIF managed by LBI as collateral for loans for the benefit of the private side. He also knew from the audit work carried out at FTIT for the year ended 31 December 1989 of the similar use that had been made of the shares from the FTIT portfolio also managed by LBI. He took no steps to make enquiries about the use of the shares of the CIF when conducting audits of the pension schemes and the CIF or to bring the use to the attention of the trustees of the pension schemes.

---

[a] see paragraphs 2.47 and 5.8. No person could reasonably have held the view CLD first put forward to us as to their interpretation of what constituted a financial transaction.

[b] see paragraph 13.7.

[c] see paragraph 5.25.

[d] see footnote to paragraph 5.25.

[e] see paragraph 5.41 and Appendix 10 paragraphs 4.1 to 4.16.

22.9 continued

- For a period of almost one month during the audit of the CIF for the year ended 5 April 1990 information received by CLD revealed that the shares of the CIF were being used as collateral for financing from Lehmans for the benefit of the private side. Mr Cowling readily accepted an explanation from Mr Trachtenberg despite the fact that it made no commercial sense and was contrary to information he had received. He failed to see the obvious and took no proper steps to verify the explanation by
    - contacting Lehmans again
    - investigating the elimination of the fees charged for the "stocklending"[a].
- CLD did not follow up in their post balance sheet work on the audit of the CIF for the year ended 5 April 1990 information provided to them in relation to use of the shares of the CIF for "stocklending"[b].
- This serious abuse continued. By 31 December 1990 shares from the pension funds to the value of about £206m were being used as collateral.

In addition to the two principal failures, there were also failures in respect of:

Investment in related companies

- In the year ended 5 April 1990, the CIF was used to purchase large quantities of MCC shares and the holding was then reduced; the transactions that reduced the holdings became known to CLD in the course of their audit of the CIF for that year[c]. CLD did not consider whether they should bring these transactions to the attention of the trustees of the pension schemes.

Related party dealings

- The Reuters transaction was unscrambled following advice from CLD that it would require disclosure if it remained in place[d], but they never brought their views on disclosure to the attention of the trustees of MGPS. In their audit work they ought to have appreciated that the transaction had been backdated to the serious disadvantage of MGPS and reported on this accordingly.
- CLD never drew any of the other related party transactions to the attention of the trustees of the pension schemes nor discussed with them the desirability of disclosing the transactions in the accounts, because they took the view there was nothing on which to report, provided the price was an appropriate price and that the transaction appeared normal; CLD did not consider whether such transactions were in the interests of the pension funds as they were for the private companies[e].

---

[a] see paragraphs 9.41 to 9.44 and Appendix 10 paragraph 6.1.

[b] see Appendix 10 paragraph 7.

[c] see paragraph 9.36.

[d] see paragraphs 2.38 to 2.43.

[e] see paragraphs 5.8 and 9.35.

RM's control of the CIF

- CLD were well aware of the risks that RM's control entailed[a] and they were aware of the matters set out above that resulted from this, but never in the course of their work discussed the issues with the trustees of the pension schemes.

CLD consistently agreed accounting treatments of transactions that served the interest of RM and not those of the trustees or the beneficiaries of the pension scheme, provided it could be justified by an interpretation of the letter of the relevant standards or regulations.

- **Mr Stephens**

As a director of BIM, he did not protest at RM's management of the assets of the CIF but facilitated some of the transactions by approving them at board meetings[b], and did not ensure that proper reports were made to the trustees of the participating schemes. In the case of the Reuters transaction, Mr Stephens signed the board minute dated 30 December 1988 and the sale agreement between Funvale and MGN even though he should have appreciated they were backdated.

22.10 There are others who bear a more limited responsibility in failing in their respective positions to ascertain what was in fact happening.

- **Mr Woods**

As a director of BIM, he did not until December 1990 protest at RM's management of the assets of the CIF but facilitated some of the transactions by approving them at board meetings[c], and did not ensure that proper reports were made to the trustees of the participating schemes. His main role related to taxation matters and he did not have a proper picture of what was happening at BIM. His responsibility is therefore limited.

- **Mr Guest**

The only matters in which Mr Guest was directly involved were Maxwell House and the unscrambling of the Reuters transaction. Although Mr Guest did not at the time have concerns about these transactions, he should have explained both these transactions to the other trustees of MGPS. In the case of the Reuters transaction, he signed the board minute dated 30 December 1988 and the sale agreement between Funvale and MGN even though he should have appreciated that they were backdated. He should have told the trustees of MGPS that the investment committee was not being provided with proper information about the investments of the CIF which were not managed externally[d].

---

a see paragraph 13.27.

b In particular the purchase of shares in Société Générale and in FTIT in November 1988 and in De La Rue in December 1989. It was Mr Stephens' evidence that though shown on the board minutes as present, he was not in fact present.

c In particular the purchase of the Société Générale shares and the shares in FTIT in November 1988, the decision to increase the investment in MCC shares on 30 March 1988 and the approval of the decision to invest in the Robert Fraser promissory note for £5m on 13 June 1989.

d see paragraph 5.8.

- **Lord Donoughue**

Although Lord Donoughue (i) asked questions about the funds lent and the collateral and received reassuring answers; (ii) understood that the auditors were satisfied with the arrangements; and (iii) was unwell between May and October 1990, he ought, as a director of LBI and LBH, to have ascertained sufficient information about the security being used for loans obtained by LBI and about the lending of funds to the private side in the years 1988-1990[a]. Had he done so he might have identified the abuse by RM of funds managed by LBI and, in respect of FTIT, acted sooner than he did.

- **Mr Chapman**

Mr Chapman should have told the trustees of MGPS that the investment committee were not being provided with proper information about those investments of the CIF which were not managed externally although he reasonably felt he could rely on the auditors.

- **IMRO**

Although IMRO has recognised the limitations in its procedures for admissions, the difficulty faced by IMRO was that they had to have evidence that would withstand open scrutiny in court if they were to refuse to admit BIM and LBI; the suspicion that they correctly held about RM was not enough to justify the refusal to admit BIM and LBI. Although they correctly held a suspicion about RM, they did not seek evidence which could have supported the refusal to admit BIM and LBI. On the monitoring visits thereafter, RM's character was not sufficiently taken into account; persons with more experience of investment management might have noticed certain matters that were amiss at BIM and LBI.

22.11 In respect of certain transactions, we consider that some criticism attaches to:

- **Morgan Stanley**

As to the knowledge of Morgan Stanley

  - we accept the evidence of Mr Bernard that it was known that the overdraft of $135m obtained by LBI was not accidental but the result of misrepresentation[b], though it was the evidence of the operational staff that they believed it was "accidental" or due to "operational difficulties"; such views failed to take account of the obvious.
  - it was known that part of the overdraft had been incurred on the CIF client account and Morgan Stanley had been told this overdraft had been used in LBI's own proprietary trading.

Morgan Stanley had the following relationship with BIM

  - BIM paid its fees
  - the account at Morgan Stanley was referred to as the "BIM account"
  - BIM was provided with a computer link to Morgan Stanley.

---

[a] see paragraphs 5.25 and 5.34 to 5.40. Lord Donoughue did not know of the arrangements with MSTC described at paragraphs 5.33 to 5.38 or of the overdrafts described at paragraphs 6.28 to 6.32.

[b] see Appendix 7 paragraph 6.51.

Morgan Stanley submitted that MSTC did not report the overdraft to BIM or any regulator because the operational staff at MSTC considered the overdraft had not been deliberately created. However $55m of the unauthorised overdraft had been incurred on trust accounts in circumstances which Mr Bernard[a], the member of the main board of Morgan Stanley responsible for MSTC, had correctly identified. MSTC also contended that in any event, they had no legal duty to report the matter to BIM or IMRO, as MSTC was not regulated under the Financial Services Act 1986 and, because KM was a director of BIM, BIM knew of it. However, even if this is a correct view of the law as it stood at the time, given the obvious impropriety of what had happened and the scale of the misuse of client accounts, MSTC as a responsible custodian and as a subsidiary of a leading international investment bank of pre-eminent reputation, ought to have reported the facts to Mr Cook as a director of BIM who was not a director of LBI and to the regulator of LBI, which was IMRO.

- **Lehmans**

Although Lehmans initially considered that the financing arrangement was for the benefit of a fund being managed by BIM, they did not, at the time of the increases in the facility in October and December 1990 make sufficient enquiry about their client, BIM and the purpose of the transaction, given the knowledge of the relevant officer of the financial difficulties surrounding RM's companies in the Autumn of 1990[b].

- **CCM**

Given the fact that the shares transferred to Lehmans were to remain under their management, CCM ought to have found out why the shares were being transferred to Lehmans and properly understood the transaction. There was no reasonable basis for their assumption that custody of the shares they managed was being transferred to Lehmans[c].

- **MIM**

Given the fact that the shares transferred to LBI were to remain under their management, MIM ought to have found out why the shares were being transferred to LBI and properly understood the nature and purpose of the transaction.

The trustees

22.12 The information provided to them indicated that the funds were doing well and the information that would have disclosed the abuses was withheld from them. No blame attaches to them.

---

a see Appendix 8, paragraph 6.53.

b In *Macmillan v BIT* (10 December 1993) Millett J reached a different conclusion on the knowledge of the relevant officer about the financial difficulties surrounding RM's companies in the autumn of 1990. In our view, Millett J's finding on the limited point in relation to the knowledge of the officer was not a necessary part of his judgment that Lehmans was not liable. Indeed, we agree with his conclusion that Lehmans did not know of the use of pension fund assets for the benefit of the private side or were in fact alerted to that use or should have been.

c see Appendix 8 paragraph 5.48 to 5.49.

Section 2: Was MGN suitable for listing?

22.13 In our opinion, for the reasons we summarise in this section, MGN, although it had a profitable and modern newspaper business, was not suitable for listing and the prospectus issued was materially inaccurate and misleading. We set out our reasons for our opinion and attribute responsibility for the failures we identify under the headings:

(1) Control over the management of the company
(2) Control over the finances of the company
(3) Control over related party dealings
(4) The arrangements for the pension schemes
(5) Financial and other information
(6) The finances of the private side

It is first necessary to refer to the responsibilities of those primarily concerned.

22.14 The directors of MGN and Samuel Montagu were under respective responsibilities[a]:

- to prepare MGN so that it was suitable for listing.
- to set out in the prospectus the information that potential investors and their professional advisers might reasonably require and expect to find for the purposes of making an informed decision in accordance with the requirements of the Financial Services Act 1986.

In carrying out these tasks the directors and Samuel Montagu had to exercise due diligence, but they were entitled to rely on the work of others, particularly CLD.

22.15 It is evident from the matters to which we have referred in the preceding chapters (and which we summarise in this chapter) that although MGN had a newspaper business that had been modernised by RM, was well run by its operational management and profitable, there were changes which were required to be made in respect of MGN's corporate governance, financial controls and pension arrangements in order to prepare MGN so that it was suitable for listing, as well as putting in place adequate arrangements for the control of related party transactions. Many of the necessary changes were not made. If the need for such changes had been appreciated, then depending on what had been discovered, the changes would either have been made if there had been time, or the flotation would have been delayed or abandoned. Since the changes were not made and the flotation proceeded there was not only a failure to exercise due diligence to prepare MGN so that it was suitable for listing, but also, as a result, a failure to make proper disclosure in the prospectus of the unsatisfactory features which required remedy.

22.16 RM was, however, determined to retain control over the management of MGN:

- That was the way he had run his other companies.
- Use of MGN's cash flow was essential for his other companies; the private side was still dependent on that cash flow, as the amount raised by the flotation did not make good the loss of MGN's cash flow.

---

[a] Set out in Chapter 7.

22.17 RM bears the major responsibility but the other directors of MGN and the advisers also bear varying degrees of responsibility as described below.

22.18 MGN[a] itself was responsible for the failure to make the disclosures to which we refer in this chapter and which was attributable to the actions of the directors we specifically criticise. However, advisers of high reputation were appointed and MGN was entitled to rely on them.

(1) Control over the management of the company

22.19 The proposed system for corporate governance was inadequate and control over the management of MGN had not passed from RM to the board:

- RM should not have been the Executive Chairman[b].
- The executive directors had been accustomed to running the company under the control of RM rather than themselves controlling the company; some had no experience of a company being managed through a board. RM had given direct instructions to his senior management, thereby by-passing reporting structures[c].
- Sir Robert Clark and Mr Clements, newly appointed non-executive directors, had not got to know the executive directors of MGN and did not attend any meetings concerned with the ordinary business of MGN until after the flotation.
- The board of the operating company, MGN Limited, had not met save for formal purposes and there was no structure in place for its board to meet or report to the main board.
- The existing resolution delegating the board's power to a committee including RM or KM had not been revoked[d].
- As to the audit committee, no chairman had been appointed, no terms of reference had been set and there were no arrangements for the organisation of meetings.
- The company did not have its own separate secretarial function; nothing had been done to see that the company secretarial department operated independently of RM and that procedures were in place for the proper operation of the board.

22.20 These inadequacies in the system for corporate governance meant that MGN was not suitable for listing.

---

[a] Our criticism of MGN as a company only relates to the disclosure (or lack of disclosure) in the prospectus.

[b] IM thought that Samuel Montagu were naïve to believe that RM would change his way of operating unless he had to; RM was fond of saying that "you can be taught by the rocks or you can be taught by the rudder" and, in IM's view, RM always had to be taught by the rocks.

[c] IM told us that he hoped that MGN could and would be run in a different way to the way it had been run by RM. He realised that, with RM as Executive Chairman, this would not be easy but, with RM involved in the USA and in less robust health than previously, he thought it was possible. However, when RM was absent, the management seemed to be in a state of paralysis – directors were so used to being told what to do by RM that their ability to take initiatives had atrophied. This assertion was strongly rejected in other evidence to us on the basis that it was the other directors who ran the business profitably.

[d] See the footnote to paragraph 10.27.

(a) Consideration of how MGN had been run

22.21 A major reason for some of the inadequacies was the failure to ascertain how MGN had been run in the past.

- Samuel Montagu told us that it was not necessary to know in great detail how RM had run his companies and it was sufficient to have a general understanding of the type of management style adopted by RM, which they maintained that they had; the running of MGN in the past was not an important factor because the structure in the future was to be completely different. On the other hand they maintained that the long form report was seriously defective, as it failed to draw attention to certain matters of which CLD were well aware, particularly the delegation of board powers and the fact that key decisions were not approved by the board.
- CLD told us that they understood that Samuel Montagu's approach was not based upon forming an understanding of all the procedures then in place and adapting or changing them; they summarised Samuel Montagu's approach thus:

  "They intended to start with a new system for a new company"

- SBIL told us that they considered it important to understand how the members of the board would interact with each other so that all understood their roles as directors of a public company and could be effective in running it. They did not consider that the historical way in which MGN had been run from day to day was necessarily important to the way in which MGN was to be run in the future since it had taken on non-executive directors and significant minority shareholders.
- Clifford Chance told us that they did not believe that in order to establish what controls were appropriate to be put in place on flotation it was necessary to investigate how MGN had operated previously, but on the other hand added that they thought it more important for the sponsor to ensure that existing internal controls were properly adapted to meet the status of a listed company.

22.22 These somewhat inconsistent approaches were in the main misconceived as it was essential to know how RM had run MGN:

- MGN was not a new company, but a company with a history that had been run by RM for 7 years. It was as necessary to know about the manner of his management and those who managed the company under him (many of whom were to be directors of the company when listed) as to know about the trading results. This was particularly so because it was proposed that RM be the Executive Chairman.
- It was necessary in order to institute new or amended controls appropriate to a listed company.
- In 1971, DTI Inspectors had concluded that RM was not a person who could be relied on to exercise proper stewardship of a publicly quoted company; their Reports supported this conclusion with a number of detailed examples. No person should have ignored this or concluded that this was not relevant without ascertaining through a proper investigation the actual facts of RM's stewardship[a]. The fact that RM was considered to have been

[a] See paragraphs 6.47 and 6.48.

successful and was courted by many leading professionals and politicians and the fact that no steps had been taken to prevent him being a director or chairman of listed companies did not mean that his stewardship had changed[a].

22.23 The most direct way of examining RM's stewardship of a listed company would have been to enquire into MCC, which was in 1991 a large listed company: as set out in paragraph 10.15, the apparent success of MCC was regarded by Samuel Montagu as one of the reasons for accepting RM as Executive Chairman of MGN. We have been told, however, that

- it would have been difficult to obtain the type of information suggested about MCC;
- such information was confidential;
- there was nothing to put Samuel Montagu on enquiry so as to cause them to seek out this evidence.

Nonetheless, by not making enquiries and satisfying themselves that RM had exercised proper stewardship of MCC, Samuel Montagu failed to investigate an obvious source of information; they could have asked RM if CLD could provide information on MCC in the same way as they obtained RM's agreement that CLD provide comfort on the private side finances.

22.24 The responsibility for the failure to ascertain how MGN had been run is as follows:

- **Samuel Montagu**[b]

The major responsibility rests with Samuel Montagu.

- The lack of information about the previous management of MGN and its system of corporate governance prior to the flotation was apparent on the face of the long form report; they should have asked that it be provided.
- They did not consider the 1971/73 DTI Reports in any detail; they did not obtain any evidence to show that the conduct described in the Reports and the conclusions of the Inspectors were no longer apposite. Nor did they make sufficient enquiries which would have reasonably entitled them to reach the judgement they formed about RM.

- **CLD**[c]

The long form reports did describe the existing management structure, but did not describe how RM ran MGN; examining the latter in detail was far more important than the former, but this was not done. Despite the terms of their letter of engagement, CLD did not include a

---

a We have referred in the footnote to paragraph 7.11 to the tributes paid by politicians on his death. He also entertained and was received by leading world figures. But that said little about his stewardship of his businesses.

b The responsibility for all matters in respect of which we criticise Samuel Montagu lies as follows: (i) Mr Galloway had day to day conduct and made the day to day decisions. He was at the time too inexperienced for the formidable task entrusted to him and he never properly understood how RM ran his businesses; and (ii) Mr McIntosh whose involvement was significant should have appreciated that Mr Galloway was too inexperienced and played an even greater role himself.

c The responsibility for all matters in respect of which we criticise the reporting accounting team lies as follows: (i) Mr Walsh who had primary responsibility for the long form reports had a greater understanding of RM's private companies than anyone else at CLD and should have brought his knowledge to bear more than he did; and (ii) Mr Wootten was also responsible for the long form reports but he never understood either the way in which RM ran his businesses or the pension funds or the consequences that flowed from the control that RM exercised.

proper description of the way RM ran MGN in their long form reports which were intended not only for Samuel Montagu, but also for the directors of MGN including the newly appointed non-executive directors.

- **Miss Maxwell**

Miss Maxwell who had undertaken the responsibility for co-ordinating the preparations for the flotation should have told Samuel Montagu and the directors of MGN about RM's conduct in October 1990 in refusing to disclose in the MCC circular on the disposal of QPI and Donohue the six per cent. holding of BIM in MCC, since the conduct it exemplified reflected on the fitness of RM to have stewardship of a public company[a].

- **Clifford Chance**

Clifford Chance said that it was not their practice at the time to read the board minutes nor was it the practice of other City solicitors. We have reached a different conclusion on the evidence as to the best practice in the City[b]; they should have read the board minutes of MGN and thus discovered the delegation resolution of 9 October 1990. It could then have been brought to the attention of Samuel Montagu[c].

(b) The new system of corporate governance

22.25 The responsibility for the failure to establish a system of corporate governance appropriate to a listed company rests as follows:

- **Samuel Montagu**

Samuel Montagu did not take adequate steps to see that control of MGN passed from RM to the board and that there was a proper system of corporate governance. It was not enough to create a new board and to appoint non-executive directors, given RM's character, given the way he had run MGN and given the fact that the non-executive directors had little familiarity with the business of MGN.

They should have appreciated that greater care and attention than usual was needed on the flotation of MGN because of RM's role and taken steps to see that all the directors understood how a listed company should be run in practice with RM as Chairman.

- **The directors**

The directors of MGN did not take proper steps to ensure that the board of MGN was in a position to control the running of the company and to control RM so that the inadequacies of the past did not continue.

---

[a] Miss Maxwell had been told by RM that the holding had been reduced to below 3 per cent by the time of the flotation, as was in fact the case. Any duty of confidence she owed to MCC was overidden by her duty to speak out in relation to the serious breach of the Companies Act that had occurred.

[b] See paragraph 5.8 of Appendix 10.

[c] Clifford Chance pointed out that no related party transaction could have been validly effected through such a committee after flotation because of the revision to the Articles of Association to which we have referred at paragraph 10.26.

22.25 continued

It has been contended on behalf of many of the directors that:

- At the time, RM was not perceived as a person unfit to have stewardship of a listed company.
- It was the primary responsibility of the reporting accountants and the sponsors to draw attention to deficiencies in the management of the company and to suggest and put in place appropriate controls suitable for a listed company.
- The way MGN had been run in the past was not a guide to the way in which it was to be run in the future.

However:

- Sufficient was known about RM for the directors each to have appreciated that the board needed to exercise strong control over RM.
- Although the sponsors and reporting accountants had the responsibilities described, it was the primary duty of the directors as directors to satisfy themselves that there were in place appropriate controls suitable for a listed company.
- Unless a very firm line was taken by the board from the outset, RM would run MGN as he had run it in the past.

Although the board owed a collective duty, the individual responsibility of the members of the board, having regard to the reasons for which they were appointed, is as follows:

- Sir Robert Clark and Mr Clements[a] (who had been appointed to the board to use their skill, experience and independent judgement in the board's control over the management of the company) bear the major responsibility amongst the directors for this. Sir Robert Clark and Mr Clements should have found out much more about MGN before the flotation and asked what had been done to pass control to the board. They should have considered whether this was adequate. We do not accept that they were entitled to rely on Samuel Montagu having put proper systems in place without themselves making due enquiry; nor do we accept that they were entitled, in the circumstances, particularly the way in which MGN had been run and RM's dominant character, to have relied on the executive directors bringing matters to their attention.
- Mr Burrington (as joint managing director) bears some responsibility, but that must be viewed in the light of the decision that RM be the Executive Chairman, his inexperience in the management of a company through a board and his lack of knowledge of the financial position of the other companies controlled by RM.
- IM knew how RM ran his companies. He had been appointed to the board because he was a member of the family. Having accepted the position, despite his inexperience, he should have acted to discharge his duties. He did not do so.
- Mr Stoney also knew how RM ran his companies. He also failed to act to discharge his duties.
- Mr Eastoe, Mr Ferguson and Mr Guest (all of whom knew of RM's style of management) knew how RM had run MGN and therefore have a limited measure of responsibility.

---

[a] Mr Clements pointed out that he was never told by Samuel Montagu that this was his duty; nor did they do so in October 1991 on the occasion referred to in the footnote to paragraph 21.51.

- Mr Horwood bears some responsibility, but that must be viewed in the light of his primary role being responsibility for SDR in which RM's management style did not impact as greatly and the fact that Mr Horwood spent most of his time in Scotland.
- Lord Williams had drawn to the attention of Samuel Montagu the fact there had been no board meetings at MGN and had attended properly run board meetings at Hollis when a listed company; he nonetheless bears a limited measure of responsibility as he should have ascertained what had been done and considered whether it was adequate[a]. Mr Haines also knew of RM's style of management. Although when appointed a non-executive director he had no briefing on his duties and responsibilities, he had accepted the position and ought to have discharged the responsibilities that went with the position. He therefore bears a limited measure of responsibility.
- Mr Wilson and Mr Laird only became involved at a late stage in the flotation and had no experience of the way in which RM ran MGN. No criticism attaches to them.

- **Smith New Court and SBIL**

Although both Smith New Court and SBIL were entitled to expect Samuel Montagu to discharge the principal obligations of the sponsor, they should have been alert to the issues of corporate governance, given RM's character, as part of the responsibilities described in Chapter 7 and Appendix 10. Neither had properly tried to understand how RM had run MGN in the past[b] nor the importance of ensuring that the necessary steps had in fact been implemented to transfer control to the board. It was not enough to create a new board, to appoint non-executive directors and an audit committee and see that the non-executive directors were briefed, given RM's character, given the way he had run MGN and given the fact that the non-executive directors had little familiarity with the business of MGN. They therefore bear a more limited responsibility than Samuel Montagu and the directors.

(c) The description in the prospectus

22.26 The operation of the board was dealt with in the prospectus.

- It described the board in the following terms:

> "The management of the [MGN] newspaper operations is conducted through its two principal operating subsidiaries, [MGN Limited] and SDR. These companies are managed independently of each other through their respective boards of directors.
>
> The respective boards review detailed monthly management accounts, including profit and cash forecasts and comparisons of performance against budget. These are then submitted to [MGN] for consolidation with those of [MGN]'s other activities and are reviewed at a monthly board meeting of [MGN]."

---

a See paragraph 10.11 and the footnote to paragraph 10.5.

b Smith New Court have said that they were not responsible for the work necessary to understand how RM had run MGN in the past; they were not aware that the work had not been done by others; nor were they aware of the matters set out in paragraph 22.19, apart from the fact that RM was going to be Executive Chairman. However, Sir Michael Richardson had (as set out in the footnote to paragraph 4.34) known RM first in the 1960s. As a result he had doubts as to whether or not RM had "changed his spots" and also changed from the "wheeler dealer" he had been in the 1960s. Since those doubts could not be put to rest by anything in the Long Form Report (which contained no information on how MGN had been run), Smith New Court ought to have carried out the duties identified in paragraph 3.5 of Appendix 10 and prompted Samuel Montagu into action.

- We were told that this paragraph was intended to refer to the way in which MGN and its two operating subsidiaries were to be run after the flotation. Save in the case of SDR, it was not meant to be descriptive of the position as at the date of the flotation because the boards of the English operating company (MGN Limited) and the board of the parent company (MGN) had never reviewed detailed monthly management accounts and they did not have monthly board meetings.[a] However the paragraph was drafted in the present tense and there was nothing to alert those who might subscribe for shares that MGN had not been run by a board.

22.27 Samuel Montagu ought to have corrected the passage in the prospectus to make it clear that it was describing what was to happen in the future.

22.28 The verification work carried out by Clifford Chance was defective in failing to identify that the description of the board gave an incorrect impression. Linklaters & Paines failed to identify the incorrect impression in their review of the work of Clifford Chance; their responsibility is very much more limited.

(d) The role of the Stock Exchange as the Listing Authority at the time of the flotation

22.29 It remains unclear to us, having seen the information the Stock Exchange possessed on RM as the Listing Authority at the time of the flotation, what analysis it made or what work it did (apart from the routine examination of the directors' cards and raising a comment on an early draft of the prospectus) in relation to a consideration of RM's suitability to be the Executive Chairman of MGN. It would appear, from the information the Stock Exchange were able to find, that no proper review was made of RM's suitability.

22.30 We were told by the Stock Exchange during the course of our enquiry that it considered that neither the conclusion of the DTI Inspectors in 1971 nor, what the Stock Exchange perceived to be, the existing widespread distrust of RM would have been sufficient to have justified a refusal to list MGN, given the equally widespread willingness of many to do business with him and act for him and the fact that he was a director of other listed companies such as Reuters and MCC.

22.31 In 1973 the Stock Exchange had considered in detail the underlying facts set out in the 1971/73 DTI Reports and concluded there were numerous examples which cast doubt on RM's fitness to be a director of a listed company. Its actions in 1977 and 1981 have been described at paragraph 1.15. It does not appear that the Stock Exchange in 1991 either itself considered the issues raised by those examples or asked the sponsors whether they had addressed them. For the specific reasons given in chapters 10 and 11, many of those examples remained apposite to the way RM conducted his businesses (including MCC) at the time of the flotation.

---

[a] Mr Haines commented in writing to Mr Burrington that this description of the MGN board and its regular monthly meetings was incorrect and was told that it was a commitment for the new main board. Mr Burrington told us that he put Mr Haines' point to Mr Galloway and Mr Galloway told him it was a commitment for the new main board. Mr Galloway had no recollection of this point being raised.

22.32 Although the appropriateness of RM being Executive Chairman was questioned by the Stock Exchange in a comment on an early draft of the prospectus, this was not followed through by the Stock Exchange; it was believed sufficient to draw the point to the attention of Smith New Court.

22.33 The Stock Exchange was given some information about FTIT (as set out at paragraph 9.52), but it does not appear to have considered whether what it had been told reflected on the suitability of RM to be the Executive Chairman of MGN.

22.34 The Stock Exchange do not appear to have been informed of the arrangements stipulated by the Bank of England as necessary when RM sought to gain control of Robert Fraser in 1990. This was because they were not a member of the College of Regulators[a]. Although the TSA (which checked the directors' cards under contract to the Stock Exchange) had attended the meetings of the College of Regulators referred to at paragraph 6.43, they did not pass on to the Stock Exchange what was said there primarily because they considered they were constrained by confidentiality under the Banking Act 1987; their obligation to the Stock Exchange was to check the cards for their accuracy.

22.35 In view of the Stock Exchange's past opinions of RM and what it knew about the conduct of RM, it should have questioned Samuel Montagu and obtained assurances that Samuel Montagu had satisfied itself that RM could be expected to honour his obligations as a director of a listed company.

(2) Control over the finances of the company

22.36 The board of MGN did not have control over the disposition of MGN's funds when the flotation occurred; RM exercised this control.

- Nothing had been done to implement the decision that MGN have its own treasurer or a separate treasury. The treasury remained under the direct personal control of RM and not under the control of the MGN finance department or the board.
- RM's sole signatory authority for an unlimited amount over MGN's bank accounts continued.
- Nothing effective had been done to curtail RM's ability to initiate treasury transactions and transfer funds from MGN.
- Nothing was done by the directors or anyone else to address the problem of MGN's finance department obtaining documentation for transfers in and out of MGN's bank accounts carried out by the central treasury without adequate explanation or to prevent such transfers.
- Mr Stoney had taken on a significant role in MGN's finances and Mr Guest was not going to fulfil the usual role of a finance director.

---

[a] As explained in the footnote to paragraph 6.43, after November 1992, information was disseminated more widely through a structured network which included the Stock Exchange.

- Although it had been decided that KM could not be a director of MGN and he had been removed from MGN's bank mandates, the banks continued to deal with him (as the representative of RM) in respect of the strategy and arrangements for MGN's borrowings.
- Improvements to the financial reporting system did not address the deficiencies to which we have referred, as the finance department could only report what was known to it.

22.37 These inadequacies meant that the company was not suitable for listing. This was exemplified by the fact that just prior to listing three substantial sums had been paid out of MGN on 15, 29 and 30 April 1991 and other monies paid in, for which the finance department had no supporting documentation.

22.38 The prospectus said nothing about the deficiencies set out in paragraph 22.36. Disclosure was not in any event a realistic option because an appreciation by Samuel Montagu of the position would have required them to take steps to remedy the deficiencies before listing or the company should not have been listed.

(a) Consideration of the existing financial controls at MGN

22.39 The reason for the inadequacies was the failure to ascertain the actual position at MGN and the control RM exercised over the finances.

- Samuel Montagu told us that it was necessary only to know that controls appropriate for a listed company were in place; what had existed while MGN was privately owned was not a significant factor. On the other hand they maintained that the long form report was misleading and inaccurate in its description of the existing internal controls and in particular failed to draw their attention to RM's sole signatory authority and the lack of financial information and documentation supplied to the finance department of MGN.
- Notwithstanding the paragraph in the long form report referred to at paragraph 11.8, CLD told us that they did not consider that knowledge of the existing controls was relevant; in any event signatory authorities were not a control. They told us that the approach of Samuel Montagu should have been (and indeed was) to determine what financial controls were appropriate and then to ensure that they were put in place.

22.40 It was essential to know what control RM exercised over the finances for the reasons given in paragraph 22.22; no assessment could be made that controls appropriate to a listed company were in place without ascertaining what the existing controls were.

22.41 The responsibility for the failure to ascertain the existing financial controls is as follows:

- **CLD**

The major responsibility rests with CLD as the long form report did not identify RM's direct personal control over the disposition of the funds of MGN, his sole signatory authority, the way in which the central treasury operated nor the deficiencies in documentation provided to the MGN finance department. We do not find it necessary to attempt further to resolve the conflict of evidence as to whether CLD sent to Samuel Montagu the management letters identifying some of these points, as this would in any event have been an insufficient discharge by CLD of their responsibilities. These matters should have been set out in detail in the long form report.

- **The directors**

Some responsibility attaches to the directors. Mr Burrington, Mr Horwood, Mr Guest and Mr Stoney were aware of RM's sole signatory authority; Mr Guest and Mr Stoney were also aware of the direct personal control RM exercised over MGN's finances and the deficiencies in the documentation provided to the MGN finance department. These directors ought to have raised these issues with Samuel Montagu or CLD.

(b) The new system of financial controls

22.42 The responsibility for the failure to ensure that there was proper control over the finances of the company in our view rests as follows:

- **The directors**
  - Mr Stoney and Mr Guest should have informed the board and Samuel Montagu that the treasury had not been separated and a treasurer had not been appointed.
  - Mr Burrington and Mr Horwood should have enquired whether the decision to separate the treasury and appoint a treasurer had been implemented.
  - Although Sir Robert Clark and Mr Clements contended it was not part of their duty, we do not accept that and consider that as part of finding out about the way MGN was being run they should have enquired what system of financial controls existed.

- **Samuel Montagu**

Samuel Montagu should have ensured prior to the issue of the prospectus that the decision to separate the treasury had been implemented and a treasurer appointed and other steps had been taken to transfer control over the finances of MGN to the board, as these were essential pre-requisites of MGN's suitability for listing.

They should have appreciated that greater care and attention than usual was needed on the flotation of MGN because of RM's role.

(3) Control over related party dealings

22.43 As referred to in Chapter 12, the Stock Exchange[a] raised several points on the related party arrangements as this was an area that concerned it. These were taken into account.

22.44 Although arrangements for regulating related party transactions had been put in place:

- No procedures were put in place to ensure that transactions with related parties were brought to the attention of the board.

---

[a] The Stock Exchange also raised other points such as the reorganisation scheme (see paragraph 15.11), the three year record (see paragraph 15.27) and marketing (see paragraph 17.3).

- No line was drawn on the intercompany account to separate what had been past transactions between private companies from what were to be future trading transactions subject to the strict control of the independent directors of MGN.

As a result of these inadequacies, the opportunity was provided to make unauthorised payments from MGN.

22.45 The responsibility for these failures rests with Mr Stoney and Mr Guest.

(4) The arrangements for the pension schemes

22.46 The following abuses of the pension schemes and the CIF existed:

- The extent of the investment in related companies.
- The practice of lending cash to the private side on an unsecured basis and the fact that the CIF was owed about £100m by the private side in April 1991.
- The nature of related party dealings between the CIF, the pension schemes, the private side and MCC.
- The use of the shares of the CIF and the pension schemes as collateral for loans for the benefit of private side companies and the fact that at 30 April 1991 the value of the shares being used was about £270m.
- The domination of the CIF by RM and the inadequacies in the investment administration of the pension schemes and the CIF.

No steps had been taken to remedy these.

22.47 The prospectus disclosed that BIM managed approximately 80 per cent. of the CIF, that it was owned by The Maxwell Charitable Trust and its directors included RM, IM and KM. It also disclosed that LBI had been appointed a manager of part of the fund and that this company was a subsidiary of HI. This description omitted information as to the way RM operated the CIF, used it for the purposes of the private side and MCC and carried out large transactions with his other companies.

22.48 The disclosure made in the prospectus about the investment of the pension funds was in relation to the position at 5 April 1990, the date of the last audited accounts. As regards the position at 5 April 1990:

- The holding in MCC shares of MGPS was given as 4.7 per cent. of the assets of the scheme and that of MCWPS as 5 per cent. of the assets of that scheme. These figures were after the reduction brought about by the arrangement with IBI and the transfer of MCC shares from the CIF to BIT on 26 March 1990, but no mention was made of these transfers.
- No reference was made to the use of the shares by the private side as collateral for loans in the year to 5 April 1990.
- No reference was made to the borrowing of cash by the private side in the year to 5 April 1990 or the fact that it was unsecured.

The disclosure of information at 5 April 1990 implied that there had been no material change between that date and the issue of the prospectus over a year later[a]. Since 5 April 1990:

- There had been very substantial purchases of MCC shares (particularly in September 1990 to support the MCC share price) and the holding had only been reduced just prior to the issue of the prospectus by the transfer of 25 million shares to Yakosa and Servex, as referred to at paragraph 13.15; no payment had been made for these shares to the pension schemes.
- There was a current holding of about £15m in MCC commercial paper.
- In April 1991 the private side owed about £100m to the CIF and no security had been provided.
- On 30 April 1991 the value of the shares of the CIF and the pension schemes being used by the private side as collateral was about £270m.

22.49 The prospectus stated:

> "The financial review [at 31 December 1990] shows that [MGPS] had a surplus of £149.3 million of assets, as valued by the actuaries, over the scheme liabilities. The assets represented approximately 144 per cent of the liabilities..."

The "pension holiday" resulting from such a surplus was taken into account in the profit of MGN for the years ended December 1989 and 1990. The existence and amount of a surplus largely depended on the ability of the private side companies to meet their obligations to the CIF in respect of the debt referred to above and their substantial debts to the banks who held shares, owned by the CIF and the pension schemes, as collateral for part of those debts. This was not disclosed in the prospectus.

22.50 The abuses of the pension schemes and the CIF which had taken place meant that MGN was not suitable for listing; the reality was that had the abuses been discovered, MGN would not have been floated. The evidence of the bankers to the private side was that they would have reported the matter to the Bank of England and that support would have been withdrawn; what happened after RM's death would have happened in April 1991[b].

22.51 The responsibility for the failure to identify and prevent abuses has been described in the first section of this Chapter. The major responsibility for the failure to identify them on the flotation of MGN rests as follows:

- **KM**
    - KM should have told Samuel Montagu of the practices in the pension funds about which he knew as we have set out in section (1) of this Chapter.
    - The instructions he gave for the payment to BIT of the proceeds of the sale of the MCC shares held by MGPS and MCWPS was inexcusable.

---

[a] The advisers other than the reporting accountants recognised that this was the necessary implication and had sought and obtained confirmation from Mr Cook that this was so. The reporting accountants told us they were not a party to this and did not accept there was such an implication.

[b] We have referred to the evidence of KM and Sir Robert Clark on this in the footnote to paragraph 16.21.

22.51 continued

- **CLD**
  - As auditors to the CIF and pension schemes, CLD knew of each of the kinds of abuses listed in paragraph 22.46 though not the specific sums involved in April 1991. Mr Cowling did not consider that any of the abuses were in fact abuses, though he should have done so. He should have drawn those abuses to the attention of the reporting accountants. He did draw attention to the investment in related companies and the use of shares in the so called "collateral swap"; he did not draw attention at all to the other matters of which he was aware.
  - The reporting accountants team did not carry out an adequate investigation into:
    - the loans of cash (about which Mr Walsh had known for some time)
    - the use of shares as collateral (which Mr Cowling had raised in his conversation with Mr Walsh on 4 February 1991[a] by the reference to "collateral swap"); the use of FTIT shares as collateral was also drawn to Mr Walsh's attention at the end of April 1991[b].
    - the investments in related companies

    They did not discover the other abuses of the CIF and the pension funds.
  - In the light of CLD's knowledge of
    - the way RM ran his businesses and the pension funds
    - the control by RM over MGPS, MCWPS, BIM and the CIF

    the reporting accountants team ought to have
    - investigated in conjunction with the trustees and manager of the pension funds, Mr Cowling and the audit team the way in which RM had exercised control over the pension schemes and the CIF
    - enquired into the audits of the pension schemes and the CIF and carried out additional audit procedures in relation to the pension funds' assets
    - considered the adequacy or otherwise of the post balance sheet events audit work and carried out additional procedures to provide adequate information about the pension funds in the year that had elapsed since 5 April 1990
    - carried out more detailed enquiries into the IBI transaction and the "collateral swap" and properly identified their significance in the long form report
  - As Mr Walsh and Mr Wootten were aware of RM's close involvement in pension matters, these two partners should have considered the pension issues themselves far more thoroughly; they should not have relied so heavily upon their assistants who had much less experience; the fault was that of Mr Walsh and Mr Wootten and did not lie with those in their team. Mr Wootten's degree of responsibility is less than that of Mr Walsh[c].

---

a See paragraph 9.41.

b See paragraph 9.56.

c See the explanation of their respective roles at the footnote to paragraph 22.24.

- **Mr Cook**
  - Mr Cook failed to discharge his responsibilities as he
    - did not draw to the attention of the reporting accountants team and the other advisers what he knew of the use being made of the shares of the CIF for the benefit of the private side[a];
    - told Clifford Chance that
      - auditable information about investments was only available to 5 April 1990 and information at 31 December 1990 was not readily available (see paragraph 13.14); this was untrue as he in fact held detailed records that contained information about the investments after 5 April 1990 (including information at 31 December 1990).
      - there had been no material change in the investments of the pension fund after 5 April 1990 (see paragraph 13.15).
    - misled the representatives of IMRO during their inspection in November 1990 by what he told them about the work done by CLD and about the way in which dealings with related parties were conducted and monitored (see paragraph 13.29).

22.52 A more limited measure of responsibility for the failure to identify abuses that they knew of attaches to:

- **Samuel Montagu**

Samuel Montagu did not properly consider the implications of the role played by RM in the management of the pension funds, particularly after they learnt of the views expressed by both Clifford Chance and Linklaters & Paines about the incestuous relationships in the management of the pension funds[b]. Had they done so they should have:

- insisted that information about the investments at 31 December 1990 or 31 March 1991 be provided; they should have appreciated that such information was readily available and rejected Mr Cook's assertion that such information was not readily available as it was obvious that a competent pension fund manager had to have up to date records of investments;
- examined the adequacy of CLD's instructions and the scope of CLD's investigation;
- required the imposition of a "ring fence" around the pension funds, which should have been no different in principle from that created around MGN. Samuel Montagu told us that they did not consider this to be necessary because there was no one person who controlled the pension funds and no obvious source of potential conflict; the pension funds were under the control of the trustees and were subject to a regulatory regime; their assets were fundamentally different from those of MGN. If, however, Samuel Montagu had become aware of the abuses, they could not have maintained this view.

---

a We accepted as regards his conduct to CLD that he had reasonable grounds for believing that they knew of the use being made of the shares.

b The fact that they only required changes to MGPT shows how little they had understood.

- **Mr Guest**

Although Mr Guest (as a member of the MGPS Investment Committee) was entitled to take comfort from the investment performance of the CIF and did not know of the abuses, he should have brought to the attention of Samuel Montagu the fact that RM had exercised control over the assets of the CIF and the pension scheme and that the investment committee of MGPS was not being provided with proper information about the investments of the CIF.

- **Mr Willett**

Mr Willett was, as set out at paragraph 9.55, aware from shortly after 20 February 1991 as a director of FTIT of the "lending" of the shares owned by FTIT to LBH and RMG, the fact that it had not been authorised, and the impact that these facts would have on the flotation of MGN. When the bid was made for FTIT, he understood the reason for it. Although he had a reason (as did the independent directors of FTIT) for remaining silent in the interests of FTIT shareholders, he should have resigned from the prospectus drafting committee as his membership was incompatible with his remaining silent about the unauthorised "lending" of shares owned by FTIT.

- **The Stock Exchange as the Listing Authority at the time of the flotation**

On the basis of what it is agreed Mr Fryer was told about events at FTIT as set out at paragraph 9.51, those responsible at the Stock Exchange for the MGN prospectus should have been given the information conveyed to Mr Fryer. The Stock Exchange, despite its concern about confidentiality[a], should have pursued further enquiries and raised questions with either Smith New Court or Samuel Montagu.

(5) Financial and other information

22.53 The circumstances in which MGN had acquired the interests in QPI and Donohue and Worship Street (namely the need of MCC and the private side for funds) were not appreciated.

22.54 The exposure of MGN under the circular loan of Can $35m in respect of the acquisition of QPI and Donohue involving RMG and MCC was not specifically disclosed or eliminated.

22.55 Samuel Montagu should have ensured that MGN's exposure was disclosed in the prospectus either as a material contract or elsewhere.

22.56 The cap and collar contracts had not been drawn to the attention of Samuel Montagu until 15 April 1991 and there had been insufficient time to procure their assignment or to discover that the banks would not agree to an assignment.

22.57 The responsibility in respect of the cap and collar contracts rests upon KM. These were significant liabilities and Samuel Montagu had made it clear they should be transferred to the private side. No proper steps were taken to obtain the consent of the banks and the assurances given by KM were given albeit there was no proper basis for them. He signed the letters containing the assurances because he knew that they had to be given to enable the flotation to proceed.

---

[a] See the footnote to paragraph 9.52.

(6) The finances of the private side

22.58 The true state of the private side finances had not been identified:

- its impact on the pension schemes and consequently on MGN was not appreciated.
- the potential strain on the "ring fence" was not realised[a].
- indemnities such as those in respect of Worship Street and the cap and collar contracts provided by the private side were unlikely to be of value.

- **KM and Mr Bunn**

22.59 The major responsibility rests upon KM and Mr Bunn for the deficiencies in the information provided to CLD:

- Despite the late stage at, and the manner in which the information was required, KM and Mr Bunn must have appreciated that CLD required accurate information about the entirety of the external borrowing of the private side. They did not provide that information and in particular did not provide information about the loans made through LBI and LBH. The information provided was materially inaccurate and misleading by reason of its incompleteness.
- Although we accept that KM and Mr Bunn were entitled to think that Mr Walsh was well aware of the longstanding practice of borrowing from the pension funds, this was a matter that they should have raised to ensure that it was taken into account, given the scale of the borrowing in April 1991. The failure to consider this as a separate liability contributed to the inaccurate picture of the finances of the private side.

- **CLD**

22.60 Although CLD were not carrying out a task that was in the nature of an audit and were thus not required to make detailed enquiries, they should not have provided comfort to Samuel Montagu and SBIL because:

- the state of the accounts and records of the private side did not permit an adequate view to be taken of the liabilities of the private side or its ability to pay its debts as and when they fell due.
- a judgment as to the value of the holding in MCC and the ability to dispose of a substantial part was critical to a proper assessment; CLD did not have the expertise to make such a judgment themselves and did not seek advice from those who did.
- the liability of the private side to the pension funds was not examined. Mr Walsh knew of the longstanding practice of borrowing cash by the private side but made no enquiry as to the extent of the indebtedness in April 1991.

Furthermore, Mr Walsh's attention had been drawn to the "collateral swap" and to the use of shares in the FTIT portfolio as collateral for private side borrowings but no enquiry was made into this. Had even the existence of these liabilities, let alone their true extent, been taken into account, no comfort could have been given.

---

[a] See paragraph 22.63.

22.61 One way in which CLD might have been able to make a better assessment of the overall finances of the private side and to have reported properly (both at audit and on the flotation) about the CIF and pension schemes would have been if they had had an overview. However, we were told by CLD that no one partner had an overview. There were five reasons for this:

- a partner who had an overview was not something required or desirable under audit procedures; audit procedures were specifically directed against this approach;
- audits were directed at recognised entities and groups and the "Maxwell empire" was not an entity or group that was recognised for accounting purposes;
- MCC, the CIF and pension schemes, and the private side were in effect three separate clients and the auditors' obligations of confidence prevented the passing of information between the partners responsible for the three clients[a];
- even if these points could have been overcome, the overview partner would not have been in a position to obtain a clear picture of the "Maxwell empire" as a whole by reason of there being no consolidated accounts and by reason of the variety of year ends;
- that in any event the partner for each client had a sufficient understanding of the assets and liabilities to discharge his own responsibilities.

It is clear that Mr Corsan had had an overview during the time during which he was the partner responsible for the private side. There was no reason why CLD could not have passed this role on to someone else. Mr Corsan's role involved one of the three partners having sufficient understanding of all of RM's UK interests to see the whole picture of those interests and understand what was happening. Given RM's business methods spelt out in the 1971/73 DTI Reports and the way RM continued to move assets between the various companies within his "empire" and between those companies and the pension funds, by not appointing a successor to Mr Corsan, CLD were not putting themselves in the best position to see what RM was doing[b]. By depriving themselves of the opportunity of having an overview of RM's businesses which he ran as one, they had to rely on obtaining a very thorough understanding of the transactions in their audit work if they were to be able to express an accurate opinion on the accounts of each entity or group of entities they audited. In any event, they failed to obtain a proper understanding of a number of transactions, as we set out in this Report.

The overall responsibility of Samuel Montagu as the sponsor

22.62 Samuel Montagu told us that they accepted, with hindsight, that MGN run and controlled by RM was unsuitable for listing. Without RM, they submitted it would have been suitable. They had had a considerable amount of direct personal knowledge and first hand experience of him for many years and the fundamental principle underpinning Samuel Montagu's whole approach to the flotation was premised on the basis that they trusted RM. Their views of him had been formed from this experience, the success of MCC and MGN and his acceptance by

---

a There were exchanges about the characteristics of RM's style and other matters. For example, in the course of the audit of the CIF for the year ended 5 April 1990, information about the holdings in MCC and the transaction with IBI was passed by the CIF audit team to the MCC audit team.

b Duties of confidentiality do not as a practical matter prevent the passing of information between partners within accounting firms. If one partner had been a consultant partner as successor to Mr Corsan, there would be no breach of confidence in passing the information to that one person as consultant.

the regulatory authorities and the professional community. If they had read the 1971/73 DTI reports in great detail they would not have acted differently. They accepted, with hindsight, that the judgment was wrong. However, as the sponsors, they had made a number of changes – a separate treasury and separate secretarial arrangements, changes to the composition of the board, including the appointment of non-executive directors and an audit committee, the education of the board and the provisions for related party transactions. The prospectus was not materially inaccurate and misleading and the six matters we have identified in paragraph 22.13 were "weaknesses" rather than "failures"; even if they had been identified they would not have prevented what occurred. Samuel Montagu considered that criticism of them on the basis that the arrangements were not fully in place on flotation demonstrated a lack of understanding of how a flotation was carried out in the City; it was the responsibility of the sponsor to draw attention to deficiencies and seek an assurance that they would be implemented; it was not their responsibility to check that they had. However, in our opinion:

- It was not merely that their judgment of RM was wrong, but they failed even to take properly into account the obvious need for a high degree of circumspection and care to which we have referred at paragraph 22.6. Accordingly, their entire approach to the flotation was fundamentally flawed.

- Although they knew that the companies controlled by RM were not in robust financial health they did not properly understand the financial pressures that those companies were under[a] and, given the company structure, the obvious risks that posed to MGN, and in particular that RM would have to continue to use the cash flow of MGN to keep the private side going.

- It is the duty of a sponsor to satisfy himself that the company is suitable for listing. Self evidently by reason of the matters set out MGN was not. Samuel Montagu bear a high degree of responsibility for that as they did not take reasonable care to satisfy themselves that it was. They did not take proper steps to see that what they had recommended had been implemented or achieved its intended purpose. They had specified the form, but had not given attention to the actuality through the implementation and efficacy of the fundamental changes they had recommended. Those changes were particularly necessary in the circumstances of the flotation of MGN. For example, their evidence was that the separation of the treasury was a *"sine qua non"* of the flotation of MGN, but they never took any step to check what had been done and that the arrangements were suitable. Had they done so, they would have discovered the truth and that the separation of the treasury was not in place.

- MGN's unsuitability for listing was the result of failures for which Samuel Montagu were responsible to the extent we have identified. Had these been discovered, as referred to in paragraph 22.15, the changes would have been made or the flotation abandoned.

---

[a] Unlike the credit rating agencies whose position is described at paragraph 22.63.

A contemporaneous assessment of MGN by the credit rating agencies

22.63 After the flotation two credit rating agencies were approached by MGN. Although a credit rating analyst is looking at the ability to service debt, this approach is nonetheless material to an assessment of a system of controls. A key element in the considerations of both Standard & Poor's Corporation (Standard & Poor's) and Moody's Investors Service (Moody's)[a] was the degree of separation between MGN and the rest of the Maxwell interests; both were troubled about this. First in May 1991 and then in July 1991 Moody's expressed concern that money could be transferred from MGN to other Maxwell companies; they relied on the closeness of the relationship between the management of MGN and the other companies, the small size of the effective management team and the financial pressure that the private interests were then under. Moody's were told of the arrangements that had been put in place at the flotation, but felt that time was needed to see if they would work.

22.64 Standard & Poor's expressed similar concerns in May 1991 but after a preliminary expression of view continued with their review of MGN. In October 1991 they made known their provisional conclusion that they were not satisfied as to the completeness of the ring fence nor its ability to protect MGN as a stand-alone operation from RM's other interests[b].

22.65 The views of the credit rating agencies (even though that expressed by Standard & Poor's was at a time when concerns about RM's companies were much greater than those current in April 1991) are a useful point of comparison in evaluating the efficacy of the steps taken by Samuel Montagu to prepare MGN for listing.

22.66 The experience of credit rating agencies provided two lessons which they applied to MGN:

- great strain is placed on any "ring fence" when a parent company is financially weaker than its subsidiary (which was known to be so in April 1991 in the case of the private side and MGN);
- it is important to see whether a system of controls works in practice.

Samuel Montagu did not regard these as material; they believed that in consequence of the work done by CLD on the private side finances, the private side could meet its obligations; they believed that the scheme for controlling related party dealings was adequate and unconnected with the private side finances; in Samuel Montagu's view it was not Samuel Montagu's responsibility to see that this scheme was implemented, since that was the responsibility of the board whom they believed would implement it.

---

a Both were approached to give in the first instance an informal indication of a likely rating.

b They proposed that consideration be given to altering the Articles of MGN to prevent the passing of any assets from MGN to the private or other Maxwell companies but, given the situation in October 1991 (as described in Chapter 1), it was impracticable to consider the suggestion.

Section 3: What had changed at MGN after flotation?

22.67 In this section we set out our views on what had changed at MGN after flotation and attribute responsibility for the failures we identify under the headings:

(1) Control over the management of the company
(2) Control over the finances of the company
(3) Other related party transactions
(4) Other financial information: the cap and collar contracts
(5) Pensions

22.68 The events that occurred after the flotation show the consequences of what was not done at the time of the flotation.

22.69 Although the newspaper business of MGN continued to be run as it had been before the flotation, the board of MGN never obtained effective control over the management of MGN and the company's finances.

(1) Control over the management of the company

(a) The position of the main board and the role of the company secretary

22.70 The board of MGN did not have effective control over the management of MGN.

22.71 Apart from the meeting on 24 October 1991 to approve the Holborn lease which was called at such short notice that three of the non-executive directors were not present, there were four full board meetings prior to RM's death. At the board meetings on

- **11 June 1991**, the members of the board:
  - allowed RM to conduct the meeting without giving them time to read the board papers which were only placed before them when the meeting started; in consequence they inadvertently approved the minute recording RM's sole signatory authority on a bank account that had been recently opened and missed the chance of questioning whether RM had sole signatory authority on other bank accounts.
  - allowed RM to delegate all the powers of the board to a committee of two, one of whom was to be RM without ensuring that the committee's powers were limited and its use controlled
- **23 July 1991**, the members of the board:
  - permitted RM to continue with the meeting when no independent director with corporate financial experience was present in person;
  - permitted RM to get the interim results approved without asking for time to consider the interim results or enquiring what the views of the audit committee were.
  - allowed RM to continue with the other matters on the agenda without requiring time to read the other papers; in consequence they inadvertently approved the minute of a meeting attended by IM and RM that had ratified one of the cap and collar contracts which should have been assigned to the private side.
- **12 September 1991**, the members of the board:
  - did not review the use that had been made of the delegation resolution when they amended it and did not circumscribe the committee's powers.

The meeting of 29 October 1991 is considered below.

22.72 Apart from the request made by Sir Robert Clark at the meeting on 11 June 1991, no steps were taken to ensure that Mr Stephens sent agenda and papers well in advance of board meetings.

22.73 The responsibility of the members of the board for the fact the board did not control the management of the company is as follows:

- **IM and Mr Stoney**

They did not bring to the attention of the board transactions with the private side and BIM of which they were aware and Mr Stoney did not inform the board meeting on 29 October 1991 of the Bankers Trust loan.

- **Mr Stephens**
- He should not have acquiesced in RM arranging and conducting the board meetings in the way RM did. Although he was in a difficult position, he should have consulted with one of the non-executive directors.
- He did not inform the board of MGN on 29 October 1991 that there had been a board meeting of MGN on 21 October 1991 to approve the loan of £50m from Bankers Trust.

- **Sir Robert Clark and Mr Clements**

They did not make it clear to RM on 11 June or 23 July 1991 that he could not conduct board meetings in the way described. They should have stood up to him on those occasions and insisted proper disciplines were applied; their presence on the board was used to convey the impression that MGN was a properly run listed company subject to the control of the board and not RM, whereas this was not the case.

- **Mr Burrington and Mr Horwood**

In view of the acquiescence of Sir Robert Clark and Mr Clements in RM's conduct, Mr Burrington and Mr Horwood were in a difficult position, but they should have discussed with them how this should have been remedied.

- **Lord Williams**

He should have enquired of the other directors or Mr Stephens what had happened at the board meeting on 11 June 1991 and protested to RM about the short notice at which the meeting on 23 July 1991 took place; he should have given more attention to ensuring that MGN was under the control of the board by conferring with the other directors.

- **The other directors**

Those present at the meetings on 11 June[a] and 23 July 1991[b] should not have acquiesced in what occurred; however, their responsibility is limited in view of the fact that no protest was made by those more experienced with the boards of public companies.

(b) The management of MGN Limited

22.74 Those who were directors of both MGN and MGN Limited (Mr Burrington, Mr Eastoe, Mr Guest, IM and Mr Wilson) should have reported to the board of MGN that RM was continuing to run the business of MGN Limited on a day to day basis through his 8.30 am meetings with management rather than through proper board meetings.

(c) The audit Committee

22.75 It never met because the non-executive directors forgot about the commitment that had been made in the prospectus that an audit committee would be convened and consider the interim results.

22.76 The three non-executive directors with experience of financial matters (Sir Robert Clark, Mr Clements and Lord Williams) should have appreciated that the interim results required the approval of the committee and should have previously taken steps to arrange this. Although it might have been helpful if CLD had drawn this matter to their attention, we do not criticise CLD for failing to do so.

(2) Control over the finances of the company

22.77 The board of MGN did not obtain effective control over the finances of MGN.

22.78 The responsibility for this is as follows:

- **RM**

The primary responsibility lay with RM who continued to control the finances of MGN in the same way as he had before flotation.

- **KM**

RM was assisted by KM who acted as his representative and continued to play the role we have identified in effecting transfers of funds to and from MGN and its pension funds. He bears a particular responsibility for the loans from Lloyds Bank[c], Crédit Lyonnais[d] and Bankers Trust[e].

---

[a] IM, Mr Guest, Mr Eastoe, Mr Haines, Mr Wilson, Mr Laird, Mr Stoney, who were present in addition to RM, Sir Robert Clark, Mr Clements, Mr Burrington, Mr Horwood.

[b] IM, Mr Stoney, Mr Eastoe, Mr Haines, and Mr Wilson who were present in addition to RM; no criticism should attach to Mr Ferguson and Mr Eastoe as they had raised concern with Mr Burrington as set out in the footnote to paragraph 20.76.

[c] Paragraph 21.44.

[d] Paragraph 21.44.

[e] Paragraphs 21.57 to 21.68.

- **IM**

Despite the fact that IM checked with RM and Mr Stoney before signing the authorities for payments to the private side, IM bears a responsibility.

- **Mr Stoney**

Mr Stoney bears the responsibility for the payments to the private side which he authorised.

- **Mr Guest**

Although Mr Guest became concerned in July 1991 about the payments to the private side and the payments that had been made without documentation being provided to the finance department and took the steps we have described in circumstances where he was in a difficult position, he should have reported the payments to the board or the non-executive directors as soon as he became aware of them.

- **Sir Robert Clark and Mr Clements**
- As they had not found out about MGN's system of financial controls at the time of the flotation, they should have made enquiries thereafter and discussed the position with Mr Guest on their own initiative soon after the flotation.

- Once Sir Robert Clark and Mr Clements had been informed in October 1991 of the payments that had been made into and out of MGN[a], they should have acted at once to investigate what had happened or immediately have raised it with RM. They should have told Lord Williams and Mr Haines and not left them or the other directors in ignorance at the board meeting on 29 October 1991. They told us that decisions regarding this were not arrived at by default but made in the exercise of their proper commercial and corporate judgement. They told us that they decided on this course because they were uncertain of the independence of Lord Williams and Mr Haines and that a private approach to RM would be more productive of a solution. In our view, there was no reason to distrust the independence of Lord Williams and Mr Haines who were their fellow non-executive directors. Moreover, the sums of money were so large and the circumstances so unusual that, in our opinion, a director with this knowledge, in proper discharge of his duties, would have required an immediate investigation of the facts and the production of a properly documented report.

- **Mr Burrington and Mr Horwood**
- Mr Burrington and Mr Horwood should have reported to the board the decision made by RM on 20 May 1991 to divide the finance director's responsibilities between Mr Guest and Mr Stoney.

- Once Mr Burrington and Mr Horwood had been informed by Mr Guest in August 1991 about the payments into and out of MGN, Mr Burrington and Mr Horwood should have informed the non-executive directors at once in addition to the steps they in fact took[b].

---

a See paragraphs 21.52 and 21.70 to 21.72.

b See paragraphs 21.27 to 21.28 and 21.41 to 21.49.

- Although Mr Burrington made subsequent enquiries, he should not have signed the transfer on 24 June 1991 without having supporting documentation.

- **CLD**
- After Mr Walsh and Mr Wootten had told Mr Steere of their conversation with Mr Stoney on 17 July 1991, Mr Steere (as the audit partner) should have overridden Mr Walsh's view and should have advised Mr Stoney to inform the board and himself raised the matter with Mr Guest or a member of the audit committee.

- After Mr Steere's meeting with Mr Guest on 10 October 1991, rather than speculating about what Mr Guest had meant, CLD should have immediately sought further information.

- **Mr Fuller**

Mr Fuller should not have been giving instructions in relation to MGN[a] as it was intended to be independent of the private side and MCC.

(3) Related party transactions

- **Mr Stoney**

22.79 The board meeting on 24 October 1991 to approve the Holborn lease should have been called on proper notice and a full explanation of the urgency should have been given to the board. Mr Stoney failed to discharge his duties in this respect.

(4) Other financial information: the Cap and Collar contracts

22.80 • **Mr Stoney**

Mr Stoney should have taken steps to see that the private side complied with its obligations to assign the cap and collar contracts or reported the position to the board.

- **KM**

KM should have seen that the private side companies honoured their agreement in the summer of 1991, given the personal role that he had played.

(5) Pensions

22.81 What happened after 30 April 1991 has been outside the scope of our enquiry.

---

[a] See paragraphs 20.28 to 20.37.

Section 4: How did the market in MCC and MGN shares operate?

(1) MCC shares

22.82 In our view the market in MCC shares was manipulated, particularly from mid 1990:

- The use of TIB and IBI in 1989 for the placing of shares in Japan although primarily undertaken to place shares in a new market was structured in the way it was to make profits for the private side; it also helped to bolster the market.
- The market did not have a true picture of the dealings in MCC shares from mid 1990:
  - The three "option" agreements made with Goldman Sachs were not options but deferred sales of shares by Goldman Sachs to RM; they were not disclosed as such.
  - The purchases made by IBI and IBF, TIB and Dr Rechsteiner (for the Liechtenstein foundations) were in fact purchases by RM, but were not disclosed as such.
  - The purchases made by these entities were so arranged that no purchaser acquired 3 per cent. of the share capital of MCC; where a single transaction might have resulted in an entity having a holding that exceeded 3 per cent., the purchases were split to avoid disclosure.
  - The fact that the CIF held 6 per cent. of MCC was not disclosed in October 1990.
  - The sale of 25 million (over 3 per cent. of MCC shares) shares from the pension funds to Servex and Yakosa for the Liechtenstein entities in April 1991 was effected to avoid disclosure on the flotation of MGN. It was done by an agency cross[a] effected by Goldman Sachs New York so that transfer was unknown to the market and to the advisers on the flotation and the holding divided in such a way that the purchasers did not have to disclose their holding.
  - The fact that by 30 April 1991 RM controlled through his family and the entities 76 per cent. of MCC[b].

22.83 We are satisfied that RM bears the primary responsibility for manipulating the market[c] in MCC shares and he did this because:

- He was obsessed with the share price which to his mind reflected on his personal standing.
- Shares represented by far the largest asset of the private side and were used extensively as collateral for the borrowings of the private side. The solvency of the private side and the loans from banks depended on their value.

---

[a] The same means were used on 26 March 1990 to effect a sale of 7.904 million MCC shares from the CIF to the private side (see paragraph 5.21).

[b] See paragraph 9.3.

[c] The events at MCC (through matters such as the use of the Berlitz shares from November 1990 as collateral for private side loans and the MCC property transactions such as the use of Corry Foundation in May 1990 in relation to Worship Street) has been outside the scope of our enquiry; we have only dealt with such transactions where necessary to explain what happened to MGN or its pension funds and we have therefore not enquired into why such events at MCC did not come to light.

    - The shares were represented as an asset that could be sold to assist cash flow and the value of the holding demonstrated a large surplus of assets over liabilities.
    - The two largest loans were collateralised by MCC and MGN shares and the amount required as collateral depended on their value.
- The rise in the MCC share price in the period prior to the flotation was helpful to the flotation of MGN.

22.84 However, the expenditure on the purchase of MCC and MGN shares placed severe strains on the finances of the private side:

- £130m was expended in 1990.
- £105m[a] was expended for the purchases made in the period between January and April 1991.
- £109m was expended in the period between May and October 1991.

22.85 KM knew of the majority of the purchases and assisted in the execution of the purchases of MCC shares made by RM; substantial responsibility attaches to him.

- KM knew of the substantial scale on which RM was purchasing MCC shares as he was asked to execute many of the transactions.
- He also knew that the purchases being made by TIB, IBI, IBF and the Liechtenstein entities were being made by RM.
- Because of the questions he was asked in 1989 about the status of TIB, he knew that the real issue was whether they were independent of RM, the family and the Maxwell Foundation. Although he told us that he considered that these entities were sufficiently independent of RM to be considered by him as separate entities, his analogy with offshore vehicles used in the acquisition of OAG and Macmillan is not, in our view, sustainable. The use of the offshore vehicles in connection with Macmillan and OAG had been disclosed. Furthermore, even if the entities used to purchase MCC and MGN shares had been technically independent of RM, purchases by the entities should have been disclosed because of the way the deals were done and the fact that the funds to pay for the shares came from RM's companies and the pension funds.
- KM must have appreciated by April 1991 by reason of the scale of the purchases being made by TIB and the Liechtenstein entities that the market did not have a true picture of the dealings in MCC shares.
- He was far too ready to ignore the advice from Miss Debbie Maxwell and Titmuss Sainer & Webb about the need to disclose the size of the CIF's holding in October 1990. He acquiesced too readily in the view that a further opinion should be obtained, but when one was not, he took no action. The result was, as he accepted and regrets, a misleading circular which was never corrected.

22.86 Mr Bunn also knew of the majority of the purchases of MCC shares and assisted in the execution of some of the purchases; a responsibility attaches to him.

---

[a] This excludes the price payable for purchases from the pension funds.

22.87 A substantial responsibility in respect of MCC shares also attaches to Goldman Sachs:

- There is, as we have summarised in this Report and set out in more detail in Appendix 7, a conflict in the evidence given to us as to the way in which transactions were effected and as to whether the deals were in reality done between RM and Mr Sheinberg or between Dr Rechsteiner, Mr Freedman and IBF, and Mr Sheinberg.
- Mr Sheinberg consistently maintained that all the deals were done between him and those directly representing the entities entering into the transactions. He told us that he believed that the entities were independent of RM, although "friends of management", and that he had relied at all times on the oral and documentary assurances he had been given as to the independence of these entities. A critique was made on his behalf and submitted to us in relation to the credibility of KM, Dr Rechsteiner, Mr Freedman and Mr Mitchell, and the unreliability of their evidence. A contrast was drawn with Mr Sheinberg's unblemished reputation, his many years experience as an equity trader and his position as a senior partner of Goldman Sachs.
- We are, however, satisfied that the deals were in reality done between RM and Mr Sheinberg and that Mr Sheinberg must have come to appreciate in due course that RM was in fact the purchaser of the MCC shares which, on the face of it, were being sold to the entities and, by reason of the scale of the purchases and the arrangements to avoid disclosure, that the market did not have a true picture. We have reached this conclusion independent of the evidence which was called into question by Goldman Sachs and accepting that Mr Sheinberg is a man of good character and unblemished reputation. Our conclusion is based upon our assessment of Mr Sheinberg's evidence viewed against the following:
    - RM was obsessed with the MCC share price. Mr Sheinberg knew this and perceived a trading opportunity to acquire MCC shares and dispose of them to RM, with the implied threat that, if RM did not buy, the shares would be sold onto the market and the market thereby rocked.
    - RM tightly controlled the finances of his empire. It is inconceivable that he would have allowed Dr Rechsteiner, Mr Freedman or IBF to negotiate the substantial deals with Mr Sheinberg (even within pre-set parameters as to price and settlement). The money being spent was regarded by RM as his own and, accordingly, he would have agreed the terms of the deals himself, particularly when a number of the purchases were made at prices other than the market price and with non-standard settlement dates. It is axiomatic that RM would have done the deals himself.
    - Mr Sheinberg and RM entered into the three "options" (referred to at paragraphs 6.14, 6.17 and 9.5) which were, from their substance and purpose rather than their legal form, a means by which Mr Sheinberg could dispose of shares on his books to RM and to allow RM to have time to pay for them.
    - The very first trade that Mr Sheinberg made with one of the entities (the sale of 3.446 million MCC shares to TIB in May 1989) demonstrated that from the outset there was clearly a close link between RM and the entities. That first trade, as Mr Sheinberg himself surmised, was only made after he and RM had agreed the purchase for BIM and then RM had asked that Mr Sheinberg call Mr Freedman to see if he was interested in buying the shares.

22.87 continued

- We have taken full account, as Goldman Sachs submitted that we should, of the fact that on the first trade, and on later trades with other entities, Mr Sheinberg was provided with an assurance that there was no relationship between the entities and RM (or the companies associated with him) that would give rise to any obligation to report the purchases as having in fact been made by the RM (or the companies associated with him). Mr Sheinberg may initially have believed that the fact that the sales were nominally being made to entities which he had been assured were independent of RM was sufficient to avoid disclosure. As the course of events set out in Appendix 7 reveals, however, it must subsequently have become apparent to Mr Sheinberg that the assurances he had been given were incorrect; Mr Sheinberg must have come to appreciate in due course that the reason for the trades and their structure was to avoid disclosure which would have revealed the involvement of RM. We consider that Mr Sheinberg must have come to appreciate by February 1991, and if not then by April 1991, that the market did not have a true picture:
  - The arrangements made for the placement of shares in Japan in December 1989 (which were organised by MCC) conferred the benefits upon TIB and IBF.
  - The sale of 10 million MCC shares to IBF in August 1990 was at a price above the market price; the shares were in fact paid for by, and delivered to, BIT although Mr Sheinberg told us that he was not aware of this[a].
  - Mr Sheinberg acted on an agency basis on the sale in January 1991 of 2.285 million MCC shares from IBF to a Swiss lawyer, Dr Rechsteiner, introduced to him by RM and knew that the substantial part of the purchase price had been provided by the seller, IBF, rather than the purchaser.
  - During 1990 Mr Sheinberg made major sales amounting to over 65 million shares to RM, his companies and the pension funds. After the delivery of the shares under the third "option" in February 1991, Mr Sheinberg sold no further shares to RM, his companies, his family, the Maxwell Foundation or the pension funds. In February 1991 the disclosed holding in MCC of RM, his companies, his family and the Maxwell Foundation was 68 per cent.
  - Mr Sheinberg made his major sales of MCC shares in February 1991 to IBF and TIB.
  - During April 1991, Mr Sheinberg sold from his book 22 million MCC shares to TIB and Servex. He accepted that he might, on 24 April 1991, have mentioned the 3 per cent. disclosure threshold when he agreed to sell 14 million MCC shares to Mr Freedman for TIB and then to sell 3 million MCC shares to Dr Rechsteiner for Servex (with each sale being made at the same price for the same settlement date).
  - Mr Sheinberg was told that the sale by the pension funds on 26 April 1991 of 25 million MCC shares was necessary as a result of the impending flotation of MGN.

---

[a] Goldman Sachs relied upon an internal IBF memorandum (referred to at paragraph 6.17) recording that MCC wanted to conceal the ultimate purchaser of the shares from Goldman Sachs; however IBF sent faxes direct to Mr Sheinberg informing him that the shares were to be held to the order of and paid for by BIT, the nominee company used by RM in trades with Goldman Sachs. Mr Sheinberg stated that he never saw these faxes, but it clear from them that no attempt at deception can have been made by IBF.

Mr Sheinberg checked with Goldman Sachs' compliance department about the reportability by Goldman Sachs of the trade; he was told that as the trade involved more than 3 per cent. of MCC shares it would be reportable if done with Goldman Sachs as a principal but not as an agent. The trade was done as an agency cross in New York. Further, as with the trade on 24 April 1991, the number of MCC shares acquired by Servex (16 million) meant that its holding in MCC would not pass through the 3 per cent. threshold and therefore have to be disclosed. Mr Sheinberg's evidence was that he chose to do the transaction in New York to avoid undue publicity for Goldman Sachs consistent with his trading philosophy; it was commonplace for traders to arrange trades so they were below disclosure thresholds. However, Mr Sheinberg must have appreciated that the reason for the sale of the shares to Servex and Yakosa (also represented by Dr Rechsteiner) was to avoid disclosure of a holding by the entity, because the shares were split between the entities in a way which made it obvious that disclosure was avoided. Furthermore, there could have been no rationale for effecting the sale by an agency cross in New York other than to avoid disclosure.

    - In July 1991, at a time when the MCC share price was under severe pressure, Mr Sheinberg spoke to RM on four occasions and as a result sold a total of over 30 million MCC shares to four further Liechtenstein foundations each of which was represented by Dr Rechsteiner.

- The matters identified above are entirely consistent with the evidence of KM, Mr Freedman and Mr Mitchell, and the reported statement of Dr Rechsteiner. Although there may be reasons for attaching little weight to the evidence of KM and Mr Freedman, the evidence of Mr Mitchell of Coutts & Co. (who was involved in one transaction[a]) is independent and consistent with the deals being done between Mr Sheinberg and RM.
- We should emphasise, however, that we are satisfied that Mr Sheinberg was not acting in league with, or on the basis of any agreement with, RM to cause the price of MCC shares to rise. It does not follow from that conclusion that Mr Sheinberg was deceived about the use of the entities[b].
- Mr Sheinberg, we conclude, was motivated by the large profits that he perceived could be made by purchasing substantial blocks of MCC shares and disposing of them to RM. The resulting trading relationship was very profitable for Goldman Sachs (£8m from MCC shares and a further £15m from other trades)[c].

22.88 At the latest by 22 October 1991 when RM paid $17.7m in respect of a purchase by one of the Liechtenstein foundations[d], the senior management of Goldman Sachs must have appreciated

---

[a] See paragraph 9.8.

[b] Goldman Sachs submitted to us that, throughout, there was a deliberate scheme by RM and KM to keep Mr Sheinberg in ignorance of the true position but, when they were dealing with the operations department to settle the trades, they were open as to the source and application of funds because they knew that the operations department would not understand the significance of what they were being told. We do not find this suggestion credible because of the obvious risks of such a scheme but, even if it were, it would make no difference to the conclusion we have reached as to what Mr Sheinberg must have appreciated.

[c] See Appendix 7, paragraph 17.43.

[d] See paragraph 21.74.

that RM had a beneficial interest in some of the purchases made by the foundations. Goldman Sachs did not pass this information to any regulatory authority whilst they sought to recover the amounts outstanding on their loans to RM's companies, although the Bank of England were informed of Goldman Sachs' intention to realise their security.

22.89 Although the Stock Exchange carried out between December 1990 and July 1991 a limited enquiry into the second and third options, this was narrow in its scope and did not reveal in fact what was happening in the market. No wider enquiry was made contemporaneously into the market in MCC shares or RM's dealings in them.

(2) MGN shares

22.90 The market in MGN shares was also manipulated by the secret purchases made by RM in breach of the undertakings in the prospectus. The same means and entities were employed that were used to purchase MCC shares and Goldman Sachs were through Mr Sheinberg involved in the same way as they were in the dealing in MCC shares[a].

22.91 Although RM must bear the primary responsibility, KM and Mr Bunn also bear a significant responsibility in respect of MGN shares for the reasons we have given in respect of MCC shares.

22.92 A substantial responsibility in respect of MGN shares also attaches to Goldman Sachs. Although we are satisfied that Mr Sheinberg was not in league with RM, we are satisfied that he must have appreciated that the purchases of MGN shares being made in May and June 1991 by TIB and Servex were purchases by RM. Mr Sheinberg told us that he had been told by RM that he (RM) could not buy MGN shares and, therefore, he would not. However, the manner in which these entities purchased MGN shares was similar to the manner in which they had purchased MCC shares and, for the reasons we have given earlier, we are satisfied that Mr Sheinberg must have appreciated that RM was in fact the purchaser when the MGN shares were purchased by them.

---

[a] For example, the sales made by Goldman Sachs on 22 May 1991 of 13 million MGN shares were made as to 10 million to TIB and 3 million to Jupiter Participations. If the whole of the 13 million shares had been bought by one person, that holding would have exceeded 3 per cent. and been disclosable (see paragraph 20.50).

23. RECOMMENDATIONS AND LESSONS FROM THE EVENTS

Introduction

23.1 Although we submitted some preliminary recommendations to the Secretary of State for Trade and Industry in 1995, we have reviewed the position in the light of the considerable developments that have occurred since then. We are grateful to the Financial Services Authority (FSA), the Occupational Pensions Regulatory Authority (Opra), the Department of Social Security (DSS), the Department of Trade and Industry (DTI) and the Institute of Chartered Accountants in England and Wales (ICAEW) for discussing with us a number of issues that we consider arise in the light of the events we have investigated.

23.2 The most important lesson to be learnt is that high ethical and professional standards must always be put before commercial advantage. The reputation of the financial markets depends on it. Legislation and regulation is, however, of great importance in underpinning those standards.

23.3 Many of the deficiencies in legislation and regulation which permitted the events we have described to occur have been rectified, but there remain some important matters which still require to be addressed or considered. We deal with these under the following headings:

	Paragraphs
(1) Pensions	23.4 – 23.17
(2) The public offering of securities	23.18 – 23.30
(3) Regulation within the UK	23.31 – 23.43
(4) The securities markets	23.44 – 23.56
(5) The audit and regulation of company "empires"	23.57 – 23.60
(6) Auditors, independence and the detection of fraud	23.61 – 23.74
(7) Corporate governance of listed companies: chairmen, directors and non-executive directors	23.75 – 23.91
(8) Technical matters	23.92 – 23.100
(9) Review of recommendations	23.101

(1) Pensions

23.4 In February 1995, we put forward some preliminary recommendations in relation to pensions in the light of the fact that the Pensions Bill, based on the full and comprehensive report of the Pensions Law Review Committee chaired by Professor Sir Roy Goode QC[a] (the Goode Committee), was then before Parliament. We have since that time considered the resulting Act and had the benefit of discussions with Opra.

[a] Cm 2342. It was followed by a White Paper "Security, Equality, Choice: The Future for Pensions" (Cm 2594)

23.5 The Act and the Regulations made under it has prohibited many of the abuses we have identified[a] such as the provision of loans to the employer, provided effective sanctions for the late completion of accounts[b] and provided duties to "whistle-blow"[c].

(a) The risk of misuse and public expectations

23.6 Although the changes to the law made by the Pensions Act 1995 and the creation of the regulatory regime under the supervision of Opra have made it less likely that pension funds will in the future be misused, the risk cannot be eliminated as no system of regulation can do so, particularly when there are about 119,000 "live" occupational pension schemes, most of which are very small. This is a risk which must be understood by the public. Vigilance by associations representing beneficiaries to ensure they are provided with full information and disclosure[d] can be an effective prevention against abuse and mismanagement.

23.7 We understand that there has been a good response to the duties imposed under the "whistle blowing" provisions contained in Section 48 of the Act[e]. However, as pensions are such a significant asset for most of the population, there are in our view some further modest steps that should be taken, at little cost, to reduce the risk further.

(b) The trustees

23.8 As it is the trustees of each pension fund under the UK system who remain central to the proper stewardship and investment of pension funds, it is upon them that the beneficiaries must primarily depend for the proper care and management of their pensions arrangements. It is therefore essential to encourage suitable people to become trustees and give them proper support in discharging their onerous responsibilities.

23.9 We consider that the work done by Opra and the DSS in raising the standards expected of trustees, providing them with guidance[f] and in encouraging education and training is greatly to be welcomed; the provision of guidance and encouragement of training is remedying one of the serious deficiencies that existed.

23.10 The statutory objectives of Opra do not, however, include an obligation to give information and guidance, though this has not inhibited them from doing so. In view of the central importance of this function to the proper running of pension trusts, we recommend that the Act should be amended, when the occasion arises, to add this as an objective. There may be cost implications,

---

a See the summary at paragraph 22.7.

b cf paragraph 13.4.

c cf paragraph 22.11.

d cf the attempts to get information by the pensioners of MGPS described at paragraphs 6.22 and 13.38.

e cf the position under section 109 of the Financial Services Act 1986 referred to in the footnote to paragraph 5.43.

f Opra published in July 1997 "A Guide for Pension Scheme Trustees" which is intended to help trustees understand their duties and responsibilities.

but we doubt whether these would outweigh the benefits obtained by providing further assistance to trustees who perform such useful and important functions.

23.11 As trustees take on such an onerous responsibility, they should be given every assistance in carrying out their responsibilities particularly in dealing with their professional advisers. We recommend that in addition to the valuable work done by Opra and the DSS, there are some further steps that should be taken:

- **Guidance on good practice:** We consider that the clear and helpful guidance published by Opra on the duties and responsibilities of trustees should be expanded to include more detailed guidance on relations with auditors[a], custodians, legal advisers, actuaries, investment managers, financial advisers and independent scheme administrators. These are the key professionals upon whom the trustees are dependent. This guidance should cover the minimum information that they should require from each adviser and the kind of probing questions they should ask. It should also set out what trustees can expect from their advisers and what they cannot and must check themselves. It is in our view important that there should be a clear understanding of the respective roles of trustees and their advisers. We understand that Opra are in the process of preparing guidance in relation to some of these professionals.

- **Model terms of engagement with professional advisers should be provided by Opra:** Although we recognise that trustees must be free to negotiate with their professional advisers on the exact terms of their engagement, there are certain points which as a matter of good practice should always be covered. For example, model terms of engagement with auditors could provide for an annual report on internal controls and the custody of assets (if appropriate) and for the attendance of the audit partner at least once a year to present a report to the full body of trustees. It may also be desirable that guidance be given on the disclosure of the fees paid to professionals, as there is public interest in controlling the costs that pension schemes have to bear.

- **Related party transactions:** All pension trust deeds should contain a requirement that all proposed related party transactions should be put before the full body of trustees for consideration and approval. We recommend consideration be given to legislative provisions to facilitate this.

- **Training for trustees:** The Goode Committee considered it was impracticable to require all trustees to attend training courses[b]. However bearing in mind the onerous responsibilities placed on trustees and the fact that few non-professionals have little relevant experience on

---

[a] Opra published in June 2000 "A Guide to Audited Scheme Accounts" for people involved with insured salary-related pension schemes. It contains helpful guidance on what the trustees must do themselves and what they can look to professional advisers to provide. In October 2000, Opra published "A Guide to appointing professional advisers". This again contains very clear and useful practical guidance on how to appoint (and dismiss) professional advisers.

[b] Recommendation 52. See also paragraph 4.5.65.

appointment, it ought to be regarded as standard practice that trustees are trained; they need to know not only their responsibilities and have the skills necessary to invest the assets of the fund, but also how to question apparently plausible explanations put forward by professional advisers. We understand that consideration is being given by the DSS to requiring trustees to make a statement in their annual report on their training policies; this is a welcome and necessary step forward towards universal training.

(c) The professions

23.12 We were surprised to discover a lack of understanding by some professionals of the fiduciary duties relating to pension funds[a]. There can be little doubt that advising and auditing pension funds requires specialist knowledge and skill. It should be a clearly expressed and specific part of the code of conduct of each relevant profession that those advising pension funds have a duty to familiarise themselves with the relevant fiduciary duties[b]. This should prove a relatively cost efficient way of bringing home to professionals this obligation in contrast to a licensing system or certification of special training requirements. The relevant government departments responsible for the professional bodies should ensure that the necessary changes are implemented.

(d) The Disclosure Regulations

23.13 In February 1995 we put forward some preliminary recommendations relating to proper disclosure in pension fund accounts of material transactions, and in particular related party dealings, during a scheme year. The basis of these recommendations was that disclosure has a preventative effect. Since that time a revised SORP entitled "Financial Reports of Pension Schemes" and Financial Reporting Standard (Number 8) entitled "Related Party Disclosures" have been issued. These require proper disclosure of related party dealings in pension fund accounts.

(e) The regulator – Opra

23.14 It would be clearly impracticable and incompatible with a system based on the use of a very large number of non professional trustees to require them to be vetted and approved prior to appointment. At present the powers of Opra in respect of trustees are somewhat limited.

23.15 Opra should be given power to prohibit individuals acting as trustees if they discover evidence that shows they do not meet "the fit and proper" standard, despite the limitations to which we refer at paragraph 23.39.

---

[a] See paragraph 5.42.

[b] Some professions have general rules: see for example Section 1.200 of the Guide to Professional Ethics of the ICAEW. This provision was in force during the period of the events we describe . The Auditing Practices Board issued in 1997 a Practice Note (Number 15), "The audit of occupational pension schemes in the United Kingdom", which replaced the Auditing Guideline 'Pension Schemes in the United Kingdom' which was issued in November 1988 and was extant during the period of the events we describe. The Practice Note contains explicit statements that auditors need to be familiar with the legal and regulatory background to pension schemes.

(f) Custodianship

23.16 A significant proportion of the shares of the pension funds that were used as collateral for bank loans to the private side were in the custody of a custodian of high reputation[a]. However under the usual form of custody agreement, the custodian is entitled and obliged to act in accordance with instructions given to him provided they are duly authorised, without enquiring into whether the action authorised is in the proper interests of the pension funds. In many senses therefore, it follows that entrusting assets of a pension fund to a custodian provides little more protection to the assets of that pension fund than could be obtained by placing them in a safe and controlling access to the key (in the same way as controlling the authority to give the custodian instructions[b]). Pure custodianship is therefore of limited value in preventing any misuse of pension fund assets. We agree in this respect with the conclusions of the Goode Committee[c] that it would not be appropriate to require trustees to place pension fund assets with independent custodians[d] under the usual form of custody agreement. Mr Paul Myners[e] in his letter to the Chancellor of the Exchequer and Secretary of State for Social Security dated 8 November 2000 has indicated that he intends to recommend that it be a mandatory requirement that assets be placed in the possession of a regulated custodian independent of the employer. Mr Myners' review considered that matters had changed since the time of the Goode Committee's Report and, in particular, custodians are now authorised and discussions with the pension fund industry suggested that the costs involved were not likely to be significant, as the custodian will ordinarily perform ancilliary services at a lesser cost than the pension administrator could provide them. Mr Myners' review also considered that independent custodians could provide a source of independent "check and balance", raising questions about unusual transactions even if not legally obliged to. This proposal is, we understand, made in the context of expecting greater professionalism from trustees, making them more accountable and imposing on them a higher legal duty in respect of their decision making. If it is envisaged that a custodian will perform services ancilliary to pure custodianship and will undertake a higher legal obligation in respect of the propriety of instructions than that which is presently found in the usual form of custody agreement, then we see merit in the proposal.

23.17 As is mentioned at paragraph 5.37, in the USA the obligations placed upon custodians under ERISA may be more onerous, as a custodian who is regarded as a fiduciary is in effect required to monitor compliance with pension plan trust deeds and must act in accordance with strict fiduciary standards. This form of custodianship is more akin to a professional trustee of a pension fund in the UK and would in essence duplicate at a cost the work done by the trustees under UK pension funds. Given the fundamental policy decision made in the 1995 Act to continue to rely upon the central role of the actual trustees in the proper stewardship and

---

[a] See paragraph 5.33.

[b] This was accepted by the custodian which held some of pension fund shares – see paragraph 5.33.

[c] Recommendation 114

[d] We do, however, consider that the involvement of independent custodians does give an opportunity for whistle blowing although this may be limited due to the nature of the custodians' obligation.

[e] He is Chairman of Gartmore Investment Management, fund managers. He was requested by H M Government to carry out a review of institutional investment.

investment of each pension fund (following the recommendations of the Goode Committee), the wider form of custodianship is presently inappropriate in the UK.

(2) The public offering of securities

23.18 In July 1995, we put forward some preliminary recommendations in respect of changes[a] that should be considered in the role of the Stock Exchange and advisers in relation to listing of new securities; we also suggested changes to the Yellow Book, after discussions with those then responsible at the Stock Exchange (which was then the UK listing authority).

23.19 On 1 May 2000, the functions of the Stock Exchange as the UK listing authority were transferred to the FSA. It is therefore not necessary for us to set out what changes we previously considered needed to be made in the internal procedures of the Stock Exchange in the light of its own internal report on the MGN flotation and the subsequent changes to the Yellow Book. Significant improvements were made to those procedures when the Stock Exchange was the UK listing authority. We have discussed with the FSA the issues that we consider still remain to be addressed.

(a) The expectations gap on the role of the UK listing authority

23.20 As set out earlier in this Report, there was some confusion as to the Stock Exchange's role and responsibilities[b]; for example, many (including leading figures in the City) told us that they regarded it as significant that the Stock Exchange had permitted RM to become the chairman of a public company, whereas the Stock Exchange told us it had no power to prevent him[c]. A misconception of the role of the listing authority can lead investors to attach undue significance to the actions or inactions of the listing authority.

23.21 The public is, in our view, entitled to a simple statement of the role and responsibilities of the UK Listing Authority so that its limited regulatory function is clearly understood. This should cover:

- Its understanding of its duty as the listing authority as regards the accuracy and completeness of a prospectus.
- The fact that it does not regard itself as under any responsibility as to suitability for listing of a company being listed.
- Its understanding of its very limited responsibility in respect of the directors.

One way of doing this is to build on the passage contained in the introduction to the current Listing Rules (the "Purple Book").

(b) A definition of the role and duties of advisors on a flotation

23.22 In 1978 the Council for the Securities Industry proposed the formulation of a Code of Conduct in relation to flotations and other new issues[d]. It met powerful opposition in the City and the

---

a We also drew attention to the view expressed to us about future flotations of companies owning newspapers, as set out in paragraph 17.7.

b See paragraphs 7.17 to 7.19.

c See paragraphs 1.15, 4.5 and 4.36.

d See the footnote to paragraph 7.2.

work was never finalised. This was unfortunate as the expressions of concern by persons such as Lord Benson were ignored and the opportunity missed to record the lessons to be learnt from corporate failures so that they were available to those who by reason of their youth or inexperience had not encountered them; they summarised their concerns as follows:

> "there should be a general requirement that those sponsoring public issues should form an overall opinion whether those running a private company are fit to run a public company. A prospectus may contain no misstatements and may yet give a wrong general impression. An entrepreneur may run a private company very successfully as a one-man show, but be unwilling or unable to submit to the disciplines, in regard to accounts, board meetings etc required in a public company."

23.23 We recommend that the unfortunate rejection by the City of such a code should now be remedied. We recommend that the FSA should facilitate the production of "Guidance" setting out a statement of the respective duties and responsibilities of advisers[a] and containing useful advice and examples of lessons that have been learnt.

(c) Box ticking

23.24 Regulation can give rise to a real risk of a "box ticking" approach. This is less of a risk where broadly based codes are used which are not prescriptive, as such codes encourage the exercise of judgment rather than a mechanical approach. An example of the risk to which we refer is that, if there is a requirement for an audit committee under a code or regulation, then the obligation can be taken as performed by establishing one, without ensuring its proper organisation and integration into the overall structure of the company[b]. The "Guidance" we have proposed should therefore emphasise that, although compliance with the detailed requirements must be thoroughly performed, advisers have not fulfilled their duty unless they stand back and analyse the issues and the solutions to see whether at the end of their task the intended result has been achieved.

(d) Disclosure

23.25 The tendency has been for listing particulars to become increasingly long. This has been accentuated in part by a properly cautious attitude to disclosure displayed by advisers. However there is an increasing risk that, although everything is in fact disclosed in detail, it is not easy to discern a fair presentation of the risk attendant in subscribing to the shares. We do not think providing for less disclosure or for a short form prospectus would be the answer, but the issue needs to be addressed.

23.26 We therefore recommend that consideration should be given to requiring directors to include in the particulars a summary "fair presentation" of the risks and benefits of subscribing to the shares; a fair presentation would require a degree of candour as it would have to draw to the attention of investors not only the specific advantages on the upside but also the specific disadvantages on the downside[c]. There are some powerful arguments against such a "fair presentation", but this is an issue that should be debated and considered.

---

a We have set out in Appendix 10 a summary of the functions and duties of advisers in 1991.

b cf what happened on the flotation of MGN: see paragraphs 10.31, 20.72, 21.72 and 22.19.

c cf the evidence of Samuel Montagu set out at paragraph 17.13. If a "health warning" had to be given, the conclusion might be that the company was not suitable for listing.

(e) Listing requirements

23.27 In July 1995, we made preliminary recommendations that there be changes to the Yellow Book to cover:

- The application of the rule relating to continuity of management to non-executive directors[a].
- More detailed requirements in relation to the pension fund[b].
- More stringent listing requirements in relation to financial controls[c].
- A requirement that the financial position of a shareholder with a controlling interest be disclosed[d].

23.28 The last of these points appears largely to have been met by the requirement in the "Purple Book"[e] that the listing particulars contain a statement explaining how the issuer is satisfied that

(a) it is capable of carrying on its business independently of the controlling shareholder; and

(b) all transactions between the issuer and the controlling shareholder are and will be at arms' length and on a normal commercial basis.

As to the other preliminary recommendations:

- We understand that the rule as to continuity of management has been relaxed to facilitate the listing of companies; whilst we appreciate the reasons for this, it imposes a higher duty on the sponsor to satisfy himself that the company is suitable for listing and a clear duty to disclose prominently in the prospectus any lack of continuity[f].
- We also understand that recent practice has been to disclose more about the arrangements for pension funds; we do not consider it is sufficient just to rely upon practice.

We therefore recommend that the listing rules be changed to make more detailed requirements in relation to both pension funds and financial controls.

(f) Reporting accountants

23.29 The Auditing Practices Board produced in December 1997 "Statements of Investment Circular Reporting Standards" which considered independence and ethical standards where a firm that is the auditor to a company acts as reporting accountants to that company. These statements require[g] that where an opinion in true and fair terms is involved, a partner other than the audit partner should be involved in the conduct of the work[h].

---

a See paragraphs 10.23, 10.24, 22.19 and 22.25.

b See paragraphs 22.46 to 22.50.

c See paragraph 22.36. A new rule (Para 2.11) was introduced into the Listing Rules in December 1993 to deal with financial reporting procedures.

d See paragraphs 19.11 and 22.63 to 22.66.

e Listing Rule: Para 3.12, 3.13 and 6.C.23.

f Paragraph 3.8 of the Listing Rules requires the directors and senior management to have collectively appropriate expertise and experience.

g SIR 200 – Accountants' reports on historical financial information in Investment Circulars, paragraph 8.

h Samuel Montagu had stipulated that the partner in charge of the reporting accountants' team was to be a person who had not been involved in the audit of MGN for the preceding five years (see paragraph 4.17).

23.30 In our view this does not go far enough, given the essential role of the reporting accountant in the due diligence work done on a public offering. It should be a minimum requirement (and not a recommendation) that the team be completely independent of the audit team of the company being reported upon and any other company controlled by the majority shareholder. However best practice that should be required by sponsors, unless there are strong reasons to the contrary, should be that the reporting accountants come from another firm so that a completely independent view is provided.

(3) Regulation within the UK

23.31 There were significant changes, particularly at IMRO after November 1991[a]. The establishment of the FSA in late 1997 has brought about much needed radical change. One of the most significant changes has been to reduce within the UK the fragmentation of regulation that was one of the hallmarks of the 1986 Act. The implementation of the Financial Services and Market Act 2000 (FSMA) later in 2001 will further strengthen the changes. There are, however, five matters on which we now wish to comment.

(a) Conflicts of interest

23.32 The approach to regulation adopted by the FSA is one of prudential supervision of each firm regulated; the aim is, having regard to business of the firm, to ensure the adequacy of the firm's capital and the systems and controls which the firm has in place to prevent wrongdoing and breaches of regulation. Wide use is made of individual registration so that individuals appreciate the personal responsibility they carry and the sanctions that can be visited on them personally. The FSA assesses the systems and the calibre and integrity of the management and expects firms and individuals to report breaches and to whistle blow. It also adopts a pro-active approach, for example by checking on individuals, carrying out visits and investigations at firms' premises, examining any complaints made about firms, analysing relationships with customers and overseeing what is happening in the market.

23.33 Even allowing for the FSA's pro-active approach, this method of prudential supervision, which depends to a significant extent upon member firms to enforce proper regulation through proper systems, must also manage the conflicts of interest that are produced by this regulatory method. We welcome the very strict and rigorous stance the FSA has taken on this issue.

23.34 It must, however, be appreciated that there remain therefore considerable risks in this system of regulation because of the inherent conflict that exists between (1) the desire of a firm on discovering wrongdoing to protect its own financial position by making recoveries of monies outstanding and avoiding damage to its own commercial reputation by keeping the discovery confidential and (2) the public interest in immediate disclosure to regulators and in taking action against the malefactor with the consequent adverse publicity to the firm and the reduced chance of making recoveries. This conflict can only be met by vigilance on the part of the FSA and by severe and public deterrent penalties against not only the individual who has failed to honour his

---

[a] See Appendix 9, paragraphs 7.1 to 7.10.

obligations but against the senior management of companies where there is a failure to whistle blow or disclose wrongdoing. It should be made costly in terms of loss of reputation to fail to disclose wrongdoing and to attempt to cover it up, if the FSA's system of prudential supervision is to command public confidence in the long term.

(b) The expectations gap on the scope of regulation

23.35 Regulation plays an essential role in maintaining public confidence in institutions that are permitted to handle and invest pensions and savings. However, no system of regulation can prevent another series of events similar to that surrounding RM's companies, though the risks of this happening should have been significantly reduced by the radical changes made to the regulatory regime by the FSA and the FSMA. The public should understand the risks. There should be no "expectations gap" and the fact that an institution is approved and regulated does not obviate the need for vigilance.

(c) Approval of a person as fit and proper

23.36 A clear example of the fact that regulation is not an assurance against wrongdoing is provided by the limitations on the scope that a regulator has for declining to approve a person as a fit and proper person to conduct investment business.

23.37 As is clear from our summary of the events leading to the approval of BIM as an investment manager, a forcible view was expressed about the integrity of RM[a], but BIM was nonetheless approved as the view was taken that there was no hard evidence to support a refusal to admit BIM[b] which would withstand scrutiny in court.

23.38 After the events we have described, IMRO introduced a system[c] of individual registration which the FSA will also implement. In June 2000 the FSA published "High level standards for firms and individuals" which contained as annexes "Statements of Principle and Code of Practice for Approved Persons" and "Fitness and Propriety". These set out the standards which it is expected the applicant must meet and maintain; if an individual fails to maintain standards and is disciplined, he may not be employable in the industry. We consider that this more robust approach[d], together with improvements in the gathering of information, go a substantial way to remedying the difficulties.

23.39 However, we do not consider that the basic problem has changed. The FSA cannot act without hard evidence which will withstand scrutiny in court. Thus an approval is more in the nature of a negative clearance than a positive approval. The public should have a clear understanding of this; there should be no expectations gap.

---

a See paragraph 5.6.

b See Appendix 9, paragraph 2.6.

c See Appendix 9, paragraph 7.6.

d See also the approach adopted by IMRO after 1993 described in Appendix 9, paragraph 7.3.

(d) The communication of information

23.40 The inclusive structure of the FSA, the ending of the fragmented system of regulation created by the Financial Services Act 1986, the establishment of a department of the FSA to deal with complex groups and the transfer of supervision under the Banking Act 1987 to the FSA has meant that the problems of communication of information within the UK are now significantly less.

23.41 We understand that since the events we describe the information exchange network established in 1992 as set out in the footnote to paragraph 6.43 has continued to expand and now has a full time secretariat and membership includes such bodies as the DTI, the FSA, the SFO, the Stock Exchange and Opra as well as a number of other regulatory organisations in the widest sense.

(e) Staffing of regulatory bodies

23.42 We have noted[a] views expressed to us about the comparative inexperience of the regulatory staff who conducted the inspections of BIM. We understand that the knowledge and experience of staff is now much better, though the retention of staff with experience sufficient to conduct a analytical review of a firm remains a challenge.

23.43 It is in the general interests of regulated firms that the public has confidence in regulation as it underpins confidence in their business. It is therefore in their own interests to make available on secondment their more able employees to ensure that regulators obtain staff who have the relevant experience of current market practices. We would encourage the FSA to make public information about the assistance given to them by firms through the provision of seconded employees. City firms and institutions should do as much as possible to see secondment to a regulator as an important step in the career of their most able employees.

(4) The securities markets

23.44 The dealings in MCC and MGN shares exemplify problems that have arisen in markets in securities because firms who deal in securities operate in markets on a transnational basis whereas regulation of markets to ensure that they are fair, open and transparent is essentially still national. This therefore gives rise to issues on which more radical thought is needed.

23.45 For example, a transnational firm can chose the regulatory regime that best suits a particular transaction and conduct business in such a way that others in the market do not have a clear picture of what is happening[b]. Although individual exchanges monitor what is happening on that exchange and there is co-operation between exchanges, there is no overall monitoring of transactions in the same security done in different markets or through different subsidiary companies of the same firm operating under different regulatory regimes. For example, although a subsidiary of a transnational firm authorised in the UK is required to report all trades undertaken in a security to the FSA regardless of the location of a trade or whether it is on or off

---

[a] See Appendix 9, paragraphs 5.13 and 6.4. For the changes at IMRO after 1991, see Appendix 9, paragraph 7.5.

[b] See paragraph 1.12 of Appendix 7.

market, there is no obligation for a subsidiary not authorised in the UK to do so; that subsidiary reports to the regulator in the state which regulates it[a]. Thus the transnational firm has a very substantial advantage over national governmental regulators which attempt to regulate its transactions in a given security to ensure that markets are fair, open and transparent; it is not in the public interest that this imbalance should continue as it can, as the dealings in MCC and MGN shares exemplify[b], be detrimental to the maintenance of fair, open and transparent markets. More effective control and accountability is therefore needed over the business transacted by the transnational firms to ensure the openness, fairness and transparency of markets in securities. As has been forcibly pointed out, this is a matter of wide public concern and interest, given the dependence of large parts of the population on the investment of their savings and pension funds in securities traded in these markets[c].

23.46 Much of the debate on transnational regulation has taken place in the context of controls over systemic risk to international financial stability and in the context of greater access to markets. It is, we believe, important that the debate also gives sufficient emphasis to the need for control over transnational firms to ensure fair, open, transparent and stable markets in which the public and investors can have confidence.

(a) Co-operation under existing arrangements

23.47 Arrangements exist for the exchange of information between regulators in different jurisdictions and for the obtaining of information from other state authorities both in the UK and overseas:

- Within the European Economic Area EC Directives[d] form the basis of co-operation and set out the terms on which information can be exchanged, used and disclosed within the European Economic Area and to states outside that area. The implementation of the Directives has not been entirely uniform and differences exist in national implementation.
- There are also other bilateral and multilateral arrangements[e], usually in the form of a "Memorandum of Understanding", which facilitate co-operation. These arrangements specify the terms on which information can be exchanged and used, including restrictions on disclosure even as between different regulatory authorities with the same state[f]. This is a

---

a The monitoring system operated by the FSA is in addition to that carried out by the Stock Exchange in London; for example, the Stock Exchange monitors compliance with closed periods.

b See our conclusions at paragraph 22.82 to 22.92 and Appendix 7.

c The FSA has adopted a broader approach to its jurisdiction and will exercise jurisdiction over actions overseas if they have an effect in the UK.

d These include the Major Shareholding Directive, the Insider Dealing Directive, the Investment Services Directive, and the Second Banking Consolidation Directive. Liechtenstein is a party to the European Economic Area Agreement which extends to the European Economic Area the operation of single market directives.

e There is also an Intermarket Surveillance Group which includes all the Exchanges in Canada and the US as well as Amsterdam and Brussels, but not Paris or Frankfurt; this is a group of self regulatory organisations. At present the FSA and the London Stock Exchange are members of it. When the FSA becomes a statutory regulator, then the information will have to be supplied to it through the SEC.

f For example, a memorandum of understanding between the DTI, the Securities and Investment Board and the Swiss Federal Department of Finance contains restrictions on the disclosure of information.

regime of "soft law" which is not enforceable or legally binding. This regime is subject to national laws and, within the European Economic Area, to the EC Directives.

- In 1999, the FSA and the 16 other members of the Forum of European Securities Commissions (FESCO) signed a Memorandum of Understanding on the Exchange and Surveillance of Securities Activities; this provides a multilateral framework for the sharing of information about business in the securities markets undertaken by firms within the European Economic Area and for bilateral co-operation[a]. However, the initial report of the *Committee of Wise Men on the Regulation of European Securities Markets* under the chairmanship of Mr Alexandre Lamfalussy (the initial Lamfalussy Report) concluded[b]:

> "However useful this work is, FESCO is confronted with several drawbacks: it has no official status, it works by consensus and its recommendations are not binding. Furthermore, the actual implementation of those decisions in different Member States is dependent upon the regulatory powers granted internally to each respective regulator – and these differ widely."

23.48 The system for the exchange and obtaining of information has at least three limitations:

- It is usually reactive and does not easily permit routine monitoring to ensure that the market has all the relevant information, although proactive exchange of information is permissible
- It can be slow, as a request for information has to be made and then a response considered. Some jurisdictions are quicker than others; for example the Memorandum of Understanding between the UK and the USA and the FESCO Memorandum of Understanding provide for urgent requests.
- Some jurisdictions prohibit the making public of information so obtained[c]. As the provision of information to the public as to the way in which a market is operating or has operated is often the most effective sanction against the wrongdoer, this is a serious restriction in such circumstances, though there are other circumstances (such as criminal investigations) where restrictions can be necessary.

The initial Lamfalussy Report observed more generally in respect of the EU:

> "There is no single template for supervision. Co-operation between securities regulators for dealing with cross-border practices and trading is only lightly covered."

(b) International lead supervisors and colleges of regulators

23.49 Steps are, however, being taken to establish the principle that, in supervising financial groups active in a number of industry sectors, it is helpful to have a co-ordinating supervisor operating on a transnational basis.

23.50 For example the FSA has regular bilateral meetings with other European Regulators, particularly those in France, the Netherlands, Germany and Sweden. It has also encouraged the establishment

---

[a] In June 2000 FESCO producced a paper (FESCO/00-0961) to contribute to the consideration by the EU Commission in formulating a Directive on market manipulation. This paper suggested that "the Directive must do more not only to enhance co-operation between supervisors... but also establish a more common approach to detection and investigation... as well as enforcement".

[b] 7 November 2000.

[c] It has been observed to us that jurisdictions with highly pervasive freedom of information rules can also pose difficulties in exchanging information.

of international colleges of regulators; for example with regard to banking supervision, it has regular meetings with the Federal Reserve Bank of the United States and the Swiss Banking Commission to co-ordinate supervisory programmes. IMRO, the SEC and the Securities & Futures Commission of Hong Kong collaborate on joint visits to head offices of transnational firms with local visits based on a common agenda. We welcome this approach.

(c) Possible longer term solutions

23.51 Other solutions in relation to issues are being addressed. For example the theme of the International Organisation of Securities Commissions (IOSCO) annual conference in May 2000 was "Global Markets, Global Regulation". It was recognised that it is impossible to regulate investment activity on a nation state basis, but progress in solving the difficulties created is clearly very difficult. Possible ideas include:

- Regulation by the home state of the transnational firm: Within the EU, a firm regulated in the home state has a "passport" to conduct similar business throughout the EU and is primarily regulated by the home state. This could be expanded gradually to a global framework, giving the home state power to compel all the subsidiaries of the firm to report to it on all business done, whatever the jurisdiction in which the business was effected. However, given the global dominance by a few firms from a small number of states, this would have considerable political implications and be difficult to achieve without a common approach to a legal framework. Furthermore such a system requires a common regulatory approach on methods of supervision and risk assessment and common standards on matters such as solvency and exposures; that would not be easy to achieve given different national perspectives.
- Supervisory regulation of an individual security from its home base. To ensure that there was proper information about the dealings in a particular security, a national exchange or regulator could be designated as the body to whom dealings in the security had to be reported; the home state for this purpose could be, for example, the state of the corporate residence of the issuer or a state chosen by the issuer. This would not be an easy system to operate; the choice of home state would at times be difficult and dealings in shares can move from market to market. Furthermore, account would have to taken of the implications arising from the fact the Stock Exchanges now compete with each other and some regulate new electronic markets which are their competitors.
- Development of the system of international lead supervisors and colleges of regulators: we have described the steps being taken to develop this system. For the foreseeable future, this may well be the only system which will be practicable[a].

23.52 We appreciate the very real difficulties that lie ahead, but this is a problem that is of considerable importance to the public the value of whose savings and pensions depend on the proper operation of the markets in securities. We can do no more than draw attention to the need for these issues to be a matter of high priority in that context for further consideration and action. The events

[a] The Final Report of the *Committee of Wise Men on the Regulation of European Securities Markets* published on 15 February 2001 recommends the setting up of an EU Securities Committee and an EU Securities Regulators Committee. They conclude "Other options are in the present circumstances impractical, including a single European regulatory authority."

relating to the dealings in MCC and MGN shares demonstrate vividly the abuse of the market that can arise; since those events the progress towards globalisation has increased and the growth in the use of the internet have increased the opportunities for market manipulation[a] and made the problems of national regulation even more difficult.

(d) Jurisdictions where there is secrecy

23.53 Another problem that arises in the transnational markets in securities is the use in the course of trading of jurisdictions where little information is publicly available about the beneficial ownership of corporate entities, trusts, foundations or other entities. In some jurisdictions, it is even possible for lawyers, bankers and other professionals to refuse to reveal the identity of a client for whom they have purchased securities without the consent of that client. There can be legitimate reasons for such confidentiality, but there can be no justification for withholding information about ownership from regulators in other jurisdictions when they are concerned about the operation of markets in other jurisdictions, even if the regulator may make that information public.

23.54 A proper application of the "know your customer" rule by securities firms should go some way to obviating the difficulties; they should, as part of that rule, in appropriate circumstances ascertain the ultimate beneficial ownership of the counterparty with whom they were dealing. We have no doubt that some jurisdictions which still maintain secrecy laws will be persuaded to change their attitude; the publication by the Financial Stability Forum[b] and the Financial Action Task Force on Money Laundering[c] of standards in different jurisdictions has highlighted the different quality and level of co-operation given by offshore centres and compliance with acceptable standards. In the case of those jurisdictions which do not co-operate, then we would suggest that consideration be given to taking steps to restrict dealings by securities firms in securities that are traded with any person in such a jurisdiction unless that person makes a declaration of the ultimate beneficial ownership of the securities the subject of the transaction.

(e) Public expectation of regulation

23.55 It is obvious from the above that protection by national regulators of the public in their dealings on markets is of less effect than it was before the advent of global markets and the transnational firms that deal across those markets. It is therefore very important that the public appreciates this fact and that as globalisation increases, so the level of protection afforded by national regulation of markets gets less.

23.56 This fact underlines the importance of progress to more effective transnational supervision of markets to ensure their fair, open and transparent conduct and of the transnational firms that

---

a See for example the report of the Technical Committee of IOSCO on Investigating and Prosecuting Market Manipulation, May 2000. It identifies common types of manipulative methods that can be used to create a false market and gives several examples.

b See http:\\www.fsforum.org.

c 22 June 2000: see http\\www.oecd.org\fatf; some of FATF's 40 recommendations might provide a useful basis for standards applicable to transnational dealings in securities, in particular recommendations 8 to 12.

operate in them to correct the imbalance that presently exists to the detriment of the proper operation of the markets.

(5) The audit and regulation of company "empires"

23.57 RM's companies were made up of several different groups of companies (in the technical sense); as there was no overall group, there was no requirement for an overall audit of the companies he controlled, despite the fact that RM operated those companies as one "empire", using that term to distinguish it from the technical sense in which "group" is used. The position of that "empire" was exacerbated by the opaque ownership structure which included offshore vehicles and the fact that many companies had different year ends[a].

23.58 We have expressed the view[b] that the auditors would have been able to obtain a somewhat clearer view if there had been one partner with an overview of the "empire".

23.59 There are and will doubtless continue to be similar "empires" subject to the effective control of one person, but where it is difficult to have a clear understanding of the overall financial position at a point in time. Such understanding is essential in circumstances such as where there is inter-company trading or financial dependence by companies within "the empire" on each other or on common sources of funding.

23.60 In our opinion, auditors should be alert to the pitfalls in acting for such "empires" and given guidance in the conduct of such audits. Regulators should also be aware of these issues.

(6) Auditors, independence and the detection of fraud

23.61 As set out earlier in this report, the auditors to RM's companies enjoyed a long standing professional relationship with RM and his companies and provided non audit services to his companies[c]. In the light of the conclusion[d] to which we came in relation to the audit of the pension schemes, we consider that there is the need for more radical thought and wider debate in the UK on the issues of auditor independence and detailed consideration of the rules being promulgated by the SEC and of the consultation paper issued by the EU Commission.

(a) Non audit services: independence and conflicts of interest

23.62 The importance of the independence and integrity of the audit of a company is self evident. There has been an increasing tendency for auditors to perform more non audit services to the company they audit; for many firms this non audit work has become a significant part of their work. The conflicts of interest to which this give rise are obvious; the only issue is how this is best dealt with to maintain public confidence in the audit and to ensure that auditors are not only

---

a See paragraphs 4.57 and 4.60 to 4.63.

b Paragraph 22.61.

c See paragraphs 4.11 to 4.17. Their business valuation unit also provided a valuation of the newspaper titles owned by MGN (see paragraph 14.22 and Appendix 14). As set out at paragraphs 3.32 and 3.45 of Appendix 14, the issue of independence of CLD was carefully considered.

d See paragraph 22.9.

independent, but are perceived by the public to be independent, rigorous and robust in their audit of a company or indeed any entity. In the light of the events surrounding RM's companies and the pension funds, public perception and confidence should be seen as of central importance.

23.63 At present, the professional accountancy bodies are required to have rules to ensure that the auditor is independent of the audit client[a]; rules and guidance on ethics are set by the professional bodies under the overall supervision of the DTI[b]. Auditors are obliged to disclose their global audit fees and that proportion of non audit revenue that arises in the UK.

23.64 In 1999, following an agreement with H M Government for the establishment of an independent framework of regulation for the accounting profession, the accountancy bodies agreed to establish an independent foundation, known as the "Accountancy Foundation" to provide such a framework on a non statutory basis, subject to a review after 5 years. The "Accountancy Foundation" is to be funded by the accountancy profession. It is in the process of establishing a number of boards, including an Ethics Standards Board, 60 per cent. of whose members are to be non accountants. It is likely that the issue of auditor independence will be a matter for that Board but, as the Board had not been established in February 2001, we were unable to obtain its view on this issue.

23.65 The questions that arise are whether (1) the present position should be left unchanged and rules on ethical guidance should form the basis of ensuring auditor independence or (2) there should be a prohibition on an auditor of a company providing non audit services, particularly consulting services, to that company, or (3) there should be additional or more clear cut restrictions on certain services[c] where there is a clear inconsistency with audit independence rather than an outright prohibition of all non audit services or (4) there should be more disclosure particularly in relation to the detail of non-audit fees and services or (5) there should be statements of the independence arrangements in place, or (6) a combination of some of these.

23.66 These questions have been extensively debated in the USA where the SEC has taken an active role[d]. The SEC has addressed the main issues in new rules[e], one of the principal features of which is to identify certain non-audit services (including some bookkeeping, valuation and legal services) which a firm cannot provide if it is to be an independent auditor.

---

a Para. 7(1)(b) of Schedule 11 of the Companies Act 1989 and Article 24 of Directive 84/253/EEC.

b This work is done in respect of the three Chartered Institutes (ICAEW, the Institute of Chartered Accountants of Scotland and the Institute of Chartered Accountants in Ireland) by the Chartered Accountants Joint Ethics Committee which keeps the guidance under review. The Association of Chartered Certified Accountants has comparable rules and guidance.

c An example might be the valuation of an intangible asset by one part of a firm which is then audited by another part of the firm.

d See for example the speech by the Chairman at New York University Center for Law and Business on 10 May 2000. He expressed concern that "the audit function is simply being used as a springboard to more lucrative consulting services instead of augmenting the firm's core focus".

e Revision of the Commission's Auditor Independence Requirements: File No S7-13-00.

23.67 The EU Commission following negotiations with Member States has issued a consultative paper "Statutory Auditors' Independence in the EU: A Set of Fundamental Principles"[a] which considers auditor independence on statutory audits, including principles applicable to the provision of non-audit services.

23.68 In the UK, the debate has included:

- The Company Law Review Steering Group (whose functions we explain at paragraph 23.76) in a consultation document published in March 2000 identified the problem in these terms:

  > Another important development is the radical change in the structure of the accountancy profession, which raises the question about the auditor's independence. In the early years of audit regulation the big accountancy firms derived a high proportion of their revenue from auditing. Today, these same firms are, in effect, financial services and consultancy conglomerates. There is a concern that potential conflicts of interest arise from combining these activities with the statutory audit function.

  However although it was recognised that the "independence issue" needs to be kept in mind, the Group concluded that, although the matter should be kept under review and invited comments, it would "not be helpful to make specific proposals on auditor independence at this stage."

  In their further consultation document published in November 2000 they commented:

  > "We received a wide range of comments on this issue, many of which expressed concern about the increasing diversification of the major accounting firms and the possible threat to the independence of the statutory audit....
  > We note in particular the new Ethics Standards Board. These arrangements should ensure that issues of auditor independence are addressed. We do not believe that further change is desirable at this stage but would wish the legislation to be sufficiently flexible to enable change to the statutory arrangements were that to prove necessary."

- In May 2000, the ICAEW established the Auditor Independence Working Party under the chairmanship of Mr Ian Hay Davison to review the issue of auditor independence[b]. In its report in August 2000, it concluded that an ethical framework approach along the lines of that currently operated in the UK was the most sensible approach to the requirement of independence.
- Simultaneously the Joint Monitoring Unit of the Institutes of Chartered Accountants published a review of compliance with the ICAEW's guidance on independence. It concluded that there was no evidence of systemic or significant failure to comply with the guidance. It made some suggestions to the ICAEW Auditor Independence Working Party which did not "cast doubt on the general soundness and relevance of the current guidance".
- The Chartered Accountants Joint Ethics Committee are in the process of re-drafting the whole of its guidance on auditor independence issues in the light of the EU Commission paper.

---

a 15 December 2000.

b The Secretary of the Working Party, Mr Tony Bromell, was quoted in *Accountancy* as saying at the time of the announcement of the working party that the difference between the bodies approach to auditor independence were not huge. "Ultimately, some form of global standard will be adopted. We are all feeling our way towards it. The only organisation which was out on a limb was the SEC" he added.

- The importance of the role of a listed company's audit committee in giving detailed consideration to the issue of independence has been stressed[a].

23.69 In addition,

- In July 2000, the Report of a Review Group on Auditing established by the Government of Ireland was published; auditor independence was one of the subjects it examined. It concluded that there was a need to introduce additional safeguards to protect the independence of the auditor from the threat posed by the provision of non audit services to client companies. It considered that these be best achieved through the development of a framework for auditor independence; they recommended full disclosure of non audit fees, restrictions on the amount of non audit fees and restrictions on certain non audit services.
- In July 1996 the International Federation of Accountants (IFAC) established a "Code of Ethics for Professional Accountants", which was updated in January 1998[b]. This set out common objectives for the accountancy profession worldwide and fundamental principles[c] that should be observed with the intention of serving as a model on which to base national ethical guidance.

23.70 The issues relating to auditor independence are important having regard to the events surrounding RM's companies and pension funds. Further consideration will be required in the UK to take account of the SEC rules and the EU consultative paper and to ensure, as far as possible, that there is a common approach with other EU States and the USA. This should contribute to a maintenance of public confidence in the independence of the audit and its value in identifying or preventing irregularities and abuses in companies and other entities and in their financial statements.

(b) Rotation of auditors

23.71 In June 1991, a senior partner of the auditors to RM's companies set out his view of the firm's strategy[d]:

> "The first requirement is to continue to be at the beck and call of RM, his sons and staff, appear when wanted and provide whatever is required."

The partner had been responsible for audits for many years.

---

a The Audit Briefing Paper "Communications between external auditors and audit committees" issued in June 1998, stated that an audit committee's role can be expected to include considering the adequacy of arrangements for external audit and supporting the independence and objectivity of the external auditors by, inter alia, reviewing the nature and extent of non-audit services.

b An exposure draft of proposed changes to the Code of Ethics for professional accountants was issued in June 2000. The proposed changes set out a framework describing the factors that could threaten a reporting accountant's independence and the safeguards that can be put in place to preserve that independence.

c The fundamental principles identified were integrity, objectivity, professional competence and due care, confidentiality and professional behaviour.

d See the footnote to paragraph 4.12.

23.72 In our view the same person should not be responsible for an audit of a listed company for more than a given number of years so that a fresh and objective view is regularly undertaken. There are two principal means by which this could be achieved:

- Compulsory rotation of partners[a].
- Compulsory rotation of firms.

The EU Consultative Paper to which we have referred provides for rotation of audit partners for public interest companies. There are benefits and disadvantages in both of these alternatives[b].

(c) The expectations gap and fraud

23.73 In a consultation document published in March 2000, the Company Law Review Steering Group(whose function we explain at paragraph 23.76) observed:

> "In reality auditors cannot be expected to detect a carefully planned and well executed fraud. This has led to a so-called "expectations gap" – that is the gap between what auditors can achieve and what users think they can achieve. Part of the work of the Auditing Practices Board is to explain and debate these issues to bring public expectation and what is possible into line, though this is a far from easy task."

In November 1998, the Auditing Practices Board issued a consultation paper "Fraud and Audit: Choices for Society" which was intended to inform and stimulate debate on the actions that should be taken to establish the right balance between the benefits to society from increasing the auditor's role in relation to the detection of fraud, and the costs and consequences that would flow from such changes.

23.74 Although we accept that a well planned and executed fraud can be difficult to prevent or detect and the primary responsibility to prevent and identify a fraud is that of the directors of a company, there is more that auditors can and should be doing to help prevent fraud:

- **Whistle blowing:** There should be a general duty[c] on auditors to inform the DTI and, where appropriate, the FSA of significant fraud or illegality at a listed company which it discovers in the course of an audit; we understand that the duty of whistle-blowing has worked well in relation to pensions and to firms regulated under the Financial Services Act[d]. Its more general extension would be highly desirable.
- **Maintenance of the independence of auditors.** We have addressed this topic above.

---

a The current Guide to Professional Ethics of the ICAEW (effective from 1 September 1997) requires audit firms to ensure no audit engagement partner remains in charge of the audit of a listed company for a period exceeding 7 years (without returning to the audit engagement partner role for at least 5 years). If this solution were adopted, it would be essential to prevent a more junior partner or senior manager who had worked with the partner assuming the responsibility, though provisions would need to ensure proper arrangements for the transfer of information and lessons learnt from experience.

b The Irish Review Group on auditing considered this topic.

c The current section of the Guide to Professional Ethics (1.306) of the ICAEW places a heavy emphasis on the duty of confidentiality which in the context of the relationship between a company and its auditor is a very important consideration. The Statement of Auditing Standards (Number 110) issued in January 1995 by the Auditing Practices Board requires auditors becoming aware of suspected or actual fraud to consider whether the matter ought to be reported to a proper authority in the public interest.

d The Public Interest Disclosure Act 1998 which came into force in July 1999 encourages whistle-blowing by employees by affording them a measure of protection from dismissal and victimisation.

(7) Corporate governance of listed companies: chairmen, directors and non-executive directors

23.75 Since the flotation of MGN, three committees have reported on corporate governance - the committee under Sir Adrian Cadbury in 1992, the committee under Sir Richard Greenbury in 1995 and the Committee under Sir Ronald Hampel in 1997. As a result of the reports of these committees, the Combined Code was produced by the Stock Exchange in June 1998. The Listing Rules were amended with effect from 31 December 1998 to require a company to state how it has applied the principles set out in the Combined Code; where it has complied with only some or none of the Combined Code provisions, it must specify the Combined Code provisions with which it has not complied and give reasons for non compliance.

23.76 In March 1998 HM Government announced a fundamental review of company law to be overseen by The Company Law Review Steering Group, a group of independent experts, which is due to report in the summer of 2001.

(a) The preferred approach

23.77 Some commentators have observed that it would have been possible for MCC and MGN under the chairmanship of RM to have complied with the provisions of the Combined Code if the provisions were applied simply as a checklist with boxes to be ticked and standard statements to be made without analysis of whether there was compliance with the spirit of the Combined Codes. We see considerable force in such comments. However, we consider that the preferred approach to corporate governance is still to deal with it by code rather than detailed legislation[a], though there is a need to underpin codes by making legislative provision[b] for them and to provide effective sanctions that can be enforced.

(b) Directors' understanding of their duties

23.78 Prior to the flotation of MGN, Clifford Chance[c] provided the directors with a memorandum on the liabilities of directors for listing particulars and the other duties of a director of a listed company; it did not (and was not intended) to deal with corporate governance. In March 1991, Inspectors reporting on Bestwood plc recommended[d] that a code of directors' duties be formulated; in the preliminary recommendations we made in July 1995 we strongly endorsed the principle of this recommendation made by those Inspectors and advised that fiduciary duties should be covered in the formulation.

---

a There are strong arguments to the contrary; we are grateful to Lord Williams of Elvel for his submissions to us on this topic.

b One method which could be used to underpin codes and similar extra statutory documents would be to give the Courts express power to have regard to them when assessing the conduct of directors.

c See a footnote to paragraph 10.23.

d Paragraph 18.6.2.

23.79 In September 1999, the Law Commission in their Report *Company Directors: Regulating Conflicts of Interest and Formulating a Statement of Duties*[a], recommended partial codification of directors duties which was summarised as follows:

> "We recommend that there should be a statutory statement of a director's main fiduciary responsibilities and a director's duty of care and skill; this statement should be set out on forms 10(2) and 288a; that when a director signs such a form he should acknowledge that he has read this statement; and that the DTI should consider how pamphlets explaining a director's duty might be made available to directors."

This recommendation is now being considered by the Company Law Review Steering Group, which, we understand, has expressed strong support.

23.80 We consider that, in addition to the statutory statement, the provision of practical extra statutory Guidance on Directors' Duties is clearly needed. This Guidance would deal with matters such as corporate governance and should be regularly updated. Not only would this provide useful assistance to directors, but leave less room for argument on the scope of duties in the case of corporate failures. We recommend that the work to prepare such Guidance be put in hand by the DTI as soon as possible.

23.81 We also recommended in July 1995 that the listing rules be amended so that the sponsor was bound to ensure that the directors understood not only their duties under the listing rules[b] but also in relation to all their obligations as directors, including those as to corporate governance and financial controls. We understand that this has been accommodated in the requirements of the Combined Code.

23.82 We recommend that when the extra statutory Guidance on Directors' Duties (which we have recommended) has been prepared under the auspices of the DTI, the Combined Code should be revised to include a reference to directors of all listed companies having undertaken to abide by the terms of the Guidance.

(c) Executive Chairman

23.83 One of the undesirable features of MGN on flotation was that it had an executive chairman and no separate chief executive. We expressed the view in July 1995 that we agreed with the conclusions of the Cadbury Report[c] that the office of chairman and chief executive should not generally be combined.

23.84 The Combined Code provides:

> "There should be a clear division of responsibilities at the head of the company which will ensure a balance of power and authority, such that no one individual has unfettered powers of decision. A decision to combine the posts of chairman and chief executive in one person should be publicly justified. Whether the posts are held by different people or by the same person, there should be

---

[a] Law Com. No. 261.

[b] This obligation is in Purple Book at Rule 2.9.

[c] Paragraph 4.9 of that Report.

> a strong and independent non-executive element to the board with a recognised senior member other than the chairman to whom concerns can be conveyed. The chairman, chief executive and senior independent director should be identified in the annual report."

23.85 The combining of the functions of chairman and chief executive at MGN should not have been permitted[a] and we doubt whether the provision in the Combined Code would have been sufficient to prevent it. We therefore recommend that the working of this provision be monitored. A possible revision to ensure the elimination of combining these offices in listed companies in all but the most exceptional and objectively justifiable circumstances should be kept under review.

23.86 If a company which combines the posts of chairman and chief executive is applying to be listed, the Listing Authority should require a comfort letter from the sponsor to the effect that, having considered the implications, it was satisfied that no detriment would be likely to arise. The view has been expressed to us that advisors and shareholders are fully aware of the risks of combining the posts of chairman and chief executive; as a result of our investigation, we are not as sanguine and consider a comfort letter from the sponsor is necessary.

(d) The role of non-executive directors

23.87 It is clear from chapters 20 and 21 that the presence of non-executive directors contributed little to MGN. It would have been helpful

- If those appointed on flotation had familiarised themselves sufficiently with MGN.
- If there had been a clearer understanding of the time they had to devote to the affairs of MGN.

23.88 In our view the way a company governs itself should (within the requirements of the EU directives and the Companies Act) generally be a matter for the shareholders and directors to decide; we do not consider that detailed legislation is therefore needed to regulate further corporate governance, though it will be necessary, as we have stated, to underpin the codes of practice. We agree with the approach of the Combined Code that a company should have non-executive directors of sufficient calibre and number for their views to carry significant weight in the board's decisions. Furthermore, it should be for each company to decide on the particular role of a non-executive director. Legislation is not required to ensure that a non-executive director familiarises himself with the company.

23.89 The key issue is how to make non-executive directors properly accountable for the responsibilities they undertake within the company (as responsibilities may differ from company to company) and thereby act more diligently in carrying out such responsibilities. Further consideration could usefully be given to this issue[b].

---

[a] See paragraph 22.19.

[b] It was submitted to us that cronyism plays far too large a part in the preservation of the present position. Companies like to chose non-executives from a narrow circle of those that they are likely to get on with; there is no wish to see the present position changed by anything that might risk disturbing the existing cosy relationships and opportunities.

23.90 We consider one way to ensure that:

- the role of the non-executive director within the particular company is defined[a];
- the time he has to devote is made clear
- the non-executive is accountable for what he does and the time he spends

is to make it a provision of the Combined Code that the annual report should also contain:

- a statement setting out the functions carried out by the non-executive directors within the company;
- a statement of the time that each non-executive director has actually spent on the affairs of the company during the year[b].

23.91 The view has been expressed to us that it is doubtful whether there would be support in the City or from institutional shareholders for our suggestion. For our part we consider that there is a strong interest in ensuring greater accountability and transparency and thereby enhancing public confidence.

(8) Technical matters

(a) Definition of realisation

23.92 As is clear from the scheme devised to enable the elimination of the debt of the private side to MGN (described at paragraphs 15.6 to 15.14 and in Appendix 15), section 263 of the Companies Act 1985 is unsatisfactory in that it fails to deal with realisation within a group context and may be ineffective in restricting the funds that are distributed within a group. We recommended in July 1995 that this issue be addressed.

23.93 As we explain at paragraph 8 of Appendix 15, in 1994, the Accounting Standards Board issued Financial Reporting Statement Number 5 under which financial statements were required to report the substance of transactions.

23.94 In July 1999, the ICAEW began developing new guidance on the determination of realised profits. A draft technical release issued in August 2000[c], provided a much clearer definition of considerations to be taken into account in assessing whether there was a "realisation" and in paragraph 12 stated:

> "In assessing whether a company has a realised profit, transactions and arrangements should not necessarily be looked at in isolation. A group or series of artificial, linked or circular transactions or arrangements that is designed to achieve an overall commercial effect (for example, the creation of a realised profit) should be viewed as a whole, and a realised profit does not arise where the end result for the company does not meet the criteria set out in this statement."

---

a The SEC issued in September 1999 useful guidance on independent directors of investment companies, particularly in relation to conflicts of interest.

b A survey published in 2000 by PricewaterhouseCoopers "Non Executive Directors: A survey of practice and opinion" provided some information on time spent; the author of the survey observed (at paragraph 55) in respect of their finding that non-executive directors were spending somewhere between 10 and 20 days on the job, "These do not seem very high figures in relation to the demands of the role as they have been described".

c Tech 25/00.

23.95 The view has been expressed to us by the DTI that this is not a suitable area for statute law because of the complexity of intra group transactions and that it should be dealt with by the new guidance being developed and the interpretation of the current law. We have considerable sympathy with that view. We understand the guidance will be finalised and available in the course of 2001. The guidance will need to deal expressly with the type of transaction that occurred at MGN.

(b) Options

23.96 The Bestwood Inspectors recommended in March 1991 that the prohibition of the purchase of options by directors should be extended to the sale of options[a]; we endorsed that recommendation in July 1995.

23.97 In 1998 the Law Commission issued a consultation paper[b] by which comments were sought as to their provisional view that section 323 of the Companies Act 1985 should be repealed. In their Report of 1999[c], the Law Commission recommended the repeal of section 323 on the basis that the mischief that it was designed to cover – insider dealing – has been dealt with by Part V of the Criminal Justice Act 1993. The Law Commission is plainly correct, but (as RM's dealings in MCC shares reveal) insider dealing is not the only possible mischief. Another mischief could be share support, in particular through the use of options during closed periods[d]. Whilst that might be contrary to the Combined Code, RM's dealings reveal that a statutory prohibition backed up by criminal sanction may well still have a real purpose. We recommend that the Company Law Review Steering Group consider this issue further.

(c) Disclosure of a director's loans secured by shares

23.98 The Bestwood Inspectors also recommended in March 1991 that the law be amended to require directors of listed companies to reveal details of any loans (say over £20,000) which are secured by shares in the company[e]. Their reasoning was that other shareholders were unaware of the risk of a director being forced to sell blocks of shares at short notice if he could not service his borrowings or if the value of the shares fell. We endorsed that recommendation in 1995 and suggested that the provision should be drafted widely enough to cover all holdings whether held directly or indirectly. The events we describe in this Report show that there is a further risk arising out of a director borrowing against the collateral of large shareholdings – manipulating the market to keep the price high to maintain adequate collateral for loans. We also recommended that consideration should also be given to extending this disclosure requirement to the use of shares as collateral by shareholders holding more than 3 per cent. of the shares of the company.

---

a Paragraph 24.5.11; section 323 of the Companies Act 1985.

b No 153 Company Directors: Regulatory Conflicts of Interests and Formulating a Statement of Duties.

c Law Com No 261.

d The Working Party appointed by the Stock Exchange to consider RM's dealings in options also recommended that amendment to section 323 be considered (see Appendix 7, paragraph 19.4).

e Paragraph 24.5.10.

23.99 This issue is not presently being considered by the Company Law Review Steering Group. We recommend that this issue be addressed.

(d) Disclosure for the purposes of a criminal trial

23.100 We were invited to make observations in 1995 in relation to the disclosure in criminal proceedings of materials obtained during the course of an Inspection prior to the enactment of the Criminal Procedure and Investigations Act 1996 which has modified the law. A large amount of material we had obtained was disclosed shortly before the criminal trial started; this caused considerable concern to those who had made available information to us, some of which would not have been available otherwise, for example, because it was the subject of legal professional privilege. When the law relating to disclosure is next reviewed, we recommend the review consider the circumstances relating to our enquiry for the reasons we have given. We would hope that any future modifications of the law will not discourage the voluntary disclosure of information to enquiries (particularly of confidential or privileged information). We also suggest that consideration should be given as to whether it is appropriate to provide safeguards in respect of information disclosed to enquiries under compulsion, though this may require a balancing exercise to be undertaken by the court.

(9) Review of recommendations

23.101 Recommendations in reports such as this are sometimes implemented, sometimes rejected, sometimes considered for long periods and sometimes ignored. For example, nearly 10 years after the Bestwood Report, the recommendations to which we referred are still being considered. There is a public interest in knowing what the response has been to recommendations made. Providing such a statement would be in accord with a modern approach to government. We would therefore recommend that the DTI publish from time to time reports dealing with, or include in their annual report, their responses to the recommendations made by enquiries such as this and, where decisions are made to implement recommendations, thc progress towards implementation.

LIST OF ABBREVIATIONS

Abbreviation	Full Name
Ansbacher	Henry Ansbacher & Co Limited
Astaire	Astaire & Co
Barclays	Barclays Bank plc
Beecham	Beecham Group plc
BIM	Bishopsgate Investment Management Limited
BIT	Bishopsgate Investment Trust plc
BNP	Banque Nationale de Paris
BNPC	British Newspaper Printing Corporation plc
BPC	British Printing Corporation plc
BPCC	The British Printing Communication Corporation plc
Britannia Arrow	Britannia Arrow Holdings plc, subsequently known as Invesco MIM
BZW	Barclays de Zoete Wedd Ltd
CCF	Crédit Commercial de France
CCM	Capel Cure Myers Capital Management Limited
Chase	The Chase Manhatten Bank NA
CIF	Common Investment Fund
CLD	Coopers & Lybrand Deloitte, Coopers & Lybrand and their predecessor or successor firms
Conrad Ritblat	Conrad Ritblat & Co
Crédit Lyonnais Laing	Laing & Cruickshank Investment Management Limited, Crédit Lyonnais Securities
Daiwa	Daiwa Europe Bank plc
De La Rue	De La Rue plc
Disclosure Regulations	Occupational Pension Schemes (Disclosure of Information) Regulations 1986
Donohue	Donohue Inc
DSS	Department of Social Security
DTI	Department of Trade and Industry

ERISA	Employee Retirement Income Security Act of 1974
Extel	Extel Group plc
Fleet	Fleet Holdings plc
FSA	Financial Services Authority
FTIT	First Tokyo Index Trust plc
Funvale	Funvale Limited
Goldman Sachs	Goldman Sachs & Co and all entities within the Goldman Sachs group
GSES	Goldman Sachs Equity Securities Limited
GSIL	Goldman Sachs International Limited
GS-NY	Goldman Sachs & Co
HI	Headington Investments Ltd
Hill Samuel	Hill Samuel Group Ltd and all subsidiaries
Hollis	Hollis plc, subsequently Pergamon AGB plc.
ICAEW	Institute of Chartered Accountants in England and Wales
IBI	The IBI group of companies
IBF	International Bankers France
ILSC	International Learning Systems Corporation Limited
IM	Mr Ian Maxwell
IMRO	Investment Management Regulatory Organisation Limited
Invesco MIM	Invesco MIM plc
Jupiter Participations	Jupiter Participations SA
KM	Mr Kevin Maxwell
KOP	Kansallis-Osake-Pankki
Lakeport	Lakeport Nominees Limited
Lazards	Lazard Frères & Co
LBG	London & Bishopsgate Group Limited
LBH	London & Bishopsgate Holdings plc
LBI	London & Bishopsgate International Investment Management plc
Lehmans	Shearson Lehman Brothers Holdings Inc and its subsidiaries

LGSI	Lehman Government Securities Inc
Lloyds	Lloyds Bank plc and its associated companies
Lloyds Investment	Lloyds Investment Managers Ltd
Macmillan	Macmillan Inc.
Magnacell	Magnacell Limited
MAPs	"Matters for the attention of partners" a summary of the main points arising on the audit prepared for the attention of a partner.
Maxwell Scientific	Maxwell Scientific International (Distribution Services) Limited
MCC	Maxwell Communication Corporation plc
MCEEP	Maxwell Central and East European Partners plc
MCPT Ltd	Maxwell Communication Pension Trustee Limited
MCPT (WS) Ltd	Maxwell Communication Pension Trustees (Works Scheme) Limited
MCWPS	Maxwell Communication Works Pension Scheme
MGN	Mirror Group Newspapers plc formerly Mirror Group Newspapers Limited
MGPS	Mirror Group Pension Scheme
MGPT	MGPT Limited (formerly Mirror Group Pension Trustees Limited)
Midland Montagu	Midland Montagu & Co Ltd
Midland Bank	Midland Bank plc
MIM	Montagu Investment Management Limited (also known as Invesco MIM Management Ltd)
MNI	Maxwell Newspapers Inc.
Moody's	Moody's Investors Service Limited
Morgan Stanley Group	Morgan Stanley Group Inc. and all its subsidiaries
MSTC	Morgan Stanley Trust Company Inc.
MSI	Morgan Stanley International
National Westminster	National Westminster Bank plc
Nikko	Nikko Bank (UK) plc
Nikko Management	Nikko Capital Management Limited
Nikko Securities	Nikko Securities Co
Nomura	Nomura Bank International plc

NPA	Newspaper Publishers Association
OAG	Official Airline Guides Inc.
OPS	Occupational Pension Scheme
Paramount	Paramount Communications Inc.
Peat Marwick	KPMG Peat Marwick McLintock
Peel Hunt	Peel Hunt & Company Limited
PFT	Pergamon Financial Trust
PG	Pergamon Group plc
PGH	Pergamon Group Holdings Ltd
PGS	Pergamon Group Services Limited
PHA	Pergamon Holdings Anstalt
PHAF	PHA Finance Ltd
PHAI	PHA Investments Limited
PHC	Pergamon Holdings Corporation
Phillips & Drew	Phillips & Drew Fund Management Limited
PHL	Pergamon Holdings Limited
PHLE	PHL Estates Limited
PHUSI	Pergamon Holdings (US) Inc
PMR	PMR Limited
PMT	Pergamon Media Trust plc
PP Inc	Pergamon Press Inc
PPL	Pergamon Press Limited
QPI	Quebecor Printing Inc
Quebecor	Quebecor Inc
Rank Hovis McDougall	Rank Hovis McDougall plc
Reed	Reed International plc
Reuters	Reuters Holdings plc
RM	Mr Robert Maxwell
RMC	Robert Maxwell & Co Limited
RMG	Robert Maxwell Group plc
RMGH	Robert Maxwell Group Holdings Limited
RMH	Robert Maxwell Holdings Limited
Robert Fraser Group	Robert Fraser Group Limited and its subsidiaries
Rowe & Pitman	Rowe & Pitman Limited, S.G. Warburg Securities Limited and associated companies
Samuel Montagu	Samuel Montagu & Co Limited

SBC	Swiss Bank Corporation
SBIL	Salomon Brothers International Limited
SBUKE	Salomon Brothers UK Equity Limited
Scitex	Scitex Corporation Ltd
SDR	Scottish Daily Record and Sunday Mail Limited
SEC	The Securities & Exchange Commission
Servex	Servex AG
SFA	Securities & Futures Authority
SI	Syndication International Limited
SIB	Securities & Investment Board
SLHI	SLH International Inc. (subsequently Lehman Brothers International Inc.)
Smith New Court	Smith New Court plc & all subsidiaries
SORP	Statement of Recommended Practice
Standard & Poor's	Standard & Poor's Corporation
Stock Exchange	The International Stock Exchange of the United Kingdom and the Republic of Ireland Limited
Teva	Teva Pharmaceutical Industries Limited
Thornton	Thornton Management Limited
TIB	Torafugu Inspection Board Inc.
Toronto Dominion	Toronto Dominion Bank
TSA	The Securities Association Limited
UBS Phillips & Drew	UBS Phillips & Drew Research Limited
United Newspapers	United Newspapers plc
V&G	Vehicle and General Assurance Company Limited
Visaford	Visaford Limited
Yakosa	Yakosa Finanzierungs AG